This is the long-awaited second volume of one of the finest general introductions to the medieval world of recent times, first published in French by Armand Colin. Extensively illustrated with many accompanying maps, each volume presents a synthesis of scholarly research and interpretation, carefully checked, translated and revised for an English-speaking readership.

Volume II begins at the turn of the millennium and covers the extraordinary rebirth of Europe in terms of demographic expansion, agrarian settlement and organisation, the establishment of towns and villages, the ascendancy of the feudal system, the appearance of formal states and kingdoms, and the dramatic controlling ascendancy of the western Church. In the East, despite the external appearance of grandeur, the Islamic countries were being torn apart by mutual rivalry, while the Byzantine Empire lost massive border territories through political and economic incompetence. As in Volumes I (350–950) and III (1250–1520) full coverage is given to both East and West, and their artistic heritage is displayed lavishly in many of the colour plates. A well-researched select bibliography is also included as an aid to further investigation, whether by general readers or by students of the period.

The Cambridge Illustrated History of

THE MIDDLE AGES

The Cambridge Illustrated History of

THE MIDDLE AGES

II   950–1250

Edited by
ROBERT FOSSIER

Translated by
STUART AIRLIE
and
ROBYN MARSACK

CAMBRIDGE
UNIVERSITY PRESS

PUBLISHED BY THE PRESS SYNDICATE OF THE UNIVERSITY OF CAMBRIDGE
The Pitt Building, Trumpington Street, Cambridge CB2 1RP, United Kingdom

CAMBRIDGE UNIVERSITY PRESS
The Edinburgh Building, Cambridge, CB2 2RU, United Kingdom
40 West 20th Street, New York, NY 10011-4211, USA
10 Stamford Road, Oakleigh, Melbourne 3166, Australia

First published in French as *Le Moyen Age 2. L'Eveil de L'Europe 950–1250* by Armand Colin,
103 boulevard Saint-Michel, Paris 1982 and © Armand Colin Editeur, Paris 1982
First published in English by Cambridge University Press, 1997, as *The Cambridge
Illustrated History of the Middle Ages II: 950–1250*

English translation © Cambridge University Press 1997

Printed in the United Kingdom at the University Press, Cambridge

A catalogue record for this book is available from the British Library

A catalogue record for this book is available from the Library of Congress

ISBN 0 521 26644 0 hardback (v. I)
ISBN 0 521 26645 9 hardback (v. II)
ISBN 0 521 26646 7 (v. III)
ISBN 0 521 59078 7 (3-volume boxed set)

SE

Contents

Contents

Colour plates

List of colour plates

Maps

Acknowledgements

Photographic agencies

Aerofilms
ANA
Atlas Photo
Bildarchiv Foto Marburg
S. Chitol
Gerard Degeorge
A. Dufau
Editions Arthaud
Foto-Enit
Fotogram M. Cabaud
Giraudon
C. Kutschera
J. Le Caisne
Mas
Perceval
Photothèque Armand-Colin
Pieterse Davison International Ltd
Rapho
Michaud-Rapho
Roger-Viollet
Scala
Yan
Yan-Zodiaque

Scholarly institutions

Cambridge, Cambridge University Collection
Cambridge, Corpus Christi College
Dijon, Bibliothèque municipale

Dublin, Chester Beatty Library
Jerusalem, The Israel Museum
London, The British Library
London, The British Museum
Munich, Bayerische Staatsbibliothek
New York, Metropolitan Museum of Arts, the Cloisters Collection
New York, Pierpont Morgan Library
Nuremberg, Stadtbibliothek
Oxford, Bodleian Library
Paris, Bibliothèque nationale
Paris, Collection de l'Ecole des hautes-études en sciences sociales
Paris, Réunion des Musées nationaux
Reims, Bibliothèque municipale
Rome, Biblioteca Apostolica Vaticana
Trier, Stadtbibliothek
Venice, Biblioteca Marciana
Vienna, Kunsthistorisches Museum
Vienna, Österreichische Nationalbibliothek

Colour plates

	between pages
Lauros-Giraudon, Mas, British Library, Victoria and Albert Museum	70 & 71
Lauros-Giraudon, Rapho, J. Dieuzaide, Barnaby's Picture Library (London)	142 & 143
G. DeGeorge (3), Roger-Viollet	214 & 215
Scala, Victoria and Albert Museum, Scala (2)	286 & 287
J. Dieuzaide, Giraudon, Domstift Naumberg, Réunion des musées nationaux	358 & 359
J. Dieuzaide, Anne Gaël (2), S. Chirol	430 & 431
CNMHS (Paris), Victoria and Albert Museum (2), CNMHS (Paris)	502 & 503

Glossary

This glossary of technical terms is confined to those referring to institutions or phenomena not explained in Volume I. Terms explained in the text or found easily in a dictionary have been omitted.

ACCOLA: land brought under cultivation by a tenant either in addition to his manse or specially granted to him, thus a part of the demesne.

ADJECTIO STERILIUM: compulsory assignation by the authorities of lands not under cultivation; an ancient practice, continued in Byzantium (*epibole*), by which the state sought to keep the fisc intact. The practice faded out in the West except in the form of distribution to neighbours of lands without known heirs.

ADJUTORUM, ADOHA: tax levied on aristocratic lands owing services.

AFORESTATIO, AFFORESTATIO: the reservation of a wooded zone, or of uncultivated land; either as part of a lord's policy of distraint of land or for straightforward local purposes of reclaiming woods or establishing a hunting reserve.

AGRARIUM, AGRIÈRE: dues paid in kind in the south of France; generally refers to land rent but it was extended to banal levies.

AIOLE: plots of land assembled in quadrangular form (Mediterranean area).

ALBERGA, ALBERGAGIUM, HERBERGE: the lord's right of lodging or requisition.

ALBERGO: the 'house' – the extended family and its main residence, in Liguria and central Italy.

ALCADE, ALCALDE: from the Arab *al qadi*; public official providing justice in Spanish towns; by extension, a member of a municipal body.

ALDEA: Christian village in reconquered territory in Spain.

ALFOZ: territory dependent on an *aldea* for its cultivation and security.

ALGARADE: Spanish cavalry raid on Muslim territory.

ALLELENGYON: payment by the office-holding magnates of the taxes of the poorest in Byzantium.

ALLMENDE: common village lands, or areas for common pasturage.

ALQUEIRAS: village with a predominantly Muslim population in reconquered territory in Spain.

Glossary

AMBROSINO: gold coin issued in Milan in the thirteenth century (from St Ambrose, patron of the city).

AMICI: the clients or relatives – by blood or association – of the head of a lineage.

APRISIO: the giving in full ownership of land occupied by its tenant for thirty years.

ARENGO: people's assembly in the northern Italian towns.

ARTI: crafts, professions; term used in Italy and southern France.

AS'AIFA: annual raid made by Muslims into Christian Spain.

ASHKENAZIM: from the eleventh century the name given to the Jews of the Rhineland and central Europe, who had a specific way of observing and commenting on the Law.

AUBAINS: strangers to a village or town.

AUCTORITAS: one of the attributes of seigneurial and royal power, based on moral or charismatic authority rather than material power.

AULA: generally a prince's reception chamber or hall of judgement; can also refer to a public hall.

AZYME: unleavened bread used by the Jews during Passover.

BACADE: transhumant flock, often of different kinds of animals, in the Pyrenean regions.

BAILE: bailey, the outer courtyard of a castle, used to shelter villagers who had taken refuge there and often the site of quarters for the garrison.

BAILLI: royal judicial and administrative official.

BALIA: people's assembly in Tuscan towns.

BAN, BANNUM: public authority, an order deriving from it.

BANCO: counter set up in a public space, used by money-changers and later by money-lenders.

BANIÈRE: banner; by extension, came to refer to a district of a town controlled by a particular family or trade; the banner itself symbolised the urban territory.

BARRI, BARRIO: suburb (Mediterranean region).

BEDE: German term referring to tax, generally a banal levy.

BERCARIA: sheepfold, pasture.

BESANT: Byzantine gold or silver coin in circulation across Europe.

BESTHAUPT: the 'best head', i.e. of cattle; the portion deducted by a lord from the inheritance of serfs, and sometimes of free men, in the German Empire and some other regions.

BONIFACHI: reclaimed land in northern Italy, usually drained or, in mountainous regions, terraced.

BONI HOMINES: people qualified to act as witnesses or assessors in a court.

BOURG: new fortified town.

BRAZO: a social rank in Spain; refers to legal status rather than to an order or class.

BRUNETTI, BRUNOS: devalued coinage in Spain and Italy, in which alloys replaced much of the silver content.

BUTEIL: the portion of a serf's or sometimes a free man's inheritance which a lord reserved for himself; could include the whole inheritance where there was no direct heir (in the Empire).

xvi   CABALLEROS, CABALLERÍA VILLANA: in Spain, mounted peasants, particularly responsible for defending the *aldea*; they owed mounted military service in the king's army.

CANADAS: paths of transhumance in northern Spain.

CANCO: Occitan or Italian form of lyric poetry.

CAPITANEI: propertied lords in northern Italy, vassals of counts and bishops, generally in charge of a public stronghold.

CARRUCA: late Latin term for a cart; during the twelfth century came to refer to an asymmetrical plough with ploughshare, coulter and mouldboard.

CASANE: commercial premises, centres for borrowing and changing money (Piedmont).

CASTELNAU: new village established around or in the neighbourhood of a castle (Gascony).

CASTLAN: holder of a castle in Catalonia; generally similar to the castellans of northern Europe in his relative subordination to the ruler.

CAUSIDICI: professional jurists, involved in the administration of a lordship or a town.

CENSE: large farm, very often leasehold.

CENSUALES: men belonging to a church, generally free tenants but sometimes subject to certain taxes; sometimes *cerocensuales*.

CHAMPART: right of feudal lords to levy a portion of their tenants' harvest.

CHARISTIKION: distribution of church property by the Byzantine emperor.

CHEVAGE: from *capitatio*, head tax, recognitive of legal alienation although it appears to stem from the manumission tax of the ancient world.

CHORION: free rural community in the Byzantine empire, basis of land tax assessment.

CHRESIS: usufructuary tenure in Byzantium.

COGNITIO FUNDI: sworn inquest.

COLLEGANZA: merchant contract of association where the sleeping partner, who provided two-thirds of the capital, did not participate in business activities but received two-thirds to three-quarters of the profits.

COMITATUS: office of a count; territory belonging to that office.

COMMENDA: merchant's contract of association whereby the sleeping partner provided all the capital and yielded to the merchant one-eighth to one-third of the profits. The word also refers to the commending of a man or a piece of land belonging to the church to a powerful patron.

COMMUNIA: common village lands, pasture area; see *Allmende*.

COMPAGNA: merchants' association in which members of the same *familia* and outsiders combined, each member contributing a share of the money required (see *corpo, sors*) for a specific short-term transaction; renewable.

CONDUCTUS: the escorting of a merchant caravan or of ordinary travellers by armed men as they crossed a certain territory; the toll levied on such an occasion by the territory's lord, particularly during fairs.

CONSOLAMENTUM: in Catharism, reconciliation administered by one of the *perfecti* to the dying, purifying the latter on condition that abstinence was maintained until death.

CONSORS, CONSORTERIE: associations of families, in the broadest sense, in Italian towns, creating local and business networks.

Glossary

CONSULS: citizens responsible for urban administration in Mediterranean regions.

CONTADO: Italian term referring to the territory of the *comitatus*.

CORPO: a company's base capital, usually coming from one family.

DEFENS: zone, generally wooded, preserved from pasture.

DELLE: district subject to regular cultivation.

DEMOSIARIOS: in Byzantine territory, a category of peasant established on fiscal lands and paying taxes directly to the treasury.

DEN: territory on which pigs were pastured (Anglo-Saxon).

DIDASCALIA: collection of Psalms and Epistles (mainly St Paul's) which constituted the basis of Byzantine ecclesiastical culture.

DISPUTATIO: scholastic exercise in which two masters or one master and his audience took opposing views of a text studied beforehand.

DISTRICTUS, DISTRETTO, DESTRIOT: the power to constrain and judge; also the actual territory where this power was exercised.

DIVIETO: prohibition of the sale of cereals in the countryside when stocks in the towns were low (Italian, 13th century).

DIWAN: government office or ministry; royal reception chamber.

DOMICELLI, DONZEAUX: originally referred to young aristocrats not yet dubbed; after the 13th century, to minor landholders.

DRAILLE: path followed by flocks during transhumance (Pyrenees).

DRYKKIA: forms of association in Scandinavia, initially on a religious basis, later professional.

ECHEVIN: from the tenth century onwards, refers to person (usually noble) responsible for local administration and low justice in town or country.

ÉCU: gold coin issued by St Louis, then regularly after 1290.

EMPORIUM: port where goods were unloaded; eventually, the taxes levied on the unloaded cargo.

EMPRIÚ: villagers' collective right of usage (Pyrenees).

ESCARTERON: association of transhumant shepherds in the southern Alps.

ESOTHYRA: zone of gardens and hay meadows round a Byzantine village.

EXACTIO: any fiscal exaction by the lord, especially *taille* (tallage), levied as the seigneurial framework was being established.

EXARICOS: Muslim slaves in Spain.

EXEMPLA: tales of a moralising cast intended to aid understanding of the Christian faith and morality; basis of popular sermons.

EXKOUSSEIA: a form of fiscal and legal exemption in Byzantium.

EXOTHYRA: forms of dry-farming cultivation in the Byzantine world; cultivation of the vine.

EXULTET: hymn for Easter eve; the roll of parchment on which it was written, often embellished with didactic illustrations.

FADERFIO (from the German *Vater*, father): elements of the family patrimony which a man established as a dowry on the marriage of his daughter (Lombard law).

FERIA: weekday; by extension, day on which a special assembly was held, hence the meaning 'fair'.

FERRAGINA: area of orchards, meadows and gardens around villages in Italy and southern France.

FERRATA VIA: Roman roadway.

FESTUCA: a length of straw or a rod symbolising the grant of a piece of land to a man, usually a vassal.

FIDEJUSSORE: one who stood pledge for the fulfilment of another's duties towards the authorities.

FIORINO: Florentine gold coin bearing the city's emblem, an iris.

FIRMA BURGI: text granting privileges to a village (in western France, England), chiefly the right to become a town.

FOLLIS: Byzantine copper coin.

FONDE: commercial court in the Holy Land.

FORAINS: strangers, outsiders in a village or town.

FORMARIAGE: fine levied in cases of marrying outside the lord's estate, payable by serfs but also occasionally by free men; known in England as *merchet*.

FRATERNE, FRAIRIES, FRÉRAGES, FRÉRÈCHES: forms of association composed of brothers who shared an inheritance or members united in pious works; such terms may refer to the joint holding of lands, to religious associations, or to political or geographically limited associations; see *consorterie*.

FRUITIÈRES: peasant associations formed for the common exploitation of land sometimes also in the pastoral economy (in the Jura).

FUEROS: Spanish charters of privileges.

GÄSTE: incomers established on new lands; can also refer to a deprived class of peasants.

GEMEINENFREI: allod-holders (Empire).

GENICIA: workrooms set aside for women's work, e.g. weaving, spinning.

GENOVINO: Genoese gold coin.

GEOPONIKA: a Byzantine collection of extracts from agricultural treatises.

GESCHLECHT: large kin-group, clan or tribe with a common original ancestor.

GHAZI: Muslim confraternities aimed at making converts by example or force.

GHIBELLINES: Italian political 'party' in favour of a central authority in Italy and thus, eventually, a supporter of the Germans (from Weibelingen, the Hohenstaufen estate).

GOLIARDS: unruly groups of intellectuals in the Paris region in the twelfth century.

GONFALONIERI: the leading men of the districts in Italian towns, hence those responsible for public order there.

GRADONI: hillside terraces supported by low walls on cleared slopes.

GROS: silver coin worth ten deniers.

GRUARII: estate officials, then public officials, responsible for maintaining and exploiting forest resources.

GUELFS: Italian political 'party' in favour of local autonomy or subjection to the papacy

Glossary

rather than to the Empire (from the Welfs, a Bavarian family opposed to imperial intervention in Italy in the twelfth century).

HANDWERK: an organised trade.

HANSE: association of merchants; originally this term referred to sea-going Baltic, German and English merchants, but it was extended to other forms of professional association.

HARDINES: kitchen gardens on the banks or flood lands of a river.

HEERSCHILD: aristocratic hierarchy in Germany; a highly artificial structure created by jurists to classify the different levels of the German aristocracy; public or private rights calculated according to Heerschild (literally, shield) status.

HÉRBERGEMENT: originally, the right to lodging/hospitality (see *alberga*); in western France it refers to new holdings of relatively free status.

HEREDITARII: hereditary tenants (northern France, Low Countries).

HERIOT: payment owed to a lord on death of estate-holder.

HERM: from the Greek *eremos*, an uncultivated place, the 'desert' of the Cistercians.

HOF: court, estate.

HOLZBAU: wooden construction.

HOMMES DE CORPS, HOMINES PROPRII: bondsmen.

HORT, HORTILLON, HUERTA: see *hardines*.

HOTE: see *forain*.

HYPERETAI: in the Byzantine Empire, urban servants attached to their master through bonds of clientship.

IMMATRICULATI: the poor entered in the register of those receiving public aid.

INCASTELLAMENTO: the establishing of fortified settlements in Italy (tenth century onwards).

INFANZONES: in Spain, a ruler's followers of high birth, usually armed and endowed with a fief.

IQTA: a grant of state lands or revenue usually in return for service.

IWAN: vaulted or flat-roofed hall, open at one end (Islamic).

JAHBADH: government banker.

JAWALI: Egyptian version of the *jiziya*, i.e. tax levied on non-Muslims.

JOCULATOR, JONGLEUR: refers not only to court entertainers at noble feasts but also to any vagrant figure on the edge of society.

JURISPERITI: professional jurists, usually distinct from notaries.

JUVENES: men who have not yet settled down, whatever their age.

KALAAT: Muslim stronghold, usually on high ground.

KARFAR: great ship of Scandinavian rulers, who were often buried in one.

KARIMI: Egyptian, on occasion Jewish, merchant.

KASTRON: Byzantine walled town.

KATEPANO: Greek provincial governor (in the west).

KEURES: fraternities (northern France, Low Countries), associations for mutual aid.

KEUTES: coarse wollen blankets, part of the levy of compulsory lodging or hospitality.

KLISOURAE: territorial units in the Byzantine Empire, smaller than a theme.

KNECHT: manservant, workman.

KOMMERKION: Byzantine customs tax.

KOOP: see *relief*.

KRAL: Slav ruler (perhaps from Carolus).

KRITES: in Byzantium, generally an area of jurisdiction, an area subject to tax.

LAMBI: flat-bottomed barges used in river traffic.

LANDFRIEDEN: charters of peace, granted by the emperor, securing public order under threat of secular and ecclesiastical sanctions.

LANDSASSEN: German peasants free to exploit their holdings.

LAUDATIO PARENTUM: practice enshrined in law and custom permitting the close relations of a person making a gift to support or oppose the action; their consent is recorded in the charter.

LAUDESI: initially, poor vagrants; came to be organised as mendicant groups, generally in the countryside, performing penitential songs (laudi).

LEDING: levy of ships, men, etc. to equip a war-fleet (Scandinavia).

LEIBEIGEN: bondsman, serf; one whose body no longer belongs to himself.

LEIHEZWANG: the practice in the Empire of the immediate re-infeudation of a fief without heirs.

LIVELLO: a form of thirty-year tenure in Italy, owing very few services but subject to heavy relief.

LOCA: shares contributed by an investor to an enterprise, giving him a right to some of the ensuing profits.

LOCATOR: person responsible for recruiting settlers for rural colonisation.

LODS ET VENTES: dues payable on sale and transfer of land.

LOGISMA: Byzantine practice of the granting of lands by the state to prosperous owners such as the Church.

MADRASA: school of higher Islamic learning, midway between a Western university and a monastic school.

MALSUSOS: Spanish term referring to the unwelcome 'new customs' introduced by lords in the eleventh century; see *novelté*.

MANADES: transhumant mixed herds.

MANANTS: villeins.

MANNSCHAFT: homage (German Empire).

MANUS: according to Roman law, authority belonging to the husband, father, master over slaves, etc.

MAQAMA: an eastern literary genre consisting of encounters between different social types, enabling the audience to draw a simple moral.

MARABOTIN, MARAVEDIS: coin, generally gold, struck in the Christian states of Spain, in imitation of the dinars of the Maghrib and circulating in the Mediterranean.

MARRANOS: Jews living around the Mediterranean, apparently converted to Christianity but continuing to practise their faith in secret.

Glossary

MESNIE: the group of relatives, domestics, clients and servants of a ruler or kin-group.

MESTA: association of transhumant stock-breeders (Castile).

MEZZADRIA: 'ad medietatem', half-share tenure (sharecropping).

MORE DANICO: 'in the Danish manner', Scandinavian customs, with particular reference to private life, especially legalised concubinage.

MORGENGABE: 'morning gift': a grant from husband to wife after their wedding night.

MUDAE: Venetian merchant fleet (generally two a year) escorted by warships.

MUNTMANNEN: 'men with little': mendicants, destitute.

MUNZ: coinage, and by extension, the right to strike it, also the mint; *moneta.*

NIZARITES: an extremist Egyptian Shi'ite sect which, after breaking away from the Fatimids, sought refuge in the Lebanon.

NOMISMA: Byzantine gold coin.

NOVELTÉS: any change or new demand introduced by a lord; see *malsusos.*

NUNDINAE: fairs.

ODAL: allod.

OPOLE: neighbourhood association in Slav regions; by extension, the district where such an association was established.

ORDO: text of a ritual ceremony such as a royal, imperial or episcopal consecration.

ORTS, ORTICELLI: see *horts.*

OSCULUM: a kiss on the mouth, the kiss of peace, exchanged between lord and vassal.

ÖSTERLINGEN: 'men of the east', i.e. the German merchants from the Baltic who were so called in London.

OYLATA: holdings planted with olive-trees.

PANNI: large cloths.

PARAGE: an association between equals; refers in the first place to associations between lords, whether related to each other or not, for the administration and exploitation of property; can refer simply to a business agreement.

PAROIKOI: free peasants in the Byzantine Empire who fell under the fiscal and economic control of the rich.

PARIAS: tributes imposed on the Muslims by Spanish rulers in exchange for military protection or for being left undisturbed.

PATARII, PATARINES: 'rag-pickers', beggars; term originally applied insultingly to those who protested against the corruption of the Milanese Church, later applied to any marginal figures whether orthodox (umiliati) or heretic (cathars).

PAZIERS: villagers appointed by their fellows to maintain the local 'peace' and, where necessary, to collect the fines of justice and dues.

PEONES: village foot-soldiers (Spain).

PERRON: large stone staircase from which the lord gave judgement.

PFAFFENSTRASSE: the 'priests' road', i.e. the Rhine, so called because of the many episcopal cities and abbeys along its banks.

PLESSIS, PLOICUM, PLOUY: an enclosure circled by a hedge or palisade.

POBLADOR: settler.

POBLACIONES: establishment or repopulation of villages in 'reconquered' Spanish territory; by extension, the franchises granted to the inhabitants.

PODESTÀ: imperial agent in Italy, originally German, then Italian and later of any origin, entrusted with keeping watch over the city fortress.

POLIDION: Greek village.

PONTIFES: associations of lay people who took it upon themselves to build bridges as a work of piety for which they were content to receive alms.

POTACIO: annual banquet of a pious or professional association.

PRÉVÔT; PRÉVÔTE: royal administrative and fiscal official; district subject to his control.

PROASTEIA: estates in Byzantium.

PRONOIA: in the Byzantine Empire, land, revenues and people granted unconditionally, usually to a magnate or military leader.

PROSTASIA: the exercise of patronage over peasants, on condition of paying a tax.

PSYCHOMACHIA: 'the combat of the vices and the virtues'; from the work of Prudentius (fifth century) onwards, a literary and iconographical theme of great appeal in the Middle Ages, with a strongly moralising strain; the *Romance of the Rose* is a notable late example.

QUADERNI: land made up of territories roughly divided into squares (Italy).

QUESTA: tax paid for protection; can refer to a variety of banal levies on the part of a lord.

QUINT: a fifth; customary portion of a succession tax.

QUOTIDIANI: domestic slaves or serfs subject to strict control.

RAT, RATHAUS: town council, town hall (Empire).

REALENGUM: royal lands in Spain.

REGALIA: totality of rights and the revenues stemming from them which formed the basis of royal authority.

REICHSGUT: imperial lands.

REICHSKIRCHENSYSTEM: 'imperial church system'; the incorporation of high-ranking churchmen into the royal administration in Ottonian and Salian Germany.

RELIEF, VERLIEF, KOOP: the rights to succession or inheritance taxes, particularly on feudal lands.

RIBA: property rent in Muslim law.

RIBAT: pious Muslim communities consisting of men gathered together in a form of fortified monastery from which they could launch missions or expeditions in a holy war.

ROCCA: natural mound with a tower on it.

ROGATA: levies of banal lordship.

ROMFAHRT: military service required by the emperor on his expeditions to Italy.

RONCIN: pack-horse demanded for war service as a substitute for serving in the host.

SAKE, SOKE: rights of jurisdiction (Anglo-Saxon England).

SALVAMENTUM: seigneurial protection; the area subject to it.

SCABINI: see *boni homines.*

SCHULTHEISS: German mayor; agent who undertakes exploitation of new lands; see *locator.*

Glossary

SCRIPTORIUM: writing-room, originally where the monks gathered to copy out manuscripts.

SEPHARDIM: Spanish or Portuguese Jews, whose interpretation of the sacred texts was less strict than that of the Ashkenazim.

SEQUIN: Venetian gold coin, the ducat; name derives from the Zecca, the city's mint and arsenal.

SERRANOS: mountain-dwellers, initially referring to inhabitants of the Pyrenees, later extended to anyone to the north of Spain who came to repopulate the lands conquered from the Muslims.

SHARIʾA: the Holy Law of Islam.

SICARII: thugs (Italy).

SKALAI: Greek business centres, generally devoted to the sale of cereals.

SOPRACORPO: the portion of a commercial association's capital provided by contributors outside the family.

SORS: the capital share provided by a 'shareholder' in a commercial contract.

SPICARIA: public granary; can also refer to a family store.

STABBAU: a structure made from planks.

STRATEIA: compulsory military service, which eventually became a purely fiscal obligation.

STUBE: the meeting-place for members of a confraternity or guild, where the annual banquet was held.

STUDIUM GENERALE: refers to the major centres of learning, before the period of the universities, where scholars could go beyond the liberal arts and study law and theology.

SUNNI: those who recognised the historical caliphate as legitimate, the majority in Islam; they claimed to follow the tradition (*sunna*) of the Prophet.

SUPANIS: in Slav lands, clan chieftains and wealthy landowners.

SYNDICS: in Mediterranean regions, those villagers nominated to supervise the legal or fiscal privileges granted by the lord.

TAGESSCHALK: domestic servant obliged to perform daily *corvée*.

TAILLE, TALLAGE: money levy, see *exactio*.

TARI, TARINOS: silver coins, occasionally gold ones, issued in the Mediterranean by Muslims and later copied by the Normans in Sicily and by some Spanish rulers.

TASCA: banal levy (southern France); can refer to several types of tax.

TAVOLA: money-changer's table.

TERTIARE: agricultural practice of ploughing land three times before sowing.

TERTARTERA: devalued version of the *nomisma*.

THEME: military unit and territory.

THEOW: Anglo-Saxon or Scandinavian slave.

TROBADOR, TROUBADOUR, TROUVÈRE: poet, especially a singer and musician who recited and performed the lyrical and epic songs of southern France.

TRUSTE: sworn association; can refer to an urban group, a craft, a dynasty.

TYPIKON: foundation charters of a Byzantine monastery.

VALI: provincial governor in Muslim Spain.

VERLIEF: see *relief*.

VIRIDARIA: orchards encircling towns in Mediterranean regions.

WASSERBURG: term used of aristocratic building on a modest scale, surrounded by ditches but not necessarily raised on a motte.

WATERINGEN: village associations responsible for inspecting the condition of dykes and land reclaimed from the sea.

WEISTUMER: synallagmatic (mutually obligatory) texts drawn up between a village community and its lord to establish their obligations and the limits to them.

WIEC: federation of Slav tribes.

ZECCA: see *sequin*.

ZEUGARIATOS: Byzantine peasant possessing only one plough-team.

The resurrection of the dead. The year 1000, burdened with millenarian fears of the end of the world, also saw the dawning of a new era: the awakening of the West. (The *Pericopes Book* of Henry II, from the early eleventh century, Abbey of Reichenau; Munich, Bayerische Staatsbibliothek.)

Introduction

'Some flickerings in the night', 'a dark age', 'a time of blood and terror': the tenth century has certainly had a bad reputation among Western historians. In studying it they are all too conscious of the lack of documents – the medievalist's daily bread. Behind it they can still make out the fading brightness of the Carolingian Renaissance; ahead glimmers a promising dawn; between these two points lies a sombre transition period, made darker by the splendours of the Islamic world and Constantinople, then at their dazzling zenith. How can we avoid the romantic image, that image of 'the terrors of the millennium', when an entire people, cowering before a wrathful God, seemed to await the inevitable ending of time, the millennium of the birth or crucifixion of Jesus? The other temptation to be avoided is imagining that any development whose origins are obscure can safely be assigned to this period.

But this 'transition' cannot be both a negative time of darkness and a source of renewal: we have to make a choice. Contemporaries, short-sighted as always, hesitated; the writers were clerics and we should be wary of their bias; the few nuanced judgements strike us all the more forcibly. 'The approach of Judgement Day', 'an ageing world in its death-throes', 'the last moments of humankind' – so some proclaimed. But others: 'a radiant morning rose upon the world', 'a delight for humankind', and the famous phrase of the Burgundian monk, Raoul Glaber, whom one cannot avoid quoting: 'The world then shook off the dust from its old vestments, and the earth was covered in a white robe of churches.' The same author, we note, then goes on to write of the horrible famine of 1033 when cannibalism was reported in Tournus. Today the problem is resolved: if texts are uncertain, excavations do not deceive; if genealogists balk at the 'gulf of oblivion' between 900 and 950, archaeologists find in that space the erecting of castles, the coming together of people as seen in new cemeteries, the rebuilding of walls and urban districts and, thanks to the pollen analysis of samples from peat bogs, the reappearance, sometimes the origins, of plants useful to man; thus it is not merely intellectual sloth that makes us suspect that the roots of medieval Europe go deep into this black hole.

The 'true' Middle Ages

This conviction is recent; it is shared by historians of land-use, by archaeologists, and by economists. But why does it not command universal assent, even where it originated, in

1

Germany, in Italy and in southern France? Because it denies the continuity which is seemingly manifested in private institutions, spiritual forces and political organisms, the study of which has for more than a century been the main concern of traditional historiography; because it is based on 'humble' objects such as agricultural tools, little cottages, rubble and skeletons, rather than on the wars of kings and the holiness of bishops; above all, because it has reduced the Carolingian experiment to an episode without a sequel; this is a bitter blow for those attached to Charlemagne's 'Palace School', an especially unkind cut for Germany. Excavations in the Rhineland, Franconia and elsewhere seem designed to cut Karl der Grosse down to size.

This is thus our first problem: is there continuity in the West between the great attempt at stabilisation and growth in the period 750–850 and the indisputable 'century of great progress' of, say, 1020–1150, the prelude to the apogee of medieval Europe in the following hundred years? It seems impossible to say that there was no continuity, especially in those fields of research dear to earlier generations of medievalists: the form of the written word, the rules of law, the Christian message, the memory of Antiquity and the prestige of royalty. That is why, in the previous volume, our account ranged beyond the deposition of the Carolingians, beyond the foundation of Cluny and the Viking and Hungarian raids. But even when novelties strike us, links can be traced right back to the early medieval period – for example, in the practice of commendation, in family structures and in merchants' activities. Nevertheless, at this stage there was, as George Duby says, no more than a 'surface agitation'; it would be unreasonable to make the meagre land clearances of the ninth century the precursors of the explosion of food production in the twelfth century; to see in the Carolingian 'villa' the ancestor of the seigneurial estate would be nonsense in economic terms, and probably in legal ones. Links? Certainly, because what humankind has created never dies away completely. Origins? No, because the quantitative difference in effort requires that we look for a cause other than natural progression.

That is why this account must change its pace. Up to this point, there was very little indication of the birth, let alone the triumph, of an infant Western Europe; the eye was drawn to the Levant, where there was still evidence of Romanisation, then it focused on Islam, Hellenism and the civilisation of Persia; in the West a first glance revealed only mediocrity and ruins. It is true that new blood was flowing through this great wounded body, but that was not apparent; it is also true that Europe suddenly reasserted itself for a time, but 900 saw it prostrate once more. So we had to look first to the East. But after 900, with the advantage of hindsight, we must shift our gaze back to the West. We are forced to do this by the plan of these volumes – to show the gradual reorganisation of the ancient worlds around Western Europe – and now we are on the threshold of this process. Of course darkness did not fall over all the East at once: Firdawsi, Avicenna, Averroes, Ibn Khaldun himself, not to mention the masterpieces of Isfahan, Granada, Palermo and Delhi, all post-date the tenth century; and an anaemic Byzantium could still produce Michael Psellos and Anna Komnena, Mistra and the manuscripts of Mount Athos. Nevertheless, in Western Europe the torch of expansion was lit; shaking itself free from its dependent posture, Western Christendom rediscovered its vitality. The 'true' Middle Ages had begun.

2

The miller and his mill. ('The Mystical Mill', capital at Vézelay, twelfth century.)

Where is the cause to be found?

So much is easily said, but problems remain. For if the West gradually took centre stage, and if this was not merely a logical progression from the early Middle Ages (a late offspring of *Romanitas* after the Carolingian still-birth), we have to find a cause or causes for this development. I mentioned this in the first pages of these volumes; the time has come to return to the matter.

The genius of the Celts, the Germans and the Scandinavians is well known; not too long ago, this genius was loudly proclaimed, even as its weaknesses were glaringly exposed. But this sort of explanation is worthy only of a Boulainvilliers or a Rosenberg; some other cause must be sought for its relatively late appearance compared to the genius of the Greeks, Persians and Indians. That population pressure stimulated a spirit of enterprise and led to possession of the land, or to a quest for sufficient living space, is undeniable; it is in fact one of the most fruitful new aspects of the period; but it is obviously only a secondary cause. Our enquiry must go deeper: why was there an increase in births and a decline in the mortality rate? The mastery of water and of the fires of the forge was undoubtedly the source of that perfecting of tools which permitted an increase in production, not to mention the practical improvements in animal traction and ploughs which historians of the 1930s, such as Lefebvre des Noettes, were tempted to look upon as the source of Western Europe's superiority. But it is always risky to rely on mechanical causes to explain

3

one culture's predominance over another; only the social or economic context can explain such success. Moreover, archaeology and a broader and more detailed examination of written sources have since clarified the problem: the mould-board plough, shoeing horses, watermills – these were all old; the earliest material evidence – horseshoes, asymmetrical ploughshares, blast furnaces – dates from the eighth, ninth and tenth centuries, but has been dug up in Bohemia, Moravia and Silesia, regions which certainly did not take a lead in the economic efflorescence of the young Europe. Furthermore, such laboriously constructed forges and mills did not become widespread until some time after 900 and they scarcely appeared before 950 or 980 in even such economically precocious regions as Catalonia, the Auvergne, Burgundy and northern Italy – in any case *after* the restructuring of society. So we must place technical progress among the effects of change rather than among the causes.

Even before this hypothesis was discarded – scarcely thirty years ago – researchers were aware that it involved a question fundamental to human history, and had turned their gaze outwards. Devotees of the 'classical' Mediterranean, together with believers in 'eastern influences', advanced the idea of imitation: the West was the child of the East. This hypothesis cannot be taken seriously for many reasons, of which three will suffice here: as in the above case of technology, a spirit of enterprise or borrowed skills can take root successfully only in hospitable soil; secondly, part of the European efflorescence, for example in naval weaponry, techniques in metallurgy, and the balancing of food supplies, could not possibly have been imitated from the Mediterranean world; and lastly, contact with the scientific heritage of the ancient world, mediated through Islam, remained very rudimentary between the time of Isidore of Seville in the sixth century and the twelfth century. There were few pilgrims from the West, few travellers from the East, only a bookish culture that remained inaccessible for a long time. Until the attempts at translation and adaptation initiated by Constantine the African, Bernard of Chartres and Peter the Venerable between 1090 and 1130, Western education was based on what had been established for centuries; there was nothing new here, or at least nothing that dates from the tenth century.

Perhaps the economic impetus came from the outside, rather than from within. We know that in formulating the idea, new for its time, that the loss of the Mediterranean had affected Europe adversely, Henri Pirenne bequeathed the controversial but fertile hypothesis of a rupture between Antiquity and the Middle Ages, an hypothesis which is now accepted. He placed this, however, in the eighth century, attributing it to the conquests of Islam pushing the West back to its own lands and forcing it to draw on its own resources for its development. It was Muhammad who created Charlemagne. While the idea of such a break is accepted, we no longer share Pirenne's valuation of its effects as negative; there is too much evidence to the contrary – for example, the persistence of links with southern lands, or the chronological gap between the theoretical 'impact' of the Muslim conquest and the practical effects of the Western renewal. Some forty years ago, however, Maurice Lombard reversed this view while retaining the idea of a north–south relationship, positive this time, and put forward the idea that Europe's flourishing was due to an 'injection' of Islamic gold which gave an initial impetus to the European economy; for good measure, the

Scandinavian and Polish lands were later seen as playing a key role, by relaying the Muslim gold north and east. Unfortunately the gold in question is amongst the very rarest finds of Western Christendom, and written sources are silent on the subject. To put the circulation of money before agricultural development is, given the economic conditions of the time, to put the cart before the horse.

It is best, then, to seek the original spark within Europe itself. A few years ago, Georges Duby, carefully sifting earlier theories, proposed an explanation that is both reasonable and plausible. There was in fact a sharp break at the end of the tenth century, because it is there that all the modern tools of research locate the dawning of the new era. But the break was not quite complete, for two main reasons. First, the Scandinavian and Mediterranean centres of gravity continued to exert their influence through their staging-posts – Catalonia, southern Italy, the Adriatic, the Danubian axis, the Russian waterways from the Baltic to Novgorod and on to Byzantium. Secondly, the Carolingian experience cannot be ignored; the process of launching raids and the consequent assembling of subjects constituted a sort of accumulation of men and resources, including precious metals, without which the later explosion cannot be explained. In explaining this acceleration of the process of 'taking off', Duby stresses the essential importance of the establishment of a period of calm in Europe, the first one of significant duration there since the incessant 'movement of peoples' from the third to the tenth century. Since what has been or will be said about the Eastern world – in its turn torn apart and trampled on after the tenth century by the Turks, the Bulgars, the Moors, the Pechenegs, the Sudanese and the 'Franks' – shows that these upheavals brought destruction and disorder, and resulted in the slow ebbing of Eastern influence, the different outcome of similar events in the West shows the sound nature of the explanation given above concerning Europe.

Climate

So I shall adopt this explanation. But it is easy to see that it is not absolutely satisfactory. First of all because we must find the reasons for this interlude of 'peace', and then because the first regions to awaken were in fact not the most peaceful: Spain, northern and peninsular Italy. Moreover, the sequence of peace (increased production, improved tools, rise in population, commercial expansion) looks more convincing on paper than it did on the ground in the eleventh century, where the historian can perceive so many clashes and contradictions. Thus our theory offers only an outline, perhaps more satisfactory than any other, but it is still only a theory.

Can we find a better one? Frankly, given the current state of research, we cannot. But we had better add certain facts to our dossier: the North Atlantic route leading from Scandinavia to Iceland and Greenland was free of ice by the end of the ninth century, and the same was perhaps true of Labrador, if we can trust the sagas which refer to the colonisation of Iceland after 840, the herds of cattle from the 'green land' (Greenland), and indeed to expeditions as far as 'Vinland'. And these are not imaginary, because eleventh-century runes have been found at latitude 72°N on the Baffin coast. The Swiss glaciers of

5

Introduction

Aletsch and Grindelwald, or the Fernau glacier in the Tyrol, in the course of their powerful advance from the sixteenth to the nineteenth century crushed conifers and broad-leaved trees which their present retreat has revealed in abandoned moraines, and which have been dated to between the tenth and twelfth centuries – a period when the Alpine forest regained those areas which in the early Middle Ages had been covered in ice. The thawing of this ice corresponds, with an inevitable time-lag, to the incursions of the sea, that is, to the encroachment of the sea on land. In Flanders, geographers and historians such as A. Verhulst have combed the sources in order to tabulate the waters' retreat, apparent in the ninth century and the early tenth century. They have also noted the phases of the 'third Dunkirk encroachment', perceptible at the beginning of the eleventh century (Emma, the queen of England, could sail right to Bruges itself in 1037), growing in the twelfth century and combated by means of drainage and dykes, despite sudden sea-flooding (*zeegang*), as occurred in 1134. Are there other, similar signs? Excavations of villages now under way in Franconia, the upper Rhineland and southern England show variations in the level of the water-table, whose fall, from the seventh to the ninth century, led to the abandonment of early medieval sites, and whose rise, in the eleventh and twelfth centuries, corresponds to fixed settlement. Palaeo-botanical excavations, increasing in Belgium and Germany these days, insufficiently used in France, provide us with evidence of the effects of such movement in the variation of species of trees and in the appearance of cereal pollens.

I am sure that the reader has seen my final observation coming: the above evidence convincingly shows that long-term climatic change affected the northern hemisphere, at least, from the tenth century onward. Its effects on central Europe seem to have been positive: a rise in the water levels, soils broken down, regular periods of sunshine; perhaps, further south, they were negative: the development of deserts and of the arid plains of the Maghrib, Spain and Sicily. Climatic experts relate these variations to phases of solar activity: the sun is subject, we know, to periods of intense emissions of electrons and positive ions, those 'spots' and persistent outcrops on its surface. While the Europeans – even the Muslims – were unable to maintain regular observation of these phenomena before the sixteenth century – especially because of their conviction, at once Aristotelian and religious, that celestial bodies could not suffer 'corruption' – these anomalies were noted in Asia, for example in the Korean Ko-rynsa. Thus over four centuries, from 950 to 1350, twenty-nine decades out of forty showed an average solar activity lower than normal, while in the preceding 300 years there were only nine such decades. However, the effects visible to people on earth from discharges in the ionosphere, described as 'veils of fire', 'tears of blood', 'dragons', etc., and noted in chronicles, are less numerous in historical literature of the tenth and twelfth centuries than in the Carolingian era. Today it is supposed that these variations in activity, caused during the crossing of dark zones in the universe by the sun and earth, lead to a displacement of atmospheric currents at a very high altitude, and thus to variations in temperature and rainfall over the land. The phase of climatic regularity from 900 to 1250, when the weather was good and relatively dry, undoubtedly favoured the ripening of food crops and use of the forests. Here the geographers stop. It is up to the historians, if they dare, to draw conclusions to explain a whole phase of human endeavour, which is my intention.

It will thus be necessary to focus our attention on the European peninsula, which was finally emerging from a long period in the womb, and it seems right, as I attempted with the remains of the Roman heritage, to set out an inventory of what we can see there.

Gathering together

The establishment of a way of life that lasted, come what may, for six centuries and linked the Ancien Régime to the Middle Ages, has always impressed historians of this period; patterns of rural and urban lordship were set at this time. Obviously and undeniably this novel system had such a complex genesis, varied so much according to region and basically is so little understood that we must pause here for a while. Nevertheless for many decades historians have been all too quick to settle the problem; one invokes the decline of the 'State', another the retreat to small territorial units, although no one knows why they were henceforth considered the only governable kind; a third does not hesitate to denounce the mores of the time and the 'trahison des clercs'. Yet none of this is satisfactory. After a decade of archaeological work in northern Europe, and of long-overdue examination of the archives of the south (often even older than those of the north), these explanations have been relegated to the level of subsidiary causes. What now strikes us and justifies us in identifying this as the main break in Western history, is the gathering together and settlement of populations.

In showing us that halls and huts in Yorkshire, Hampshire, Thuringia, the Harz and Westphalia, or the cemeteries of the early Middle Ages, isolated on the fringe of the community, ceased to be occupied between the eighth and tenth centuries, archaeology has given us proof of the break between a rootless type of habitation, flimsy and temporary, and what we call a 'village', grouped around the dead and a religious place that is henceforth also fixed, 'the white robe of churches' described by Raoul Glaber. Of course this assemblage could occur around a venerable sacred site, in some cases very near an ancient ruin or a Carolingian *villa*; what counts is the coming together and settling down. The problem of toponomy need scarcely detain us; the name given to a group of huts follows its successive moves and sticks to it, especially if it is taken from the name of a person or totem. Such a name tells us how that group recognises itself rather than where it lives. For a long time it was thought that such a practice could only concern 'wild', 'barbarian' areas, and that in the ideal *Romania* of its admirers everything ran along ordained lines. Unfortunately, Brittany and Gaul, under the scalpels of the excavators, have passed into the other camp; worse than that, where archaeology falters the researchers into French and Italian sources have shown us that the entire system of land-use and its Christian layout, *corti* and *massae*, *pievi* and *oracula* from the sixth to the eighth century, was shattered and disappeared, right in the heart of the Romanised West.

I think, without taking sides, that we have to admit that populations were entirely resettled. I acknowledge that there was enormous variation in practice, which allows some

7

historians to cling on to the idea of continuity. In one case there will be a controlled settlement, accompanied by the siting of a village on a hill – the *incastellamento* characteristic of central Italy and Provence; in another, the 'cellularisation' will occur more spontaneously, around a *rocca* in Languedoc or Lombardy, a *castelion* in southern Italy; elsewhere it will be a new creation, sometimes the settling of immigrants, but more often the coming together of the inhabitants of some scattered hamlets, forming a *castelnau* in Aquitaine, an *aldea* in Castile, a *bourg* in Normandy or Poitou, and a *burh* in England; in more northerly regions, this settlement will take the form of a crystallisation around a *curtis*, a *Hof*, a 'manor' larger than the others, often already possessed of a chapel. And I am not even taking into account the German 'palaces', around which clustered workshops and cottages, *capmas* in the Auvergne, which absorbed some of the nearby dwellings, and above all the Scandinavian camps.

This particular phenomenon, so diverse, so important and so long-lasting, has marked our countrysides right up to the depopulations of the present; neither the short phase of readjustment in the fifteenth century, nor the way individual dwellings developed in the eighteenth century, altered this fundamental pattern. On the other hand, we cannot be certain about the chronology: 900–50 in Italy, at least a generation later in Provence and northern Spain, scarcely before 1020 or 1050 in south-west France and on the Atlantic coast of Europe. By contrast, developments were probably much earlier in England, the Rhineland (the ninth and early tenth centuries) and in my opinion, between 950 and 1000 in northern France, central Germany and Poland. In order to establish both a more accurate chronology and a firm typology we need to be better informed about the three obvious reference points for this settlement: cemeteries, churches and castles. Excavations of cemeteries, however, pose problems in that they often remain in use, and burial in wooden coffins or directly in the ground deprives us of many more human remains than there are for the early Middle Ages. With regard to churches, it is essential to know about the process of their construction, but in ninety cases out of a hundred, subsequent building has wiped out the evidence. Similarly, the lords' dwellings – the castles – were often built of wood on a mound of stones gathered for the purpose, and oblivion and fashion, if not an anxious monarch or a greedy peasant, have all too often seen them worn away or demolished.

Expansion

Demographic pressure in Europe cannot be measured, of course, until much later, in the fourteenth century, except in certain cases; even these provide only reference points, not a measure of development. So we have to assemble widely scattered evidence – fragments of genealogies, allusions in chronicles, witness lists, and archaeological investigations of burial grounds and the appearance of new sites – to get some idea of this development. I will return to this matter when we come to the mid-eleventh century, and the picture starts to become clearer. But in this period, the movement has certainly got under way everywhere: the key evidence is the breaking up of the old type of large familial structures, a change which antedates the appearance of Gregorian reform or the re-emergence of Roman law. We sense that the movement began in southern Europe, around 970 or 990,

Settlement in the towns. Near Saint-Gaudens (Haute-Garonne), a circular salvamentum.

but the scarcity of written sources before 1025–50 is such that north of the Loire and the Danube one would hesitate to date it. The indications provided by the archives of Farfa, Bobbio, Santa Giulia in Brescia, Saint-Victor in Marseilles, Cluny, Saint-Julien de Brioude or Seo de Urgel are plain; but more than this we cannot say.

We have no idea as to whether this population growth was due to genetics or to some combination of causes. There was a drop in the mortality rate which may have been a result of the first respite from famine; nevertheless famine recurred throughout the eleventh century, as in the general famine of 1033, together with epidemics caused by nutritional deficiencies such as the typhus and scurvy epidemics of 1090 in Germany and Lotharingia. This would seem to indicate a continuing gap between potential production and need.

I mentioned the obvious link between this growth in population and family structure. Here is a second major trait of the history of the people of Europe: large organisational structures grouped into a *gens*, a *Geschlecht*, a clan, in which everyone was related by blood and sometimes also simply by duty – these were a reality in both legal and economic terms, which marked the whole of the early Middle Ages. Not that the married couple did not have its place, even its rights, especially lower down the social ladder; that is, the further one gets from the level where the defence of material interests or even moral ones required the solidarity of the entire family; but control over the couple was always maintained. Thus it was a novelty, which the Gregorian Church encouraged, to validate the autonomy of the couple, and thus of the woman. This was no trivial development in social history.

Moreover, if it is now legitimate to speak of Europe, it is because the expansion of its territory is evident henceforth. The entire northern section of the continent is absorbed into the body of Europe; undoubtedly there is evidence, in the tombs and treasures of Scania and Gotland that Iceland, the British Isles, the Danish straits and the lands of Baltic Russia were linked by intense activity in the ninth and tenth centuries, but this seems to have been quite separate from what was going on in Germany or the Low Countries. The trading posts set up on the Baltic shores, at Hedeby or Trelleborg for example, had an aggressive rather than a commercial function. However, between the conversion of St Olaf at the beginning of the eleventh century and the attachment of England to the Continent by the Norman Conquest in 1066, the British Isles and the northern seas were gradually absorbed into Europe. This was also the period in which the isolated Polish world, which had commenced a process of urbanisation and, in its *gorods*, the development of original craft industry, found itself brutally invaded by German settlers and nobles, and forcibly incorporated into western Christendom. By its very nature this process is uncertain, but without being specific we can say that in its expansion, from the first German attack over the Elbe around 985 up to the regaining of Toledo just 100 years later, the 'West' gained all around its perimeters a belt of lands that increased its extent by a half.

Stability

In approaching the third and last new characteristic in my picture, I am designedly using a controversial term. Actually, I think the time has come to explode the old cliché of 'feudal

The certainty of the Last Judgement: the weighing of souls. (Capital from Saujon, in the Saintonge, twelfth century.)

anarchy'. It is a 'Jacobin' concept, very strong in France, but almost unique to it, which identifies any period in which the power of the State is weakened as one of disorder and impotence; hence the exalted status of Rome and the Carolingians in the eyes of those who hold such a view. But this is to fail to see that a power is only real in so far as it is adapted to the physical, mental and social structures over which it claims to hold sway. In an essentially rural world, where even surplus produce could not travel far without improved means of communication, without local élites capable of maintaining generally accepted laws, and without reasonably accessible higher authorities, obviously horizons were narrow and real authority rested at a local level. However, it is exactly this restricted grouping – a few villages – which made up the 'seigneurie', a very tight social structure, and not until this was dissolved were State powers really restored. It would be quite erroneous to present these small human groups, turned in on themselves as they were, as merely cowering together in a state of fear and ignorance. They not only had active relations with neighbouring groups – and I have already mentioned this constant interchange – but they also grasped the existence of much larger groupings (counties, the king's authority, and the notion of a Christian world). Above all, they developed networks of horizontal association to strengthen the networks of vertical dependence, woven from fear, need and respect.

Associations built on piety, on blood-ties, but also on neighbourhoods, ways of getting a living, professional activity: we are moving away from the time when a man deprived of family or of recognised status was an outcast. He had the possibility of comfort, mutual assistance, a 'profession' in universities, of brotherhood under the 'banner' of his district. He was no longer simply from such-and-such a place, son of so-and-so; he was also a member of the Brotherhood of St Eloi, registered as a silversmith, a sworn citizen of Laon, client of the lords of Coucy, head of the St Vincent district, and perhaps also sergeant of the watch, brother of a canon, provided with a fief, etc. This is one example out of a thousand to be found above or below him on the social pyramid.

This very rigorously organised framework, much more restrictive than that around the alienated man of previous centuries, or the modern citizen, held in place – as long as the

11

notion of reciprocal service remained strong – a society conceived along lines very different from our own. It is this which makes it difficult for us to apply our own social criteria to the period from the tenth to the thirteenth century. The concept of 'orders', which we will shortly discuss, certainly takes account of the fundamental idea of the fixed place allotted by God to all men when he created the world, whose balance depends on each member carrying out his own task satisfactorily, to everyone's advantage. Conversely, the idea of 'class' is not useful with regard to groups that were undoubtedly intermingled, despite differences in origins, activities and interests; this has allowed too many historians, burdened with an outmoded vocabulary and determined to shut their eyes, to deny all 'class struggle' in this period. We never come across allusions to the dictatorship of the proletariat, declared R. Morghen confidently, as if it were 1890. This is why social movements, heretical or not, with or without specific aims, but which in any case were in opposition to the established order, must be examined and explained in the light of social demands, whether we are looking at a handful of intellectuals who were burnt at the stake or peasants who raped an estate-manager's daughter. Obviously once the principle of consensus was broken after the mid-thirteenth century, we can no longer doubt the nature of the 'emotions' that were unleashed.

One last remark: if this society held together it was also because it was steeped in a common moral attitude – we might be tempted to feel some nostalgia for this, but what good did it do that a Greek heresy should lead to a 'national' secession, or that the existence of Muslim rites should unleash a bloody settling of accounts? What henceforth separated West and East was a spiritual harmony that touched every aspect of life, in a way that was foreign to the East; this unity was to have its effect even in the sphere of art, and its expression as Romanesque, then as early Gothic, was to be one of the original manifestations of a morally independent Europe. Of course one can, in the name of intellectual progress, regret that the occasional 'heretical' movements did not much affect the faithful masses, and that they were the concern of isolated intellectuals, or that they had a social rather than a dogmatic content and merely wore the habit of doctrinal deviation. Nevertheless, if religious knowledge did not go very deep, spiritual knowledge was vast: from the oath, which was enough to bind a person absolutely, to the certainty of the Last Judgement, via general acceptance of the mysterious and unknowable, there was one Europe of which it can be said that, despite the traditional description, it cannot be called truly 'Christian', but that it arose from and believed in the sacred.

Façade of Saint-Etienne, Caen, one of the masterpieces of Anglo-Norman architecture. Built around 1070–80, in the second Romanesque period, it was part of the Abbaye aux Hommes founded by William the Conqueror. The horizontal alignment of the windows and the strong lines of the buttresses form a balanced base from which the towers spring up.

PART 1

Dawn in the West:
c. 950–*c.* 1100

Europe in the year 1000

Lévi-Strauss once said: 'If the West produces ethnographers, it should be racked by potent remorse, forcing it to confront its own image in that of quite different societies.' For some years now, we have gained a different impression of the Middle Ages, with characteristics that are most marked at the end of the period.

Nobles and peasants

At the end of the tenth century, power in the Frankish Empire, however divided that empire was, still seemed to belong to the characteristic social group of Carolingian civilisation – namely, the imperial aristocracy made up of some hundreds of families of Frankish, Swabian, or more rarely Saxon, origin, related to each other, and, at least for the more powerful among them, to the royal line.

The imperial group

These princely alliances were increased by polygamy on the part of the magnates, a custom that was practised openly despite the prohibitions of the Church. Thus the family of Boso, who was to be crowned king in Provence at the end of the ninth century, prided itself on having supplied women to the royal house for several generations. It was not until a century later that an unsympathetic cleric was to insist on the 'concubinary' aspect of their genealogy.

Another characteristic of the families of the *Reichsaristokratie* – as German historians have named it (and clearly shown by the *Libri Memoriales* (commemoration books) of abbeys in the Germanic lands) – was that the kinship-groups spread out into a large network of relationships, rather than a 'lineage' in the medieval and later sense of that term, that is, a kin-group strictly organised along the line of succession from male to male. We may wonder how far back the genealogical consciousness of these families could reach with any precision. Indeed, did they want to be particularly accurate? Without the support of written records, collective memory would quickly arrive at a time which was no longer historical, or even pseudo-historical, but legendary and mythical. The Hohenstaufen, even after their accession to the imperial office, knew only a few stages in their genealogy, but this scarcely mattered: an ancient mausoleum, which was in fact probably Roman, in their Weibelingen lands gave them the opportunity to trace themselves back, through one Clodius-Hlodio, to the legendary Merovingians. Similarly the Bishop of Bamberg, Gunther, proud of his name and family, had no need of a written genealogy to boast that he was a descendant of the Burgundian or Frankish kings from the *Nibelungenlied*. A warrior-bishop, he did not hesitate to lead an armed pilgrimage to the Holy Land, a forerunner of the Crusades which were to serve as an outlet for the energy and aggression of the all too pro-lific knightly families. Gunther's boldness was, in the eyes of his contemporaries, simply the confirmation of claims associated with the names which his family had chosen to bear throughout the tenth century: his own, which was that borne by a sixth-century Burgundian chieftain, the unlucky founder of the kingdom of Worms, and that of Siegfried, the Wälsung, King of Xanten. Such arrogance clashed with the pride of the Carolingian line, in so far as these families claimed to equal or surpass it. Prestigious names, therefore, according to individual preference were shared out amongst all such families like a common inheritance, according to their alliances.

The cohesion of this class obviously had a material foundation in what, paradoxically, incited bitter internal rivalries: the offices of the Empire, the government of some province, the command of some frontier, or the mastery of some great abbey. The competing ambi-tions of the magnates led them into intricate manoeuvrings through which, supported by their kin and friends, they sought in turn to dominate Paris or the Viennois, Bavaria or Burgundy, Lombardy or Alsace, the Auvergne or Catalonia. The official and unofficial annals, composed in the great northern churches, limit the nobility to that social class alone, and in fact scarcely refer to any other class. This is not surprising, since we are dealing with the discourse of Frankish kingship, modelled and remodelled by clerical members of the *Reichsaristokratie*, habitués of the palace where they foregathered almost every year. Medieval historiography has long been the victim, and sometimes the willing victim, of this Carolingian self-centredness, supposing the history of the period to be merely the story of the exploits and crimes of the Roberts, Bosos, Williams and three – or is it four? – Bernards. Far behind them, in the background, there are a few supporting actors, their loyal clientele or humble followers. There is no mention of the peasants, con-

A princely alliance. Rudolf, Count of Rheinfelden, then Duke of Swabia in 1057, married Mathilda, sister of Emperor Henry IV. When the latter came into conflict with Pope Gregory VII, Rudolf rose up and was elected King of Germany (1077). After several victories, he was killed at the battle of Merseburg in 1080. (Tomb slab in Merseburg Cathedral.)

sidered by the aristocratic authors of the annals and capitularies as the faceless mass of 'the poor', fit for protection and succour, an object of their generosity and charity and thus subject to their power. This was the result of ideological blindness, and ideological necessity.

The upheavals of the tenth century were to dispel this illusion, or at least to make it less tenable; as the Empire disintegrated and the class which claimed to govern it fragmented and 'regionalised', the haughty voices of the aristocratic annalists fell silent. They were replaced by lesser figures, hagiographers or local chroniclers, less lofty but often sharper observers of social reality. Their texts give the nobility a rather different image from that imposed on us by the annals – indeed, a variety of images.

Aspects of the nobility

In fact, images of the aristocracy differ from region to region, and it is unlikely that this is a matter of historical chance. In the land that appears in contemporary texts as 'Francia', which may be very roughly defined as being between the Seine and the Rhine, and in 'Frankish' Burgundy between Autun, Mâcon and Langres, lived many lesser nobles, whether as warriors installed to garrison the estates of the great ecclesiastical immunities, as clients of the magnates, or as petty independent lords whose only service to the magnates consisted in being governors or counts of the lands where they resided. Thus, at Saint-Riquier in Ponthieu, the eleventh-century chronicler thought that the abbey's vassals belonged to the nobility in the Carolingian period, and this sentiment was shared by the people, because the chapel in which they gathered was called the Chapel of the Nobles. At the Abbey of Waulsort, in the diocese of Liège, the same social group had its own 'cemetery of the nobles'. When the early tenth-century author of the *Miracles of Saint-Bertin* wrote about those men who 'commended themselves' to lords and thus became their vassals (because they did not have enough family land of their own), he incorporated the two social levels in a single term – 'the nobility of the land'. The same lesser nobility can be found in Burgundy. A serf of the Abbey of Fleury, in the Orléanais, ran away. He grew prosperous, and styled himself a free man. He married a woman whom the author of the *Miracles of St Benedict* described as 'noble'. But the abbot of Fleury laid claim to him as a serf, and it was decided that the case would be settled by trial by combat. The serf, either because he was a poor fighter or because he was frightened of God (who always gave victory to the just side) tried to confound the champion sent by the monastery by reversing roles. He claimed that the latter was not a free man and thus unfit to fight. The champion replied indignantly, 'I am free, and in fact from an old noble line. I'll teach you how much Benedict enjoys God's favour.' The boundary between these petty nobles and the dependent peasantry was so fine that we can come across some astonishing cases. For example, at the end of the tenth century a knight was in dispute with the Abbey of Saint-Bertin over a rich property in the region of Beauvais. He claimed to have inherited it from a man whose heir he proclaimed himself to be, 'by the bond of kinship, and above all because he had been his serf'.

For many people, it was at this level that social boundaries operated: on one side were all the free men, that is, all the nobles. Nobility was freedom and both were constantly under threat. This was a very old, undeniably Germanic tradition. It speaks through the writer who relates the origins of the Lombards; in his account of how they had always remained independent despite their small numbers, he writes, 'they had fought for the glory of liberty'. Nobility at this level, among the Franks, was less a matter of being connected with the royal house than of courage and independence. Alliances and connections followed on from that, as a reward for bravery displayed.

By contrast, in the Midi the circle of the nobility appears to have been much more restricted. Catalonia offers a good example of this. There, nobility was granted only to the great lords, descendants of the Romano-Gothic aristocracy and members of the comital assembly. This was the general trend south of the Loire, with the exception of the small property-holders who still lived in towns. Just as in Roman law, there was a distinction between nobility and freedom. For here nobility was rooted in the memory of the great Gallo-Roman families, who had formerly been able to send at least one of their members to sit in the Senate in Rome, and who, therefore, long after the fall of the Eternal City, were known as senatorial families. In the provincial assemblies presided over by the Frankish ruler, the impoverished descendants of this senatorial nobility strove to preserve their 'Roman' character, whatever that term had come to mean. When the Frankish Empire finally broke up in the tenth century, these 'princes of the provinces' reassumed the old titles of Roman officialdom, such as *illustris* and *clarissimus*, as well as, to some extent, the names of their ancestors – Pons, Calixtus, Maurice, Abello, to mention only the most venerable.

Their consciousness of being aristocratic was heightened by the fact of literacy, which gave it a much stricter form than that assumed in the north. Chance has preserved for us a genealogical fragment, used by an eleventh-century forger of the Abbey of Saint-Yrieix in the Limousin to lend credence to an alleged grant to his monastery. Here six generations are traced out with precision, from the fifth to the seventh century, where almost everyone bears the traditional names of the senatorial aristocracy; where appropriate, those who were bishops or martyrs are carefully picked out. Two centuries later, a great landowner in the Auvergne, Gerald of Aurillac, describing himself as from Aquitaine, counted among his ancestors two sixth-century nobles, Ariès of Limoges and Caesarius of Arles. Other clues, small as they are, are no less revealing. In early tenth-century Provence, there was a great family which held most of its lands north of the Ventoux, in the region now called les Baronnies, though some of these lands belonged to the Abbey of Nyons. The eleventh-century descendants took their surnames from this area: Mirabel, Montauban, Mévouillon. They were also known as the princes of Orange, since they held power in that town, and the dazzling fortune of that name is well known. In the tenth century, one son of the family was customarily given the name Pons. This name echoes that of a very old abbey, founded on the ruins of the old city of Cimiez and restored in the tenth century, where rested the body of one St Pons. Maria Rusticula, the seventh-century abbess of Nyons, had made a special cult of him, and had brought his relics to Arles. But further up the Rhône, in Vienne, there was a legend that Pontius (Pons) Pilate had come, repentant, to the city to end his days there. The significance of a name as illustrious as this for the tenth-century Provençal lords is easy to comprehend.

Such scattered allusions to a past with nothing Frankish about it are not only found in far corners of the Midi. Thus, the counts of Anjou, who came from the Gâtinais, and whose names and ancestors – where these are known – reveal their connection with the imperial aristocracy, claimed as their ancestors a local man, that is a noble of the region, rather than a high aristocrat of the royal entourage. The name of this forebear, Tertullus, again evokes the Gallo-Roman period. It is equally curious to see the efforts made by the followers of these counts, installed by them in the castle of Amboise, to establish a connection with one Sulpicius 'Mille Boucliers' (of the Thousand Shields), despite its violating the principle of patrilineal descent. The nobility of this figure, in these regions of the Loire, irresistibly called to mind the ancient senatorial family of the Sulpicii of Bourges, and Sulpicius Severus, the aristocratic biographer of St Martin of Tours.

Naturally these ancestors, even if they did exist historically, had a legendary aspect. But the social model which they offered, and which the best of their descendants among the lay aristocracy strove to imitate, was one of order and moderation, not of prowess in battle. The life of Gerald of Aurillac or the tale of the lords of Amboise speak a very different language from the heroic violence which is the substance of so many Germanic or Scandinavian sagas. What makes for sanctity and nobility in these texts is a blend of outward moderation – a sense of proportion and of law – and of inward detachment which recalls the stoicism of the ancient Roman nobility. Above all, their disgust with violence and their distaste for blood, along with their interest in letters, made such figures typical of the southern aristocracy, and baffled their northern contemporaries, in whose eyes they were neither clerks nor laymen: Gerald, the founder of the Abbey of Aurillac, who was admired so much by that 'Romanised' Frank Odo, abbot of Cluny; or Peter, 'clerk from the Auvergne, of the highest family, rich in offices', described with a fascination equal to Odo's by Bernard, master of the school of Angers:

That year, as I was returning from Rome, this same Peter was also returning, surrounded as usual by an escort of his nobles riding excellent mules, with their kingly trappings . . . He had red hair, was of medium height, broad-shouldered, and gave a general impression of agility. He followed the extreme custom of many of his countrymen who, although they are generally moderate in their habits, wear a beard with their short hair. And because he was bearded, I did not take him for a clerk.

But Peter's learning alerted Bernard: 'I asked him if he were a clerk; he replied that he was an abbot. People like him are called abbots not because they are monks, but because they control abbeys.' The rest of the story shows, on the one hand, Peter's involvement in the secular world of his time – he had numerous knights at his command and was exposed to frequent attacks from no less numerous enemies – and, on the other, the distance which he maintained between himself and that world. Although he was brave, a good soldier and 'broad-shouldered', he preferred to give his enemies the slip rather than to fight them. This affable lord did not enjoy fighting. It was a task for lesser individuals. Here we are at the opposite pole from the world where Gunther of Bamberg, albeit a bishop, enjoyed listening to the songs of the heroic exploits of Dietrich the Amal in preference to the Psalms.

As long as these cultural models remained opposed, and nobility did not mean the same thing for everyone, it is difficult to speak of a fusion of these two aristocracies, one of which continued to bear the name of Franks, however inaccurately, while the other insisted on being called Roman or Aquitainian. Nevertheless, a process of fusion did take place. Let us now turn to its elements, before attempting to assess the results.

Fusion

Among the southern nobles, a key element in this process was the undeniable 'Frankicising' of their names. The significance of this phenomenon becomes clear when we see what names were taken over in this way: Gerald of Aquitaine, referred to above, had the same name as his father, but in the previous generation this name had been borne by a Frank, the governor of the Auvergne. Gerald's successors were called Bernard and William, and these two names were to recur regularly in the name-pool of the southern nobility. Conversely, 'Roman' names borne by the 'Frankish' higher aristocracy, or by the petty nobility of the north, are, if not non-existent – since genealogies are never completely reliable – at least extremely rare. The predominance of Frankish names reveals the political dominance of the imperial aristocracy.

Did this mean cultural dominance? It is debatable. At this stage of the Middle Ages names were distinctive and generally singular, rather like our Christian names. A son did not therefore inevitably carry his father's name, or a daughter her mother's. But these individual names were not assigned at random; they were always the name of a relative and usually a close one. Many historians have thus drawn the logical conclusion that the Frankish names of the local aristocracy in the Midi were the outcome of numerous marriage alliances with the imperial aristocracy. This is possible but not certain. There is in fact another relationship by which names can be transmitted, that of baptism. The Frankish governor of the Auvergne could be godfather to the offspring of a family from Aquitaine, and give him his own name. Such a practice would explain the fact that there are fewer Germanic names among women: since these godparental relationships were political affairs, they mainly concerned men.

But it should be said that even among men, Germanic names did not totally predominate. In the great southern families, sons continued to be given 'Roman' or even Gaulish names. In Gerald's family there was a Benedict, among the lords of Orange there was usually a Pons, an Abellonius among those of Castellane, and a Maurice in the ranks of the lords of Montboissier.

Among the Frankish aristocracy, in certain houses, there was also a converse attempt at 'Romanisation'. This was apparent in the palace, where men from the south often occupied key posts among the clergy and also in the government of the southern provinces. Let us return to the example of the Williams. At the end of the ninth century, Bernard, Marquis of the Auvergne, paid Gerald the compliment of sending his son and heir to be reared in his house. Some Franks in Bernard's entourage had learned Roman law. Bernard's son tried, without success, to marry off one of his sisters to Gerald. The Romanophile tradition of this family was an old one: it had earlier supported St Benedict of Aniane, whom some figures in the Frankish court had wished to put to death as a dangerous spokesman for the Romano-Goths of the Narbonnais. The pro-southern sympathies of this Frankish house were closely connected with its ambition to control the Midi, and with the impressive numbers of 'traitors' to Frankish power which it had produced in each generation. The attempts at assimilation were not therefore a more or less 'spontaneous' process of fusion, but a quite specific policy on the part of one section of the imperial aristocracy, correctly identified by other Franks as a threat to their collective power.

Nevertheless, even those great Frankish families who were most directly involved in the process of assimilation still needed their links with Francia during the ninth century. In the second half of the century, when that same Bernard of Auvergne fell into temporary disgrace, he took refuge in the north, in a quiet part of Lorraine, the Ornois, west of Metz, and lived there in apparent security. His son William, Count of Auvergne and Duke of Aquitaine, who enjoyed semi-royal public powers in the Midi, at the beginning of the tenth century still held on to an estate at Einville-aux-Jards, in Lorraine. He then gave it up for the Cluny lands in the Mâconnais. This exchange was perhaps more symbolic than it appeared, as he was relinquishing the heritage of his Frankish ancestors, a portion of the harsh soil of Lorraine, in order to found an abbey that was to become the true successor to Roman Gaul.

At about the same time, the head of a powerful, rival Frankish house, which held Rodez, Cahors and Toulouse, and was aiming to control the whole of the province of Narbonne (present-day Languedoc), took a Roman name for the first time, adding the name Pons to his traditional one of Raymond. A century and a half later, his descendants had forgotten their origins and described themselves as following Roman law. This was one form assimilation took in the southern provinces.

Changes were also taking place in the Frankish lands. The kinship network of the high aristocracy, more or less integrated with the the royal house, broke up in the tenth century into separate lineages described as having issued from royal stock, and purporting to continue it. This pattern passed from the princes to those of their followers who held public fortresses and fiscal estates. Thus the Lotharingian Adalbero, Bishop of Laon, declared that 'noble lines are descended from the blood of kings', and this maxim well expressed the feelings of the great lineages of Francia on the eve of the eleventh century. The kinship of the high aristocracy was henceforth modelled on that of the royal line, to the extent that the magnates and their followers established themselves in definitive and hereditary control over public properties.

The imperial aristocracy as such then ceased to exist as a social class. Its descendants, the territorial princes, were of semi-royal status, even when they did not take a royal title. But in putting down roots in the midst of their subjects, they snapped the links that bound them to each other. This was the end of the Empire, of the power of the 'Frankish people' and of the frequent military expeditions which renewed the subjugation of dependent peoples and kingdoms. Regino, abbot of Prüm, one of the most famous monasteries of Francia, was not mistaken when he wrote, in one of the last great chronicle compiliations: '888: each kingdom decided to create its own king drawn from its own entrails.' Despite their Frankish origin, the independent princes of the tenth century were indeed created by the kingdoms which they headed, and these kingdoms were nothing other than local aristocracies. The emotion concealed beneath the dry statement by the abbot of Prüm is revealed by his contemporary, Ekkehard of Saint-Gall, when he sighed for the time when 'the Gauls and Aquitainians were proud to be called the serfs of the Franks'.

The end of the Empire and the creation of independent principalities outside Francia meant that the great Frankish houses were absorbed by the local nobilities, and that the latter rose to power. The significance of this power was not slow to be revealed when the old public institutions, some elements of which were still preserved by the principalities, gave way beneath the blows of a united and strengthened aristocracy, which was seeking complete mastery of the peasantry. Seigneurial power gradually penetrated the most humble and most remote cells of rural society. The dislocation of the old power structure which was then taking place should not obscure the fact that through this crisis another structure was forming, infinitely more solid and durable because it was more deeply rooted. We must descend to that level now, to the everyday existence of the majority of people, namely, that of the peasantry. There, in thousands of villages and hamlets, the destiny of the feudal society of the future was being played out. There, in the space of a few generations, a uniform and profound transformation took place: the end, in nearly all the territories of the West, of peasant liberty, and the establishment of seigneurial justice, basis of the power of

24   the feudal aristocracy.

The free communities of the south

Nineteenth-century historians, of whatever political persuasion, imagined medieval society sometimes as idyllic, sometimes as turbulent, but always with essentially the same structure. It was composed of two great classes – nobles and serfs – or perhaps three if the Church was considered as an autonomous class. Such historians knew of the existence of certain people whom they persisted in calling, in unconscious identification, 'small free property-holders'; but they placed them in a sort of social no-man's-land, somewhere between the glittering aristocracy and the numberless herds of servile peasantry. They were basically isolated cases, referred to in order to set the writer's mind at rest, rather than a true social group deserving of analysis. As the years went by, these free men on the fringe of society revealed themselves as more numerous than had been thought, and even became familiar figures to some historians, in particular to the Spanish, without however losing the rather anachronistic label which had been attached to them. Recent studies have made it impossible to continue to confine the free peasants to this minor status, or even, by trying to update the old notions without really modifying them, to see them as either an intermediate group whose rise was due to the troubles of the tenth century, or by contrast, as a relic of a previous era. Free peasants, described in our sources as allod-holders – those people in possession of an allod, an ancestral estate – at the beginning of our period, still formed the largest class of the peasantry and belonged to a society of thousands of free village communities, some of which were well organised, while others were already under threat.

Let us start by establishing their existence, and distinguishing the situation in the north from that in the Midi, as we did in examining the structure of the nobility.

The general features of allodial communities in the south are quite well known now, and many examples can be found stretching from the Ebro to the Tiber. The documentary evidence is especially rich and revealing for the west of Spain, where historical circumstances granted these communities a longer existence, and where the practice of written law was maintained longer than elsewhere.

The 'occupants' of a village, its 'residents', were grouped into 'clans', and these clans in their turn formed a 'neighbourhood'. When important decisions had to be made, all the 'neighbours who had property in the village' (village here means territory) came together in a 'council'. Everyone went along; thus for example, 'all of us who are of the community of Rio de Polos', or 'in the great council of Agusyn, from the greatest to the least', or again, 'all of us who are the council of Berbeia, men and women, old and young, all of us together, we who are the inhabitants'. Sometimes it even happened that two or three villages held a combined assembly. When the communities confronted magnates in the course of law-suits, whether over common lands, rights to grazing land, forests, rivers, salt-mines or mills, the councils were represented by 'delegates'.

But at some stage the councils were opened to the nobles when also resident locally, and they sometimes deigned to mix with the more lowly inhabitants of the village. This was not surprising, as the opening up of the village councils was to be a trump-card in the hands of

25

ETAEQUITATE SCMETTERRIBILENOMEIUS· INSAECULUSA

The residence of a northern noble in the ninth century. The distribution of food to the poor is blessed by God, whose hand is visible; the chapel is crowned by a cross; guards armed with lances and shields ensure its defence. (*Utrecht Psalter*, Utrecht, Bibliotheek der Rijksuniversiteit.)

the secular and ecclesiastical magnates. They set in motion, in these regions as in the rest of the south, though perhaps more gradually, an irresistible policy of expansion.

Continuing our journey eastwards, we find in Catalonia the same 'residents' communities'; they also had their own properties, and purchased common rights to forest, pasture or stream water. They had their representatives and were even capable of resorting to forgery to maintain what they saw as their legal rights. It is easier to detect among them the leading figures of the community, called by the same name throughout the whole of the south, the 'good men'. They were the judges in the judicial assemblies of the district, which were presided over by the holder of public authority or by his delegate. They were the recognised experts when it came to assessing the value of a piece of land for exchange, or for the payment of a fine or debt. They were privileged witnesses in the lawsuits over boundaries. They were the spokesmen and guarantors of the community. The detailed study of these fortunately preserved Catalonian charters has revealed an interesting piece of information about these allod-holders: they were armed.

The same conflicts appear in both the north-east and the north-west of the Iberian peninsula. We have the records of some fifty-five judicial assemblies of a public court, under a count or viscount, in Catalonia before 1020. In thirteen of them, village communities took part in trials to defend their property. It is interesting to see that the legal definition of these common properties varies according to the point of view of the source: when the villagers of Pallerols in Cerdanya claimed a piece of pasture land, they declared that it was part of 'their allod', their common ancestral property; but the count and his lawyers, in the tradition of Roman law, thought that such lands came within the public domain, and that the peasants had only a right to their collective use, a right called the *empriù*. The consequences of this difference of opinion were not confined to the realm of legal theory.

In the tenth century, this official point of view was still very far from being generally accepted. It is sufficient to read the privileges which the counts were forced to grant to the frontier communities. The counts found themselves agreeing to some astonishing declarations. Thus, the people of Cardona, specifying the conditions under which the military defence of the border would be undertaken, made the following addition: 'If necessity dictates that more be done, you [that is the members of the community, as the count is meant to be speaking here] acting together shall make all the arrangements, as it pleases you and as you see fit.' A little further on, they referred to the prospect of the neighbouring aristocracy encroaching on their rights, and proposed a remedy: 'and if some wicked man, dangerously puffed up with pride, attacks one of those who live here, or wishes to live here, and takes over his property, let the latter be compensated sevenfold, and let all the inhabitants assist him . . . And if some wicked man, be he lord or patron, wishes to increase the burden of taxes, let him by no means do such a thing . . . And if some wicked man rises in anger against you and attacks you, you in turn are to rise up and combat him with all your strength, and kill him. And if there is one among you who does not participate in this, he is to be proclaimed by your council as an outsider in your midst.'

Each word of this text deserves attention: the free people of Cardona were perfectly well aware of the ways in which village communities could lose their liberty: through the greed of magnates who deprived the weaker members of their land in order to lease it back to them at a rent and thus turn them into dependants. These magnates, who appeared sometimes in the guise of haughty lords and sometimes in the guise of friends, always ended up making their protection and 'friendship' a matter of payment, through increased taxes. If this did not bring results, they would expose the villagers to the attacks of their strong-arm men, or wear them down by guerilla tactics. To all this the people of Cardona had only one reply: solidarity and armed struggle. They also knew that the maintenance of this solidarity involved refusing anyone privileged authority within the community: 'And if anyone of you wishes to be more than the others, he shall be treated just like a boy.' We are at a turning point. Within the space of a generation, the balance was to tip in favour of the magnates. The lively political awareness of those pioneers who had gone out to resettle the frontier regions had perhaps originated in bitter experiences in their home villages in the interior.

If we cross the Pyrenees, we find the same kind of community around Carcassonne, Béziers, Nîmes and Arles. Although there is less evidence here, what there is can be equally illuminating. Here, peasant households were grouped around a large piece of common land. The families sent their herds to common grazing lands, cut wood on common land – land of the 'free men'. Here too, the community functioned as a single legal identity. A

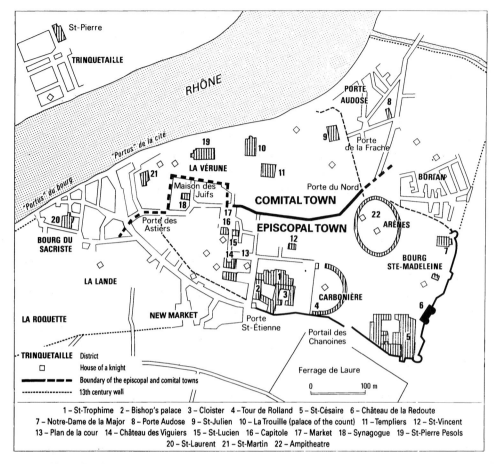

St-Pierre

TRINQUETAILLE

RHÔNE

PORTE AUDOSE

8

'Portus' de la cité

19

9

Porte de la Frache

10

LA VÉRUNE

11

21

Maison des Juifs

Porte du Nord

BORIAN

'Portus' du bourg

18

COMITAL TOWN

17

22

20

16

EPISCOPAL TOWN

ARÈNES

Porte des Astiers

12

BOURG DU SACRISTE

15

7

14 13

BOURG STE-MADELEINE

LA LANDE

1

3

2

CARBONIÈRE

4

6

LA ROQUETTE

NEW MARKET

Porte St-Étienne

5

TRINQUETAILLE District

Portail des Chanoines

☐ House of a knight

━━━ ━ ━ ━ Boundary of the episcopal and comital towns

Ferrage de Laure

·············· 13th century wall

0   100 m

1 – St-Trophime 2 – Bishop's palace 3 – Cloister 4 – Tour de Rolland 5 – St-Césaire 6 – Château de la Redoute
7 – Notre-Dame de la Major 8 – Porte Audose 9 – St-Julien 10 – La Trouille (palace of the count) 11 – Templiers 12 – St-Vincent
13 – Plan de la cour 14 – Château des Viguiers 15 – St-Lucien 16 – Capitole 17 – Market 18 – Synagogue 19 – St-Pierre Pesols
20 – St-Laurent 21 – St-Martin 22 – Ampitheatre

Map 1. Arles in the twelfth century.

record of one court-case tells us how the men of Costebalen, near Nîmes, had sold one of their 'common allods' to the neighbouring village of Quart. When objections were raised to this, the two groups met together with the people from the village of Luc, who were also interested in the matter. We also catch glimpses of the communities in records of boundary disputes, when the agents of public authority – in the person of counts or viscounts – became involved. With them presiding, there was an assembly of all the 'village-folk' of Aspiran, that is, all those who lived together there; a similar inquiry at Bizac reveals the 'village-folk' to be some 200 in number. In the Narbonnais, too, around the year 900, the nobles did not think it beneath them to mix with the crowd of peasants, the 'lesser folk', the 'large crowd of common persons of both sexes'.

We can add to this, along with some slight evidence from Provence, the examples from across the Alps provided by the rich sources of the Church in Lombardy. The allod-holders of Cologna Monzese are the subjects of a detailed monograph. The common picture that emerges from such surveys shows us that the southern great estate, while not quite a secondary structure, was certainly far from being dominant. The great estate did not hold unchallenged sway and its rented farms had the allodial lands of free men as neighbours.

The spread of 'feudalism' in the north

The relative abundance of evidence for the south ought not to mislead us. At the beginning of the ninth century the southern communities were probably not much more numerous than their northern counterparts. But the considerably less widespread use of writing in the northern region makes them more difficult to discover, and often they only come to light by chance – as, for example, when the administrators of a great monastic estate, confident of what their lordship entailed, decided to note down the two days of labour due in the name of public service from the free men who lived alongside their tenants. In the area of Saint-Bertin (Saint-Omer) there were, in the territory of the village of Guines, forty free men to only sixteen tenants of the abbey; at Wizernes, twenty-one free men and eighteen tenants are recorded. In fact, these two villages were mainly populated by yet another category of peasant, but we shall come to this later.

It was from these groups of free men that the public authority in Francia tended to recruit those guarantors known as the *fidejussores*, who were bound by oath and held responsible in their person and property for the carrying out of public services. We have a good example of this at Ardin in Poitou, but these *fidejussores* and the communities which they represented must have been fairly numerous as they are mentioned regularly in charters of immunity. 'Gathering the oath-takers' was a normal administrative measure carried out by the king's representative in lands where a group or groups of allod-holders could be found, and this shows that we are dealing with free communities: slaves did not take oaths. When the place of the king's local agent was taken by a great religious establishment, it fell to its lay representative, the advocate, to deal with such matters. Sometimes it happened that the list of these jurors was written down in the estate records; this was the case at Saint-Germain-des-Prés at the beginning of the ninth century.

Nevertheless, the situation of the free peasants in the north soon revealed itself as more precarious than that of their southern equivalents. This was not so much the case for the wealthier and more aggressive among them; these figures, as we have seen, were regarded at Saint-Bertin as members of the 'nobility of the region'. But the problem did apply to those people whom the Carolingian clergy, with a compassion tinged with scorn, called 'the poor' (*pauperes*). Some early ninth-century capitularies did try to protect them and shield them from the magnates' manoeuvres. A perusal of these texts reveals that the devices used to bring about the dissolution of village communities in fact were part of the system which united them – 'public work' – but misused in order to bring about the opposite of what they were intended to do. Let us briefly survey them. The king's representative, the count, was meant to allocate fairly the obligations of 'public service', whether military service or taxes, among the different social groups of the county, i.e. the great estates or the free villages. To make the weight of such service fall more heavily all the count had to do was to alter the allocation. He could defy the express prohibition of the capitularies and regularly take recruits from the same village, or the same farm, thus crippling its capacity for agricultural labour. He could keep billeting himself and his followers, as he had a right to do after his tours of inspection, in the same hamlet and thus gradually bankrupt it by requisitioning supplies. He could use false weights and measures when he levied public dues.

But what if the allod-holders refused to obey his orders? He could fine them to the tune of 30 or 60 sous, a huge sum for a lowly peasant. If the household or households penalised in this way could not pay the fine, the 'judgement-finders' of the village, the *scabini*, were asked by the count to price the properties of the defaulters and put them up for sale. Who would buy them? Often enough the local noble, the count's friend. To try and avoid such a sale, the peasants could search out this man and borrow from him, often with interest, the necessary cash for paying the fine. But if their next harvest was a bad one, they would be unable to repay him and would have to go back to the *scabini* and go through with the sale. Sometimes it happened that their benefactor was generous and did not charge them interest. But in return for this 'favour', he might ask his peasant debtors to hand over to him the ownership of their land, either at once, or on the death of the head of the family, in order to receive it back from him and hold it of him as their lord. Wouldn't this be the best way to guarantee future good relations with his friend the count? Naturally, the choice victims of such proceedings were the families of widows or orphans, who were less able to resist such benevolent pressure.

Sometimes the peasant household would refuse to play its allotted part. The kin-group would gather together and set off to lodge a complaint at the general assembly of free men just outside the city walls, beside an ancient shrine. The count would refuse to judge the case, which he should have done if he were observing the capitularies; he would pass it on to the district assembly, which was under the supervision of one of his own appointees, this deputy being none other than the local noble. But what if the peasants insisted on carrying on with their case before the general asssembly? Scorning custom, the count would change the date or site of the assembly, which would be packed with his own creatures. When the villagers wanted to put their case themselves, as they did at the end of the tenth century, in an assembly held at the palace of the King of Burgundy, the nobles laughed them to scorn. That court was not for the likes of them: they should have stayed at home. Free, but badly off, such people were confined in a narrow social network, their horizons limited to their own villages or those nearby. The great assemblies were beyond their reach. If they did go to town, it was not to argue for their rights but to buy and sell, and such activities benefited those who taxed them.

Pressure grows

Some of those tactics were not new, but they seem to have become more effective in the second half of the ninth century, when Viking raids hit the areas abandoned by magnates. The countryfolk now tried to defend themselves, and it is significant that royal legislation, hitherto concerned with protecting the poor, now began to order their subjection. In 857 a royal decree denounced the popular militias, the *trustes*, which the peasants had formed against 'bandits'. Such formations might in fact seem rather praiseworthy; at any rate they were in accordance with Frankish custom, as recorded in Salic law. We learn from the annals for 859, from a passage tight-lipped with embarrassment, that the peasants of the country between the Loire and the Seine had joined forces to fight the Vikings but had been crushed . . . by their own king's horsemen. In 884 a new warning was given to villagers who had formed 'what are known among the people as guilds' (i.e. sworn leagues in the old Germanic tradition) 'to resist those who are preying upon them'.

Confronted with the failure of resistance, many became demoralised. Since some form of protection had become indispensable, they sought it in the arms of the Church, agreeing to an annual payment for their 'head'; they were *chevagiers* (*chevage*: head-tax, poll-tax); others gave a candle to the altar of their patron saint, and were *luminiers* (*luminaire*: candle) or *ciriers* (*cire*: wax). In other words, they were now subject to a patron. This phenomenon is well known. To estimate its scale and rate of growth we have to examine estate records. We know that, in the villages close to an estate centre, the farms of the dependent cultivators often lay cheek by jowl with those of free men and those under protection. The population living on the estates of Saint-Germain-des-Prés at the beginning of the ninth century can be divided up approximately as follows: slaves 7 per cent, freedmen (i.e. those released from slavery) 3 per cent, tenant farmers 77.5 per cent, and those under protection only 12.5 per cent. The low proportion of slaves is noteworthy. In the same period, if the estate records of the Abbey of Saint-Victor in Marseilles can be trusted, the Midi was a land of servitude; here we find the slaves accounting for 44 per cent. But the men under protection are missing or unknown. A couple of generations later, on the lands of Saint-Rémy of Rheims, in Champagne, slaves were still in the minority (13 per cent), and the relatively high number of freedmen is revealing (15 per cent). Tenants were still in the majority (47 per cent), but those under protection amounted to 28 per cent of the Rheims *familia*. Further north at this time, at Guines and Wizernes, there were 100 men under protection for every twenty tenants. The question is whether these differences reveal a geography or a chronology of dependence. If we adopt the latter hypothesis, we see that the social category which expands from the mid-ninth century onwards is that of former freeholders who have become men under protection. Their status was ambiguous from the start.

Until the beginning of the eleventh century those who had placed themselves under the protection of the great churches thought of themselves as free men, even if they were no longer completely free. But over time their masters, even the churchmen, tended to look upon all their dependants, slaves, tenants or men under protection, as 'their' men, without bothering too much about nuances. Gradually, therefore, that numerous class of dependants was formed from which the turbulent *ministeriales* would later rise. The size of this class gives us a striking impression of the pressures then operating in the northern countryside. The end of the Carolingian period saw the establishment in the north, on public estates (especially the Church estates), of what was to become 'banal' lordship – a territory where all the peasants were subject to a lord. In effect, the only 'free men' were the 'nobles'. In the tenth century, the crisis of feudalism burst over the Midi, as we shall see; in the north, feudalism was established.

The Bayeux Tapestry, no doubt intended to hang from pillar to pillar in the nave of the cathedral where it was presented officially on 14 July 1077, recounts the conquest of England by William, Duke of Normandy. On an immense piece of linen 70 metres long, with embroideries in eight different coloured wools, it celebrates in fifty-eight scenes of varying length the saga of the Conqueror, and its images of daily life provide a veritable encyclopaedia of material civilisation in the eleventh century. Here the Normans set fire to an unfortified manor house.

The great transformation

In western and southern Europe after 950 or 980 the sense of the legitimacy of royal power, a sense still very much alive in the Midi, lost its strength. The façade of royal power no longer troubled the aristocracy, and the south became a land without a king. Until then, traditional institutions, especially the public assemblies, had somehow managed to survive despite the independence of the princes. But now the aristocracy staked its claim to domination. The legitimate power of command, the *ban*, which had for a long time been more or less justified by collective necessities was to become a daily constraint, in the hands of the lord.

32   The reality and depth of this crisis has been doubted; it has been seen as a picture of monastic propaganda. We must therefore re-examine the available evidence and trace step by step the itinerary which we have already followed in our survey of the communities of allod-holders in the south. The way in which these texts converge will then emerge clearly.

From the Ebro to the Alps: civil war

Until the beginning of the eleventh century peace within Catalonia had been preserved, after a fashion, even if there had been an increasing shift in the balance of power among the various groups there – the magnates, the communities and the churches. Around 1020 relations between the latter and the lay aristocracy seem to have deteriorated. After 1035 an openly hostile situation developed. Magnates crammed their halls with mounted warriors, monopolised the command of public fortresses, which had previously been places of refuge for the local population, and installed garrisons of robbers under their orders. They went on to take control of the countryside more completely by building new castles. Once they were entrenched in these strongholds they employed threats and terror to impose their power everywhere. This process is only revealed to us when the interests of a church or another magnate were at stake. Then a catalogue of grievances was drawn up in which the wrongs that no court could then redress were preserved in writing.

In this way we know of the 'grievances and complaints' of one of the two counts of Pallars, Ramon, against the other: 'He rode to Tendriu and plundered it . . . he rode to Puigmanyons, and killed several men there with his own hands, and he killed men at Peracalç, he killed men at Beranui as well . . . At Santa Coloma he rounded up all the men who had taken refuge by the altar . . .' The unfortunate Ramon also had complaints to make about his other neighbour, the Count of Urgel: 'He rode out against me and slew my viscount and others of my men; he cut down or burned my crops, and plundered my land.' Eventually Ramon took steps to re-establish control. As an old man he was to confess 'the sin which I committed when I led Saracens against Christians, which was the cause of the death or capture of many Christians'.

Worn down like this by a succession of raids and counter-raids, the allod-holders, despite their resistance, lost their liberty. In this region the only ones who managed to remain independent were the 'rustics' of half a dozen remote mountain villages in the Andorra valley. Although he had waged war on them, the Count of Urgel had failed to make them render tribute to him. He made over his claims to lordship to the bishop of the diocese. At the same period, the great castellans were eliminating the peasant liberties in the southern border zones.

The same process was at work in Narbonne and Béziers. Let us listen to the Viscount of Narbonne's grievances against an archbishop who was more interested in acquiring power than in praising God: 'The archbishopric of Narbonne was formerly held by my uncle, Archbishop Ermengaud, and in his time it was one of the best sees in the lands between Rome and the Spanish marches . . . [on Ermengaud's death one Guifré, a relative of his from a noble family, gained the bishopric]. He behaved like the Devil himself . . . he set up castles against me, he marched against me with a great army and waged a cruel war on me in

Depiction of a town under siege. The town pictured in this eleventh-century Catalan bible is basically circular, enclosed by a partially crenellated stone wall. This is a schematic image, based on old iconographic conventions, because at this period cities were in fact just as likely to be made up of flimsy wooden buildings. The towers represent the town buildings. Amidst this fairly abstract architecture, the movements of daily life are observed in a lively way: people burdened with faggots, a woman carrying a jar, fearful inhabitants crouched in the shelter of the ramparts. (The Farfa Bible, Vatican Library, cod. lat. 5729.)

which almost a thousand men on each side were killed.' To gain control, Guifré went to any lengths to attract horsemen to his service. He gave away church property to them. He used the money accumulated from fines for breaches of the peace to pay the wages of his mercenaries. It does not really concern us here that the viscount was not quite the innocent victim he claimed to be; his grievances were based on events that were too well known to be pure invention.

In these same crucial years, the families of the counts of Carcassonne and the viscounts of Béziers strove to subjugate the countryside around the Etang de Thau. They allied themselves with a formidable castellan from the Nîmes area, Bernard 'le Velu' (the Hairy), lord of Anduze. In the course of their campaigns they damaged property held by the Abbey of Conques, and this means that we now have a frank account of their operations around Loupian:

A certain knight, Bernard 'the Hairy', laid siege to Loupain with a thousand mounted troops and almost as many infantry. Encircling it with a trench, he laid waste everything around it with fire and sword. Those people who had foreseen such evils had gathered up their property and sought refuge behind the walls which protected our church of Pallas; all they had left behind were their empty huts. Frustrated in their desire for plunder, the knights went around the neighbouring districts and brought back to their camp everything they could lay hands on.

Nevertheless, the monks of Conques were not hostile to the lord of Anduze. In fact they tended to look upon him as a just and righteous man, since he had favoured them in a lawsuit. But good relations with the local lord did not spare them the attentions of his over-zealous henchmen, one of whom had no hesitation in setting about the monks with a troop of fifty horsemen in the hope that they would lose their appetite for reclaiming monastic property in the area.

The ambitions of the lords also shattered the peace in the plateau of the Auvergne. There,

a certain knight called Amblard (the Lord of Nonette) came into conflict with his neighbours, who claimed to be as powerful as he was and would yield to him in nothing . . . Knights from both sides fell upon each other and with fire and sword laid waste the dwelling places and provisions of the country people. And since this happened in several places, the peasants, who feared lest their own cottages be burnt, put out their hearth-fires so that anyone who wanted to plunder them and burn their huts to the ground would not be able to find flames to light their torches.

On the whole, however, knights only attacked Church lands after laying waste the rest of the countryside, and then in desperation. The complaints of the churchmen, far from being exaggerated, are therefore likely to give only part of the picture. In fact, even when they themselves were not under direct attack, it was difficult for churchmen to be unaware of the sufferings of the countryfolk around them.

Everyday violence

Thanks to such wars, insecurity became a feature of everyday life – and was almost accepted as such. We can get some sense of this from the testimony of a figure close to the peasants, Renaud the monk, who looked after the small Provençal priory of Villecroze for the monastery of Saint-Victor in Marseilles. When he was an old man he recounted to the monk who was writing the biography of the late abbot (Isarn) the tale of the disputes which he and his abbot had had with the head of a local noble household, Pandulf, lord of Salernes and Pontevès.

There was once a man called Pandulf, who lorded it over all his neighbours as much by his power as by every sort of wickedness. In his fortress stronghold . . . he hanged two fine young men who had come to request some money from him and secretly had their bodies thrown into a great cave. A little later, this crime was discovered by the monks living at Villecroze and the corpses were brought back to the monastery for Christian burial . . . Some time afterwards, a man was returning from Châteaudouble. A band of Pandulf's ruffians set upon him, hurled him from his horse and took it away . . . My lord abbot at once sent me to Pandulf, who was going around the district, to try and reason with him; the abbot himself set off to beg Pandulf's wife to return the horse. But he sought a meeting in vain: that shrew, with her usual peevish disposition – so unbecoming in a woman – saw to it that he had no hope of recovering the animal. For his part, Pandulf, knowing full well that I had set out to find him, skulked along the back roads, or so it seemed to me, in order to avoid me. In the end, vexed more by my failure than by weariness from the journey, I returned home and busied myself with setting an adequate guard over all our possessions, particularly over our herd of pigs. But what can guard against these diabolical men, these – if I may call them so – human devils? Throughout the

35

day the thieves hid themselves in the nearby forest, and at nightfall, when we relaxed our guard, they suddenly sallied forth out of the woods and made off with our herd of pigs under cover of approaching darkness.

One gets the impression that these knights were merely having some sport. But such games could sometimes drive peasants to the end of their tether. Renaud remembered another affair that very nearly turned out badly:

There was a powerful layman called Adalard, who was arrogant and wicked, whose constant demands weighed heavily on the tenants of a farm at Lagnes, which belonged to the monastery; he forced them to yield up to him their pigs, their sheep, anything that took his fancy. If these poor folk did not carry out his wishes, he would take what he wanted by force . . . Once, when the holy man (Isarn) was there, messengers came with the news that the sacrilegious bandit had plundered a village the previous night, and was now settling down to feast on what was left of his ill-gotten gains. The whole household around Isarn was outraged, and shouted to the neighbours to come and help them. Snatching up their spears and shields, they prepared to rush upon their enemy. But the man of God, shaking with emotion, his hands outstretched, opposed their going, vehemently arguing against their right to carry out this wicked action, and saying that they would have to kill him before they could set out . . . Then he sent his own escort to the robber, as messengers of peace, to try and arrange a meeting with him.

Between the aggrieved peasant communities and the plunderers from the castle, the Church took up the ambiguous position of mediator. We shall come back to this point. But exhortations to good behaviour were not always enough, and sometimes the bolder souls decided to take matters into their own hands.

[In Rouergue] in the village of Conques, there lived a certain Hugh; sharing the vanity of the local magistrate, whose illegitimate brother he was, Hugh boasted of his membership of this gangster aristocracy, and was hated by everyone. There was a villager called Benedict, who stood up to his arrogance, and whom he persecuted with extreme malevolence; he used to insult him all the time, and pester him with quarrels on any pretext. Benedict took these insults badly and at last, overcome by rage, he struck him down and killed him. Then, fearing the dead man's kinsmen, he ran away, leaving all his property behind; his wife, who did not want to leave his side, fled with him. Their five-year-old son remained behind in the house, since they could not take him with them on their flight.

The peasants believed that the child would be safe in the village, while they were forced to live as outlaws in the forest, hunted for vengeance. They little reckoned with the arrogance and cruelty of these upstart nobles: the dead man's family wreaked its venegeance on the child by gouging out his eyes and leaving him for dead. The people of the village picked him up and carried him to Sainte Foy, who restored his sight 'amidst the rejoicing of everyone, young and old, men and women'. A small victory for the village over the castle.

But neither active nor passive resistance on the villagers' part could check the increasing acts of violence. Evidence of this appears in the *Miracles of Sainte Foy*, whose cult extended over an immense area, in Agennais, Périgord, south Limousin, Quercy, Rouergue, Albigeois, in the southern Auvergne and the region of Nîmes and Béziers. If this collection is compared with earlier works of the same type, the increased frequency of attacks and confiscations becomes clear. In the first two books of the *Miracles*, 26 per cent of the saint's interventions were the result of such affairs; they cover the period 980–1020. Books III and IV, which deal with events between 1030 and 1076, show that the proportion had climbed to 36 per cent. Both these percentages are still too low. There had been so many opportunities for Sainte Foy to work miracles of setting peasants free that the monks could not remember the names of the humble majority of the victims. But their abandoned iron fetters so cluttered up the church that they were taken away and melted down, so that the metal could be put to other uses. Even if descriptions of these fetters were largely imaginary, which is unlikely, they symbolise the torment of the contemporary peasantry. Each age gets the miracles it needs.

Law as the façade of force

It would be wrong, however, to think that such greed and brutality were founded only upon force. When the lords and their followers rounded up horses, mules, donkeys, pigs and sheep, they claimed to be simply exercising lawful constraint; horses or other beasts of burden were the mounts that could be requisitioned by the king's envoys, according to the old Roman system of the *cursus publicus*. This is what lies behind the references in the late tenth-century Auvergne councils to 'public horses'. The beast of burden was the tithe which the fisc claimed from public pasture land; or it could claim that the king's envoy and his escort be fed, or that the army be supplied – in short, everything that could be subsumed in the old Germanic word *haribergon* (modern French *héberge*: lodging), or 'the refreshment of warriors'. One blanket word suffices for all this: *exactiones*, a word which described the public taxes and which at that time acquired the meaning which it has in modern French or English: 'to levy more than is due to authority, or even what is not due'. It was, after all, one thing to supply board and lodging to an 'envoy of the lord king', but it was something else again to suffer regular harassment at the none-too-gentle hands of the knights of the local castle.

It mattered little. The great local landowner was well within his rights when he asserted that he was carrying out 'public functions' because he had become the 'public power' – such is the vocabulary of the period – which had been delegated to him by the count, who was himself the delegate of the king. The lord, therefore, had been appointed judge over the very people he was subjecting to pressure. He had taken over the ancient stronghold where the local population used to take refuge in times of danger, and where its places of worship and assembly were as often as not located. Then the lord and his gang fortified the remaining hills, with the result that the landscape was criss-crossed by a network of watch-towers.

This 'feudal' insecurity, as revealed in the proliferation of castles, began when the great invasions came to an end. After 1030, the number of fortifications in Bitterois, as in Provence, quadrupled. Of course it could be argued that all these towns, mounds, stockades and ditches were – just as in the past – protection for the 'poor', for the 'unarmed'. But at the same time, one would have to explain why insecurity was now so much worse than

A circular keep on a mound surrounded by a large ditch: entry was by a steep footbridge leading to a narrow opening. Stone replaced wood in the twelfth century. (Restormel, Cornwall.)

it had been when the Viking, Hungarian or Saracen raiders had roamed the land. The reason for this was the contemporary increase in what we might call 'competing forms of protection'. While it is true that the lord (and his men) defended the countryfolk who were his dependants, and who lived in what had become the territory of his lordship, it is also true that he was defending them against another lord, his neighbour, who, with his own following of strong-arm men, sought to extend his sphere of power.

Naturally, some historians have found it difficult to abandon the comforting image of an eleventh century peopled with good lords, the strict but fair shepherds of a flock of backward peasants. To believe these writers, all the 'captures', 'predatory acts', 'wrongs', 'acts of violence', 'acts of force', 'rapine', 'levies', 'exactions' and 'demands' – in short, all the 'wicked customs' which the lords promised from time to time to abandon – were nothing but the inventions of the monks who were jealous of the powers of the secular lords. The whole thing is a great historical bluff, which was originally intended to convince the lords to give up their own legitimate powers, but which has ended up misleading modern historians, or at least those who have some sympathy with the peasantry of the time. But in fact it only takes a little knowledge of medieval Latin to see that most of these words, which run through the charters of the period, had passed from the vernacular into the Latin of the monks, and not the other way round. It goes without saying that the monks and bishops, or at least the more intelligent of them, incorporated these terms into their own discourse, which was not an innocent one; but they did not invent them.

38

The Church and the keeping of the peace

At the end of the tenth century, some churches appeared to make a stand against the lay aristocracy, with the intention of keeping the violence of the time in check. Thus began the movement known originally as the Peace of God and then, as it took root and spread, as the Truce of God. This deserves examination at some length, both in order to define more precisely the chronology and geography of the feudal crisis, and the better to understand the essential part the Church played in its resolution, leaving aside for now the movement's place in the history of the Church itself.

The lands of the Church had long been a temptation to the great laymen, who were always on the look-out for land to support their large families. Sometimes farms were isolated, far from the estate centres administered by monks or canons, and it would happen that, giving in to the magnates' pressure, the church that owned them would hand over their administration to these magnates, by a contract known as *commenda*. This type of contract was not confined to relations between lords and clerics: a widow, too weak to keep hold of her land, or another great landowner living at a distance, sometimes had to 'entrust' (*commendare*) a village to a powerful local noble. Kin-groups or even entire free communities could entrust or 'commend' themselves to the lord. Through the device of this contract many villages in the tenth century came under the control of the aristocracy, a control described in contemporary texts as 'wardship', using the term that referred to the guardianship of minors. This explains the frequency of such 'commendations' in the lands south of the Loire during the eleventh and twelfth centuries. Once the farms had been 'entrusted' to him, it was inevitable that the lord would take advantage of his position, and even without public powers or office having been delegated to him, he claimed the right to levy taxes in order to fulfil the obligations to public authority for which he himself was responsible as a landowner or administrator. After this, his way forward was clear. Denouncing such seigneurial exactions, a monk from Marmoutiers, near Tours, said accurately: 'As for these customs, there is no need to define or list them, for the chief of them is this "commendation" we have mentioned, and from that all the others flow.'

It is likely that such seigneurial pressure on communities drove many peasants in the tenth century to turn to the churches for refuge. This was certainly the case north of the Seine, and there are also examples in Catalonia. The protection offered by a saint was more honourable and, at first, more compatible with liberty. After all, the lordship of the Church was less arbitrary than secular lordship; at least, so the clergy of the major churches claimed in the twelfth century, when contemporary reformers accused them of being too devoted to wordly matters and of behaving like masters, not brothers. The peasants chose us as masters, was their reply, and we could not refuse them.

The lords' pressure on land-holders now came to bear on the Church, as they pursued on to its lands the men and women who had thus hoped to escape their grip. But it was no longer a case of obtaining from some co-operative abbot a *commenda* over some distant estate, or over land granted to the Church by the family. Now the target was the very heart, the main bulk of Church estates, the belt of territory around the great shrines. The

39

Bishop Ermengol of Urgel takes his oath of fealty to Count Guifred of Cerdana. (*Liber Feudorum Cerritaniae*, eleventh century, Barcelona, Archives of the Crown of Aragon.)

churches of the south could not accept this without putting their own existence at risk. Hence the appearance of a movement at the end of the tenth century, guided mainly by the monks of Cluny and by some of their allies among the bishops, which aimed at checking the aggression of the knightly class and proposed that bounds be set to it.

Great assemblies gathered round the holy relics of local saints, the precious reliquaries within which the magical bones were enclosed. Taken from the crypts and brought out into the open air, they inspired fervent popular emotion. Some magnates, friends or kinsmen of the monks, would also be present. Knights were asked to pledge 'peace', that is, to take an oath to observe certain prohibitions. Chief among these, as one might expect, were prohibitions on violence designed to protect the Church's lands and weaponless clergy. But it was also forbidden to seize peasants and hold them to ransom, except when a crime had been committed, which excused public officers exercising justice. The *Miracles of Sainte Foy* reveal that such illegal confinements were common, and that they constituted one of the knights' favourite methods of exerting pressure. Similarly, restrictions on levies for the host were designed to reduce 'exactions' to a bearable level. The Peace assemblies tried to bring some order to a very specific situation, as described in the texts quoted above.

The movement appears to have started in Le Puy, with a local council held perhaps in 987. Then the reformers tried to extend it westwards, towards Poitou, with a council held at Charroux in 989, and southwards the following year, with a council in Narbonne; in 994 a general council, or what was intended to be one, gathered again at Le Puy and, on a larger scale, at Limoges in the west, and to the east at Anse, in the Lyonnais. The 994 assemblies display the movement's real sphere of influence, after the ambitious attempts at expansion from 989–90 onwards.

They perhaps also mark a turning-point in the process of what one might call 'seigneuralisation', perhaps already under way for several years in these central regions: the beginning of its radical phase. In the 1020s, the crisis deepened; the movement for Peace was then taken up again openly by Cluny, which tried to extend it north of the Loire, into the sphere of influence of the Capetian king, whom the Cluniacs wished to see re-established in the Midi. Around 1040, the supporters of the Peace went one step further, by systematising a measure they had already sketched out in 1022–3: no longer focusing on certain places or particular categories of people, they defined certain times as 'non-violent', sanctified periods that were consecrated to the annual celebration of the great religious feasts. This was to protect the broad fabric of social life: these feasts assembled masses of people in the familiar places of pilgrimage, and the peaceful journeys they undertook had been a perfect occasion for ambushes and captures. The forbidding of the use of arms in these periods meant protecting something essential to society.

The peasants and the Peace: a 'revolution'

The Peace and then the Truce of God, promoted by the most active sector of the southern Church, were both underpinned by popular fervour and by some great castellans, who seem to have felt outdone by their own knights. This common alliance was not maintained without friction. In Limoges in 1038 the peasants, encouraged by a rash bishop, formed Peace militias and launched attacks on castles. This sort of behaviour was more than the Church had bargained for and was doubtless exceptional, but it shows what pressure the peasants could bring to bear on the Peace assemblies.

In the central region – Auvergne, Burgundy, and around Vienne, and to a lesser degree in the rest of the Midi, but not in Catalonia and the west (where powerful feudal principalities had been constructed) – the monks of Cluny, and those bishops and lords who supported them, were forced to rely on the countryfolk. And they had to speak to those folk in the way that they had been hoping for, speaking not only of the unity in Christ of God's people, but of equality; they sang, to use the ironic expression of an adversary of the movement, Bishop Adalbero of Laon, 'the song of our first parents', that of father Adam and mother Eve, the song of a time when everyone worked, and noble genealogies did not exist. And the Bishop of Laon, appalled, denounced the 'rural councils' and the peasant militias, which he saw as grotesque, with their cavalry mounted on donkeys – buffaloes or camels would do just as well, he snorted. The world was topsy-turvy, soon bishops would have to pull ploughs, and fighting men wear cowls and observe a cloistered silence, and peasants would be crowned; the king himself, proclaimed as servant of the poor, was thus no more than a 'serf given the rank of king'. Such mockery says a great deal about the popular implications of the Peace movement, about the fears that it might assume an even more radical form, and about the feeling that a powerful subversive movement could well reverse the whole dominant ethos of nobles or clerks. We can of course distinguish within this

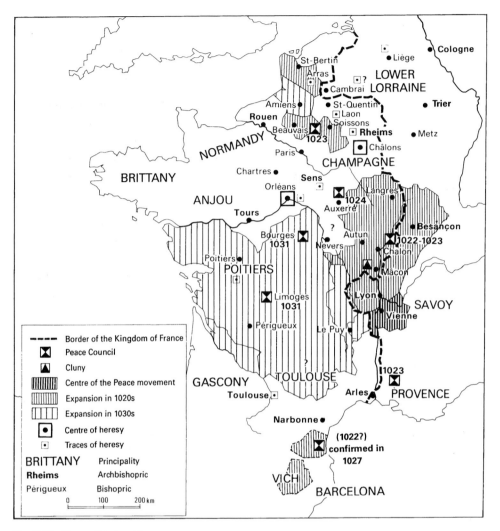

Map 2. The Peace of God and heresy.

deep-rooted agitation the wave of 'heresy' which swept over peasants and townspeople alike. Some have argued – as we shall see – that the religious dimension should be stressed above all. But, from the movements of 1020–5 in northern France up to the great 'pre-Gregorian' revolt of the Patarenes in Milan in 1050, there are too many resemblances with the movements for Peace for us not to recognise that other factors were at work.

Wearied at finding no end to the weeping and suffering, country prophets rose up in the villages of France, challenging the harsh conditions of an evil century with a dream of a world without evil. Let us take, for example, the village of Vertus in the area of Châlons, some years before the turn of the millennium. A peasant named Leutard lived there. He had separated from his wife, because he had been moved by the Spirit.

One day he found himself alone in the fields, going about some farming task. Tired by his labour, he went to sleep; and it seemed to him that a great swarm of bees entered his body by his secret passages, and then burst out of his mouth with a loud noise and stung him repeatedly. After this had been going on for some time, and he was almost maddened by their stings, it seemed to him that they were speaking to him and commanding him to do many things that were impossible for a man.

And the Burgundian monk who has left us an indignant account of the affair describes Leutard standing up during mass, tearing down the crucifix, that image of the woes of God and man, and stamping on it. He then spoke, fluently and at length; 'his renown soon attracted no small number of people'. A generation later, despite repression, 'Manichaeanism', that ascetic dialectic of Good and Evil, won over many village groups in the region.

There again, the rebellious talk of the eleventh century pointed to the storms and revolts of the twelfth. It was at Mont Guimer, not far from Vertus, that the northern heretics would take refuge, when their religion reached the Rhine, the coasts of Flanders and the plains of Picardy, when their bearded prophets, dressed in long black robes with hoods, indefatigable wanderers, went barefoot to preach on roads and in squares the intangible glory of the Father and the world without Evil. In fact the Cathar religion – although this will not please its ill-informed admirers – was undoubtedly stronger in the north, at the beginning, than in the Midi.

The northern bishops: against the Peace

But let us return to the eleventh century. In setting themselves at the head of the country people, and giving voice to their concerns, the Cluniacs had certainly opened up a path that was dangerous to the ruling class, of which they themselves were the most enlightened part. The northern bishops denounced those whom they considered to be irresponsible innovators. It is no accident that the harshest critic of the Cluniac path was a bishop from between the Seine and the Rhine, Adalbero, son of a great Lotharingian family. The position of the Church, and indeed the social situation in general, was very different in these regions. We have seen that the crisis there had perhaps started earlier and was slower to develop. Above all, the bishops and abbots had long been (as they themselves phrased it) the 'strongest pillars of royal power'. The contrast with the Midi was particularly striking in the monastic church. Unlike their southern sisters, devoted solely to prayer, the great northern abbeys had been veritable strongholds of Carolingian power. Their vast estates formed solid blocs of territory where the abbot, through the intermediacy of the advocate, his representative approved by the king, dispensed justice to the free men, raised recruits, and maintained a seasoned and disciplined cavalry. These territories enjoyed the privilege of immunity, which is to say that they were linked directly to the royal palace, and placed outside the control of the count. The immunity of Corbie, at the end of the ninth century, thus covered an area of 1,700 square kilometres; that of Saint-Riquier included most of Ponthieu, that of Saint-Bertin was the hinterland of Boulogne; the immunity of Saint-Vaast in Arras was so large that it removed half of the diocese of Cambrai from the

The Church as supporter of royal power. King Harold, leader of the Anglo-Saxons and William of Normandy's rival for the English succession, receives the orb and sceptre with the blessing of Archbishop Stigand. (Bayeux Tapestry.)

German Empire to which the bishopric itself owed obedience. Around Paris, the estates of Saint-Denis covered the Vexin, and those of Saint-Germain-des-Prés the area south of the Seine.

In these regions, the Church's estates were not competing with those of the laity: they were far and away the dominant ones. The problem for the noble houses here was not to extend their power but to take over these lands in order to build up a lordship which would otherwise remain out of their reach. The justification for this seizure was provided by the transformation of the office and role of the advocate. We have seen that the advocate was a sort of lay lieutenant of the abbot, subject to him and through him to the king. Chosen from among the local dignitaries, it was difficult for him to throw off this submissive role. But in the tenth century, when the great Frankish houses became independent, the responsibilities of the advocate had been taken over by the count, thus escaping the control of the head of the monastic community. And the count redistributed this office by dividing it up amongst his supporters, who became 'sub-advocates'. The estate was correspondingly divided up for their profit. When the allod-holders, who lived on the formerly immune territories, committed a crime, they were brought before the abbey court by the advocate, who called them to account, or, in the vernacular, 'reprimanded' them (*tancer*). Thus it was said of the local lords who had become sub-advocates that they had the *tancement* of a village, and this northern *tancement* was a sort of equivalent of the southern *commenda*. By a different route, the same point had been reached.

But this appropriation did not provoke the brutal confrontations that it had in the south. It was not so much a change in structure as an individualising of the aristocratic hold on the mass of former public estates. Such 'privatisation' corresponded to the general change of direction among the Frankish nobility, who ceased their foreign ventures. Above all, the great northern churches had not abandoned all their powers to the castellans. The abbots, and especially the bishops, with their following of domestic vassals, their traditions of command and their habit of regarding themselves as the representatives *par excellence* of royal power, felt they were strong enough to keep society on the straight and narrow.

Thus it made no sense for them to rely on the communities of allod-holders. It seemed to them that society was completely divided between noble houses and serfs, the labourers in the fields. In Western Europe this alleged 'Indo-European' division into the three orders – priests, warriors, farmers – was quite recent. For Adalbero of Laon and his like, all peasants were henceforth serfs, and as such destined for hardship, labour and 'travail' (in the etymological sense of the word 'pain'). 'This burdened race possesses nothing without hardship. Who can measure the effort of the serfs, their journeys and innumerable tasks? To provide wealth and clothing for all, that is the serf's lot.' But as Adalbero was a man of the Church, he thought it timely to remind people that 'no free man [i.e. himself and his nobles] can live without the serfs . . . The lord is fed by the very serf whom he prides himself on nourishing.' A good estate administrator should remember this and treat the productive class well. Reflecting on this, the bishop could conclude tranquilly, 'There is no end to the tears and complaints of the serfs.'

We must remember that, among these so-called serfs, there were many former clients of the Church. The northern bishops had not thought of making any alliance with the peasants, but only of making them obedient, obviously for their own good. We can understand why the bishops would look askance at the country assemblies, founded as they were on the display and adoration of relics which could look like idol-worship. The Christian tradition in the Midi was strong enough to cope with this. As we shall see, however, the situation was quite different in the north, at least until the beginning of the tenth century. What was the point in awakening old demons in order to claim the leading place in society? On the whole, the northern bishops already enjoyed that privilege. Unluckily for them, the 'burdened race', which they were calmly inviting to persevere in its efforts, was developing along lines hidden from the bishops' gaze, like underground rivers, from the end of the tenth century. The sudden emergence of rural prophets would show the bishops the danger of their conservatism.

It was in these conditions that, during the 1060s, the northern bishops and some princes, such as the counts of Flanders and the dukes of Normandy, decided to adopt the Truce of God, but adapted it to their own customs. Its aim was not the protection of the weak, but the limitation of the feuds which were decimating the knightly kin-groups, and

45

threatening not only the cohesion of the new nobility, but also the type of social order which they were imposing in their principalities.

In the final analysis, the Peace and the Truce had less of a transforming impact on society than might appear at first glance. Once the communities of allod-holders were broken up, country society split into two classes, one of serf farmers, the other of squires who were proud to be allied with the old noble houses, which had become numerous and intrusive. This development was well advanced before it receives its first mention in our sources. The Peace legislation, in so far as it took into consideration the new vocabulary arising from the crisis (for example, the opposition between knight and peasant), actually legitimised the social categories that it masked, even as it claimed to moralise their role. It defined them. The transformation of seigneurial warriors into noble Christian knights permitted them to be something more than mere brigands: a strong, hierarchical ruling class, whose physical and ideological position was founded on the bonds of the fief. The knight held his fief of the baron, the baron of the count, the count of the king. Society had become feudal.

The role of the allod and the fief

The feudal crisis, to state the obvious, not only entailed the setting up of a new relationship between the rulers and the ruled – a relationship epitomised in the stark arrangements of seigneurial justice – but also implied profound mental transformations in the collective consciousness of the groups concerned. There was, of course, the great creative movement which, in the literature of the new knightly class, brought forth and transformed elements of legend and gave birth to a new culture proper to the feudal imagination. This also marked the beginning of the manipulation of the ancient epic themes for political ends. This is a rich field of study, but it does not much concern us here, in that it heralds the recognisably modern elements of the future, rather than clarifying the period of transition formed by the tenth and eleventh centuries. We must try to clarify another subject here, unfortunately more obscure but essential: that of the beliefs, customs and rites of the allo-dial communities whose decline we have witnessed in the preceding sections. These can only be glimpsed as fleeting shadows just at the time they are dissolving – a paradox familiar to ethnologists, who know that they can only understand a culture when it begins to fall apart.

In order to grasp something of peasant thought in these two centuries of change, we must give up almost entirely the use of the material favoured by medievalists, the texts written down in Latin. Not only because they are generally the work of clerks who were *a priori* hostile to such thought, but also because medieval Latin, forged over centuries of effort as a 'univocal and categorical language' was not adapted to portraying the world of a peasantry attached to the very ancient past. While Latin can transmit expressions which are valuable evidence, it is rarely capable in itself of showing us the life which animated them. It is quite different with the texts in the vernacular, which are much closer to the conceptual system used in 'popular' thought, in what the clerks of the Middle Ages disdainfully called 'rustic speech', 'the language of the simple', used by the 'illiterate', the 'idiots', in the original sense of that word. It is true that this form of discourse was rarely practised in front of them, and for a reason. When they chanced to hear it, they could not help but testify to its eloquence and the fascination it exercised over the rural masses, as we have seen in the accounts of the eleventh-century prophets. It is this repudiated discourse which we will try to restore, at least in part, in the two essential, overlapping spheres of law and religion.

From cultural diversity to class conflict

Throughout the Carolingian period, groups born in the ethnic patchwork resulting from the decline of the Roman Empire had managed to preserve their distinct legal traditions that were rooted in their original cultures, albeit adapted to their new circumstances. Each person followed the 'law' of his cultural group, and thus considered himself to be 'Frankish', 'Burgundian', 'Gothic' or 'Aquitainian' (that is, 'Roman'). The name given by jurists to this phenomemon – the personality of laws – should not disguise its collective quality. Clearly the personality of laws did not mean that legal usage was always and everywhere different. That depended on the region, and on social class. Where the majority consisted of a peasantry who had long since absorbed the few non-native elements, a diversity of laws would not make great sense, and the local petty nobles who 'pronounced the law' knew what was to be done around Cambrai as around Narbonne; those subject to their justice never moved away, and they married men or women from the neighbouring hamlet. The problems of conflicting laws, such as we know today in the field of international private law, would not exist at this level, except in the cultural borderlands where there were large groups of heterogeneous peoples.

At the level of the imperial aristocracy the problem was quite different; there, political calculations, the enormous networks of matrimonial alliances and distant governments encouraged social mobility on a scale unknown to peasant groups. Unfortunately, almost all the legal documentation – the law-codes apart – tells us only about the noble houses. This explains an apparent contradiction in the texts.

Until the mid-tenth century, the aristocrats had maintained the old distinctions of law: in Angoulême and in Clermont, which in the thirteenth century were lands where Roman law did not apply, there were still cultivated nobles who knew about it; on the other hand in Vienne, or Narbonne, which were later to use Roman law, a minority continued to use 'Salic law', that is, Frankish custom. In 918, when there was a great assembly of jurists at Alzonne in the Toulousain, the specialists in different kinds of law were carefully distinguished from each other: eight Roman 'judges', eight Gothic *rachinburgii*, and only four Frankish *scabini*. Toulouse, in the Aquitaine of Roman tradition, had also been the capital of the Gothic kingdom, and the marquis who governed it, the offshoot of an ancient Frankish family, in 933 still held to the 'Salic law'.

Nevertheless, in 864 the Carolingian king could still speak of the southern regions as 'those lands where Roman law is observed'. He thus alluded to the law largely pertaining to the peasant population. Conversely, in the north, Roman law tended to disappear, even amongst the aristocracy. In a lawsuit between two abbeys, no judge able to apply Roman

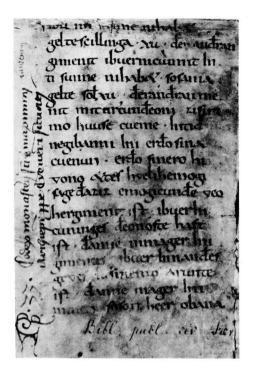

Frankish law: fragment of a manuscript in Old High German. (Trier, Stadtbibliothek.)

law could be found in Paris, although it had to be used in ecclesiastical cases. This shows that around a great town of 'Francia', free men of sufficient standing to pronounce the law no longer knew 'vulgar' Roman law but only Frankish custom. In order to find Romanists, in this case, the proceedings had to be held in Orléans and the Roman judges had to come in from a specific region, the Gâtinais.

So when the Archbishop of Lyons, Agobard, in the same period complained of the variety of judicial systems applicable to the tangled kin-groups in his city, it should be noted that this concerns a special case: aristocratic, urban groups, in a frontier town, where Roman traditions rubbed shoulders with Burgundian, Frankish and perhaps, given the links with Italy, Lombard traditions. Agobard's testimony shows how, in Lyons, the variety of 'laws' hindered the unity of 'God's people' (in fact only the aristocracy is concerned); he nowhere claims that this variety existed, to the same degree and with the same inconveniences, in the surrounding countryside. The solution he proposes is revealing. He suggests reducing judicial practice to two systems: one 'Frankish', which was the most widespread barbarian law, and that of the royal house; the other 'Roman', which was the law of the Church and of the majority in the Midi.

It was only from the tenth century that Agobard's wish was realised, and probably to an extent beyond his hopes. In this period, a text from Poitou speaks for the first time of 'the custom of the province'; in 1095, another cites 'the custom of Bordeaux'. In 1095, the Count of Toulouse, who was certainly of Frankish stock, was considered to be living under

48

Roman law. From this period onwards, there was no longer a question of 'Roman' or 'Frankish' custom but of the custom of the region. The law was not that of a 'people', that is of an ethnic and cultural group, however artificially constructed, but that of a region. From being 'personal', custom became 'territorial'. Thus a geography of customs was established, which owed much to the political geography of the eleventh century, but which was based on the double substratum of the majority revealed in the ninth century.

South of the Saintes–Lausanne line lay the lands of 'written law', i.e. Roman law. Local customs, already Romanised, were strengthened there from the twelfth century onwards by jurists, specialists in law who were in the service of princes. These southern jurists, influenced by the Italian schools, introduced in the early part of the century the Roman law of Justinian, which applied in Italy especially in Rome's dependencies. In the north, in the lands of 'custom' in the narrow sense, where the base was non-Roman, the jurists soon began to record local custom, which until then had been oral, and gradually to transform it into a vast *corpus* of law that was also 'written', reworked and given a bias towards the monarchic, starting with the 'custom' of Paris. The purpose of this effort was not so much to improve customary law by making it fixed (in any case, its malleability in its oral state should not be exaggerated) as to place it under the control of royal power and its agents at the expense of the groups that had hitherto produced it.

The customs as recorded show us that in the north there existed a class division, visible in the law, between nobles and 'peasants'. From the twelfth century, each of them had their distinct customs and 'law'. Of what did this distinction consist?

Allodial society

When we encountered the allod-holders for the first time, I spoke of the unthinking anachronism which had led to their being called 'small landowners'. It is time to justify this criticism. Some eleventh-century southern scribes, when they wrote down a charter, would often use either the vulgar Latin term *allodium* – which in old French became *alluet* – or the classical Latin term *proprietas*, without distinguishing between them. Their mistake, in these areas and at this period, was probably not as serious as the confusion to which it gives rise today. Property and allod in fact mean exactly the opposite: the one really belongs to an individual, who has, according to the old definition, 'the usage, profit and abusage' (that is, the right to give it away or to destroy it); the other is *all-eaht*, 'the possession of all', a term brought into French territory by German immigrants and which eventually reached the Midi.

Two associated concepts are involved in this latter idea. One is that of the dead, the ancestors: in the old barbarian law-codes, *allod* was rendered in Latin as *terra aviatica*, the land of the forefathers. When one of those who had a share of the land had to give it up, in the exceptional cases of fine or banishment for example, he had to make *chene-chruda*, or as the Anglo-Saxons would say *kin-hredde*, 'free himself from his kinship'. In Scandinavia, where the identical category of *odal* existed, it was this possession by dead relations that justified the current possession: if there was a lawsuit, each party listed those of his dead relatives **49** who had once lived there, 'inhabiting' the land, each trying to remember the greatest number and the furthest back. This ancient occupation of an allod was demonstrated by the place-names, as the Icelandic sagas show: some farm where an ancestor had lived, some ford where a relative had died, weapon in hand, some gully where another had been drowned; above all the tumulus of the ancestors, an irrefutable proof, which gave rise in Scandinavian law to the expression *haug-odal* 'allod with tumulus'. From within the earth, in mounds or mountains, the dead, the 'Black Elves', continued to watch over the 'possession of all'. And, at each death, all the survivors had to have their part in this power, their part of this soil. We shall see that in the tenth century the dark spirits of the departed were far from having been chased out of the countryside by Christian preaching or by the work of bishops.

But the regime of the seigneurie, as we have seen, was the enemy of the allodial communities. Under its pressure, allods diminished. A few all too rare figures show us the pace of this decline. In Catalonia, the study of wills, which were numerous in this Romanised region, shows that between 990 and 1000, 80 per cent of the property bequeathed was allodial; then the curve descends: 1000–25, 65 per cent; 1025–50, 55 per cent; 1050–75, 35 per cent; 1075–1100, 25 per cent; 1120–30, 10 per cent. Around Bordeaux in the twelfth century the percentage of allods seems to have been the same (10 per cent). In the country around Chartres, from the mid-tenth century, allod holders also gave bits of their lands to the cathedral; this fact in itself, in a non-Romanised region, marks the first erosion of the system. The pace seems to have been the same as in Catalonia: 940–1030, 80 per cent; 1030–60, 45 per cent; 1060–90, 38 per cent; 1090–1130, 8 per cent. If we move to the borders of Picardy and Flanders, we get an entirely different impression: in the land of Hesdin, which covered about 250 square kilometres, 61 per cent of the land transactions of the period 1090–1150 still involved allodial holdings; another stretch of country in the region sported the name 'pays d'Alleue'. Elsewhere the same sort of name only indicated villages, such as les Allues in Savoy, les Alluets near the forest of Yvelines, les Alleuds in the Ardennes, in Anjou and near Niort, in Poitou.

For a long time, however, it was thought that there remained more allods in the Midi than in the north. In fact, this impression disguises a fundamental difference both of structure and nature. The lands called allodial in the north remained grouped together; the allods were less frequent, we might say, but greater in extent, and it was certainly in the nature of a real allod to remain a collective piece of land. There were thus whole cantons where groups of free peasants had succeeded in maintaining their independence and their customs. The pays d'Alleue in Ternois, which we will discuss below, and the famous 'kingdom' of Yvetot are striking examples. The southern allods, on the other hand, were small in size, and thus they crop up more often in legal documents. This in itself indicates that people in the Midi applied the Frankish term to a different reality, to heritable property free of rent, but which, as in Roman law, could be bought and sold. The difference becomes clearer if one examines a map of the customs followed by families in the thirteenth century when they confronted this central problem: the succession to land, and the part accorded to each of the descendants in this succession. Only the north interests us here, since the customs of the peasants of the Midi are disguised by the second layer of Roman law. On the other side of the feudal crisis, chronologically speaking, the survivals of the allodial system are important.

Rustic inheritance under discussion

On such a map, drawn up according to the work of historians of customary law, we see three areas where custom has brought a variety of solutions to the problem of equality between heirs.

The first region under customary law is found in Normandy. In this land they were strictly egalitarian. At the end of the twelfth century, the *Très Ancien Coutumier* of Normandy declared: 'If the father divides between his children during his lifetime, and each of them holds his part for a long time during his father's life, after his death these shares are not tenable.' It states, a little further on, that after the father's death, 'all the heritable gifts which he has made to a child's advantage must be returned in full so that they can be shared out. No one can, by donation, tradition, sale, or any other means, do better than any of those who await an equal part of his inheritance after his death, or favour any of their progeny.' The wishes of the deceased did not hold good for the allod; it returned ineluctably and equally to the relatives. Those who had received something from the dead man put it back into the common fund: it was obligatory. Of course the eldest could choose the best piece of land, 'the main herbergerie', but only on condition that the youngest relatives were recompensed.

The same prohibition on leaving a 'best inheritor', a *lief kind*, an *enfant chéri* as they were called in Flanders, was found almost throughout the north, but with various nuances. In the west – in Anjou, Maine, Touraine, Poitou and some parts of Brittany – the return was obligatory, but was restricted to the part that was in excess of the common share, as judged by trustworthy men. The same solution was adopted in most of Champagne around Châlons and probably in Flanders. In all these regions, custom had similar characteristics: a kin-group regime, no sharing according to the will of the dead man, representation *ad infinitum*, and the concern to pass on the inheritance as a whole.

This system, which has been described as pernickety egalitarianism, was also an individualist system: each man could dispose of his own plot as he wished. He could marry and settle away from the others; he could leave his property in pursuit of adventure; he could remain unmarried, and live with his brother or sister. Often the plots remained grouped together, and the children lived together in order to work them, as is seen in Scandinavia, where there was an identical system. But if each man had his portion, then he also had a say. That was what made a man – or a woman – free. Rather than individualism, which implies dividing things up (and which was often avoided), we should once again be speaking about freedom.

A second region under customary law seems to have been developed from the two great customs of Paris and Orléans. We can say, leaving aside certain doubts about their origin, that these customs were a matter of options. Children who received property, generally

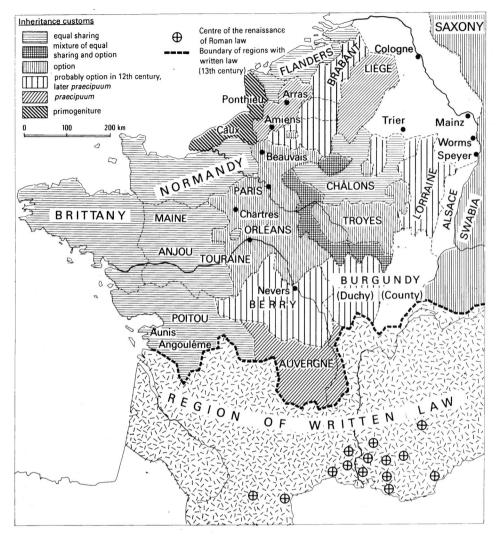

Map 3. Customs and survivals of the allod.

upon marriage, had the choice between keeping it or returning it to the common 'fund' until it came to dividing that up; they could be 'inheritors' or 'partners', but not both. This solution seems to have spread or to have been in use around Troyes, in Vermandois, Lorraine, Berry, Nivernais and the duchy of Burgundy. This could represent a decline from the first system of absolute equality – an impression reinforced by the existence of intermediary customs, as in the long strip extending from the custom of Sens, between the egalitarian zone of Châlons and the twin blocs of Troyes and Orléans, or even the custom of Rheims. Reciprocal enclaves were just as frequent, in Lorraine, Dunois, Noyon. Such a system in theory might allow some advantage to one heir. But it should be noted that the custom of Paris, for example, vigorously affirmed the principle of equality; and often it was said that if the advantage was 'unreasonable' or 'extreme', 'trusty judges' should be called in to assess the surplus, and return it to common possession. This was also the solution, as we have seen, that was adopted by customs in the first bloc. The option system perhaps tended, in the long run, to move away from equality, but it did not deny the principle. Moreover it provided for equality among the children who were not established, who remained together living in the 'hall'.

Finally, there were inegalitarian zones. In Ponthieu and the lands of Caux the dominant practice was primogeniture; in the Amiénois and in the region of Arras, custom permitted *praecipuum*, the practice by which one heir was authorised to take in advance more than his equal share.

A correlation between these three systems – egalitarianism, option and *praecipuum* or birthright – and the main ways of working the land in these various regions is possible in some cases. Egalitarian customs prevailed in the allodial regions – as in Normandy, peopled by Scandinavians, and the lands of Hesdin, in the north-west part of the Artois. On the other hand, in the south-east part, around Arras, we know that from the eleventh century onwards, the former free men had been reduced to the status of dependants of the abbey. In the region of the option system, around Paris and Beauvais, the lands concerned were those of the 'villeins', people who were not serfs, nor free, nor nobles, it was all one here in the thirteenth century. But these lands are no longer considered to be allodial, they are 'villein holdings'. We can thus better understand, perhaps, the interest in the option system, which encouraged the children to remain grouped around the house, precisely because at first the property given as a marriage portion had to be smaller than the portions for inheritance. In Orléans, the very oldest dispositions simply excluded the children who were established, because they had already received something. This was an area where the seigneurial regime bent peasant custom without really being able to break it. Finally, the regions where birthright prevailed certainly show landholding of the classical estate type: one man alone was in charge; in cases of age or sickness, he had to divest himself of this responsibility, and the name of one of his sons, sometimes the eldest, sometimes the youngest perhaps, would be inscribed on the estate roll in his place. The strip of 'inegalitarian' lands in the north thus probably represents an area where the great estates were indeed preponderant. In a few specific cases, as in Uccle in Brabant, on the border of two zones, custom distinguished expressly between two categories of peasants: the *mesniemen*, members of a *mesnie* (a domestic society) and the *voegtmen*, the men of the advocacy (that is, as will be recalled, the former free men); the *mesniemen* had an inegalitarian system, the *voegtmen* a system of return.

A glance at the areas covered by these two opposite systems, at that where the egalitarian allodial system dominated, and at that where the inegalitarian estate system triumphed, is enough to make us doubt how widespread the latter was. In fact, the region in which the allodial system was predominant is impressive. The example of Scandinavia, where the wealth of source material enables us truly to appreciate the implications of the system, shows that equal shares in inheritance and judicial assemblies of free men were integral parts of the same social structure, which was not compatible with strong lordly power. The apparent 'individualism' of this system was in fact part of a network of strong collective and associative habits. Social equilibrium was the result of a balance struck between kin-groups, rivals and allies, and the limits on any one person's power, as illustrated by many of the Norse sagas. The peasant revolts of the twelfth century, by making original equality the basis of their claims, in the regions where seigneurial power was becoming more oppressive, were still defending the remains of a social model, not merely a dream.

The beginnings of the fief

In the same period, the world of the nobles had beome in essence a world of fiefs. We have seen how many knights had risen from the ranks of the peasantry to swell the aristocratic houses during the ninth and tenth centuries. Their land was part of the great seigneurial estate and became an independent working, a holding, thus risking confusion with the smallholdings of the tenant farmers and the master's farms. To hold in fief was a way, if not of escaping dependence, at least of choosing the most honourable interpretation of it: fidelity rather than obedience. Just as the *all-öd* implied a concept of the relations of a human group to the land, so its later form, the *feoh-öd*, was really a way of thinking.

Feohu, faihu, from which our word 'fief' comes, is a key notion of ancient Germanic tribal culture. It designated the very first of the runes, the head of the original tribe, then no doubt the most prestigious, 'the family of Freya'. It is significant that the first ideogram in a conceptual series which would dominate archaic culture should be consecrated to the goddess and to a gift. 'Feohu', says the gloss, 'is consolation for all men; however, each one must distribute it generously.' Materially speaking, *feohu* was a precious object, on which had been painted (*faihan*) one or several magic characters, perhaps in fact the rune of the goddess Freya. These paintings obviously disappeared with time, but in the third century, when runes were incised in metals, partly to serve as an alphabet, the term 'painting' was still used to describe the procedure. Many of these early inscriptions, engraved on precious objects such as brooches for cloaks, or boxes of bronze or bone hung from a belt, were dedications and expressed a link of affection: 'Alu gave this', 'Hariberga gives to Liubo, with love', 'Boso wrote these runes, to you Deotha, he gave [this gift]', 'Arogis and Alaguth made [this gift] with love', 'Joy to Godahid'.

This 'painting' made the *feohu* much more than a simple present, which was designated by another rune, *gibu*. By the sign, the *feohu* became what ethnologists would recognise as a gift that conferred an obligation, but it might be better to see it as a gift created from a relationship of friendship. It was thanks to this 'generously distributed consolation' that peaceful sociability was maintained, placed under the sign of the loving and generous Freya. Peace was made by offering compensation to hostile clans for their dead, dear to their hearts, consoling them for their loss. When one of his friends, Edgetheow, killed the Wulfinga Haetholaf, king of the Danes, Hrothgar decided to intervene between the parties: 'By *feohu* I settled this feud, I sent to the Wulfingas ancient noble gifts.' In Jutland, a Saxon clan had been treacherously attacked by Frisians and Jutes, led by King Finn. His palace was burned down. Then they made peace, and promised to reconstruct a hall, with a high seat,

In the presence of his wife Almodis, Raymond Berengar I, Count of Barcelona, hands over 2,000 ounces of gold (represented symbolically by the coins in his left hand and on his lap) to Viscount Bernard of Béziers to purchase rights over the counties of Carcassonne and Razés. (*Liber Feudorum Major*, eleventh century, Barcelona, Archives of the Crown of Aragon.)

which they would hold in common with the Jutes. They would be on an equal footing with them: 'to give the *feohu*, the son of Folcwalda [King Finn] always did honour to the half-Danes [the Saxons]] . . . he would honour them with circlets, precious gold worked objects [bracelets worn by warriors], exactly as he did to please the Frisian kin-group, in the drinking hall. And the two parties pledged their faith in a firm peace.' Similar alliances are also found among the Lombards: the *faderfio*, 'the father's gift', was given to the new couple by the father of the bride; the groom himself brought the *metfio*, the 'gift of meeting'.

Whether large or small, the *feohu* involved friendship, or re-established it; it 'consoled', wrote the scribes who recorded in Latin, it 'softened' and 'reassured'. It helped the person whom the others considered to be their leader to maintain a harmonious balance in the tribe. And there was nothing worse for a chieftain than to be *feoh-leas*: without fiefs to give. A few rare indications show that this idea of gifts conferring an obligation survived in Carolingian society.

At the same time in the service of Carolingian royalty there spread an ancient institution of the later Roman Empire, the *beneficium pro stipendio* (benefice as reward), which was used to establish the warrior bands that formed the core of the Carolingian army, especially the knights of the great northern churches. This form of salary was aimed at allowing a man to concentrate, undistracted by worries, on fulfilling a task: it comprised a parcel of land intended for the support of a soldier, no more and no less. One of the most famous bishops of the ninth century, Hincmar of Rheims, justified the institution by saying: 'If one does not raise the calf, one does not hitch the ox to the plough.' The Church here inherited the aristocratic disdain of the senatorial nobility for soldiers, seen as both beasts and butchers. The great lay landowners also gave a *beneficium* in land, but this was something else again, a recompense for a deserving domestic servant. Sometimes, the term referred to the recovery of an allod by a powerful man, who then returned it as a *beneficium*, on generous terms, to the former allod-holder.

Then, in the tenth century, the term *feù*, brought into the Midi by Frankish garrisons, began to mean *beneficium pro stipendio*. It was said that land was held in *feù*, and this land came to be called *feudum*, i.e. *feoh-öd*, 'possession of a gift which carried obligations'. The neologism, because a *feoh* was never a piece of land, was used in the north, in the Vermandois and in Hainault, from the beginning of the eleventh century. Possibly it was even older. The German warriors or peasants who had long been settled in the old Western Empire interpreted sale as a gift or counter-gift. The price was for them a *feoh*, the land sold could be for them another *feoh*, its counterpart. The notaries of northern Italy dealt with these 'barbarians', and had been forced to understand their customs, and had energetically blended their own writings with old barbarian rites: 'If the vendor is a Frank, whether Salian or Ripuarian, if he is a Goth or an Aleman, put the charter on the ground, and on the charter place a knife, a marked stick [with runes], [or] the magic staff; put down also a clump of earth and a twig, and the inkpot [in Alemanian usage, there is a *wandilanc*] and lift the charter off the ground. Then, holding it, recite the traditional formula as given above.' The notary would not put all these objects on the parchment; the marked stick – *festuca notata* – was known to the Franks, who also used sticks in the *renunciatio parentillae*, leaving an allod; the transfer was called *ant-daelang*; the Alemanni worked the transfer by means of the magic staff, *want*, which was the *want-daelang*; the clump and the stick signified the land; as for the inkpot, probably it represented the notary's own contribution to the ceremony. This kind of ritual, which went on for a long time in the north, was not necessarily very old; it may even have been a creation of Merovingian society. No matter: in the twelfth century, the northern knights were still invested with their 'fief' by means of a stick and a wisp of straw. And when they wished to part from the lord who had given it to them, they 'threw away the straw', somewhat like their forefathers in the *renonciatio*, when they separated from the allodial group by throwing down some sticks. The rite persisted, albeit adapted or transformed.

The *feoh-öd*, unlike the allod, could never be shared. The allod kept a sense of eqality among the kin-group; the fief, this Germanic form of tenure, organised the family around a single individual, who held the fief. When, in the north, the only remaining free families were absorbed into the aristocracy (their allods having been yielded to the magnates and returned to them as fiefs), the nobles enforced their own law and turned their back on the old Germanic custom of equal division. Normandy, whose Scandinavian origins were still felt in the twelfth century, was an intermediate stage in this evolution. Equal division still applied there among both 'villeins' and 'nobles' if it was a matter of ancestral lands – *socagia* – defined as hereditary by the *sokemen*, 'the men who attended trials' (that is, those who had the right to go to the judicial assembly of free men). Fiefs themselves were not divisible. But, everywhere else at this time, the distinction shifted from land and became applied to men: peasants divided their land, nobles did not, or very rarely. The law of their fiefs was extended to the rest of their property. Or rather, the structure imposed on the 'noble' family by seigneurial society had transfomed its relationship to its patrimony.

Noble succession, contrary to allodial succession, created or aggravated inequality between heirs. First, it created inequality between children declared legitimate and those declared illegitimate by excluding bastards and abandoning (to the Church's solace) multiple marriages and the ninth-century marriages 'in the Danish fashion'; second, it aggravated inequality between sons and daughters, the latter 'contented' with their dowries, however meagre; and third, it introduced inequality between the sons themselves through inheritance by the eldest or through *parage*. Noble succession also enhanced, within the limits of the system, the power of the head of the patrimony over those of his relatives who lived on it, by extending his freedom to grant or bequeath the least parts of it; the material well-being of the youngest member, for example, could depend upon his favour.

Thus the noble family came to shape itself, and express itself, as a single male 'line', a 'lineage' in the medieval sense, where each individual had to serve the head of the line and depended on him, without his death changing this pattern in any way. Naturally this model was not realised everywhere to the same degree. But the general tendency was the same everywhere, from the north to the Midi. Perhaps, however, the frequency of *seigneuries en parage* in the Midi – where lesser knights shared the revenues of a village in tiny parts – was the sign of the model's being less successful in these regions.

Thus it is quite right to call the nobility of this period a feudal nobility: it was so by its very family structure, which was henceforth profoundly different from the peasant structure, at least where the peasantry remained more or less free. The allodial family had given way to the feudal family. Some historians reject the use of this adjective, seeing it as less a descriptive term than as an echo of the revolutionary propaganda of the eighteenth century: one might ask what else they would call a society dominated by such a class.

Ceremonies and obligations

Whatever the part played in the development of 'feudalism' by the conscious policy of the princes or by the strong trend towards the formation of private followings, Christian Europe was slowly given over to the practice of vassalage, which evolved into feudal practice, between the end of the tenth century and the beginning of the twelfth. It is true that in the French Midi, a written agreement, the *convenientia*, gave it a firmly contractual character, whereas in central Italy the 'personal' element mattered less than the 'real' element of the fief, while the reverse was the case in Germany. It is also true that many regions were merely brushed by this development, or touched by it very late, as in Aquitaine or Picardy, while others such as Normandy and England were entirely feudal. But even where the noble allod held good, or where the 'feudalised' part of the aristocracy remained a minority before 1200, a common social code now affected the whole of the nobility.

Harold takes his vow to William, one hand on each of two reliquaries. The scene takes place at Bayeux; probably Harold was recognising William as King of England on the death of Edward the Confessor. (Bayeux Tapestry.)

By the beginning of the twelfth century the ceremony was fixed, composed of bits and pieces which were to be combined into a single model that would be reproduced everywhere: the vassal made a short declaration, kneeling, without his weapons, in recognition that he was the man of another man, and put his hands together and placed them between the hands of the other man (*immixtio manuum*), then the 'older' (*senior*) would raise the 'boy' (*vassallus*) and kiss him on the lips as a sign of accord (*osculum pacis*, rejected in Germany because it seemed to establish an unseemly equality between the two men). This was the 'homage' (in German, *Mannschaft*), which accompanied a mutual oath sworn on some relics. The physical aspect of the double contract 'of mouth and hands' revealed a relationship, almost a form of kinship, that henceforth bound both men: vassals owed respect, and on occasion had to provide lodgings and financial aid (which they soon sought to limit to particular cases). They also proffered advice by which, we should not forget, the vassals were able to control their common master to some extent. They did not always have to perform military service themselves; sometimes it was limited to a tour of guard duty at the lord's castle, those dreary weeks of 'residence' when there was nothing to do but play chess or flirt with the girls; sometimes, however, active military service was an integral part of homage, as in Normandy, England and the Holy Land. As for the lord, he had to be a father to his man, defend him, give him gifts, receive him at his table, bring up his sons and marry off his daughters. But in this ideal model, the fief tended to become, like the old public *beneficium*, the salary for feudal service, without any distinction being drawn, at least in law, between the holding of a simple knight and the high offices held by great laymen or churchmen. In all cases, investiture took the form of the presentation of an object that was more or less appropriate to the nature of the fief, a clump of grass or a wisp of straw, a rod, a banner, an abbatial or episcopal cross, a bible, keys, or even the bell-rope from a church. Here too, rites that had been distinct were blended in a formal ceremony whose deliberate archaism should not disguise its recent character.

58

A servant offers a cup of wine to his master.
(Lectionary of Rheims cathedral, eleventh century,
MS 294.)

The permanent nature of feudal-vassalic relations between the aristocratic lineages was reinforced by the hereditability of fiefs, which satisfied both sides. We have already seen how difficult it was to reclaim a fief after the ninth century, even on the death of the holder. Of course the law permitted the two parties to break their contract, renounce the oath they had sworn, and the lord would then declare that the fief had been seized into his hands. History is full of struggles of this sort; it was then necessary to try to carry out the sentence or prevent the fief's passing into other hands. On this level, and many others, the introduction of these practices into the Church created very complicated situations: the grant of a fief to a convent deprived the lord of land which would henceforth yield him no service; his only resort was financial compensation; equally, it was impossible to extort from the Church, since as an institution it never died, the payment for the right of succession to an office (the 'relief') on the death of an individual bishop or abbot. These properties fell into the 'dead hand' of the Church. Heredity became strengthened among the laity; its almost unchallenged introduction after 1100 no doubt explains why a large number of allod-holders did not hesitate to 'take back as a fief' the allods which they had ceded to a lord, confident that they would be able to hold on to them.

The cohesion of the unified aristocracy at the end of the eleventh century nonetheless meant that there were tensions within its structure because of the rigid nature of the system. The princes and most of the eminent lords rejected the idea of dividing fiefs: a notable example is the Ottonian dynasty, which firmly maintained the principle of non-divisiblity of lands attached to public offices, the *honores*. It was doubtless this kind of anxiety that led to the development of the birthright principle, i.e. favouring the eldest son, ensuring that the lord had a single holder for his fief. This principle meant that lineages followed a policy of restricting marriages for the sole profit of the eldest son, populating castle halls and the roads with disinherited and discontented younger sons, who were rarely

59

tempted by the life of a monk or canon. Thus there was a relative 'proletarianisation' of the nobility, together with a risk of the line dying out if the main branch was weak. The systems of multiple tenure under a single responsible person, such as *parage*, frequently encountered in the West, also generated tensions and difficulties. This was the price the new 'feudal' aristocracy paid for its strength and its dominance over the other classes of society.

It is tempting to reserve the term 'feudality' for the group of relationships between nobles and the structure they formed; we can thus distinguish 'feudality' from 'feudalism', which designates the structures of domination – and exploitation – of men by the 'feudal lords'. It is a useful distinction, but not always a clear one: 'feudalism' in effect is simply the return into English of the German form which was a translation, in German historigraphy, of the French word *féodalité*. *Feudalismus* was thus used by Marx and Engels, who gave the word a more critical and materialist character. Then the divergence arose between feudality, the subject of a more traditional and legalistic approach, and feudalism, which was studied from the angle of relations of production.

Whether or not we use the distinction between feudality and feudalism, it is plain that the fief was also a structure of government. The modern reader is sometimes misled by the nuances of medieval language: this castle, or stronghold, and the land belonging to it, were for the nobleman his fief, which he held from his lord. But for the peasant who lived there, the lord was this enfeoffed noble, the land an estate, what we would call a *seigneurie*, although the term was rarely used in the period. The lord of the land exercised his many rights over the peasants living on it (the *manants*), rights derived from ancient public laws of command but adapted to his use, i.e. made stronger and wider.

Thus land rent became widespread through the entire peasantry. Thanks to his troop of armed horsemen, the lord of the castle, also armed with the power of the *ban*, was able to extort extra labour from the country people, a development that – as one might imagine – was not at first a welcome one. On this level, feudalism was the supreme development of manorialism. In so far as it forced the peasantry to produce a surplus, it can be seen as the origin of the take-off of the European economy, and in fact of 'economic progress' – that 'European miracle'. But it should not be forgotten that the workers of this miracle were reluctant peasants. They were urged on by those of their number who agreed to work for the master at the expense of their fellow villagers, and who formed that class of greedy and arrogant seigneurial officials who dreamed that their own humble origins would be forgotten and that they might rank with the nobility; but they became bourgeois, rather than members of the feudal nobility.

Feudal lordship, sanctioned by the Church, became a stable and regulated part of the landscape after the violent crisis that produced it had passed. As such, feudal lordship could be accepted by the peasantry as a force for stability, and as a lesser evil. The great peasant revolts of later centuries, which threatened it in the name of primitive equality and freedom, i.e. in the same terms by which it had been challenged at the time of its origin, were to reveal the limits of this social consensus. And yet feudal lordship was established, and this cannot be explained solely by the terror inspired by the knights. Some things are mightier than the sword. The disssolution of the communities of allod-holders is not merely a problem of political or military history, but also a problem of cultural history.

The castle as tool of protection and domination: an aerial view of Hedingham Castle (Essex), an eleventh-century castle in the Norman style.

The taming of the savage mind

In evoking the cluster of ideas that surround the notion of the allod, we have already touched on the other fundamental aspect of the independent peasant culture in the north: what has long been called *religio pagana*, peasant religion. Here we have an exceptional text available, which throws a strong light on the religious world of a large group of refractory peasants: *The Corrector and Physician* by Burchard, Bishop of Worms. Although this is a clerical text, it goes into matters more deeply than the conventions of the genre might lead one to expect. The references which he gives allow us to establish a link between pagan culture, as it was preserved at this time in northern Europe, and French folklore, which was here basically Frankish.

Burchard's work, which was included in his large collection of canon law around the year 1000, is a penitential – a detailed questionnaire with a list of penances to be undertaken by the repentant sinner, thus 'corrected' and 'cured' at least in theory. This manual, the most complete of its kind, was compiled by the bishop of the small diocese of Worms, among the 'red hills of the Rhine'. But from the outset the text goes beyond this narrow compass. Burchard was aided by his friend and neighbour the Bishop of Speyer. He was himself a product of the venerable Abbey of Lobbes, in the diocese of Liège, where he perhaps found one of his basic texts. His vast compilation was probably intended for all his colleagues in the provinces of Cologne and Mainz, and through them for the priests of the region, at a time when the network of parishes was only just developing, and when the religion of the local priest was sometimes as suspect as that of his parishioners.

Burchard's work was the culmination of a very old missionary effort which went back to the evangelisation of the barbarians of the British Isles, the Anglo-Saxons, by Theodore of Canterbury (669–90), encouraged both by Rome, which had sent him, and by the monastic Church in Ireland, on which he relied for support. One of the first penitentials goes back to his time. A little later, the torch was taken up again by two illustrious offspring of the Anglo-Saxon nobility: Egbert, Archbishop of York (732–67), and Winfrith, who passed through the Frankish kingdom and, under the Roman name of Boniface, was energetically employed in restoring the Christian religion, which was weak in the region at that time. He became Archbishop of Mainz (746–55). It was probably he who inspired the Carolingian ruler Carloman to promulgate a capitulary in 743–4, now mostly lost, at Leptines or perhaps at Estinnes, very near Lobbes. The list of headings, which has survived, shows – by the care with which it details forbidden practices and by the vernacular equivalents it gives 'of sacrilege concerning the deceased, that is to say *dad-sidas*' (vision of the dead) – that it was a serious attempt at providing information. The task undertaken by Boniface was to be pursued over more than a century by his spiritual heirs, the great Carolingian churchmen Halitgar, Bishop of Cambrai (823–30), Hrabanus Maurus, Archbishop of Mainz (847–56), and Regino, abbot of Prüm, who worked for the Archbishop of Trier, Ratbod, between 899 and 915. This entire missionary tradition was taken up and completed in the work of Burchard, who revised, developed and added to this material, in a style that was much less cursory and allusive than that of his predecessors.

Hrabanus Maurus, Benedictine scholar and Archbishop of Mainz, offers his book, *De Laudibus Sanctae Crucis*, to Pope Gregory IV, ninth century. (Vienna, Österreichische Nationalbibliothek.)

The magic of the wise women of the Rhine

Once the scattered fragments of the collection are gathered up, the cultural panorama thus partially revealed is quite extraordinary. We will pass over the questions about wizards, soothsayers and poisoners; they do not tell us anything very new, and there are such people all over the world, throughout history. Equally, we shall leave aside the banquets and merrymaking where people 'acted as a stag or a calf'. These 'carnivals' in December or Lent – the 'swinish feasts of February' denounced by the council of Estinnes – were repeatedly forbidden by the Church councils of the early Middle Ages. More or less Christianised by the twelfth century, they became tolerated by the Church. The bishop's questions reveal the widespread existence of other interesting practices.

Burchard knew exactly what he was fighting against: not against marginal, scattered 'deviations' from Christian worship, but against a religious system hostile to his own. In order to combat the worship of the stars, especially of the moon, he repeated the clauses of an old Spanish council, which he had found in Regino's work, but he did not repeat them uncritically: 'if in fact you are still observing the pagan traditions which fathers have always bequeathed, as an inheritance, to their sons down to this day'. This clear-eyed statement precedes the prohibition of the rite of help for the moon when it was clouded over (the 'Victory to the Moon' – prohibited in Estinnes and described a hundred years after that by Hrabanus, who declared that many people in his diocese practised it openly).

Thus the word 'inheritance' is appropriate here; but on looking closer at Burchard, we might ask whether it came from mothers rather than fathers. In this 'pagan tradition', in the collective rituals which expressed it, women played the central role. Look at them in their daily activities. In weaving, when they were gathered in the shade and warmth of their shelters, they cast spells to make their material tough, or to make their enemies' material weak; at the Octave of Christmas, when they should have been resting from work and honouring the coming of the Saviour, they were instead starting on the business of weaving and sewing so that their work overlapped with the beginning of the new year.

The household bread was also their concern; in the house, the woman ground the grain in her handmill. If she wished to get rid of her husband, she would grind some grain sticky with honey, which she had previously smeared on her body, and grind it in the opposite direction to the movement of the sun. If, on the other hand, she wished to make herself loved, a friend would knead this mixture on her buttocks. When the family wondered about the future at New Year, the women would watch the way in which the bread rose. And when a child was feverish, women would put it briefly in the oven, like one of their loaves.

The women laid the table for meals. At certain times of the year, probably in autumn, they would lay three places for the three Fatal Sisters, in order to earn their good graces. It is not difficult to recognise the Norns in this (the three Fates – Urd, Verdande and Skuld), and we are reminded that they were so powerful that they could confer on the newborn the gift of transforming themselves later into other shapes, such as that of a wolf, 'which is fool-ishly called by the people a *werwolf*', a man-wolf. West of the Rhine, the word passed into Romance language as *garou*. We shall return to these enchanted wolves. Notice that a part of this everyday magic could not help but be public: even if the bread of death or love could be hidden, a child in the oven or a meal for the Three Sisters could not.

As for the dead, they were watched over by the community, with dancing and 'diabolical, pagan' songs, and much drinking. The women placed their carding-combs on the coffin. Then the moment came to take the body away: quickly they ran for water, filled a jug and sprinkled the lid. When the pall-bearers crossed the threshold, they watched that the bier was carried low, no higher than knee-level. In front of the hut a wagon was dismantled and the pall-bearers had to pass between its two sides. In the empty room, where the corpse had rested, grain was burnt. Without these rites, the living would be threatened by the dead.

Some of the deceased were more dangerous than others, harmful in their despair: the stillborn child who had not been given a name, and the mother who died in childbirth. A woman would put a stake through them in their graves and thus fix them to the ground, because stillborn children would certainly become blood-drinkers, or werwolves. And it was the werwolves who devoured the moon when it was clouded over during an eclipse; at least the people in Hrabanus' Mainz diocese believed this.

And lastly, the weather. It was the women of the village who were responsible for the rain, if not for good weather. They assembled the little girls, choosing one, whom they stripped. The procession went down to the fields carrying the little girl and kept walking until they came across some henbane, 'which is called *bilse*', noted Burchard. This was one of the most powerful aids of Frankish sorcerers, one of the formidable group that included bel-ladonna. The Anglo-Saxons called them henbane, nightshade, thornapple and mandrake. *Bilse* (the pain-herb), used green in a mixture of clay and alum, soothed the pains of childbirth. It could also be used as an abortive agent; and in another passage, Burchard denounces abortifacient drinks. But *bilse* could do more: to her who mastered it, it gave vision; to her whom it mastered, it gave death – an ambiguous power, in which Good and Evil were indissoluably mixed. Let us go back to the ceremony, with the procession stopping by this sacred herb. The little girl goes nearer, she picks the plant with the little finger of her right hand, then binds it to the little toe of her right foot. We can imagine what these small female fingers and toes represent. The women then go on their way, still carrying the little one; they go to the river and plunge her in it. They get into the water themselves, they beat it with sticks, and splash the chosen child. They sing and weave spells. Finally, they pick up the little girl and return to the hamlet, by the way they came, keeping the river in view. All this is out in the open, public. These 'pagan acts' took place in broad daylight, a few dozen leagues from the cathedrals of the Rhine.

These songs and dances and processions, scandalous as they might be, were only the manifest part of the 'inheritance'. There were more terrible aspects: the hard core of evil, the masters (or rather the mistresses) of these rites and culture. The astonishing shamanistic practices of these witches of the Rhine are denounced in a Carolingian capitulary utilised by Regino of Prüm, and repeated by Burchard who added some even more revelatory passages.

Some women say that they had to do this, out of need or because commanded: some nights, they had to mount a beast, with a troop of demons who had the appearance of women, whom the foolish call Holda (the Kindly Ones), and they join their company . . . Some wicked women believe and teach that in the hours of night they ride on a beast in the company of the pagan goddess Diana or Herodiana and an enormous crowd of women, and that in the silence of calm nights they traverse immense tracts of land, and that they obey her orders as they would a mistress, and that they are called to her service on certain nights. And an enormous crowd, deceived by this false opinion, believe that it is all true.

We shall see later what might be concealed behind this twinning of 'Diana and Herodiana' in hesitant Latin, which later texts 'correct' in order to make an identification with the biblical Herodias. Anyway, it is established that the nocturnal rides of these women in the middle of the Rhineland were led, not by the 'Devil', that wicked catch-all, but by female spirits and a 'goddess'.

This flying company came up against other hostile groups: 'Some women believe this: in the silence of the tranquil night, you go out through closed doors with other members of this devilish company, and you rise up in the air until you reach the clouds, and there you fight with other women, sometimes wounding them and sometimes being wounded.' In the night mists, women joined in magical defensive battles, repelling the sorceresses from enemy villages. But the same power that protected could also kill:

many women believe this and say it is true: that in the silence of the tranquil night, while you are stretched out in your bed, your husband sleeping beside you, you can, while your body remains there, go out through closed doors, and can cross immense tracts of land with other women . . . Without visible weapons you can kill even people who have been baptised and saved by the blood of Christ, and

65

you eat a part of their cooked flesh, and then you put in place of their heart some straw or a stick or something like that, and even if they [the hearts] are eaten, you can make them [people] live again, you can permit them to live.

Two centuries previously, the Frankish kings, forcibly imposing Christianity upon the Frisians and Saxons, had condemned to death 'those men or women who eat human flesh', without finding out exactly what was eaten. It was apparently the heart that the magicians particularly wanted in order to have power over their victims, as over the living dead. The council of Estinnes had already denounced 'those who believe that women swear allegiance to the moon in order to have power to take out the hearts of human beings', and the person writing down the text used the same word to indicate the tie that linked these women to their mistress as that for vassals vowed to their lord's service. These ogresses were not isolated: 'May it please Heaven', cried Burchard (or his source), 'that they should die alone in their perfidy and that they should not attract many other people to their sickness.'

'An enormous crowd . . . many women . . . many people. . .' We should not be deceived by this: the way of thinking revealed by Burchard's inquisition began its slow decline in the tenth century. Of course it was still alive among the German-speaking peoples of the mid-Rhine, the small farmers who were free or quasi-free in Franconia and the Palatinate, and amongst their more recently converted neighbours in Saxony and Frisia. But to find a place where paganism was still dominant, one would have to go as far as the Danish Marches, to the northernmost isles in the world, to vast Scania, 'womb of peoples', from which the ancestors of the Rhenish peasants had come.

A little more than two centuries previously, paganism still ruled west of the Rhine, and even in the cities: in Metz, where blonde princesses were buried with their long hazel wands; in Tournai, where the men of the mayor of the palace threatened the bishop when he dared to rebuke them, and made fun of him. The councils of that time admitted the collapse of the Church. Then the power established by the Carolingians had forced paganism into retreat, tracking it down to its strongholds: to the marshes of Frisia where the *Upstalboom* (the Tree of the High Seat) was to be found; the forest of the *Teutoburgerwald*, occupied by the Saxons, where the *Irminsul* stood, the tree of Odin. In these sacred places where the forward thrust of the Roman legions had been broken, the Christian law of the new Rome was now supreme, at least in theory. Burchard, that latterday Carolingian, inherited this great civilising mission; he was its culmination. And we should remember that the source of our information, his detailed inquiry, was the instrument of a more efficient repression.

After him, because of him, the rites that had still been public in some places became clandestine; a whole occult system, in order to survive, was gradually buried. The savage mind, now under siege, weakened and dissolved into mist.

The geography of the shades

Herodiana and the Holda troop suffered the same fate as Melusina further south, being gradually relegated to the unthreatening level of folklore. It is this area which we will now explore.

Representation of the great funerary goddess, Hel, of ancient Germany. (Tombstone, island of Gotland, seventh century.)

The wits of the late twelfth century knew something about the creatures who rode through the night. These 'new philosophers' rarely left the world of the cloisters. Their humble origin, their travels, their desire to please princes who were partial to 'curiosities' meant that their discourse included elements that had been rejected by their predecessors. But they did not linger long on this subject, either because their information was vague, or because it remained dangerous. One of them, William of Paris, a twelfth-century version of the encyclopaedists, who showed off his omniscience, limited himself to telling his readers: 'Concerning night rides, which in France are called *Hellequini*, and in Spain the Ancient Army, I cannot give you satisfaction. Because I have no intention of saying what they are. And in truth, it is not certain that they are evil spirits.' Master William was not willing to assign the night rides to the Devil's party, but neither did he wish to elaborate on the subject. His peers in belles-lettres, Orderic Vitalis and Peter of Blois, were no less allusive when they spoke of the Helletini, or Herletigni.

The Germanic forms underlying these vernacular words are clear: *Helle-kin* or *Helle-tegn*, which is to say the kin-group of Hel, the company, or, as one is tempted to translate it, the vassalage of Hel. Later, by a tautology similar to that which created the 'loup-garou' (wolf-werwolf), people spoke of the *mesnie-Hellequin*, using the same term – *mesnie* – employed for a noble household. Thus they lost sight of the great funerary goddess of ancient Germany, Hel, who was enthroned far to the north in the marshes of Nebelheim, foggy lands, surrounded by her dogs, wolves and snakes. Hel was well known to the Icelandic compilers of the thirteenth century, who were familiar with most of Germanic pagan thought, but who, as Christians, had made her a devilish figure to fit in with their concept of a later Odin, 'Father of All', who seemed to pave the way for Our Father. But the sagas always sang of the *Disir* or the *Wael-kur*, crows which fed on corpses, she-wolves which stalked their human prey, sombre escorts. At their side the dangerous dead rode in the sky, the 'black elves', surrounded by dark clouds, and the *trolls*, sorcerers or sorceresses capable of taking any form. This terrible cavalcade still had friends, whom it protected, as in Worms, by fighting in their place, or by giving the newborn gifts that would rule their lives.

Hel and her people dominated many northern lands: in Scania, Halland; in Jutland, Helleland; at the mouths of the Rhine, in Holland; and among the Angles of Britain, in the Holland of the Wash. But a detailed toponymic study by Scandinavian researchers has revealed many other traces of their rites and habitations, notably in Lorraine, and even well to the west of the Rhine.

But the most surprising traces of Hel are to be found in the folklore of certain regions in northern France. In Flanders, Lorraine, Normandy, Anjou, Maine and lower Brittany, faithfully transmitted through well-intentioned changes, we find that the hunt still rode in the nineteenth century, being referred to as *Helquin, Heletchien, Herlequin* or *Hierlekin, Hannequin* or *Hennequin,* or even the hunt for humans (*Hellemen*) – terms which evoke dogs, terror, a crowd. In Normandy, where the imprint was strong, we know that in many districts the hunt was led by a female, Mother Harpine, alias Cheserquine, alias Proserpine, which probably means a killer from the army of corpses, *Here-beana, Hraes-here-beana,* a name very close to the Herodiana of Burchard of Worms.

But in some districts in Normandy, ideas differed: the hunt was led by a male figure, Hugbercht, the 'Brightness of Hugi', the classic periphrasis for describing Odin. Thanks to a holy bishop of Liège, who died in 727, Hubert the Hunter had been sanctified. The same divergence may be observed south of the Frankish regions, around Touraine, Berry, Burgundy and the Varais, where the hunt was also led by a male. In Poitou, the Marche, the Bourbonnais and in lower Maine, regions the Swabians had once settled, the wild hunt changed its name. There it became *Gallry, Galeria, Valory, Galière, Gayère,* i.e. *Waelhere,* the Army of the Charnelhouse; disquieting apparitions prowled about, often in the shape of crows – *Galopine* or *Galipote, Wael-beana* or *Wael-boda,* Female Slayers or messengers from Odin, the lord of Valhalla. This rivalry for the mastery of the Army of the Dead, the 'ancient Army', was found again east of the Rhine: in Saxony the hunt was led by a great sorceress, Werre or Holle, while in central and south Germany it was led by a hunter. The Icelandic masters, wishing to accommodate everyone peacefully in their folk pantheon, explained that the lordship over the dead was shared between Hel or Freya and Odin. But on the ground, their devotees did not confuse the two; mastery by one of the gods excluded the other.

Apart from this, the hunt had common features. Thus the spirits rode out into the night sky, accompanied by dogs or by wolves with red eyes. The spirits of the dead were among them, and, it was sometimes insisted, the spirits of dead children. To those who greeted them, who responded to their cries – which were those of the chase, Houvari, Hallali, but also perhaps the cries of general clamour, Haro or Charivari – they threw prey. People rarely dared to call them by name, because human flesh was involved. To greet the hunt was to declare yourself its friend; to eat the prey it offered was to join it. Of course this common core gave rise to many variations in folktales, which should be studied in themselves, taking

68

account of the likely developments – making the leaders male and devilish, moralising the infernal gift, ill-acquired property. But the Wild Hunt as it has come down to us, when it is described in a Germanic vocabulary, allows us to glimpse the mental background of the flights denounced in Burchard's manual. It also makes clear that these practices extended over a much larger area than simply the diocese of Worms: in fact, over all the lands where the *Hellequin* rode, the women's hunt led by the great sorceress of the north. And we can sketch a mental geography of the society of the dead, which reveals much about the society of the living, both female and male.

The silence from the southern regions is probably explained by the fact that peasant religion had long since succumbed to pre-Christian influences, such as the mystery religions and solar syncretism of the later Roman Empire, and then to the various currents of Christianity itself. The Church could therefore be much more conciliatory as regards pagan traditions that were of a more assimilable kind. Tolerance towards the quasi-idolatrous representation of the saints was, as we have said, still a southern trait at the beginning of the eleventh century, and it was on this type of culture that the Peace movement was founded. We have seen how this inspired the contempt of northern bishops. From the twelfth century, the Devil became omnipresent, but one can still see that he concealed different figures: in the north, Hel or the King of *Wal*; in the Midi, a dubious St James or St John, looking towards Spain. At the same period, the resistance of the northern ruling classes to 'popular' cults gave way: French royalty merged with the cult of St Denis, while the German emperor introduced into Cologne the cult of the Magi, which originated in Italy, in Milan and Pavia.

The choice had been made at the beginning of the eleventh century. The King of France hesitated between three influences. First, that of the northern Church, in the Carolingian mode, embodied by Fulbert (Bishop of Chartres); second, that of the ascetic clerks of Orléans, won over by 'Manichaeanism'; and third, that of the Cluniacs, masters of the holy images. Fulbert aligned himself with the Cluniacs, and King Robert, under their combined influence, consigned his heretical friends to the flames. Amidst the feudal crisis, under pressure from crowds of peasants, the real choice in the war of ideas came down to two paths: either a fairly orthodox Christianity, which could be considered a compromise in the southern manner between a strong monastic Church and a watered down and domesticated rural paganism; or medieval Manichaeanism, which violently rejected the cult of the dead and graves, together with everything fleshly, and which, breaking with a wicked world, turned towards the hope of the existence, somewhere, of a world without evil.

Curiously enough, the rise of prophetic movements was also rooted in peasant society. The monks of Chartres and Burgundy had begun by accusing these nocturnal gatherings of being sabbaths, where people had taken dreadful potions, including the ashes of newborn babies, in order to fly, and where people outdid each other in fornication. But this was a hasty slander for want of solid information and is unsupported. Even if it borrowed from the ancient 'savage' culture certain symbols, such as bees, Manichaean preaching was fundamentally different. This was perhaps the reason for its undoubted success in the towns and in the Midi. From this point of view, the claim of these heretics to be 'the true

69

Christians' does not seem exaggerated, even if they did deny the crucifixion. They were a kind of herald of an ascetic and 'purified' rational current from within Christianity, and perhaps the attraction of heresy for the literate of the eleventh century, and its success amongst merchants and money-lenders in the thirteenth century, bears more than a superficial resemblance to later rigorous Christian movements that were also successful among intellectuals and bankers. Above all, it must be remembered that these dramatically opposed currents – Manichaeanism and what we might call monastic 'hagiolatry' – both developed in opposition to 'paganism'; the one by denying it, the other by diluting and transforming it. From the tenth century, the religion of the towns ceased to be restricted to cities and nearby territories, it invaded the countryside and even the wilderness. But until the end of the Carolingian period – as the testimony of Hrabanus Maurus shows – large sections, perhaps the majority, of the peasantry in the north were still focused around their ancient culture.

In order to appreciate the real import of this change, we must return to the material world: not just pigs, sheep and wheat – primitive production and accumulation – but to something more fundamental, the worst thing according to the Manichaeans: namely reproduction.

'Primitive reproduction'

In the era which saw the decline of allodial communities and peasant religion in western Europe, the 'wilderness' retreated. Pioneers from the old villages cleared the moors and forests in the process known as assarting, and drained the marshes. It used to be thought that the abbeys, seen as little islands of knowledge in the sea of medieval barbarism, were the driving-force behind the widespread movement which pushed so many groups of peasants into their assault on the woodlands, and made the countryside into roughly what it remained until some 100 years ago. In fact, it now appears that the churches, far from promoting such clearance, only joined in gradually. The aristocracy did not favour it either, at least at the start. It was forbidden to clear forest land in the estates of the Carolingian kings, perhaps out of respect for the hunting tradition, and also because these small clear plots in the wilderness were bad for the business of the estate stewards or the agents of royal power. This is recognisably the sort of thinking one finds on *latifundia*.

What compelling reasons drove the countryfolk, despite opposition, to leave the ancient routine of their fields for the hard work of bringing new land under cultivation?

New land, free land

The classic reply – overpopulation – has the virtue of obviousness. It establishes a causal relation between the gradual disappearance of wilderness and the type of life associated with it, and the growth of population. We will look at this process, originating in the demographic changes in peasant families in the tenth century, and measure its consequences in the following section.

Miniature from an English manuscript, late tenth to early eleventh century
(Sacramentary from Winchester; Rouen, Bibliothèque municipale)

Miniature from a Spanish manuscript, late tenth century (The Escorial *Beatus*, from the monastery library)

Miniature from a Spanish manuscript, early twelfth century (The Silos *Beatus*; London, British Library)

Leaf from St Mark's Gospel, Constantinople, late twelfth century (London, Victoria and Albert Museum)

When modern historians have looked more closely than their predecessors at land-use in the ninth century, they have been struck by impresssive disparities: densely cultivated lands here, empty farms there. Sometimes one comes across densely populated lands, as at Palaiseau or Verrières near Paris, or around the Abbey of Saint-Bertin in Flanders, sometimes nearly empty villages. This phenomenon sometimes occurs within the same area. At the end of the century, in an Ardennes village belonging to the Abbey of Prüm, 116 families were settled on 34 farms, while other holdings were deserted. This situation is explained when we see some families in Lorraine preferring to cling to their original holdings rather than occupy new ones, which their lord had offered under the usual contract. It was better for them to gather around the old fields because the dues and services owed to the master were thus lighter for each. To take back into cultivation abandoned ground also meant much extra work. In such a system, the clearance of land on the estate was not to the peasants' advantage.

When pressure was too strong, the tenants did leave. The serfs themselves did not hesitate to follow suit. Thus in the Châlonnais, a whole group who had tried to escape from the monks of Saint-Rémy were taken and given in service to the Courtisols estate. The tenants were, in theory, always free and thus more difficult to keep. At the beginning of the tenth century, the Saint-Rémy monks were forced to admit that the free man who cultivated one of their estates could leave it, on condition that seven witnesses among his peers testified that he could no longer hold the land because of his 'poverty'. In the Midi, the situation of the great landowners was no better. Some holdings belonging to the Abbey of Saint-Victor in Marseilles, in lower Provence, were empty, while the neighbouring villages were peopled by allod-holders. The explanation of these absences is provided in the notes made against the names of some families by the monastic overseer: 'to be searched out'.

In the Auvergne, the tenants of a great landowner, Gerald, founder of Aurillac, departed from his lands with their tools and baggage, because he had installed a master between them and him. The warriors in Gerald's household looked on this with displeasure: it set a very bad example. Others did not have any scruples about forcing free men to work on their estate. In the Châlonnais, formerly free men were fixed in servitude on one of the estates of the fisc by royal order.

In Cambrai, a vassal of the bishop claimed to make a whole family similarly subservient. In the Midi, the heirs of great landowners tried to bribe judges in order to return the emancipated men of the deceased to slavery. Depopulation and the relative overpopulation of land thus had the same cause: the struggle of tenants to improve or maintain the contract linking them to their master, and the choice they made: either to leave, or to group themselves around the same piece of land if they stayed. In the great estates, what was lacking was not land, but men. It was not from them that the movement for land clearance came.

For a long time, on the margins of some great estates, it had been accepted that outsiders, strangers, (*forains* or *hôtes*), could clear small pieces of land, 'cultivated on the side', a little addition to the actual estate. The dues were very light. In about the tenth century, the number of these adjoining estates can be seen to grow in the various estate registers of Saint-Rémy of Rheims. They increased in Picardy over the same period.

71

au illaqqailua illyili
fortaffe opif uacuari

sacri eloqi
rium tanc
ut utruise
hunc neq: n
deprimac?
tif uacuii t
pc eiuf setit
concepaon:
eas ad folai
carii nocti
Nonnulle u
tif miferuu
liuf peneria
mil inuena
fouif locum
ne quoq: n
signficaaoi
uirgaf pop
linaf. & ex
ticauit eaf
hif que exp
apparuit. I
uiridiapma
modu. colo:
& fubdimir;

Despite what is said, did the monks
encourage forest clearance? In this
Cistercian manuscript from the
early twelfth century, a lay servant
lops a tree with his pruning knife,
while the monk prepares to fell it
with an axe. (Dijon, Bibliothèque
municipale, MS 173.)

72

Was this erosion of marginal areas simply the beginning of the great clearances, the only part revealed by contemporary documents? If we accept this analysis, we must note that the assarting began at a time when the best-recorded parts of the agrarian landscape were those punctuated by empty spaces. What pushed people towards clearing the land was less what we call 'overpopulation' on the estates, for we have seen in the estate system that this worked in the peasants' favour, and more the increasing pressure exercised by the lords over lands henceforth divided up and taken in hand by them. People cleared land in order to remain free or to regain freedom, not to avoid overcrowding. This was, in any event, the reason given by the Norwegians for venturing into Iceland, or by the Pyreneans who brought into cultivation the no-man's-land on the Catalan border. Some particularly determined fugitive slaves went to live in the harsh solitude of the Alps in order to be free. The same desire for liberty drove the heretical peasants, minorities in the west, into the forests of Maine or Anjou, and to establish their heretical outposts there in the twelfth century. And later, this desire remained the bait which attracted inhabitants to the new villages that had been given privileged status, when the lords, trying a new tactic, granted favourable charters, a necessary compromise in a world where 'wildernesses' were becoming rarer. Whatever we might think of the deeper causes of the movement, the fact remains that for the people of that time, it was the 'franchise' – freedom – which led to the populating of land, not the other way round. But let us return to peasant demography.

The Church, technology and food

One of the most harmful consequences of nineteenth-century historians' pictures of the early Christianisation of the countryside was the tendency to assume that the Church's teachings on marriage, sexuality and procreation had a very real impact on the secular culture of the ninth and tenth centuries. Applied to the field of historical demography, this *a priori* assumption paradoxically led to a mechanistic view of population increase. In fact, the canons of the Church did not noticeably change in the period that concerns us. If, as was thought, the peasants dutifully observed the canons, then the demographic surge could only be attributed to factors extraneous to their mental universe. Reduced to its essentials, the analysis is as follows: peasant couples at the end of the tenth century and in the eleventh century had more living children

The spread of the wheeled plough marked a great advance in rural life in the West. This scene from the bronze doors of the basilica of St Zeno in Verona (late eleventh century) is certainly the first to picture it. Cain, after having killed Abel, becomes a ploughman.

because they ate more, and they ate more because they produced more food, and they produced more food because they had better techniques of production. Since the regime of the seigneurie was established in this period, it took only a small step to grant that the local lord was filled with the spirit of enterprise, and thus to make feudalism into a motor of social progress and present it, despite its flaws – which had fortunately been exposed in the modern period – as a generally positive state in the evolution of human society. The ideology in play here is as obvious as it is disavowed.

Not that we should deny the importance of food, of production techniques, and more generally, of what we call the material forces (for want of a better term) in social relations. What is questionable is the analysis which presents techniques as operating in an unmediated and undifferentiated way on the development of these relations. We know the all too influential saying: 'Give me the yoke and the watermill . . .' which condemns technical inventions to 'appearing' in the course of history like so many *dei ex machina.*

The analysis of medieval demography is weakened by a second assumption: more or less consciously, the most critical historians have borrowed from the Third World and its often atrocious poverty the elements of a 'demography of pre-industrial societies', a 'primitive demography'. Everybody knows, however, that these societies are extremely old, and that their poverty is not unrelated to military or economic imperialism. And we might consider that the successes and splendours of ancient conquering kingdoms – so dear to traditional historians – by no means implied that the quality of life was improved for the peoples concerned. In this reckoning, happy peoples have no history, or rather, not the sort of history we are used to studying.

In the opposite camp, many ethnologists have recently argued that the food of hunters

73

and gatherers was much better than that of nineteenth-century farmers – indeed that the Stone Age was an age of abundance. Such abundance obviously presupposes that there was very little settlement. This condition had not totally disappeared in the early Middle Ages, before the clearings were made. In many areas the forests or marshes were still extensive, and the population was scattered. In the 'common lands', in the 'free lands', hunting and gathering were still practised and, together with widespread stock-breeding, provided a necessary adjunct to agriculture. What can the slender dossier on the tenth and eleventh centuries add to this debate? Let us quickly review three elements: morbidity, famine and under-nourishment.

The period from the ninth to the twelfth century was certainly not free from epidemics, but it did not experience the great 'plagues' that occurred in the preceding and following centuries. As regards ordinary morbidity, recent research based on the systematic study of miracles of healing points clearly in some cases towards sicknesses that might have arisen from malnutrition, but the proportion of these ailments amongst the cases recorded in accounts of miracles is the same for the ninth and tenth centuries as for the twelfth and thirteenth centuries. Thus the 'historical turning-point' of the eleventh century does not mark any progress. We can hope for confirmation or invalidation of this analysis by the study of historical pathology undertaken by archaeologists, even though its conclusions have recently been disputed as regards prehistory.

Research into famines seems to add even more surprising data. The admittedly rudimentary statistics for western Europe reveal twenty-six years of famine in the ninth century, ten in the tenth century, twenty-one in the eleventh century and thirty-two in the twelfth century. Paradoxically then, the tenth century marks an improvement in production, while economic growth and the population boom were accompanied by a worsening of the food supply.

Such variations prompt us to ask whether the peasants always, and fatally, had too little to eat. Again recent studies throw new light on the subject. They indicate that levels of prosperity or penury differed considerably between tenant families within the same region. They also suggest that diets varied a great deal. Previously, historians had contrasted a Roman-style diet, based on cereals and continued in the monasteries, with a 'barbarian' diet, which used much more milk and cheese, meat and fish, and which is clearly detectable in, for example, seventh-century Anglo-Saxon laws. It is probable that both models lasted into the ninth century. In the great ecclesiastical houses, and perhaps on royal estates, people's diets were largely bread-based, a real 'barracks' diet. This enormous quantity of wheat was drawn on the one hand from the estate itself, and on the other from the smallholdings of sharecroppers, who had to contribute a portion of their harvest, and from the free households, who paid for the milling when they brought their grain to the estate mill. The area of the smallholdings or little allods that could be cultivated was not very large; in order to contribute their due amount, and to feed themselves, the peasants who lived there would have had to produce yields of surprising size for the period. It is more likely that their diet was less cereal-based than that of the servants of the great estate. The knights' raids on the herds of pigs and sheep that grazed in the semi-wilderness were perhaps more a means of restraining the free men by destroying one of their sources of food, and thus their economic liberty, than simply the result of gluttony on the part of seigneurial households. The same goes for the increase in the number of hunting or fishing reserves, the *défens*; their establishment was one of the main causes of the Norman peasant uprising at the end of the tenth century, as the peasants had been accustomed to Scandinavian freedom in this area. The peasant, at least in the north, was not only cornered by this inroad on his animal diet, but also by that on his cereal foods. From the eleventh century, the lord forced him by order (the *ban*) to use the estate mill. What had sometimes been convenient now became a rule. The small domestic mills, which we have seen in the hands of women in the Rhineland, were forbidden. The lord could thus also control the harvests and, by means of an extra levy, come down heavily on those households whose ploughing, and thus whose production of wheat, was inadequate, either from necessity and real poverty, or by choice and their way of life. We can see that the seigneurie was far from being an enlightened supporter of peasant activity; rather, it was simply a parasite on that activity. In this guise it effectively encouraged them to produce more, but not under conditions that necessarily increased peasant families' consumption. The growing number of famines in the twelfth century does not lead to optimism in this respect. The present state of research leads us to believe that basic food consumption in the period under examination was not improved, and may even have deteriorated. We must look elsewhere for the origins of the economic take-off.

The creation of a 'natural' demography

If we examine closely the demography of the ninth century, we see that it is perhaps 'traditional', but certainly not 'natural'. The detailed study of estate records, despite inevitable uncertainties, has nonetheless given us some significant data. First of all, it seems to be established that the serfs tried to marry outside their class, that is with free people or, if need be, with people under some form of protection: this is the case for some 70 per cent in the estates of Saint-Germain-des-Prés, and some 30 per cent in those of Saint-Rémy of Rheims. But it was the male serfs who made these mixed marriages rather than the females: the ratio was four to one. These proportions are all the more significant when we look at the cases of marriages between freed and free, which are divided equally between women and men. The reason for the rarity of marriages between a female serf and a free man is that, unless there was a particular arrangement on their estate, their children were serfs, whereas the children of a male serf and a free woman were free – at least in theory, as the master, always on the look-out for workers to people his lands, kept a close eye on them. Moreover, we know from a twelfth-century document from Liège that the masters overcame the scarcity of marriages amongst female serfs by making their male serfs marry them, with the declared aim of possessing their children and thus profitably perpetuating their slavery.

The refusal among a considerable number of servile peasants to pass on the burden of servitude continued after marriage, and that is what interests us here. It seems clear that serfs had fewer children than free people, and, above all (and here the figures are quite reliable) they had more male children – fewer daughters – than their free neighbours. We could formulate the axiom that the more a family was free, the larger its holding would be and the less likely it was to have many male children, even while its level of fertility was better than that of the serfs.

Such variations are not to be explained away by 'natural' conditions. The explanation involves two factors. First, that the excessively high proportion of male children born to serfs is the result of female infanticide. Ignoring the old rule of *partus sequitur ventrem* ('the child takes its condition from the womb that carries it'), the serfs imposed a policy of favouring sons over daughters. In the short term, their interests coincided with those of their masters, who wanted above all a male labour supply for the *corvée*. In the long term, the effect of the scarcity of girls in the estate's population could only be disastrous. The second factor, the differing levels of fertility, is the result of a restriction on births brought about by the practice of either contraception or abortion, both denounced by Burchard of Worms.

But these practices required, then as now, a level of knowledge. Who made up the abortifacient potions, for example, if not those gatherers of henbane, those same wise women who advised their companions when they wanted to seduce men or poison them, and who were responsible, if the birth turned out badly, for driving a stake through the body of the stillborn child. In so far as these same women led groups of other women, and often, through these groups, entire communities, then real birth-control could exist, together with some balance between the land and the people who lived off it. But from the moment that the power of these wise women was broken and their knowledge went into decline, such control deteriorated into a wretched rag-bag of methods, into an 'accident in bed' whereby the baby was smothered, or into the sort of furtive sorcery that was denounced to the parish priest. It was now dangerous or impossible not to increase and multiply. The female magicians, now seen as 'witches', took to the road through the great forests, like the peasants who balked at the seigenurial yoke. It was there, on the margins, that the remains of their culture lasted longest; elsewhere, the way was free for a 'natural', or almost natural, population growth.

Despite this, even in the twelfth century, children in certain remote villages were not simply accepted as they appeared. This is clearly seen in an affair which brought down the wrath of the Lyons inquisition in the thirteenth century, and which unfolded in the Dombes, a combination of clearings and forest. There, as elsewhere, some newborn babies were sickly and insatiably hungry; worn out by diarrhoea, they in turn drained their mothers. It was believed that an evil spirit had slipped into the child's place – or body – at birth, a spirit from the woods, the waters or the earth, or perhaps the spirit of a child of these elements. Therefore the true spirit of the newborn child had to be recalled, and the spirit of the 'changeling' returned to its own. To do this the mother, accompanied by an old woman who knew 'the ritual behaviour', went to the woods, in this case the wood of St Guinefort. After having made offerings, especially of salt, and after putting a nail in a tree, they would pass the child nine times through a fork in the tree. A similar rite was denounced by Burchard: a channel was hollowed out under a hillock, and the newborn child was passed to and fro over it; the spirits of the earth were called upon in the same way as the mothers from the Dombes called upon the spirits of the forest. The infant was then exposed to two candles, and the woman would retire after having conjured the spirits to take back 'their' child and to return her own. Predators such as wolves would discover these tempting victims, and must have haunted the woods. Often the candles would set the straw cradle alight, or the weak child would die of cold. The two women would return when the candles had burnt out. If the child was still alive, it underwent the further trial of being dipped nine times in the cold waters of a nearby stream.

This 'exchange' took place under the auspices of a rather unorthodox 'saint': Guinefort, a dog hostile to snakes – perhaps worms – and protector of the newborn against them. The invocation which has survived in folklore sums up the radical choice prayed for by the mothers: 'Saint Guinefort ou la vie ou la mort' ('Saint Guinefort, [grant] either life or death'). Those babies that were too sick would probably not survive the exposure. Those that survived must have had, as the inquisitor Stephen of Bourbon remarked with heavy irony, 'a strong constitution', which was precisely not the case. Stephen, who did not wish to understand what was going on, saw all of this as infanticide. But J.-C. Schmitt's fascinating study devoted to this affair rightly underlines the fact that, in the peasants' eyes, the infants who died were not mortal babies taken away, but those of 'demons'. For the mothers it was, moreover, a matter of regaining their true children rather than getting rid of an unlucky intruder. Their belief in the changeling explained the sickness and allowed them, one way or another, to deal with it: the selection was seen as a rescue, a last resort. It was not undertaken lightly: sometimes the woman could not go through with the whole rite, and would return to snatch the child from the wolf's jaws.

This remarkable example should not give rise to any illusions. The thirteenth-century inquisitors were no longer confronting a dominant culture, only its stubborn, passive remnant. The inquisitors from Lyons could travel to the Dombes without difficulty, assemble the local people to preach to them, cut down the sacred wood and condemn those who frequented it to the loss of their goods, practically to banishment. All this was easily accomplished, thanks to the powerful overlord of the region, the lord of Villars. Such draconian measures, however, were not enough to suppress completely the worship of Guinefort. Even at the beginning of the nineteenth century, mothers who had an ailing or feverish child would go to the wood and take some gifts for the hermit who lived there. But this 'mendicant' had asked the bishop's permission for the cult, and the practice was not felt to be dangerous, merely annoying. 'The local people', said the priest to the bishop, 'are quite superstitious, some about one thing, some about another.' This was no longer a peasant culture, only fragments of superstition.

Once the storms of the feudal crisis had passed, the power of the Church over the countryfolk was firmly established, thanks to the lords of the manor. The modern era begins. We should be wary of judging the preceding centuries by its light, of adding to the distortions that peasant culture suffered in ecclesiastical texts, thus masking its wildness, its irreducible strangeness relative to our own culture. It was an irrational era, in which the northern lands were still dominated not by Jesus Christ, or by Mary, full of grace, but by the ambiguous star of night, shining Bertha Bigfoot, leaving behind her the traces of marsh birds, followed by her faithful train of wizards 'of the two hearts', warriors and knights of

The dominant culture and the unofficial culture: the Church condemned the practice of magic. The fall of Simon Magus, a capital at Autun, early twelfth century. According to the Acts of the Apostles, Simon, known for his spells, proposed to St Peter that he should buy from him the power to confer the Holy Spirit (from which the word 'simony' derives). St Peter indignantly refused.

the skies, with their long hazel wands, their charms 'of human bones, of ashes and dying coals, of hair, of the pubic hair of men and women, of herbs, snails, snakes, everything interlaced with coloured strands', with their dream potions and hallucinatory visions. This must remind us of Talayesva of the Hopi and, even more 'primitive', of the wizards Yaqui, Tarahumara, Bororo, Acheh, Yanomani, drugged visionaries fighting the storm. A great gulf separates us from these figures of the past, a gulf created by a series of Church councils, by the work of rational, terrified clerics, by the patient grinding-down of people's spirits. Writing has immortalised the exploits of Roland, who split human bodies in half just like pigs being sliced up for the winter; but what are they beside the prodigious flights of the wise women of the Rhine? It was a time of exotic practices in the very heart of Europe.

The eleventh century saw the battle won between ecclesiastical culture, the culture of the towns, and an independent peasant culture. The trees – whether kindly or threatening – were cut down, or stood uncertainly under the shadow of the axe. Patches remained, perpetuating the untamed past in a debased form. The little wood of Saint Guinefort, for example, is small beer compared to the vast 'lands of Hel'. And what would have remained of it after Stephen of Bourbon and the lords of Villars had gone? Yet this victory by the Church could not have been accomplished without profound changes on its own part. The clerks of the eleventh and twelfth centuries obviously inherited an ancient theological tradition, which we could call imperial Christianity. But they too were at a turning-point in history, creators of new religious forms which were much more popular and thus much more fruitful.

2 The birth of Christian Europe: 950–1100

Between the end of the tenth century and the beginning of the twelfth, the West, hitherto merely a geographical expression, became a reality with the birth of Christendom. The peoples who shared Latin as the language of their liturgy became conscious of a unity beyond their differences. This was a watershed since, after the disintegration of the Carolingian Empire, there had been no political or spiritual power with sufficient prestige to exercise authority across the boundaries of different kingdoms. The papacy had been under the thumb of the Roman aristocracy since the end of John VIII's pontificate in 882, and was going through one of the darkest periods in its history; even the Empire restored by Otto I in 962 was neither extensive nor cohesive enough to act as a focus for those who did not accept the slide towards feudal disintegration. This Empire's power made itself felt only in the lands of Germany and, to a lesser extent, in northern and central Italy. Even in these regions, the power of the emperors was frequently put to the test by uprisings and rebellions, resulting in the sharp curtailment of the universalist claims of these sovereigns and of the clerics in their entourage, who were the main supporters of the ideology of the *renovatio imperii*. In fact it was on another basis, the basis of religious association, that the West was to rebuild its awareness of belonging to a cultural community that embraced the previously scattered peoples.

The power of faith

Throughout the early Middle Ages, the sphere of influence of Latin Christianity had continued to extend northwards and eastwards, in the same way as Frankish ascendancy was maintained over the other Germanic peoples. In Charlemagne's time all the inhabitants of the Empire were supposed to have been baptised, and those who refused – especially the Saxons – were forced to adopt the faith of the ruler. After the second wave of invasions in the ninth and early tenth centuries, there was a redoubled effort to incorporate the new outsiders into a homogeneous religious bloc, which stretched from Ireland to Italy and from the Pyrenees to Germany.

On the fringes of Christianity

Among the new invaders, the Vikings were conspicuous in the speedy adoption of the beliefs of their new subjects, both in France and in England. This was the price of admission, as it were, to enter fully into the community of 'civilised peoples', whose way of life and forms of political organisation exerted such a fascination over those who had previously been living on their borders. The same was true of the Slavs and Hungarians. It is no accident that Christianity was established among them, as among the Scandinavians, together with the apparatus of the State, particularly the institution of the monarchy. The Church preserved and glorified the memory of those clan chieftains who were fascinated by the title of king and the prestige that went with it, and who knew how to make their warrior tribes accept the religion of the West: Poland's Miesco I, Hungary's St Stephen, Bohemia's St Wenceslas and Norway's St Olaf all founded both their independent national states and their local Church, with the support of missionaries sent by emperor or pope. But, by ordering the baptism of all their subjects and by defending the new faith against the pagans, they were accepting at the same time the incorporation of their people within a larger community: the community of Christians who celebrated the mass in Latin and who acknowledged the pre-eminence, as yet ill-defined, of the Bishop of Rome. Thus the period around the year 1000 witnessed the appearance of new metropolitan sees (Prague, Magdeburg, Gniezno, Esztergom, Lund, Nidaros, etc.) which were also missionary centres, from which the Catholic faith penetrated the most remote rural areas as the eleventh century wore on.

This development, however, encountered checks and difficulties. The conversion of Scandinavia, for example, was a long-term undertaking. It was begun by German clerics, and continued by monks from England and France, but it was really only in the twelfth century that Sweden, Iceland and Finland were bound within the framework of Roman ecclesiastical organisation. Futher east, it was not until the fourteenth century that the Lithuanians, northern neighbours of the Poles, adopted the religion of the west. In the Slav lands, there were sharp disputes between Latin missionaries and their Greek counterparts. In Serbia and in Moravia the boundary between rival versions of Christianity only became fixed after a complex series of moves and counter-moves. These conflicts over ritual and borders involved the two ecclesiastical hierarchies in Rome and Constantinople in an increasing hostility which contributed to the schism of 1054. Both before and after that date, pope and patriarch behaved as rivals, each seeking to draw the newly converted peoples into his sphere of influence. This was what happened with the Bulgarians, who **81**

A parish assembly in Sweden. In a decorative and stylised manner very different from the Bayeux Tapestry, this tapestry from Skög (*c*. 1100) depicts the holding of a service: the priest is at the altar, the bells are being rung; from both sides great lions rush towards the church. (Stockholm, Statens Historiska Museum.)

eventually went over to the Byzantine camp, and above all with the Russians. When Vladimir, Prince of Kiev, was baptised in the waters of the Dnieper in 987, Russia's religious destiny swung decisively to the East.

The growth of parishes

In lands which had long been Christian, the Church's hold over the faithful was strengthened by the creation of a dense network of parishes which, assuming different forms in different regions, was one of the most important achievements of the first feudal age. Indeed, from the end of Antiquity the Church had organised itself on the basis of dioceses, which in turn were grouped in ecclesiastical provinces reflecting the administrative structures of the late Roman Empire. Although they seemed threatened with dissolution at the end of the Merovingian era, these institutions had endured and had become even stronger under the Carolingians. The latter had increased the power of bishops and had transformed the metropolitans into archbishops with authority over their suffragans. But these hierarchical structures hardly touched the main body of the faithful and the humble priests who, outside the towns, had very little contact with prelates. Parishes scarcely existed and, in many regions, the faithful had to gather in a mother church (*pieve* in Italy, *minster* in England) for religious ceremonies and receiving the sacraments. Such churches were either old episcopal foundations or former monastic missionary centres.

Between the eighth and twelfth century, the West was to witness a great increase in the number of country churches which enjoyed parochial rights. This proliferation was allied to the gradual establishment of the seigneurial regime and feudalism. The masters of the land, soon to be all-powerful, built places of worship on their estates the better to oversee the people placed in subordination to them. Not only did these lords themselves choose the priest to be in charge, they came to look upon these churches and the property with which they endowed them as their very own. There were, of course, certain drawbacks for the ecclesiastical hierarchy as the links between parish and bishop were weakened, if not broken, and its property was often misappropriated or divided up by the lay patrons who brought it under their jurisdiction. But this system of the 'proprietary church' (*Eigenkirche*), as legal scholars and historians have labelled it, did not have simply negative consequences. The fact that everyone – from the king, the great abbots and lords of the manor down to the humblest landowner – could create and own one or more shrines indubitably helped bring about the appearance of that 'white robe of churches' which covered the West by the year 1000. In the same period, the territorial boundaries of parishes were becoming fixed and in many regions tended to coincide with the boundaries of manors or village lands. Like contemporary secular society, the eleventh-century church rebuilt itself on the basis of the smallest component part.

Every effort of the eleventh- and twelfth-century reformers was aimed at removing these now numerous places of worship from the power of the laymen and submitting them to the authority of the Church hierarchy. The lords concerned did not yield easily. The clergy did succeed in making them feel uneasy and impressing them with the threat of canonical penalties. But rather than restoring their churches to the local bishops, as the papacy would have liked, they often preferred to give them to monastic communities in return for prayers for the repose of their souls and those of their ancestors. Moreover, among the shrines founded or supported by aristocratic families were a good number of ecclesiastical establishments, such as abbeys, priories, and rural and urban collegiate churches. In theory, the latter churches had no pastoral function and were simply centres for prayer and celebration of the liturgy. But in practice, these communities, however modest, could not remain indifferent to the world around them. Through such communities the chances of contact between the faithful – lords and peasants – and the Church increased. Thus religion impressed itself deeply on the minds of men, and if the exact nature of the process now escapes us, its reality is undeniable.

God in the world

For the laity, the church, whether a parish church or one attached to a monastery, was a place apart, invested with a sacred aura. A place of refuge, and as such inviolable on pain of excommunication, it was defined firstly by its possessing the relics of one or several saints, who would punish anyone who dared to profane the site. But, as we shall see, it was also a gathering place for the men and women of the village or district. In times of invasion or attack, the population would take shelter there; when decisions had to be made concerning the life of the local community, the meeting was held there, a meeting which came to be known in some parts of France as the *général* of the parish, that is, the assembly of the heads of households. Finally, the church was the place where the sacraments were celebrated, where sentences of excommunication and interdict were promulgated, and around

83

A country church in Catalonia: Santa Maria de Barbera (late eleventh century). An intact example of the early Romanesque art of the south which owed much to Byzantium.

which were gathered the remains of the dead, henceforth buried in consecrated ground in the adjoining cemetery.

Yet terms such as 'Christianisation' or 'conversion' are not without a certain ambiguity. With the exception of the Jewish minority, the inhabitants of the eleventh-century West were indeed all baptised and thus could claim to be Christians. But the substance of their faith might not have stood up to rigorous scrutiny from a theologian or canon lawyer. The religious faith of the age was not rooted in dogmas, which were barely understood by the faithful or even by the majority of clergy, who knew only the Pater Noster and the Credo. Rather, it was rooted in certain fundamental beliefs which held universal sway. Everyone believed in an after-life, that is, in the existence of other realities which were ultimately more important than those here below. The Church taught – and here its message was clearly understood – that the eternal destiny of man was played out on this earth. The result for the faithful was not a fear of death, which was too familiar to inspire real fear, but a concern with making a good end, by renouncing *in articulo mortis* some ill-gotten gains or

The combat of the Vices and the Virtues: two virtues dressed as knights strike down two vices, reflecting the theme of the *Psychomachia*, a popular work of the fourth-century Christian poet, Prudentius. (Capital in the church of Notre-Dame-du-Port in Clermont-Ferrand.)

a scandalous liaison. Aware that their way of life was not a moral and still less a religious one, the laity sought to atone for their sins by increasing their gifts to the Church and to the poor, so that they might obtain the support necessary for their confrontation with the heavenly judge. Convinced that the prayers of monks were especially valuable, they sought to establish links of 'fraternity' with the latter by having their names inscribed on the memorial lists of a community, thus gaining long-term benefits from their intercession. And it was not just the feudal aristocracy who behaved thus; even money-lenders, when they sensed the end approaching, did not hesitate to disgorge their profits and ask the clergy to make due recompense to their victims.

For men of this period, the world was a battlefield where the forces of God, identified with Good, ceaselessly confronted the forces of Evil, embodied in the Devil. Being fundamentally dualist, they believed in the reality of the latter just as much as in the former. These were not merely abstract considerations: Satan was at work in the created world and in everyday life: he would appear to people in various guises, seeking to tempt them; he would mock them and sometimes even beat them black and blue if they resisted. But God was no less present – primarily in events themselves, which were really signs that had to be correctly interpreted. Both natural disasters and unnatural phenomena appeared to them as manifestations of the wrath of heaven and as warnings given to sinners by a God who, with his perfect knowledge of the deeds of mankind, was identified with immanent justice. But they were also a reflection and consequence of the sin which held sway in human hearts, where vice and virtue were locked in perpetual struggle – this was the theme of the *psychomachia* illustrated in countless Romanesque frescoes and illuminated manuscripts. A person could only emerge victorious from this combat with the aid of heaven. For God did not hesitate to intervene actively on the side of those who begged for his help; he would then show himself in miracles, whose function was to re-establish order not only in the human body and spirit, by restoring them to health, but also in society at large by freeing captives,

85

The journey of the relics of St Benedict. St Benedict, who died in 547, was buried in Italy in the monastery of Monte Cassino, which he had founded. In about 672, the head of the Benedictine Abbey of Fleury, on the Loire, learnt that Benedict's body was lying under the ruins of the monastery which had been destroyed by the barbarians. He despatched a number of monks to rescue the bones of the saint, whose name the abbey then took (Abbey of Saint-Benoît-sur-Loire).

delivering the condemned – in short, by shielding the faithful from all the violence that surrounded them. People in this period were all firmly convinced that such miracles were real, or at least possible. This was not surprising in a world where the boundary between the natural order and the supernatural was not strictly defined, and where problems, because they so often seemed to have no human solution, could only be resolved through divine intervention.

Was it not offensive to the majesty of God to claim that he could be made to intervene whenever people found themselves in insurmountable difficulty? In fact, people of this epoch preferred to turn to more accessible intermediaries, the saints, whose relics they believed had beneficial powers. We can scarcely imagine the role that these fragments of bone, preserved in chests or precious caskets, could play in the life of this era. The most solemn oaths were sworn over them; they were carried in procession to ward off the plague, or to obtain a good harvest, or to drive away the enemy from a village under siege. They were the goal for pilgrims who flocked to the sanctuaries where they were preserved and worshipped. The Church encouraged this devotion and increasingly moved relics from place to place, providing occasion for ceremonies in which the lay rulers always sought to take part. These 'translations' attracted huge crowds, and miracles often occurred in the process; this could only increase the faith and enthusiasm of the faithful. From the late eleventh century, the Church endeavoured to channel popular piety towards more worthy objects. Besides local saints, whose origin and history were often obscure, there developed the cult of the great figures of Christianity's history: St John the Baptist, the Apostles, and above all, the Virgin Mary. The bizarre and even absurd forms which this devotion took – in one place they venerated a drop of the Virgin's milk, in another, the head of John the Baptist, which another church also claimed to possess – should not obscure the importance of this development, which was aimed at focusing on the person of Christ and his first disciples a fervour which otherwise tended to be dispersed among countless intercessors. The extra-

The Devil as devourer of men. This monstrous devil, gripping his human prey in his claws before swallowing it, resembles the ravening wolf-gods of peasant folklore. The Church cast out demons by exorcism. (Capital in Saint-Pierre-de-Chauvigny, Vienne, twelfth century.)

ordinary popularity of the pilgrimage to the shrine of St James at Compostela, which in this period became one of the most visited shrines in the West, testifies to the success of this endeavour.

Signs and rituals

Religious life at this time was scarcely inward-looking, except among the élite of monks and prelates. Beliefs were expressed not so much in words as in visible and tangible signs. Moreover, people's psychology made them swing from one extreme to another. Such fever also affected moral behaviour: the same individual could display the most horrible violence or complete degeneration, followed, often very quickly, by a spectacular conversion whose distinguishing marks were a rigorous asceticism and a flight from the world, which was suddenly scorned as passionately as its pleasures and values had been desired. People were fascinated by these violent transformations, which resulted in many a knight renouncing the pleasures of combat in order to spend the rest of his life celebrating divine office in the peace of the cloister. This is one of the factors that explain the increasing number of hermits – a phenomenon that becomes particularly noticeable during the second half of the eleventh century in many parts of Christendom. The depths of the forests and 'desert' regions were sought out as refuges by very different types of men, who all believed that the only way to salvation was to break completely with a society busy enriching itself and with the structures of a church that was slow to reform. This voluntary return to the wilderness and solitude was a clear sign to those who came into contact with them that they were now men of God. The hermits acquired a religious prestige that soon led flocks of disciples to join them; an ever-increasing number of visitors begged them to perform miracles for the sake of a suffering humanity. If they acceded to these requests – as was often the case – then they were instantly perceived as saints, but their enhanced reputation cost them their tranquil solitude. Some were moderate in their pursuit of asceticism and were content to don the habit of the penitent or lay brother, placing themselves in the service of a hospital or of a religious community vowed to fraternal charity and work.

For most of the population, however, religion was still a matter of prescribed observances. The distinction between the sacraments – of which the Church had yet to draw up a definitive list – and other holy ceremonies was not clearly perceived. If everyone understood the beneficial effects of baptism and penance, the benefits of confirmation and communion do not seem to have been so plain to the faithful, and the clergy was still pondering the nature of marriage. On the other hand, much importance was attached to blessings, sprinklings of holy water, and expiatory or supplicatory processions. Exorcism, that is the rituals used to drive out the Devil, was certainly carried out by bishops. But in cases of madness or possession, it often seemed better to take the afflicted person to a famous shrine. The Church itself helped to maintain this ambiguity by trying to give the elements of secular life a sacred character. Under its influence, ceremonies such as a royal coronation or the dubbing of a new knight became infused with a religious content that they had not originally possessed, or at least not to the same extent. As for the faithful, they tended to find the most physically demanding religious acts – fasts, abstinence, pilgrimages – the most significant, and to place less importance on regular church attendance or prayer. This was not surprising, as only the clergy, or at least those of them who knew Latin, had any direct contact with the Scriptures, as the Church was opposed to translation of the Bible into the vernacular, lest it be profaned in the process, or wrongly interpreted.

Hopes for the year 1000

Towards the end of the tenth century there developed in the West a reaction against religion as generally practised (in which agents mediated between the people and the sacred, and where the supernatural was perceived in concrete terms). This reaction was evident in various centres of religious agitation, which had only one feature in common: the intensity of spiritual fervour. These trends are clearly visible in the early heresies which flourished in France and Italy around the year 1000. At Vertus, near Châlons-sur-Marne, a peasant called Leutard destroyed the crucifix in his parish church and urged the faithful to stop paying tithes to the clergy. In Ravenna, the grammarian Wilgard amazed his hearers by informing them that the legends related by the authors of Antiquity contained as much truth as the texts of Christian revelation. In Aquitaine around 1020, in Orleans in 1022, in Arras in 1025, and in Monforte in 1028, heresies were uncovered and condemned. Contemporary chroniclers thought that they were seeing a resurrection of the Manichaeanism of the ancient world. For these radical sects, not only were works and manifestations of piety of no use in the quest for salvation, but the Church itself had no purpose; some went so far as to question the role of Christ as mediator. These trends have often been presented as the harbingers of an evangelical revival, or as a protest against the weight of the feudal structures which were then settling into place. In fact they were something else entirely: the men and women who rejected all the material and earthly aspects of religion and of the human condition (since they also condemned marriage and procreation) intended to assert that it was possible for initiates to enter into a direct relationship with God and to act here below under the impulse of the Holy Spirit. This ideal was lived out within small, enclosed communities in which values denied by the majority were recognised and practised: for example, brotherhood (in the castle of Monforte, lords and peasants lived as equals), purity, and the freedom to act in accordance with inspiration from within. Without explicitly calling the temporal order into question, these zealous groups were particularly attractive to people who felt excluded from the new warlike, materialist society: women, peasants and some literate clerics who found their own times repugnant and preferred to seek inspiration in the ancient cultures of the Mediterranean, not just in the Bible, but also in the apocryphal gospels and heretical writings of the early Christians.

These isolated dissident movements were soon quelled by the Church and the lay powers. Driven to suicide or condemned to the stake – which they welcomed with joy, as it delivered them from their fleshly condition into the heavenly home for which they had longed – the heretics of this period do not seem to have had any direct heirs. But it is striking to note that aspirations and beliefs very similar to those held by these victims of repression did surface among some of their contemporaries.

Within the monastic movement in particular, and even on the part of some bishops, there was a concern to rescue the Christian faith and the Church from the influence of the surrounding society, which seemed likely to pervert them. Clerics such as Ratier of Verona and Gerbert of Aurillac (who became Pope Silvester II, 997–1003) desired to express by reasoned argument 'that which God is not' in order to counter the ever-present threat that he would be identified with the objects through which he chose to reveal himself. Others were moved by a desire to liberate spiritual forces from the world's grasp. The ideas of Abbo of Fleury or Odo of Cluny concerning sexuality and marriage were not in fact far removed from those of the heretics of Arras or Monforte, who would not countenance procreation. There was a similar trend as far as relations with secular powers were concerned. If some monks like Helgaud of Fleury, author of the *Epitome of the Life of King Robert the Pious*, still exalted the figure of the sovereign, others freely admitted that the Devil was the begetter of temporal power, under whose influence the 'simoniacal heresy' had been introduced into the Church. This was the deplorable custom of buying and selling for cash both ecclesiastical offices and the sacraments. What separated the eleventh-century reformers from the heretics of the year 1000 was their rejection of pessimism; the heretics were convinced of the fundamentally perverse character of the social and religious order around them. The outstanding figures of the new monasticism – St Romuald, St Peter Damian or William of Volpiano – certainly did not regard their society any more indulgently, convinced as they were that man could only achieve salvation by breaking with the world and its prevailing values. Military violence, sexuality and money were the three things rejected by all the spiritual movements of the first feudal age, whatever their ultimate aims. But these men of action avoided the temptations of both passivity and messianic fantasies. Inspired by a profound faith in Christ and his Church, they preferred to work at creating the Kingdom of God in the here and now by setting up fervently devout communities, anticipating and witnessing to a new order. Through their perfect devotion and purified eucharist offered to God, the all-important relationship between God and man would be re-established.

The Church guides society

During the early Middle Ages, the Church had exerted a profound influence on Christian society but had not tried to become its leader. Besides, the barbarian kings would not have allowed it, and even the Carolingians, no matter how respectful they were towards pope and clergy, fully intended to be masters in their own house. Of course the two powers did not ignore each other, indeed they collaborated closely: rulers had chosen their most trusted counsellors from the ranks of bishops and monks, and the royal palace under the Merovingians, as under the Lombards and Anglo-Saxons, had been a breeding ground for prelates. After the empire was re-established in 800, there was an even closer bond between Church and State. Charlemagne summoned and presided over synods, and promulgated capitularies that reformed the clergy and liturgical practices. The pope and bishops were asked to support the monarch's efforts and to pray for the success of his ventures. This ecclesiastical ideology, which made the king the head of the Christian people – who were likened to the people of God in the Old Testament, ruled over by the kings of Judah – retained its vigour in the Holy Roman Empire under the Ottonians and Salians. The system reached its peak around the year 1000, when Otto III installed himself in Rome with his friend and colleague Gerbert of Aurillac, whom he made pope as Silvester II. On the model of the Byzantine East, where the patriarchate of Constantinople was usually granted by the emperor to one of his followers, the Roman Church in the West looked like the private church of the German monarchs who, in the time of Henry III, wrested it from the clutches of the local aristocracy and placed worthy figures at its head.

Ideologies and utopias

This parallel between Byzantium and the West was short-lived, and more apparent than real. From the end of the ninth century it had been clear that the central power was no longer able to maintain order within Christendom, especially in France and Italy. Its inability to provide defence, when confronted by the second great wave of invasions by Vikings, Hungarians and Saracens, led to the Empire's breaking up into territorial principalities whose leaders swiftly came to think of themselves as autonomous sovereigns. In the tenth and eleventh centuries, society's move towards feudalism resulted in public authority in many areas being transferred into the hands of the masters of castles, who were soon able to ensure that their descendants inherited the lands and offices previously held by the sovereign, and to dispose of them as they chose. In Italy, the restoration of some order by the Ottonians and the periodic expeditions of German sovereigns to Rome concealed for a while the scale of these changes. But in France, where the accession of the Capetian dynasty (987) had failed to alter the course of events, the clergy, who alone were able to reflect on the transformations they witnessed, found themselves confronting a new situation in

1000. They did not all react in the same manner. The ideologies which they sketched out were important, as they left a lasting mark on the mind of the ruling classes and helped to direct the evolution of Western society by proposing a voluntarist interpretation of it.

The most famous of these 'interpretations' of feudal society is the one that, following G. Dumézil, we refer to as the 'ideology of the three orders'. This finds its clearest expression in a few texts of ecclesiastical origin, of which the best known is the poem written in *c.* 1015 by Bishop Adalbero of Laon for the benefit of his friend, King Robert the Pious. In it he presents earthly society as a debased reflection of the kingdom of Heaven. Echoing the Trinity, the structure of the world is simultaneously one and three – a trinity in unity. While all baptised Christians certainly formed a single people, they were in fact divided into three classes: those who prayed (the clergy), those who fought (the lay aristocracy), and those who laboured (the peasants and artisans). Between these three groups there existed – or ought to exist, according to Adalbero – relationships of subordination and links of solidarity. The men of the Church were at the top because they fulfilled the noblest function, interceding with God for men; then came the lords, who did not spend time on menial tasks but wielded power and justice; finally there was the mass of serfs, subject to the preceding groups and whose *raison d'être* was to provide everyone with their material needs. But each category had an indispensable role to play, and none could survive without the others.

This pattern of three orders, influenced by a social model present among various Indo-European peoples, is interesting on more than one level. First of all, we can see it reflecting the transformations which had affected the West since the Carolingian era. Adalbero was very much aware that the laity could no longer be considered an undifferentiated category, now that the aristocracy constituted a military class which exercised the real power, and that serfdom was a condition which had spread throughout the countryside. But the acknowledgement of the separate status of the labourers was a device aimed at overcoming the social tensions which were keenly felt at this period, as feudal structures were established. To divide society into three and stress the necessary solidarity of the orders was surely a means of avoiding a confrontation between the *potentes*, holders of power, whether clerical or secular, and the *pauperes*, the labouring masses who were deprived of their rights and of means to action. Lastly, by assigning a specific function to each social group and making it an order (*ordo*), Adalbero was aiming to freeze the social structures of his time by giving them a sacred character. If a tripartite society was God's will, it became sacrilege to think of changing its structures or its operation.

Of course we might wonder if such a conception of social relationships was in fact widespread, and whether it would exert any real influence at a time when, even among the clergy, there were not many people capable of handling such concepts. The manual workers, bent over their ploughs or work-benches, had doubtless never heard about such things; for them, as far as we can tell, there existed only two categories of people: the lords and the rest, among whom they counted themselves. Whether the former were ecclesiastical or lay lords, they behaved in much the same way towards their dependants, and showed a common scorn for that inferior part of humanity that had to earn its bread, and theirs too, by the sweat of its brow. But what the majority thought hardly counted. What did

The ideology of the three orders.

Those who pray: in the midst of celebrating the eucharist, the priest turns towards the hand of God, thus showing that he wishes to be faithful to God's will. (St Augustine, Commentary on the Psalms, late eleventh century, Bibliothèque du Mans.)

Those who fight: Norman knights cut the Anglo-Saxon host to pieces. The sword was the aristocratic weapon *par excellence*, but the Anglo-Saxon nobles are using Danish battle-axes. The horses are saddled and shod, their riders use stirrups and spurs. The combatants are protected by coats of mail and helmets. The kite-shaped shield was in use from the tenth century. (Bayeux Tapestry.)

Those who work: the grape harvest. The whole family, including the women, takes part. The scene is in southern Italy, where the vine clings to the trees. (Miniature of 1028, Abbey of Monte Cassino.)

count were the élites, who were not slow to adopt this convenient scheme, even if it meant changing its internal structure. This can be seen in the twelfth century when the knights endeavoured to wrest first place in the hierarchy from the clergy. Perhaps the influence of this compartmentalising taxonomy finally made itself felt outside the ruling classes. Despite some rebellions and several attempts at individual social advancement, the prevailing general opinion was that everyone should know their place and stay in it. In contrast to modern society, medieval society was in principle hostile to change. Those who wished to change the existing situation even slightly were regarded as unscrupulously ambitious and subversive, since they were questioning the order of the world as willed by God. Thus popular rebellions, such as that of the Normandy peasants at the end of the tenth century, were always energetically suppressed by the lords, whose consciences remained clear because they viewed such movements as mere displays of sacrilegious presumption and madness.

Monasticism: a perfect society

At the same time as Adalbero was composing his famous poem, other churchmen, especially the monks of Cluny, were also trying to find a remedy for the ills afflicting their society. It was not obvious to the men of the millennium, as it is to us with hindsight, that the anarchy and climate of violence then affecting the greater part of Christendom, but especially France, in fact marked the birth of a new order, 'feudalism', which was to prove capable of maintaining the relatively smooth functioning of western society for some centuries. Rather, contemporaries were aware of the decay of ancient structures, of the violation of traditional rights, and of the increasing usurpation of properties. Some of them drew pessimistic conclusions and were disposed to see in the convulsions of the social order the forerunners of the final catastrophe. Numerous clerics penned treatises on the imminent coming of the Antichrist.

These fears and hopes – for the ending of the world also signalled revenge for the just – were not only expressed in writing. Art also became a vehicle for them – from the Spanish miniatures of the *Beatus* of Liebana to the tympanum of Moissac, this iconographic commentary on the Apocalypse nourished in people's minds an eschatological tension that was to reach its high point in the first half of the eleventh century, and was later revived on several occasions. We no longer believe in the 'terrors of the Millennium'; but the appearance of the world at that time gave many sensitive souls the impression that they were living through the last days. Fleeing from a society seemingly incapable of regaining its balance, they sought refuge in the 'wilderness' or in religious communities where the Benedictine Rule was fervently observed. Under the influence of Cluny and reformed abbeys such as Monte Cassino in Italy, Gorze in Lorraine and Le Bec in Normandy, monasticism entered an outstandingly fertile period and these 'citadels of prayer' swiftly became the major spiritual centres of Christendom. Their influence was bound up with the intensity of their praying and the quality of their liturgy. As the chronicler Raoul Glaber wrote about Cluny, 'There the life-giving sacrifice was celebrated so continously that not a day passed when such celebration did not snatch souls from the Devil's grasp, and this was done with such devotion, purity and respect that you would say it was the work of angels rather than of men.' These last words are significant: cloisters and abbeys achieved, even if imperfectly, a genuine community of minds and hearts – expressed in the unison of plainsong – together with a peace so tragically absent from secular society, and true brotherhood. There it was not a matter of abstract speculation: in the eleventh century, monasticism in its prime offered an alternative to temporal society. The great abbots of this period, from Odilo of Cluny to Desiderius of Monte Cassino, were wise enough not to try to 'monasticise' the world around them. They thought of their monasteries as so many 'Noah's Arks', which it was proper that the élite of humanity should enter for its salvation. Hence their attempts to put a religious habit on all those whom they saw as particularly gifted. In the same spirit they sought to extend their influence and possessions, so that an increasing number of the clergy and the faithful could benefit from the salutary influence of their communities. This is the explanation for the formation, quite new at this time, of powerful congregations (historians even refer to 'monastic empires') like that of Cluny which, by the end of the eleventh century, stretched from England to Lombardy, and from Spain to Hungary. By means of the centralised network of abbeys and priories, religious and moral pulses were transmitted throughout the West, making a powerful contribution to the creation of a homogeneous Christendom.

From the peace of God to the war for God

What was the point of reforming the monasteries and restoring regular observance there if all such efforts were periodically threatened by the turbulence of feudal society? Thus, in some regions where central power was in an advanced state of decay, some prelates and monks sought to re-establish a minimum of order and security in the society around them. This was quite a revolutionary step and was clearly seen as such by contemporaries. Bishop Adalbero of Laon, who still regarded the King of France as an arbiter among the three orders, was unsparing in his sarcastic criticism of the abbot of Cluny – whom he called 'King Odilo' – who had assumed the leadership of the peace movements around the year 1000. Again, in 1033, another prelate, Gerard of Cambrai, refused to allow into his diocese a movement which challenged the prerogatives of his sovereign, the German emperor. It seemed to him to be dangerous for the Church in so far as it might become a substitute for the legitimate authorities by assuming political responsibilities foreign to its vocation. These were the reactions of traditionalists who were steeped in the ecclesiastical ideology of the Carolingian era, which saw the sovereign as the spiritual and temporal head of the Christian people. But in the lands between the Loire and the Pyrenees, where there was no longer any authority able to check the prevailing anarchy and violence, churchmen were not slow to initiate specific measures aimed at restoring a minimum of order and concord. So from 989 onwards, as we have seen, they summoned peace assemblies. The lords of the areas concerned, from Catalonia to Burgundy, were made to promise that they would no longer attack churchmen or unarmed lay folk. By taking under their protection the defenceless rural masses, pilgrims and merchants, women and children, churchmen were sanctioning the increasingly evident distinction between the peasants and the new aristocracy of the *milites*, the 'knights'; the Church certainly took the part of the poor, whom some bishops – as in Bourges in 1038 – even encouraged to attack castles to force troublemakers to respect the agreements that had been made. In stressing the sacred character of ecclesiastical personnel and property, the Church was also protecting itself and securing for its members a privileged status in feudal society. Responding to the feelings of the populace, who of their own accord sought refuge near churches, monks increased the sacred enclosures marked out by crosses. Thus the presence and power of spiritual factors was evident even in the organisation of public spaces and settlement.

The success of the peace movement between 990 and 1020 in western Christendom encouraged the clergy to go further. At first, they had sought 'to confine violence to one section of the Christian people: those men who bore sword and shield and travelled on horseback' (G. Duby). But the stabilising of the new ruling class, and above all the climate of eschatological tension as the Millennium of Christ's Passion approached, enabled the Church to increase its demands. It proposed to the faithful, haunted as they were by the prospect of Judgement, an ideal of purification and asceticism: communal self-deprivation in order to ward off the divine wrath whose portents were increasing, if contemporary chroniclers are to be believed. The Church demanded that laymen, especially knights, abstain from what gave them greatest pleasure: war. Henceforth the peace movement's aim was different. It was no longer a social contract but a contract with God, intended to drive off sin in the world by an intensification of penitential practices. This was the meaning of the Truce of God, which found its definitive expression in the councils of Arles (1037–41). From this time lords were prohibited from waging war in the period from Wednesday evening to Sunday morning, just as clerics were strictly forbidden to pay cash for ecclesiastical offices and to have sexual relations.

These new prohibitions were not fully observed by either the warriors or the clerics. But they did not become merely dead letters either, and it is worth trying to uncover the reasons for the relative success of these great assemblies held under the aegis of monks and bishops. One of the elements of this response is certainly to be found in the close ties that had developed between reformed monasticism and the knightly aristocracy. Most monks in fact had come from that social class, and the abbots of Cluny in particular were quick to propose a religious ideal adapted to its way of life and capabilities. As early as the tenth century Odo of Cluny glorified the figure of St Gerald of Aurillac (d. 909), a lay aristocrat who had remained in the world and had attained a high degree of perfection there by practising virtues previously regarded as belonging to the just king: piety, respect for clerics, justice, generosity towards the poor. This symbiosis between the world of the monasteries and the world of the castles is not in itself sufficient explanation. In order to impose their code, the clergy relied on the faithful's belief in the power of the saints. It was upon their relics that the peace oaths were sworn, and it was their vengeance with which perjurers were threatened in the most explicit manner. In fact monks did not hesitate to pronounce curses upon the incorrigibly violent, curses that were dreaded as much as their prayers were sought. By

95

means of such threats, canonical sanctions – to be deprived of a Christian burial was the gateway to hell – and processions with the bodies of the saints, they did succeed to some extent in overcoming resistance and in establishing around themselves the minimum peace and security which society needed.

More was needed, however, than the threat of heavenly thunderbolts. The violence of feudal society may have been contained for the moment, but it threatened to break out again unless a way to harness it could be found. Both Cluny and the papacy were well aware of this and, from the mid-eleventh century, encouraged Christian knights to go to the aid of the small kingdoms in northern Spain, menaced by the advance of Islam. In the 1060s, Pope Alexander II launched new initiatives: not content with extending throughout Christendom the local measures in support of the Truce of God, he appealed to the knights to cease shedding Christian blood, but to combat the enemies of the Faith on Christendom's frontiers. His message was repeated and amplified by Urban II at the Council of Clermont (1095). The preaching of the Crusade sharply focused the energies of the laity, particularly the knights: by setting out as penitents and pilgrims to free the tomb of Christ, warriors would find a field of action suited to their faith, while Western society would be relieved of its most disturbing elements. The Church, as a consequence of its work for peace, was at the head of this movement: at the call of preachers and hermits, the crowd of Crusaders set out for the first time along the road to Jerusalem.

New paths of perfection

Not everyone wanted, or was able, to leave for Jerusalem, or even for Compostela. Furthermore the shedding of blood, even the blood of infidels, did not appeal to everyone. Could the monastic life not offer other ways of salvation to souls in need? The way of Cluny, whose empire spread across the world, did not seem the best to everyone; the power of a St Hugh (d. 1109), whose abbacy lasted sixty years, seemed too close to the power of a pope: he was beside Gregory VII at Canossa as a witness to the penitence of the emperor, who was his godson. The monks did not benefit personally from the enrichment of their monastery, and their lives were obviously irreproachable; nevertheless, the enormous abbey church begun under St Hugh (and which remained the greatest religious building in the Christian world until the construction of St Peter's by Bernini), called attention to the black monks' policy of systematic recruitment among the aristocracy, and to their phenomenal wealth. Furthermore, the Cluniac freedom from any episcopal control and the excessive concentration of power in the hands of the abbot of Cluny irritated the secular clergy. Even a former Cluniac such as Pope Urban II – and Callixtus II repeated this more sharply – reminded the abbots to moderate the scale of their establishment; the bad government of an abbot such as Pontius at the beginning of the twelfth century warranted even more severe criticisms.

In fact Cluny did not deserve its fall from grace. But its lofty intellectual activity, together with its conviction that nothing was too beautiful for God, and its belief that a certain moderation (a key word for St Benedict) in austerities gave greater strength and joy to the praises it raised to God, all failed to answer the faithful's increasingly powerful desire for

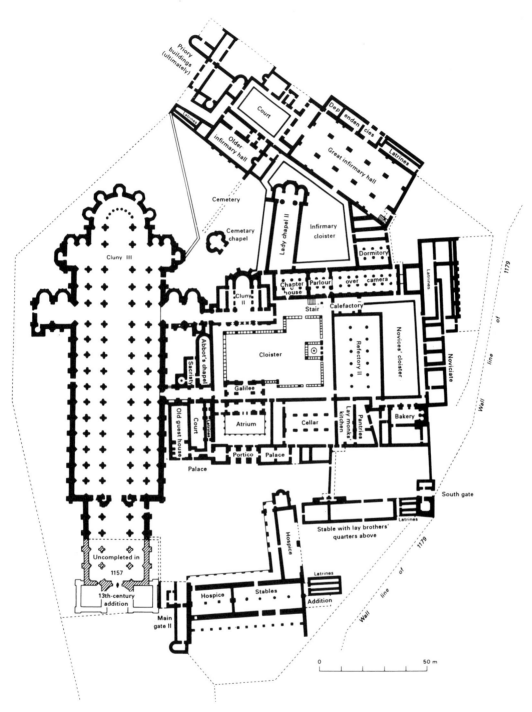

Plan of the Abbey of Cluny

Three hundred monks were permanently based here, together with hundreds of lay brothers (*conversi*) and novices, not to mention the indispensable lay personnel. This was a true town with the church at its centre. Eventually the church became too small and was rebuilt from 1088 to 1121.

change. Famous monastic schools such as Fleury, Corbie and Saint-Gall had already seen their constituencies dwindle, and their recruitment was suffering. The established Church wanted the faith to penetrate souls too, and looked for ways by which the monks' example could be transmitted: it was convinced that they should be 'witnesses'.

So let there be penance and poverty: but should there be preaching and counselling, or contemplation and prayer? Between 1039 and 1100, during one of the richest periods of medieval spirituality, there was a flood of attempts to answer this question. Some opted for a rejection of the world and for meditation. Such a movement often began as the work of a solitary man, a hermit weary of the world or a visionary ascetic, but disciples flocked to them; and the Church, which was suspicious of isolated figures, was happy to incorporate them into a formal structure. The list is a long one: at its head was John Gualbert at Vallombrosa in Italy (1039), followed in the west of France by Bernard of Tiron, Vitalis of Savigny and Gerald of La Sauve Majeure (1079). In this series, Stephen of Muret holds an ambiguous place; he settled at Grandmont near Limoges in 1074, but his 'good men' went about in the outside world, helping the underprivileged. How could the virtues of poverty, withdrawal and contemplation be reconciled with obedience and stability? St Bruno, with Urban II's support, offered a solution to the problem of squaring the circle: after one attempt in Champagne, he settled in the Préalpes in 1084; the *Chartreuse* (Carthusian monastery) was a 'community of recluses', each man isolated in his own hut, only gathering together on Sundays, helped in absolute silence by 'lay brothers', and subsisting solely by their own efforts. This was a hard life of sacrifice: the Carthusians had created only thirty-nine houses by 1200. As for choosing the path of preaching, this was to run into opposition from the bishops, whose sphere of activity it was. In 1043 in Livradois, at La Chasse-Dieu, Robert de Turlande, a former cathedral canon, founded a community along classic lines but with the aim of taking the word of God into the countryside. However, with just fifteen abbeys by the end of the twelfth century, it achieved only moderate success. Despite a startlingly successful beginning, this also proved true of the idiosyncratic initiative of Robert of Arbrissel, a mystic who held crowds in thrall at the end of the eleventh century, and who was followed by widows, female sinners and younger daughters at odds with their families. This scandalous situation, which still raises eyebrows, was firmly steered by the bishops towards respectability; in 1100, Robert established his penitent women at Fontevrault, in Anjou. But suspicion continued to check the success of an original women's order.

Perhaps all this was going too far. Was it not possible to tap the praiseworthy aspirations of those somewhat weaker figures who were deterred by the propect of pastoral work and mortification? The end of the eleventh century witnessed the beginnings of the successful establishment of chapters of regular canons: 'canons' because they preserved some freedom of action and kept an eye on the things of this world, and because they taught, preached and gave counsel; 'regular' because they lived in a fixed collegiate house or abbey, and because they were obliged to be obedient, to say the monastic offices, and to live as a community. From the twelfth century most of them were described as following the 'Rule of St Augustine', although that illustrious Church Father had never in fact drawn up a rule as such for the friends and disciples around him. This was a way of life that did not lay too much stress on mortification, that was fairly moderate in its vows, and was therefore a tempting prospect for many less adventurous souls, especially the more humble folk and for townspeople. Since the foundation and endowment of an abbey was often beyond the means of an aristocractic family, many nobles, seeking to emulate the kings and princes whose family burial sites were in holy places, founded collegiate churches in order to glorify the family name. The movement, at least in its first spontaneous stages, without lay pressure, began in Mediterranean Europe, at Avignon, in Provence generally, in Spain, and along the Garonne around 1050–65; but it flourished especially north of the Loire: at Arrouaise in Picardy (1090), at Marbach in Germany (1094), around William of Champeaux at Saint-Victor in Paris (1100). The most successful attempt was that of Norbert of Xanten, formerly chaplain to Henry V, a wandering preacher until 1118, when he founded at Prémontré, near Laon, an abbey of canons which rapidly enjoyed great success.

The basic elements of this religious life were prayer, singing, copying of texts and working the land. Such activities were not common in the world of warriors. Was it possible to continue to fight, but in a sacred cause: to become a 'Christian soldier'? St Bernard, himself from the warrior caste, understood this. Aware of the need of the Latin states of Syria to maintain an experienced standing body of soldiers to protect the liberated Holy Sepulchre, he encouraged, in 1119, Hugh of Payns from Champagne – and, in 1120, Raymond of Le Puy from the Auvergne – to set up troops of well-trained knights, soldiermonks: the Templars and Hospitallers. This was a strange form of monastic life, not so different in fact from the armed fanatics who sprang from the Muslim *ribats* of Tunisia or Egypt. The 'military orders' were organised for war, with knights, sergeants and commanders. For almost a century they seemed sufficiently successful to stifle any question whether their role as warriors of a militant faith in Lebanon was actually compatible with their possession of lands and headquarters in Europe.

The Cistercian spark

Perhaps there were too many paths from which to choose. Warrior, labourer, ascetic, preacher – all these potential roles reflected the aspirations of the late eleventh century, as the number of recruits clearly demonstrates. The most tormented and exacting souls continued their search.

The saintly Robert, monk and then abbot at Saint-Michel-de-Tonnerre, did not find the Cluniac regime satisfying; in 1071 he withdrew to contemplate various plans; in 1075 with some disciples he created a new monastery at Molesme; but he was weak, and let the community become lax. In 1090 he abandoned it, being tempted by asceticism, and returned in 1098 only to be sent packing by his own monks, apart from a handful whom he established in a 'wilderness' granted by the Duke of Burgundy, in the forest of Cîteaux. The papacy compelled him to return to Molesme in 1099. His Cistercian foundation seemed fated to wither away when, in 1112, the Englishman Stephen Harding welcomed into it the decisive and unexpected reinforcement of the young Bernard de Fontaine, accompanied by thirty other young men whom he had won over to the idea of a retreat from the world.

The development of the Cistercian order, which in 1118 settled on its own rule, the *Carta Caritatis* ('Charter of Love'), seemed to mark no radical departure from the Benedictine Rule. On the contrary, the monks wished to follow it to the letter: extreme poverty, plain surroundings, heavy manual labour. The aim was to obliterate the individual will, to renounce all harmful contact with the world, to practise penitence in the 'wilderness', and to practise charity (which required regular consultation about each other's wishes). Here there was no social snobbery, no pact with the world outside; conversely, there was no arrogant rejection of control by the secular Church, or the pope, no 'empire'. Instead there was a 'general chapter' that annually brought together all the abbots and promulgated decrees. A support group of lay brothers, not admitted to the choir of the church but acting as labourers in the fields, admitted the most impoverished and the least literate; but everyone was accepted, from the king's brother to a vagrant. This clearing of an old road rather than the creation of a new one certainly attracted vocations and inspired donations, but there was also the extraordinary activity of St Bernard. The explosion of fervour from which the order benefited was due to him. A man who harangued princes and preached Crusades, tireless defender of a militant faith and belief, devotee of Mary, mystical philosopher and warrior of God, he burned with a feverish eloquence and played a major role in kindling a smouldering religious vitality into a blaze. His sermons were more those of a soldier-monk than of a kindly shepherd; he heaped criticism on the free thought of Peter Abelard, and on the generosity of Abbot Peter of Cluny; he often provoked fury by his insufferable and harsh interventions. Nevertheless, when he died in 1153, public opinion, and the papacy, canonised him before a year was out.

The order spread very quickly: La Ferté (1113), Pontigny (1114), Morimond, and Clairvaux (1115), where St Bernard became abbot. By the mid-twelfth century the Cistercians had more than 400 abbeys over the whole of Christendom. Rejecting tithes, rights over men, and the use of machinery, they adapted the best techniques for economic management without making profit their prime consideration. They offered an example of what a 'traditionalist' organisation could achieve, avoiding the vices which had flawed other monastic movements. The generosity of the faithful matched their example, and it is no paradox to say that it was suffocated that way, so that 'spark' is an apt description of this brief movement. Of course disillusionment did not set in immediately: around 1300 there were more than 650 Cistercian abbeys, for both men and women; but from 1160 onwards, the business of buying and selling and the flood of donations sustaining the labour force opened the gates to profit-making, diverting the order from its mission and reducing it to conformity.

The primacy of the spiritual

If the monks were among the first to aspire to reform society, their desire to remain apart from the world limited the effectiveness of their contribution. From the mid-eleventh

In 1125, Stephen Harding, abbot of Cîteaux, visited the Abbey of St Vaast, one of the richest abbeys in the West, to establish a link with his own monastery. The relative poverty of the Cistercian abbey, on the right, is noteworthy. The presence of the Virgin, to whom the two abbots offer their monastery, testifies to her importance in the spiritual life of Cîteaux. (*Commentary of St Jerome on Jeremiah*, Bibliothèque de Dijon.)

century certain clerics, sometimes from a monastic backgound but raised to positions of authority in the ranks of the secular clergy, realised that the Church's only hope of surviving the threat of dissolution posed by feudal society was to free itself from the 'protection' of kings and lords. In opposition to the latter, who disposed of sacred matters as they pleased (from episcopal offices to churches and altars), they asserted that it was necessary to return to a distinction between the two powers, and to rescue the clergy from its subjection to laymen. This claim was already implicit in the tripartite outline of Adalbero of Laon, who had placed the specialists in prayer (*oratores*) at the head of the three orders. But with the reformers, from Humbert of Moyenmoutier to Gregory VII, who struggled for the 'liberty of the Church', it took a polemical turn.

A clergy in need of reform

These reformers saw the secular authorities, with the German emperor at their head, as oppressors who had wrongfully appropriated the property of the Church and were selling ecclesiastical offices to the highest bidder. This had resulted in the clergy's going down the slippery slope of worldliness. Such a situation was not only morally scandalous but actually a threat to the salvation of souls. Some of the faithful, too, were up in arms against this state of affairs, which was beginning to be perceived as an abuse and a scandal. In Milan, the greatest city in northern Italy, a clerk called Ariald stirred up a section of the population after 1057 by preaching against the archbishop and local clergy, whom he criticised for their corruption and loose morals. Moving from words to actions, he and his supporters attacked priests who were simoniacal, who were married or who had concubines; their services were boycotted and strong pressure was brought to bear on them to abandon their female companions. Condemned by the archbishop, the Patarenes – as their enemies called them, from *patarii*, beggars – soon gained the support of the papacy, especially of Gregory VII, who took the movement under his wing. Similar demonstrations occurred in many towns in Lombardy and in Tuscany, where the battle against unworthy priests was waged by monks and hermits, who were admired by the laity for their ascetic rigour and supernatural powers. One of them, Peter Igneus, walked through burning coals, emerging unscathed, in order to force the simoniacal Archbishop of Florence to resign his responsibilities, which he duly did.

Out of these upheavals, which took different forms in different regions, but in which moral concerns always played a decisive role, a new conception of the priesthood emerged. Laymen, who constituted the majority of the protestors, by no means sought to supplant the priests whom they dragged from the altars, at least in the movement's initial phases. On the contrary, it was because of their exalted view of the ministry that they wanted the priests' way of life to match the sacred character of their office. Surely an example ought to be set by those to whom Christ had entrusted the task of preaching his word and instructing the people? For the supporters of reform, the status of the clergy was not defined simply in institutional or canonical terms, but according to spiritual and moral requirements. If the clergy did not meet those, the sacraments they conferred had no value and could produce harmful effects in those who received them.

It is in this mental and religious context that we should place the successful activity of the wandering preachers who grew in number in the late eleventh century. In France, Germany and Italy, hermits and even monks came out of their retreats to address passionate speeches to crowds. Their personal asceticism was impressive and was enough to establish their sanctity for most people. For many lay people, an encounter with such 'men of God' as Robert of Arbrissel, Peter the Hermit and Vitalis of Savigny aroused their enthusiasm. Perhaps for the first time, they were confronted with the Gospel as preached by someone who lived according to its precepts. As a result, they sometimes turned violently against those who should have brought them this message, the priests whose lives were in flagrant contradiction to it. In an apparent paradox, the spiritual awakening of the laity ended up in demonstrations of virulent anti-clericalism. In some cases this led to a questioning of the very structure of the Church, as in the examples of Tanchelm in the Low Countries and Peter of Bruys in the French Midi shortly after 1100.

The elevation of the clergy

Obviously the papacy did not wish to rely on such measures to achieve reform. Having regained its moral standing with the pontificate of Leo IX (1049–54), and having won its freedom after 1059, when free election of the pope by the cardinals was instituted, the Roman Church regarded itself as 'the head and axis of all the churches', and wanted to make its own view of the relationship between spiritual and temporal power prevail. This vision achieved real coherence in the thought and actions of Pope Gregory VII (1073–85), who did not hesitate to unleash a political and religious conflict which shook the whole of the West in order to gain his objectives.

Gregory and his supporters argued that it was spiritual power (namely, the Church with the pope at its head) that should control Christian society. Creation had fallen as a result of sin and was dominated by Satan, but it longed for a conversion that would free people and things from the power of evil. Since the world, that is sin, had penetrated the very bosom of the Church, what had to be done first was to expel everything that smacked of worldliness, beginning with the secular grip on the Church. Such was the real meaning of Gregory VII's 1075 condemnation of lay investiture, which had permitted the emperor and kings to appoint bishops and abbots. But, not content with rejecting the traditional ascendancy of secular authorities, the Roman Church asserted that the balance of power was to be rearranged to its advantage. The popes then arrogated to themselves the right to condemn sovereigns, and even to depose them if their behaviour was not in accordance with these principles, as in the case of the Emperor Henry IV in 1075. The Church's claim to lead Christendom resulted in a strengthening of pontifical authority in society, which now, under the Church's direction, was called upon to realise the lofty aims the Creator had assigned to it: to set up a Christian order here below, anticipating the Kingdom of God on earth. The Gregorian eschatological sense was no less well developed than that of the monks of the previous generation, but it was played out on a bigger stage. The time was past when they could be satisfied with gathering together a chosen handful in a few abbeys. Henceforth the whole of Christendom, as far as possible, had to be made in the image of the heavenly Jerusalem.

At the time, these hitherto unheard of claims provoked a strong reaction. In many regions the bishops, creations of local power or at any rate accustomed to respecting it, felt closer to the prince than to a pope whose authoritarianism they had good grounds to fear. As for the kings, the majority refused to acknowledge themselves as vassals of the Bishop of Rome. The German Empire in particular rightly felt that a threat was posed to its very existence. Heir to the Carolingians and Ottonians, the German sovereign was not prepared to lose his sacral aura; it was of the utmost importance to him to be able to count on the loyalty of the clergy, to whom he often entrusted political offices, and to keep control over

103

appointments to the hierarchy. Between these two visions of the world and the Church, confrontation was inevitable. The result was the seemingly endless Investiture Conflict (1075–1122), which set the Church and the empire at loggerheads. It was a tragic conflict, racking the consciences of clergy torn between their old loyalties and the demands of reform. After years of fruitless confrontation on the diplomatic and military level, marked by famous episodes such as the shrewdly timed penance of the German monarch at Gregory's feet in the fortress of Canossa (1077), and the miserable death of the pope, who had taken refuge with Norman troops from Campania in an uneasy alliance, it was high time for a compromise.

In 1111 Emperor Henry V cunningly proposed to Pope Pascal II a solution whose merit lay in its simplicity. Since the main object of contention was the investiture of bishops and abbots – that is, the ceremony during which the king handed over to his candidate the pastoral staff and ring, symbols of a power both temporal and spiritual – it was enough for the prelates to renounce the rights and powers which the sovereign conferred on them for the problem to be solved. If he no longer held property, sources of wealth, and sovereignty delegated by the public authorities, the bishop could then be freely elected by the clergy and consecrated by his peers. For a moment Pascal was tempted by this proposal, which would return the Church to apostolic poverty and leave temporal matters in the firm grasp of lay power, and at first he accepted this compromise. He soon had to back down, however, in the face of indignant protest from the majority of German bishops, and a good number of the Italian ones. In their eyes, the Church had to possess substantial resources, especially at a time when authority was increasingly coming to rest on economic foundations, and when landed lordship was the only basis of government. Moreover, one of the fixed aims of the 'Gregorian' reformers had been to identify religious offices so closely with the rights connected to them that any dealings in ecclesiastical incomes would be seen as simony. Pascal's refusal was significant: in the eyes of the majority of the clergy, asserting the primacy of the spiritual was not meant to result in a poor and submissive Church, but rather in a Church powerful enough to overawe rebels and sinners, and rich enough to fulfil its obligations to the religious orders, the sick and the poor.

Since the lay powers did not want to lose out on all fronts, the Church was forced to accept a compromise that was not particularly satisfactory in principle, but in practice revealed itself as advantageous to both parties. The agreements that were concluded with the kings of France and England at the beginning of the twelfth century, and then with Emperor Henry V at Worms in 1122, were based on the distinction between the spiritual and the temporal which is commonplace to us but which was quite new at the time.

Both the freedom of the Roman Church and the independence of the pope with respect to the emperor were recognised. The emperor abandoned the practice of investiture prior to the consecration of a bishop; no longer did a layman appoint the bishop and confer authority upon him. But for all that, free elections were not restored and, with some regional variations, the choosing of prelates remained to a large extent in the hands of sovereigns. Like an old married couple who, having been torn apart for a long time, rediscover the advantages of living together, the Church and the lay powers recognised their necessary interdependence. The links that bound them were too close and too subtly woven

Benedictine monks. (MS of Hrabanus Maurus, Abbey of Monte Cassino, Vatican Library.)

to be snapped. It suited the interests of both parties to establish that relationship of mutual aid and collaboration between *sacerdotium* and *regnum* which, with some ups and downs, was to live on to the end of the Ancien Régime. In the short term, however, neither the papacy nor the Empire had given up the intention of dominating Christian society and, on this level, the Concordat of Worms merely marked a truce in a conflict which was to flare up again and again.

At the moment when claims for the primacy of the spiritual had been frustrated in the political arena, they were asserted with greater success within the Church itself. 'To the laymen, the affairs of this world, but to clerks, the things of the Spirit', Humbert of Moyenmoutier had already asserted in the heroic era of Gregorian reform. This willingness to confine the faithful to the temporal sphere scarcely veiled the real intention, which was to submit them to the clergy's authority and reduce them to the role of passive agents. Only kings and nobles, because of their social and political importance, managed to escape the Church's supervision to some extent. Whereas Gregory VII had admitted that laymen could set themselves up as judges of unworthy priests and, if necessary, force them to abandon their offices, his successors, aware of the risk of subversion, endeavoured to shield the clergy from the criticisms of its flock. The teaching of the Church, which had not been clear on this point, was sharply defined at the very end of the eleventh century: sacraments administered by clergy guilty of dubious or even scandalous behaviour lost none of their validity as long as the priests concerned had been regularly ordained and invested with their office in accordance with canon law. The authorities replied to those who challenged these new rulings by hardening hierarchical divisions and reminding the faithful of their specific obligations: paying tithes, respecting the property and the men of the Church, and distributing alms. Thus the movement of religious reform in which, in many regions, lay people of all ranks had taken an active part, ended up by elevating the office and role of the clergy in both Church and society.

The eleventh-century 'renaissance'

The clergy, or at least some of them, had another advantage over the laity in that they held the monopoly of learned culture, which meant the use of writing and knowledge of Latin. **105**

This state of affairs can be explained by both the 'barbarisation' of the West in the wake of the great Germanic and Scandinavian invasions, and by the decline of urban civilisation. But certain measures taken by the monarchy and Church under the Carolingians were also an important factor. At a time when even the clergy had only a faint knowledge of Latin, and when the type of script varied markedly from one region to another, Charlemagne and his advisor Alcuin had decided to promote not the vernacular, which even in former Roman territories was already far removed from Latin, but the language of the Church Fathers.

From the heritage of antiquity to ecclesiastical culture

In the eyes of these men, to be able to read and understand the works of St Augustine or St Jerome it was necessary to have a grounding in the works of classical authors. It was within this utilitarian perspective that the study of classical literature regained its lustre. At the same time, the simplification and standardisation of scripts led to Caroline minuscule – a script perfected in the late eighth century at the Abbey of Corbie – spreading to all the *scriptoria* (writing-rooms) in the abbeys and cathedrals. Schools were then established, especially in the principal episcopal towns, to produce an educated clergy. But the parish schools, whose foundation was envisioned in some capitularies, do not seem to have seen the light of day – and in any case, this attempt to raise the cultural level of the West rapidly came to a halt with the fall of the Carolingians and the disintegration of their empire. As a result, until the beginning of the twelfth century, the monks were to remain the chief repositories of learning.

The Rule of St Benedict, which became standard for all western monks in the ninth century, assigned an important place to the *lectio divina*, to which the monks and the community devoted several hours each day. In addition, each monastery had some choir monks who were able to read and sometimes able to write. Knowledge of Latin and some of the rudiments of literature was for them a way of approaching the word of God and the Rule, the reading of which was the centre of their existence. In monastery schools, novices were taught to read the Psalms and gained familiarity with the rules of Latin grammar. Whether the pupil was a future monk in the abbey boarding-school or a young lay aristocrat in the abbey day-school, he would study extracts from the Old and New Testaments and work on biblical commentary, a form of spiritual meditation on sacred texts designed to uplift the soul.

For those who lived in the cloisters, Scripture was not a means to knowledge or information but an instrument of salvation. Hence the infinite respect which surrounded it and which is revealed in the way the sacred books were copied, illuminated and preserved. Hence also the ambivalent attitude of the monks towards the culture of Antiquity, the study of which often posed problems of conscience. Odo of Cluny, for example, wanted to read some lines of Virgil one day, but he had a dream in which he saw a magnificent vase out of which crawled snakes who wrapped themselves all around it; this led him to abandon his plan. Others were bolder and plunged unhesitatingly into the works of Cicero or Ovid. But they could do this secure in the knowledge that they were finally directing the rich

St Benedict writing his Rule. The quill pen and horn inkstand on his monk's desk are clearly visible. In the *scriptoria*, the copyists' workshops, a new synthesis of classical tradition and Christian spirit was developed. (Pen and ink drawing in a codex from Zwiefalten, 1138–47; Stuttgart, Württembergische Landesbibliothek.)

107

pagan heritage towards its true destination: the worship of God in the Church. Thus, even when the ecclesiastical culture of that time decked itself out in humanist trappings, it was concerned with a very different source of inspiration and it reinterpreted the authors of Antiquity in the light of Christian revelation. Nonetheless, monastic culture was deeply marked by this alien heritage which it endeavoured to assimilate. It owed to that heritage its exclusively literary character as well as its cultivation of fine language and formal elegance. As Gerbert of Aurillac (the future Pope Silvester II) wrote, shortly before 1000, 'Philosophy does not separate knowledge of manners from knowledge of speech. And so I have studied simultaneously the art of right living and the art of speaking well.' In the cloisters and *scriptoria* there developed an original synthesis of the classical tradition and the spirit of Christianity, a synthesis founded on the conviction that if it was grace alone that raised up the soul, it was culture that refined and adorned it and prepared it to proclaim the glory of God.

The era of the 'masters of the schools'

It would be misleading to imagine, however, that the learned culture of the tenth and eleventh centuries was the culture of a large number of people. In many regions Carolingian educational establishments had foundered amidst the crises and invasions of the late ninth and early tenth centuries. In Normandy, for example, it was still difficult around the year 1000 to find clerks with an adequate knowledge of Latin. But the collapse had not been uniform throughout the West, and some centres retained enough energy to provide impetus for a fresh start when the general situation became more favourable. This is what happened in the Empire, especially in its Germanic lands where the cultural re-awakening occurred earlier than elsewhere. There the Latin language had not been contaminated by the vernacular and its rapid development was aided by the religious policy of the Ottonian monarchs, who were anxious to raise the moral and religious standards of the clergy. This is the context of the short Latin comedies by Hrotsvitha, abbess of Gandersheim in Saxony, who took her inspiration from Terence, and the composition of liturgical sequences by Notker, the monk who headed the abbey school of Saint-Gall, and who also translated some classical authors into German. In the monasteries of Reichenau and Tegernsee at Weissenburg, and St Emmeram in Regensburg, the early eleventh century saw the production of some noteworthy texts, often inspired by vernacular literature (for example Ekkehard's *Waltharius*, and the *Ruodlieb*). This movement spread to Lotharingia. In the cathedral schools of Liège, Toul and Metz, in the abbeys of Gembloux, Lobbes and Stavelot, clerics studied grammar and musical theory; some, such as Sigebert of Gembloux, wrote chronicles and historical narratives whose influence extended as far as Italy and Poland. But this remained an essentially academic culture. It had a vital role to play in transmitting the Carolingian heritage and through that, the heritage of the Romano-Byzantine world. But fresh inspiration was to come from other centres and different regions.

From the late tenth and early eleventh centuries the intellectual tide flowed towards
France, where monastic life was flourishing. This was not so much because the atmosphere

The Romanesque basilica of St-Benoît-sur-Loire (Fleury), constructed 1067–1108. Founded in the seventh century, by the time of Charlemagne the abbey was famous throughout the Christian world as an intellectual centre. Theology and the liberal arts were taught there; manuscripts were copied and illuminated; chroniclers recorded the history of their time; and its masters took an interest in agriculture and medicine.

was particularly favourable for study, since at that time the structure of feudal society was being laid down, often in a violent fashion. But in a few cathedral towns such as Rheims and Chartres, or in great abbeys like Fleury (Saint-Benoît-sur-Loire) and St Martial of Limoges, there was a rebirth of cultural activity. At Chartres, for example, the pupils of Bishop Fulbert (d. 1029), an Italian educated in Rheims, were to become the architects of the theological revival in the next generation: Adelman of Liège, Berengar of Tours and Lanfranc of Pavia. The situation of these clerics, 'masters of the schools', is revealing. Before becoming master at Rheims at the end of the tenth century, Gerbert had been sent to Catalonia, on the borders of the Muslim world, to learn the art of debate (dialectics), which was not taught in monastic schools, and more importantly, the subjects of the **109**

Quadrivium (arithmetic, geometry, astronomy and musical theory). Men travelled from far and wide in order to consult Fulbert at Chartres, one of the few men of his time with a knowledge of medicine. There is also the case of Abbo of Fleury who tried to complete at Rheims the studies that he had begun in a monastery, but could not find anyone to teach him music. In desperation, he had to turn to a priest from Orléans who agreed to teach him, but in secret and for a fee. These few examples reveal the extremely isolated and fragile nature of those schools, whose brilliance depended on the personal influence of one or two masters. They were not so much beacons of culture as flickering sparks.

The development of critical thought

Nonetheless, as time went on, the signs of a genuine renewal of cultural life began to multiply. In 1079 Pope Gregory VII revived the legislation of the Carolingian era which obliged each bishop to maintain a school in the chief church of his diocese where the clergy could be instructed. While the papal commands did not produce immediate results, in those regions where political and economic conditions were favourable (as they were in northern France and Italy), scholarly institutions were developed and attempts were made to reconstruct libraries and archives. Under the supervision of the chancellor, a canon of the cathedral chapter, who generally acted as head of the school, masters (*magistri*) began to provide regular instruction, usually at an elementary level, in the cloisters and buildings adjoining the cathedral. As well as clerks destined for an ecclesiastical career, other students came for instruction and benefited from the same privileges and liberties.

In the eleventh century, however, monasteries remained the most flourishing centres of culture. In Italy, the monastery of Monte Cassino experienced a period of exceptional brilliance under Abbot Desiderius (1058–86). The influence of neighbouring areas such as Byzantine Italy and even the Muslim world, filtered through the ports of Amalfi and Salerno, encouraged the copying and illuminating of manuscripts whose stylistic quality and originality found their finest expression in the famous *Exultet* rolls. Classical literary form was revived in the *scriptorium* of Monte Cassino, where the future papal chancellor, John of Gaeta, learned the polished epistolary style, the *cursus*, which he was to introduce between 1089 and 1118 into documents emanating from the papal bureaucracy. Another region with a thriving culture at this time was Lombardy. From here came masters such as Lanfranc who in 1045 established in the Norman Abbey of Bec a school which gained a reputation as one of the finest in the West. There he trained men who were to play an essential part in the life of their time, men such as St Anselm (1033–1109), another Italian, who succeeded him as abbot of Bec and as Archbishop of Canterbury, and Bishop Ivo of Chartres, the famous canon lawyer. With these two figures the scholastic culture of the eleventh century took a great leap forward; it was no longer a case of 'masters' transmitting a fossilised or rarefied body of knowledge, but of original thinkers applying their intelligence to solving the essential problems of their time. St Anselm began using dialectics, that is formal logic, in his exploration of the divine mysteries. Of course for him faith remained the basis of any speculation, but such speculation could help to explain the content of faith by applying reason to the facts of relevation (*fides quaerens intellectum*). But the problem of a fundamental reality and the development of concepts, expressed in the contemporary term 'universals' such as 'Good', 'Truth', and of course God, was to divide those who believed in pre-existing postulates (realists), who had the Church's backing, from those who saw in all these only a form, a *nomen*, which required demonstration by reasoned argument (nominalists). To the ecclesiastical hierarchy, the latter view was too dangerous to escape condemnation, and its adherents were driven either to the stake or to the recantation of their belief (Berengar of Tours).

This new approach to the relationship between philosophy and theology culminated in the ontological argument, the first attempt at a purely rational demonstration of the existence of God. For his part, Ivo of Chartres set himself the task of studying the delicate question of the relations between Church and State. He contributed to the ending of the Investiture Conflict by defining a fundamental distinction between things temporal and spiritual, a distinction he formulated while pondering on the notion of episcopal authority, which was at the centre of the conflict. In fact, cultural development at this time was stimulated by the great disputes which were shaking the ruling circles of Christendom but which also had tangible repercussions lower down the social scale. The dispute between those who supported Church reform under the papacy's leadership and those who upheld imperial ideology produced a widespread literary polemic on such basic questions as the foundations of sacerdotal and royal power, the position of the pope in the Church and the relationship between clergy and laity. The papacy's need to ground its new claims in the solid base of tradition resulted in the systematic scrutiny of old legal collections and encouraged the compilation of canon law texts. The attempt was made to eliminate documents of dubious origin, and those that had been corrupted by Celtic or Germanic additions, retaining only those texts which conformed to Roman tradition and which contributed to the glorification of the Apostolic See. Even this initially rather disorganised attempt at classification and repossession reveals that culture was no longer the private preserve of pedants, or simply a scholarly exercise, but had become an instrument of analysis with direct relevance to society.

An ignorant laity?

The Carolingians' choice of Latin as the religious, and hence cultural, language of the West opened up an ever-widening gap between clergy and laity. To the clergy, at least until the twelfth century, the laity appeared to be ignorant and illiterate. And in fact, around the year 1000, even in the ranks of the high aristocracy only a few outstanding women, such as empresses, queens or great ladies, had managed to acquire the rudiments of Latin by going through the Psalter with a clerk in their entourage. In the course of the eleventh century, this situation began to change and some sons of the nobility, and not only those who were destined for a clerical career, gained a knowledge of Latin, at least at an elementary level, either with the help of a tutor or by attending the external schools of the monasteries. This trend, however, affected only a very small minority and, even among the knightly class, the

111

majority remained completely ignorant of learned culture. But this is not the whole story: ignorance of Latin, or refusal to learn it, did not present an insurmountable barrier to the development of a secular culture, which eventually found expression in a literature of its own.

The real problem lay in the sphere of writing. Most lay people of the eleventh century, apart from those in areas such as Catalonia or Italy, could not write their name at the foot of a charter. Even the writing of Countess Matilda of Tuscany in a charter of 1106 for an abbey of Pavia is clumsy and stiff beside the professional neatness of the rest of the document, drawn up by a clerk in her entourage. Far from constituting a standard means of expressing human thought, outside ecclesiastical circles the written document appeared as something exceptional. Not only was it of no use to most people, it was also incomprehensible since it was written in Latin, that is, in a dead language which could express contemporary realities only in an approximate fashion. One could even describe this period as one of a reaction against writing in so far as it had lost any practical application. Within the Capetian lands, for example, the number of charters from the eleventh century is very low. They were hardly anything more than *aides-mémoire* whose clauses were less important than the names and status of the witnesses, who guaranteed that what the document stated would be carried out.

The decline of the written document was by no means unconnected with the appearance of new political structures. The weakening of royal and imperial authority, as well as the increase in centres of power which accompanied the setting up of feudal structures, led to the eclipse of laws and even of attempts to apply them as the Carolingian capitularies. Henceforth the legal relationships between men were determined by 'custom', the content of which varied across time and place according to whatever balance of power existed between a given lord and his dependants. In France, once the comital courts had disappeared, there were no more public tribunals; judgement was a matter for local lords and the little group of friends and counsellors around them. The clergy vehemently denounced the 'bad customs' introduced at will by the powerful, customs all the more formidable in that they were often not recorded in written form. But even within the Church itself, the canonical texts were far from constituting the only source of law: in cases of proof, there was increasing recourse to the 'judgement of God' in the form of the ordeal, which left to fire or water the task of discriminating between true and false, just and unjust.

Does all of this mean that contemporaries, since they were ignorant of Latin and seldom had recourse to written documents, were entirely lacking in culture? Far from it; they had in fact a culture of their own, quite separate from that of the Church, but we know little about it as it was essentially a culture of speech and gesture. As far as relations between men were concerned, this period witnessed the establishment of a symbolic ritual that was purely secular: that of homage and investiture. For an agreement or a treaty to be ratified, a meaningful ceremony had to be performed in front of competent witnesses: the man concerned had to place his clasped hands between the hands of his lord and receive from him a wisp of straw or an abbot's crozier. If a clerk was present and a written record was drawn up, its purpose was merely supplementary, to help preserve the memory of the ceremony.

Feudal homage of the nobles of Perpignan to Alfonso the Chaste, King of the Asturias. (*Liber Feudorum Major*, twelfth century; Barcelona, Archives of the Aragonese Crown.)

It was the same with rites of passage, of which the most important was dubbing – transmitting a life-force with a blow – and the test of the quintain. From its earliest mention in written sources, dubbing appears to be fulfilling an important social function, and its significance increased as the class of *milites* (knights in the service of the lord of the castle) imposed their own system of values throughout the entire aristocracy.

It is difficult to know, in such a context, what might count as entertainment. There is some evidence to suggest that there existed a highly developed oral folk-culture. Unfortunately we can only grasp it through the distorting lens of clerically produced texts or later literary creations such as *chansons de geste*, saints' *Lives* and miracle-collections which do not allow us fully to grasp the significance of actions and practices which they simply note in passing.

In order to reach these people, who seemed to be largely outside their influence, the clergy developed a vernacular literature. From the tenth century there appeared texts in Romance dialect that functioned as an adjunct to the liturgy, texts such as the *Sequence of St Eulalia*, or the tropes composed in Conques, St Martial of Limoges and Fleury. Parallel to this, the eleventh century saw an upsurge in the production of hagiographical texts. Using

113

a biography brought back from the East in 977, a Norman clerk composed the *Song of St Alexis* around 1040 and some twenty years later a monk of Conques wrote the *Song of Ste Foy* in assonantal lines. Finally, in Burgundy and Aquitaine the first *chansons de geste* were committed to writing (*The Song of Roland, Girard of Vienne*, the William of Orange cycle). These texts took up the epic traditions of the Carolingian age and breathed a new meaning into them: the victory of the Christian faith over the infernal forces of Islam. These works, which were to enjoy huge success in the twelfth century, offered idealised models of behaviour. The gallant knight Roland prays and makes confession when he feels the end approaching; he dies faithful to his lord in contrast to Ganelon, the treacherous vassal. Through this literature of entertainment, the work of clerks living among laymen, the Church sought to christianise the mentality of the new aristocracy and to give a sacred aura to the order of knights by offering it a religious ideal.

The first expressions of a Western consciousness

The fact that a new spirit was abroad within western Christendom is revealed by the flowering of works of art, especially buildings, many of which survive as testimony to the creative dynamism of what was in fact a deeply troubled era. In order to explain this apparent paradox historians have had recourse to a variety of solutions: the need to rebuild after the wave of invasions in the ninth and tenth centuries; the rise in population, the impact of which was felt particularly keenly in the countryside; and the development of monasticism which meant an increase in the numbers of shrines. All these factors are important but the main stimulus probably came from the fragmentation of power within feudal society. Following the example of the great church-building monarchs, the new regional leaders competed with each other to raise up to the glory of God religious structures designed to bear witness to their own power. Thus in Normandy, the development of Romanesque architecture paralleled the rise of the ducal house, and from the Abbey of the Trinity at Fécamp to the Abbaye-aux-Dames at Caen, the founding of abbeys marked the progress of the ruling dynasty. Similarly in Christian Spain, which was a mosaic of small kingdoms clinging to the southern slopes of the Pyrenees, the political fragmentation encouraged the building of churches and royal monuments: San Salvador de Leyre in Navarre, San Juan de la Pena in Aragon and San Isidoro in León.

At first, these new eccelesiastical buildings were not accompanied by any artistic innovation. Between 950 and 1070, in the German Empire, Ottonian art contented itself with repeating and perfecting Carolingian architectural formulas. In the Mediterranean lands, the first phase of Romanesque art was an empirical synthesis of elements borrowed from the past. Even if some buildings – such as the Catalan abbeys of Ripoll and St Michel de Cuxa, and the church of Sant'Abbondio of Como in Lombardy – were artistically successful, they only reveal the strength of Roman traditions which had never been completely broken in these regions, and the power of Eastern influences, not only Byzantine but also Anatolian and Syrian. On the artistic as on the intellectual level, the second millennium 'began not with a revolution but with a revival of the ancient world' (H. Focillon).

Romanesque art of the year 1000: the Abbey of Saint-Martin-du-Canigou, founded in the early eleventh century; its monolithic columns and thick eastern wall recall its original framework, which was soon vaulted. At an altitude of 1,000 metres its square bell-tower dominates the splendid surroundings.

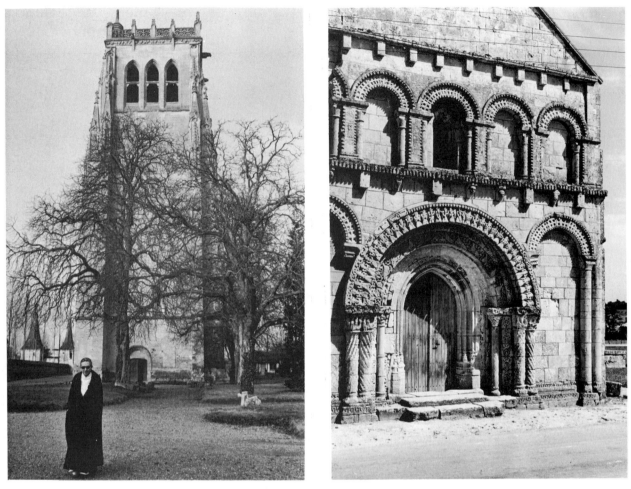

Left: The Benedictine Abbey of Bec-Hellouin, founded in the eleventh century. Right: Doorway of the Romanesque church of Avy-en-Pons (Charente-Maritime).

Relief sculpture at the Abbey of Moissac.

The cloister and abbey church of Moissac (late eleventh century).

The Eve of Autun, the work o
the sculptor Giselbert (mid-
twelfth century), a fragment c
the former lintel of the north
portal of the cathedral.

Nonetheless, in some places new solutions and techniques were appearing which, while originally intended to improve the existing type of church, in fact brought about basic changes in the overall design, structure and decoration of ecclesiastical buildings in the West. And so the classical plan of the basilica gained a projecting transept; chapels came to radiate out from the apse. Nearly everywhere new solutions were attempted to the problem of roofing vaults with carved stone, as can be seen at Tournus and Nevers. In fact, Romanesque art proper was born after 1070, with the emergence of original formulas which combined tradition and individual experience in a significant new synthesis.

This particular style first saw the light of day in areas which hitherto had seemed old-fashioned in comparison with the Mediterranean and the Rhineland: Normandy, Burgundy, Aquitaine and Apulia. There, great buildings, distinguished by large ambulatories with radiating chapels, were constructed with naves of three to five aisles under a single covering of stone. The same stone was used for the walls as for the roof. Columns evolved into pillars whose regular placing meant that the walls were, so to speak, rhythmically divided and which acted as sprung vaulting ensuring an organic link between the different parts of the building. Despite the impression sometimes conveyed by the surviving sources, these experiments were not carried out in modest village churches. On the contrary, the first full flowering of Romanesque art was rooted in the great monastic shrines, famous pilgrim churches and urban cathedrals. One of the chief centres was the Abbey of Cluny, whose builders knew how to combine Roman, Lombard and Byzantine forms into something more than the sum of these parts. Under the influence of the Cluniacs the new art spread and flourished in areas which had hitherto been on the fringes of western Christendom and which had remained faithful to traditions which were by now exhausted, as in south-west France (Aquitaine and Languedoc) and northern Spain. Saint-Sernin of Toulouse, Conques and Moissac still stand today as testimony to the tremendous success of this transplanting of styles which linked these areas with the remainder of the West and with Rome and which, on an artistic level, were the hallmarks of Christendom.

Elsewhere, in southern Italy, the Auvergne and Périgord, artistic creativity was stimulated by external influences whose transmission was made possible by the revival of trade and the increased mobility of men who now did not hesitate to journey to the Orient as pilgrims, merchants or Crusaders. Thus regional styles were formed and spread, from great buildings to humble ones. Such styles may have been formed within territorial principalities but never coincided precisely with their boundaries. Romanesque art progressed by 'a regional synthesis of international styles' and each of the 'schools' which art historians have managed to distinguish combined the new imported forms with the living elements of their local culture, their own powers of invention and their folk traditions. Contrary to the view of Marc Bloch, this was not simply the reflection of the feudal and ethnic diversity of the West, nor was it the result of a mass of individual efforts which had somehow spontaneously achieved an artistic breakthrough. Instead it would be more accurate to see it as the sign of the spiritual and artistic awakening of the different regions of the new Christendom through a series of contacts with the main currents of international culture. Romanesque art reveals all the richness and creative dynamism of feudal society. That society is often viewed as the outcome of a negative process of political disintegration. Such a view, however, fails to recognise feudal society as an active attempt at reorganisation which liberated creative forces hitherto buried in obscurity.

It is no accident that this was the time when the art of sculpture was revived in the West and the long-absent human figure reappeared. The Eve of Autun, in her artfully naïve nakedness, stands as the most perfect expression of this renaissance. In the columnar statue, the human body was no longer confined within a grid of geometric abstractions but was able to rediscover its true proportions and form. In its rediscovery of the plastic and monumental values of the human body, Western art firmly turned its back on barbarian traditions and Eastern influences. Around 1100, in this artistic sphere as in others, Latin Christendom asserted itself through confrontation. Islam and Byzantium, which had given it so much, were now faced with a self-consciously independent West. Diverse but united: such were the Westerners who answered the papacy's call by swarming eastwards in 1096 and to whom their adversaries were to give a single name: the Franks.

3 The establishment of states

Until recently, historians of previous generations were happy to confine their interest to the framework of political life, and they gave pride of place to the history of the State, which represented the sum of history: dynasties, wars, treaties. At best, it was a study of administrative structures within which men acted. This pattern of thought was inherited from both the Ancien Régime and nineteenth-century nationalism: we are unhappily indebted to this for the dry accounts of reigns spanning a variety of historical periods, which were nonetheless presumed to be homogeneous. We also owe to it the complete lack of interest, not to say repugnance, aroused in a child or adult when confronted by a history of the Middle Ages, full of sound and fury, signifying very little to the potentially curious. When, after the first quarter of the twentieth century, the focus turned towards economic and social history, the Middle Ages came back to life; add to this the interest in collective mentalities and daily life typical of our own uneasy society, and it is not surprising to find the Middle Ages in the forefront of public interest. The 'history of battles' has given way to the 'history of social structures'.

There is still so much to discover in these areas of research that it seems unlikely that the pendulum will swing back; however both 'political' history and even military history are regaining ground. But these are no longer merely chronological lists; they have become rooted in the study of social groups or in the study of thought. That is why the reader is urged to pause here, briefly but necessarily, at the level of events. Otherwise, in what follows concerning the great expansion during the central Middle Ages and what has come before (the setting the scene for this drama), we run the risk of vagueness and obscurity. Besides, Europe was not born in villages, or in men's minds alone: Europe's profile today still bears the mark of the establishment of a political order which the future was not to efface.

The northern world joins Europe

The essential feature of medieval political geography between 900 and 1100 is the bringing into the feudal and Christian mainstream the marginal lands which had, until then, been quite isolated: a world of Nordic seas closer to Islam or the Greeks than they were to

Map 4: Europe in the year 1000.

Germany; a southern fringe which had been occupied for centuries by these same Greeks or Muslims; and finally, a shadowy host of Slavs to the east, confronting the evolving Germano-Celtic world. As was said at the beginning of these volumes, their major theme is the grouping around the European core of marginal cultures, some of which had been dominant for a long time, as in the Mediterranean for example, while others had become mere appendages, as in the East. It is important, therefore, to examine the progress and the early stages of this movement, which in the period 1000 to 1200 was only in its first phase. Soon we will need to examine more closely its economic and social dimensions, but for now let us attempt to sketch the *dramatis personae*.

The secrets of the northern mists

For a priest venturing towards Denmark or Sweden, like those sent out by the Carolingians or Ottonians, the impression of entering an utterly strange and hostile territory must have

Scandinavian jewellery: a hammer of Thor from Erikstorp, Ostergotland, tenth century. (Stockholm, National Museum of Antiquities.)

been as strong as it had been for the explorers of Antiquity. Moreover, from these harsh and misty regions there burst forth the unpredictable expeditions of pirates whose violent behaviour was compared to that of animals by their victims – Saxons, Frisians and north Germans, whose ancestors, however, had probably come from the same regions long ago.

Fishermen, woodcutters, hunters of seals, whales and bears, intrepid sailors who launched their boats in the roughest seas, blind to danger, fearsome, axe-wielding warriors, these men of the North seemed unlikely to establish any peaceful, orderly contact with Christendom. Moreover, there seemed to be no established political authorities, only coastal chieftains. Such was the superficial picture, and it remained the stock image until almost fifty years ago.

Since then, archaeology has so completely transformed our knowledge that a whole new world has appeared before us. In tombs of the eighth to tenth century in Jutland and Gotland, Uppsala, Oslo, Bergen and Tonsberg, works of art were piled up together with gold and silver coins, fragments of jewellery and coins (which had come from Turkestan, Iraq, the Greek world, even from China). Futhermore, on the southern and north-western shores of the Baltic, the remains of trading posts such as Hedeby and Birka, dating from the early ninth century, and of the great fortified military camps (Trelleborg, Jomsborg), reveal a level of activity and organisation of which contemporary Christians were unaware. Dating from the eleventh or twelfth centuries, the sagas testify to commercial voyages and warrior ventures from Greenland to Byzantium, from Lapland to the Caspian Sea. The Viking raids are quite naturally included in the context of this wholesale expansion, although their causes remain obscure. Probably because the Vikings were willing enough to accept amber, Irish slaves, iron or wood offered by the Swedes – whom they called the Varangians – in exchange for precious metals or furs, the Slavs of Lithuania and White Russia did not experience the troubles suffered by the Anglo-Saxons and Franks.

The settlement of Norwegians in Ireland (from 800), in Iceland (870), in the 'Danelaw' in England (after 870) and in Normandy (from 910), made the North Sea and Baltic into a unit within which the same nautical, technical and farming skills were spread; many historical puzzles such as the landscape of the Pays de Caux and of Kent, or the way land was divided on both sides of the Channel into measures of *delle* and *furlong* can be solved by

Aerial view of the ruins of Norse settlements in the Orkneys, north of Scotland.

reference to this fact. The same may be said for the forms of social organisation and the terms used for them: the Danish mass levy of troops, the *leding*, recalls the Anglo-Saxon *fyrd*; the *althing* of the free men of Scandinavia recalls the English *witenagemot*; the Norse *jarls* point to English *earls*, and so on.

This situation lasted for a long time. Perhaps the conversion of the Scandinavians to Christianity – albeit a very slow process (the continental Saxons, for example, had only recently accepted the new religion themselves) – established, through a place such as Hamburg, a fragile link between the continental mainland and the men of the North; but the Christian faith was the faith of the princes, still coloured by the magical beliefs fostered by the long winters, mists and forests, where such beliefs were well rooted. King Cnut travelled to Rome in 1034 to kiss the hand of the pope, but he was notorious for skewering small children on his spears. Politically, the settling of accounts between such 'kings', who were begining to define the boundaries of their spheres of action, was neither important nor long-lasting before the year 1000; its sole interest lies in the fact that it sometimes took the form of naval battles worthy of Antiquity. But the impression remains that a significant part of the isolated, scattered population was untouched by all this.

Such developments culminated in the attempt by the Danish king Svein 'Forkbeard' to move out from the Danelaw and conquer the whole of England (1002). He died, leaving the task to be completed by his son Cnut (1014). Since the latter enjoyed good relations with the 'jarl of Rudhu' (the Duke of Rouen), with the Count of Flanders, and with the emperor, and since, for good measure, he occupied part of Sweden, history has granted him the title **123**

The Normans landing in England, 28 September 1066. They reached the coast at dawn; here they are shown lowering sails and masts, and unloading the horses; the derigged ships are already lined up on the sand. (Bayeux Tapestry.)

'Great'. The northern world really seemed to form a unified whole, from London to Novgorod, the trading post in Russian territory. More importantly, within this framework of political unity the final stages in the process of peasant settlement took place. We know all too little about the process in Denmark, but excavations in England such as the one at Chalton, show that settlement was assuming its lasting forms, often close to the *burhs* established by Alfred and his successors in the late ninth and tenth centuries during the struggles against the Vikings.

1066 and all that

The title of a humorous survey of English history, this phrase sums up a fact of great importance for the West: the beginning – for the end is not yet in sight! – of England's firm attachment to the Continent.

The death of Cnut in 1035 meant the break-up of his short-lived empire: trouble broke out in the north, in the south Hedeby was sacked by the Germans, in the west an Anglo-Saxon king was restored, while Normandy was developing into a strong and henceforth 'Frankicised' power under the firm rule of Duke William. By 1030 or even earlier, links were forged between both sides of the English Channel: mutual exchanges took place in the fields of ecclesiastical personnel, religious foundations and recruitment of warriors. English historians are sharply divided on the question of the part played by the Anglo-Saxons and the Normans in the subsequent history of their country; to a continental historian, this appears an artificial dilemma as the social structures in question are not fundamentally very different: free men, most of whom had entered into some relationship of commendation (*vassi, thegns*), an aristocratic hierarchy – strongly military in both cases (counts and earls, viscounts and sheriffs); similar military customs and practices (*feorm, firma*; bodyguards for rulers, etc.); *burhs* and castles erected in tandem. Of course this does not mean that all the developments were foreseeable, but even the unexpected ones could only have surprised ignorant contemporaries, though those may have been numerous.

The outline of events is well known. On the death of the last Anglo-Saxon king, Edward, who was as chaste as he was ineffectual, the English leaders elected as king in 1066 one of their own number, Harold, who bore a typically Danish name. Over the next three years there was a great settling of accounts: first of all Harald, King of Denmark, landed in the Danelaw; but Harold of England confronted and killed him. Later, in 1069, Svein, King of Norway, tried his luck in England, but without any more success. Between these two episodes, the main drama had been played out: delayed by unfavourable winds, Duke William invaded the south; with his exhausted troops, Harold met him at Hastings and fell in battle. William 'the Conqueror' now conquered his kingdom, no easy task as it took him nine years of dismissals, expulsions and above all the bringing over and settling of men from Normandy, Brittany and Picardy on the island. His difficulties led him to harden the still fluid ties of personal dependence in England, especially by severely curtailing the rights of the free English and by extending the feudal military system upon which his authority in Normandy had rested.

125

All this was more than a successful landing, although that in itself was not a trivial accomplishment. As a result of both sides of the Channel being joined under the same power, the British Isles were to turn towards Europe. If the Norman dukes had been more aware of their Danish origins, perhaps this shift in orientation would not have come about. But, in the society of Rouen and Caen, the legacy of a shared past with the northern world amounted to only a few customs of family law (legal concubinage, for example) which may account for the blending with the native population, who represented the majority some 150 years after Rollo set up his duchy. Furthermore, as we shall see, the accidents of inheritance brought England into the hands of the Angevins in 1154 (two generations after William the Conqueror), and this could only strengthen its continental ties.

The northern world was not broken up, however: around 1100, English merchants were encountering their Danish counterparts in Novgorod and, for their part, Baltic ships belonging to the 'men of the East' (Österlingen, from which the word 'sterling' may be derived), were still coming to London, if not Rouen. But by then the Scandinavian states seemed to be losing their dynamism. The development of royal power, the work of conversion and organising the Church passed into the hands of the Germans, as did the trade and control of the straits. Henceforth the members of the German 'Hanse' were the power-brokers in these lands. Northern Europe was now firmly bound to the continent.

The ever-open eastern frontier

It is difficult to date the arrival of the western Slav peoples in central Europe; certainly it was some time after the movement south and south-west, towards the banks of the Danube and Bohemia, of the Scandinavian peoples and their Germanic kinsfolk, the Goths and Lombards, which occurred around the third or early fourth centuries. But the arrival of the Lombards in the plain of the Po appears to coincide with a strong penetration by the Slavs into the Balkans between 540 and 620; contemporaries remarked on this. The Slav tribes were then established from the Baltic to the Adriatic, where they remain to this day, and in that way they were brought into contact with the Germanic peoples who had settled there after the period of invasions: Saxons, Thuringians, Bavarians, and soon enough, their Frankish masters. Then from the end of the eighth century a fierce and apparently implacable hostility set in between these two ethnic groups. The Middle Ages did not settle it, any more than the following centuries, particularly our own; we must, however, uncover its origins.

An astonishing maturity

In the aftermath of the Second World War, Central European historians and archaeologists – the Poles in particular – turned away from the traditional study of chronicles, charters and the ruling élite, which had been an area of study heavily influenced by the Germans. Instead, they worked hard at reclaiming the material culture of the Slavs before Germanisation. The results repaid the effort: this territory – which Western historiography saw as being stuck at a primitive stage of evolution in all spheres until the time of the Teutonic *Drang nach Osten* – now revealed undeniable signs of a highly developed culture and economy that were certainly in advance of anything shown by the eastern Germans who were their neighbours to the west.

The excavations of the burial grounds of Bohemia, Moravia and Poznan have revealed traces of continuous use from the eighth to the eleventh century and possibly beyond – evidence that these regions were rapidly settled. In addition, study of land-use such as that of Spicymierz on the Warta provides evidence of the early grouping together of agrarian lands and settlements in the ninth and tenth centuries, precocious even in relation to the Italian *incastellamento*. Furthermore, these sites have yielded up the oldest metal furnaces and ploughshares found in Europe for the period between the eighth and tenth centuries. The sites of villages and modern towns such as Poznan, Gniezno, Opole, Gdansk, Biskupiec and even Prague reveal the building of strongholds around which gathered workers of metal, leather and fur, probably in the service of the local lord, which shows that society was already stratified. In addition, trading centres, *gorods* or *grods*, have bequeathed us extraordinary remains of stockades, streets and wooden façades from the tenth century, of which there is no equivalent in the West.

It is possible that such developments were helped by existing links between the worlds of the Baltic and the Danube. In the tenth century many Jewish merchants from Islamic lands, from Spain and Iraq, followed the great river which, between 940 and 975, seems to have been an axis of communication under Germano-Slav control. This control lasted until the invaders from the steppes, the Pechenegs, settled on the lower Danube. Ibn Yakub, for example, who visited Prague and Cracow c. 940–50, saw Frankish and German silver, Byzantine and Muslim gold, grains and metals all in circulation. In this period the double role of the northern Slavs seems to have been the collecting and selling of grain – wheat, barley and millet – and acting as intermediaries between the Baltic and the Danube. But the southern peoples, for example the Serbo-Croats and Styrians, who were established in the former province of Illyricum, could not profit from this increase in wealth. Thus their development was slower, their activities, such as piracy in the Adriatic, were cruder, and in the tenth century their resistance to Byzantine pressure was weaker, especially as regards Christianity.

By contrast, the Czechs and the Poles – even if fragmented into a score of tribes (which the none too well-informed Carolingian analysts sought to classify pedantically) – display from the ninth century onwards signs of vitality and well-established settlement that may be linked to an increase in population. It was this double lure, of men and wealth, rather than a desire to convert or occupy, which explains the endless raids of the Carolingian princes across the Elbe. These great raids fed the traffic in slaves, a word originating from the generic term 'Slav'. Nonetheless, the strength of the Sorbs, Liutizi, Wilzes, Poles and other Abodrites does not seem to have been affected, since, as a result of Carolingian setbacks at the end of the ninth century, many groups of them managed to settle beyond the Elbe and even beyond the Saale, very near to the silver-producing regions of the Harz mountains, or further north in Holstein and Hanover. The most threatened area of eastern

German penetration eastwards: Emperor Otto II at Verona invests the Czech Bishop of Prague, Adalbert, who was to attempt the conversion of the Slavs. (Twelfth-century bronze door at Gniezno, Poland.)

Francia was obviously Saxony; it is therefore not surprising that at the beginning of the tenth century, Duke Henry and later his son, Otto I, after succeeding to the throne, took defensive measures. In 955, the same year in which he blocked the Hungarian advance, King Otto inflicted defeat on the Slav forces at the Recknitz and pushed them back across the Elbe.

The early relations of Germans and Poles

Conversion to Christianity and the end of Hungarian raids divided the Slav peoples in two, exposing the weaker southern Slavs to the warriors of the Ostmark – the future Austria – and to Archbishop Arn of Salzburg. In the north, a 1,000-year conflict was beginning. The period before 1020 or 1050 is particularly interesting as it is a time in which the Slavs seem to have had the upper hand. Doubtless Otto I and his three successors all saw themselves as emperors in the Carolingian model, with a mission to conquer and convert, and thus took the offensive several times. But what success they had was really due to the infiltration of the missionaries sent out by Adalbert, Bishop of Prague, or Pilgrim, Bishop of Passau. The setting up of episcopal sees, from Poznan in 968 to Cracow in 1000, was a definite German success, and we have noted above the conversion of Duke Miesco, *amicus imperatoris*. But the sees soon came to be occupied by Poles, which strictly limited German influence.

In fact, politically speaking, the Germans had hardly moved from their base on the Elbe. True, Otto I had planned to establish 'marches' along the contact zone – Nordmark and

Sorbenmark, for example, open towards the east with a view to conquest – but they were actually defensive. This was the time when Slav society was assuming its definitive form: the village communities (*opole*, rendered in Latin as *vicinia*), reveal a strong peasant structure. Gradually the different tribes came together and formed *wiec*, which were placed under the control of clan chieftains, great landowners known as the *supanis*. Each of them surrounded himself with a band of armed supporters, bound to him by an oath of loyalty, a feature that parallels the organisation of vassalage in one of its early stages. Finally, at the top, the tribal chieftains appointed a king, a *kral*, a term whose etymology seems to be based on the royal name of so many Carolingians, Karl. This development gained formal recognition at the end of the tenth century: at Gniezno in 999 Boleslav Chrobry received from the hands of Emperor Otto III a gold circlet which made him a prince in alliance with, but not subject to, that sovereign. This ceremony confirmed his belonging to Europe, as a similar ceremony did for Stephen of Hungary. There was no question of submission to German power. Quite the contrary, in fact, since Boleslav was to take advantage of Henry II's difficulties to occupy Pomerania, Mazovia, Upper Poland and even, for a time, Bohemia. Just like a Western ruler, he concocted a more or less mythical ancestry, going back to the fabulous figure of Piast, a peasant-king. Poland was born.

Unhappily for the Slavs, this was not a strong enough obstacle to German expansion. Such expansion was driven by population pressure, the hunger for new lands and contempt for its neighbour. After a relative lull in the eleventh century, the twelfth was the great century of the German offensive, that slow-moving assault that was intended finally to push back the Slavs bit by bit to the Oder, and beyond. This was an essential stage in the history of the region's settlement, and as such will be discussed below, but for now we should note that a major feature of modern Europe was already in place.

In the south: prelude to reconquest

By the end of the ninth century, the proud boast of the Abbasid caliph that the Christians could not float a single plank on the Mediterranean was not far from the truth, at least as far as the West was concerned. From Spain and the Balearic Islands, from the Maures and the shores of Corsica, from conquered Sicily to their bridgeheads in Campania, the Saracens held the coast, having sacked Tarentum, Bari, Rome and the entire coast of Languedoc. In Spain they held in check the mountain dwellers of the high valleys of the Pyrenees and the Asturias. Moreover, at the beginning of the tenth century, as we have seen, the Hungarians reached the Apennines and the Cevennes. This was a disastrous situation. But it was in this very darkness that the first signs of a revival glimmered, and then flared up; this phenomenon requires explanation.

Indomitable Spain

Confined in the eighth century to inaccessible lairs in the Pyrenees, from the river Rhune to Le Perthus, or clinging to the coast of Galicia and Asturias, handfuls of peasants and shepherds still thought of themselves as Christians. The emir of Cordoba hardly seemed to care about these mountain eyries. Only the feeble Carolingian advance in upper Catalonia seemed at all worrying. It is debatable whether the Muslims in fact evacuated the settled populations of the area who were in contact with these small groups, creating a depopulated zone, a buffer region watched over by a string of garrisons securely set up in *kalaats*; what is probable is that, because of the transhumance system, herds, which had no religion, regularly crossed this no-man's-land, which suggests that some men must have remained there.

Although the emir 'Abd al-Rahman III was well enough aquainted with history to have had himself proclaimed caliph at Cordoba in 929 (after he learned that the Fatimid had done the same in Cairo), he seems to have had a shakier grasp of geography. For if he and his entourage had been more knowledgeable, they would have realised that the Christians of the north represented a very real power, as events were soon to prove. First of all, and without there being a great influx of warriors – of which there is not much sign before 1020 or 1050 – the Christians of Spain had behind them the world of the Franks, and a sea free of Saracen pirates. From there they could expect horses, fish and grain; their own valleys, with wooded slopes, were rich and easy to defend; it was here also that the greater part of Iberia's metal lay, notably iron in Asturias, in the Basque country and in Catalonia. The cultivation of the vine was accompanied by those communal planting agreements that were so favourable to binding together peasant communities. These groupings were solid, and were given added stability by the hard life of the mountains: it is worth recalling now that it was here, at Oloron, Jaca and Pamplona, that the rights of villagers were early proclaimed. Moreover, these handfuls of people were made more indomitable by their cultural, linguistic, even ethnic origins than by their faith: these were the Basques, the likely heirs to the Iberian legacy, and their brothers from Navarre, Goths and Sueves, penned up there since the sixth century. They all formed the warrior fraternities whose courage Charlemagne had experienced at Roncevaux. Last, but by no means least, there was a binding force in the law which had come down from previous centuries, the *lex gothica*, a product of Roman law and of Visigothic custom. This unified the mountain peoples, all very different from each other, and revealed to them their common identity in the face of Islam.

Their progress was at first very hesitant: each year, in the summer months, when the animals had gone up to the high mountain pastures, men were mobilised by order of a 'king' (often only a tribal chieftain), and launched raids (*as'aifa*) southwards as far as Vigo, Sahagún, and even Valladolid on the Douro; to the east, the lower Ebro was easily gained. Their successes, which were easy enough in populated territory, saw some chiefs taking the title of 'king' – of Asturias (then of Castile) at Burgos (884), of León at Oviedo, then at León itself (912), and of Navarre at Pamplona (925); but in the east, around Barcelona, the title of 'count' continued to be used because this was, in principle, Carolingian territory. These advances did not really threaten the new caliphate, but they were sufficiently worrying for the vizier al-Mansur, and later his son, to drive back the Christians brutally between 985 and 1008, taking Barcelona, Urgel and Compostela. Certainly, the hour of the *Reconquista* had not yet come.

The turning-point came in the period 1020–60. First of all, Islam's resistance weakened, the caliphate died out, leaving its authority fragmented into tribal kingdoms, the *taïfas*. At the same time, lured by the relics of St James of Compostela, by the prospect of gaining land or of making a reputation, armed pilgrims and acquisitive younger sons crossed the Pyrenees via Le Perthus, the Somport pass or Roncesvalles. These people came from Toulouse, Provence, Burgundy and even Brittany; some followed the pilgrim road, which was dotted with Cluniac shelters all the way to Compostela; others committed themselves to the service of some public authority, infiltrated the ranks of the clergy or set up *barios francos* – townships at the foot of some count's castle-walls. Moreover, there were speedy and simultaneous changes in the social make-up of all the small Spanish states. After a great crisis between 1020 and 1050, local authority came to function at a very low level: the lords of castles, the *castlans*, could surround themselves with armed retainers (*infanzones*) who had some land, and in the name of the king raise an army of villagers who fought on horseback (*caballería villana*), a phenomenon that caused outrage beyond the Pyrenees. These troops were seasoned warriors, fully confident of gaining booty or land; the highest ranking would receive a *tenencia*, a public office from the king or his lieutentants; others would gain control of a *kalaat* taken from the infidel. And all this activity was blessed by the Church which, since Gregory VII, had promised salvation to those who waged holy war.

Such war began in earnest in the 1060s, and especially after 1075 when the kings, having regained power, increased their strength with each campaign by reserving the cities for themselves, or by collecting the tribute (*parias*) paid to them by the Muslim chieftains who had been conquered or who needed mercenaries. Thenceforth the *realengum* (royal property) became an essential basis of the Spanish monarchs' power: what else could enable them to make so many grants of land to new arrivals, pay for garrisons and repair castles? Moreover, the restoration of trade, especially in Catalonia, after 990–1000, brought Muslim gold into circulation amongst the Christians, in the form of 30 kilograms for each yearly tribute to the Count of Barcelona. Rich in treasure, dealer in slaves, *poblador* and *bastidor* in the reconquered territories, the Spanish prince of the eleventh century was very probably better off, better served and more envied than any other Christian king.

With these assets came the knowledge of how to use them. From 1009 to 1065 the *reconquista* may have been limited to large-scale raids (the *algarades*) which reached as far as Cordoba, but it got under way properly with the formation of a united kingdom of Castile and León, flanked by a Portuguese kingdom created by and for Burgundians, and by a kingdom of Navarre, uncertain as to which side of the Pyrenees its destiny was to be found, and soon by a kingdom of Barcelona and Aragon. Coimbra, Salamanca, Segovia and Soria formed the line reached by 1070; in 1085 Toledo was taken, an action evoking the Romano-Gothic past; by 1120 Saragossa and Tortosa had been taken. Half of Spain was in Christian hands, though Islam's power was not completely destroyed, as we shall soon see; moreover, the problems posed by the *poblacio* of the reconquered territories were vast, costly and complex. But History had decided: at the dawn of the twelfth century, there could be no doubt that the cross was to reign over the Iberian peninsula.

Unconquerable Italy

From the Etruscans to our own time, who has been able to boast that they control Italy, not to mention the Italians, a quick, lively and subtle people, the inhabitants of a land which, from the Middle Ages, has been exposed to the best and worst elements of a mixture of cultures? Among the never-ending attempts of their neighbours to impose an order upon them which they did not seek, the Italians endured from the tenth century to the thirteenth the wearisome Teutonic efforts, whose course I will trace here. The outline is known, and the result foreseeable. Because Charlemagne had been there, because the Greeks in the south could not forget Justinian, because the Church in Germany could only be controlled once the pope was subdued, and also because – why not? – Italy was rich, beautiful and the ideal playground for a warrior, the German sovereigns, from Otto I in the 950s to Frederick II, who died three centuries later, dedicated themselves to the task of binding Italy to Germany.

The German sovereign had both the motivation and the means to do this. It was in Rome that he could assume the imperial crown, in Italy that he could confront the infidel and negotiate with the Byzantine emperor, and it was in Italy's ports that products emanating from an economy north of the Alps were sold. Moreover, there was the Brenner, the only Alpine pass free of the grip of ice in winter; he could demand from his warriors the duty of *Romfahrt*, and then journey to the Eternal City with the promise of booty as a lure, and with German bishops in attendance. But difficulties, foreseeable or not, quickly arose. First, there was the cost and work involved in constantly having to reorganise enterprises because the Italians were too well versed in the law to submit to it; once the emperor had departed, they ignored all the agreements that had been concluded. Then there was the double danger of revolts in Germany, encouraged by absences lasting perhaps many months, and of illnesses and epidemics in Italy that decimated companies who were used to the very different rhythms of life in the north. Finally, there was resistance which, it was thought, would be easily disposed of through cunning (but in fact Italian cunning proved to be superior), or through violence, which only served to make the resistance more stubborn. At the head of the opposition ranks, especially after the Gregorian reform, stood the pope himself, while the imperial anti-popes kept popping up only to be swiftly eliminated like the straw men they were; then there were the towns that covered this old Roman territory: these were not *Königsstädte* where the emperor and his bishop held unchallenged sway; on the contrary, the representative of the former and the latter himself were usually expelled if they were not docile. The towns thus had to be besieged, indeed destroyed; this was a vain process because if Milan was razed, Alexandria sprang up not far away. As for the Mezzogiorno, it was soon left to its own devices. Otto II had already been trounced there by the Muslims, as was Henry III later by the Greeks. After 1050–80, as we shall see, the indomitable Normans were there, posing a fresh threat.

Unceasing German efforts failed, one after the other. Usually the sovereign would manage to hack out a path to Rome, with increasing difficulty in the twelfth century, but the viscounts and *podestàs* whom he had left behind in the towns would betray him or

Castel del Monte, the castle which the enigmatic Frederick II, emperor and king of Sicily, had built in 1240 in Apulia. This powerful structure stands on a lonely hill; its eight octagonal towers hem in an interior court.

abandon their posts. Conrad II in 1037 and Frederick Barbarossa in 1154 both realised that what was needed was a transformation of the social structure, at least in the Po valley. Conrad II had the idea of binding the lesser vassals directly to the princes or to himself in order to by-pass the middling aristocracy of the *capitanei*, the most dangerous element, but without much success. Frederick Barbarossa, at Roncaglia, tried to set up a whole social pyramid in the German style with himself at the apex; omitted from this, the towns made him realise that their militias did not deserve the sarcastic comments of the German knights (Legnano, 1176). One solution remained: to become Italian. Frederick II was Italian by virtue of his birth, his tastes, his residence, his intelligence; but this was only to reverse the problem because, for him, Germany proved to be ungovernable from Italy.

Thus it was not this series of fruitless episodes which contributed to the making of modern Italy, but two sets of unconnected events: an explosion of urban growth, which was quite predictable, and the settlement of the Normans, which was completely unexpected.

The reshaping of rural settlement, a process known as *incastellamento* which has been somewhat neglected in writings on Italian history, is less visible than the urban development which created an image of the southern city and a way of life that is still recognisable. It was not that these cities were particularly advanced: many northern centres can be shown to have attained maturity before Italian ones. But in Italy this process touched all   **133** aspects of the urban world: people's positions and structures of government, economic activity and the urban landscape. This justifies the commonly held view that the 'typical' city of the Middle Ages is Florence or Genoa rather than Bruges or Cologne. A particular aspect of this expansion, often at the expense of the Germans, was that all social groups in the city, even if they engaged in fierce struggles for power, contributed to some degree and at some time to the movement for the liberation of the cities. The various social groups comprised first the old nucleus of the *cives,* an entirely theoretical survival from the city of Antiquity, who were proud to be called *quirites* or *curiales* as in the time of Augustus (although in fact they were descended from the *ministeriales* around the bishop, viscount or *gastald* of Lombardy); then the *populus,* who had the illusion of being free but nonetheless did play an active part, with the artisans grouped together as *arti;* the lords' agents who preserved the old title of *arimanni* or 'warriors'; and finally, the aristocracy with its extended *familia,* whose origins and wealth were basically rural but which had come to the city, stayed there, built towers and family chapels and hired soldiers to defend the people of its 'houses' – *case, alberghi, consorterie.* These ranks were very homogeneous, kept to their own districts and were very concerned with matters of finance and justice. In northern Italy from the end of the eleventh century, in Verona, Parma, Genoa and Cremona, *universitates civium* sometimes resembled organs of self-government, but generally the setting up of 'consular' or 'communal' structures came later, either as a result of dynastic accident (Venice 1035), or of a popular rising (Milan 1055), or of a privilege granted by a prince (Genoa 1081); but it must be realised that urban vitality in itself was not dependent on such developments. We shall see below how the Christian counter-attack by Pisa, Lucca and Genoa in the Tyrrhenian Sea began after 1013, was well under way after 1050 and was at its height at the end of the eleventh century. It has been noted that the 'merchants', apparently such typical figures of medieval Italy, played a very restricted role in the movement of urban emancipation, though this in no way prevented the launch of bold commercial enterprises.

A Norman adventure

While it is only natural to count Venice or Genoa amongst the finest jewels of which Italy may still boast, the distinctive situation of the Mezzogiorno deserves our scrutiny. Rome seems to have paid little heed to the special qualities of the southern regions, including Sicily, which had nevertheless experienced the impact of Greece before Rome itself had; the 'sanctuary' that Hannibal found there was bound to attract its attention. But it may be that the climatic and physical conditions which weigh so heavily on modern-day southern Italy only took full effect after the southern shore of the Mediterranean had dried up, a long-term phenomenon to which we have already referred. It could be said, in short, that the Mezzogiorno was born with Justinian and his successors when the 'Roman' reconquest found itself rapidly confined to the area south of Rome, after the sixth-century Lombard invasion, which extended its grip as far as Benevento and Troïa.

The divergent and, as it were, 'oriental' character of the region obviously increased after

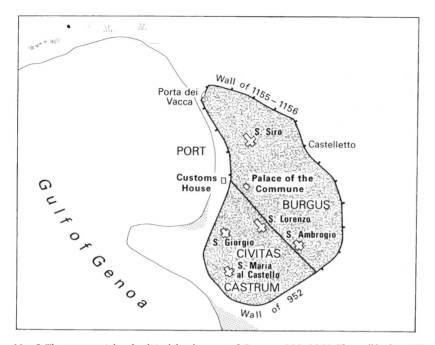

Map 5. The commercial and political development of Genoa, c. 900–1160. The wall built in 952 protected the port against Saracen attacks and encircled the castle and the bishop's town. The wall of 1155 took in the commercial centre, which stretched northwards, and the political centre around the Palace of the Commune. In the eleventh and twelfth centuries Genoa grew rich first by the raids of its sea-going buccaneers, then from the commerce of its merchants during the Crusades.

the Muslim seizure of Sicily and some parts of Calabria and Campania. The Greeks remained in Naples and Apulia, but what is known about the commerce of the inhabitants of Amalfi, Gaeta and Salerno reveals that, in the tenth and early eleventh centuries, the merchants of these towns carried on a triangular trade in which Egypt and Byzantium played an equal part. Even after the Byzantine emperors had restored their authority in these regions around the year 1000, local rivalries naturally existed from Gaeta to Bari. Men were needed, and if able men were passing through, they were recruited: this is what the people of Salerno thought of when a large troop of Norman pilgrims landed there in 1016 en route for the Holy Land.

Here we have a typical example of the 'unprogrammed' historical accident. The brave warriors of the Bayeux region worked wonders and were so well paid that they relayed news of their good fortune to a crowd of younger sons, illegitimate sons and other marginalised figures who had no prospects in Normandy. They rushed to the scene from 1025 onwards, sometimes in the pay of the Greeks, sometimes of the Italians. Some of the more skilful managed to gain lands and titles, such as the Count of Aversa (1030) and the Duke of Melfi (1043). The Hauteville family led the movement and worked for its own ends: its head, Robert Guiscard, carved out a principality for himself in Apulia, chased out the Greeks, shamelessly made a captive of Pope Leo IX and had himself recognised in 1059 as Duke of

135

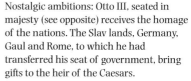

Nostalgic ambitions: Otto III, seated in majesty (see opposite) receives the homage of the nations. The Slav lands, Germany, Gaul and Rome, to which he had transferred his seat of government, bring gifts to the heir of the Caesars.

Calabria and Apulia. Sicily was the next target, the German emperor was defied, the eastern emperor's lands saw Norman landings and in 1130 Roger II assumed the title of King of Sicily and Naples; to legalise this, he in turn had to catch a pope, Innocent II, in 1139.

In itself this episode is remarkable enough when one considers the successful attempts to fuse the three cultural zones that met there – Islam, Byzantium and post-Carolingian Europe. Roger's great-grandson, Frederick II, who was born in Palermo, was the incarnation of this extraordinary and – to contemporaries – scandalous cosmopolitanism. But as well as this episode, which was relatively brief, the whole history of the Mezzogiorno stemmed from the above events. The specific physical characteristics of the region and its particular culture were fixed by them, held in a mould that was the result of political chance but which was strong enough to stiffen them against the influence of the North. In this light, if one considers the difficulties experienced by southern Italy, both past and present, as a result of domination by the Normans, Swabians, Angevins, Aragonese, Spaniards, French and Bourbons right up to unification in 1871, one might conclude that the bright idea of the people of Salerno in 1016 was not so bright after all.

The anxieties of power

In its time, the 'Peace of God' movement, which reached its height after 1030, was harshly criticised, strangely enough by distinguished and undeniably virtuous prelates. Lamenting the baseness of his age, Bishop Adalbero of Laon turned to the example of the king; in resisting the encroachments of the 'Peace' within his diocese, Bishop Gerard of Cambrai

The emperor, who dreamed of the rebirth of a Christian Roman empire, is surrounded by archbishops and courtiers carrying arms. (Gospel Book of Otto III from the Treasury of Bamberg, 998; Munich, Bayerische Staatsbibliothek.)

invoked the figure of the emperor. Both prelates objected to the self-reliance displayed in the peace movement, which took no account of the fundamental support of the Christian world – that is, the prince in his role as the natural and unique defender of the peace, a role which the prince, at the behest of bishops and pope, had sworn to fulfil at his coronation. Adalbero and Gerard were either fifty years behind the times or three centuries too early; in their day the monarch's power had not yet recovered from the disintegration of the Carolingian Empire.

The dream of empire

It has been claimed that German brutality played an essential part in frustrating the emperors' designs in Italy. It is doubtful whether the kings of France or anyone else would have been more successful. The Carolingian emperors did not last long enough (800–55, in effect) to show whether an 'empire' was possible in Europe, given the resources of the time.

The reason should perhaps be sought in the very concept of the *dominium mundi* as it was expounded by Carolingian thinkers and taken up by the Germans, especially after the re-emergence of Roman law. In principle, the supreme sovereign had to win the obedience of the other princes, the *reguli* ('kinglets') as Barbarossa was scornfully to call them; this created a problem from the start because such rulers were no longer the brothers and kinsmen they had been in the ninth century. Without referring to 'national pride', which would be anachronistic, one might expect that the rulers in distant lands such as Spain and   **137**

Map 6. The Empire in the tenth and eleventh centuries.

Scandinavia, or those convinced of their regional independence, such as the rulers of France and Poland – or indeed those rulers who did not care to lower themselves in the eyes of their unruly subjects, like the kings of England – would all be more than hesitant. But even if the emperor were to content himself with a few symbolic gestures on their part, to deserve his title he nevertheless had to combine the three elements of *actio* in the Roman manner: physical power (*potestas*), moral and judicial authority (*auctoritas*), and supreme military command (*imperium*).

Many avenues were explored in the 850 years after Otto I won the imperial crown for the Germans. He himself founded a Christian empire, in the Carolingian manner: the rites (*ordo*) of his coronation, the way in which he dealt with the pontiff, the attempt to exercise systematic control over bishops (the *Reichskirchensystem*), the creation of *regna* around himself, of lands nominally in subjection – all these elements were essentially Carolingian. This attempt to revive the past could not work; despite his personal successes, and the hegemony exercised over west Francia, Otto lacked the support of a system of commendation which alone could have relayed his authority, his *verbum*, right to the base of the social pyramid. His second successor was Otto III, son of a Greek woman and pupil of Gerbert of Aurillac, whose impetuous nature led him to the other extreme when he tried to replace the Carolingian dream with a Byzantine one; along with Gerbert, whom he appointed pope, he sought to usher in a *renovatio mundi*, to suffuse the world with religion. He established himself in Rome, *Aurea Roma*, set up a senate, and busied himself with the affairs of other kings. His death at twenty-one in 1002 sounded the knell for this grand but unrealistic conception. What remained was the traditional path, the feudal strategies increasingly adopted by princes everywhere: to hold fiefs and castles, to control bishops and vassals, to have warriors and treasures at one's disposal and through them to inspire fear and obedience. Moderate rulers sought to establish themselves in Germany before trying to extend their power. More ambitious rulers, such as Henry V or Barbarossa, were doomed to frustration.

Despite their best efforts, German kings were never able to amass the resources which would have made possible the fulfilment of their ambitions. First, the shadow of Italy fell over Germany, paralysing any action begun north of the Alps, draining purses and straining loyalties. Second, the king never had at his disposal a personal landed base which would have released him from the necessity of begging for assistance, which always came dear: the *Reichsgut* extended into some 1,500 localities but only an insignificant number of castles and monasteries; as for the episcopal properties which Otto I had used as a prop for his authority, the Investiture Conflict which was concluded at Worms in 1122 deprived the emperor of their use. This serious defeat explains in retrospect the king's desperate efforts to ward off a resolution of that conflict for as long as possible. As for local loyalties, the kings had increased the requirements of military service but they had been forced to pay for this by granting away many rights, including that of justice, the *regalia* which local lords desired to possess. Finally, torn between the demands of their imperial mission, especially in Italy, and the humdrum realities of Germany, the emperors failed to translate their universalist claims into reality. One last point, perhaps a fundamental one: out of the three successive

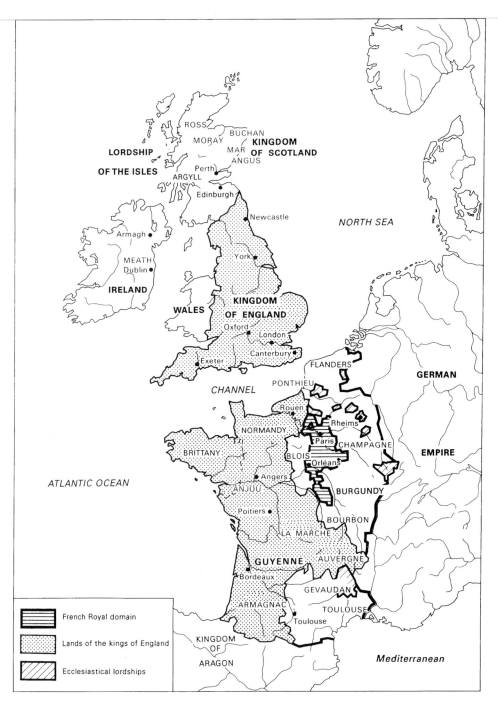

Map 7. The Plantagenet Empire in the twelfth century.

dynasties – the Ottonians, Salians and Hohenstaufen – not one lasted a hundred years. Time was one of the resources the emperors failed to win.

England's misalliance

The Anglo-Saxon kings and their Scandinavian successors had controlled, since the eighth century or even earlier, a compact kingdom, sparsely populated, predominantly rural, distinctive in culture and structure. As a result of the disaster which overwhelmed it in 1066, Anglo-Saxon kingship arouses little interest amongst continental historians. English historians, however, while accepting that their country was heavily Normanised, are highly conscious of the extraordinarily firm foundations on which later kings would build. First, there is an impressive legal heritage that could bear comparison with the capitularies of the Continent; secondly, a strong and straightforward royal administration with its coronation ritual, its council of bishops and secular office-holders, and its sheriffs (representatives of the king in the shires). But there were also public rights which were regularly claimed and acknowledged, especially the mass military levy of free men, the *fyrd*, and the right to shelter and requisition, the *feorm*. As for the social structure into which feudal commendation was introduced, it included a whole range of practices of varying origins, the very distant ancestors of the privileges protecting the individual of which England is justly proud: hundred courts, manorial courts, and so on. We noted above that there was nothing that would have been alien to William the Conqueror: in fact, once he had subdued the English, he actually added an extra feature to these splendid royal resources, the 'Forest', i.e. private royal property, augmented by spoils of conquest, almost a quarter of England for himself and his family. As for the principle of commendation, he hastened its development by systematically granting land *in capite*, that is, in direct subjection to himself.

The flaw in this achievement was of course the fact that England and Normandy were divided by the Channel; nonetheless, at the time of his death (1087) William was regarded as the most powerful ruler of his age, favourite son of the Church and defender of the peace. William's territories were re-united under one ruler at the beginning of the twelfth century by his third son, Henry I, whose powers seemed comparable to those of his father. But clouds were already gathering: the English, quite rightly, felt that they had been too readily shunted out of positions of power; in the north, the Celts of Scotland and, in the west, the Celts of Wales kept up constant pressure on the Normans. In the south, the Capetian King of France stirred up his vassals in Anjou and Flanders against a ruler who had not only refused to perform homage for Normandy, but had even defeated him in battle in 1119. This time, too, future developments were affected by chance; since Henry left no legitimate male heir, a war of succession broke out and dragged on until 1153, in the process severely damaging the powers of the crown. The victor in the struggle was neither English nor Norman: it was Henry Plantagenet, Count of Anjou, married to the duchess of Aquitaine, whom Louis VII of France had recently divorced because she had failed to provide him with a son.

This was one of the great elements of medieval history which, for over three centuries, was to set France against England. Eleanor was in fact perfectly capable of bearing sons: she

141

provided her second husband with four in succession, and so the Plantagenet line was assured. One man was thus master of the entire European Atlantic coastline, from the Clyde to the Pyrenees; he held London, Rouen, Tours, Poitiers and Bordeaux; and as he himself was king of England, he made all sorts of difficulties about paying homage to a Capetian king of France. When displayed on a map, this power looks impressive, and this is the traditional view of it in France; moreover, it was supported by strong English institutions, by feverish activity on the part of Henry II, by his legal reforms and assizes, and by a variety of court officials (such as the Exchequer, and the sheriffs and seneschals who were dotted around the Angevin Empire), not to mention the wine of Bordeaux, the negotiations with Barbarossa, and an English pope (the only one so far). But we should be more cautious: the 'triumph' of 1154 is one of the most deceptive in English history. What sort of relationship could exist between a Basque and a Yorkshireman? What common interest could unite a lord from the Welsh marches and a castellan from Périgord? This heterogeneous mass, where the king's authority fluctuated, in some places subject to written law, in others to custom, where English, northern French (*oil*), Breton, Poitevin, southern French (*occitan*) and Basque were spoken, and which was not united by any economic logic, which it took a king a month and a half to travel through, whether or not he was accompanied by his army – all this could not be governed, nor was it. Add to this the extraordinary nest of vipers that was the Plantagenet family, and the annoyance – to put it mildly – of the English at having to fight or pay up because of some obscure dynastic tussle between Anjou and the Marche. All it needed was for the king to falter, as John did in 1212–13, and the English nobles could wring from him a concession, the Magna Carta. Given all this, it is not paradoxical to assert that when the Capetian monarch Philip Augustus scattered John's allies at Bouvines in 1214 and followed up his success by swallowing the entire region between the Seine and the Loire, he was doing England some service. For, just as the German emperor was bound to Italy, so England had been bound to the Continent and had suffered for it.

The splendours and the wretchedness of the king of France

Captured by one rebellious vassal after having been defeated by another (923), restored to the throne by the goodwill of a third (936) before coming under his thumb, and then under that of Otto I of Germany, and seeing the remnant of his fiscal lands between the Aisne and Paris crumble, the western Carolingian king seemed to have outlived his time. Gradually the area covered by the charters of such kings as Charles the Simple and Lothar shrank; bishops began to act independently and, after 955, Aquitaine no longer responded to Carolingian commands. Nonetheless, the interval between the passing of the last German Carolingian in 911 and the quite accidental death of Louis V in France in 987 had its positive side: in the face of the struggles of Anglo-Saxon kings and the uneasy conscience of the Ottonians, it helped make the 'king of the Franks' an exceptional figure, even after the enthronement of Hugh Capet, descendant of the new-style 'mayors of the palace'. More than any other king, the king of the Franks represented stability, peace, security, the anointed of the Lord. In the depths of his material and moral wretchedness,

Trier cathedral, showing the influence of Carolingian and Ottonian architecture, mid-eleventh century

Vézelay, the nave and choir of the abbey church, completed by the beginning of the twelfth century

The abbey of Conques (Aveyron), completed around 1130, belonging to the second phase of the Romanesque

Salisbury cathedral, 1220–54. early English Gothic

he remained an anointed king, and even south of the Loire, charters were dated by the year of his reign.

At first glance, he appeared to have very little in his favour: the loyalty of the clergy who supported him was suspect and they may have favoured the emperor; his *fideles* who were also his vassals respected not so much the man as the dignity of his office; the great lords of Burgundy, Toulouse, Anjou and Poitou, moreover, were themselves struggling against the growing power of the castellans, officials, viscounts and, after 1050, even that of the petty lords. Only the Count of Flanders and the Duke of Normandy succeeded in making themselves obeyed in their own territories, thanks to the peace-keeping institutions which they headed; the natural defender of the peace, the king, had enough trouble trying to win respect for himself whether in the valley of the Chevreuse, or the Oise, or on the road to Orleans, which bristled with hostile castles – Coucy, Montlhéry, Houdan, Le Puiset, Étampes.

On closer inspection, the king does not appear so badly off: first of all, his aura protected him and it was in his kingdom that the papacy, under pressure from the German Empire, knew it could find safe refuge. The emperor himself did not dare challenge the heir to the prestigious Merovingian title; at Yvois in 1023 he even agreed to meet him and acknowledge him. As for the royal demesne, whose lands and rights the traditional textbooks have mournfully declared to be too few, it was in fact far superior to the resources of the majority of vassals, indeed even to the *Reichsgut*, rooted as it was in the richest and most populous part of the kingdom; taxes, garrisons and monasteries extended from Montreuil to Le Puy. Thus the king 'lived of his own' and if this was unspectacular, it did guarantee him men, supplies and money.

It must be admitted, of course, that from the reign of Hugh Capet's son, Robert the Pious, the Church lamented the king's inability to make himself obeyed at a distance; after 1050, his immediate following consisted of only petty vassals, friends and lords from the Ile de France. But the king still controlled the former organs of the Carolingian palace: the chancellery, the treasury, the chapel; he carried out his 'sacred' office, his religious *ministerium* with the help of courtiers (*palatini, curiales*), who were sometimes of humble origin, but who guaranteed the continuity of the *Res publica*. Here there was no need to formulate some specific system of government, nor to wear oneself out, like the emperor in Germany, in continuous struggle with a competitor, who also had universalist pretensions; here there was no enemy of the faith to hunt down and chase from village to village in order to win salvation, at the cost of an empty treasury, as was the case in Spain; nor even the threat of civil war, as there was in the British Isles. The king of France had his troops, his granaries and his servants; he was irreplaceable and no one, not even the Duke of Normandy, thought of supplanting him. He could draw on the support of the Church, as in Germany, on the feudal levy, as in Spain, and on the family, as in England. There was only one area which made him vulnerable to the blows of fate: his dynasty had to survive.

And survive it did; this point alone highlights the fundamental reason for the ultimate triumph of the Capetians. Thanks to the male offspring being of an age to reign when required, and to their brotherly co-operation and longevity, son succeeded father for an

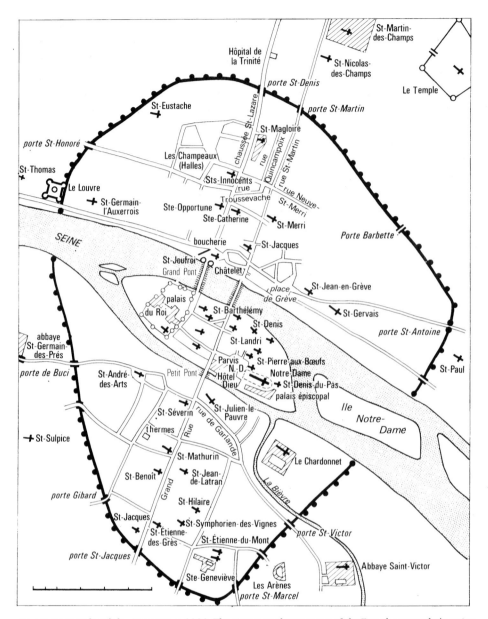

Map 8. Paris under Philip Augustus, *c.* 1200. The city was to become one of the French monarchy's major assets: a royal residence visited not only by satellite kings but also by the great vassals of the richest and most populous kingdom in the West; a major centre of consumption, and indeed of industry, if not commerce; and finally, one of the intellectual and religious capitals of Christendom, whose university attracted scholars and students from every land. Paris was the only Western city at this time able to offer all these attractions.

unbroken span of 350 years. Members of the dynasty did not have to be brilliant to be able to reap the harvest of such endurance. In fact, the Capetian kings do not have a particularly good reputation: timid, unimposing, lacking flair. Robert the Pious appears sluggish; Henry I a very pale character; Philip I, undermined by the Church, resembles nothing so much as a grasping peasant; Louis VI fought, but without much success; Louis VII made one miscalculation after another. Two centuries elapsed before the marriage of Philip II (Augustus) with a princess of Carolingian blood conferred on the dynasty its henceforth unchallenged role as successor to the Carolingians; the moment had come to break out of the royal demesne and impose obedience. With Philip Augustus French royalty proper is born, better equipped than any other with the resources that soon enabled it to become the premier monarchy of Christendom.

This survey has been a brief but necessary prelude to the more detailed examination of the fabric of Europe, which at last had come into being: between about 950 or 1000 – when the last embers of the Carolingian world were fading and were being replaced by the feudal structures by which men were to live for the next six or seven centuries – and the mid-twelfth century, the scattered pieces of the mosaic of Christendom fell into place. But some of the joints were not well made: particularly in southern Italy and along the German–Slav divide. Still, all the players were now in place: the Celtic fringe, the Nordic world, the bulk of Germans and Gauls with their Slav or Muslim borders, the Iberians and the Italians. What more was needed for the outline of modern Europe to take shape? Some advance to the east, north and south, given that the west was blocked by the ocean. But that leap forward cannot be understood without reference to this laying of foundations.

4 Explosions within Islam: 875–1100

From the last quarter of the ninth century to the end of the eleventh, Islam experienced both a great Isma'ili interval and a revival of the damaged Mediterranean economy. The ideological crisis of the Islamic monarchy, already apparent in 812, together with its inability to establish a stable relationship between legitimate central power and the naked force of the army generals, the provincial governors, opened a breach through which flooded the millenarian movement of the masses, who adhered to the ideas of the Isma'ilis. The generals and soldiers had always drawn money from the State but now their pressure on fiscal resources increased, though it would be inaccurate to depict them as 'feudal lords' who were to circumscribe the freedom of an 'urban bourgeoisie'. At bottom, nothing changed in the countryside, where age-old patterns of dependence continued; in urban society, however, there were re-adjustments. Under the hegemony of the military leaders and their bureaucracy, the position of intellectuals was strengthened, thus preserving, in the face of the power of the emirs, a widely supported principle of 'dissidence' on moral, religious and political questions. The intellectual movement's importance was underlined by the rise of the Isma'ili party and its search for a synthesis between the world of Medina and that of Greek science. The basic equilibrium of the Islamic world was not shattered; the network of commercial routes was eventually to be disturbed only by the slow rise of the Western powers.

Failure in the East

Civil war in the time of Ma'mun, the lack of agreement with the Shi'ites and the weakness of the empire's government beyond Khurasan all served to dash the hopes of the Islamic monarchy; Abbasid power, while engaged in its struggle to impose a state ideology, was challenged fiercely in Baghdad, and its authority depended solely on the provincial governors to whom it had conceded virtual autonomy.

Crisis at the centre

Since the time of Harun, Ifrikiya in the west had its own dynasty of emirs in the Aghlabid family, and paid only an annual tribute to Baghdad and Samarra; in the east, after 820, the sons and grandsons of Tahir were the real pillars of support for the Abbasid dynasty, for if Tahir himself had displayed some independence in his immense eastern governorship, his descendants were guarantors of peace and stability in the empire. From their capital at Nishapur, they governed Khurasan, Kirman, the provinces of the Southern Caspian and Transoxiana where they established governors from the Samanid family. Nonetheless there was constant disorder: the sons of Tahir co-operated with the vizier of Baghdad in 822 in subduing the high valleys of Transoxiana, crushed Kharijite rebels in Seistan and then had to struggle against Coptic rebellion and against the Zaydite infiltrations into Tabaristan.

For their part, the Alids tried to profit from the rapid Islamicising of Iran by setting up dynasties on the frontier regions from where they could threaten the heart of the caliphate; in 834 there was a short-lived attempt on Khurasan and another one after 864 with the support of the traditional dynasties of the South Caspian mountains of Daylam. The seething forces there could see that power within the caliphate was moving inevitably towards decentralisation: Mazyar, a descendant of the former lords of Tabaristan, became a Muslim. Recognised by Ma'mun, whose client he became, he returned as governor, converted the ruling classes, built 100 or so mosques and consolidated his power in the mountains by wiping out rivals from other families and within his own clan. The region groaned under the oppressive fiscal burden he imposed on it and for this he was denounced to Ma'mun in 827. But he was confirmed in his office and seized the chance offered him by the rapidly proceeding Islamicisation of Iran and the rise to power of the Tahirids to break with the tribal past for his own profit. He set up an emirate of a wholly new type with a guard of 1,200 slave mercenaries and a treasury of 96,000 dinars and 18 million dirhams. But this premature experiment collapsed in 839: the army surrendered without a fight when confronted by the force sent out from Samarra. Mazyar's career had no connection with any Mazdakist or communist traditions; he had, admittedly, stripped many of his enemies of their property but he had not attacked them on a class basis; it was simply a matter of local risings.

Confusion now reigned among the Tahirids; Sijistan had to draw on its own resources. Now there arose a rebel power of humble origin in Iran, the first in Islam's history to make the shocking break with the unity of the empire, and with the tribal, military and religious traditions of legitimacy. An army of volunteers gathered around Ya'qub al-Saffar, who proclaimed himself emir of Sijistan in 861, overcame the Kharijites and incorporated them into his own army, launched an attack on Afghanistan, plundered the heathen temples and captured the great silver mines of Andaraba. He extended his power over the Tahirid provinces (Kirman, Khurasan) and paid the Caliph Mu'tamid handsomely for recognising his conquests. The revolt of the Zanj enabled him even to march on Baghdad, but he was defeated at the city gates by the regent Muwaffaq. On his death in 878, the succession passed smoothly to his brother Amr, who obtained official permission to rule Fars, Khurasan, Kirman, Sijistan and Sind in exchange for an annual tribute of 1 million dirhams, which rose to 10 million in 889. Captured by the Samanids in 900, Amr was sent to Baghdad, where he was executed; this marked the end of a remarkable personal power which Iranian patriotism had supported in its hostility to the Abbasids. Memories of their

147

good government and the renown of their victories were to play an essential part in the Persian renaissance, which blossomed in the poetry composed at the Samanid court, and at Ghazna.

These upheavals did not bring about the restoration of Abbasid authority; the dynasty suffered from a lack of vigorous leaders and generals with the exception of the regent Muwaffaq, who was not himself caliph, and his son who in 896 was to crush the Kharijite rebellions and resist the Carmathians (Qaramita) of Iraq. Muwaffaq's main triumph had been his defeat of the major revolt of the century, that of the Zanj, which had threatened the caliphate in the very heart of its power, in Iraq. Much like the Iranian movements of the previous century, the Zanj embodied a harshly exploited minority's hopes of implementing a Medina pattern for its own benefit. They were blacks brought in as slaves from the seventh century onwards to the marshlands which separated Kufa, Wasit and Basra, and were employed as labourers to break up the layers of natron which made the soil of lower Iraq unfarmable. Their first revolts date from 869 and their situation, which was exceptional in medieval Islam, as well as their numbers (Tabari speaks of 15,000 slaves), created a force which was given coherence by Shiʿite propaganda. The weakening of the caliphate's authority as it struggled with the revolts provided an opportunity for a pretender, Ali ibn Muhammad, of disputed descent but recognised by the Bedouin tribes, to unleash a slave revolt in 869, which soon involved the whole region; the towns of the Ahwaz were taken and burned, and then it was Basra's turn, destroyed in 871.

The strong sense of unity felt by the rebels enabled them to resist the Turkish army of the Abbasid generals and to establish a warrior state in the marshlands, a military community of the Zanj and their Bedouin allies. Their commander, Ali, had proclaimed himself *Mahdi* and surrounded himself with a caliph-like court which, however, included no Zanj. The rebel leader minted coins, and his dirhams bore Kharijite legends; he built a capital, Mukhtara, with *diwans*, a hippodrome and palace workshops, although the State's economy was dependent on booty and taxation of the subject regions, whose social structure was unchanged. The high point was reached in 878, when there was collaboration with the rebels of the East, and an attempt to link up with the Carmathians, resulting in a military power which enabled the 'master of the Zanj' to attack the Baghdad region and prevent the pilgrimage to Mecca. Muwaffaq needed five years and 5,000 men to crush the insurrection; it was necessary for the regent and his son to take the field in person, and suffer wounds, before the walls of Mukhtara were breached in 883. The fierce resistance of the Zanj was not the product of blind despair: those soldiers who surrendered were incorporated into the regular and homogeneous units of the Abbasid army. It is in this that the messianic character of the rebellion is revealed, for if its basis in social conditions is evident, it was nevertheless easily absorbed into the Muslim world, while its explicit references to activist Shiʿism heralded the great Ismaʿili movement of Iraq and Syria.

After the death of Muʿtadid, in 902, the emirs and viziers subjected the caliphs, who were skilfully chosen for their youth and feebleness, to close supervision, making submissiveness the dynasty's only hope for survival. Since the caliphate offered the only principle of legitimacy in the Dar-al-Islam, its continued existence was absolutely necessary to the rulers

Descendants at war: the various Islamic dynasties which fought among themselves from the eighth century came from a common root, founded by the Prophet. In this seventeenth-century Turkish family tree, one can see at the top the direct ancestry of the Prophet, which legend said went back to Seth, son of Adam through Noah. The figure of Muhammad is traditionally veiled. Around him are the first four caliphs: Omar, Abu Bakr, Ali and Othman. (Turkish manuscript *Zubdat al-Tawarikh*; Dublin, Chester Beatty Library.)

who came and went amidst the struggles for power. The caliphs were forced to play one emir off against another; their first attempts failed: Muttaqi, who sought the support of leaders in the West, was deposed in 944 and Ta'i, who made a similar attempt, was deposed in 991. The long reigns of Qadir and Qa'im covered the periods 991–1031 and 1031–75: protected by the Fatimid threat which forced the Buyid emirs into alliance, they counted on the mounting rivalry of the great emirs. Thus they received gifts and homage from both the Ghaznavids and the Seljuks; they strove to ally themselves with traditionalist opinion ('Sunnism') that was then in the process of formation: thus Qadir permitted the condemnation of Mu'tazilite puritanism, had the Isma'ilis denounced, and accepted a profession of faith which bound him closely to the traditionalists. The caliph had his supporters: purists and religious men who dreamed of a restoration of his authority, notably the bold Mawardi who protested in 1018 against the usurping of the title 'king of kings' by the Buyid Iranian

149

emir. Strengthened by the backing of this party, Qa'im offered lengthy resistance to the claims of the Seljuk Turk, Tughrul, finally reaching a compromise agreement with his successor, Alp-Arslan, on the condition that his higher spiritual authority was preserved. Falling back into the role of arbitrator and paying close attention to the climate of opinion created by preachers, the Islamic monarchy remained, however, a potential power and resource.

Emirs and viziers: constant upheaval

The key elements of the political structure of the Islamic monarchy remained the viziership, the army and the taxation system; but they were no longer the exclusive preserves of the ruling dynasty and they gradually became the basis for what were in effect provincial governments. The latter, however, did not attain the status of organised, peripheral, quasi-federal states; with the exception of the Samanid emirate they served only as springboards for capturing the central power and the position of supreme emir. These developments, however, do reveal the extreme flexibility of the administrative apparatus and how it could serve ambitious generals and provincial governors. The provinces continued to be watched over, and taxed, by the *diwans* but the old practice of delegating power permitted the build-up of a financial and military base for taking control of the capital and dividing up the authority of the caliph.

At first, however, at Baghdad and Samarra the viziership came up against other forms of government: under Mu'tasim, for example, the viziership was subject to a 'chief minister', the 'Great Qadi' Ahmad ibn Abi Du'ad, who watched over political and ideological trends within the empire; under Ma'mun, power was in the hands of the Tahirid emir at Baghdad, who held the important posts of prefect of police and military governor; the reign of Mutawakkil saw the reappearance of viziers linked by some spiritual bond to the family of the caliph, especially to a prince or to the caliph himself. The viziership, after the assassination of the caliph and civil war between his sons, which led to the first appearance of a 'regent' in the person of the Turk Utamish, came under the control of the regent Muwaffaq, only to regain its power in the first half of the tenth century as the emirs struggled among themselves.

The viziership was then fully caught up in factional rivalries and itself became the object of a lengthy struggle between two rival clans of administrators: the 'Nestorian scribes' who belonged to the families of Banu al-Jarrah and Banu Makhlad, and the Shi'ite financial experts of the Banu al-Furat, whose support for extremist sects did not prevent them from serving the Abbasid monarchy and taking a full part in the intrigues which reached a peak after 950.

The struggles for the viziership and the rivalries among the emirs increased the instability of the dynasty. They made long-term policies impossible and exhausted the energies of governors and military commanders in a seemingly sterile and tedious free-for-all. But on the governmental level, continuity of offices, of personnel and of administrative authority ought to be noted. Thus the machinery of administration remained a sound instrument, reproduced in the great provincial commands, in Samanid Bukhara, in Ghazna, Shiraz, and among the Buyids, preserving the requisite information concerning districts under its control – an ever-decreasing number due to the granting-out of fiscal resources as *iqta* – and the mathematical skills necessary for fiscal efficiency. Thus the *Kitab al-hawi* provided the officials with formulae for calculating which areas were to be taxed, the basis of assessment for the land tax, and the part allocated to the currency handlers and the cost of collection.

The Abbasid viziership was itself the object of imitation by the emirs. The Samanids crowned their bureaucracy with a vizier, a treasurer and a master of the post, and they also preserved the concurrent offices of grand chamberlain and commander of the army. The Ghaznavids, for their part, copied the viziership by setting up a powerful military registry office, which checked that the army records matched the actual number of troops or made up the balance. Among the Buyids, who attached the viziership firmly to the emirate and granted the caliph's vizier only the semblance of administrative power, a series of skilled rulers such as the powerful Ibn Abbad in the Iranian provinces kept up effective government. This latter figure, who became a minister after being a secretary, was a highly cultivated man. In his *Epistles* he has left a manual of chancery but also of politics and government (in which he reveals quite clearly his antipathy to the cities' claims for independence and the activism of the 'Young Ones', of the *Futuwwa*). Besides this, he wrote numerous works of Mu'tazilite theology and of history, lexicography and grammar as well as a *diwan* of poems. The Iranian viziers played a large part in the Persian literary renaissance, as seen in the part played in the development of the sciences in the Dar al-Islam by Avicenna (Abu Ali Husayn known as Ibn Sina, 980–1037), son of a Samanid official at Bukhara and a philosopher and doctor from his youth, in fact a universal man, who wrote his books in the intervals of his activities as counsellor and vizier to the Buyid princes of Hamadhan and Isfahan.

The development of a professional army gradually increased the independent status of the officers: the Abbasid revolution marked the end of the period of tribal domination when agreements had been made and disputes settled according to the old customs of the Bedouin world. The formation of an army of paid professionals, that is, a military body united by dynastic and ideological loyalty, could have come to grief in conflict between the princes and the officers from the Abbasid east. In fact, however, the recruiting of homogeneous contingents allowed a different *esprit de corps* to come into play, which warded off the risk of a *coup d'état* produced by an increase in separate and rival units. The most reliable warriors were the Turks, whose language isolated them from the religious conflicts and who, after 830, formed the backbone of this new army, the heavy cavalry. They were not the only people to be recruited: there were also Arabs from the Jazira, Kurds, black slaves in Egypt, Hindus on the eastern frontiers – all of them, like the Bedouin cavalry and the Iranian foot-soldiers, armed with axe and javelin. The Daylamites, with their expertise in fighting in mountains and marshes, gave way to the Turks who introduced new tactics such as feigned retreat, mounted infantry and mounted bowmen, and who eclipsed their rivals in the eleventh century.

151

Defensive strategy and professional army. Foreign mercenaries, mainly Iranians and Turks, continued to be the strength and the weakness of Islam, while shrewdness prevailed in the arrangement of urban defences, such as this low archway in Mosul, designed to block cavalry. (Detail of Iranian lancers, ivory; Seattle Art Museum. Detail of Turk with an axe, incised in gold; Paris, the Louvre.)

The burden of this army (whose actual strength can only be estimated at between 50,000 and 100,000 men) was increased by its great expense. This was high (the revenues due from fiscal districts were estimated at between 1,000 and 1,200 dinars for a horseman, between 1,300 and 2,000 for an emir) and was supplemented by payments in kind and by special grants on great occasions, such as the proclamation of a caliph, gestures which army pressure made absolutely obligatory. Altogether, under Mu'tadid (892–902) the main army required 5,550 dinars a day (2 million dinars a year); the estimated total cost for an army of 50,000 men, including the expenses of equipment and upkeep, amounted to some 5 million dinars, almost half the empire's budget, which, at its height, was **152** 16 million dinars. The Office of the Army, *Diwan al Jaysh*, with its immaculately maintained registers – which recorded the names of the soldiers together with their genealogies and physical characteristics in order to ensure that the strength of the army on paper matched its real strength on the battlefield – tended, therefore, to absorb the State's entire fiscal energy. So, under the Ghaznavids, the head of the Military Registry Office became one of the chief figures of the emirate and under the vigorous direction of the Buyid emirs, the army took over all aspects of the fiscal system.

The iqta: a distinctively Islamic development

In fact it was the needs of the army, and particularly of the Buyid army, which led the emirate to set up a new system of assigning fiscal revenues. Historians have sometimes been tempted to see in this the beginnings of an Islamic version of feudalism. But this new development, the *iqta*, has really nothing in common with the Western feudal model. If, for the time being, it did strengthen the authority and influence of those holding the concessions, especially the Turkish officers, it never eroded the public nature of state power, it did not lead to the creation of great hereditary estates, and it did not bring about a change in social relations. In the ninth century the *iqta* consisted of a distribution of tithed properties in the control of the Office of Estates: the holder collected a land tax from the peasants and passed on a tithe to the State; he was responsible for irrigation work and for land development, and could thus increase the difference between his revenue and his payments. The estate remained subject to the law of the land, and the holder could only increase his power by offering expensive 'protection' against banditry and the abuses of the fisc to neighbouring rural communities, who were gradually taking their place in the system of tenant farming. The limitations of this type of 'great estate' are obvious: even once it was consolidated, the holder had no right to dispense justice; it enjoyed no privilege with regard to Muslim law; and above all, it was not exempt from the laws of inheritance, the effect of which was to break it up and make it difficult to reconstitute.

Other legal methods of collecting the land tax lay behind the new *iqta*: contracts which handed over to military commanders or tax-farmers the exclusive right to levy taxes – free from any control by the government bureaucracy – in return for a yearly payment. These contracts, which were particularly common in frontier regions, were systematised by the Buyids in Iraq, and subsequently introduced into Iran by the Seljuks in the form of the 'revenue' *iqta* whereby the holder, the *muqta*, was given the responsibility of levying a tax which in theory corresponded to the balance owed him by the State. All the fiscal revenue of the district went to him and fell outside the jurisdiction of the fisc, a feature which encouraged the exercise of maximum financial pressure. The State did, however, maintain a careful watch on the service that was due and the personal relations between an officer and his men did not assume institutional form. Each soldier, whether a simple cavalryman or an emir, was in effect the holder of an *iqta* that corresponded to his pay. For the peasants, the burden of the land tax combined with usury, violence and the tightening of feudal ties all served to worsen their position: they declined to the status of tenant-farmers and legally dependent 'clients'. The frequent combination of the offices of governor, financial administrator and *muqta* in the person of a single officer or vizier saw the creation of immense

153

zones of authority and control over fiscal revenues, and this would lead to the formation of great estates. These 'lordships', however, were often unstable: exploited to the point of exhaustion, the *iqtas* were returned to the fisc and they subsisted only while their holder enjoyed employment and favour from the prince.

Although the entire Muslim world did not undergo this process, it did occur in Buyid Iraq, where the plundering which it entailed simply increased the rate of desertion and forced the Seljuks to undertake rigorous reform. Nizam al-Mulk was to apply the Buyid system but he restricted the *iqta* to officers and compelled them to exchange their jurisdiction every three years in order to avoid the erosion of the fisc's capital. Samanid Khurasan and Ghaznavid eastern Iran retained the traditional practice of paying wages from treasury revenues, supplemented by taxes on trade with the Turkish lands and by booty gained in frontier wars. The Seljuks extended their type of *iqta* and the whole of Iran was to experience the establishment of great command zones granted to the Turkoman chieftains and Seljuk princes. Finally, in Egypt which, under the Tulunids, seemed to be some vast new type of *iqta* in itself, the Fatimids kept a close eye on the officers to whom they had granted fiscal jurisdiction, while in Syria they relied upon the granting of fiscal revenues along with political and military command as a means of keeping the country under control. The expansion of the *iqta* thus reveals throughout the eastern world the omnipresent twin concerns of ensuring the regular payment of soldiers' and administrators' wages and of decentralising power, the obsession of caliphs and emirs. The rise of the military, so visible in the Buyid State, did not lead to the creation of a stable hierarchy; it remained linked to the fortunes of the dynasties, and these fortunes in turn rested on personal authority and on the *esprit de corps* of the supporting group.

The unstable and revocable character of the power of the soldiers is clearly seen in the way forms of 'protection' mushroomed and then disappeared under the Buyids: for example, the client system for the peasant faced with taxes (whether in the shape of the legal fiction of payment in kind which effectively robbed him of his land, or of a straightforward tax payment), the 'racket' practised by the police with regard to traders and estate owners, and the State's handing over of the public task of protecting the highways to what were essentially private enterprises which then collected tolls and taxes. The bringing together of these revenues and the power underpinning them permitted the development of a network of local powers, sometimes in concert with the *iqta*, which were more or less recognised by the State, but which were to be swept aside and replaced as a result of the Seljuk invasion. Thus, far from achieving a stable, hierarchical structure, crowned with ideological consensus, the rise of such *de facto* authorities was checked by their lack of strong roots and the dissent of the intellectuals, who were drawn to different models, focused on a caliph or a messiah, and which could inspire and mobilise the masses.

Good performance of the peripheral lordships: the caliphs put under guard

Stability, peace and long duration were the characteristics of the great peripheral dynasties, which thus ensured the smooth transmission of power from caliph to caliph. Thus

Egypt, for example, from 867 was entrusted to Ahmad ibn Tulun, a Turkish officer, son of a slave-mercenary from Bukhara. In 872, he gained financial independence and his relationship with Samarra consisted only in the sending of a tribute of 1.2 million dinars; he defied the regent Muwaffaq when the latter had him recalled. In his struggle with Muwaffaq, Ibn Tulun turned for support to the Caliph Mu'tamid whom he had intended to receive in 882 after the latter's abortive attempt at flight, and then went on to conquer Syria and the frontier regions. It is obvious that good administration and internal peace required continual involvement in the politics of the caliphate and this resulted, in the case of Ibn Tulun, in an armistice: in 884 Muwaffaq agreed to his appointment for thirty years, and to a tribute of 200,000 dinars, raised in 893 to 300,000 dinars. Egypt was reconquered in 905, only to be lost in 936. In the face of Fatimid pressure, Baghdad then recognised the power of the prefect of Damascus, an Iranian general who took the princely name of Ikhshid, the title of the former kings of Farghana.

Although its existence was necessary on a local level, the power of the emir was unwelcome to the caliphate and quickly became dangerous; only the Samanids – Ahmad, then his sons Nasr and Isma'il, the latter's son Ahmad and Nasr II (son and successor of Ahmad) whose reign, which ended in 943, marks the dynasty's apogee – seem to have been untouched by the ambition to dominate the caliph. From 900 they controlled the Iranian territories apart from Fars, which they ruled through the intermediary of their own Turkish governors. Their administration, modelled on Baghdad, shows the ease with which the empire created the instruments of its own decentralisation: a vizier, a grand chamberlain, a treasurer, a master of the Post and a commander-in-chief of the army with the Persian title of *sipah-salar*, a powerful bilingual bureaucracy which administered great towns – Samarkand, Bukhara and Nishapur – and controlled the profits of a vast trading traffic: furs from Russia and Siberia and, above all, Turkish slaves.

While the Samanids kept out of the hornets' nest of Iraq, three principal forces were involved in that drama: the Turkish generals of the caliph's guard; the Hamdanids, Arabs from the Jazira; and the Iranian condottieri from Daylam, the powerful dynasty of the Buyids. The first-mentioned displayed an extraordinary talent for assimilation together with great energy, but they never succeeded in controlling the caliphate for long; they were simply military commanders who struggled fiercely among themselves for the title of 'emir of emirs' in which henceforth effective power resided, but they founded no lasting dynasties to which they could bequeath their power.

Only the Arab Hamdanids of the Jazira showed a staying-power which made them, for the sixty years between 930 and 990, serious contenders for the supreme emirate. Their integration into the tribal world of the Bedouin and Kurdish nomads enabled them to tap the energy and *esprit de corps* of the clans of the Mosul region for their own profit. After taking part in the factional struggles among the Kharijites in the period 860–90, the Hamdanids along with their tribal forces entered Abbasid service. Made rich by their victories over the Carmathians and the plundering of Fustat in Egypt, after 930 they strengthened their authority in Mosul, eventually gaining the supreme emirate in 942. Their leader took the name of Nasir al-Dawla. The case of the Hamdanids shows the essential fragility

155

of purely military power: Nasir al-Dawla enjoyed the power and profits of central authority for only one year before he was expelled. He withdrew to Mosul and would agree or refuse to pay tribute (of between 2 million and 7 million dirhams) depending on the fluctuations in the balance of power between himself and the Buyids. Rivalries among the Hamdanids and violent tribal conflict among the Arabs of the Jazira (some of whom preferred to emigrate to Byzantine territory and become Christian rather than submit to the Hamdanids) spelled failure for attempts to reconquer Baghdad, although a brother of Nasir, Ali (known as Sayf al-Dawla), was able to set up a vast frontier command stretching from Syria to Armenia, which he defended energetically against the Greeks. From 931 to 967 the campaigns of Sayf al-Dawla meant that the Hamdanids were the sole defenders of Islam in the face of Byzantine efforts at reconquest, as the caliph, the Ikhshid of Syria and the Buyids abandoned their responsibilities. On the death of Sayf al-Dawla, a Hamdanid principality remained in Syria but it paid tribute to the Byzantines and its power was gradually eroded in the north (Aleppo and eventually Antioch were lost after a struggle). It lasted until 1002; it was administered by emirs' officers, Turkish commanders and slave chamberlains, who ended up as its true masters.

The case of the Hamdanids admirably illustrates the characteristics of the emirate: an exclusively military power which generated its own organs of government, but a power prone to factions, whose survival nevertheless depended on tribal and familial cohesion. By contrast, the caliphate sought to neutralise competitors by setting them against each other. The caliphate thus outlasted the emirate which had no theoretical basis for replacing it; but being too deeply involved in the struggles between the emirs, the princes of Baghdad were to suffer death (932), deposition and blinding (934, 944 and 946). The Buyids installed in the capital oppressed the Abbasid dynasty, but, in spite of their Shi'ite beliefs, did not dare annihilate it, perhaps because they feared to see it replaced by a more energetic Alid caliphate. Persian 'condottieri' from Daylam, the three sons of Buya, who were all officers, took control of the army in north-west Iran; masters of Fars by 935, they entered Baghdad in 945 and divided their forces according to the prudent principal of solidarity. Ahmad received from the caliph the title of regent and became his master; Hasan was the governor of Fars while supreme authority rested with the eldest Ali, Imad al-Dawla, who was installed at Shiraz.

Baghdad was thus downgraded; if it remained a great metropolis, it was isolated by the Carmathian wars, and it was challenged by powerful economic centres in Iran such as Rayy, Nishapur and Shiraz, which gave the Buyids the opportunity to impose their will on the emir of Baghdad. This was a very flexible 'confederation', where authority passed from hand to hand within the family. In fact, these developments have been seen as a restoration of the Sassanid empire: the use of the title 'king of kings'; the reappearance of Persian regalia, such as the throne, crown, robe; the astrological sign of the Lion; Pahlavi inscriptions on medals; Persian names for princes, especially propitiatory names; and, finally, a theory of twin power (the Prophet's legacy for the Arabs and the caliph, royalty for the Persians). This, however, was a form of double consciousness: the Persian symbols were intended for the court and the Daylamite army, whereas the Buyid, on coinage and in

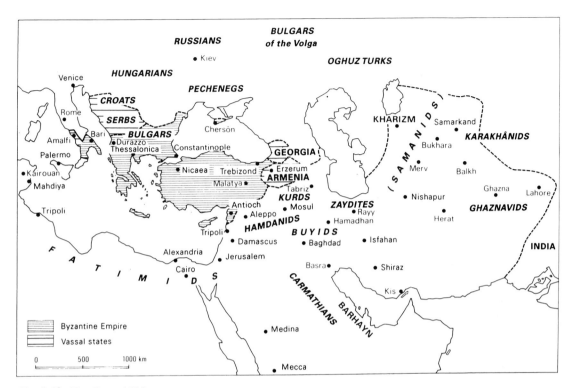

Map 9. The Near East *c.* 1000.

prayers, took other titles intended for the Muslim community. There was rioting when his grandson, despite his weakness, wrested the title of *shah-an-shah* from the caliph in 1027.

The Buyid government gradually put an end to the anarchy: agreements were patched up with the Hamdanids, the Samanids and above all with the Kurds, whose tribal and nomadic expansion meant that there was a multitude of local dynasties. Security was restored along the Khurasan road and great projects were undertaken in Iraq such as the rebuilding of Baghdad and irrigation programmes. Neither brief civil wars nor rivalries among the Buyid princes, whose positions in command had increased, jeopardised the position of the emiral dynasty until after 1012. Their estates, reunited by Imad al-Din in 1040, were broken up by the advance of the Oghuz Turks under the leadership of the Seljuk clan. On the death of Imad al-Din in 1048, his son, Khusrau Firuz (the two Sassanid names are worth noting), took the near-blasphemous title of the Forgiving King, Malik al-Rahim, but his power was continually shrinking and in 1055 he had to share power with the Seljuk Tughrul only to be deposed soon afterwards. The caliphate knew how to play on the rivalry among Buyids, Ghaznavids and Seljuks in order to ensure its own survival; it adopted an official ideology largely inspired by Hanbalism, the first form of Sunnism. The 'profession of faith' of the caliph Qadir, repeated and broadcast by his son Qa'im, was thus in opposition to Shi'ite popular feelings, which the Buyids had developed and given form to (for

157

example, anniversary feasts for the martyrdom of Husayn (the son of Ali) and for the designation of Ali by the Prophet, the building of a great Shi'ite mosque at Baghdad, the forming of a group of descendants of Abu Talib, and the father of Ali). But in fact it was the gradual disappearance of the Daylamite regiments who came to be replaced by Turkish slave contingents which undermined Buyid military power and put the dynasty at the mercy of its army.

The Turks arrive on the scene

The rise of the Turkish emirs in the East heralded a powerful migratory pressure which was to change the population and structure of the Iranian provinces. These developments were first seen in the formation of a huge independent emirate by Alptakin and Sabuktakin, the Samanid governors of Ghazna in Afghanistan, whose military activities on the Indian frontiers took the form of a holy war with expeditions designed to plunder the heathen temples. After being divided among the sons of Sabuktakin, this territory, which included Khurasan, was reunited by Mahmud (998–1030) and then came under the firm rule of Masud (1030–40). Thus began an emiral dynasty much like many others, which experienced typical succession disputes and whose strength rested on the individual ability of the great generals who launched powerful attacks on India. They were not out to make converts; they confined their activities to destroying temples (particularly Somnath in 1026) and exacting heavy tributes. The revenue from this, together with the fruits of their plundering, enabled them to purchase recognition from the caliph, charters of legitimation and honorific titles, which entered into the prayers of the faithful and featured on coins and *tiraz* cloth. Their administration and army did not differ in any respect from those of the Samanids, but they were purely Turkish and spoke Turkish despite deep acquaintance with the culture of Iran (at Ghazna, they welcomed Persian poets, including Firdawsi). Their unconditional support for the Abbasids strengthened the caliphate and delivered a sharp check to the development of Shi'ite extremism, especially to the Isma'ilis in Sind. They opened the way to the uncompromising Sunnism of the Seljuks.

This explosion of Turkish power, which was doubtless due to a rapid increase in population among the peoples of the steppe, had been held in check for a long time, thanks to struggles between the tribes and persistent large-scale immigration to the Muslim Empire of slaves captured in raids by the 'soldiers of the faith' or sold by hostile tribes. Muqaddasi gives a figure of 12,000 for the number of men handed over each year by the Samanids to the caliphate. Even if this figure is exaggerated, the careers of certain individuals confirm the importance of the great slave markets at Isfidjab and Shash (Tashkent) where Sabuktakin was sold; a military career awaited the boys while the harems, especially the caliph's, welcomed the girls. The transformation that occurred must have resulted from the conversion of the Turkish tribes; now formed into Muslim societies, admittedly with large pockets of paganism and still adhering firmly to local traditions, they now acquired stronger political structures: local emirates and tribal confederations. These military states – which seem, curiously enough, to recall the Hegiran model – represented a decisive military force, animated by a tribal *asabiya*, and the fierce military virtues of pre-Islamic times. From the outset, they prevented their emiral dynasties from recruiting armies of slaves and the great march eastwards was the march of large tribal groups who took with them their nomadic way of life, and whose meagre resources meant that war would be an important, or indeed essential, activity. In Transoxiana, Bukhara fell in 992 to the Qarluq, led by the Ilig-Khanids (or Qarakhanids) of Kahgar and Khotan; in 1034 Khurasan fell into the hands of the Turkomans or Oghuz Turks, who had previously been in the service of both the Ghaznavids and the Buyids.

Under the leadership of the Seljuks, the brothers Tughrul and Tchaghri, this was a numerous but compact people: in 1040 they had 16,000 soldiers at the battle of Dandanqan, near Merv, which ended the Ghaznavid sway over western Iran. Skilful deployment of a policy of terror (the sack of Rayy ensured that all towns opened their gates to them), the establishment of relations with the caliph Qa'im and respect for the obligations of Islam all resulted in the rapid extension of the power of Tughrul. While the caliph was in no hurry to recognise him (he was not given an honorific title until 1050, nor an audience until 1057), the Seljuk declared himself to be his client and turned the caliph's weakened position to his advantage by using it to justify his march on Baghdad, which he entered as a pilgrim in 1055. He had no trouble in wiping out all his rivals, who had rallied hastily to the Fatimids in the hope of finding support against him. By 1057 Seljuk power filled the East: Tughrul, the 'Cornerstone of the Faith' and 'Power' (*sultan*) was at the head of a people in arms, whose settlement, once the first shock of their arrival had passed, contributed greatly to Iran's prosperity; the Oghuz Turks settled in Transoxiana, in Azerbaijan and on the banks of Lake Van, from which they expelled the Armenians. The transformation of the ethnic make-up of these regions was to be definitive; a new nomadism was introduced into Anatolia, and the need for pasture combined with the dynamic energies of the Turks meant that intense pressure was to be brought to bear on Asia Minor. When the Byzantine barrier unexpectedly collapsed at Manzikert in 1071, unplanned and uncontrolled Turkish settlement on a vast scale took place throughout the hitherto sheltered province.

Within the Islamic world the Seljuks, in the face of repeated revolts by their Turkoman troops who were attached to traditional ways of administration which the emiral power had abolished, consolidated their authority: they strengthened the title of 'king' by using 'sultan', along with other impressive titles; they arranged marriages for the caliph (who nonetheless resisted and continually postponed a recognition which would deprive him of any freedom of manoeuvre and of any influence over Tughrul); they undertook a campaign in Iran, where Transoxiana was reconquered by Alp-Arslan, son of Tchaghri; and then, from 1073 to 1092, under Malik-Shah (a noteworthy name: being 'king' in both Arab and Persian) the administration was reorganised by Nizam al-Mulk. This Persian vizier, 'tutor' and spiritual father (*atabeg*) to the caliph, has bequeathed an account of his principles of government in his *Siyasat-Nameh* (*Book of Government*), written in 1091. At the height of the Seljuk dynasty, this collaboration between a Persian vizier and a Turkish sultan shows the reality of a Persian renaissance on the literary, linguistic and even, to some extent, the 'national', level.

Iran's cultural resurgence

This renaissance unfolded in a completely Islamicised Iran: the only missionary activity was on the part of the Shi'ites, such as the Isma'ili Nasir-i Khusrau, who wrote an admirable account of his journeys, the *Safer-Nameh*, and who was a man of many parts: militant, gnostic philosopher and great Persian writer. The reawakening of Persian literature did not signify any sense of separatism, only the assertion of particularly Iranian glories together with, perhaps, some claim to a supremacy confirmed by the rise of the emiral dynasties and the winning over of the Ghaznavids and Seljuks to the culture of Iran. The first element in this revival was the emergence from middle Persian dialect – the *dari*, which had replaced the ancient Pahlavi literary language – of a new language, 'New Persian'. This had absorbed a strong Arab lexical component and subjected 'the Iranian syllabic metre to the Arab quantitative prosody'. Some poets, first at the Samanid court and then at the court of Ghazna, had prepared the way for the restorer of the Persian language, Firdawsi. Born in Tus in 940 of a legal family, he wore himself out for his work, combining dynastic annals and the collections of oral traditions already put together by the governor of Tus and forming from this the material of an immense historical poem. This *Book of the Kings* (*Shah-Namah*) glorifed generous kings, the heroes of Iran, including Rustam, as well as the the virtues of the Sassanid aristocracy (purity, action, self-denial), in the course of a pessimistic story in which the eternal struggle of Good and Evil recalled pre-Islamic philosophy, but whose gloom matched contemporary Islam's speculations over its own future. But if the future of Islam was problematic, Islam's science was in a flourishing condition as the seeds sown in a sort of pre-renaissance during the ninth century were now bearing fruit. Branches of knowledge that had been slowly ripening in the Houses of Wisdom were now capable of delivering mature syntheses as can be seen in the work of figures such as Abu Bakr al-Razi (d. 923), known in the West as Rhazes, and above all Ibn Sina (d. 1037), known as Avicenna. The investigations of blood circulation, bone tissue, infectious diseases and surgery that were contained in medical encyclopaedias of ancient and Persian knowledge and experimentation led to them being used in Europe up until the fourteenth century; and the optical work of al-Khazin (d. 1039) lasted as a basis of knowledge until Kepler.

Amidst all this it is perhaps rather curious that in neither religious nor civil architecture was there work of comparably high quality. This may have been because the problems of war made building a risky activity but the fact remains that the only two exceptional buildings of this period, the mosque of Ibn Tulun at Fustat (*c*. 878–90) and of Malik-Shah at Isfahan (*c*. 1090), highlight an important gap in art history. But the picture looks very different if we turn to the so-called 'minor arts' which flourished from this time onwards. 'Minor arts' is a greater misnomer in Islam than in any other civilisation, as fabric, panelling and carpets were not merely decorative objects but were items worthy of being given as gifts or as a sign of favour, and wealth was measured by the number of such items, rather than by houses or dinars. The wooden carvings of Egypt and Syria depicted miniature scenes of secular life: the hunt, dances, concerts and drinking parties; in Egypt, the tapestries and carpets were adorned with the figures of birds and hares in procession, and in Iran with the ancient motifs of strapwork, wheels and ovoid forms; fabrics and silks bore designs

A 'fixed star': Andromeda. Despite the Seljuk invasion, Iranian intellectual influence remained great. This miniature representing the constellation of Andromeda is taken from a manuscript of 1009 inspired by the works of the famous astronomer al-Sufi who worked at the Buyid court. (Arab manuscript Marsh 144; Oxford, Bodleian Library.)

of ever-increasing complexity and mystery; earthenware was glazed in brown or many colours. All these objects henceforth revealed an originality in which the influence of Iran, both in its taste for the fantastic and in its severity of expression, was paramount. In this respect, the Turks could only increase eastern influence within the Dar al-Islam; they accentuated the two fault-lines which were to be responsible for breaking the Muslim world into three pieces: the one which the Isma'ilians opened, and the one which was to separate them from the West.

The survival of proud cities

The power of the caliphate was in crisis: torn apart by the intrigues of officers and princes, weakened by doubts over the dynasty's legitimacy, shaken by Iraqi revolts and by the rise of

161

new emiral powers. All these developments meant that the fiscal base of the Abbasid Empire was constantly shrinking. Iraq's revenue declined from 100 million dirhams at the beginning of the ninth century to a figure which hovered between 30 and 40 million in the tenth; revenue from the provinces of Upper Mesopotamia fell from more than 10 million dirhams in the period before 900 to 3 million in 959, going down to 1.2 million by about 965. It was the treasury of the caliphate that was first affected by the concession of the *iqta*, and much more seriously affected than the provincial tax systems (similar decline is not to be found in Syria or Iran). The dynasty's impoverishment can be seen in its temporary abandonment of the very high standard of the caliphate's coinage. The dinar, of excellent quality under the Umayyads and the early Abbasids in Baghdad and Samarra, saw its standard (the purity of metal) tumble from 96–8 per cent to 76 per cent under Muntasir and experience long-term decline under the Buyids, the Samanids and Ghaznavids (between 50 and 87 per cent, except at Nishapur where the standard remained steady). Its weight also declined: the gold dinar fell from 4.25 grams to below 4 grams. This underlines the importance of manipulating the currency, the desperate financial expedient of weak dynasties. All the conditions seemed ripe for an urban crisis which would strike the large centres first, for their consumption depended on fiscal revenues.

The teeming world of Baghdad

In fact, however, it is the vitality of Muslim society that can be seen at the turn of the tenth century – in the diversity of urban activities, in the confident survival of the capital cities and in the increase in the number of commercial centres linked with the supply and trade networks that provisioned the Abbasid capitals. The revival of urban activities on the Mediterranean coast and the increase in the number of major cities under Fatimid dominance echoed the prosperity of the cities of Iran such as Nishapur, which flourished in spite of the constant civil wars and the great insurrection of 860–950 and the factional struggles which prolonged it. The success of Baghdad is the most immediately striking feature among these developments: the grafting of a healthy economy on to the former seat of the caliphs along with the development of municipal functions.

The nature of production in the markets of Baghdad was essentially that of a large-scale workshop; the craftsmen had established themselves near the centre of consumption: weavers from Tustar, and carpenters, plasterers and masons from Mosul, Ahwaz and Isfahan, all recruited by the Buyids. As is typical in all artisanal production, textiles were a staple commodity in Baghdad; in 985 a planned tax assumed that a total value of 10 million dirhams would be generated by the capital's production of silks and cottons. In fact, the amount raised was not all that large; according to Ya'qubi, writing in 889, local taxes brought in 12 million dirhams, and the hoped-for revenue in 985 (1 million dirhams) was only slightly higher than that raised in the town mills from the traditional consumption tax. But this was an indication that the metropolis of the caliphs was no longer merely swallowing up what was brought to it. At Karkh, many covered halls were to be built to accommodate the sale of raw materials for the textile industry; and

From the tenth century, Baghdad's status as capital was increasingly notional. Nevertheless, it was still being fortified in the eleventh century. Now only a few remains of the walls exist, such as this gate by the Tigris.

embroiderers there produced high-quality fabrics, especially veils (*taylasans*). The presence of the Buyids along with the caliph's power meant increased construction – new markets, new hospitals (such as that of Adud al-Dawla in 982, converted from the former Khuld palace) and many palaces – and support for building activity and public works. The emirs paid particular attention to repairing the embankments of the Tigris which protected the town against floods. Descriptions of Baghdad reveal the remarkable activity and sophistication of the markets. In his panegyric on the city, Ibn Aqil recalled the riches of the bird and flower markets. He also stressed the importance of the booksellers' district where the intellectuals tended to gather; the scale of manuscript production is recorded in the catalogue of Ibn al-Nadim, the *Fihrist*, dating from *c.* 1000. While these commercial activities seem to reveal the diffusion of rather modern-looking cultural models (buying flowers and birds is still popular), the presence of military contingents encouraged the existence of large specialist markets (*suqs* for weapons, horses and hay) around the emir's palace of *Dar al-Mamlaka*. As a consumer, the army played an important role in the town's development.

The movement towards the east of the capital continued, resulting in an extraordinary increase in its area; under Muqtadir (908–32), it exceeded 8,000 hectares, but much of the land was largely unoccupied: gardens (the *Harim* of the Tahirids, and the *Zahir*, an orchard of some 32 hectares belonging to the caliph), vast cemeteries, military camps and parade grounds at the gates of the round city and at Shammasiya, not to mention the ruins of former palaces. The sheer scale of the city made a deep impression on contemporaries; in 993 a count was taken of 1,500 baths, 869 doctors and 30,000 boats; 33 mosques and 300 shops were destroyed in the fire of 971 in the Karkh district, when 17,000 people **163**

A *madrasa*. A centre of religious and legal teaching, this institution remained closely linked to the schooling given by the mosques. This is the al-Firdus *madrasa* in Aleppo which remains one of the best examples of the classical *madrasa* style.

perished. Within this immense area, gaps appeared as the result of emigrations prompted by famines or the upward spiral of prices. Baghdad faced the threat of splitting apart into hostile districts, separated by the abandonded areas; these districts were defined by their strong popular sense of identity: Sunnite (in Harbiya, near the tomb of Ibn Hanbal, and at Bab al-Taq on the east bank) and Shiʿite in Karkh. The visible signs of this constant factional conflict were demonstrations, riots and the despatch of troops. The two banks of the Tigris confronted each other, each one with its *qadi* and prefect of police. The caliph–emir diarchy set the centre of the caliphate, the *Dar al-Khilafa*, in oppositon to the emir's palace, the *Dar al-Mamlaka*, built for the Buyid Adud al-Dawla in 980 in Mukharrim, where the military markets were located, near the parade grounds of the Daylamite troops.

Despite the eruption of violent rivalries between the religious parties and between districts (in 1002, 1007, 1015–16, 1045 and in 1051, 1055, and again in 1072, 1076, 1082 and 1089), there was some sense of a common identity in the capital and this was part of its strength. A Baghdadi patriotism was in existence as early as the sieges of 812–13 and 865; on great occasions political co-operation could result in the temporary suspension of sectarian hostilities: in 1049 Shiʾites and Sunnites made a common piligrimage to the *martyria* of Ali and Husayn. Although no truly municipal body existed, stable political life was sustained by two intellectual circles: alongside the 'secretaries', who maintained the effective Iraqi administrative framework right up to the time of the Mongol invasion, there were the teachers, the *ulama*, who were the city's moral and intellectual backbone. They were mainly lawyers and party men, but in no sense did they live in an ivory tower: their wide-ranging knowledge and curiosity, as seen in the extraordinary breadth of culture of a figure such as Ibn Aqil, brought them into contact with a variety of social milieux. For example, since the time of Harun, *ulama* and poets had held meetings in the book market in Shammasiya. The existence of parties, of religious and intellectual factions ensured the circulation of ideas and authority among the *ulama* and the groups of volunteers who maintained a struggle against signs of immorality or heresy in their districts. In the absence of any municipal representation, these academics provided a multi-faceted political authority, in contact with all the factions of the town.

Intellectuals, factions, 'youths'

In Baghdad, Hanbalite traditionalists gained ascendancy through their constant struggles with Shi'ites and Mu'tazilites, long before Tughrul or Nizam al-Mulk established their new *madrasas*, or 'houses of wisdom', to counter Shi'ite teaching. The chief events of the capital's political history were religious controversies and recantations: the execution of the dissident Mansur al-Hallaj, the 'carder of hearts', on 26 March 922; the anti-Buyid riot of 1031 led by the volunteers for the holy war, who were marching through on their way to fight the Byzantines; the capitulation of the *qadi* Saymari, who abandoned Mu'tazilism; the riot of 1067 against the Mu'tazilite Ibn al-Walid, and the exile and later withdrawal of Ibn Aqil. The arrival of the Turks left Hanbalist dynamism unchanged, and their Sunnism should not be seen simply as a stark, militant force: Tughrul and his vizier were tolerant figures and Nizam made the *madrasa* Nizamiya, which was his own foundation, a centre of legal and philosophical learning in Baghdad. In the second half of the eleventh century, the *madrasa* was to play an increasingly important role in the towns of the Islamic world. Appearing first in Iran, around 1020, as a place designed to accommodate visiting scholars investigating traditions, it developed into a centre of learning, staffed by paid teachers (on the model of the 'chairs' which already existed in the mosques), with colleges which were the personal foundations of generous patrons, and with students who received a bursary. It thus increased the number of professional intellectuals, consolidated their social role, allowed for democratic recruitment and created a class of judges and censors who were quick to appeal to the law when faced with abuses of power.

An urban independence resembling that of Baghdad can be seen in the factional struggles in Iran. Here again we find that the organisation and development of the urban community was taken in hand by religious groups: in Nishapur the Shafi'ite school, which had links with mystics, confronted the Hanafites who had close ties with Mu'tazilism. The struggle between these factions resulted in the constant oscillation of local power, as displayed in the choice of *qadi*: he was Hanafite under the Samanids, Shafi'ite under their governors, and Hanafite again under the Ghaznavids. In both Nishapur and Baghdad the emiral dynasties periodically became involved in these conflicts and financed the building of *madrasas*, persecuted the leaders of hostile parties, put them on trial and made them recant. These conflicts disappeared under the Seljuks, who brought the rivalry to a provisional close by ensuring the triumph of the Hanafites and letting the opposing schools be destroyed. Were social conflicts being played out through this long struggle? The mystics had settled in the poor district of Manashik and perhaps they channelled the hostility felt there for the powerful inhabitants of Hira, the merchants' quarter. But this was of peripheral importance; what really mattered was the conflict between a variety of inherited legal and philosophical viewpoints which sustained an equivalent number of warring clans.

In Iran, as throughout the Muslim world, the rise of many factional groups was accompanied by the decline of central authority: in 897 the caliphate had prohibited the demonstrations through which urban identities were asserted, and which found their expression in conflicts between cities at a provincial level (Tustar versus Susa, in Ahwaz), between factions in a town (Manashik versus Hira in Nishapur), or between supporters of different families. Thus in Qazvin, in north-west Iran, two families shared power and administered the town, each one centred on an hereditary *ra'is*. A third force, consisting of great landowners, intervened in their struggle while the administrative and military authorities appointed by the emir tried to arbitrate and prevent the conflicts worsening without encroaching on municipal autonomy. These factional struggles proved to be fertile soil for the growth of armed groups which attempted to restore public order in the absence of effective policing. The militias of 'Youths', *ahdath*, mobilised to serve the local *ra'is*, evolved smoothly from their ambiguous position as irregulars on the fringes of the underworld to running protection rackets in the *suqs* and enrolling in the urban security and 'volunteer' corps which accompanied the regular army, and could sometimes even deputise for it. In Qazvin, around 970, the 'rogues' confronted the 'noble' Ja'fari.

The organisation of the urban 'Youths' reveals a combined military and political force. It had its roots in a long tradition of rebelliousness among the 'young men' who lived in isolated bachelor communities. These forms of association disturbed the authorities and they can be seen to have been active in the great cities from the eighth century onwards, playing a role, for example, in Baghdad's resistance to Ma'mun. The groups of 'Youths' increased in number in the second half of the tenth century in Iran and in Baghdad, as well as in Syria where they joined the anti-Fatimid faction. In Egypt, they sprang up in Tinnis amidst the Copt population, only to be wiped out by the caliph's forces after protests from leading Christians. The spread of such groups of 'Youths' – who constituted both an age cohort frustrated by the concentration of wealth in the hands of the established generation and a community of outsiders and dependants in a society where authority was assumed to rest with old age and hierarchy – was apparent even within the minority religions, no matter how tightly structured. Documents from the Jewish Genizah reveal the disquiet felt by the leading members of society in the face of factions and troublesome groups who banded together in 'associations', disturbing the authority of the 'Old Ones'. Everywhere the virtues of the 'Youths' were extolled: generosity, physical strength, heroism and solidarity; in Persian, they were described by a term meaning 'young hero'. But the religious basis of these factions was changeable and merely provided a façade for the ubiquitous urban conflicts.

Isma'ili digression

In the crisis of confidence which affected the Abbasid dynasty, the philosophical and political movements which developed out of Shi'ism provided an ideology and a programme of action. While the ideology was complex – combining cosmology, an interpretation of history and law (as in every Muslim movement), together with its own traditions (*Sunna*) – the political programme took the form of a millenarianism firmly based in a philosophy of history, dominated by a 'Master of Time', and permitting its adherents to live out an Apocalypse of Salvation and Victory.

Islam's profound ideological crisis

The principal movement was that of the Isma'ilis or *Batiniya* ('the people of the secret'). Despite the complexity of its doctrines, its internal quarrels and its failure on a practical level, it attracted wide support. The masses, whether Iraqi Bedouin, Berbers from North Africa, townspeople or country folk from Iraq and the Yemen, rallied to its slogans in their anger at injustice in high places, thus rediscovering the original inspiration of the community of Medina. But intellectuals and scholars also broadly supported Isma'ili philosophical and historical concepts. In fact they brought to a logical conclusion the intellectual edifice developed by Muslim scholars in contact with Hellenistic thought. They integrated into Islam the cosmological speculations of the Pythagoreans and Neoplatonists in the shape of a bold theory which asserted the primacy of knowledge and reason but which also involved a gradual initiation into the Truth, leaving some leeway for political errors. This reinforced the hegemony of the intellectuals over first the 'party' and then the State.

The 'Isma'ili party' was the fighting wing of Shi'ite Islam; it was born in the atmosphere of the Abbasid revolution and the endless conflicts between the cliques of the Alid princes, in Baghdad and Samarra. It was confident of having in its ranks an *imam* endowed with supernatural powers, but it was difficult to identify him, and this difficulty together with the hope of the sudden return of a *mahdi* who would avenge the persecutions they had suffered split the Shi'ite movement into several factions. Such uncertainty in the end drove most of the supporters into some form of union with the Abbasids: a theory of 'occultation' (*ghayba*) took account of past history but fixed its hopes on a fairly distant horizon. There had been a succession of twelve immaculate *imams* since the Prophet; their martyrdom was the proof that they had succeeded legitimately; the twelfth, 'hidden', invisible, would return to inaugurate the 'Age of Truth' which would precede the Last Judgement and permit a settling of scores. Although they assumed a position of lofty detachment, the Shi'ites did develop the cult of the martyred *imams* and the hope for the *mahdi*; they dominated the intellectual and religious worlds and even influenced the Abbasid dynasty, but to little practical effect. The militant fringe groups, on the other hand, who followed the traditional policies of Shi'ism, supported the immediate establishment of the Rule of Justice, which would mean both the spreading of justice in the world and the restoration of the legitimacy of the House of Ali. But their success, while indisputable, was marginal: the emirate of Tabaristan, which lasted till the early twelfth century, and the emirate of the Yemen, founded in 897, a more solidly based but isolated creation.

Isma'ilism, originally the movement of the clique surrounding Isma'il ibn Jafar and his son Muhammad, and which developed in an atmosphere of constant rebellions, achieved an astonishing breakthrough with a bold synthesis: a militant party, it took on the rigour of the Shi'ite movement and attracted activists; as a secret movement of initiates, it was capable of endurance, of rising from the ashes and shielding its secret leaders. Its *imams*

167

were not so much 'hidden' as well concealed, so well concealed in fact that the roll-call remains uncertain and from the eleventh century their enemies claimed that the Fatimids of North Africa did not belong to the family of Ali. The first of them, Ubayd Allah al-Mahdi, was actually descended from another line, that of Ma'mun the Oculist, which had provided the underground Fatimids with 'spiritual kin' who had represented them and organised the party and revolutionary movements. According to an early source, the *mahdi* would be an *imam* from this apocryphal line, but would have adopted Qa'im, son of the hidden *imam* and a legitimate Alid.

Doubt has been expressed as to the existence of these two types of *imams*, the 'Active Ones', merely temporary guardians, and the 'Silent Ones', permanent and authentic. But even if it cannot be confirmed, this theory does make sense of the uncertainty over their genealogy, which the Fatimids of Mahdiyya and Cairo never succeeded in explaining in their secret messages to their followers, and of the importance of mystical kinship and the bond formed by education (the true line of descent was from master to pupil). The secret designation and transmission of the imamate was meant to prevail over the claims of ultimately insignificant and transitory physical kinship. It was this point which split the movement time and again.

The gradual introduction of Neoplatonist concepts brought a cosmological dimension to the history and political philosophy of Isma'ili Shi'ism; its character was to possess its adherents totally, fully justifying revolutionary action, as an inexorable fulfilment of the law of the world. This culminated in the compilation between 961 and 980 of the *Epistles of the Brethren of Purity*, an encyclopaedia of all branches of knowledge, which took into account both the rational knowledge and the revelations of Antiquity and combined them into a generalised imamism. Although the Isma'ilis did not adopt a full-blooded version of metempsychosis, they did believe that the transmigration of individual souls occurred in the course of Seven Cycles of a thousand years, each one presided over by a prophet: Adam, Noah, Abraham, Moses, Jesus, Muhammad and the Qa'im, 'the resurgent one'. The existence of the *imam* was thus necessary; he was continually present and provided a link between God and man and proof of the 'recall' of souls.

In this unitary, symbol-laden philosophy, action was an essential component: only moral, mental and political effort could free the light of the soul from its material burdens. And the next step was initiation into esoteric secrets, the *batin*.

Even before the new Law was proclaimed, political activity was taking place through a hierarchical underground organisation which has been compared, with some justice, to the grades of freemasonry. Within the spiritual city in action, social functions corresponded to human faculties and to virtues: 'divine' *imam*, 'truthful' kings, 'virtuous' judges, and 'pious and compassionate' workers provided a framework for the 'community' which represented reason enthroned. The presence of manual workers does not mean that all this masked social revolution: although open to popular elements and aspirations, this was nevertheless an eschatological movement led by militant intellectuals.

Up until 899, the underground Isma'ili movement remained united under a central leadership based first in Ahwaz, then in Basra and finally on the edge of the Syrian desert, in the town of Salanuya. It took the form of a 'revival' similar to the Abbasid revolution and quickly spread throughout the Muslim world: one missionary introduced the movement to Rayy around 877, another established a state in the Yemen and along its merchant routes in 881; the same family succeeded in setting up a revolutionary principality in Sind in 883, while Abu'l-Abbas al-Shi'i converted the Kutama Berber tribe in 893, and after 891 lower Iraq came to form a great dissident zone, where the rebels, established in rural communities, shared their booty as well as their livestock, tools and property. These quick gains turned out to be the prelude to a violent split: the leader of the Isma'ilis of Sawad and Kufa, Hamdan Qarmat, heir to a venerable tradition of Shi'ite militancy, broke with the concealed *imam* Ubayd Allah, who thus lost the support of Bahrayn. For his part, the leader of the Syrian Bedouin who had rallied to the movement proclaimed as *mahdi* a mysterious 'Master of the She-camel' and won a series of astonishing victories in Syria (in 902 and 903) and Iraq, until his death in 907. He also broke with Ubayd Allah, who barely escaped assassination by fleeing to the Yemen. After 907, the movement continued in Iraq under the leadership of former Carmathian commanders, who continued to proclaim the coming of a *mahdi*; an immense political and scholarly labour undertaken by the Carmathian 'missionaries' from Iran succeeded in reuniting the different factions in the common hope of the *mahdi*'s arrival.

The establishment in Bahrayn of a 'Carmathian' centre, where messianic expectation was combined with military action, disturbed the whole of the East: the messianic era, proclaimed in 928 on the basis of astrological speculations (the conjunction of Jupiter and Saturn) began with an expedition against Mecca in 930, when pilgrims were massacred and the Black Stone was removed. In 931 (the year 1500 of the Zoroastrian era) the Carmathians, imbued with the cyclical cosmology of Neoplatonism and backed by many Iranians, acknowledged a magus from Isfahan as *mahdi* and proclaimed the passing of the Age of Islam. But this failed; the *mahdi*'s attempt to restore fire-worship led to his death. Now demoralised, the Carmathian movement fragmented; some of its members found service as mercenaries in the armies of the Emirate states while others remained in their Bahrayn stronghold and awaited the *mahdi*, though they were to remain aloof from the Fatimids and they renounced the antinomianism that had characterised the messianic period of 928–31. Playing a part, along with the emirs and the Turks, in the destruction of the empire of the caliphate, the original revolutionary Carmathians hardened into a more conventional élite community. Around 1045 Nasir-i Khusrau described this state, which collectively owned 30,000 black slaves and was governed by a council of the descendants of its founder, as a welfare state, an echo of the peasant communism of the rebels of ninth-century Iraq.

The triumph of the Fatimid Alids

The storm generated by these movements checked but was unable to hold back the accession of the Fatimid imamate: the *mahdi* Ubayd Allah had prepared his 'Hegira' in the Yemen. When the Yemenite 'missionaries' went over to the Carmathians, he was forced into making a long and dangerous journey to the Maghrib heartland among the Kutama: he was imprisoned in 903 and led to Sijilmasa, from where his supporters liberated him in 909, after the conquest of the capital of Aghlabid North Africa, Raqqada. The *mahdi*'s triumphal entry in 910 marked the fulfilment of messianic hopes, but the accession of the Fatimids, who took their name from the daughter of the Prophet, was the accession of a dynasty whose legitimacy was challenged and whose doctrine was subject to continuous revision. While in hiding, the *imams* had considered themselves as merely the guardians of the imamate; in 953, in order to win back the dissident groups, especially the intellectuals who were loyal to Neoplatonist doctrines, Mu'izz had to bring in their cosmology and declare that Muhammad ibn Isma'il was indeed the longed-for Qa'im, regarded as the ancestor of the Fatimids. These very real problems of theory, along with constant family conflict, go some way towards explaining the terrible eschatological crises of the eleventh century.

No account of the ebb and flow of Fatimid history can ignore the importance of its messianic impulses, including the early drive to universal monarchy, which was never fulfilled and was in fact eventually abandoned. The course of the dynasty's history was erratic. Its attitude appears illogical: from 909 to 969 all its efforts were concentrated on the East, on the conquest of Egypt, while a tight grip was kept on the Maghrib and Sicily. There was a first expedition in 913, with further attempts in 919, 921 and 935. The Isma'ili attempts foundered on the resistance of the Iranian emir, who bore the title of *Ikhshid*. The establishment in 920 of the capital, Mahdiyya, on the coast symbolised the impending break from North Africa and the intention of carrying the war by land and sea to the East. Aggressive propaganda directed against the Abbasids and the Umayyads of Spain stressed the legitimacy of a family destined for universal rule and 'joined to God by a tightly woven spiritual link'. The Fatimids presented themselves as the authentic caliphs, the champions of Islamic morality in the face of drunken and debauched Turkish emirs; they were monogamous and lived in austerity; they claimed to defend the rights of religion: in 951 they managed to get the Carmathians to restore the Black Stone. When the Sicilian Jawhar finally entered Fustat in 969 and the following year founded the new dynastic capital, Cairo, 'The Victorious', the Fatimids appeared to be establishing themselves as the leaders of an élite brotherhood. The religious isolation of Isma'ilism seemed complete. Jawhar undertook to respect the rites and law of the Egyptians: he took a pragmatic and tolerant stance, characterised by openness towards the Christian and Jewish minorities and sought to convert people only by means of preaching and education. Moreover, after the Syrian conquest of the Carmathians, the war effort came to a halt; no serious attempt was made to break the power of the Abbasids or to dislodge the Buyids.

In fact the dynasty experienced violent internal conflict: in 965 Mu'izz tried to rectify Fatimid doctrine and genealogy in order to disarm Carmathian criticisms and to reaffirm the family's Alid origins. The end of his reign was marked by a contested succession. Jawhar's autobiography reveals that popular expectations and beliefs had penetrated the very heart of the Isma'ili hierarchy. The dynasty presented itself to outsiders as that of all Muslims; but it willingly employed Christians as ministers (after Ibn Killis who was of

A mounted warrior. (Arab manuscript 3929; Paris, Bibliothèque nationale.)

Jewish origin but a convinced Isma'ili, Egypt was governed by Isa ibn Nasturis who was a Copt). It was eaten away by its own messianism and the need to postpone endlessly the realisation of the eschatological hopes on which its success had been founded. Tension exploded with al-Hakim, the '*imam* for the year 400'. Proclaimed caliph in 996 on the death of al-Aziz, he was the son of a Christian woman and the nephew of the Melkite patriarchs of Jerusalem and Alexandria, Orestes and Arsenios. As he was only eleven, power was divided and disputed by the leader of the Kutama Berbers and the eunuch Barjuwan, whom al-Hakim got rid of by murder in 1000. The approach of the 400th anniversary of the Hegira in 1009 generated seemingly contradictory decisions, reflecting the tensions felt by al-Hakim. From 1003 to 1007 he re-established the traditional ethical rules of Islam, and prohibited promiscuity, alcohol, extravagance (the killing of working oxen, for example, and ostentatious dress) and he restored the rules about dress for minorities. To this fighting stance, that of a *muhtasib*, which was very popular, was added fervent Shi'ite and Isma'ili propaganda (between 1005 and 1007), which was met by the proclamation of an Umayyad anti-caliph in Spain: declarations against the Companions of the Prophet, lessons in the House of Wisdom, the opening of the sect to converts. In 1008 persecution of Christians and other minorities began: confiscation of *waqfs*, churches, destruction of the symbols of religions subject to Islamic rule, actions that became a part of the *muhtasib* tradition, torture or forced conversion of some of the highest officers of the State, including the caliph's maternal uncle, the patriarch Arsenios. Finally, in 400 (1009), in an apocalyptic atmosphere, churches were destroyed, notably the Church of the Holy Sepulchre. No doubt the caliph and his entourage expected radical changes in the new century, the messianic culmination of History in the abolition of all other religions and a return to unity.

The failure of this persecution, which ceased in 1014 and was partly dispelled in 1021 with the restoration of property, reconstruction of buildings and the authorisation for forced converts to return to their faiths, allowed the return of Shi'ite propaganda. The new initiates affirmed that al-Hakim was indeed the *Qa'im*, the awaited 'Resurgent'; amidst rioting, from 1017 to 1019, and without the caliph's admitting the existence of such a movement or taking the place it gave him, they organised a sect within the *da'wa*. The bizarre behaviour of this modest, generous and rash caliph was doubtless a reflection of confidence in his destiny, as confirmed by the movement; his random actions were seen in the context of veiled purpose, visible only to the initiated, but his habit of solitary rambles at night provided an occasion for his murder in 1021. The Isma'ili movement and the Fatimid dynasty were shattered on emerging from this failed apocalypse. The revolution continued, but on the peripheries, in Iran, Yemen and India; in Egypt, the followers of Hamza continued their preaching and established the Druze community. As for the dynasty, it became sluggish, but was shaken by a last schism in 1094 over the succession, which gave birth to the strange brand of Isma'ilism focused on the figure of Nizar.

The secession of those who recognised Nizar as the rightful *imam* led to the creation of an asylum-state in the mountains of the Lebanon, and the combination of the traditional 'concealment' of the Shi'ites with a hitherto unknown spirit of sacrifice permitted the consolidation of an independent region around the fortress of Alamut. The Isma'ilis terrorised the Sunnites with grisly murders. The line of the ruler of Alamut was to last until 1256. His descendants hesitated between several policies: to continue terrorism within the apocalyptic perspective (two Abbasid caliphs were victims of this); to set up an Alid mini-caliphate by proclaiming themselves descendants of Nizar (as the Fatimids had done with Isma'il); or to adopt Sunni law and make themselves a marginal emirate. Such uncertainty between messianic hopes and reality is reminiscent of that which had given the Carmathians their marked originality. But these hesitations did not prevent the Nizarites of Alamut and central Syria from continuing to perpetrate their series of murders, with such a contempt for death that their enemies attributed their attitude to the use of hashish, and called them *haschischiya*, or 'assassins', as it was translated. They contributed to the dissolution of the Muslim world, whose structure crystallised around the personalities of military and political leaders, and where personal parties and opposing intellectual loyalties occupied the whole political ground. As long-term neighbours of the Assassins, the Christians of the Holy Land quickly seized on the advantage of having the support of their leader, the 'old Man of the Mountains', without of course attempting to understand his philosophy.

Open sea, open pathways

The growth of a new kind of large-scale trading underpinned urban activity and has left much evidence, both archaeological and archival. It reveals a new element of the Islamic world: in this expanding but essentially unchanged map of economic regions, a Red Sea–Mediterranean axis was fixed, one that was turned towards the West. In fact it was the West – Muslim and Christian – which was henceforth the driving-force of this great transformation: first, as we shall see, there was change in al-Andalus (Muslim Spain) where, out of a rural, tribal and military society was born an entirely new urban world, perfectly

Arabised if not totally Islamic, which adopted the style, fashions and refinements of Baghdad. Thus the Genizah documents from Cairo enable us to grasp that al-Andalus was the ultimate destination, via Sicily and Tunisia: it was along the Fustat–Mazara (Mahdiyya)–Almeria axis that the products of traditional Muslim consumption flowed. This trade enlarged the structures and geographical extent of the Abbasid East, without transforming it or breaking it up. At the same time, through the activities of new agents such as the merchants of Amalfi and later of the north Italian maritime republics, the Frankish world was drawn into the trade in products and luxuries of the urbanised and sophisticated East.

Reconstruction of a Mediterranean axis

The rapid development of this east–west traffic gave life to a sea that had been deserted. During periods of Muslim weakness and reduced military activity, it had simply become the frontier between naval powers and the hunting ground of pirates. This late development of the Mediterranean as a transport route was no doubt facilitated by the weariness of two rival powers, the Fatimid caliphs preoccupied with their internal problems and ready for long truces with Byzantium, and the Macedonian emperors of Byzantium who were content with the reconquest of the Syrian marches and concerned only to maintain their strategic superiority. They apparently did not try to interfere with trade along the coast of Cyrenaica from reconquered Crete, although this route was particularly vulnerable. But it may be observed that in this reawakening of the Mediterranean, Byzantium and Islam continued as two separate worlds, very rarely connected by economic links. The main point of contact between them remained Trebizond, on the road from Armenia; as Istakhri confirms in 940, the Muslims went there to obtain brocades and other materials which came from Greece.

The scale of this new Mediterranean trade is remarkable: in the eleventh century, ten or so ships per season were counted at Fustat, having come from Mazara and the West. Each carried 400–500 hundred passengers, that is, as much or more than the caravan which, at the time of the *hajj*, followed a parallel route from Sijilmasa and Kairouan as far as Fustat, whence it joined the mass of pilgrims to Mecca. The Sicilian and Tunisian trading posts distributed the products of an internal exchange between the two parts of the Muslim Mediterranean: Andalusian and Sicilian silk, products of the Iberian mines, especially copper, antimony (khôl), mercury, and also Spanish saffron, lead, good quality paper, Sicilian and Tunisian cotton for Egyptian flax, which was imported by the West in great quantities, and whose production price (2.5–4 dinars per 100 pounds) was already doubled on the Fustat market, and climbed to an average of between 7 and 11 dinars, occasionally reaching as much as 17.5 dinars in Sicily and Tunisia.

Added to these products were Egyptian pottery, oil, rice, glass and even broken glass, sent to the Italian glassworks which, albeit using inferior techniques, were to imitate Egyptian products, using their cast-offs. There were also spices and drugs from Egypt and Syria and of course products from the Far East in transit. Fustat thus marketed sal ammoniac from

Ship setting out for the Indies. After the conquest of the continental trade routes in the ninth and tenth centuries, trade by sea entered a prosperous era. Sea routes developed from the Persian Gulf to the Indies and Far East, despite the hazards of the voyage. (*Séances de Hariri*, thirteenth century; Paris, Bibliothèque nationale.)

Wadi Natrun, tragacanth from the desert, nutmeg, lacquer, brazil wood, and, above all, pepper. The price of pepper doubled or tripled between Fustat and the Sicilian and Tunisian trading posts, from 18 to 34 dinars and up to 62 dinars per 100 pounds. Tripoli exported Syrian sugar, rose jam and preserved violets. Clearly these were all expensive, precious products and the enormous gains in price amply offset the risks of the sea-crossing and the uncertainties of an abruptly saturated market. There is a striking absence of heavy products such as grain and cattle. The demand of Western consumers, however, helped to give an industrial character to Egyptian production of sugar and paper: while the normal mode of artisan production remained the family workshop or an association with several partners, the refinery had already become a powerful industrial unit which required an investment of thousands of dinars.

The rapid growth in trade with Amalfi gave a new dimension to this traffic. Up to the ninth century, southern Italy does not appear to have had commercial links with either Egypt or hostile Sicily; it had been hit by Muslim military expansion, impoverished, ruralised and was only a minor consumer of goods. The tenth century, however, saw the development of Campania; the clearance of the Amalfi peninsula and the spread of Muslim gold – the *tari,* a quarter of a dinar, which was lightweight and easy to use, and went hand-in-hand with commercial ventures. The first sign was in 871, when an Amalfi man from Kairouan warned the prince of Salerno of an imminent Aghlabid attack; in 959, a 'Greek' market existed at Fustat, in the old centre of Babilyun, and the name 'Greek' (*Roum* in Arabic) was used to describe all foreign Christians, although there was no Byzantine presence in Egypt. In 978, a first contract confirms the presence of an Amalfi merchant in Cairo, and a text of Yahya of Antioch relates that on 5 May 996, after the Fatimid fleet had been burnt in Cairo, the Berber troops threw themselves on the '*Rooms* of Amalfi', 160 of whom were killed; the *Dar Manak,* the Italian trading post, was pillaged, the Nestorian and Melkite churches burned down, and 90,000 dinars' worth of merchandise was lost. In this unusual affray several points attract our attention. First, the crowds appear to have confused merchants from Amalfi with those from Byzantium, since they attributed to the former sabotage that clearly profited the latter. Second, there was the apparently quite normal presence at Fustat (south of the caliph's city of Cairo and thus in the heart of Egypt) of merchandise and ships not confined to the Mediterranean ports – ships whose light construction enabled them to pass through the Delta. No doubt this involved the creation, near the caliph's palace, of a compulsory trading area to permit surveillance of the foreigners and the exercise of the caliphate's purchasing monopoly, which we can identify as the *Dar Manak,* probably the entrepôt for the Westerners. Finally, the commercial activities of Amalfi had shifted eastwards and were apparently considerable: 160 dead indicates the presence of several crews. This traffic was still in its early stage, and the Amalfi interests were traditional: spices and drugs in exchange (probably) for the products of intensive agriculture then under way in Campania – hazelnuts, chestnuts and wine. And we can attribute their eastward expansion to Amalfi familiarity with Sicily and Fatimid Tunisia: Jawhar, who conquered Egypt for the Fatimids, was a Sicilian convert, and the spread of the *tari* in Campania had accompanied the plantation of vines. The hypothesis of a trade in wine, certainly attested in the thirteenth and fourteenth centuries, is quite acceptable. The Amalfi merchants brought to Egypt turned wood, cheeses, honey, wine and several kinds of valuable materials (voiles, brocades), which were perhaps Byzantine. The merchants were already so numerous that Italian vocabulary began to enter into commercial Arabic: from 1030 'quay' was called *isqala* (from the Italian *scala*) in Fustat, and as far back as 1010 'bale' was known as *barqalou* (from the Italian *barcalo*). The successes of the Amalfi merchants were continued into the eleventh century, with the expeditions of Mauro and his son Pantaleone. Around 1070 they restored St Maria Latina in Jerusalem, and its hospital became the Hospital of St John, the home of the military order which fought against Islam

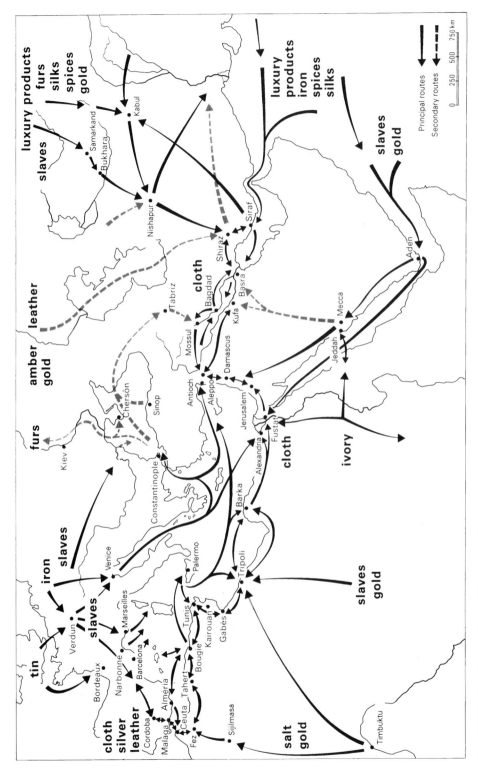

Map 10. Islamic trade from the ninth to the eleventh century.

to the last breath of the crusading spirit, in Palestine, Rhodes and Malta. The renaissance of Alexandria was slow and late: its growth was limited firstly by the penetration of foreign merchants as far as Cairo, then by competition from other ports on the mouth of the Nile – Damietta and Tinnis. The Fatimids did not re-establish the Mint there until 1076, and Alexandria did not become the obligatory port of call for the Italians until Saladin's time, at the end of the twelfth century.

This early and far-reaching opening up of Egypt to trade with Amalfi, evidence of the growth of Christian Europe and its increasing demand for luxury products, was accompanied by a real commercial revolution in this ancient trading area – a revolution in which the Fatimids were, or made themselves, the protagonists. Undoubtedly they had consciously sought a monopoly over the eastern routes. They were already masters of the routes across the Sahara; these came to life in the ninth century and were opened up in the tenth century with the formation of African states founded on trade in gold and slaves, linked with the Muslim commercial and state structures of the Sahel (kingdom of Ghana, city of Awdaghast, kingdom of Bornu-Kanem). The Fatimids also tried to take over the eastern commercial routes of Eritrea and northern Syria, reactivated by the Hamdanids. If this last point is more doubtful and if an exclusively commercial aim only corresponds to one part of the dynasty's complex policy, one point is certain: commercial traffic was definitively turned from the Indian Ocean towards Egypt, the Red Sea was reactivated, and the Persian Gulf abandoned.

The Indies route

This transformation occurred in two episodes: from 870, when the rebel Zanj cut the spice and teak route between Basra and Wasit; and in the tenth century, when the relative decline of Iraq, marked by the ruin of Basra and the great Carmathian rebellions, resulted in ships retreating to the coast of Fars. There, the port of Siraf supplied the city of Shiraz, while Hormuz was linked with Kirman and Sijistan. This was the period of Siraf's prosperity, as revealed by recent excavations. But insecurity increased in the Gulf where the Carmathians had set up a pirate state, based in Bahrayn; Siraf had to be protected by vast fortifications and quickly went into decline. Around the year 1000, its inhabitants left the town for the island of Qays and many merchants took their trade to the new commercial capital, Aden, which was already very active by the end of the tenth century. An example was the 'millionnaire' Ramisht, who died in 1140, and who covered the Ka'ba with Chinese silks as a sign of his commercial triumphs. While the outlets to the Gulf were large but depended on the fragile prosperity of the Abbasid cities and capitals of the emirates, the new caliphate's capital was constantly growing in response to its own needs and to consumer demands that went out across Egypt and monopolised the produce of India, eastern Africa and China. The 'Samanid' routes in eastern Europe and the Russian steppes were all affected by a common crisis, the main evidence for which lies in the fact that the latest coinage found in eleventh-century treasuries bears the dates 1002, 1013 or 1014. This was a sign of the dislocation of the trade in furs destined for Samarkand and Bukhara, no doubt because of the Turkish

177

A stop for the night: the caravanserai. Land routes were dotted with buildings like these, usually fortified, especially in open country, where the merchants and their caravans could stop and rest on their journey. (*Séances de Hariri*, thirteenth century; Paris, Bibliothèque nationale.)

pressure on Transoxiana and Khwarazm; perhaps also because the fabulously rich new political centre of Iran was now Ghazna, on the border with India, and for half a century the Samanid zone was only a peripheral province, and no longer required the products of the taiga. But according to evidence provided by place-names, it was from 970 that Nishapur and Khurasan experienced the diminution of their long-distance links, and so we may relate this early decline to the upheavals in the Turkish steppes.

The development of the Egyptian spice route has been described from traditional sources, which are in agreement with the Genizah documents. The route began as a link between Aden (entrepôt for pepper, cinnamon, ginger, cloves, camphor) and Upper Egypt (linked via

Rare evidence that routes existed in Upper Egypt, which was reputed to be dangerous. This perched mosque (thirteenth century?) was actually built on the ruins of the famous temple of Luxor, then almost entirely covered by sand. The uncovering of these ruins by Maspéro in 1883 was only permitted on condition that he respected the mosque.

Aydhab, an inferior anchorage) and the Wadi Allaqi of the gold-hunters; it was then extended to Aswan along a dangerous road, exposed to raids by the Beja tribes, and then followed an Aydhab–Aswan coast road; finally, the re-opening of the port of Bernice and the adoption (c. 1060–70) of a shorter route, which took the caravans to Qift (the Coptos of Antiquity), saw the spice route emerge on the northern Nile, near Qus, the metropolis of Upper Egypt. From there, the great barges (*usharis*) carried products in transit peacefully by river to Fustat. If the merchants took this route going northwards – difficult via the Red Sea because it was infested with pirates– they avoided numerous points of conflict between Aswan and Luxor. This was dangerous country, torn between Arab tribal groups – the Qays of the far south, the Yamanis from Sa'id, and threatened by Beja raids. Later, around 1360, **179** the opening of the port of Quseyr further shortened the land route, giving a decisive advantage to the Sinai peninsula and the road from Suez to Cairo.

Great open-air entrepôts marked out the Egyptian route towards Aden, and merchants gathered at Akhmim, Qus and Dahlak. On the Indian route a large community was formed, and thanks to the Genizah we know a lot about its Jewish participants and its commercial infrastructure: this was the beginning of the great Karimi trade, which reached its peak under the Mamluks, but at that time the Red Sea was reserved as a Muslim merchants' monopoly. Under the Fatimids, who carefully protected naval traffic and built a Red Sea fleet for the purpose, a merchant community united Muslims, Jews, Christians and Hindus in the management of a vast trading enterprise. This trade been estimated at 3,000 bales of spice and precious merchandise. Enormous fortunes were amassed from the eleventh century onwards by the ship-owners, the *nakhudas*, and by the merchants. In the thirteenth century, the fortune of one merchant was estimated at 1 million dinars, between 30 and 100 times the wealth of a Cairo merchant; and under the first Mamluks, there were 200 such river merchants, each with his itinerant slave-factors. A *ra'is* directed, or rather presided over, an informal 'corporation' of merchants strengthened by the kinship links which united them.

Egyptian trade with India, however, did not exhaust the former's reserves of cash and precious metals: Egypt learned to increase and diversify its exports – silks, linen cloth, chemical products (alkali, sal ammoniac) – and to re-export, via the Red Sea, 'Russian' cloth, metals (Spanish copper, lead), silver dishes and carved Sicilian coral. From India, Egypt imported brazil wood for dyeing, pepper, musk and laquer – for which, according to the accounts of 1097–8, Egypt paid 90 per cent in goods and only 10 per cent in gold. We can deduce that the balance was not too unfavourable to Egypt, even if the authorities were moved by preoccupations completely contrary to mercantile notions, and mainly sought to encourage the supply of capital. Indeed Fatimid taxation discouraged exports: it surtaxed surplus in relation to the value of imported goods, as is revealed in the *Kitab al-minhaj fi'ilm kharaj Misr* (The book of the easy road to knowledge of the taxation of Egypt), an Ayyubid fiscal treatise by al-Makhuzumi,which uses Fatimid documentation. The Fatimids hit commerce with an extremely heavy tax – some 20–30 per cent *ad valorem* – which nevertheless did not discourage merchants, proof of the irrepressible demand for luxury goods. They also imposed a monopoly on the sale of Egyptian alum to the West, which did not become really important until the twelfth century.

Forms and foundations

The revival of Mediterranean traffic was further sustained by the economic reawakening of Syria and Palestine. As early as 969, the treaty between Byzantium and the residents of Aleppo, renewed under the Greek protectorate, allowed for the levy of a tax on goods coming from Greek lands. Urban uprisings around 990, notably in Tyre, are the signs of new life here, and probably of the enriching of an ambitious 'patriciate'. Around 1030–40, the Genizah documents show that there were a number of 'western' merchants (Jews from al-Andalus and the Maghrib, perhaps) in Tyre, Sidon and Tripoli; it also shows renewed maritime activity in these ports and in Ascalon, Acre and Latakia, and, before long, links with Cyprus, Antalya and even Salonica. Long truces, the Byzantine protectorate in Aleppo, the proximity of Antioch and Tripoli's independence – administered from 1070 to 1109 by a *qadi* family, the Banu Ammar, a sort of merchant family seigneurie – had all helped to open this door to Byzantium, and to the West in general. In 1047 Nasir-i Khusrau described Tripoli with its merchants' *khans* and the port busy with ships from 'Rum' (perhaps Byzantium and/or Amalfi), Muslim Sicily and the Franks' lands (no doubt northern Italy). We should not attribute this Syrian revival to traffic coming from the Gulf, however; the dark picture that can be painted before the arrival of the Seljuks and even in the second half of the eleventh century means that Syria had not become once more the emporium of Indian trade, as it had under the Roman Empire. Instead, it was the new developments in agriculture, especially sugar, in the plain of Tripoli and the irrigated coastal strip, that provided the merchandise for export. The loads sent in 1039 from Tripoli to Mahdiyya in Tunisia by the merchant Jacob Abul Faraj included rose jam, lacquer, cotton garments, tragacanth, and, on other occasions, mastic, candied violets and sugar.

The new commercial energy resulting from the reopening of the Egyptian isthmus gave a larger role to religious minorities; they had always taken part in trade, or at least the ecumenical communities had – the Melkites, the Nestorians in particular, and the Jews of two rabbinates; long-distance trade was easily grafted on to existing relations rooted in enforced communion and a common education plus the effort made to maintain them (especially among the rabbinates of Iraq and Palestine, which set up Academies everywhere) and a centralised jurisdiction. The Jewish family model combined marriage within the local and family groups with a search for prestigious alliances with distant families. Their intellectual model stressed that travel was necessary for learning and encouraged itinerant studies and pilgrimage; both were in accordance with the technical requirements of a commercial structure based on kinship and friendship, whereby commercial activity operated on a family basis. The model also bound employee to employer through a system of apprenticeship and education. At Fustat, we observe the powerful family group of the Banu Taherti, originally from the Maghrib (from Tiaret), the sons of Barhun and of Tustari, also Jews, but originally from Ahwaz and who moved from trade to the administration of the Fatimid princes' private property.

It would be wrong, however, to think that the Jews monopolised the main trade in the area of the Genizah. The same mistake has led to the over-rating of the famous Jewish 'bankers' of Ahwaz, Joseph Ibn Fin'as and Harun Ibn Imran, agents for the vizier Ibn al-Furat; they have been seen as pioneers of large-scale banking, whereas their function was that of *jahbadhs*, handlers of money for tax collectors, certainly able to make large investments, but not from a dignified position, given their disdained role as underlings. In Cairo, or rather in Fustat, the role of minorities in commercial activity was limited. Although they numbered in their ranks such great merchants as Ibn Awkal (active from 1000 to 1038) and Nahray ibn Nissim of Kairouan, the large majority of their merchants were miserable wretches, brokers and peddlars. Jewish religious rules concerning rest on the Sabbath and

181

A Jewish marriage. Religious minorities enjoyed much tolerance from the Muslims. The Jews in particular played a large part in Islamic political and economic life. But few documents of this period enable us to glimpse their daily life. This fifteenth-century manuscript, however, is an excellent illustration of the marriage rites. (*Yahida Haggadah*, Jerusalem. Museum of Israel.)

forbidden foods constituted a serious obstacle to long voyages, and in any case minorities did not generally own ships, at least not in the Mediterranean (some Jews acquired them in the twelfth century in the Indian Ocean), and Christians' movements – like Italian movements – were watched, at least on the Ethiopian routes, and they were no doubt forbidden, like the Christians from the West, to travel via the Red Sea. Moreover the Fatimid tax system ceased to discriminate between Muslim merchants and *dhimmis* as regards merchandise: if the Fatimids did not go out of their way to ensure Muslim commercial hegemony, it was probably because the balance was still in their favour. Even when subject to tithes, they would not have been penalised as heavily.

The structures of the commercial world grew more complicated as traffic increased: it was no longer simply a matter of going on buying expeditions; different kinds of trade had to be linked up, administered from a distance and carried on over periods of the merchants' absence. 'Exchanges' multiplied: at Fustat there were stores ('houses' for cotton, silk, sugar, rice, etc.) where a space was cleared ('the circle') for public sales. The proxies who represented the merchants and administered their stocks gradually assumed an official position as sworn agents and arbiters of trade. From being simple representatives, they took on administrative powers, gaining commissions and also taking on the office of tax farmers; their *dar al-wakala* (the 'agency house' of the Levant ports) served both as an exchange and as the official quarters of the notary; several of these notaries and proxies would be present in the large ports. They served as a postal address and as a centre of merchant activity. Thus at Aden, from the end of the eleventh century to the end of the twelfth, the Jewish family of Hasan ibn Bundar kept the *dar al-wakala* where the Jewish merchants on the Indian route would meet. Their house was an obligatory staging-post and their influence was so palpable that after 1150 Hasan's son became the *nagid*, the official head of the Jews in the Yemen.

The resumption of trading relations from one end of the Mediterranean to the other, at the same time as towns were developing rapidly and gold was abundant, has rightly given the period from the late tenth to early eleventh century the reputation as a Muslim 'Golden Age'. Without the flourishing of western Islam at that time, these hundred years or so of omnipotence would not have been so brilliant. We must return, in the direction opposite to that taken by the Fatimids, along the western road and look at the aspects of and reasons behind this success.

The splendour of al-Andalus

The tenth century is usually considered to represent the political apogee of western Islam, when the two rival caliphates of Kairouan and Cordoba suddenly supplanted a declining eastern Abbasid caliphate. The establishment of a Fatimid regime in Ifrikiya corresponded to the overturning of political balance in the Maghrib, with the destruction of the emirate of Tahert and the efforts – eventually unsuccessful – of the Shi'ite caliphs of Kairouan to extend their influence over the western Maghrib. The proclamation of the caliphate at Cordoba represented the restoration of Umayyad authority and central power over the whole of the Andalusian lands, the end of a long political crisis that had affected Muslim

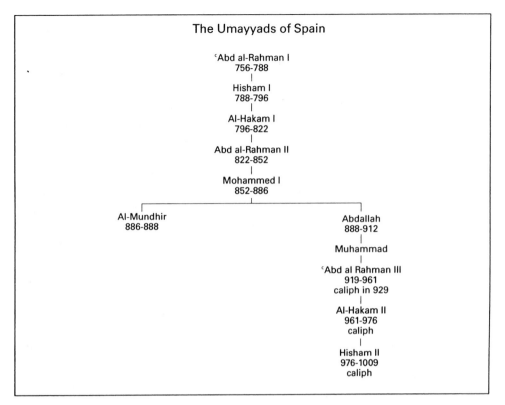

The Umayyads of Spain

'Abd al-Rahman I
756-788

Hisham I
788-796

Al-Hakam I
796-822

Abd al-Rahman II
822-852

Mohammed I
852-886

Al-Mundhir
886-888

Abdallah
888-912

Muhammad

'Abd al Rahman III
919-961
caliph in 929

Al-Hakam II
961-976
caliph

Hisham II
976-1009
caliph

Family tree of the Spanish Umayyads.

Spain during the last decades of the ninth century and the beginning of the tenth. The emir 'Abd al-Rahman III, in giving himself the title of caliph, claimed a prestige equal to that of the newly established Fatimid caliphs in Kairouan (910). Shi'ite propaganda was still capable of arousing movements in al-Andalus that threatened the Umayyad regime, as was seen at the beginning of the century (901) in a curious episode that, in its early stages, was surprisingly like the episode of Ubayd Allah with the Kutama tribe. A political–religious agitator of a similar kind encouraged the Berber tribes of central Spain in a great expedition, a holy war against the Christian town of Zamora on the frontier of the kingdom of León. The invasion ended in wretched failure due to the defection of the Berber leaders, who having at first supported the rebellion, came to fear for their own authority. The rebellion had failed, but it could have shaken the regime.

Muslim Spain opens up

Emir 'Abd al-Rahman proclaimed himself caliph in 929. Two years previously, taking advantage of the troubles of the Kairouan Fatimids in the central and outer Maghrib, he had occupied Melilla on the eastern shore of Morocco. In 931, an Umayyad fleet succeeded in conquering Ceuta. Shortly afterwards, the most powerful of the Berber leaders in the region, Musa ibn Abi al-Afiya, who had been a supporter of the Fatimids, allied himself with the Umayyads. The greater part of the western Maghrib thus became a sort of 'protectorate' of the Cordoban caliphate, although Umayyad positions of influence had to be defended, throughout the century, against attacks from Fatimids and Zirids. The struggle spread to maritime areas. In 955 a Sicilian squadron attacked the port of Almeria, destroying a large section of the war fleet that was based there. In reprisal, an Umayyad fleet set out the following year to pillage the coast of Ifrikiya, sacking Marsa'l-Kharaz and devastating the area round Susa and Tarbarqa.

Besides Almeria, the Cordoban fleet then had another important base, with an arsenal (of which the foundation inscription, dated 944–5, has been preserved), at Tortosa, and ports of call in the Balearic Islands, where we know that an Umayyad governor (*amil*) resided from at least 929, and where Cordoba sent a *qadi* for the first time in 937. In volume V of the *Muqtabis*, Ibn Hayyan gives an important account of the Mediterranean strategy of the Umayyad caliphate around the mid-century, mentioning several treaties signed in 940 by the government in Cordoba with various Christian princes of Mediterranean Europe, among them the count of Barcelona and in all likelihood the king of Italy, Hugh of Provence (*Undjuh*).

According to this source, this Undjuh had sent an embassy to Cordoba to ask for safe passage for the merchants of his lands when they were in al-Andalus. The treaty giving them the requested guarantees was communicated 'to the commander at Fraxinetum and to the governors of the Baleares and the coastal ports of al-Andalus'. At this time, the Saracen colony of Provence, which seems to have developed independently over a long period, was under Umayyad control. These treaties rapidly came into effect, because in 942 Amalfi merchants came to Cordoba for the first time to trade. In the same year, a Sardinian embassy also asked for a peace treaty with the caliph. It was at this time that there were increasing signs of the renewal of long-distance links in the western basin of the Mediterranean, starting from centres on the Muslim side that had begun to develop around the end of the previous century. The main centre was constituted by the neighbouring localities of Pechina and Almeria, on the south-east point of the peninsula. The town of Pechina had been founded in 884 by Andalusian sailors from the eastern coast in search of secure ports of call for the trade with what is now the coast of Algeria. During the anarchic period of the late ninth and early tenth centuries, the town grew quickly, as a sort of small, independent republic, and was already an important cultural and commercial centre when Umayyad authority was established there in 922. 'Abd al-Rahman III made it the main base for his fleet of warships and from 955 undertook considerable work on the port of Al-Mariya, situated a few kilometres from the original urban nucleus which had developed slightly further inland, on the banks of the Andarax. The new creation soon became much more important than Pechina, which at the end of the century declined into a medium-sized town, while Almeria became the busiest port and one of the largest towns on the peninsula.

We have very little precise information about the economic base of the growth of

Cordoba, view from the bridge over the Guadalquivir. This ancient town enjoyed a brilliant revival under the Arabs in 711, then under the Umayyads, who made it their capital. The proclamation of the caliphate at Cordoba by Abd al-Rahman III in 929, thereby strengthening his authority over the whole of al-Andalus, made the city a dangerous rival to Kairouan.

Pechina–Almería. Al-Razi, writing a little before the mid-ninth century, speaks of ship-building and the manufacture of silks and brocades. It may be, however, that one of the main factors in the town's prosperity was originally the trade in slaves seized by pirates when they raided Christian coasts. Eastern geographers of the tenth century mention white slaves (*saqaliba*) as one of the main Andalusian exports, and one of them, giving details of the methods of castration practised on some of the slaves, indicated that the operation was carried out by Jewish merchants in a locality close to Pechina. In this case it concerned slaves brought by land from Frankish territories, but it is likely that Pechina, given its geographical position, was also the focus for Saracen trade in the western Mediterranean basin. In the same period there is evidence of links between Tortosa and the Frankish world, as revealed in the written record of a journey into western Europe in 965 by a Jewish merchant of that town, Ibrahim ibn Ya'qub. At the same time as Pechina was developing, other trading posts or ports of call appeared on the Maghrib coast, also founded by Andalusian merchants, such as Ténès (875) and Oran (902). All along the sea route from al-Andalus to Ifrikiya, new ports sprang up in the tenth century because of Andalusian trade, like the ports just mentioned or others that were already in existence but not mentioned until then, such as Tabarqa.

The Saracen sea

It seems, then, that at the very end of the ninth century and throughout the tenth the western Mediterranean was once again the focus for long-distance trade. For a century and a half it had been virtually abandoned to anarchy and piracy, but it now became subject to the political and military control of official Umayyad and Fatimid fleets. The two facts were no doubt linked: the authorities established in the great political capitals could not suddenly suppress these raids that were leaving from their coasts because they formed part of a legitimate holy war and certainly yielded revenue to the public treasury; but it is very likely that once they acquired a certain international status, the authorities could not tolerate uncontrolled activities of this sort. It is probably significant that the Saracen base at Fraxinetum, which Cordoba controlled politically by the mid-tenth century, disappeared at precisely the apogee of the Umayyad caliphate, around 970, without the latter doing anything to maintain it.

The maritime power of the Fatimids was considerable. They had inherited a large fleet, created by the Aghlabids, with control over Sicily and traditional links with the central Mediterranean, which was maintained throughout the early Middle Ages. But it was in their own time that Ifrikiya became for a while the pivot of Mediterranean trade. Mahdiyya, founded in 916 by the first Fatimid caliph (who wanted to make it his new capital), played a primarily military role, and did not supplant Kairouan, with which the princely city of Mansura was linked from the middle of the century; but the choice of a coastal site for the first Fatimid capital is interesting. Also significant on this score was the project investigated by the caliph Mu'izz, before his departure for Egypt, for a grand canal to link Mansura to the coast. This project was revived under the Zirids, three-quarters of a century later, but

187

White slaves. Besides its great political prestige, Cordoba had the distinction of being one of the great centres of assembly for prisoners, mainly Franks, who were either sold on the spot or sent to slave markets in other Islamic regions. (*Cantigas d'Alfonso X*, thirteenth century; Madrid, Escorial.)

to no avail. The 'foundation' of Algiers by the Berber leader Buluggin ibn Ziri, around 960, must also reflect the increasing activity in the central Maghrib related to trade with al-Andalus. In the course of the tenth and early eleventh centuries, routes linking the towns of the Maghrib interior with those on the coast were developed, as were routes between ports all along the coast and the towns of the Andalusian coastal regions; and bisecting these, of course, was the great sea route linking Spain and Ifrikiya.

In the third decade of the eleventh century, small kingdoms were formed in what is thus called the *taifa* (small kingdom) period; they included Tortosa, Valencia, Denia, Murcia and Almeria, on the eastern coast of the peninsula. This was not simply the consequence of a negative political event (the collapse of the caliphate of Cordoba), but resulted from the earlier development of large urban centres, capable of becoming political capitals, in a region where there had only been small, sleepy towns up to the tenth century. We do not have the information to establish in each case exactly what economic and political factors were involved in this urban development, but it is clear that, in general, economic activity preceded the promotion of a city as a political centre. Denia, for example, does not make an appearance in Arabic sources before Razi mentions it in his geographical survey around the mid-tenth century, and then merely as 'a good port'. Around 1011, during the *fitna* or period of anarchy which paralysed central authority in Cordoba, a ruler of Slav origin settled there and established autonomous power. No doubt using the existing naval resources in what had been a base for Saracen pirates in previous periods, and with more peaceful maritime activities beginning to develop, he rapidly extended his authority over the Balearic Islands and even tried to take over Sardinia in 1015, but was repulsed by the Genoese and Pisans. This Mujahid al-Amiri was one of the most remarkable of the *taifa* kings in eleventh-century al-Andalus. He was an enlightened patron, founding in his capital a school for studying the Koran that enjoyed a great reputation in the contemporary Muslim world, and attracted to his court learned men of various kinds. The documents from the Cairo Genizah show that Denia was then one of the main ports of the peninsula, along with Almeria and Seville, with direct sea connections to Egypt. The rulers of Denia also had diplomatic relations with the counts of Barcelona, where the main Muslim gold currencies circulating in the first half of the eleventh century were the dinars of the Hammudid principality of Ceuta-Malaga and those of Amirid Denia.

In the course of the tenth and eleventh centuries, two quite different political and economic island centres also developed, whose rapid growth reveals the new vitality of the western Mediterranean: Madina Mayurqa (Palma in Majorca) and Palermo. Integrated into the Muslim world at the beginning of the tenth century, the Balearic Islands seem at first to have served mainly as a base for pirate activity directed against Christian coasts. The source which relates the conquest of these islands also reveals that the conquerors soon built mosques there, and *funduqs* (storehouses) and baths; that is to say, a region that previously had been totally non-urban gained the fundamental elements of the religious, economic and social life of any Muslim town. Another sign of the rapid urban development of the new capital of the 'eastern isles' was the remarkable growth of intellectual life. From the tenth century, Majorcan doctors of jurisprudence – *fuqaha* – merited inclusion in the biographical and bibliographical lists of scholars. In the second decade of the eleventh century, Palma was the seat of a controversy between two of the most renowned Andalusian intellectuals of the time, Ibn Hazm and al-Baji, which created a stir. The high level of culture on the island is revealed by the fact that this debate was conducted in public. Created an independent state between 1070 and 1080, the Balearic Islands were the object of a 'crusade' by Pisa and Catalonia in 1114–15, which ended in the sacking of the capital. The Catalans wanted to put an end to the home-base of piracy which so annoyed them, but for the Pisans it was a matter of weakening or destroying a commercial rival. We know that Majorcan power was revived several decades later, under the independent Almoravid dynasty of Banu Ghaniya, in the second half of the twelfth century.

As for the remarkable development of Palermo, it began when Sicily became part of the

Muslim world, as a result of the conquest by the Aghlabids in the ninth century. 'County-town' of a province run from Kairouan, the town claimed the role of administrative and military capital as it developed as an inevitable relay post between Sicily and Ifrikiya on the one hand, and Sicily and the southern merchant cities of Italy on the other. In the Fatimid era, Sicily acquired increasing autonomy under the Kalbi governors, who were in fact independent after the departure of the caliphs from Kairouan to Cairo in 973. The detailed description of Palermo around the mid-tenth century, which we owe to the geographer Ibn Hawqal, shows us one of the greatest cities of the Muslim West, its *suqs* buzzing with commercial and craft activities. As we have seen, the Genizah documents show the importance of the commerce which linked the capital of Sicily not only to Christian countries and the Maghrib, but also to Muslim Spain and to Egypt in the first half of the eleventh century. According to the Genizah letters, Palermo was the focus for imports of henna, indigo, pepper and Egyptian flax, while almonds, cotton, hides and above all silk were exported to Ifrikiya, Egypt and the Middle East in general. Moreover Sicily sent large consignments of wheat to Kairouan, Mahdiyya and the urban centres of what is now Tunisia. No doubt there were some secondary ports, like Mazara on the southern coast, which faced Ifrikiya and were active to a certain degree, but it is interesting to note that whereas what is now Palma was then called 'Madina Mayurqa' (that is, simply the principal 'town of the eastern isles'), Palermo on its island site – albeit on a different scale – absorbed practically all the island's economic activity because it was the capital. Indeed, in the Genizah documents the word *Siqillya* came to mean Palermo itself; Palermo had totally eclipsed the old Byzantine capital of Syracuse, which was by this time rarely mentioned.

An active, community-minded, rural world

The economic and social history of the countryside of the Muslim West in effect only survives as a list of products drawn from the works of Arab geographers, accompanied by vague accounts of the 'prosperity' of one region or another. Doubtless it is useful to know that a large quantity of oil was produced in the Seville region, or wheat in the Beja region in Ifrikiya, or cotton in Sus, and that the specialisation of such and such a region would be integrated into the general network of exchange between town and country, but one would like to be able to get beyond this simple cataloguing to an understanding of the situation of rural producers and the notion of land-ownership. What we do know about Andalusian agronomy in the eleventh century shows the sophistication of cultivation methods in the Muslim part of the peninsula, as much in the irrigated sector as in *secano* (dry-farming) agriculture. These techniques were not radical departures from the antique methods, but they built on the best of the latter, enriched by experience and rationalised. Moreover they integrated the eastern contribution, especially concerning the use of water; and by intensifying traditional methods they obtained the maximum yield possible within the structure of traditional Mediterranean agriculture. We can scarely say more as regards techniques, and we are not certain as to how far the agronomic example of Seville and Toledo was followed. This intensive agriculture was certainly practised in the *huertas* (irrigated gardens)

The eternal problem of irrigation led to increased technical research. Here a wheel with a broken rim is turned by two buffaloes. (*Séances de Hariri*, thirteenth century; Paris, Bibliothèque nationale.)

around urban areas, and on the great estates belonging to the aristocracy. But what happened elsewhere? To whom did the land belong, and what was the socio-economic condition of those who cultivated it?

With regard to Spain, most authors generally agree that the general pattern was one of great estates and smallholdings. The great estates belonging to the state or within the Arab framework were built up at the time of the conquest, although there remained a large sector of native aristocractic property-holders. Even in the Visigothic era, land was mainly worked by sharecroppers, who were virtually slaves, and this method was generally maintained in the Hispano-Muslim estates without any sudden changes. E. Lévi-Provençal, who wrote a standard history of al-Andalus through the fall of the caliphate, writes for example:

The peasant, hereditarily attached to land which in law he did not possess, no doubt kept more or less the same position as he had under the Visigoths, that of a serf attached to the estate, linked to his master by a tacit, permanent contract of share-cropping in virtue of which he had only the right to

191

keep a small part of the harvest for himself . . . a quarter, a third, in exceptional cases, a half. But even as a free man, or one considered to be free, the Andalusian peasant was no less restricted, outside his daily labour, by conscription and requisition, not to mention the tax on the produce from his land owed to the fisc. One imagines that he usually led a mundane if not a miserable existence, without even always benefiting from any real protection on the part of his master or patron.

The most recent studies do not challenge this general notion of land-ownership and work patterns, although they tend to modify the pessimistic nature of the preceding judgement with regard to the material condition of the workers. Thus, although the *muwallad* (native Muslim) settler was not the owner of the land he cultivated, which belonged to the State, to the ruler or to a great landowner, his situation was improved relative to that of the Visigothic era by the transformation of the slave regime into a system of share-cropping whereby the sharecropper received a larger proportion of the harvest. Moreover, while the fiscal levy was very heavy under the caliphate, in the decentralisation of the *taifa* period the tax burden tended to be lighter, and this favourable situation for the rural economy helps to explain the remarkable development of Andalusian agriculture during this period. 'The development of Andalusian intensive agriculture . . . seems only to have been possible thanks to the decentralisation of the eleventh century.' And: 'The predominant social type in rural Muslim (Andalusian) society was the *sharik* (sharecropper or tenant farmer), whom some authors have seen as a kind of serf, but who was in fact a free man, with a perpetual tenancy, for which he payed a fixed rent.'

The sources supporting this opinion are mainly Christian documents from the twelfth century, written after the reconquest, which demonstrate the existence in eastern Spain, especially in the Ebro valley, of a category of Muslim peasants called *exaricos*, whose situation corresponds to that described above. It would be unwise, however, to rely on texts from the Christian era (which deal with a fundamentally altered socio-political structure) in order to reconstruct the society of the Muslim period. Arab texts concerning the condition of the rural Andalusian population in the tenth and eleventh centuries are few and far between. On the one hand we have agrarian contracts for sharecropping preserved in notaries' formularies, and on the other, in sources concerning the *taifa* period, some indications of the extent of landholdings by this or that ruler, who is said to possess a third or a half of the land in his country, as well as complaints about punitive taxation that the governments of the period imposed on their subjects. In this regard, there is a particularly interesting text by Ibn Hayyan, an eleventh-century historian, who accuses the first two Slav rulers of Valencia in the *taifa* period, in the years 1011–17, of having reduced the inhabitants of the region to a miserable state by their impositions, and forced them to abandon their villages or rural areas (*qura*). The rulers had not hesitated 'to appropriate the villages from which people had emigrated and converted them into private estates (*day'a*)', and then had sometimes taken back the former inhabitants as tenants on the lands that they had once owned. This text, which clearly describes a process of manorialisation of land previously held by free peasants within a rural community framework, suggests that at the end of the caliphate the common pattern of landholdings was not the *latifundio* but the small or medium-size peasant property within a framework of villages or *qura*.

Doubtless there was pressure towards an extension of the estate sector, but the *repartimientos* of Valencia and Murcia at the time of the Christian reconquest certainly seem to indicate that again in the thirteenth century the independent peasant landholder in the *qura* owned the greater part of the land under cultivation. In the same region, other documents from the same period show the vigour of the rural communities or *aljamas*.

This questioning of the traditional picture of rural society which is made possible by studying documents from Valencia could no doubt be extended to other regions of Muslim Spain. We might think that the gardens and estates in the immediate environs of the towns would belong mainly to the wealthier urban classes, but there is nothing to say that the numerous villages scattered throughout the Andalusian countryside were not principally the sites of property-holding on a small to medium scale. In the Levante region and the greater part of Andalusia, the frequency of 'family-name' toponyms suggests a form of collective land-ownership; the sources, however, give us little indication as to the actual duration or nature of such property-holding organised according to kin-group. These land-owning structures of a communal kind have left a mark on the toponomy in regions which were influenced by Berbers at the time of the Muslim conquest, and one sometimes finds traces of these Maghrib origins in later sources. Thus, for example, the *qarya* of Bani Uqba (today Beniopa, near the town of Gandía, south of Valencia) was described at the end of the eleventh century as the place of origin of an educated man belonging to the Berber tribe of Nafza, which seems to have made a particularly strong impression on the region of Valencia. Vestiges of weakened tribal organisations or simple communal village structures probably played a more important role in the social life of rural Andalusia than we would believe from reading accounts of rural life in Muslim Spain; up to now scholars have only seen dependent peasants and labouring masses passively submitting to the rule of the State and the masters of the land.

The nearby Maghrib

It was the same in the Maghrib, in fact even more so, since the power and the extent of tribal or village structures was that much greater. Here, too, the written sources enable us to study only the formal relationships between the urban landowners and the tenant farmers who, according to various agrarian contracts, farmed their properties. But, particularly in the central and western Maghrib, the most widespread form of land-ownership was that of communities of settled farmers or breeders of livestock who were to some extent nomadic. Thus the description by al-Idrisi of the 'town' bearing the name of the Miknasa Berbers – Meknes – reveals a primitive territorial organisation based on division by clan in groups arranged by paternal affiliations which corresponded to the 'tribes', each established on their own land: Banu Ziyad, Banu Tawra, Banu Atush, and so on. These little rural areas or tribal segments initally had in common an 'old market' (*al-suq al-qadima*), 'where all the Banu Miknas tribes assembled'. In the Almoravid period, such areas underwent urbanisation, with the construction of a fortified emir's residence, bazaars and baths, as well as palaces surrounded by gardens, doubtless belonging to the ruling aristocracy. But if the

193

primitive conditions of communal ownership had undoubtedly been altered in the centre of the 'town', outside that area the old tribal use of land was still to be found, if we are to believe al-Idrisi, who goes on: 'Where the Banu Atush dwellings ended, the encampments and dwellings of a small Miknasa tribe called the Banu Burnus began . . . The inhabitants grew wheat, vines, many olive trees and fruit trees, and fruit there was very cheap.'

The extent of the landed estates was no doubt much larger in Ifrikiya, at least until the Hilali invasion. But there too, great estates had certainly not led to the disappearance of tribal or village forms of land-ownership. Al-Andalus, Ifrikiya and the regions of the Maghrib where an urban monetary economy had spread and where there was state organisation, pose two problems which it is almost impossible for us to resolve, given the present state of knowledge: one is the nature and method of rural taxation, and the other is the existence and scale of land grants or concessions to individuals of the right to collect taxes. In both al-Andalus and in Ifrikiya fiscal land existed, often not easily distinguishable from the ruler's own estates. Estates could be carved out of it to be given to individuals. Moreover, the central power (*sultan*) could also concede in *iqta* unclaimed land (*ard mawat*), which allowed the extension of the estate sector and the cultivation of new lands by wealthy individuals.

Furthermore, under al-Mansur, the government in Cordoba seems to have handed over responsibility for the direct collection of certain taxes to the military. These practices were certainly followed in the *taifa* period, at least in the kingdom of Grenada, where the military leaders received not only estates of their own, but also, it appears from the memoirs of Abd Allah, 'fiefs' (*inzal*) made of up villages where they probably collected taxes. We still do not know exactly what the state levy was on agricultural produce, or the relative size of the lands on which the land *kharaj* was collected, or to what areas only the tithe applied. It is likely that, despite individual cases of abuse, rural taxation tended to conform to what was laid down in the Koran, and that alienation of tax rights was made mostly in the form of charters (*sijill*) granting to a political or military leader the overall state prerogatives in an area (in other words, it was a delegation of government (*wilaya*) which did not fundamentally challenge the essence of socio-political relations). Such concessions or grants, like the taxes which did not conform to the Koran (the existence and unpopularity of which are more evident in urban than rural areas), in any case had only a precarious existence and, condemned by law and popular opinion, were strongly challenged whenever central power was restored. The model of a state organisation which worked only through the sultan's agents and the social groupings of village, tribe and town, without any intermediary 'feudal' or 'seigneurial' class, retained a hold on the collective imagination, and was feasible – as for example when the Almoravids in al-Andalus dispossessed the *taifa* kings, abolished the illegal taxes and restored the unity of the community and the power of the State.

The birth of western Islam

In the economic world of the western and eastern basins of the Mediterranean described above, Sicily and Palermo were merely part of an Ifrikiyan orbit centred on the two capitals Mahdiyya and Kairouan. Other urban centres such as Tunis, Sfax and the interior towns essentially played the part of staging-posts on the roads leading to these metropolises. Especially after the extension of Fatimid authority over the central Maghrib – and even for a time over the western Maghrib – they were also the destinations of the caravans carrying gold and slaves from the Sudan, as well as ships carrying Andalusian merchandise destined for re-export to Egypt and Syria. Despite the new life on its Mediterranean side and the rapid growth on its margins of two economically important and politically independent centres – Palermo, on the border of the Christian world, and Sijilmasa, in contact with the Sahara and black Africa – the western Muslim world around the beginning of the eleventh century remained strongly centralised around the two great urban conglomerations of Cordoba on the one hand, and Mahdiyya–Kairouan on the other. There appeared to be a political and economic balance between them, although we see the two powers competing for influence over the western part of the Maghrib, where the situation was confused by political and tribal divisions.

The gold of the Sudan

Fierce conflicts took place in this part of North Africa, between the Algerian meridian and the Atlantic, in the tenth and early eleventh centuries; the Fatimids intervened, then the Zirids, the caliphate of Cordoba, the Idrisid emirs of Morocco, and the great tribal confederations peopling the central and western Maghrib. These have often been interpreted as struggles for control of the final stages of the great Saharan routes, by which the gold of the Sudan was brought to the Maghrib. Maurice Lombard argued in 1947 that the health of Fatimid finances, a condition of their military success in Egypt, could be explained ultimately by the fact that the Shi'ite caliphs of Kairouan, by destroying the state of Tahert and simultaneously extending their authority to Sijilmasa, had managed to control all the outlets and routes for Sudanese gold. On the other hand, at the end of the century it was the Umayyads of Cordoba who, through their Zanata Berber allies (masters of the Nakur–Fez–Sijilmasa route), had re-routed most of the gold traffic towards Spain, this fact being the main explanation for the prosperity and power of the caliphate of Cordoba in the era of al-Mansur's 'dictatorship' (c. 980–1002).

These theories are based on a very 'monetarist' view of economic history and on the idea that the great urban-based states of the medieval Maghrib were principally founded on the development of long-distance commercial activities, with little reference to the local social and economic context. 'Each state acquired more power in so as far it managed to concentrate the greater part of the gold trade, the principal factor in its strength and economic importance.' It was for this reason that the caliphs of Cordoba 'clung on to Ceuta, their African bridgehead, and endeavoured to maintain, either directly or by an alliance system, their links with Sijilmasa', while 'by a series of massive attacks on Fez, Tlemcen, Tahert and especially on Ceuta, the Fatimid rulers, and then their successors, sought to prevent the caliphs of Cordoba from exercising their influence over Sijilmasa and thus controlling part of the gold trade'. The seizure of the place where the trans-Saharan route emerged into the western Maghrib would thus provide the most satisfying key to explain the rapid development of the great empires which successively dominated the Maghrib: the Fatimids in the

195

The traffic in gold from the Sudan to the Maghrib and Egypt took the great Saharan roads and long contributed to the wealth of the caliphate of Kairouan. But, beyond the economic, political and social milieu, about which much is known, there was the often dangerous reality of the land itself, as is shown in this aerial view of a part of the south Tunisian desert.

tenth century, the Almoravids in the eleventh, and lastly the Almohads in the twelfth century. Conversely, the extension of Cordoban Umayyad influence over the western Maghrib and the re-routing of most of the gold trade to Spain on the one hand, and on the other, the growth of independent states or autonomous military lordships on the western and southern marches of the Zirid state (the Hammudid state and the great 'fiefs' of southern Ifrikiya), help to explain the economic and social difficulties and the weakening of the Kairouan state even before the arrival of the Hilali in the mid-eleventh century. Thus the great 'financial crisis' of 1050, which saw the withdrawal of Fatimid currency from circulation and its replacement by a new, much devalued Zirid dinar, can be linked to the Kairouan government's need to 'make the most of the gold reserves existing in Ifrikiya, once the influx of Sudanese gold dried up, which had fed and enriched the country for centuries', the gold route now being 'dominated and increasingly reshaped, either by the Umayyad conquest or by the development of new Djerid powers'.

The town: hostage to trade and money

The historians who developed these arguments have reacted against the general explanations of Maghrib history contemporaneous with colonisation, which are based on the opposition of ethnic groups (Berbers and Arabs, Zanata and Sanhaja) and of nomadic and settled ways of life. They were right to insist on the fact, already emphasised by F. Braudel, that in this medieval Muslim West, towns often developed without relation to the surrounding countryside, but later organised that countryside around themselves – the reverse of what usually happened during the Middle Ages in the West, where urban prosperity was deeply rooted in a rural environment already favourable to it. The example of Almeria mentioned earlier, whose rapid growth in a region that was not naturally encouraging was due in the first place to trade, and then to political factors, was not at all exceptional. Even more remarkable was the growth of the towns on the northern and southern fringes of the Sahara, such as Sijilmasa and Awdaghast. In the latter there was some gardening, the land carefully dug over and plants watered by hand, but this was far from meeting urban demand, and food imported from far away reached fabulous prices.

Obviously these are only isolated examples, but the growth of the large Andalusian towns, the Ifrikiyan capitals, Palermo, and towns in the central Maghrib, also relied to a great extent on pre-existing trade and on trade encouraged by the rate of urban growth itself, without which these enormous cities – with perhaps hundreds of thousands of inhabitants in the largest ones – would have been unable to survive. The town authority profited indirectly from such trade by collecting the customs duties – the ruling classes and the ruler himself directly participating in commercial activities, there being no aristocractic prejudice against them. The fiscal returns from commerce and manufacture greatly contributed to the maintenance of an administrative and military system which forced the country-dwellers to pay tax. The wealthy classes in the towns and the ruler himself, either by financial means or by force, appropriated most of the land of the *fahs* (rural areas) around the town and employed on their estates agricultural workers or tenant farmers according to various kinds of sharecropping contracts. However, a great part of a town's provisions were imported from more distant rural regions thanks to the wealth generated by trade and manufacture (thus Kairouan, for example, imported wheat from the plains of Beja and Sicily, figs from various regions as far away as the Algerian coast, dates from Tozeur, and nuts from Tébessa).

The development of towns was thus linked both to major trade networks and to the ability of political power to maintain state institutions which were only partially dependent on a regional economic base. This means that the great urban bodies were often quite fragile. Even in the case of much smaller towns, we sometimes see in the records the ambiguous nature of rapid urban growth unrelated to rural surroundings. Thus the chronicler who relates the foundation of Achir by Ziri ibn Manad in 935–6 says that he summoned masons and joiners from Msila and Tubna to build the new town, and that the caliph of Kairouan sent his lieutenant in the central Maghrib other craftsmen and materials, especially iron. Once the fortress was built, it was filled with scholars, merchants and lawyers. But the most interesting details concern the circulation of currency established in the region as a result of the city's foundation: until then, transactions had not been made in money but in kind, especially in cattle. Ziri minted money and began to pay his troops in cash, with the result that a great quantity of dirhams and dinars henceforth circulated in the rural area around the new capital.

This redistribution of money to the administrative and military sectors through state institutions was an important factor in the social and economic life of the Muslim West in the tenth and eleventh centuries. The development of *iqtas* was much less important, though at the same period it was undermining the political and administrative organisation of the Abbasid East. There are some curious passages on the subject in the work of legal scholars, pondering the legality of individuals using monies coming from the collection of non-Koranic taxes, redistributed by the State in the form of salaries paid to soldiers and government servants, and injected into the economy in general by means of the purchases made by these people in their turn. Thus Ibn Hazm of Cordoba gives a picturesque description of the impure product of illegal tributes collected by the Andalusian *taifa* rulers in the eleventh century as comparable to a fire, its warmth increasing after the soldiers received their pay, 'because they then used it for their purchases from traders and craftsmen, in whose hands it is converted into scorpions, snakes and vipers. In their turn, the traders buy what they need from other subjects, so that gold and silver coins are in the end like wheels going round amidst the fires of hell.'

It would be hard to evoke more clearly the importance of currency circulation and the very 'monetised' nature of life in these states of the Muslim West in the Middle Ages. One of the most important facts of economic history in the tenth and eleventh centuries is the progress of gold currency in al-Andalus and the Maghrib, which was the way these countries aligned their monetary structures with that of the eastern world. Until that time, the Andalusian and Moroccan workshops had only minted dirhams, and it seems that the gold coins issued by the Aghlabid rulers had mostly served to pay the tribute to the caliph of Baghdad, internal circulation being based on silver. When the caliphate was proclaimed, the Umayyad rulers of Cordoba began to mint dinars, which seemed to be aimed at restoring the prestige of the dynasty. Nevertheless, there was not an abundance of gold in al-Andalus during the first decade of the Umayyad caliphate. Until around 940, in fact, there were few mintings, and the main issue was fractions of dinars. In the course of the next decade, issues increased, perhaps as a consequence of the difficulties the Fatimids had in the Maghrib at the time of the great revolt of Abu Yazid (943–7), which allowed the Zanatas, allies of the Umayyads, to confirm their authority over the western Maghrib. After this, the minting of gold coins keeps a rhythm which is not always easy to relate directly to political events in the Maghrib. In all likelihood, it was the extension of Cordoban influence over northern Morocco and the alliances with the Zanata tribes from the Algerian–Moroccan high country that played an important part in the formation of a 'Hispano-Moorish' economic and monetary grouping, which began to take shape in the era of al-Mansur and went on to make its presence felt in the political and cultural life of the Muslim West under the great Almoravid and Almohad empires from the end of the eleventh century.

A single region, from the Ebro to Senegal

It is very difficult to say exactly what role the 'control of the gold routes' played in the history of the Muslim West. Even when the largest number of dinars were minted in al-

Andalus, minting gold never replaced the minting of silver. For example, for the last five years of al-Mansur's government (998–1002) we have only 92 specimens of Umayyad dinars and 7 fractions of dinars, but around 1,500 dirhams. If we take the number of known specimens of each coin, and draw a graph (which, in the absence of more precise evidence, gives a very rough idea of the variations in production), we observe remarkable parallels over the last twenty years of the tenth century, which suggests that the coinage in both metals was determined by a complex of economic, fiscal and political factors which are now obscure, but which influenced the issue of gold as much as of silver. With regard to gold then, it seems wrong to ascribe primary importance to the possibilities of direct supply through political control over arrival points and trade routes, since this factor was not important for silver, whose rate of issue was basically the same. We can observe, moreover, that, at least in the written sources, the diplomatic and military efforts undertaken by the government of Cordoba to maintain its dominance in Morocco are mainly detectable in the massive outpouring of dinars, in the form of payment for the army and presents and grants to the vassal Berber leaders. Finally, how did this Sudanese gold get into the State coffers? In part, possibly, through the minting process itself – but there was not much of this in the Maghrib – more probably from the collection of taxes on trading activities within the region dominated by the caliphate.

Relations in this direction became greatly intensified in the second half of the tenth century and at the beginning of the eleventh. Two great trading routes ran more or less parallel along the furthest reaches of the Maghrib: one went westwards along the heights of the Atlas mountains to the straits of Gibraltar via Aghmat and Fez; the other followed the high plains (now within the Algerian–Moroccan region) and from Sijilmasa led to the area of Tlemcen and Oujda (the town founded in 994 by the Berber emir Ziri ibn Atiyya, ally of the Umayyads of Cordoba, and chosen as his residence), and from there to the coastal ports such as Tabahrit or Arshgul. Al-Bakri's account, which mentions the numerous links between the western and central Maghrib ports and their opposite numbers on the Andalusian coast, shows how thickly woven was the commercial web binding the two coasts in the eleventh century. Northern Morocco and western Algeria were then prosperous agricultural countries, providing large quantities of cereals, fruits, livestock, honey, and some more specialised products, such as cotton from Gharb and sugar from Sus. Ibn Hawqal indicated in the tenth century the existence of sugar-cane plantations in Morocco, and al-Bakri, in the following century, emphasises the low price of sugar in the same region, because it was so plentiful. All these products increasingly tended to be exported to Spain, no doubt in exchange for industrial products, of which textiles were probably the most important. Throughout eastern al-Andalus, in large centres such as Valencia, Murcia and especially Almeria, but equally in smaller towns which appeared quite rural, such as Bocairente and Chinchilla, there was abundant silk production, of varying degrees of luxury. Most of it was exported to the East, to the Maghrib and also to black Africa via Morocco, Sijilmasa and the western Saharan routes. Evidence of this silk production in Almeria and the Valencia region was noted by al-Razi from the mid-tenth century, and it was probably to this trade that al-Udhri was referring a century later when he mentioned

199

Spanish Umayyad dinars. (Paris, Bibliothèque nationale.)

the commercial links that joined an eastern Spanish village such as Játiva to the *bilad al-Sudan* and to Ghana.

If we suggest too neat and 'mechanical' a relationship between economic prosperity, the provision of gold and the political power of the medieval Muslim states, we will have difficulty understanding the major disruption represented by the disappearance of the Umayyad caliphate of Cordoba. At exactly the moment when its political power reached its height, extending over the western Maghrib as well as Christian Spain, the central authority collapsed in crisis in 1009–31, and political power was transferred to the great provincial towns, promoted to the rank of capitals of the *taifa* kingdoms. The whole area over which the Umayyad caliphate had exercised control became politically fragmented. On both sides of the straits, in Tangier and Malaga–Algeciras, the Hammudids exercised authority over a principality which was built from the shrunken remains of Cordoban ambitions in Morocco. These former generals of the Umayyad army, who were Idrissid in origin, minted gold coins of the type made by the caliphate, and these circulated throughout the peninsula, especially in Christian Spain where they were known as *mancusos ceptinos* (i.e. from Ceuta). In the first half of the eleventh century, dinars continued to be minted at Valencia, Denia, and above all in Seville, and smaller gold coins in the other *taifa* kingdoms (for example, Toledo and Saragossa). It would seem that African gold was still reaching the peninsula: from 1018, and in greater quantities after 1037, a number of *mancusos* were issued in Barcelona in imitation of the Hammudid dinars, struck from ingots imported from Ceuta.

A graph of gold circulation in Catalonia in this period would show that, after a vigorous increase from 980 to *c.* 1015, gold imports took a downward turn between 1020 and 1050, attributable to political factors (the temporary weakness of comital power, which led to a lessening of Catalan influence in Muslim Spain), then clearly went up again between 1050 and 1080 with the interventionist policy of Count Raymond Berengar I, who imposed heavy tributes (*parias*) on his Muslim neighbours. The end of the century saw a sharp fall once again, relating to the arrival of the Almoravids and the presence of El Cid in Valencia, both of which stopped the collection of the *parias*. It seems difficult, looking at this sequence of events, to accept the idea defended by several authors that there was a sudden fall in the imports of African gold in the peninsula as a consequence of the caliphate's crisis.

On the other hand, the fact that this occurred at the same time as Cordoban power in the western Maghrib reached its height prevents us from linking the power of western Muslim states too closely with control over the African gold routes. According to the hypothesis mentioned earlier, the re-routing of Sudanese gold to the Iberian peninsula was one of the causes of the economic and social difficulties experienced by the eastern Maghrib from the first half of the eleventh century, even before the arrival of the Hilali. That seems contradictory, given the fact that the Andalusian crisis occurred at the very moment when Cordoba was clearly at the peak of its political influence over the western Maghrib.

No one denies, however, that the quantity of gold in circulation in *taifa* Spain generally tended to decrease after the era of the caliphate, especially in the second half of the eleventh century, when the lack of precious metals is demonstrated by the very poor quality of the surviving coinage at the end of the *taifa* period. Its poor quality, moreover, contrasts with the descriptions in written sources of the luxury of the princely courts in Muslim Spain of this period, and with the envy aroused among the northern Christians by the monetary wealth of al-Andalus. It is likely that the *parias*, which involved considerable withdrawals from circulation, were an important contribution to the decline in quality, the consequences of which are difficult to measure. The economic and social history of the *taifas* remains, in fact, almost unknown. For a long time it was considered as an era of decline, but now this is being reviewed; historians think that political regionalisation in fact may have encouraged economic growth and a degree of social equilibrium between the urban classes and rural producers, who had been partially relieved of the heavy centralised taxation of the caliphate period. This interpretation may not correspond to the actual situation, but it must be recognised that the dismembering of the caliphate did not challenge the tendency towards social unification that was noted in the tenth century. Indeed, although politically fragmented, Andalusian society 'was culturally and socially more homogeneous than it had been under the Umayyads'. This social homogeneity and the influence of the legal scholars, the *fuqaha* – especially in urban areas – was to encourage after 1086 the extension of Almoravid power over the peninsula, a power already imposed on Morocco in the preceding twenty-five years. This political unification of the Maghrib and Muslim Spain was the logical consequence of the development begun at the end of the tenth century, and represented the creation of a vast economic and cultural region, the 'Hispano-Moorish' region which continued to exist in the twelfth century with the Almohad empire.

The Almoravid venture is one of the most surprising in Islam's history. Berber nomads of the Sanhaja confederation, they wandered south of the Atlas mountains and served as intermediaries between the lands of gold and salt, Awdaghast and Bambouk, and the oases of Tuat and Draa; they had been converted at the end of the ninth century and had helped to spread Islam as far as the Niger. Around 1048 a Moroccan *faqih* called by the Sanhaja chiefs Abd Allah ibn Yasin founded on an island of Senegal a military community (*ribat*); the members of this little group, the 'people of the *ribat*', al-murabitun (hence 'Almoravids'), struck out towards the Sudanese lands of Ghana, and in the other direction towards Sijilmasa and the Tafilelt; in the north, their commander Yahya Umar crossed the Atlas mountains around 1055; his cousin Yusuf ibn Tashfin set up camp in Marrakesh in 1060

201

and pushed on to Fez (1062), Tlemcen, Oran, Algiers (1084). The fall of Toledo into the hands of Alfonso of Castile made him cross the straits: although he only managed a powerful holding action against the Christians at Sagragas (1086), he nevertheless unseated the *taifa* emirs (1090), and then after the death of El Cid took over Valencia (1102), and his son took over Saragossa (1110). This reunification of the whole of al-Andalus and its attachment to north-west Africa gave a political dimension to the economic region then in process of formation.

We can paint a glowing picture of the social and economic conditions of the lands dominated by the Almoravids in the late eleventh and early twelfth centuries. The submission of Morocco and al-Andalus was generally achieved in a peaceful fashion. The new regime's taxation, at least in its first decades, must have been relatively light and in accordance with the Koran's demands, taking into account the political propaganda aimed precisely at respecting Islamic standards in this area. Urban growth continued and increased, with the expansion of the newly created Marrakesh, the unification of Fez (which hitherto had been divided into two separate cities), and the development of commercial activtity at Sijilmasa, Tlemcen and the large Andalusian cities such as Almeria. Al-Himyari describes Almeria: under the Almoravids, there were some 800 workshops for silk manufacture and more than 900 warehouses that doubled as inns for travellers and traders (*funduqs*). The town also produced copper and iron utensils. Ships coming from Egypt and Syria called at its port, and the largest private fortunes in al-Andalus were to be found in the town. The economic unity and the expansion of the Almoravid empire was symbolised by the issue of masses of gold coins, minted in the main economic and administrative centres (Sijilmasa, Aghmat, Fez, Tlemcen, Seville, Granada, Murcia and Valencia), quantities of which circulated in the Christian Mediterranean world where they were known as *marabotins.* Cordoba was thus at the height of its splendour: its library rivalled those of the East; its mosque, extended under the vizier al-Mansur in the early eleventh century to its present size, demonstrated a combination of Iberian and Arabic taste in its furnishings; finally, in its *madrasas*, whose renown had spread to the awakened Christian West, there was a slowly maturing philosophy. And it was this philosophy which was to prove to be one of the most powerful resources upon which Europe would draw in its own intellectual flowering.

The twilight of empire: Byzantium, 950–1070

5

While the mid-tenth century may not mark a turning-point in Byzantine history, it is clear that towards 960 the empire acquired a new international standing. After an initial phase of reconquests punctuated by some reverses and even disasters, its pose on every frontier was that of eternal victor. The period of the great military emperors – Nikephoros II Phokas (963–9), John I Tzimiskes (969–76) and Basil II (976–1025) – has come to be considered a time of heroic endeavour

A stable empire?

This phrase is, however, a misleading one in so far as it suggests the irresistible pressure of a warriors' quest driving towards restoration of the old Roman Empire. At closer quarters, the enterprise appears less dazzling and more thoughtful. In fact, the years 960–76 saw the accomplishment of a policy to which little would be added later. It involved establishing, forward of the old 'natural frontiers' of Byzantium – i.e. the Taurus mountains in the east and the Rhodope mountains in the west – a line of defence intended to ward off any future direct attack on imperial territory, as defined by the first Macedonian rulers.

From Damascus to Sicily

In the East, the conquest of Crete (961), then of Tarsus and Cyprus (965), gave Byzantium a maritime hegemony, which enabled it to disrupt Muslim power; simultaneously, the empire attacked northern Syria and Nikephoros Phokas took over Antioch in 969. Tzimiskes then went further: his campaigns of 974 and 975 enabled him to enter Damascus and subjugate almost all of Palestine, except Jerusalem. But to speak of a 'crusade' is to go too far, and it must be remembered that these great emperors had been swept beyond the aims that they had set themselves. Behind the legend of Nikephoros Phokas' having renounced a final assault on Antioch because of a prediction that it would herald his death lay the calculations of a realist, an emperor little tempted by useless conquests. Moreover, the emirate of Aleppo was crushed not by annexation but simply by being broken up, together with a treaty of submission, and it must be remembered that if Tzimiskes advanced deep into the hinterlands of Asia Minor, this was originally because of an attack on Antioch in 971, launched by the new Muslim enemies, the Egyptian Fatimids, who were challenging the entire balance of power in the region.

Nor did Byzantium pursue a policy of uncontrolled expansion in the West. In Italy, where the Muslim threat had more or less been averted since 956, Byzantium preferred accommodation rather than confrontation with the new German Empire: when Otto the Great advanced as far as Benevento in 968, Nikephoros Phokas sent an ambassador to make proposals of peace and alliance. In fact, in the crisis unleashed by German aggression up to 972, Byzantium's concern was once again to preserve its lines of defence, in this case the Lombard principalities of Salerno and Benevento. The marriage in 972 of Otto II and Princess Theophanu was the expression of a profound desire to maintain the status quo. Similarly, as clumsy as Nikephoros' policy was towards Bulgaria – an orthodox kingdom under the protection of Byzantium, with whom there had been peaceful relations for forty years – it does not seem that the emperor ever intended to destroy it. While he did entrust Sviatoslav, prince of Kiev, with the task of 'chastising' the Bulgarians, he allied himself with the latter as soon as he saw that the Russians were establishing themselves there. It was definitely the Russian and Pecheneg danger rather than any desire for conquest that led John Tzimiskes, after Sviatoslav was crushed in 971, to annex the greater part of Bulgaria and to incorporate it into the adminstrative structure of the empire. Along the Danube he created a permanent line of defence. His actions won the praise of the historian Leo the Deacon, who judged that 'he prized peace far above war, because he knew that, if the former brings health to the people, the second, on the contrary, brings about their destruction'.

The most famous of the Byzantine emperors, Basil II, was no exception: a thorough analysis of the vocabulary of eleventh-century texts concerning the reign of an emperor who was almost always at war would show the predominance of words with defensive connotations. We can agree with Psellos that Basil spent his time 'repelling barbarian incursions and defending the frontiers'. Did he not say to his soldiers, who wearied of the stern discipline he imposed on them, 'Without this we would never be able to cease waging war'? During his reign the slackening of operations in the east demonstrates that Basil did not envisage anything more than slight adjustments to a near-definitive frontier. Whereas the Syrian expeditions of 994 and 999 were responses to Fatimid attacks and ended in a long truce, the conquests and annexations in Caucasian Georgia and in Armenia, which ended in 1023, were chiefly aimed at reinforcing imperial defences in the face of the growing threat of the Seljuk Turks. For most of his reign, Basil's war effort was in fact concentrated in the Balkans; Tzimiskes' conquests had not reached the territories to the north and west of the Isker, and it was in these regions that, owing to the troubles stirred up by revolts at the beginning of the reign, the Bulgarian–Macedonian empire of Samuel was born. In the course of its major expansion, towards AD 1000, this straddled the Balkans from the Adriatic to the Black Sea, breaking up the Danubian line of defence and cutting Byzantium's land links with the West, to which the port of Dyrrachion was the key. Thus

Basil II, the 'Bulgar-slayer'. (Greek MS, *Psalterium*, eleventh century; Venice, Biblioteca Marciana.)

the empire was engaged in a struggle for its survival from 986 to 1018, the date at which, after bloody wars, Bulgaria and Macedonia were finally incorporated into the Byzantine world whose rampart they were to form for almost two centuries. At roughly the same period, Basil was consolidating his hold on southern Italy which, freed from Muslim raids thanks to aid from Venice and Pisa, and unified under a military governor known as the *katepano*, proved its real loyalty during the revolt of Melo the Lombard, between 1009 and 1018. Melo's conqueror, the *katepano* Basil Boioannes, was thus able to construct a line of defence in the province, first by gaining the submission of the Lombard principalities, and above all by building along the exposed northern frontier a line of fortifications whose effectiveness was demonstrated when the German emperor Henry II failed to take the chief citadel, Troïa, in 1021. This work should have been completed by a reconquest of Sicily, begun in 1025, but it was cut short following the death of the emperor.

The limits of perfect equilibrium

That the work carried out between 960 and 1025 was intended to result in the definitive stabilisation of the empire is confirmed by the massive administrative changes which both supported and embodied it. Since the era of Romanos I Lekapenos, small districts had appeared on the fringes of newly conquered land, grouped around one or several fortresses, which, although they were also called 'themes' should not be confused with the older, great Roman 'themes'. Playing the role of the former *klisurae* (frontier fortresses), especially during the reign of Nikephoros Phokas, they were intended to transform the imperial frontiers, in the east as well as in the west, into a firmly fortified line under a common administration, where among the defenders – who often held property there – there could be forged an heroic spirit that did not in fact exclude understanding of and even friendship with the enemy, such as can be discerned in the 'epics of the frontiers', of which the best known, *Digenis Akritas*, was composed just at the turn of the tenth century. Nevertheless, behind this line of defence, the imperial administration was adapting to a peace that it believed would last. The function of the *strategos* (military governor), which had embodied the powerful union of civil and military powers, gradually declined, doubtless varying from region to region, until by the end of the eleventh century, even the word 'strategos' had reverted to its original meaning of an army commander on campaign. On the other hand, the old title of *krites* re-emerged; its holder was responsible for the district's judiciary, administration and finances. As for the military tasks, these belonged to the *doux*, the head of a detachment (*tagma*) from the central army and who, up to the end of the eleventh century, was not attached to any specific administrative unit. The essential point to note here is the return of a strong civil administration, an expression of the general feeling of the first half of the eleventh century that the empire had finally arrived at that state of perfect equilibrium which had always been its ideal.

It is true that this equilibrium lasted considerably longer than is generally admitted: the empire kept on course at least until the 1060s, and in a mainly peaceable spirit, which owed nothing to the predominance of a so-called 'civilian nobility'. It is remarkable that it was a military emperor, Isaac I Komnenos (1057–9) who refused to annex territories freely offered to him, since 'for such annexations, a great deal of money is needed, and valiant men, and sufficient reserves, and when those are not available, augmentation becomes diminution'. Thus one can say that the policy of Basil II's successors, at least until the extinction of the 'Macedonian' dynasty in 1056, conformed to the pattern set in the mid-tenth century, which was chiefly aimed at defence and the consolidation of frontiers. This can be seen in Michael IV's campaign against the Bulgarian rebels in 1041 as well as in the reaction to the Russian invasion of 1043. The same goes for the victorious campaign of George Maniakes in eastern Sicily, even if that was nullified by his revolt, or the annexation of the Armenian capital of Ani in 1045. In the case of the two latter campaigns, they were intended to put the finishing touches to Basil II's plan, which was unfinished in exactly those two areas.

Such a deliberate and sustained policy ended up forming a mentality that was arrogant yet pacific, based on the deep conviction that the Byzantine edifice was henceforth perfect and indestructible. Thus the occasionally aggressive attitudes of individual rulers were generally disapproved of as breaches of doctrine: when Romanos III Argyros attacked the emirate of Aleppo in 1030, without provocation and in violation of treaties, Psellos gave the Muslims the better part, and could not find words hard enough for the emperor's behaviour. Moreover it is symbolic to see the emperor, 'repenting of what he had done', henceforth devoting himself to the painstaking management of the public finances. Anna Komnena, at the beginning of the twelfth century, best expressed this state of mind: 'It is the mark of bad princes', she writes, 'when things are calm, to push their neighbours into war through their own actions. Because peace is the goal of war.' So saying, she produces a formula with which Basil II would not have disagreed.

Such a view was only tenable on condition that nothing changed in the world or in the empire, and the Byzantines surely believed that such would be the case. But in addition to internal changes, to which we shall return, there were serious reverses on almost all fronts from the middle of the eleventh century. In Italy the Normans, originally employed as mercenaries by the Lombard princes, had reached the Byzantine frontiers by 1050; in 1053, they crushed both Argyros, the Byzantine governor, and his ally, Pope Leo IX, and the tempo quickened when Rome invested Robert Guiscard with the Byzantine provinces. Despite meeting strong resistance, which illustrated these distant areas' genuine feeling of belonging to the empire, the Normans conquered Calabria in 1060 and, with the fall of Bari in 1071, imperial power was finally expelled from Italy. As for the Danube, already crossed by the Pechenegs in 1048, the Uzes swept over it in 1065, and Constantine X Doukas was forced to settle these Turks in Macedonia. Finally, in the East, the peace with the Fatimids did not compensate for the progress of the Seljuk Turks, who began raiding Armenia in 1048. Although defences held up well, and the Turks suffered heavy defeats, after the capture of Ani in 1064 their expeditions took them to the very heart of Asia Minor. At the end of a campaign in which there were some early successes, Romanos IV Diogenes was finally crushed and taken prisoner at Manzikert, in Armenia, on 26 August 1071.

The empire did not simply pass from triumph to adversity in the period 960 to 1071: the **207**

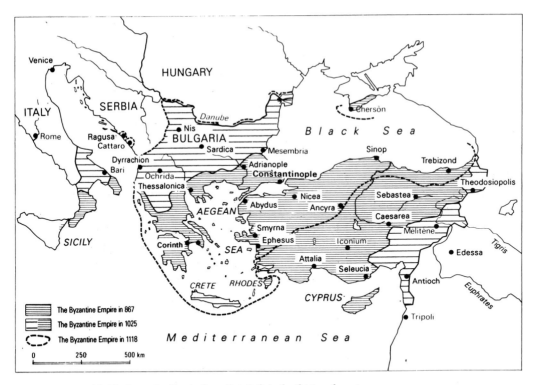

Map 11. The Byzantine Empire from the ninth to the thirteenth century.

fact is that its very centre of gravity was shifting slowly from the eastern provinces (which, at the end of the tenth century, still played the chief role in its destiny) to the Balkan territories which, significantly, had been the main theatre of war since the time of Basil II. We will soon see the reasons for this, but for now we may note how fundamental this change was – from an empire that was mainly based in Asia Minor to one becoming an increasingly European state.

We may pause in this year 1071, when the defences in both East and West collapsed simultaneously, to consider the domestic factors in such a long period of equilibrium and such a rapid fall.

Population growth around the Aegean

It is clear that the empire could not have flourished as it did without a strongly growing population, even if our documentary evidence for this is severely limited. The possible role played by the Christian doctrine of 'increase and multiply' should not be over-emphasised. Of course the large patriarchal family, of which Job's was the model, was a recurrent image in illuminated manuscripts and literary texts: the epic *Digenis Akritas* recounts that in the hero's family there were 'twelve uncles and six cousins'. But such stereotypes are so frequent that nothing can really be inferred from them. The same is true of the role of 'incitement' played by canon law, which theoretically favoured early marriages, the marriage-age being set at twelve years for girls and fourteen for boys; all that can be safely said is that such marriages were frequent, as shown by the decision of the Patriarch Luke Chrysoberges in the twelfth century that a virgin married 'before the age' and deflowered should be separated from her husband. Indeed, we know how much these doctrinal factors were worth when confronted by more material needs: among the rich classes as among the poor, a desire to preserve the inheritance led to marrying off children while very young and to reducing the number of inheritors, following the example of the imperial family, which was far from prolific in these two centuries.

Obviously, more weight must be given to the fact that there was renewed security within the frontiers. Since the beginning of the tenth century, Arab incursions had no longer affected Asia or Europe, and in Europe the Hungarian and Slav raids were only a memory. Undoubtedly there were military losses in the eastern wars as well as in the Bulgarian campaigns, and in civil wars (rebellions by Bardas Skleros and Bardas Phokas between 976 and 989), but they cannot be quantified and they were certainly not accompanied by major losses amongst the civilian population. Wars were rarely fought out on imperial territory, and there is no reason to suppose that the Bulgarian expansion in Samuel's era was particularly bloody. What can be said for certain is that the Asian and European parts of the empire did not experience in this period the same demographic trends.

Asia Minor, whose fortunes had been at a low ebb in the mid-ninth century, now flourished in the absence of any troubling external factors until about 1060: an important indication is the flowering of urban centres, shown by the increase of episcopal sees as well as by archaeological evidence. Still, it is important to remember that urban prosperity does not enable us to assess the rural population; indeed, urban growth can even be a sign of an increasing exodus from the countryside. Thus in the tenth and eleventh centuries Anatolia was the region where estates were being concentrated most intensively, proving that exploitation of the land was increasingly profitable, but not that the local market was greatly enlarged. Asia Minor, in fact, seemed to become a sort of 'colonial' marketplace, burdened with feeding the rest of the empire. It follows that such a system, by dispossessing a number of peasants, could only have accelerated the exodus to local towns, and perhaps towards the European provinces. Thus we must be cautious in our assessments. Towards 1060 Asia Minor became underpopulated, according to two indicators: first, the policy of overseas colonisation undertaken from the end of the tenth century in eastern and central Anatolia; and second, the picture left us by the chronicles on the eve of the Turkish invasion, depicting a region with large empty spaces and without resources, dotted with isolated fortified towns, staging-posts for the imperial armies. This disturbing picture lets us understand how, once the frontier defences were breached, there was nothing to stop the enemy fanning out: before and after 1071, the Seljuks found no obstacles from the Taurus mountains to the Aegean Sea. Admittedly Anatolia presents considerable regional variations: the depressed interior contrasts with the more robust coastal districts, no doubt making some progress, especially round the Aegean; and the eastern areas with their

A fortress in Anatolia. The Byzantine emperors tried to protect vast stretches of Anatolia by building a fairly loose network of forts. They could not contain the Seljuk invasion once the frontier defences had been overrun.

scattered populations contrast with the more densely occupied western provinces, against which the Turks battered in vain for nearly three centuries.

The situation was very different in Europe. Of course the progress of towns such as Thessalonica, Serres, Demetrias, Corinth, Thebes, Patras and Sparta – to which we will refer only this once – should never be over-estimated: towards the end of the tenth century, the *Life of St Nikon the Metanoeite* allows us to see Sparta as merely a small town, entrenched behind its walls. However the progress was genuine, and the Arab geographer Idrisi, in the twelfth century, stressed the richness of the Peloponnese, where he counted at least fifty 'cities', of which he considered sixteen to be important. Futhermore, this development was taking place in a very different context: except in Thrace, in Bulgaria and in the Albanian plains, the fragmented country of the Balkans was not conducive to the construction of great estates, so that a free peasantry was better able to survive. This meant that the countryside was more populous and the towns relatively small. The demographic health of the Hellenic population is particularly notable, as is shown by the settlement of a number of Greeks in neighbouring or conquered lands, particularly in Bulgaria. Even before 969, Hellenisation was so strong in the Bulgarian kingdom that it has been seen as one of the causes of revolt there and even of the social protests of the Bogomils. After the annexation of 1018, there was a colonisation movement in Bulgaria which demonstrated both the dynamism of the Greeks and a certain passivity amongst the Bulgarians whom Basil II, nevertheless, tried to protect against this excessive expansion. We should emphasise here that we would look in vain for a similar movement of the Greek population towards the provinces conquered at this time within Asia Minor.

There is another marked variation between the European and Asiatic areas. Since the era of Leo VI, Europe had rarely witnessed the arrival of these colonies of foreigners which the emperors had established in order to fill empty areas, especially after the eighth century. The sole important exception, the establishment of the Pechenegs in Bulgaria and Macedonia after 1048 and especially after 1064, only confirms the relative demographic weakness of the northern Balkans. By contrast, Asia Minor had been the chosen area for migration, voluntary or forced, at least since the reign of Nikephoros Phokas. There was an effort to repopulate the frontier regions – Syria, Cilicia, Mesopotamia – from which Phokas and his successors had systematically deported the Muslim population for security reasons. In Mesopotamia, especially in the region of Melitene, the imperial government after 965 encouraged the immigration of Syrian Jacobites, as shown by the appearance of fifty-six monasteries between 936 and 1072, and around thirty episcopal sees not mentioned until then. In 1096 Melitene still appeared to be a mainly Syrian town, with perhaps 70,000 inhabitants, although in 934 it had been deserted. While this policy had the advantage of reactivating very depressed areas, it should be stressed that it did not achieve its aim of reinforcing the frontier: the installation of these Syrian communities, whose relations were still living in Islamic territory, had rather the effect of blurring the frontier by creating a sort of no-man's-land. For other reasons the Armenian colonisation, which increased after 990, had no better results. Doctrinally less suspect than the Syrians, the Armenians established military colonies in reconquered Syria (Tartus, Shayzar) and merchant colonies from Antioch to Attalia, but their main activity was in Cappadocia, from Sebastea to Caesarea. These migrations, no doubt first triggered by the population growth in Armenia, were increased by the first Turkish attacks, taking Dvin in 1021; and Basil II, concerned about populating almost deserted regions, encouraged them with his policy of religious tolerance and substantial gifts of land to Armenian nobles, whether refugees or emigrants. Once again abandoned land was returned to good use, but the degree of autonomy given to the Armenian groups ended in the reconstruction of the semi-feudal social structure of independent Armenia on imperial territory, which made it an autonomous area that could not easily be controlled by the regular administration, especially when, after the big Turkish attacks of the 1070s, the Armenian immigration turned into a massive exodus. It should be remembered, however, that the Armenian contribution was beneficial to the rest of the empire. From the tenth century there was no Byzantine town that did not have its Armenian colony, which both increased the population and added a certain dynamism; the upper echelons of administration and the throne itself were not barred to the Armenians, the best example being the emperor John Tzimiskes.

In an area where so much remains uncertain, there are two solid facts. First, the overall demographic balance of the empire seems positive, at least up to the middle of the eleventh century. A factor in this is the absence of any great epidemic in the period under consideration, the only known cases of 'plague' being in Sparta around 990 and Constantinople around 1010. On the other hand, it is significant that a serious epidemic struck in 1053–4, **211** particularly affecting the capital and adding to its current difficulties. We may also note that at the same time, the demographic curve of the Muslim world was turning downwards, which in itself, even without any great expansion of the Byzantine population, was enough to tip the balance in favour of the empire. Secondly, and most importantly, towards the end of the tenth and especially in the eleventh century, the European half of the empire decisively gained over the eastern provinces in terms of population, which resulted in a transformation of traditional geopolitics. Furthermore, these new trends were irreversible. In the twelfth century, the Asian lands conquered by the Turks continued their steady decline in population, whereas Europe made moderate but steady progress, as the Balkans were not affected by the great catastrophe of 1071. Moreoever, although impossible to quantify, they clearly profited from the surge resulting from the Turkish and Norman invasions. Towards 1080, Byzantium seemed to have become an Aegean empire.

Achievements and anxieties

This increased population was predominantly rural and, as was the case everywhere in the Middle Ages, the resources of the countryside were the empire's principal assets.

Agriculture remains vital

Despite the scarcity of documentary evidence in this area, we can declare that Byzantine agriculture was quite traditional: there is no trace of that 'agricultural revolution' which characterised the Muslim world from the eighth century onwards, nor anything that resembles the great land clearances which in the eleventh century enabled the Western world to make decisive progress. This traditional character explains why the *Geoponika*, a collection of texts on agriculture compiled in the reign of Constantine VII Porphyrogenitos, became one of the most copied of Byzantine texts. Made up of extracts borrowed from the Greek and Latin agronomists, it was nevertheless perfectly suited to the products and techniques of the tenth and eleventh centuries.

The produce from the land is easily listed. Besides the omnipresent cereals, there were vegetables (peas, green beans, vetches) to supplement meat, which was often scarce, and fruit, the most important of which was the vine, along with apple-trees, cherry-trees, almond-trees and especially fig-trees. It could even be argued that, in comparison with Antiquity, the variety of crops was much poorer: surprisingly enough, the olive-tree is scarcely mentioned at all in surviving documents, its cultivation only being noted in northern Syria. On the other hand, there was a considerable increase in the cultivation of mulberry-trees in the eleventh and twelfth centuries in Greece and the Peloponnese, which reveals the importance of the silk industry from Sparta to Corinth and Patras. But Byzantium remained impervious to the large-scale 'industrial' cultivation that the Arabs had introduced to the Mediterranean: sugar cane, for example, did not arrive in Crete until it was taken over by Venice in the fourteenth century.

212   It is true that such crops, like those of many vegetables from Persia and India, require an

abundant and regular supply of water all year round. The Byzantine world was probably generally well provided in this regard – it contained hardly any areas of true desert and it was traversed by many permanent rivers. But there was nothing comparable to the Nile and and the rivers of Mesopotamia, and in fact the greatest rivers flowed through regions of seasonal rains which would not permit year-long cycles of growth. It must be admitted, too, that technology was primitive, so that although all the texts sing the praises of the beneficial power of water, large valleys and estuaries with badly drained lands were off-putting rather than attractive. Villages and cultivated lands were usually close to running water, but this was nearly always a stream or a small river that could hardly supply the water needed for extensive irrigation. Of course the texts, and especially the treatises on the weather, show that irrigated lands were the most valued and thus the most important; but these lands were at best 'gardens' that formed the heart of arable cultivation. No technical innovations were involved: they were worked with spades and irrigated using only the force of gravity, which meant that neither the slopes nor the plateaux could be transformed into profitable ground. Moreover, the scarcity of good land meant that cattle, goats, sheep and even pigs were pastured in the uncultivated borders and forests, and as the Byzantines do not seem to have been acquainted with the techniques of land improvement adopted in Islamic lands, there was no question of any intensive cultivation on land that was not irrigated. Thus there was a clear division of Byzantine lands into two elements: the *esothyra* – land close to the villages devoted to gardening, with the occasional field for mowing, and some fields for high-yield cereals – and, beyond those, the *exothyra* which only grew dry grains and vines, with clusters of trees scattered throughout.

It is obvious how fragile this kind of agriculture is. While the abundance of irrigated or semi-irrigated crops allowed the Muslim world at least to soften the blow of any natural disaster, especially droughts, the Byzantine peasant, with his little gardens, had no way of compensating for the lack of grain from dry lands in a bad year. This situation had at least two consequences: first, the Byzantine Empire, with relatively little urbanisation and consisting mainly of rural, subsistence-based communities, rarely produced sufficient food for itself from its own land; secondly, the basic crops, especially cereals, reached high prices because their production was limited and risky. It follows that Byzantium, even at the height of its power, was always dependent on foreign supplies, especially as its population grew. In this regard the vast Danubian plain was indispensable to it, and this helps to explain the Byzantine expansion towards Bulgaria where, in the eleventh century, a plough capable of turning over heavy soil was coming into use. The profitability of cereal cultivation explains the growth of large estates, especially in regions such as Thrace, the Albanian plains and particularly Asia Minor.

The balance of food supplies was all the more precarious in that the Byzantine Empire had no policy for a planned economy. At least this is the strong inference from the *Book of the Eparch*; we have no proof that it was still the case in the period under consideration. Private initiative was therefore the rule. The peasants themselves, when they achieved a commercial surplus, took it by wagon to the urban markets. But this was on a large scale only in the richest regions: thus Michael Attaleiates shows us in the 1070s the Thracian

Backward agriculture. Unlike Islam, where agricultural development went hand-in-hand with research into new techniques, Byzantium held on to the old ways for far too long. These stereotypical rural scenes from an eleventh-century manuscript are surprisingly similar to those from manuscripts of the sixth century. (Greek MS known as the *Oppiano*; Venice, Biblioteca Marciana.)

peasants selling their wheat from their wagons in the market of Rhodosto. The estate owners of course did the same, only on a larger scale: again in Thrace, in the same period, the same author tells us that landowners set up a string of coastal ports from which they sold their produce. At a time when, as we shall see, Italian commerce was making inroads on the empire, it is easy to imagine that even when there was local scarcity, the landowners would not hesitate to sell to foreign buyers or to those from other parts of the empire.

The decline of village communities

We are convinced that these particular agricultural conditions explain the increasing social imbalance that characterises the Byzantine countryside in the eleventh century. The years from 950 to 1070 undoubtedly saw the increasingly rapid disintegration of the free rural community, the *chorion*, even if it remained the very basis of fiscal assessment for administrative purposes (as the surviving fragments of the 'cadaster of Thebes' clearly show right at the end of the eleventh century). It must be remembered that in the country the tension between free and dependent peasants, to which we shall return, was certainly

Madrasa in the citadel of Baghdad, *muqarnas* along the gallery, end of the Abbasid era

Mirhab in the al-Firdus *madrasa* at Aleppo, mid-thirteenth century

Interior view of the cupola of the tomb of Zubayda, Baghdad, early thirteenth century

Isfahan, west *iwan* of the great mosque of Masjid-i Jami, twelfth century with fifteenth-century ceramic panelling

less important than the contrasts in wealth within the *choria* themselves in defining the levels of greater or lesser resistance. Undoubtedly an act of 1073 best fixed the social pyramid in the village: at the top, the peasant who had two teams of oxen, then a peasant who had just one (the *zeugaratos*, the average peasant able to live off his own means), then came the peasants who had only one ox, and finally the indigent, among whom a few might have a donkey, but most would have had no draught animal at all.

The old communal system, however, which depended on the principle of the *chorion*'s solidarity in the face of taxes, was increasingly ill-adapted to the new economic and demographic conditions. It relied on a situation where the number of people, their need for food and the technical means of obtaining it were balanced, which was no longer the case by the tenth century. The gulf was widening between those farmers who were well provided with labour and were productive, yet lacked sufficient land, and those who, being badly equipped at the start and less productive, had got to the stage where they could not pay even their own share of the taxes. We know that the system of escheatment (*klasma*) with respect to the *chorion* of lands abandoned by such peasants, and their sale by the State, was one of the means by which the powerful (*dynatoi*) increased their estates and eventually dismantled the very fabric of the communes (often done by the traditional large landowners or, more frequently, by the most active members of the *chorion*). Moreover, even if they had not departed, many of the poorer peasants were made to give the usufruct (*chresis*) of their land to their powerful neighbours or to put themselves under their protection (*prostasia*) in return for payment of a rent. Other forms of take-over are not clear from the legal and fiscal texts, which are more interested in types of ownership than in ways of working the land. Thus tenant farming and sharecropping were common for peasants confined to their own land; growing richer again by means of these temporary contracts, they ended up naturally enough acquiring the land that they had made productive. The *chorion* was further weakened by the State's grants (*logisima*) to lay or ecclesiastical landowners; the latter, especially the monasteries, also received many donations from individuals for religious reasons.

Faced with this situation, the State pursued the policy launched by the first Macedonian rulers, but it was clear by the end of the tenth century that it was a lost cause. The principle had always been to protect the *chorion* at any price, but the government could not avoid a serious contradiction: while it decreed severe measures to protect rural communities (the basis of taxation), it could not tolerate the escheated lands (those not belonging to the *chorion* because abandoned) becoming unproductive in fiscal terms – and yet it forbade the powerful to take them over. This explains the installation on these lands of 'public' peasants (*demosiarioi*), who had nothing to do with the *chorion* and who paid their taxes directly to the State. The State thus contributed to the undermining of an institution it wished to save, all the while populating the countryside with isolated peasants who, when its control weakened, did not even have the weapon of solidarity with which to resist the assault of their most powerful neighbours. Such a contradiction is illuminated by the Novel issued by Romanos II in 962. To deal with the specific problem of the small peasants who had to pay back the price of lands illegally purchased from them, but who had not the means to do so, two solutions were put forward: either the land was to be separated from the commune and the two parties would come to an arrangement, or the commune would substitute for the seller and, while waiting for the debt to be paid off, would enjoy possession of the land in question. In both cases, the results could only be disastrous: either the peasant would run off, or the *chorion* would not have the means to make good use of the extra land or, even if it had, it would mean increased financial obligations, involving the extension of fallow land and new problems for the commune.

Keeping faithfully to its policy of never wiping out old structures even while building up new ones, the imperial government did not wish to establish a new general law for the peasantry to replace the moribund commune, so that it unintentionally supported what the powerful were doing, the latter having every opportunity to exploit various titles to land in order to build up increasingly large estates.

Attempts to resist the powerful

While the State was fully aware of the danger, all it could do was to take prohibitory measures aimed at freezing the situation, a role that was always dangerous and even desperate in that it relied on the constant exercise of rigorous control. We have to remember that such measures would have been considered decisive at a time when, the imperial machine having reached perfection, no one could imagine its coming to a standstill. Thus rulers such as Nikephoros Phokas and Basil II took extremely strong measures in order to settle the limits of great estates, secular as well as ecclesiastical. By his Novel of 967, which has long been interpreted – quite wrongly – as being favourable to the powerful, Nikephoros was actually trying to settle things once and for all. Henceforth, the powerful could only acquire from the powerful, and the weak could only buy from the weak; at the same time, this apparent friend of the landed aristocracy brandished an almost unheard-of legal threat against them: anyone 'stirring up trouble amongst the weak' could have even his patrimony confiscated. For his part, Basil II in 996 vigorously reaffirmed Romanos Lekapenos' policy: the powerful could retain only those legally established acquisitions made before the reign of Romanos, and henceforth had no power to invoke any order in favour of fraudulent purchases. Interestingly, the emperor stressed that the peasants were threatened not only by the powerful, strictly speaking, but also by the 'weak who had become powerful', such as Philokales, a real village tyrant, whose buildings he commanded to be razed. As for the powerful ecclesiastics, Nikephoros Phokas referred again to the policy of Lekapenos in his famous Novel of 964. Noting the 'apparent mania for acquisition' which possessed the monasteries, the emperor painted an eloquent picture of the monastic estates, composed of 'innumerable acres of land, extravagant buildings, herds of cattle, oxen, camels, and other beasts in even greater numbers', and strictly forbade any more donations of land which, as the monks lacked the means to work them, would only increase the amount of fallow land. Henceforth, the only gifts allowed were money and labourers, which would enable the often neglected monastic estates to be brought back into cultivation. In 996, Basil II completed this measure by forbidding the monks to add to their possessions the oratories piously founded by farmers at a distance from the community. Finally, around the year 1000, Basil was no longer content with this simple status quo: by the system of *allelengyon* he even struck a blow at the interests acquired by the powerful by making them pay the taxes of defaulting peasants.

At the end of his Novel of 964, Nikephoros Phokas wrote: 'I know perfectly well that, by promulgating these dictates and rules, I would seem to most people to be decreeing unbearable things, and things contrary to their opinions; but this does not concern me because, like Paul, I desire to please not man, but God.' The opposition must have been very strong indeed: Tzimiskes, who had taken power in 969 by assassinating his predecessor, had to agree to revoke temporarily the decisions of 964. After the death of Basil II the secular magnates managed to get the *allelengyon* suppressed by Romanos Argyros. But all this does not mean that the struggle against the powerful had ceased, even if no more legal decisions were taken. Again in 1057–9, Isaac Komnenos confiscated a large amount of monastic property in order to reorganise the army, taking up the fight against these monks who 'were drunk with a rapacity that had reached the level of a passion'. The effort was not sustained, however, and long periods of indifference allowed the great landowners to make fresh progress. This was certainly the case between 1025 and 1056, even more so under the reign of Constantine X Doukas (1059–67) 'beyond all measure the friend of monks', according to Attaleiates. Thus the fragility of a purely repressive policy was proved; postulated as a function of the unchallenged authority of the State, it merely annoyed the powerful without giving the peasants any new defences.

For not only did the country people gradually lose control of a share of the land, but they also found their personal status to be under threat, even if, in the strictly legal sense, the Byzantine peasant would remain a free man right up to the end of the empire. Even the most protected categories, like that of the *stratiotai*, tended towards extinction: from the era of Nikephoros Phokas the *strateia* was permanently altered into a purely fiscal obligation, which could only promote growing confusion between the *stratiotai* and the ordinary peasants, the more so because the *stratiotai* usually owned the stratiotic land as well as land of common right. As this system revealed itself to be increasingly inefficient, Constantine Monomachos (1042–55) finally authorised the *stratiotai* to redeem their obligations by paying a forfeit. As for the *demosiarioi*, their separation from the community made them even more vulnerable: from 974, two of Tzimiskes' acts show that the magnates, hungry for labour to cultivate their expanding estates, did not hesitate to lure them on to their land as *paroikoi*. It is easy to judge what resistance, under these conditions, could be offered by the isolated free peasant, who was no longer protected by the declining commune and who could no longer avail himself of a special link with the State: forced to sell or to abandon his land, crippled by debts to his powerful neighbours or to the *chorion*, he could only look favourably on an offer to come and establish himself on land where he could start afresh. Moreover, the State gave priority to the defence of those directly dependent on it, *stratiotai* but above all the *demosiarioi*: the acts of Tzimiskes referred to, in 974, were promulgated 'to restore the *demosiarioi* to their condition', the monasteries having carried them off and, adopting an act of Constantine VII Porphyrogenitos, a chrysobull of Constantine X in June 1060 again forbade the transformation of '*stratiotai*, *demosiarioi* and *exkoussatoi* ('exempt

217

A chrysobull. This was the name given to official acts to which were added a gold seal (bull) with the emperor's effigy. Here it concerns the grant of a privilege to a monastery on Mount Athos in the eleventh century. (Acts of Lavra I, Mount Athos, January 1057.)

Putting down a boundary line. Faced with the abandonment of land by peasants overburdened with taxes, the State tried to limit its gifts of uncultivated land in order to put a brake on the increasing greed shown by great landowners, both secular and ecclesiastical. (Seraglio Octateuch; Istanbul, Topkapi Museum.)

ones') into *paroikoi*. As for the others – peasants who had become landless and who were henceforth to be called 'free and not liable for the fisc' – even more was to be done to slow down the movement which was sweeping them on to the great estates. Thus in 1044 Monomachos limited to twenty-four the number of *paroikoi* to be procured by the monastery of Nea Mone, on Chios; and in the act of 1060, Constantine Doukas forbade the monks of the Lavra to exceed 100 *paroikoi*. Again in 1079, Nikephoros III Botaneiates permitted the Lavra to have 100 *paroikoi*, provided that they were descended from those that were already in the monastery.

These great estates, particularly the ecclesiastical estates which were growing markedly in terms of land and men after 1025, were trying to obtain other privileges. Until the eleventh century the government would grant them, but they were purely fiscal and remained exceptions. A more dangerous movement appeared under Constantine Monomachos: in 1045, he gave legal exemption to Nea Mone, forbidding the agents of the State access to the monastery's property. In the second half of the century, a grander type of exemption, both fiscal and legal, was given the name *exkousseia*, but again it must be emphasised that this was never an administrative category, and was always considered simply as a privilege. This was the sense of the chrysobull by which Nikephoros III, in 1079, guaranteed to the Athos monastery of Iviron that it would answer only in the duke of Thessalonika's court. In the same period, some of the laity, especially those in the process of installing *paroikoi* on their lands, succeeded in obtaining exemptions, but they were always fewer and smaller than those granted to the monasteries. On the other hand, the laity had another advantage: by the system of *charistike*, under-used church lands or those fallen into disuse could be made over to lay owners to restore, a procedure still favoured by the patriarch Sergios II in 1016. After 1027, however, there were protests against the abuse of *charistike*, and in 1071 a synod reacted against the custom of making over to the laity what were actually productive church lands.

In trying to understand the period around 1070, we should avoid 'catastrophe theories': it must be remembered that the Byzantine peasantry was still composed of free men, except for the slaves, who rarely worked the fields, and that the *paroikoi* enjoyed considerable rights over the disposition of the land they cultivated. In certain respects, to the degree to which the *chorion* disintegrated, the State itself was given means of more direct control over lands and men, in particular thanks to the institution of *demosiarioi*. In general, until the latter half of the eleventh century, this control remained effective, as is shown by the placing of quotas on the numbers of *paroikoi*. But the thirst for land and labour, accentuated by the increasing profitability of agriculture, made inevitable the eventual triumph of the large landowners over a peasantry deprived of its former communal structure, especially as State control was seriously weakening. This was certainly the case after 1040. But such control was already very uneven in the tenth century: in the provinces furthest from the capital, and especially in Anatolia, it was merely theoretical. This explains the indignation with which Basil II, in 996, noted that families such as the Phokas and Maleinos had held illegally acquired property there for a century. Massive confiscations, like those of the Maleinos lands by this same emperor in 1001, were harsh but ultimately ineffective measures. All told, it is certain that the equilibrium of the empire, both economic and social, was being seriously disturbed; and it was the vulnerability of its eastern regions that was the cause for greatest concern.

The invigorated artisan class

In this rural context, the role of the towns is too often misunderstood because it is over-valued. If Byzantine civilisation is indisputably urban, it is also the case that the towns are less important in economic terms than the rural regions.

If we stick to the texts, it would be difficult even to define a specifically urban Byzantine economy. In fact, there is virtually no economic activity that cannot be found in both town and country. Take the case of metallurgy, and especially forges: these were small scale and were scattered almost everywhere, though with obvious concentrations near the metal sources. In the country there were travelling blacksmiths, 'village runners' (*koinodromoi*), who made and repaired ploughing implements. The great estates, secular and ecclesiastical, had such workers: the *Life of Athanasius of Athos* (the founder of Lavra) mentions the existence of a monk-blacksmith. Constantine Porphyrogenitos, too, mentions the making of shields and lances in the themes of Hellas, Nikopolis and the Peloponnese. Textiles, ceramics and glass could also be discussed in this context, but it is clearly impossible to establish the relative importance of town and country in this regard.

Nevertheless, what does seem new in the tenth and eleventh centuries is the obvious emphasis on the manufacturing role of the towns, which were beginning to show signs of product specialisation. Archaeology shows that this period saw the high point of the metallurgical industry in Corinth, where production was very diversified: ploughing implements, maritime equipment (such as anchors), ironwork (iron and bronze keys), weaponry (daggers, lance-tips dated to the mid-eleventh century), and also a range of remarkably delicate surgical instruments. From the same period, Cherson in the Crimea has yielded up a rich collection of crucibles which permitted the casting of clamps, nails, bolts, picks, billhooks, fish-hooks, needles and cooking-pots. It was no doubt the same in Pergamon, which specialised in producing iron arrow-tips, even though the dating of the strata is less certain there. In this context, as in so many others, it is annoying not to be able to talk about Constantinople, where any serious archaeological work is impossible and where, as we know, security regulations forbade the exercise of any trades involving fire within the city walls. It is possible that there was metallurgical industry in the outlying districts. We know in any case that there were locksmiths in Constantinople because in 969 Tzimiskes went to them in order to get wax imprints of the keys to Nikephoros Phokas' chamber, and the capital was obviously the largest centre for goldsmiths in the empire. Metal-working reached a peak in the eleventh century, when the technique of cloisonné enamelling was perfected, as shown by the pieces kept in St Mark's Treasury in Venice and by the Holy Crown of Hungary, which dates from the reign of Michael VII.

A similar concentration is seen with regard to ceramics. The attractive production of fine clay, both polychrome and varnished, reached its peak in Constantinople in the tenth

This magnificent piece of silver work is an eleventh-century reliquary, reproducing the octagonal form of the original sanctuary of St Demetrios at Thessalonica. (Moscow, Kremlin, Armourers' Museum.)

century and then expanded throughout the empire, from Preslav as far as Athens and Corinth, without its ever displacing the coarse, reddish-brown, common pottery (used especially in cooking) which we know well from Corinth but which must have been made everywhere. In the middle of the tenth century, however, there was a new development: while Constantinople-style production became more common, Corinth began to make finer pottery, with a white clay base and decorated with modelled reliefs. Similar progress was made in Athens and Sparta, while Thessalonica became the main centre of red-clay ceramics, which continued to predominate. In the twelfth century, pottery production in Constantinople declined to such an extent that it began to import more and more pottery from the provinces.

The textile industry, which in Byzantium – as throughout the medieval world – was of fundamental importance, underwent an important change in the eleventh century with the arrival of cotton. Especially in Dalmatia and the Peloponnese, cotton was now added to **221** materials known since ancient times (wool, linen and silk). Even if much of the material was produced in the home, the towns had become true centres of industry. In both the imperial and private workshops of Constantinople, as also in Greece (Sparta and Corinth, and particularly in Thebes), silk was the most commonly worked textile. The development of dyeing, which Eustathios Romaios in the eleventh century considered as a separate craft, was often the province of Jews, as was the case in Corinth, where an epitaph for a dyer called Elias has been discovered.

Such facts suggest that urban development was stronger in Europe than in Asia Minor, even taking into account the smaller body of evidence for the latter. In this period, the facts show that the decisive impetus occurred between 960 and 1070, and that production, which is a sure indicator, is actually a consequence rather than a cause of urban development. In fact, as we shall see, the Byzantine town always remained primarily a place of exchange, which was one of its main weaknesses; it should also be noted that Byzantium's regained mastery of the seas was one of the principal sources of its urban growth. This increased importance of the sea certainly played a major part in the relocation of the heart of the Byzantine world around the Aegean basin; at the same time the old caravan traffic, focused on Anatolia, did not seem likely to revive, except along the Armenian axis once the Turkish invasions had stopped. It was certainly not only for reasons of greater proximity that merchants from Italy (Amalfi and Venice) in the tenth and eleventh centuries headed towards Constantinople and the Greek ports of Thessaly and Epiros.

The static town

Even so, this urban revolution in no way revolutionised the structures of the empire. The urban fabric remained remarkably stable. A number of factors, primarily the displacement of certain commercial and strategic axes, may explain the disappearance of old towns and the development of new centres, but neither of these events were common. For example, Philippi in Macedonia fell into decline after 965 when Nikephoros Phokas fortified the town for the last time, while in Albania the town of Deabolis grew up on the new Macedonian route, as the old Via Egnatia slowly fell out of use. Yet, in general, the distribution of urban centres was much the same as in the fifth century. We may note, however, that this period was characterised by a change in the relative importance of towns; of course, it is impossible to say whether the reform of the theme system was the cause or the consequence of this change, but it certainly accompanied both urban expansion and decline. In particular, the breaking up of large themes might lessen the importance of their former capitals, while other centres, even old ones, which had long been lying in their shadow, might take on new life and perhaps even overtake them. This redistribution of urban functions occurred throughout the empire but, although the catastrophe of 1071 brought it to a standstill in Asia Minor, it continued in Europe up to the end of the twelfth century.

Such general stability was accentuated by the usually modest size of Byzantine towns. Indeed, the rising demographic curve should not obscure the fact that the empire had only one very large town, Constantinople, and also that it seems certain that even in the eleventh century the capital never had more than 400,000 inhabitants. Moreover, towns like Thessalonica or Melitene, which may have had over 60,000 inhabitants, were regarded as very large centres, and a few thousand inhabitants were enough to give the name of town to a place that we would consider a large village. Although the absence of epidemics meant that towns could rely on a degree of natural growth, and although there was undoubtedly an exodus from the countryside, the concurrent existence of a large number of urban centres must explain the generally modest scale of their individual growth. Nevertheless, this modest scale is an indication of great strength, in that it is a sign of harmonious relations between town and country at a time when, in the neighbouring Muslim world, the development of enormous metropolises meant the extinction of other towns and rural areas. Naturally there were some changes in the relationship between town and country. The renewed security of the ninth century had encouraged the great landed proprietors to establish residences in town, while remaining in close contact with their estates. With their inhabitants living mainly off the land's resources within the walls and surrounded by an upper class that was deeply rural, it can be argued that Byzantine towns were formed by the countryside rather than dominating it. In the tenth and eleventh centuries there was certainly a reverse movement: while the old aristocracy had definitely acquired an urban mentality which was confirmed by the exercise of state functions, a new social stratum – which owed everything to the State and at first had nothing to do with the land – was developing in the capital and in the provinces. These two elements, which the pattern of alliances and social complicity had brought together by the eleventh century, were henceforth the principal means by which the town sought to dominate the rural areas. However, for a while at least, the multiplicity of urban centres especially in Europe and around the Aegean prevented this imbalance from worsening because each town's area of influence was necessarily very narrow. The looser distribution of Anatolian towns, however, allowed them to dominate larger districts, whence came the possibility of building up greater estates.

Nevertheless, Byzantine towns continued to be merely points of local administration for a centralised body, either lay or ecclesiastical; they were not the seats of any autonomous institution which could evolve within the community or be taken over by the most powerful citizens. The exercise of state functions did give considerable social standing to some people, but they were so varied and they overlapped so much, especially after the re-establishment of a balance in favour of civilian offices, that no single figure could assure himself of a position of hegemony in an urban centre. Nevertheless, landed wealth and offices enabled men to acquire various clients hoping above all for protection (*prostasia*) against the taxation burden imposed by the State, which became increasingly heavy, especially at the beginning of the reign of Constantine X who generalised the system of consolidated taxes. Around the local worthies (this is roughly the sense of the word *archontes*) there were groups of 'servants' (*hyperetai*) whom the powerful referred to as their 'followers', and who gave them, according to Kekaumenos, great 'influence over the people of the province'. The authority of the State was certainly never in doubt, but rather than being exercised directly over the whole population it was increasingly being filtered through these groups. Given the growing inability of the centre to ensure administration and security, there was a great risk of these groups' becoming self-defence organisations, and independent ones at that.

The seed of such evolution lay in the urban fabric itself: by indulging in private foundations which had become numerous by the eleventh century (and around which neighbourhoods grew up with shops, workshops, hospitals, places to live, often all exempt from taxation) the churches and the rich robbed the towns of all that remained of their ancient unity and transformed them into bodies with many centres, each with a different status and corresponding to a grouping of clients, which made the overall administration of the town extremely difficult. Of course this evolution, supported by the growth of population, contributed to the reconquest of urban areas often abandoned since late Antiquity. Thus the agora at Corinth was reoccupied between the ninth and twelfth centuries by a group of chapels and monasteries which attracted housing and workshops. But how could it escape notice that these nodes of habitation, acting as fixed points for landed inheritance and made so attractive by the frequent presence of institutions offering assistance, were in danger of making it impossible for the State to master the urban areas, just at the time when it was losing control of the countryside?

Around 1070, the domination of the aristocracy over the towns was not inevitable – just as the failure of a nascent merchant class also did not appear inevitable. But, here again, everything could break up if the State's capacity to intervene was decisively weakened.

Gold circulation and government loans

Little attention has been paid to 'tertiary' activities in Byzantium. The uncritical use of literary sources, emanating almost always from the upper classes and the Church, have led to a general image of a society in which, save for work on the land and the exercise of Church or State offices, no one could gain money without dirtying his hands. Of course, it is good form to despise 'trade', and a Psellos in the eleventh century haughtily abused those whom he called 'the people of the agora'. A little later, Kekaumenos went so far as to advise absolutely against lending money with a view to commercial investment, emphasising that it was a good way of making enemies out of friends and that, moreover, there was a strong chance of not getting the money back. Nevertheless, beyond these matters of principle, the legitimacy of work and its just rewards were hardly in doubt. The *Book of the Eparch* had already forbidden certain owners to bind their workers by excessively long-term contracts, which would prevent their finding better employment, and recognised the right of workers who found themselves unemployed to break their contract. Psellos himself, in his *Life* of Saint Auxentios, portrayed some workers who 'having been laid off work, had shut up their workshops', a thing so scandalous in itself that the saint busied himself with finding work for them again. As for the mother of Anna Komnena, the Empress Irene Doukaina, she advised the poor to go out and look for work, instead of 'going around, begging from door to door'.

Commerce, however, was not a job like others because in a superficial sense it consisted simply in making money from money, often leading to confusion with usury, which the Christian religion flatly condemned. We note that, in practice, lending at interest must have been widespread: Kekaumenos would not have advised against it so insistently had it not been a common, even a much sought-after, activity. Besides, it was authorised by the law itself. The Code of Justinian, whose measures here do not seem to have been repealed, fixed the tax on interest at 4 per cent for the 'illustrious', at 6 per cent for the ordinary citizen, at 8 per cent for the merchants, and at 12 per cent for maritime loan contracts (which were particularly risky). These investments are illustrated in the eleventh century by the treatise on jurisprudence written by an anonymous student of the judge Eustathios Romaios, the *Peira*, which shows that ready money was not only invested in land but was often put into buildings (houses, shops, workshops), into trade, and into maritime ventures which, in return for high risk, gave very high returns. It was such a common activity that the State itself, by the sale of offices and honours, encouraged for its own profit the investment of private capital. Indeed all dignities and offices could be bought, in return for sums proportional to their importance, and their possession gave the right to an annuity (*roga*) for life, again proportional to the investment. The *Peira* informs us that the normal rate on investment was 6 *nomismata* per one pound (equal to 72 *nomismata*) of capital, i.e. 8.33 per cent, but the future rentier could always invest a larger sum than necessary for his costs, which would allow him to obtain a higher annuity, the extra capital bearing higher interest: one pound could thus return up to 7 *nomismata*, i.e. 9.72 per cent. Beyond the honorific aspect of titles, behind the often theoretical exercise of functions that were sometimes imaginary in any case, the institution of the *roga* demonstrates the existence of a particularly attractive form of genuine government stock; in order to draw on private capital it appealed as much to the thirst for vainglory as to the desire to put money in the most secure place. Certainly the powerful eleventh-century empire could give all the assurances desired in this respect. It was, moreover, this security factor that enabled the State to draw on savings while only agreeing to relatively modest interest rates; between private persons there must have been higher rates, but the greater risks of those transactions may have led many to prefer the 'gilt-edged investments' which the State annuities provided. In any case, ignorance of the system's workings prevents our fully comprehending the wealth of a treasury which, despite decades of continual war, could be valued on the death of Basil II in 1025 at the enormous sum of £200,000 of gold. It is nonetheless evident that, as everything rested on the confidence of the investors, the whole construction could collapse if the fate of the empire was in doubt.

The existence of what we may call State stock, and the avidity with which it was acquired, proves anyway that there was abundant capital and that money was circulating. It seems that hoarding money was never less popular than in the eleventh century. Some texts, particularly saints' *Lives*, also show that currency was in circulation in distant provinces, that peasants could be paid in money on the completion of some jobs (haulage, building works), that their wives did spinning and weaving to add to the household resources, and above all that produce from the country was exchanged either for money or for manufactured goods in the town markets. In the countryside itself, the existence of rural fairs shows that the peasants participated in some commercial activities. Moreover, Kekaumenos advised local officials to organise these fairs well away from towns, and Anna

Comnena mentions them, at the end of the century, in the vicinity of Dyrrachion and Avlona. Monasteries must have been chosen as the sites for markets where a crowd of pilgrims might gather: this was the case at the monastery of Bachkovo in Bulgaria, at the end of the eleventh century. These fairs were not only a meeting-place for small local producers, but also for traders 'from all regions' in search of the best prices, occasionally carrying considerable sums (up to 1,000 *nomismata*). This was true of those merchants who, according to the *Book of the Eparch*, penetrated deep into Asia Minor in order to buy livestock. As for the big urban fairs, like those in Ephesos and especially in Thessalonica, not only did they swarm with Greek merchants from all the provinces of the empire – from the south of the Peloponnese (Monemvasia) to eastern Anatolia (Cilicia) – but they also attracted a crowd of foreign traders. In the Christian world of the twelfth century, they were clearly the only fairs on an international scale. This whole hierarchy of markets thus shows that an exchange economy irrigated the entire empire (with important local variations of course), and that this internal circulation, far from being turned in upon itself, was relatively well connected to the international market, whether through the fairs or through the strategic position of Constantinople. By according internal trade its rightful place, we are able to correct the traditional picture of an empire whose main commercial activities were confined to international trade.

The spectre of depreciation

The monetary history of the tenth and eleventh centuries confirms this remarkable flowering of trade. Until recently, however, it was generally maintained that there was a grave crisis which had begun under Nikephoros Phokas, worsened in the 1040s and then became quite catastrophic in the second half of the eleventh century. Within a hundred years, Byzantine currency, until then the standard for the Mediterranean world, had lost both weight and alloy, thus demonstrating the increasingly severe difficulties faced by the treasury. This is the outline which now requires a thorough examination.

John Skylitzes and John Zonaras recount how Nikephoros Phokas had introduced a new, lighter currency – the *tetarteron* – which was to replace the *nomisma*. This innovation, they suggest, ended in an organised racket because the emperor, while making state payments in the lighter currency, continued to demand tax settlements in the heavier currency. In fact, it now appears that this had nothing to do with establishing dual circulation of gold pieces. Nikephoros was really aiming at the complete replacement of the old *nomismata* (*hexagia*, *histamena*) by the new, whose gold content was, moreover, only slightly less (22 carats instead of 24). Such reform was undertaken in a specific international context: as trade grew, the overweighted *nomisma*, especially in relation to the dinar, consequently increased the price of Byzantine goods to an unacceptable level; thus it was not by chance that Phokas' reform created a currency comparable in weight to the Fatimid dinar. But it was primarily concern over the internal market that would have inspired the emperor: confronted with a great increase in trade at a time when the resources of the empire's mines scarcely compensated for losses through lending and when, in this open economy, gains on

A gold *tetarteron* and a copper *follis* of John I Tzimiskes (969–76). The former was made slightly after the monetary reform undertaken by Nikephoros Phokas and weighs no more than 4 g instead of 4.46 g. The *follis*, from the same period, still bears traces of previous mintings. (Paris, Bibliothèque nationale, Coin Room.)

the foreign market no longer outstripped the flight across the frontier of over-valued cash, the whole system was in danger of seizing up for lack of precious metals. Of course gold was not in itself commercial, but in this bi-metallic system, where each *nomisma* was worth twelve silver *miliaresia*, it was the number of gold pieces which came to determine the number of silver pieces, which in their turn were the basis of internal and external transactions. In consequence, to produce lighter gold pieces while preserving their nominal value was equivalent to considerably increasing circulation without adding to the mass of gold minted; this must, in the medium term, facilitate trade. Unfortunately, Phokas' reform was either not understood or sabotaged: instead of exchanging currency, people hoarded the old coins, which led to a slowing down of commercial activity, a shortage of merchandise, a rise in domestic prices and general discontent that was certainly not unconnected with the abrupt fall of the emperor in 969.

This failed reform also had long-lasting negative effects; Phokas' successors let the circulation of both *nomismata* and *tetartera* continue, and from the beginning of the eleventh century these were thought of as a debased currency, which allowed all sorts of combinations and privileges. For example, from the reign of Romanos Argyros, the Athonite monastery of Iviron managed to pay its taxes half in *histamena*, half in *tetartera*. Thus, all the ills which the reform was supposed to have cured continued to exist: a shortage of coins, high living costs, inadequate competition, and the exodus of gold – to which was now added the disarray on the money market.

These difficulties explain the new monetary policy put into action in the 1040s under Constantine IX Monomachos. This time it had nothing to do with the weight of the coinage; the precious metal content was to be progressively decreased. Of course this was not entirely new: some coins under Basil II had their content reduced to 87 per cent gold, but henceforth it was a steady and systematic process. By the end of Monomachos' reign, the gold content was of the order of 81 per cent. Furthermore, as the alloy consisted principally of gold, there was a growing tendency to add copper: thus some *tetartera* had no more than 72 per cent gold, the rest being made up of 24 per cent silver and 4 per cent copper. Finally, this depreciation in gold was accompanied by a more gradual depreciation of silver, no doubt intended to maintain the relation between the two metals, and also to restrain the flood of silver abroad, especially to the Muslim world where the silver deficit had become endemic in the tenth century.

It must be emphasised, however, that this depreciation did not correspond to a Treasury crisis, which is not really evident until after 1070, under Michael VII and especially under Nikephoros III Botaneiates (1078–81). The mass of coins in circulation seems to have remained stable, prices did not rise enormously and the rate of circulation was not much modified. It is therefore difficult to explain the loss of 20 per cent in the weight of gold except by an increase in the volume of transactions averaging 0.5 per cent per annum. This is demonstrated by the production and growing circulation of small change, *follis*; we note that not only was its circulation in Corinth ten times greater in the eleventh century than in the ninth, but also that the demand for *follis* preceded the depreciation of gold – which clearly proves that basic commercial activity had provoked a growing need for gold, and had thus engendered the devaluation. It is thus apparent that devaluation, far from being a sign of crisis, instead reflects prosperity and expansion to which the currency was adapted and which it then helped to sustain. Confronted by market expansion, a desire to maintain the silver and gold content could only have accentuated the scarcity of coins and, consequently, curbed economic prosperity. These findings allow us to challenge some commonplaces: far from displaying an Olympian disdain for contingencies, the Byzantine State was able to show remarkable pragmatism in reacting to changes it was well equipped to detect.

Moreover, Byzantium was not a closed world, and its economic evolution was chiefly played out against the background of Mediterranean history; it devalued at the moment when, for similar reasons, the north Italian denier and Muslim coinage were also depreciating.

Commerce and the 'nouveaux riches'

We can thus be certain that trade expanded between 950 and 1060 – which makes it all the more annoying not to be able to identify those who were responsible: the merchants and the entrepeneurs. Of course it is possible to argue that we hear so little about them because they form a developing class, dynamic and even aggressive, whose expansion could only be to the detriment of the old ruling class, whose power-base was the indissoluble link between landed fortune and remunerative offices. It is the members of this latter class, however, who dominate the culture and who have thus passed down to us almost all the written texts of this period. Apart from recriminations, one can expect nothing from them that would give us clues as to the social composition and the stage of development of those who were seriously encroaching on their privileges.

Still, even this invective allows us to grasp the nature of the new means of advancement. Looking back over the career of Emperor Michael V's father, Psellos tells us that this Anatolian peasant, after having worked as a caulker, had become a naval entrepreneur, which shows how very profitable maritime traffic could be. As for Kekaumenos, the very vigour with which he advises against becoming a tax-farmer indicates that this was a common means of getting rich. In general, it was trade in all its forms that engendered this new class, which was probably a very diverse one with many members. Its strength is attested by the importance given to notaries, who were specifically in charge of drawing up and validating everything to do with monetary business. The notaries were carefully watched over by the State, their services had tariffs, there were special schools to train them, and they were given honours – all this is further proof of the care taken to assure subjects of the proper management of their financial interests.

It was natural that this new class aspired to a place in the State machinery currently monopolised by the old ruling class. In Leo VI's reign, an old cantor from St Sophia somehow became rich enough to buy for sixty pounds the post of *protospatharios*. Obviously the system of venal offices and government bonds could only favour the integration of the *nouveaux riches* into the apparatus of power itself and consequently into the most privileged group, the senatorial class. According to the *Peira*, the office of *protospatharios* was precisely the starting-point of a senatorial career. It is hard to see how the State could have refused the money of the *nouveaux riches*, who simply asked to put it into its hands. It is thus to be expected that, from the tenth century onwards, a certain 'bourgeois' element began to infiltrate the civil service. In the next century this became the basic path to advancement and these infiltrators pushed so hard towards the top that it became impossible to preserve the exclusiveness of the senatorial class. Even before 1040 it is very likely that the bourgeois were already a part of the civil service; when Psellos congratulated Michael IV on not having impoverished some senators in order to replace them with others, he was denouncing both current and ancient practice, which must have allowed the bourgeois occasionally to achieve this ultimate promotion. It was Constantine Monomachos (1042–55) who was to give solid form to what might be considered a social and political revolution: he opened up the Senate to the group of merchants' sons and provincial *petits-bourgeois* who, as civil servants, henceforth made up the bourgeoisie of Constantinople. This is what Psellos meant when he said that 'he opened the Senate to almost all the riff-raff and vagabonds of the market'. Psellos unconciously stresses that this gesture had been eagerly expected by the bourgeoisie as an act of simple justice when he confesses that, after this advance, 'the entire capital rejoiced that such a liberal prince should be at the head of affairs'.

Given this background, we are now in a better position to attempt to understand the struggles for power that characterise the second half of the century. The conflict was not between the so-called civil and military nobility, whose interests were closely linked within the old senatorial class, but rather between those whom Psellos called the 'civil body' (*politikon genos*) and the old senatorial class (*synkletikos genos*), supported by their military allies (*stratiotikon genos*). In the scheme laid down by Monomachos, however, power increasingly devolved to the new class. Under Michael VI Stratiotikos (1056–7), himself an aged patrician, the high officials were recruited from the bureaucracy – that is, from among the bourgeois of Constantinople. The *coup d'état* which brought the general Isaac Komnenos to power in 1057 was a desperate reaction on the part of the old ruling class; when the new basileus undertook to wipe out the work of his predecessors, Psellos clearly shows that this immediately and irrevocably alienated the 'mass of the people' (*demotikon plethos*). Isaac's fall in 1059 reinstated the bourgeoisie. Again, it is Psellos who emphasises that 'the mass of the people inclined towards' Constantine X Doukas, who then succeeded to the throne and took his predecessors' work to its logical conclusion, achieving the integration of the

229

bourgeoisie into the hierarchy of honours and offices, and breaking down the barrier which still separated the 'people' from the old senatorial class: he 'transformed separation into amalgamation'. This integration of the bourgeoisie with the State had some influence on the financial successes of the reign, which saw a new prosperity for the Treasury. And if this policy, steadily pursued until 1081, foundered under renewed attack from the military, it must be said that the domination of 'bourgeois businessmen', not very aware of the problems of defence, was partially responsible; this peaceful mode of rule, vital for business expansion, presupposed that the empire's frontiers would remain uncontested – but the Turkish invasion changed all this after 1067. The external catastrophe, however, showed how solid was the new socio-political system. A military emperor, Romanos IV Diogenes, came to the throne in 1068, but he did not envisage changing the political system, even to support a war, as Isaac Komnenos had attempted to do in 1057. His fall in 1071 was not merely a consequence of his military defeat; it was the result of a coalition of civilian interests which was to remain dominant until 1081, even under the emperor from the highest nobility, Nikephoros Botaneiates. It remained for the dynasty of the Komnenoi to grasp that a genuine policy of defence required fundamental modification of the administrative and social structure.

The analysis of foreign trade illustrates clearly how business became fundamentally important. By the tenth century the customs system, both internal and external, had been perfected and was staffed by state officers (the *kommerkiarioi*, whose ubiquitous presence is revealed by the seals they have left behind) responsible for levying customs duty *(kommerkion)* throughout the territories and along the frontiers of the empire. Firmly situated at the crossroads of the great trade routes which converged on its straits, the empire proved for more than a century that it had the means to control and regulate business. Economic interests played a growing part in treaties drawn up with foreigners: in 960, the accord with the emirate of Aleppo made detailed provision for the Greek merchant traffic which centred on Antioch. As for the treaties with the Russians, especially that of 971, they minutely regulated traffic with Constantinople; numerous Russian attacks on the city up to 1043 show how firmly the empire kept hold of the key to the straits. The crisis of 1043 is also very significant in that it originated in a brawl between Greeks and Russian merchants in Constantinople, during which a merchant from Novgorod was killed.

Byzantium also knew how to force recognition on its western flank. The traffic in its Italian ports, especially at Bari, was far from negligible: subjects of the empire until 1071, the merchants of Apulia travelled to Constantinople and beyond, as far as Asia Minor. Moreover, the chief Italian maritime republics, Amalfi and Venice, were officially subject to the empire, and until the end of the tenth century their colonies were subject to the same customs regulations as other merchants in the empire. The customs officials, sure of their strength, had never let them off lightly in any case: before 992, the Venetians, between entering and leaving, had paid up to thirty *nomismata* for each ship-load. At that date, Venice obtained its first privilege from Basil II, which set the entry tax at two *nomismata* and the exit tax at fifteen. This provided the base for its future expansion, but the taxes were still high enough to prevent the West from entirely dominating the Byzantine market. Of course

A school of philosophy. The eleventh century saw the opening of a number of such schools, in the provinces as well as in Constantinople. The imperial government left them for too long in the hands of private foundations and, without a coherent strategy, teaching remained traditional and reserved for a small élite.

it was disturbing to see so many foreigners flooding into the empire while the Byzantine merchants seemed rarely to step across the frontiers. In fact, this was not surprising: just as it had created a foreign policy of equilibrium and set in motion an internal socio-political revolution, the concept of an empire absolutely in control of its destiny, confirmed by the general prosperity, encouraged the Greek merchant class to wait for its clients, rather than to go out to solicit them. Master of the main trade routes in the north and east, the empire was in a position of quasi-monopoly. From its point of view, it was already a great privilege for the foreigners to be allowed to come in and spend their money in its markets. This passive mentality, however, became very dangerous the moment the empire no longer held all the keys to major commerce. No doubt it is wrong to claim that trading prosperity did not give rise to a true commercial spirit in Byzantium. It would be more accurate to say that, contrary to what is commonly thought, it was the traffic inside the empire that took precedence over international trade. It gave rise to a merchant class which, although dynamic, had a limited viewpoint and could not measure up either temperamentally or technically (Byzantium never had a proper banking system) to the Italian traders, whose entrepreneurial skills were of a different order.

The final glow of the ancient world

With regard to the reign of Basil II, Psellos admits that he is puzzled. The emperor, he writes, 'pays no attention to the scholars; in fact these same men, I mean the scholars, he holds in absolute contempt: it has amazed me that, with the emperor so contemptuous of the culture of letters, there should have been in this age such a flowering of philosophers and orators'. At the beginning of the twelfth century, Anna Comnena also highlights this apparently insoluble paradox.

231

An attempt at acculturation

We must guard against a tendency to over-estimate Byzantine culture. Superior as it was to that of the West in this period, it was nonetheless restricted to a relatively thin layer of society. The average education, such as it appears around the mid-tenth century, was traditionally private and paid for, which could only be directed at a certain social élite, consisting principally of the offspring of the officers and dignitaries of the court and the Church; moreover, this kind of school was mainly found in the capital and was often completely lacking in the provinces. Around 940, Abraamios, the future St Athanasios of Athos, had to leave Trebizond in order to be educated in Constantinople. Even if they seem too low, the suggested figures for the population at school in Constantinople – 200 to 300 pupils around 920–30 – give the impression that very few people would have progressed beyond a rudimentary education. Towards the middle of the century, however, the number of schools certainly increased under the reign of Constantine Porphyrogenitos, and the State, taking note of this new phenomenon, felt the need to establish some control over them. Of course the schools remained private institutions, but we see the appearance of the office of 'supervisor of the schools', apparently a position given disciplinary powers, while imperial consent again seems to have been required for all new teaching. Such a development is easily explained. At a time when the bureaucracy became the chief means of advancement, the schools were the breeding-ground for the future officers of the State, and it was natural that it would keep a close watch on the nature of their education.

There is almost no information available about schools in the second half of the tenth century. At the beginning of the following century, we note that their number increased appreciably and that the provinces seem to be better provided for. But, contrary to what we might have supposed, state control has noticeably relaxed. The schools of Constantinople, about which most is known, were a heterogeneous group, still private and fee-paying, but of widely varying types: St Paul's school was a State foundation, financed by the State, but the schoolmasters of St Peter and the Diaconissa were appointed by the patriarch. Moreover, the schools were very far from achieving uniform standards: while St Peter's school gave its pupils schooling up to university level, most of them did not go any further than teaching rhetoric and philosophy, and some did not even progress beyond lessons in writing and grammar. We should also note the disquieting fact that St Peter's, the most prestigious school, was greatly dependent on the Church, which suggests that the State did not show much interest in education.

This lack of interest was also shown at the level we would call 'higher' or 'tertiary' education. Constantine Porphyrogenitos himself attempted to dust off a university that had fallen asleep at the beginning of the tenth century. But this advanced education in philosophy, rhetoric, geometry and astronomy smacked more of a palace coterie than a university, and soon fell back into such obscurity that it disappears from view in the second half of the century. When Matthew of Edessa, a rather unreliable source, writes about 'the philosophers and scholars of Constantinople' under the reign of Tzimiskes, we cannot be sure that he was alluding to public higher education. In fact, as we have already seen in the example of St Peter's school, it is very likely that it was in these private institutions that the cultivated men of the eleventh century had their schooling. This kind of school could be opened freely, and this was what the future bishop of Euchaita, John Mauropous, did in 1028. One of the most learned men of his time, with several masters (*didaskaloi*) under his orders, he dispensed a mainly oral education aimed at advanced students who had often already entered the public service and who themselves could help to teach the beginners. This was what Psellos did, undoubtedly the most brilliant pupil of a school that produced several other great names of the period: Constantine Leichoudes, John Xiphilinos and Niketas of Byzantium. We can believe Psellos when he says, in his funeral elegy for the patriarch John Xiphilinos, that his time had known orators, jurists and philosophers, but lacked an audience and a leader. We have seen how disorganised higher education was, but also that it affected merely a 'happy few', most of the students going no further than secondary education and having been little encouraged to progress further because, if we are to believe Psellos, the rulers had no interest in recruiting people with a 'complete culture' who were consequently less easy to manage.

The 'reform' attributed to Constantine Monomachos should thus be seen in proper perspective. The most recent research indicates that Monomachos did not create the advanced school of philosophy of which Psellos must have been the chief ornament. The title of 'Consul of the Philosophers' which he bore from the 1050s to around 1075 gave him a vague right to survey the existing schools of philosophy, but it is likely that this was a purely personal honour. As for the history of the law school under Monomachos, that is more interesting as it represents a failure. In the tenth and the early eleventh centuries, legal knowledge was entirely dependent on the corps of notaries, who had absolute control over the schools where it was taught; we do not even know whether the teachers, appointed by the notaries, were still confirmed by the eparch of Contantinople. In any case, the State had no means of controlling either the content or the level of teaching of those who increasingly made up its ranks, namely the sons of the Constantinople bourgeoisie. This was not an acceptable situation and the emperor wanted to answer it with his Novel, probably promulgated in 1047. Henceforth, a 'guard of the law' (*nomophylax*), in the first place John Xiphilinos, was in charge of teaching the law and supervising studies; pupils were to have a theoretical and practical knowledge of the law, but also to learn Greek and Latin and be initiated into other disciplines, in order to prevent lawyers from falling into 'pure sophistry'. Henceforth notaries had to undertake this course, and the *nomophylax* had to certify, when they entered college, their legal and literary capacities: whoever contravened this regulation was dismissed forthwith. The reform was thus intended to regain control over the legal professions which were most deeply involved in running the State. This is why the emperor promised the students of the new school that they would be put at the head of the imperial provinces where, as we know, civilian offices began to take on a new lustre. But this reform was bound to be defeated: not only was the *nomophylax* the only teacher in what it is difficult to call a faculty, but the texts have left us no significant clues as to his activities, no doubt because he soon came up against the opposition of established lawyers and notaries to whom learning, in this period of economic expansion, counted less than efficiency and experience.   **233**

A State cannot be so uninterested in teaching that it can entrust it to others with complete confidence. It should be remembered that private schools in Byzantium were traditionally secular and did not provide religious instruction. This meant that, at least until the middle of the eleventh century, the emperor had no fears that the Church – whose field of action was jealously restricted by Byzantine policy – could influence the nature of the knowledge inculcated in the State's agents, or even their concept of power, at least in the short term. In the future, however, the danger was greater. From the tenth century onwards a number of ecclesiastical dignitaries took schools under their protection and subsidised them, and we know that, in the eleventh century, St Peter's, the main school in Constantinople, very much depended on the patriarch. Of course the risk of the clericalisation of culture and administration was still slight, as the growth of the middle class left the clergy scant room for manoeuvre, but any loss of energy on the part of the new ruling class could give the clergy a means of infiltrating the machinery of State and establishing a different set of ideas.

Furthermore, it is impossible to understand the part played by the private schools without keeping in mind the achievements of the encyclopaedism of the tenth century. The work of Constantine Porphyrogenitos had already resulted in bringing within everyone's range a series of 'practical' compilations upon which the average intelligent and cultivated man could rely for building up a course to a sufficiently advanced level. The existence of such a series would certainly explain the increase in schools at the turn of the century, in which industrious schoolmasters without specific qualifications could henceforth elaborate knowledge that was easily accessible. Still, these compilations remained large and rather unmanageable. In the eleventh century, however, things changed when it was realised that all the knowledge judged to be neccessary might as well be combined in one enormous manual, where it would be arranged in alphabetical order: this was the *Souda*, the 'compilation of compilations', in which the dictionary order offered definitions as well as grammatical details and biographical information. From then on, provided one knew how to read and speak, one could act as a teacher armed only with this lexicon, which represented a basic culture – suitable for shopkeepers and office employees alike.

The state and the public both got something out of this sort of teaching, which the private schools must have discharged with sufficient competence to make state intervention unnecessary. The majority of parents and pupils no longer asked for anything more. Psellos, who was probably a master at St Peter's school, says that most of his pupils were only interested in the subjects that they needed for their careers. Moreover, except for a very basic introduction to the scientific *quadrivium*, this meant an essentially literary education, based on orthography, grammar, law and above all rhetoric – in short, a scribe's training. The best expression of this desiccated culture is *schedographia*, a purely technical exercise which consisted of enlarging on a certain number of oratorical themes (*topoi*) while trying to use the maximum number of known words. The initiation of *schedographia* competitions between various schools in the capital, and the appearance of manuals for teaching it shows that ability in this 'science' was vital to getting on in the world. We might, along with Psellos – who nevertheless taught it to his beginners – despise such a meaningless skill, but we should not overlook its positive aspects; not only did this 'new rhetoric' help to improve the written language, which reached a high standard by the end of the eleventh century, but this second-rate culture reached large areas of the population. To be capable of reading well, writing well, expressing complex ideas in a perfectly clear manner – all this is as essential to good administration (whose directives then had a better chance of being correctly handed on and understood from the offices in the capital to the humblest executors) as it is to shopkeepers and those who handle money or goods, for whom clarity and precision are in themselves guarantees of a sound contract. These distinctive tools, forged in the eleventh century, gave Byzantine administration an undeniable efficiency, even when its central power began to falter. As they became more common, these skills also enabled the bourgeoisie to swell the ranks of the administration and manage its affairs better.

In the tenth century, when learning was less widespread but of a higher quality, the very scarcity of educated men meant that almost no one took a disinterested view of acquiring knowledge; the State, which badly needed them, almost automatically advanced such men. In the following century, when there was a large pool of basically skilled people, it was only personal inclination that drove certain people to pursue a much higher level of learning. This élite, whose members may once have been poor (as was true of Mauropous and Psellos), was able to launch itself into the deeper waters of its ancient culture in a manner that was totally unlike the preceding century, as soon as its income was assured (generally through some state employment). This explains the return of genuine classical philosophy, above all of Platonism, which Photios had made compatible with Christianity at the cost of sacrificing its deepest meaning. Psellos came to a genuine understanding of the spirit of classical philosophy even though he remained a genuine, sincere Christian and even though he would have tended to see Plato from the perspective of Neoplatonists such as Plotinus, Porphyrys Iamblichos and especially Proklos. But once this was achieved, there was a danger of a new awareness of the incompatibility of the latter with Christian doctrine. Thus a crisis loomed just at the moment when the church was defining an increasingly specific doctrine for its members. In the mid-eleventh century, for the first time in Byzantium, a true church education was organised, based on the 'Three Teachers' (the Psalter, the Apostle, the Gospel), which only admitted as philosophy those of Aristotle's books that were compatible with Christianity. In this crisis, it goes without saying that Psellos' successors could not count on public opinion, which was little concerned with speculative problems and always ready to support the Church authorities.

A confident Church

This was still a subterranean development and on the whole, the eleventh-century Church was revitalised neither in its political role nor in its doctrine. Its main preoccupation was to preserve and increase its inheritance, which it could not do without being generally submissive to the power of the State. The patriarchs, for the most part, were mediocre individuals, and when they were distinguished, they were always former State administrators, such as Constantine Leichoudes or John Xiphilinos. Obviously such pontiffs would not be inclined to dissociate themselves from the established power, even on ethical grounds. Xiphilinos' silence when Romanos Diogenes was treacherously captured and blinded in 1071 is eloquent. Michael Keroularios, patriarch from 1042 to 1058, was the exception that proves the rule: having taken orders after a failed plot, this ambitious fanatic went on to play a decisive part in politics, at times in conflict with the empire's best interests (as in 1054), but he never succeeded in rallying the whole Church behind him, and the people never saw him as the embodiment of the Church. When he was dismissed by Isaac Komnenos in 1058, there was no protest.

Moreover, theology remained very traditional: when they were not lawyers, like Leichoudes and Xiphilinos, the patriarchs were pietists to a man, like Alexios Stoudites. This is an important point when one approaches the history of the so-called schism of 1054. We should recall that at this time Rome and Byzantium were so little disposed towards a split that they were establishing an anti-Norman alliance for the defence of southern Italy. It was exactly this alliance with Rome that Keroularios did not want at any price, because it depended on concessions to the pope and would prevent his obtaining what he had always dreamed of: recognition of the equality of the two sees of Rome and Constantinople. There can be no doubt, then, that it was from Keroularios' entourage that texts emerged unexpectedly in early 1053, reawakening the old quarrel between the two churches, which now turned on questions of ritual (unleavened bread, the Saturday fast, and especially clerical celibacy). This provocation was certainly intended as a reminder of how deep the gulf had become between Orthodoxy and Catholicism, but the dramatic gestures of 15 and 20 July 1054, the bull of excommunication pronounced by the papal legates followed by the anathema proclaimed by Keroularios against the legates and their associates, did not really settle the fate of their relations. Not only were these gestures invalid, because Leo IX was dead by that time, but also contemporaries saw them as merely an episode. While Byzantine sources were silent, Rome did not despair of finding some common ground. In 1058, Pope Stephen IX sent Desiderius of Monte Cassino on a mission to Byzantium, and it was only political circumstances that made the great abbot, on hearing of the pope's death, turn back on his way to Constantinople. We know that Gregory VII himself believed for a long time in the possibility of an entente with Byzantium. At the end of the eleventh century, the two faiths certainly regarded each other with increasing suspicion, but no one had uttered the word 'schism'.

Events on the fringes of the two faiths are a better indication of the fact that, in the eyes of contemporaries, they were not fundamentally different. The case of southern Italy is well known. We know that Greek monks such as Nilos of Rossano were welcomed and honoured by princes and the Latin clergy. Nilos himself celebrated the office in Greek at Monte Cassino and maintained very good relations with Rome, where there were lots of Greek monks. The problem of obedience, which poisoned the relations between pope and patriarch, was doubtless only a faint echo when it reached a mixed population where the two rites co-existed and were each respected. At the other end of Christendom, in Russia, we can see the same phenomenon of co-existence. We now know that the conversion of the Russians had been undertaken by Latin clergy from central Europe, Scandinavia and

Germany, and that it was at Kiev around 987 that Prince Vladimir was baptised. His marriage to the Byzantine princess, Anna, in 989, cannot be considered a 'conversion to Orthodoxy', even if it was followed, as was normal, by the progressive establishment of Greek priests. The strength of the local clergy, Western by tradition, is further attested by the slow progress of the Russian church towards the Orthodox ranks; it was not until 1037 that a Greek bishop was sent to Kiev, and this was not marked out as a metropolitan see depending on Constantinople until a proclamation dating from Alexios Komnenos' reign (1081–1118). Furthermore, while its religious destiny was to be exactly the opposite of Russia's, Hungary provides another example of the essential harmony existing between the churches at this time: King Stephen I, a champion of Rome, throughout his reign encouraged only monasteries of Greek foundation, of which the most famous was Veszprémvolgy; others were founded, especially under Andrew I, and Greek monasticism did not disappear from the country until the thirteenth century.

The Byzantine Church in the eleventh century is a fair reflection of the Byzantine Empire itself, of its culture and even of its economy; from the absence of aggressive behaviour and the slow pace of change, to its claim to have attained moderation in everything, we gain an impression of success and accomplishment that was to take a long time to dissolve.

Art at its peak

The Macedonian period's high place in the history of Byzantine art does not depend only on the fact that it has left us more manuscripts and mosaics than any other period. It also saw the flowering of an aesthetic that had achieved maturity. Perhaps we can find in it the justification of the turbulence of iconoclasm. In wiping the slate clean, the emperors of the eighth century had opened the way to a syncretism which had been blocked by artists' unchanging reverence for the classical. Not that this disappeared: in the draping of robes, the musculature of athletes, the taste for perspective, the way symbols were used, Hellenistic inspiration was apparent. But while the artistic experiments of the tenth century had roots in the past, they took full account of the present – in the capital, in Armenia, in Cappadocia and in the Bulgarian world. On the eve of catastrophe, an original art was born. With the first hints of what was to be the 'Romanesque' also emerging in the West, the division between the two parts of the Christian world was no longer merely political.

We shall not consider architecture here, decidedly the weak spot in Eastern art; the small churches in the shape of a perfect Greek cross, which sprang up throughout the empire in the eleventh century, are modest beside the giants of the sixth century. At least they permitted the faithful to see at a glance the whole iconographic plan of the building, and it could be maintained that this was the indeed the main purpose of such a compression of doctrine: to present the whole celestial hierarchy and its human equivalent in one cycle that did not fail to include the imperial figure itself. This is the Christ Pantokrator, terrible yet benign, enthroned in the central cupola, with the Virgin comforter at the cross of the apse. Against the golden background of mosaics in Nea Mone on Chios, in the monastery church of Daphni in Attica, and in St Luke of Stiris in Phocis, the figures stand out with a power of expression and virtuosity of colouring that surpass the stereotypes of Ravenna or St Sophia. In the following centuries, the Bulgarian and Russian artists, together with those of Palermo and Torcello, had only to copy these expressions of majesty and serenity.

Society, whether monastic or urban, was hungry for luxury. The painters' workshops in the capital, the less well-known ones of Mount Athos, Mount Olympus in Bithynia and of Patmos, have left us illustrated manuscripts that are counted amongst the masterpieces of world art: lively and immensely detailed illustrations to treatises on medicine and agriculture, entire sumptuous pages devoted to the Gospels, scenes in collections of sermons by Chrysostom or Gregory of Nazianzus, psalters and sacramentaries where the artist used a technique of shading in colours, the finest nuances of light colours, rose and beige, applied with such a delicate touch that one could say that Impressionism was born in Byzantium between 1020 and 1080.

Naturally these were exceptional works which belonged to the élite. It is difficult to believe, however, given the care and quality of everyday writing, that the different social levels had nothing in common. Perhaps historians, who know that bad times were fast approaching, are disproportionately moved by this last gleam and are driven to exclaim, 'Too late!'; still, they must salute this last demonstration given by Byzantium on the verge of its ruin.

A fantastic animal from the Romanesque bestiary. This aquamanile, containing water for washing hands, takes the form of a dragon swallowing a man. (Lorraine, twelfth to thirteenth century; New York, Metropolitan Museum of Art, the Cloisters Collection.)

PART 2

The Rise of Europe: 1100–1250

The beginning of European expansion 6

Now we see creativity unleashed: the audience of Ivo of Chartres, the builders of Cluny, the conquerors of Toledo, the Crusaders in the Holy Land – all the people who lived between 1075 and 1100 are the heirs of those who toiled at the millennium, the first Europeans. It is with Europe that we are now concerned; not merely isolated pockets of scholars or warriors, poor scattered inhabitants wandering amidst the ruins of Antiquity, who could be toppled from whatever power and prestige they held by the men from the South (from the world of Byzantium or Islam), but also, from now on, villagers, merchants, knights, the 'bourgeois', who were shaking off the old Mediterranean tutelage. In all of this we see a great turning of the tide which gradually gave primacy to the Germanic and Celtic regions. Not that we should see in this a defeat of Spain, Italy or the Slav regions: indeed, around 1260 or 1270 we find Westerners in Cairo, in China, in Baghdad, Caffa, in the Rif and in the middle of Russia, and these were not only French and Germans. But it is exactly here that the major matrix lies: Bonaventura was Italian, Raymond Lull was Spanish, Roger Bacon was English, Albert the Great was German, Adam de la Halle was French; Marco Polo was Venetian, Jehan Boinebroke was from Douai, Alfonso the Wise reigned in Castile, St Louis in France, with Charles of Anjou in Naples and the Courtenays in Constantinople. It is this explosion outside Europe simultaneously with the encounters within Europe of hitherto isolated groups that makes the change decisive. Between 1080 and 1280, between the building of Vézelay and of Cologne, the frescoes of San Savinio and of Giotto, St Anselm and St Thomas Aquinas, the *Song of Roland* and Rutebeuf, a Catalan *fuero* and a Silesian *weistum*, the guild of Saint-Omer and the statutes of the Florentine Arte della Lana, Catalan mancusos and Venetian ducats, there was a quantitative rather than a qualitative change. During these two centuries we see European politics and economics get under way – or 'take off', as a modern economist would put it. Although the following presentation of individual areas artificially breaks up what was a unified process, we must throw light on this development's principal aspects in succession, turning back sometimes to their roots around the year 1000.

Virgin territory was occupied, groups emigrated, villages doubled in size on a long-term basis, towns enlarged their suburbs. These are not compensatory phenomena; they occur simultaneously and can only have one common factor – a steadily growing surplus population. It is in fact the largest and longest-lasting growth in population that the continent experienced until the end of the eighteenth century. The problem of this population boom is far from being resolved: it must be our starting-point.

The population increase

Medieval demography before 1400, or even 1350, has a bad reputation: today's statisticians snigger at it, 'modernists' pull a face – here and there is a glimmer, some limited data, an 'estimate'. Nothing can be achieved, however, without counting heads. And we have many more ways of approaching the task than is generally believed: the composition of families in a twelfth-century biography, witness lists, the surface area of towns, the extension of lands and, for the thirteenth century, censuses in the form of head-counts of tenants. A courtly romance, a *chanson de geste* or a customary may often be a better source of information on marriage-age, fecundity, sexuality and longevity than later sources. And if the burial grounds of this period are not as rich a source as the cemeteries of the early Middle Ages, because the dead have mingled with those of previous centuries as the ground settled, at least the tools, furniture and iconography provide valuable supplementary evidence.

Counting up

Let us assemble the data. American historians are the only ones to have made a guess at the overall population figures for the whole of Europe, although they do not all agree: Russell estimates 23 million inhabitants in 950, 32 million around 1100, and more than 50 million before 1300; Bennett, who is more precise, suggests 42 million in 1000, 46 million in 1050, 48 million in 1100, 50 million in 1150, 61 million in 1200, and 69 million in 1250. Furthermore, there are many estimates for each region. However, there is one solid source of information – the *Domesday Book*. The existence of this record, together with early management accounts, royal and manorial, explains the privileged place of England in medieval economic studies. The village-by-village inquiry, instituted by William the Conqueror shortly before his death, proved to be so accurate and solemn that almost from the outset it acquired the name it still bears: *Domesday Book*, the book of the Last Judgement. From its pages we get a population figure for England *c.* 1085 of 1.3 million (covering English, Normans, Danes and Bretons in almost the whole of England, *stricto sensu*). This is really the only fixed point in regional documentation, and it is by extrapolation and calculation that the Italian scholar Cipolla has arrived at the figure of 5 million inhabitants for Italy at that time, and that the German scholar Abel has come up with a figure of 6.2 million for France.

In order to find valid data at this level, we must unfortunately go forward to the fourteenth century. But it is obvious that without such a finishing point it would be impossible to approach the principal matter, that is, the rhythm and volume of Europe's population growth. Before 1350, there are a few figures available, gathered either from general documents such as the *Etat des feux* (survey of hearths) based on part of the French kingdom, or from geographically narrower lists, concerning such and such a *contado* in Italy, for example, or from specific texts, usually fiscal, from England, Spain and France: 3.5 million souls in the British Isles, 12–16 million in the kingdom of France, 8–10 million in Italy. What actually matters is the difference over two centuries, or perhaps three, if we take the year 1000 as the likely beginning of this growth. Over these 200–300 years, comparison reveals that the population of Italy doubled, the population of England tripled, and in France the population multiplied by two and a half; the limited data we have for Germany or the Slav countries seem to show growth rates equalling or surpassing those of the distant Mediterranean regions. Whether there had been fewer people in these areas at the start or whether the number had grown faster in later years does not much matter. The result emphasised above is revealing: northern Europe caught up with and then surpassed the south. This is even more marked if one follows the microchronological variations closely: one can see that the 'spate of people' rises in Germany and Scandinavia well after 1250, a time when it seems to have halted in the west and south.

It is actually possible to define this situation more clearly: for example, by carefully sorting, arranging and examining specific cases of the number of children per household, the proportion of sterile couples, those whose children died, or the proportion of celibates. The figures suggested by Russell for the whole of north-west Europe seem too high; we will stick with the estimates by Slicher van Bath, W. Abel, L. Génicot, R. Fossier and A. Chédeville for the region between the Loire and the Rhine, which give us the following margins for the average number of children per fertile household:

1050–1100	1100–1150	1150–1200	1200–1250	1250–1300
4.2–5.7	4.8–5.3	4.3–5.2	5.3–5.4	5.2–5.75

If we estimate at less than a third the proportion of men and women without children, we can then establish an average annual growth rate, for a mixture of social classes (though that presents problems), for the twelfth century of 0.46 per cent per annum in England, 0.48 per cent for west Germany, 0.44 per cent for the Meuse region, and 0.34 per cent for Picardy. This is a much lower average growth rate than that experienced by the Third World today but, because it lasted for an exceptionally long time – just over 200 years – the population doubled or in some cases tripled.

One important area of calculation remains, that of longevity or 'life expectancy'. Russell, using the criterion of life expectancy, which we know has little relation to reality, merely notes that this key indicator must have risen from twenty-two to thirty-five years between 1100 and 1275. As what we know of the age at death of the powerful during this time provides us with a very stable average age of natural decease – between forty-eight and fifty-six years for monarchs, even older for men of the Church – and as there is no reason

Funeral ceremony. King Edward is buried in the Abbey of St Peter's, Westminster, which had just been consecrated. Eight members of the royal family carry the corpse, draped in a shroud; the choirboys ring handbells; clerks and bishops sing the funeral office. The hand of God hovers over the scene. (Bayeux Tapestry.)

to think that these figures apply only to this social class, there would appear to be only one explanation of the rise in longevity: a fall in mortality rates.

On the one hand this can be seen in the mortality rates of children under ten years of age, who in the twelfth century, as the cemeteries of Sweden, Poland and Hungary reveal, constitute 20 to 40 per cent of excavated skeletons; on the other hand, there is the mortality rate of mothers, difficult to pin down except in the genealogies of noble families, but light can be shed on this problem by observing doctors' and scholars' use of the records of Arab or ancient obstetricians in Salerno, Palermo and Valence before 1100.

This last points us, ill-equipped as we are, towards a neglected research topic of fundamental importance: the high death rate among adult women, typical of a society without preventive medicine, perhaps balanced by the high death rate of young males, which occurs in all centuries, at least in Europe. The relation of their ages, or even the basic numerical relation between the two sexes when they marry is an important feature in society: more numerous, the girls are marriageable at a younger age, and the left-overs populate the convents; less numerous, even though the puerperal mortality rate remains high in this period, the men wait and choose. A large proportion of single men, in search of an establishment, these *juvenes* ('young men') of about thirty – warriors, artisans or ploughboys, whatever – form a real 'class' in the towns and villages, impatient, independent, unattached and untamed. But when they finally 'settle down', they are sometimes ten or fifteen years older than their wives. This matrimonial 'model' has wide-ranging implications – social, emotional and even economic – in the areas of literature, religion and law. These are well known and form a striking contrast with our own times, in such areas as the relations between husband and wife, father and child, child and maternal uncle.

Can this population growth be explained?

Within the period 1050 to 1250 we see population growth reach a peak almost everywhere; if it is difficult to quantify, it is even more difficult to detect its origin or cause. After

1000, or a little before, why did the population rise in Europe, even if the first sign was a drop in the death rate rather than what some have called a 'baby boom'? Let us say straight away that all the hypotheses advanced in current research are serious, plausible and not to be discounted, with the exception of the one reason invoked by contemporaries, that God's hand was over his people. Furthermore, the men travelling the roads or tilling new soil were countrymen, from all regions; as for the towns, they also had their pioneers, and we must reject the notion of some single, local cause. The better condition of skeletons, the undeniable spread of technology, the increase in the volume of grain all show that the state of permanent famine was receding in the twelfth century. Scholars have looked for a technical cause of the improvement in living conditions and the rise in the birth rate. But what was the origin? What were the stages? What was the driving-force?

We should take care, however, not to be too optimistic. Serious subsistence crises struck the whole of Europe in 1005–6, 1031–3, 1050 and 1090. After such warnings in the first half of the eleventh century, famine did no more than relax its hold: the years 1123–5, 1144, 1160, 1172, 1195–7, 1202–4, 1221–4, 1232–4, 1240, 1246–8, 1256 and 1272 were all bad, although not catastrophic; but as they only affected isolated regions, this sombre list shows above all that the rural world remained effectively compartmentalised, without negotiable stocks and without counterweights.

As another possible cause of population growth, scholars have also suggested an easing of the upheavals and violent eruptions which Europe had suffered from the third to the tenth century: with the exception of the passing Mongol alarm in the thirteenth century, then the last Turkish expansion, it is not until our own times that we (at least, those of us with our eyes open) can see Europe inundated, slowly and peacefully, with people from the north-west Mediterranean and from Africa. This *pax Christiana* thus created a favourable context; but then why the decline in the fourteenth century, well before the 'traditional' calamities? Should we be looking at the structural aspect? The way men were organised – their incorporation into the seigneurial scheme – is undoubtedly contemporary with the demographic increase. Was it the cause? Or was it rather an effect? Or should we simply link the fate of men to the caprices of the atmosphere and to such elements as temperature, hygrometry, the generation of life itself? Amidst all these possibilities, of which the last at present escapes any rational estimation, historians have modestly advanced some well-researched facts as points of reference – but no more than that – which are worth pausing over.

One, rather grandiosely labelled the 'nursing revolution', has been detected as early as the thirteenth century. By sending their own babies out to paid nurses (i.e., to mothers whose children had died soon after birth), and then employing various methods to dry up their milk supply, many women found themselves able to conceive again without the long interval enforced by breast-feeding (up to eighteen months); the opportunity for more closely spaced births thus increased.

Another concerns infanticide, or simple contraception or abortion procedures (which there is no space to go into here, except to say that their use declined in the thirteenth century). This is of particular interest where first-born baby girls are concerned. It has been said that the killing of such children was one of the causes behind the stagnation of

1.

A traveller takes to the road. (*Bible of Saint-Sulpice*, Bourges; Bourges, Bibliothèque municipale, twelfth century.)

population growth in the early Middle Ages. Besides the role of the Church, there was undoubtedly a re-evaluation of the female sex, which we will discuss later. Beyond this, the remarriage of widows, apparent in many a noble family-tree of the late twelfth century, allowed the birth rate to increase by means of successive marriages, even if they were increasingly less favoured.

Disconcerting mobility

More than fifty years ago Marc Bloch perceived the 'Brownian movement' which affected this mass of people – and which our own unsettled time understands better than did our fore-fathers, people who had been settled since the Renaissance. The causes of this incessant movement are no clearer than those of the population growth: uncertainty about the morrow, fear of shortage, insecurity of all ranks (for example, of a warrior at the mercy of his leader), together with the lack of material comfort, the threat of hunger, the fragility of all earthly attachments, the feeling that life on earth was simply a halfway-house on the road to life everlasting, after the Judgement. More recently, although their work concerns later periods, historians have stressed how little the seigneur-ial system favoured the weak, casting out and throwing onto the roads the marginal, the poor, the 'exiles', and that this mobility must be firmly linked to the very structure of society and of the family. The result at least is not in doubt; it encour-aged the two poisons from which the system itself perished: the proletarianisation of people without ties or special skills, and the circulation of cash, replacing service with the market.

On the Roman roads, more or less dilapidated but still usable, and on the web of paths sometimes retracing even older roads, there was a continual traffic of younger sons of noble families in search of adventure, bands of young warri-ors returning from a tournament, caravans of merchants, monks escaping their monasteries, students on the way to the schools, princes and their trains, exhausted by the voyages imposed on them by their duty to be seen and heard, wander-ers and pilgrims, missionaries and church dignitaries travel-ling towards those spots where faith was weakening or towards the sees awaiting them a hundred leagues from their birthplace. There is scarcely a romance, a *chanson de geste*, a poem, a chronicle, a miniature which does not show us this throughout Europe. But it is more difficult for the historian to grasp the essential detail: the movement from village to village. Here and there a witness list will show the provenance of these 'strangers', 'guests', 'entertainers', those who simply came from elsewhere, even if only a league away. It is this internal movement which is fundamental, and largely explains what follows: the filling-in of vacant land suitable for cultivation, the enlargement of patches where food could be grown, contact between village groups who had been isolated until that time. But such movements over five, ten or thirty kilometres were made by individual families or small groups, along footpaths, forest tracks, through wilderness, probably not all at once or permanently, and never to an extent that overall figures can be suggested. Of forty-seven heads of families in an English fen village in 1247, three had come recently from over ten kilometres away. As for their children, twelve boys had gone into the Church, seven had gone to the town, twenty-four had left the village in search of their fortunes; only twenty-three were still there, waiting to marry. As for the girls, twenty-seven had married outside the settlement and had returned. These are plausible figures, and are similar to those that can be established a little later for Picardy or Beauvais.

Ceaseless clearing of the land

Largely in progress by the year 1000 (if not before), man's domination over the land reached its peak between 1100–25 and 1250–75 for most of north-west Europe, extending to 1300 across the Rhine, but declining from 1200 in the Mediterranean area. This presents us with a new difficulty in research: although there is no lack of charters permitting clearance (one in every three documents from Picardy between 1150 and 1180 is of this kind), the most frequent form of land reclamation, at the beginning and end of our period, was by individual initiative or at least on such a modest scale that no written document was involved. So we must study place-names, at least those names indisputably linked to the struggle against vegetation or water: for example, *ried, rod, schlag* in German, *hurst* and *shot* in English, *sart* and *rupt* in northern French, *artiga* in southern French. An alternative, despite the fact that the struggle against forest continued in later periods, is to examine the soil or rotted vegetation of woods and undergrowth, an area which attracted the attention of Gaston Roupnel over sixty years ago. Finally, we can pin our hopes on the findings of palynology, where the proportion of tree, grass or grain pollens have permitted firm conclusions to be drawn from such regions as the peat bogs of Hesse, the Ardennes, Lüneburg, Kent and the Valais. But in spite of these hopes and certainties, we have to recognise that nothing comes close to giving us a figure for the overall gain in new land between 1100 and 1250: from perhaps 10 per cent in the regions already heavily cultivated in Celtic Europe, or among the uncultivable lands on the Mediterranean coastline, to 40 per cent or more at the expense of the Scandinavian or German forests. This is merely an 'impression'. It is equally difficult to pin down the exact significance of the increase in our archival sources of documents concerning land exchanges, a practice designed to improve one's patrimony.

Man and virgin land

First of all, we must understand the inherent contradiction in the medieval system of production, a contradiction which was never resolved. 'Common' land, as it was called, which surrounded land that had more or less been brought under control, was not just a frontier, a public zone (*haya*), eventually to be made into a refuge, but a basic part of the economy: cattle and pigs grazed on it, people – albeit of different classes and with different purposes – hunted there, picked fruit, plucked edible roots or berries or leaves, gathered firewood, and carried out all the contemporary necessities. If it went beneath the plough, it meant destroying these resources for the sake of gaining corn; but the pressure of population demanded extra capacity. This is why the medieval economy, during the two or three centuries of its principal expansion, remained in a state of precarious balance and also geographically varied. As long as it was possible to reconcile the *necessitas*, the basic minimum for each inhabitant, with the additional needs of the master, the price for his protection, his justice and his power as a 'noble', the system could function come what may; it is precisely the breaking up of this system which marks the end of the chronological period under consideration.

This hunger for land has left clear signs. We will not go back over what the twelfth-century land contracts teach us. The fact that we see the Church's patrimony and such rare secular property as can be glimpsed being re-established on more profitable bases, sometimes even altering its location, in a variety of regions (Catalonia, Lombardy, Sabine, Bavaria, Flanders, Auvergne, Provence) is not indisputable proof of the gaining of land, though it is perhaps evidence of a concern for profit which is difficult to label as a cause or an effect. But the increasing number of small peasant freeholdings – 'allods' – that crop up in our documents as we approach 1100 is a sign of the creation of new plots of land; this period, in fact, saw the universal taking in hand of old lands. If these plots are not allods, they are held on fairly liberal conditions of tenure, in any case on a long lease, like the thirty-year *livello* in Italy. This documentary evidence is almost entirely from the first phase of land conquest, which was a hesitant process, reliant on individual effort, while the pre-1100 pollen deposits indicate a retreat of beech trees and the appearance of cereals.

But after 1100 we can be more sure of our facts, because written documents give us a better notion of what was going on: the quarrels between lords over the levying of a *novale* tithe – one collected on land that had hitherto been unproductive – in France and in the Rhineland; a falling-off in the number of animals grazing in forests, according to the *Domesday Book*; claims in central Italy of use by peasants deprived of woods that had been levelled, walled off and cultivated; finally, everywhere, albeit at different periods, contracts for land clearance or marsh drainage. Such material enables us to grasp the dimensions of the struggle. The attack on fertile lands which had often been abandoned to forest, for want of sufficiently powerful tools, constitutes the essential element because this clayey alluvium on a chalky base – marl – is our best soil today. But the relatively early date of the assault, perhaps before there had been much technical progress, suggests that a preliminary phase of investigation of rich pastoral areas might have preceded any sowing activity. Do we then

Russian woodcutters clear land in the Novgorod region in the eleventh century (Moscow, Academy of Sciences Library).

only have to wait until 1140 or 1160 for the retreat first of scrub and then of the denser coppices in the country of Brioude or Thouars, of the Bouconne around Toulouse, of the *silvae* of Perche, Picardy, the Harz and the Rhineland? Wheat is sown, but in Bavaria vines are cultivated, and in England in the Weald and in Sussex, the *open dens* remain largely given over to pasture. This mixture of newly acquired food-producing territory and a pastoral zone was well suited to the drained areas: this is the main phase of dyke building, with barriers such as the *turcies* on the Loire from 1160 to 1270, and the Aunis and Brière dykes; channels, drains, *waterstraat*, appear from the Charente to Frisia, as in the fenland of eastern England around Ely. Attacks were made on the lower Rhône, the Camargue, the lagoons of Languedoc from 1080 to 1160, and slightly later on the areas fed by the Po. Too often the thankless, interminable, wearying conquest of valleys and slopes has been forgotten, the typically Mediterranean work on irregularly flooded, stony, steeply sloping and ravined territory: the *bonifachi* of the Lombard plains, the *gradoni* of Umbria, the *orts* of Provence, the Spanish *huertas*; such work cannot be dated but was a titanic achievement, with earth carried in baskets, stones lifted off one by one. This conquest initially benefited olive-trees, vines and chestnut-trees rather than wheat, whose meagre roots could not draw nourishment from the soil.

Aspects and effects of the conquest

All the same, nothing is accomplished in the relatively short span of a decade or by using just one method. If we screen out the inessentials from our sources and concentrate on their common features, we can observe that the southern regions (the Po valley, Catalonia, **251**

Provence and the Auvergne) are the first to stir, perhaps before 1000, and definitely before 1040. Not until the middle of the century, or even 1100, do Poitou, Aquitaine, Normandy and Flanders become active. The twelfth century sees activity in the Paris basin, Bavaria, around Lorraine and in central England; the end of the twelfth century and the start of the thirteenth see it in the English Midlands, Saxony and Franconia. Everywhere this conquest of nature seems to have been made in two stages, separated by three or four decades, doubtless because of the effort to restore order after the first stage; each of these stages lasts for two or three generations. They may have been preceded by individual pioneering efforts, isolated or even excluded from the general group, and unrecorded in any texts, followed by furtive and tenacious work by peasants, illegally whittling down what remained of the seigneurial woods, if the wave of court actions in the thirteenth century is any guide. All this is likely, but our sources are silent about such proceedings. As the regions which were the last to come to life are our best wheat lands today, and, even by that time, were densely populated areas, we have to accept that the attack on the oak woods or the maquis, which required labour and technical skills, did not take place until control was gained over the ancient clearings.

In this effort of conquest, what seems to have been of definitive importance is less its extent than its effects on society. Whether on their own (illegal) initiative, or whether recruited for the task, the *sartatores* (the assarters or woodcutters who worked long and hard, with little prospect of making any profit for up to three, five or even ten years) made or imposed advantageous contracts, which spread to the old landholdings too. These contracts involved the reduction or cancellation of days of 'service' in the form of labour or plough-work; the development of tenure in return for part of the crops grown (*terrages, champart, agrière*), without this being a system of sharecropping in the strictest sense (*métayage, ad medietatem, mezzadria*) in which payment of half the crops grown was common practice; even where the system was well established – as in Italy or Aquitaine – less than a quarter, or indeed a sixth, was levied. This scheme must have seemed sufficiently advantageous to both sides before 1200, because we see it spreading across the whole of the West in a few generations; that it had been accompanied almost everywhere by individual liberty is thus not surprising and the collective 'manumissions' awarded by a lord to those of his men who were still serfs coincides with these clearance projects.

Of course it is the lords that we see in the documents; we have to wait until the mid-thirteenth century, a little earlier in England, to find sources that will allow us, if not to measure precisely the part of the humblest men in the extension of arable land, at least to glimpse its effect on the intensification of small-scale peasant production. Here we are at the boundary between the economic and the social. The practical conditions of clearance or drainage, where a 'contract' lets us glimpse them, reveal two major features. In the first place a division of labour, not only according to specialised skills – still chiefly an urban phenomenon – but also according to responsibility and profits: the sponsor, all too often the Church (and our sources are predominantly ecclesiastical) who collects the tithes; the lay entrepreneur (*locator*), who may be the local overlord or a wealthy peasant, who receives the 'profits of justice', and often, directly, the rent for the land; the tenant, who keeps the basic product; and the workhand, who is paid, so that we see a cash economy taking hold in the village. Thus on the borders of the old lands, or more often, in the midst of fallow lands or woods, medium-sized lots were established alongside each other, often worked directly or by day labourers, units of production which were soon imitated on the older land. Of course these new *mas*, these *albergues* as they were called in southern France, *hébergements* or *heriberg* north of the Loire, *maneria*, *censes* in Normandy or Picardy, these *bercariae* or *vaccarie* beside land reclaimed from the sea, could be seigneurial islands: thus the estates cleared by the Cistercians and Premonstratensians were intended to be isolated, indeed closed. But there are also more modest peasant lands: in Latium, for example, it has been shown that at the end of the twelfth century the borders of average-sized lots belonged to other tenant farmers or landowners who controlled comparable lots. Not only did gaps between lots cease to exist as the spaces closed up, but also the structure of this patchwork shows that more and more patches were in the peasants' hands. It is this phenomenon that explains the long-held hope, especially in Germany, that a study of the size and shape of these plots would allow the identification and measurement of new lands; such *Siedlungsgeschichte* has in fact only come up with results as regards settlement before 1200 or 1250, to which we shall shortly return.

Limits

Always concerned to push back the origins of what they recognise to be a constantly changing phenomenon, scholars have detected signs of opposition to clearances before 1100: protection of oaks, proceedings against misuse, hunting reserves appearing from Poitou to Latium. In fact, these controls on excess are really part of the care with which landholding was organised, as we shall see. There are other, much later signs which show us the limits of the enterprise. Let us look again at the lawsuits in which inhabitants of the community were opposed by the master of a wood who feared that it would be misused: limitations on pasturing, gathering and picking might be designed to increase seigneurial taxation rather than to protect ground-cover; there is a noticeable increase in these in our sources after about 1225–30, perhaps at the time when the furtive, individual efforts were slowly giving way to collective enterprises.

There are, however, clearer signs. A slow but indisputable rise in the price of arable land is apparent at the beginning of the thirteenth century. In Germany between 1200 and 1250, where the start of clearances was slower and more land was available, the price of a plot of land rose from an index of 100 to 175; in northern France an acre rose from two livres to four and a half livres; in England between 1200 and 1230, the price of a plot rose from two and a half sous to four and a half sous. Currency devaluation would obviously alter this impression, as it only concerns prices expressed in accounting units; looked at in terms of the value of the precious metal involved, the average rise in north-western Europe appears much closer to the German rate. But there is another element to bring into consideration: the reclaimed lands were often used for vine cultivation, or as grasslands, or for the cultivation of plants used in dyeing; so it is even more striking that the price of grain

253

In this aerial view of Farlow (Shropshire) taken in 1952, existing hedges show the boundaries of lots and successive clearances. (Cambridge University Collection.)

rose faster than that of land, which indicates a need, reflecting the demands of food production or the search for commercial profit. We can establish that in England there was at first a very slow rise (measured in terms of silver ounces), followed between 1220 and 1239 by a slight fall, then by a sharp rise:

1180–1199	1200–1219	1220–1239	1240–1259	1260–1279
100	108	104	114	190

We can see, between 1240 and 1280, a marked shift from making land available to making it profitable. Evidence would seem at first to suggest some concern with organisation: placing land into reserves or districts and thereby denying people and animals free access. Such *aforestatio* also had an impact on the fringe activities of foraging in the Mediterranean as well as the north. The reason behind this form of exclusion could simply be ecological. In the Thierache region or in the many seigneurial woods in Champagne around 1245–50, and later in central France (around 1290 in the royal forests), exclusion reflects the desire to facilitate the regeneration of certain tree species and to control the length of time between each felling. The Cistercians often set an example in this way – indeed forest regulation originated with them, to be taken up by the Capetians after 1317.

254

All this was well and good, but the setting aside of copses by a lord for the hunting of 'great beasts', or for sport or military training, appears less justified. Around 1270, the consumption of butcher's meat was growing in towns; the lord's apparent preference for venison, which thus required him to close off his woods to cattle, was a class reaction; it undoubtedly harmed the peasants by forcing them to herd their livestock on over-grazed land. If the issue was not about the profits to be gained from hunting, as in the case of churchmen, it was about the sale of woods or the collection of fines for poaching: between 1240 and 1280 the proportion of the revenues from the woods of Saint-Denis in the abbey's budget rose from 5 per cent to 9 per cent. And this was not all. Not only could the forests perhaps be forbidden ground for cutting or gathering wood, sometimes even for pasturing, but the lord could also attempt a counter-attack and withdraw from cultivation those lands already won. This problem emerges around the middle of the thirteenth century. Previously, many members of the landed aristocracy had tolerated, or indeed actively encouraged, the development of *communia* – broadly speaking, 'common lands' – which were generally a clearing or on the edge of a settlement, and which were granted to a community. Many such privileges drawn up in Picardy, Hainault, Lorraine and Franconia between 1210 and 1240 take great care to specify the rights of each party. Thus they must have been contested already; and lords added acts of force to legal proceedings: in 1235, at Merton, the King of England had to promulgate a ruling forbidding the seizure of such communal lands, let alone their 'enclosure'; this was the first act in a crucial drama in the British Isles.

From all these scattered elements one very characteristic trait stands out: the fragility of the medieval agricultural–pastoral system, which we remarked upon earlier. Although established before 1100, this system did not weaken until after 1240. In the meantime various remedies had been adopted to compensate for this fragility: a better internal organisation of the structures of production, an increase in production, the opening of a trade sector. But before we consider those areas which made the twelfth century the 'great' medieval century, we must look briefly at quite another solution, much simpler and always available: taking from one's neighbour what one lacks at home.

European expansion

The first kernel of Europe was formed by conquest and more or less brutal conversion to Christianity: France, Germany, northern and central Italy. On the periphery, various powers remained outside this process: the Greeks in Italy, Berbers in Spain, Celts and Anglo-Saxons, the still scattered groups of Slavs, the Scandinavian masses. At the beginning of the twelfth century things had already greatly changed: Poland and Hungary had become Christian, and the political and commercial relations which linked these regions with the Byzantine Empire had brought them into the European world, even if it was still not possible to say this of the Russian or Lithuanian lands which were still beyond the range of Christian missionaries. In the north, the Scandinavian peoples played the same role in the vast area from Iceland to Novgorod or Kiev; the northern seas were their domain, and once their politics had stabilised, they were integrated into Christian Europe. Above all,

England's conquest in 1066 by William of Normandy connected the island to the continent, while the conquests of Sicily and southern Italy in the same period (by the Normans who accompanied Robert Guiscard and Roger) loosened the ancient links with the East. Finally, the fate of the Spanish had fallen to the Christians: the line of the Tagus and the Ebro was firmly held against a return of the Maghribins. In central and northern Europe, from the Spanish *meseta* to the Mezzogiorno, there were lands for those who had to leave their villages and were ready to take risks.

Drang nach Osten

For over 1,000 years Germans and Slavs have fought each other for possession of the alluvial wheat fields of Saxony, Silesia, Bohemia and Poznan, for the shores and fish of the Baltic, for the timber and pelts of Pomerania or Prussia, for the routes to the Danube and the Black Sea. The first phase of this struggle, i.e. the period up to 1100, was fairly evenly balanced and was marked by a process of Christianisation much less drastic than that experienced by the Saxons, as well as by the ebb and flow of alternating attempts at conquest. Such thrusts resulted on the one hand, after 1000, in a growing awareness of Polish unity, which was to drive kings such as Boleslav Chrobry as far as the Elbe or Prague around 1005, and, on the other hand, in the construction on the German side of a solid rim of 'marches', military territories with open eastern frontiers, where warriors and pioneers had a free hand: Nordmark or the Billungs' march, the Sorbs' march, the Nordgau facing Bohemia, and the Ostmark which was the cradle of Austria. We can see how explosive this situation was thanks to Polish archaeology over the past fifty years, which has succeeded in revealing the vitality of communities of Polish townspeople, craftsmen and soldiers, who were by no means prepared to yield peacefully to any attempt to push them beyond accepting Christianity and having the acts of their rulers written down in Latin.

The decisive attack was launched at the beginning of the twelfth century. It was to last for two centuries but was at its most spectacular during the twelfth century because it involved almost the only example of clear-cut racism to be seen in the Middle Ages. From 1100, not only were the eventual immigrants, whether German or Flemish or Frisian, lured by the promise of land and money to be gained by despoiling the 'pagans' – however Christianised – but they were incited to contempt and hatred by the descriptions of them, especially the Poles, as 'repulsive beasts'. Was this merely the excesses of propaganda? It was much worse – St Bernard did not hesitate to promise heaven to those who would rid the Empire of these hateful neighbours. Because the peasants had military support, the end result was a political extension of the Empire and a resettlement of Slav groups eastwards. And because all the commercial and industrial activity was concentrated on the plains of the Oder and Vistula and henceforth drained towards the Baltic or the Elbe, these areas served as a hinterland to be exploited by the north German Hanse ports and thus contributed to a weakening of the relations between the Byzantine or Mediterranean world and northern Europe.

256   It is easy to follow German progress, steady and irresistible in the twelfth century. It

depended on ambitious and avaricious princes such as Albert the Bear, who established himself in Brandenburg around 1130–5, and Henry the Lion, who founded Lübeck in the north (1143–61) and occupied Lusatia in the south (1158); this was followed by the absorption of Silesia (1160) and Pomerania (1180). If the Polish princes more or less maintained their authority around Poznan and Cracow, the law of the German towns held sway over the whole of Greater Poland and even Masovia and Galicia in the thirteenth century. The monk-soldiers, knights of the Teutonic Order, took over and cut off Poland from all contact with the sea after 1208 and especially 1231, spreading out with fire and sword over the lands of Gdansk (Danzig), Prussia, Courland and Estonia as far as Lake Peipus, where they were stopped in their tracks in 1242 by the attack of the prince of Novgorod, Alexander Nevski.

It is more difficult to imagine the material conditions of the conquest. In order to attract the peasants, the customary duties imposed in the seigneuries of central Germany were somewhat lightened: the lots given out were very large, the dues were to be paid mainly in money, the communities were strongly autonomous, law and protection were more certain than in the west; and a study of place-names shows the proliferation of sites created or renamed in the German mode. This raises a problem not easily solved: the coherent identity and marked technical skills of the Polish population make it unlikely that assimilation was rapid and peaceful, yet the texts are silent about any violence. The presence of *Kietze*, kinds of reserve or areas of assembly in Lusatia and Brandenburg, the persistence of Slav terms, and of the Polish language in Silesia, are no doubt illustrations of the local survival of some of the evacuated and reassembled population; but the rest doubtless disappeared, massacred or driven eastwards.

Towards the Arctic circle

The Scandinavian venture, which has already been discussed at length, is certainly one of the most spectacular features of the ninth, tenth and eleventh centuries. From Greenland to northern Syria, from London to Palermo, the Normans played a central role in many spheres: nurturing new commercial contacts, forging new river and sea routes, developing new navigation techniques. And they expelled the Greeks eastwards and connected the Baltic zone and the British Isles with the Frankish world. By 1100, however, this epic phase was over. What remained was no less important: settlement and exploitation.

The situation in the far north was fundamentally different: no one lived amidst the ice, the glacial moraines, the volcanic ashes or in the middle of the woods and forests of Greenland, Iceland and northern Scandinavia. There were a few Lapps in the vicinity of the Lofoten Islands, and the first Eskimos settled in the north of Greenland from their home on Baffin Island. But there was not a soul in Iceland when the Norwegians set foot there in the tenth century. Even on the Scandinavian peninusula, except for Denmark and its environs which were more densely populated, there were only a few groups of fishermen and hunters around the fjords and on the islands along the Norwegian coast. There were some more concentrated settlements around Birka and Uppsala in Sweden, but no human group

257

– or almost none – beyond 65° north, the latitude of Iceland; nor had Christianisation gone beyond that line. Not until the twelfth and thirteenth centuries did men, hungry for land and metal, penetrate the inland forest and push northwards, at first in seasonal hamlets, then in groups of autonomous villages, where the strength of collective obligations was unequalled anywhere else on the continent: the perils of the sea and of forest fires bound the local communities strongly enough for State power to be confined to the level of military service, which was basically defensive after 1100.

It is almost impossible to trace the stages of this conquest in any detail: the sagas tell stories of distant voyages, not of daily struggles, axe in hand. One thirteenth-century runic inscription on the west coast of Greenland (latitude 72° north) is the most northerly witness to the Scandinavian advance into the north Atlantic. Iceland had some 40,000 inhabitants around 1200, but alluvial arable land was cultivated all round the island. In Scandinavia, even the south coast of Finland was peopled by Swedes after 1150, as were the shores of Lake Ladoga; a few ecclesiastical settlements north of Oslo and in Jämtland, north of Uppsala, demonstrate how slowly and sparsely the interior was settled. The coastlines of the Gulf of Bothnia and northern Norway were probably not permanently settled before the fifteenth century. For the rest, the particular geographical constraints of human settlement in such conditions meant that there could not be a great number of immigrants. This is one of the arguments advanced by British historians, who suggest that the eleventh century Danish settlement along the length of the north-east coast (although the evidence provided by place-names or family names should not be over-estimated) was a form of population overflow, like the overflow of Norman warriors into England or Sicily a little later. But these are factors in the eleventh century. After 1100, it was only southern Italy and Sicily in the time of 'King' Roger II which saw the arrival of Norman colonists, established around Catania and Amalfi – hardly evidence of a population explosion; the leaders may have been Norman, but Latins, Greeks, Lombards and Berbers composed the bulk of the population.

The Reconquista

The Poles were killed off or driven out, the Scandinavians did not encounter a soul in their icy wastes, but the Iberian peninsula underwent yet another type of expansion. If the *población* accompanied reconquest, and was fed by immigrants from across the Pyrenees as much as by the surplus population of Asturias or Catalonia, there was no question here of either empty spaces or a decimated population. It is astonishing to see how Spanish historiography has presented as an avenging expulsion or as a natural return of the Christian tide what was in fact a long-term, sensible, humane, even liberal process of fusion between different faiths and races, which does great honour to the people of medieval Spain and Portugal. Only in the last few decades have Spanish scholars followed the paths traced by other scholars, particularly French ones, over the past fifty years or more. The reconquest is of course a victory for the Cross as well as a political and 'national' undertaking, but above all it is a work of co-penetration and synthesis which even today, despite the upsets of the sixteenth and seventeenth centuries, makes the peninsula unique.

At the time we take up the story, the starting-points, the narrow gorges of the Pyrenees, the Cantabrian lairs, had mostly been cleared: Santarem, Toledo, Guadalajara, Saragossa and Tarragona marked the limits of the four kingdoms around 1118–28. Portugal fixed its capital at Lisbon in 1147; León and Castile had a choice of 'royal' towns among Leon, Burgos, Salamanca, Valladolid or Toledo; Aragon–Catalonia had been recently created; and the fourth kingdom, Navarre, henceforth had no links with Islam. In the thirteenth century the decisive push took place, after a new Maghribian attack by the Almohads had threatened the progress of the Christians. The Andalusian passes were forced in 1212 at the battle of Las Navas de Tolosa, and within a generation La Mancha and Levante, the valleys of the Guadiana and the Guadalquivir, the Algarve and the Balearic Islands were conquered; Valencia fell in 1238, Murcia in 1243, Palma and Badajoz in 1230, Cordoba in 1236, Seville in 1248, Cadiz in 1265. Pinned down in Granada and Malaga, the Muslim remnant, under Castilian control, slowly died out.

The speed and decisiveness of this advance is worth stressing, as it poses difficult problems for the historian. It is certain that the firmness of the foundation provided by the Pyrenees and the Cantabrian chain has long been under-estimated: the resources of timber, iron, meat, grain, the strongly cohesive mountain and warrior communities (easily assembled and led in the direction of plunder), together with the contact (intensifying around the year 1000) with Muslim currency – all this provided a very solid platform on which to build something more ambitious. But men from other regions were necessary to the effort, and in the eleventh and twelfth centuries such men hastened to Spain from Burgundy, from Languedoc and Aquitaine, contributing both to the economic over-shadowing of Islam and to the strengthening of the autonomy of groups of peasant conquerors. It cannot be merely the accident of surviving sources that we see in Spain, before any other region, privileges, franchises, *fueros* being accorded to both towns and villages, leaving to the inhabitants the armed defence of their houses, sometimes even permitting peasants to fight on horseback (*caballeria villana*), an unparalleled instance in the West at this time. Mills and forges in occupied zones were also permitted to be equipped for defence. Perhaps in the first place, in the eleventh century, the 'reconquered' lands formed frontiers that were open both to merchants and to herds moving to new pastures, and whose redevelopment required a supply of men; some Spanish historians remain convinced that such zones were empty.

Yet the post-1150 advance, which saw neither massacres nor expulsions, was not made on virgin soil; towns and villages were wealthy and populous; they kept growing without being disturbed by the reconquest, however rapid its pace. A gradual amalgamation must have taken place; the princes and the nobles had the wisdom, while they regrouped the various faiths into separate neighbourhoods or villages, not to force peoples' consciences, and to let exisiting rights and laws survive. It is this attitude that has led to the belief that there was only a very superficial 'Arabisation' of Spain, and that a strong contingent of Mozarabic Christians survived in Islamic territory. But besides the implausibility of Islam's being merely skin-deep, after five centuries of occupation (longer than the Roman occupation of Gaul), the juxtaposition of *francos*, *mudejares*, Jewish and Spanish quarters in towns

259

The site of Toledo. The capital of an autonomous Muslim kingdom at the beginning of the eleventh century, it was governed by tolerant princes, who allowed the establishment of the famous Jewish schools there. Alfonso VI took it over in 1185 and made it the residence of the kings of Castile, which it remained until the sixteenth century.

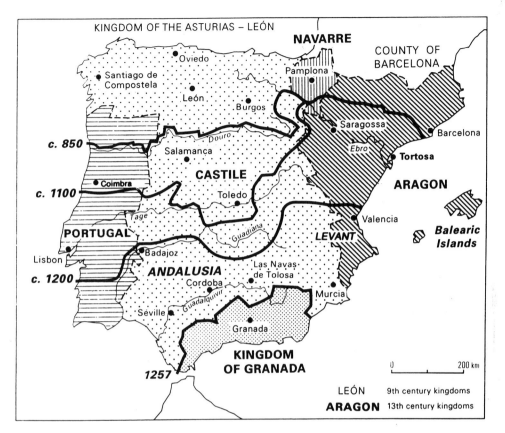

Map 12. The *Reconquista*.

is, like the place-names in the plains, a good demonstration of the variety of tenants and the diplomacy that was necessary to prevent the conquered from rising up in revolt. There still remains a great deal of work to do in the investigation of whether the conditions of tenure in the Christian *aldeas* were really better than those conceded to the Muslim *alqueiras*.

We can estimate that, in the space of these two centuries (during which the population of Europe increased enormously), between 15 and 40 per cent more land was brought under cultivation within Europe, either from previously untouched land, or at the expense of peoples who had once been located on the borders of western Christendom (or quite outside it). From the centre, this extension eventually covered some 1 million square kilometres to the north, south and east – a doubling in size of the land area available for food production. Nevertheless, even this prodigious territorial expansion of western Europe was not enough to absorb all the energies unleashed since the mid-eleventh century, as can be seen from the fact that this intra-European expansion is accompanied by expansion overseas.

261

The conquest of the sea

The wealth of fish available in the great rivers of northern Europe and the geographical advantages of the great fertile crescent reaching from the Basque country to Prussia meant that most of the Germanic and Celtic peoples naturally turned away from the sea. But the harsh soils of Armorica and western Britain forced the peoples of Armorica, Wales and Scandinavia to turn to deep-sea fishing and navigation, from ria to fjord. But while Cornish pewter, the riches of Thule, and Baltic amber had astonished the ancients, and the Veneti had embarassed Julius Caesar, the cold seas did not play the vital role in north-west Europe that the 'Latin sea' played in the south: there, towns and seafolk lived by the sea alone, the arena for the trading of goods and the wanderings of men. Driven back from the coasts and being 'unable to float a plank upon the sea' (as Ifriqiya boasted), Christendom was cut off from its traditional base of wealth, condemned to the hoe and pasture. Byzantium, as we have seen, had to some extent cleared a way for itself, reasserting some control over the road from Bari as far as Cyprus or even Antioch; but in the west, the Saracens of La Garde-Freinet, of the mouth of the Ebro, of the Balearics, indeed of all the islands, 'clambered like goats' through the Apennines, the Alps and at times the Pyrenees; and Pirenne, as we know, saw in this incursion the gaping chasm that separated this period from Antiquity.

Life on the northern seas

The ocean stretched away to the west: boundless, heaving, swept by rains and squalls, it would remain unexplored for a long time to come. Even if the few coins from Spain found in England, or even if the signs of Basque sailors in Compostela or Ireland suggest that they must have passed the Isle of Sein or cut across the Bay of Biscay, we do not have evidence of extensive traffic on the open sea. Fishermen from Asturias, Porto, Bayonne, and in particular from Brittany, did not venture far from their coasts. Trade, in such items as salt from Bourgneuf (which was in demand as far away as Germany) or wine from La Rochelle after 1115 and Bordeaux after 1172 (which went across to England), was still plied only along the coasts or across the Channel.

As we might expect, it was only the Scandinavians who braved the dangers of the Atlantic: from the ninth century, they had attacked the Moroccan coast near the river valley of Sebou, passing through the straits of Gilbraltar; those who went to Sicily followed the same route, as did those in the twelfth century who helped to drive the Moors from Lisbon. But we do not know exactly the route they followed and, before the establishment of the Italian–Flemish axis, well into the thirteenth century, these remain isolated examples. The Atlantic remained unyielding.

On the other hand, the seas bordering the Atlantic Ocean had already become familiar parts of the maritime domain well before 1100. The Frisians of the *terpen* (perhaps for over 1,000 years), the Jutes and Saxons, and above all the Scandinavians had all criss-crossed the Channel, the Irish and the North Seas, the Baltic and the ice-free regions of the Arctic. The marked differences in water temperature, colour and saltiness of these regions, as well as the long absence of any real hostility from the coastal populations, had permitted the slow development of deep-sea navigation and fishing techniques, which had paralleled the art of boat-building, so making this area one of the cradles of maritime technology. Nautical specialists attach importance to the Nordic development of different types of boats, which they date to 1100. The Swedish *knar* and the Danish *snekka*, long vessels with twenty oarsmen on each side, could certainly brave the deeps of the northern seas: these are the vessels of the Scandinavian sagas, which went out to conquer Iceland, anchored at Greenland, and reached Labrador. But fighting ships or fishing boats, without decks and swift rather than stable, could never lend themselves to trade in, say, salt from the Vendée, wine from Gascony, grain or wood from Poland, let alone to the tenth-century trade in furs, herring or whale-meat between Rouen and Pomerania. Such vessels were gradually replaced by large, bulging ships, almost as high as they were long, with a capacity of 300 to 500 tons, with decks, aftercastles and crow's nests, and capable of sailing some 180 to 200 kilometres a day. This was the Baltic *hogge* or *kogge* (cog), the merchant ship *par excellence*, ancestor of the later sailing ships and caravels. At the beginning of the eleventh century, when they were fighting for maritime supremacy, Cnut the Great of Denmark and St Olaf of Norway (1026) only had *snekka*, war- and expedition-ships, as did William the Conqueror when he attacked England in 1066. The destruction of the Danish trading post of Hedeby by the Germans in the same year is a sign of a shift in the control of the northern seas; the cogs used by German merchants from the beginning of the twelfth century have been found at Bergen, Lund and near Sigtuna (1104–10). Henceforth the Baltic, and soon the North Sea, was to be a zone of German influence.

This did not happen all at once. It is convenient and probably fair to attribute a symbolic role to the founding of Lübeck in 1158–61, thanks to the rival but complementary efforts of the two leading figures in the Germanising of the land east of the Elbe, Henry the Lion of Saxony and Albert the Bear of Brandenburg. The creation of the Hanse League by German merchants, from Gdansk to Bremen, and the free passage through the Danish straits obtained before 1175, made it possible to control the *Osterlingen*, from the mouth of the Thames to Riga (1200) and Novgorod. The trade in salted herring and milk products, in pitch and in grain, sent to Flanders and London from 1210 onwards, and the trade in the other direction of wool, pewter and wine taken to the Slav countries, became the concern of the inhabitants of Hamburg and Lübeck, while in Lithuania after 1236 it fell to the Teutonic Knights, those Templars of eastern Europe who divided their time between business transactions and conversion at sword-point. All this was no more than an expansion or development of older activities. It was not until the extravagant twentieth century that the shoals of herring in the North Sea were exhausted; in the Middle Ages, they sustained the daily life of a large part of Europe, and if herring fishing is less prestigious than the spice trade, I for one find it more interesting.

The western Mediterranean counter-attack

The intolerable Muslim pressure on the southern flank of Christian Europe was, of course, no recent phenomenon around the year 1000. The contraband trade in wood, slaves and arms carried on by the Venetians and the Catalans, despite formal papal condemnations in

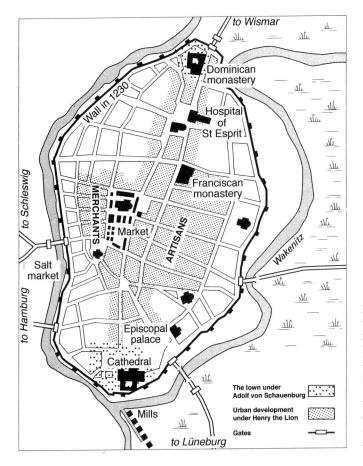

Map 13. Plan of Lübeck. In the centre of the town is the market, entirely in mercantile hands, with little shops, streets of traders and specialist craftsmen. Given the absence of long-established monasteries in this recently colonised town, Dominicans and Franciscans quickly settled there from 1225.

970, 992 and 1005, and the fairly light trading between Byzantium and Venice, established since 992 with some customs agreements, were inadequate substitutes for a free flow of European products southwards or eastwards. In the latter direction, the Danubian route, re-opened after the conversion of Hungary around 1000, was some help and was used by some German merchants. But if we are to believe the accounts of Jewish or Byzantine traders, this was a difficult route, fraught with dangers on the river and along its banks. Moreover, the hostility of the Bulgars at the end of the voyage (the most delicate stage of the journey), the Iron Gates and the Balkans, severely constrained mercantile effort, as did the Pecheneg raids after 1050 in the sub-Danubian regions. And for a Provençal or an Italian, such a path seemed inaccessible. Thus there was no doubt that the south had to be opened up.

There was a double obstacle to this. First, there had been little extension of nautical skills in the Mediterranean. Swift galleys were still being built along ancient lines, with two masts (better for racing than for trading), together with the *dromon*, with their two rows of twenty-five oarsmen, and a length of 40–50 metres. The latter, being adapted to the low swell of the Mediterranean, could serve as freight vessels but were slow and of small tonnage (scarcely 300 tons). In terms of maritime technology then, this region had seen very little progress, perhaps even a decline, compared with Roman times. Besides, these vessels were the same as those sailed by the Byzantines and Muslims, so the West was in no way superior; worse still, the shipyards of Barcelona, Saint-Gilles, Genoa and Gaeta were continually threatened by attack from Corsica, the Balearics or Sicily. Only the Venetians in the Adriatic and the Greeks from Bari could operate without too much danger; the Slav pirates of the Illyrian or Albanian coast were less formidable than the Saracens.

The second obstacle arose from the scattered nature of possible bases for a Christian counter-attack up to the end of the eleventh century. The political and military powers seemed to have other concerns, or to favour other methods. The Saxon emperor had certainly helped to destroy the nest of vipers in La Garde-Freinet in 975, but in Italy he had failed, and even suffered a considerable defeat at the hands of the Arabs of Sicily; henceforth he was wary of the sea while the Byzantine Empire was content to hold on to its Neapolitan and Tarentine beach-heads. In Provence, Languedoc and Lombardy, there was nothing to be done; and in Catalonia the Count of Barcelona managed his affairs, on a modest scale, on *terra firma*. In Valencia there was a semi-Christian maritime power, that of Rodrigo Diaz Campeador, but 'El Cid' was in the service of the Moors, when he was not working just for himself. Alfonso VI of Castile achieved a great deal around 1092, but by attacking from the interior. In these conditions, the Christian counter-attack could only be the result, at least in the first instance, of the initiative of individual cities against piracy.

The reconquest of the Tyrrhenian Sea is a major event in the history of medieval Europe, but it is one of the least well-known and least studied. Some points of reference stand out, but the motives, methods and evolution of this process are a vast and shadowy area. One thing is clear, and that is the institutional framework in which these events unfolded. After the Hilali invasions of Ifriqiya between 1045 and 1058, and despite some attempts at co-ordinating their actions, the Zirids of Kairouan and Mahdiyya had given the local leaders in Sicily and Sardinia their head, as they had also done with the raiders setting out from the fortified *ribats* on the north coast, near Bougie; after 1014 the Hammudids of Tahert were more concerned with the penetration of the Sahara than with privateering. At the same time, the explosion of the Cordoban caliphate after 1031 into fifteen rival emirates removed the Spanish danger from the seas, with the exception of Beni Modschedid's control over the Balearics. Moreover, this was the very time when the city communes of Italy were stirring, not only those in the Byzantine area such as Amalfi, Salerno and Gaeta, which had kept in touch with the eastern routes, but also the northern cities such as Pisa, Genoa and Lucca. We cannot detect a coherent organisation of local powers, however, until after 1035, which leaves us to suppose that the first signs of aggression were the work of pirates, acting on their own account: first of all the Pisans, who were to be found in Corsica and Sardinia around 1013–15, getting as far as Bône in 1034; then the Genoans, who established themselves all along the Ligurian coast. The main push, however, came after the mid-eleventh

Traditional Mediterranean galley. It was the fastest vessel in the Byzantine fleet, before the Italians adapted it for trade. It had only one deck and used oars rather than sails. (Miniature by Pietro da Eboli, *Liber ad honorem Augusti*, twelfth century; Berne, Bibliothèque de la bourgeoisie.)

century, when it was greatly assisted by the arrival of the Normans, who happened to gain a foothold in southern Italy after 1017–30, as mentioned above. These pilgrims-turned-mercenaries who became conquerors on their own account gradually eliminated the Greek leaders and local potentates from Aversa (1038), Apulia (1042–60), Calabria and Campania (1060–70), Gaeta (1073) and Salerno (1077), dominating Amalfi and Naples before annexing them (1127–30). During this latter period the decisive line was crossed: Sicily, key to the Mediterranean, became a Christian land once more. This was a hard-fought conquest, however, both because of the small number of Norman and Italian warriors who aided Roger and Robert Guiscard, and because of stiff resistance from the strongly Muslim local powers: Messina (1061), Palermo (1072), Trapani (1078), Syracuse (1086), Malta (1090). The fall of El Cid; the audacious raid by the Genoans which led to the burning of the great Tunisian port of Mahdiyya in 1087; the breaking of the Muslim hold on the Balearics in 1113 by the joint efforts of the Pisans, Genoans, Catalans and Provençals (efforts which had to be renewed in 1131 after the Almoravids sprang up) – these were all stages in a movement which saw the step-by-step dissolution, in less than 100 years, of a

Muslim domination of the seas which had lasted for four centuries. Furthermore, the situation was actually reversed as, once he became 'king' of Sicily, the Norman Roger II threw his men into the fray and kept them in Islamic territory for several years, at Sfax, Djerba and Tripoli in 1148 and at Mahdiyya in 1156, so cutting the maritime link between Almeria and Damietta, the main axis of Islamic trade in the West. Thus a basic pillar of the Muslim world was removed as the western sea was lost to it.

The eastern passage

Having become a Christian lake once again, with its ports from Malta to Otranto in Western hands, the Tyrrhenian Sea was too small for an expanding Europe. Certainly, the gold of Africa, the coral and oils of the Maghrib, the wool and pelts of Andalusia were no longer inaccessible mirages, but the demands of the Western aristocracy, and eventually of the bourgeois, necessitated access to the East. This was quite another story, however, because coastal navigation was more difficult along hostile territory, and distance multiplied the risks; and neither the Byzantines nor the Fatimids of Egypt, nor the Hamdanids and Seljuks of Syria and Anatolia were weak adversaries, and lacked neither organisation nor experience. The enterprise had to be undertaken with due caution.

Pilgrims had never ceased going to the Holy Land, and as the land route had been forbidden to them in the tenth century and after, they made their way on Greek vessels, or better still, on Venetian ships. On the way, sanctuaries such as Monte Cassino, St Michael of Gargano or St Nicholas of Bari offered resting-places. Apart from the short period at the beginning of the eleventh century marked by the fanaticism of al-Hakim, who destroyed the Holy Sepulchre, individual pilgrims could travel with some degree of security, though this varied according to their means. The spiritual awakening which preceded the reform of the Church gave impetus to the pilgrimage to Jerusalem, as to other places, and in 1033 (which marked the thousandth anniversary of the Passion), a host of pilgrims of both sexes and all conditions headed for the East, a windfall for professional ferrymen. In fact, those who personally chartered boats, like the Normans who stopped in Campania on the way, were the exception. Western historiographical tradition has made a lot of the obstacles to the voyage created by the Seljuks, once their power over the Middle East was secure. They have long been seen as the spark inflaming the army of faith, but there is an element of contrivance in this: the problems they posed amounted to little more than some administrative harrassment or financial exactions, which were exaggerated by some discontented travellers on their return, such as Peter the Hermit; in fact, the Turkish occupation of the Holy City was short-lived (1070–89) and did not check the attraction of the East.

A particular difficulty obviously stemmed from the Byzantine presence on the route, complicated by the historic rights which the empire insisted were preserved over eastern lands lost to it since the seventh century. The prevailing opinion in the West was that the 'Romans' had a duty to protect pilgrims and thus to reassume control over the East. Neither the Saxon emperors of the tenth century nor the Salian rulers of the eleventh challenged their role as sword and shield of Christendom. Even after the official rupture between the sees of Rome and Constantinople in 1054, the Western Church did not take advantage of the schism to deprive the Greeks of this mission, though ignorance and the growing feeling of a great disparity both on an economic level and in terms of moral concepts between the two halves of the former Roman world did not create the best conditions for a rapprochment against a common enemy, whom they each perceived quite differently anyway. The abrupt Greek withdrawal as far as the Straits under Turkish pressure, and the unexpected assault by the Pechenegs in the north did not greatly affect the West. Only the Normans in Sicily and Apulia saw an opportunity in that: in 1071 Robert Guiscard armed a fleet in the Adriatic, and waited only for the prize of his daughter's marriage to a son of the emperor Michael VII. But when the latter died, and believing the moment of the Komnenos dynasty's difficult assumption of the Greek throne to be opportune, he embarked from Durazzo with the pope's blessing (1084), advanced on Epiros and pushed as far as Thessaly. Local resistance, however, together with the arrival of Alexios Komnenos, and threats from the Venetians whose new treaty with the Greeks (1082) committed them to the status quo, forced him to return to base. It is thus very unlikely that the Greek emperor would have asked for help which, around 1090, he would not have known what to do with and which would have been risky; for its part, the West hardly seemed aware of Byzantine misfortunes.

Contemporaries therefore looked elsewhere. Italian traders had certainly maintained links with the East since the tenth century. From 980 there were a great many Venetians in Constantinople and Amalfians in Cairo and Alexandria. Here and there they obtained fiscal privileges and, sometimes, a market; the fortune of the celebrated Pantaleone of Amalfi, who founded a hospice in Jerusalem around 1060–70 and traded in the Italian–Aegean–Delta triangle, shows both the relative security of transport and the slow but sure re-emergence of maritime trading routes, which had been so long unused between the Muslim Near East and the Christian West. Moreover, in 1088–90, when Alexios Komnenos was driven to manipulate the currency and devalued the *nomisma* by two-thirds, the West eventually benefited: Eastern products became more accessible and thus more tempting. Besides, as the imperial tax system resigned itself to exempting all or a part of the rights of *kommerkion* on commodities sold to a foreigner, himself exempt, it may be said that by the end of the eleventh century European traders were attracted eastwards by strong economic incentives. The renewal of contacts was thus felt to be increasingly desirable and possible. But of course the political *status quo*, which Venice championed, formed the basic condition of this renewal and clearing. Here piracy was not endemic on the scale of the western basin: moreover – and even if we have no evidence for this prior to 1100, the practice was doubtless older – western convoys, notably the Venetian *mudas*, were escorted by war-galleys. Thus everything was moving towards positive evolution, slowly but entirely peacefully. This was what the pilgrims thought, as did the merchants, Greeks and Muslims. Such expectations were to be rudely shattered.

Adventure in the Holy Land

The Crusades can still provide the stuff of Christian dreams and Muslim nightmares. This great adventure which, for two centuries, served as backdrop to the fantasies of Europe, has deposited in our collective consciousness a thick layer of memories, both pitiful and glorious, of picturesque anecdotes, and of ambitions, respectable or otherwise. A realist would be quick to condemn the eventual failure, on almost every level, of this European probe into the very heart of Islam; it has even been written jokingly that the one concrete result of the Crusades was the introduction of the apricot into Europe! And after all, once trade was broken off, the ports lost, the missions scattered, what Europe retained of its contact with Islam seemed to have come its way from Spain or the Maghrib rather than from Iraq or Egypt. Be that as it may, beyond the indisputable waste of men, of effort and of money, the Crusades constituted a great episode in at least the psychological history of Europe, a great memory – and it was not only St Louis, dying in Tunis, whose last word was 'Jerusalem'.

After having rejected as too simplistic the traditional explanation that the maxim 'God wills it' was sufficient cause to send out the poor and barefoot to the Holy Places, historical research has revealed more sophisticated causes to be equally unconvincing. I have come to the conclusion that politically, militarily and economically the armed expedition to the East lacked a *raison d'être*. Today we see ourselves back at the point reached by historians in the 1920s: the Crusades were an unjustified and inexplicable urge. The abortive enquiries of historians provide one conclusion at least: an effort lasting two centuries cannot be due simply to the inflammatory words of one pope, whose authority, moreover was contested by half of Europe. The notion of the Holy War, or rather of the propagation of the faith by force, which had its place in Muslim thought, was no stranger to the Christian psyche; it had underlain many bloody conversions in the Carolingian era, for example, and had served the Germans as a pretext for seizing good land in Poland and Lithuania. One would not be too surprised to find this spirit underpinning the Iberian *Reconquista*. As I said earlier, however, the driving back of the Berbers and then the Moors to the south was touched with a spirit of piety, but its main concerns were economic rather than religious, as is shown by the generally very lenient attitude of the Spanish princes before 1250 or 1300. This rejection of intolerance is reminiscent of the Byzantine attitude on the other side of the Mediterranean basin; neighbourliness is not too far from understanding. Such a vision was evidently not shared by other peoples in the Christian world. The nobles of Burgundy or Languedoc who placed themselves at the service of the Castilians at Barbastro or Toledo between 1063 and 1085 were angered by their clemency and challenged it; after all, the popes Alexander II and Gregory VII had promised them special grace, the status of St Peter's protégés, if they would fight for the Cross; were they not the warriors, the *bellatores*, the knights of Christ, *milites Christi*?

The fundamental explanation is to be found here. If salvation could be obtained by sailing to Palestine, and, if one were a warrior, by 'thrusting a sword into the belly of the Infidel as far as it would go' (in the charitable words of St Louis) in, for example, Sicily or Spain, the Crusade (the armed explosion of men of all conditions) would not have assumed the form it did. Something more is required than the advantages promised to the Crusader or the sermons which enthused the crowds – a general psychological pressure, which is one of the elements in the formation of Romanesque Europe. The simultaneous awakening of

Leaving for the Crusades: those departing (with the cross on their chest or shoulder) and those staying behind. (Twelfth-century fresco in the Templar chapel, Cressac, Charente.)

Return from the Crusades: a 'missing person' returns to his wife. Count Hugh I of Vaudémont accompanied Louis VII on the Second Crusade in 1147. The following year, knights returning to Lorraine brought news of his death. In fact he returned to Vaudémont sixteen years later, and died shortly afterwards, worn out by exhaustion and privation. (Funerary mounument from the second half of the twelfth century, Eglise des Cordeliers, Nancy.)

piety and productiveness accompanied the grouping together of men in the seigneurial framework, and the establishment of a society ruled, at least theoretically, by God. The 'peace movements' are the clearest signs of this to historians today: the God of battles, the avenger and punisher, could not be left alone to defend his people and guide them to salvation. Since the kings defaulted – and none went to Jerusalem, all being occupied elsewhere or excommunicated – the faithful would have to take their own salvation in hand: professional soldiers by taking up arms, clerks by their prayers, workers by their toil. 'Peace' was conceived as the maintenance, by force if necessary, of God's rule; and among the 'institutions of peace', the armed pilgrimage occupied a key place. It was this which Urban II, inciting the southern barons in 1095 at Clermont to fulfil their obligations in arms, had not foreseen. He probably hoped for an expeditionary force from Provence or Toulouse, which could perhaps save him from the clutches of the emperor Henry IV along the way (but a veil is usually drawn over probable intentions which have never had the chance to be revealed). What emerged, however, was a general levy that completely escaped his control. From every corner – Normandy, Flanders, Ile-de-France, the Rhineland, Burgundy, Aquitaine, Lombardy, Sicily – inflamed by hermits, illuminati, and adventurers, came a mixture of the ambitious, the marginal, the younger sons; men of war and peasants who believed that this was the royal road to the Judgement, peace and salvation by blood and sweat, under the astounded gaze of clerks and merchants. Others were affected, too: the Jews, who were the

270

first to suffer as they were conveniently at hand along the Rhine or the Rhône, and the peoples of the East who were not expecting anything like this.

Older estimates of 100,000 men have been replaced by a figure of some 4,000 or 5,000 men on horseback, and 60,000 on foot, with women and children. These figures, which seem modest to us, struck contemporaries with amazement and fear, particularly with regard to the bands of peasants whose reputation for pillaging preceded them. It is not my brief here to follow the march and activities of the Crusaders from the first departures in spring 1096 to the bloody capture of Jerusalem on 15 July 1099, but it is important for the history of the West to note certain points. Three points in particular, even before 1099, are immediately striking. First of all, it was impossible to form a unified movement under a single direction. The papal legate Adhemar of Monteil was outflanked from the start; the theoretical leader, Raymond of Toulouse, was challenged; the highest-ranking baron, Godfrey of Bouillon, duke of lower Lorraine, was too narrow-minded; the attitude towards the Greek emperor was incoherent, the roads to be followed diverged; worse still, political calculations quickly emerged. For the Normans of Sicily, Bohemond of Tarentum and Tancred, it was a chance to renew Guiscard's designs on the Balkans; for Baldwin of Boulogne, or Raymond of Saint-Gilles, an opportunity to build up fiefs on the spot. From the outset these political calculations, grafted on to European dynastic ambitions, vitiated the *raison d'être* of the enterprise. Second, it soon became obvious that a task of this nature could only be undertaken by professional soldiers, and they soon suffered from fighting tactics which, like the customs, food and climate, were very different from their own. The heat, thirst, leprosy and harassment by sniping archers quickly caused more damage than sieges or attacks. As for those on foot, they had been massacred on their first contact with the Turks across the Bosphorus. Under such conditions, two separate strands evolved, and their separateness has not been sufficiently emphasised: one strand was the particular 'Crusades', led by the princes when a major event triggered exceptional military effort; the other was the general 'Crusade', the annual coming and going of pilgrims, merchants and adventurers at each season when the sea-crossing was possible. The third point arises from the last one: the overland route along the Danube – taken by travellers in 1096, then by reinforcements in 1100, and later by princes such as Louis VII and Conrad III and finally by Frederick Barbarossa – was seen to be so long and so perilous that the main effect of the expeditions was to make the sea the chief means of transport for men, beasts and supplies. In this regard, the adventure to the Holy Land was a fundamental stage in the reclaiming of the eastern Mediterranean for Christendom.

Europe and the twelfth-century Crusade

While the extent of the military effort it required is remarkable, the First Crusade also had unexpectedly far-reaching effects. We know that it resulted, some twenty years later, in the wresting from Islam of all access to the sea, from Cilicia to the Delta, and in the placing of the lower valley of the Nile under Greek and Frankish control, between 1153 and 1169. If we consider, moreover, that up to 1146 the Christians (Armenians and Franks) maintained control of the passes of the Taurus and of the upper Euphrates at Edessa, and up to 1185 control of the Gulf of Akaba, along whose length ran the pilgrim road to Mecca, we can grasp the scale of the threat to Islam. But we must qualify this with the fact that, on the one hand, the 'states' grouped around the King of Jerusalem were never able to count on the mastery of the interior of the fertile crescent (Mosul–Aleppo–Damascus–Petra), so that with the exception of Jerusalem, they had to cling to the coast; on the other hand, these States faced problems of a truly 'colonial' nature. Once the Holy City was retaken and the Crusaders had departed, there remained no more than 2,000 soldiers to the 'kings' and Frankish princes in the Holy Land, and this made absolutely necessary a constant traffic in horses, arms and reinforcements, even after the creation of the resident orders of monk-soldiers (the Templars and Hospitallers after 1110 or 1120), and the building of gigantic fortified refuges, the 'kraks' which are still so admired by architects. This vital traffic, which linked the 'colonies' to the West, could only be lessened in one way: by assimilation with the local Syrians or Armenians (through intermarriage, for example). But at that time this provoked discord and misunderstanding between the young champions of Antioch or Acre (who married locally, wore native costume and were careful to maintain good local relations) and the enthusiastic pilgrims who had come out to slaughter and returned home (if they were lucky) indignant and cheated.

The creation of the Frankish states in the Holy Land had other, more beneficial effects, particularly for Italian ship-owners and merchants. The Genoese were the first to see this, having had a foothold in Syria since 1065. They rented out ships and, in 1097, gained concessions in quays, markets, customs receipts at Antioch, Arsuf, Caesarea, Acre and Tripoli. Pisa, overtaken by its rival, quickly caught up; in 1099 it placed a patriarch in Jerusalem, gained a foothold in Jaffa and Latakia and kept up links with Egypt. Beaten by such speed, the Venetians adapted themselves, as always: a third of the cities of Haifa, Sidon, Tyre and Beirut, with their revenues, came their way between 1101 and 1110. But others were pouring in, from Marseilles, Montpellier, Saint-Gilles and Barcelona before 1136, when the Normans of Sicily attacked Tunisia. In general, this dense network of connections which placed Eastern maritime trade in Western hands depended on Greek neutrality or assistance, as the Komnenos emperors were shrewd enough to perceive. In return for the control they exercised over Antioch, they accepted the presence of Italian trading posts within their very capital: Venice had been there since the eleventh century; and Pisa and Genoa obtained identical privileges in 1111 and 1155 respectively. Greek–Italian complicity explains the penetration of Egypt in the mid-twelfth century. This rapprochement, however, was not undisturbed. Pilgrims criticised this sort of collaboration with increasing harshness, denouncing the debasement of the Holy Land and the duplicity of the Greeks. From time to time something soured relations: for example, after the unimportant loss of Edessa, the West took fright in 1147; at the call of St Bernard, the Capetian Louis VII and the German Conrad III took up the Cross; they rightly rejected the hypocritical proposals of the Norman Roger II of Sicily, who dreamed of occupying Byzantium. This Second Crusade failed miserably amidst military and psychological errors; for his part, Roger had to evacuate Corfu and Boeotia, briefly occupied (1148–9), but in the west the Greeks were blamed. Another warning-note was sounded when the third emperor of the Komnenos dynasty, Manuel, planned to set foot in Italy and disembarked at Ancona (1155). This merely increased Western anxieties. As a final complicating factor, Islam, hitherto suppressed and powerless, seemed to be rousing itself: in crushing the Fatimid schism and seizing Egypt, the Kurd Salah ad-Din (Saladin) suddenly upset the political scene (1171) just when the Almohads were creating an empire in the west, from Senegal to the Tagus.

Henceforth in the East, attention focused either southwards upon Egypt, or northwards upon Byzantium. The period 1170–1230 was of crucial importance. All trading activity, blocked in Mesopotamia and beyond, was now to turn towards Cairo, Alexandria and Damietta, as the Christians had realised it would by 1150. It became much more profitable for the Italians to go there in quest of seasonings, alum, spices or precious stones. From 1154, and particularly in the 1170s, trading posts were opened there by the Pisans, Genoese, and merchants from Salerno and Palermo, and Venice agreed a firm peace with Saladin, the man who held in his hand the routes from Chad, Abyssinia, the Indian Ocean and the Persian Gulf. Relations were good, even if every Christian ship had to be dismasted on entry into port; it is said that there were 3,000 Latin merchants in Alexandria. Why worry unduly about a work of pious reconquest which concentrated on Palestine? When, after having cleared the Red Sea and the pilgrim route, Saladin captured the Frankish army at Hattin and launched himself on Jerusalem (1187), this did not worry the Italians. In the North, however, it had much greater impact. The prestigious Third Crusade was launched, with the aim of retaking the Holy Sepulchre; it had as its leaders the emperor Frederick Barbarossa, the Capetian Philip Augustus and Richard of England, who gained there his name 'the Lionheart'. The results, however, were wretched. Frederick drowned before he set foot there (1190), Philip soon departed, content with the consolidation of Acre, and Richard pushed slowly towards the Holy City, but failed to take it. When he left in his turn (1192–3), the Franks held a string of coastal towns but were virtually in the hands of the Italians, with the empty title of 'king' of Acre, disputed by the Germans and the French. The situation was clear: the 'Crusade' could now only be a business affair.

The Greeks had not come to their aid, and to the Western mind their subtle strategy was nothing but treason. The Empire, once more being disturbed in Asia Minor, was gradually losing its grip: it alternated concessions with repression, allowing Italian pirates to establish themselves in the Aegean, but inciting the crowds against the Latins in the capital, who numbered 50,000 according to Eustachios of Thessalonica. The jealousy and contempt of the West was met with hatred by the Greeks, confined to humdrum local trade by the exorbitant privileges granted to the Italians, their pride wounded by continual Latin embassies, starving and suffering from a siege mentality. And there were sudden, violent acts: the arrest of the Venetians in 1171, the massacre of the Latins in 1182; the Normans, who attacked the Adriatic islands, burnt down Thessalonica in 1185. The end of the Komnenos dynasty created an anarchic situation and the son of Barbarossa, Henry VI, let it be known that drastic measures must be taken.

Where, then, were the 'keys to Jerusalem'? In Cairo or Byzantium? With the descendants **273**

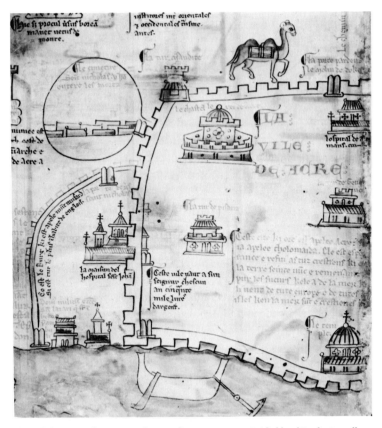

Plan of the town of Acre on a thirteenth-century map. Guided by this, the traveller would know how to reach the gate to the Saint-Jean Hospital, for example, recognisable by its roofs surmounted with the Cross of Lorraine. (Royal MS 14 c VII; London, the British Library.)

of Saladin, steady friends to the Italians but infidels? Or in that Christian land of the East where the law had been laid down so long ago?

Decline and failure

When Pope Innocent III called for a new effort in the East, the ambiguity of Western intentions was evident; the rulers declined and then changed their minds; princes such as the Count of Champagne and Baldwin of Flanders accepted but dawdled. As for the Italians, the idea of an attack on Egypt or even on Ayyubid Palestine did not tempt them; they would have preferred to see the route across Asia Minor freed – from the Black Sea or from northern Mesopotamia, which they did not control in spite of their settlements in Crete, Cyprus and Cilicia. Did the request made by the dethroned emperor Alexios IV in 1202 contain an express petition for a long stay in Constantinople? The argument for Constantinople was advanced by the Venetians who rented out their ships. Can one speak of a 'hijacking' of the

274

Crusade? After all, restoring Venetian control in Zara and in the Adriatic could be justified; moreover, if the target was Anatolia, Byzantium was of course the port of call. The outcome is well known. Against the background of a total lack of understanding, of particular circumstances and interests, and of extremely unequal strengths, relations between Greeks and Latins deteriorated. On 13 April 1204 the Crusaders attacked Constantinople and took the city for the first time in its history. The Italians arranged a thorough sacking in their own interests, and made a vast profit: five tons of gold for Venice alone! The criminal nature of this was obvious, and events should have stopped there, but they were pushed to the level of sin: the Greek Empire was declared defunct, the Count of Flanders was proclaimed emperor, and the mainland and islands were divided up between Venice and the French crusaders.

This was a solution; but it was a particularly bad one. It doubled the number of reinforcements needed around the Aegean; it sharpened the rivalries amongst the Italians (the Genoese felt themselves especially hard done by); it provided no solution to the problem of Anatolia; and, on top of all this, it did not even finish off the enemy, as one Greek Empire fell back to Nicaea, another to Trebizond, there was a 'despotism' in Epiros, and the populations of Achaea, Thessaly and Thrace did not wholly submit. The Bulgarian advance, and the Egyptian pressure on a sea now free of Greek control added to the incredible mess that was the 'Byzantine solution'.

Would the 'Egyptian solution' be any better? Disappointed, Innocent III played that card, but he was a solitary player: the Italians were openly hostile, the West was weary; the call went out to the East. The expedition to the Delta led by Pelagius the legate and John of Brienne, king of Jerusalem, was a fiasco (1215–19). Negotiations were tried: the emperor Frederick II, more attentive than most of his contemporaries to the Muslim world – seduced, so he said 'by the call of the muezzin in the night' – compromised with the Egyptian sultan. By a surprising treaty in 1229 he obtained the formal retrocession of Jerusalem, and went there, albeit excommunicated, to become 'king' of the city thanks to a disreputable dynastic subterfuge. Unfortunately this solution remained dependent on the Eastern status quo; the disruptions caused by Mongol pressures meant that the Christians had to withdraw again in 1244. They resorted once more to armed expedition. Perhaps for the first time a specific plan and a guiding will co-ordinated all their efforts. Louis IX of France, driven by piety but also tapping the newly militant faith that had shaken the world of the poor, the wanderers, the 'children' and the 'shepherd boys' in search of a new road to salvation, led a second Egyptian expedition (1249). This resulted in a fresh defeat, with two contrasting effects. On the one hand a military *coup d'état* opened Egypt to the aggressive ambition of the Mamluks, making any future attempt at intervention much more unlikely; on the other hand, the 'Passion' of the king, prisoner for a time, laid one of the foundations of his future 'sanctity'. Instead of a sea attack, perhaps the Delta could be gained from Tunisia. St Louis allowed himself to be convinced of this mad plan by his brother, Charles, who had become the new lord of Naples and Sicily, in succession to the Normans and the Germans, and for whom it would be advantageous to have a wedge driven into the heart of the Mediterranean.

The sad failure of this last effort is well known. The king died outside Tunis, struck down by plague and gnawed by doubt (1270). The affair was settled: the Mamluks could gather in the towns and fortresses of Palestine and the Lebanon, a process they completed with the recapture of Acre in 1291. Thirty years previously Constantinople, defended only by Venice, had fallen back into Greek hands. The West did keep its outposts in the Black Sea, in the Aegean, in Crete, Cyprus and the Morea. In the ports of the Levant, and even in Egypt, Western rights persisted. In short, the sea remained theirs, but the hope of reconquering the coast was no more than an illusion; it survived for 100 years or more as a tenacious memory, with the hope of Jerusalem being once more a Christian city never extinguished.

For a time – and this third solution, earthbound as it might seem, must take its place here – Europe dreamed of a grander strategy: to take eastern Islam from the rear. The building up of Mongol domination in Asia had probably not been long known or understood in the West. But the stories spread by pilgrims returning from the Holy Land, by the few merchants who had ventured as far as the edges of the Gobi, and hard facts such as the anti-Muslim raids of 1220–3 in Iran, Georgia and the Ukraine, had given birth to the notion of possible collaboration with the Tartar khans. It was said that Nestorians played an important role at Qaraqorum, the Mongol capital, and there were reports of Mongol princes being baptised. Was it not from those lands that 'Prester John' would come to the aid of the Cross? The Franciscans were more easily convinced than the merchants, who had heard other rumours of horrific and indiscriminate massacres perpetrated by these hordes. St Louis firmly believed in it, and missionaries left for Asia from 1232 or 1235. The double-edged nature of the venture soon surfaced, however. The great raid of 1238–9, which reached as far as the Russian principalities of Yaroslav in the north and Kiev in the south, revealed a total indifference to religious considerations. Worse still, in 1241–2 the horsemen of the Golden Horde sacked Cracow, Olmütz and Serbia before returning to base; Andrew, the king of Hungary, defeated and panic-stricken, proclaimed a new threat from the Hun. But illusions persisted in France. Had the Mongols not just beaten the Turks in Anatolia (1242)? They sacked Baghdad, destroyed the ancient Abbasid caliphate, advanced into Syria (1256), and held the Mamluks in check (1260). The Capetian king sent out two more missionaries, John of Plano Carpini (1245–7) and William of Rubruck (1252–5); their hopes were strengthened by the relative ease by which merchants travelled in the vast commercial zone established from Asia Minor to China. The long journeys of the three Polo brothers, Niccolo, Marco and Matteo, who wandered through Asia for thirty years (1260–95) are still famous. But all this was pure illusion: the Mongols understood nothing of the desires and mentality of the Europeans. They were nomads, who lived by raiding and attached little importance to State religion, adding to a basic animism whatever belief they pleased. As for an alliance, to them such a term meant only submission. This was a dialogue of the deaf, to which the death of the saint–king put an end. Besides, without entering the realms of hypothesis, it is hard to imagine what real help the Mongols could provide, being so far from their bases, and who, because of their climate and customs, were far from easy to bring into lasting submission.

The crusading episode had a profound effect on the psychology of medieval Europe, polarising the various millenarist tendencies and elevating pilgrimage to the level of martyrdom; but these were moral effects which do not concern us here. On the other hand, we must understand that on the earthly level of its material structure, the Christian Church experienced its effects strongly, and initially positively. For at least a century, even if they had not always been able to involve all those whom they wished, the papacy and the secular hierarchy had leaned heavily on the lay powers, draining off the aristocracy's warrior force to their own service. A number of the fratricidal episodes in European political life had been curtailed by the crusading movement, and the prestige of the See of Rome had certainly been increased, at least until 1204. What is more, the cost of armed expeditions or even of pilgrims' journeys had involved expenses which had meant a considerable transfer of wealth to the Church. The pawning of land for ready money, when this land was not redeemed, enriched the ecclesiastical world, particularly the regular clergy – the monks who played little part in the actual operations of the expeditions, but who alone held indispensable liquid assets. But we must set against this profit a debit which became ever heavier in the thirteenth century: the collusion in material or political interests between the papacy and the princes had discredited to some extent the military activity in the East. It became evident, especially after 1245–50, that the ambitions of the Angevin princes of Sicily, or the pressure brought to bear on popes by Genoa or Venice had little to do with the the interests of the faith. A low point was reached when, despite having been excommunicated for his Italian disputes with Gregory IX, Emperor Frederick II won Jerusalem (1229), which forced the pope to put the whole of the Holy Land under interdict. To such absurdities was added a strong suspicion that the Church was bent on enriching itself. The idea developed that it cared more about lending and hoarding than about ministering and comforting: the Templars later paid for this suspicion with their lives.

The warrior aristocracy had lost a great deal of blood in the military episodes in the East; without claiming that it was decimated, we should not under-estimate the losses through combat or long-term captivity suffered by the youth of France, especially in the twelfth century, and by that of Germany later, in the thirteenth. Even the simple armed pilgrim, prepared to fight his way to the East if necessary, often lost his life there. Inexperience and recklessness played a part here which they did not in European combat. Obviously no exact figure can be calculated but the study of noble genealogies shows a sudden break that has no equivalent in Western battles. In August 1119 at Brémule, where two kings engaged (Louis VI of France and Henry I of England), there were five deaths, whereas two months previously, more than 500 Normans had perished near Aleppo at the 'Field of Blood'. On the other hand, a large-scale movement of people is not likely. A number of aristocratic families established one of their younger sons in the Holy Land, but this hardly amounts to a colonial population. The aristocracy's losses in personnel were matched by financial losses. Besides the fact that properties that were temporarily pawned were often permanently lost, we have a lot of evidence for the large sums involved in the 'passage'. These naturally varied according to the rank of the pilgrim and the distance travelled, but they made up between 20 and 200 *livres tournois* at the beginning of the thirteenth century, which can be estimated as the value of between 10 and 100 hectares of good land (at the lowest estimate, this was much more than the landed capital of three to five hectares which was the minimum necessary for a peasant couple at the time).

There is no doubt, however, that the crusading movement, although it ended in territorial and military failure, gave the West a major economic boost. I have referred here mainly to the Italians, but if this survey were to be extended to the beginning of the fourteenth century, we would see Provence and Catalonia playing a prominent role. Moreover the essential point is not the identity of the agents but the fact that commerce with the East was renewed. By 1150, or certainly by 1200, the double restraint preventing the growth of the European economy had been loosened: Muslim piracy was no more and Byzantine taxation had disappeared. It is pointless to ask ourselves what would have been the catalyst for Europe had the situation not evolved in this way. It can be countered that Nordic expansion owes nothing to this, that the wealthy Europe of the sixteenth century was mistress of only half the Mediterranean. But the essential point remains: the reconquest of this sea was fundamental to the growth of Europe, a fact which must now be examined more closely.

The leap forward 7

The establishment of a new framework for existence perhaps justifies our following its stages over the decades. Each stage prepares the way for the progress of the next one. When we reach the moment at which the tree bears fruit, we must be able to see everything together in bud because it all springs from the same root; the eye cannot take all this in at once any more than the pen can describe everything simultaneously. Thus I have to resort to a sort of rational dislocation, imposed by the need for narrative, which disguises the unity of the whole; I have to cut up into sections things that only make sense as an ensemble. I am forced to do this, and the order I have adopted is simply for ease of presentation. It remains obvious that such factors as woodland clearance, the overcoming of dangers at sea, the human push forward and the evolution of consciousness, the growth of cultivable land and the expansion of towns can only be explained in relation to each other. At least the reader should grasp that everything was moving in one direction: towards growth. For a century and a half Europe, at last provided with the means of action, was escaping the weight of its past; it was 'taking off', as economists would say; and this great 'leap forward' is the major stage in its medieval history.

The explosion in food production

One of the eternal paradoxes for the medieval historian is the lack of detailed documentation of a major phenomenon, as we have already noted in the case of population growth. This time it is the progress of food production that escapes us: a regrettable gap at a time when, despite the shortage of evidence, we can make out not only the likely effects but also the certainty of such progress. The interest that those responsible showed in exploiting the land is one indication: in the mid-twelfth century, St Bernard advised establishing an abbey 'there where the seed yields a hundredfold', advice, however, which could not be fulfilled even in the modern era. Abbot Suger looked for and found sound beams for the structure of Saint-Denis; German entrepreneurs attracted forest-clearers to Silesia by promising fat

279

harvests and eternal salvation into the bargain; Philip of Alsace, Count of Flanders, oversaw the construction of Gravelines, and the stud farms of the lord of Rohan became good business at a time when warriors everywhere rode stallions. Another indication, although somewhat later, comes from the writing of agricultural manuals. Because most of these were English (*Fleta*, and Walter of Henley's *Husbandry*), the notion persists that England was in advance of continental Europe, but it is not clear that this was so. As for figures, we have nothing firm before the mid-thirteenth century, merely fragments from Cluny, Flanders, Ramsey, Winchester, Bavaria and from the regions near the Mediterranean where the natural conditions are not typical. We have to draw on acts of sale, records of alms, early taxation lists which allow a rough calculation of productivity. Archaeology, so promising for the early Middle Ages, is silent here, while iconography becomes stereotyped. However, we know that wheat, which in the ninth century on the royal estate of Annapes gave a twofold return, yields fourfold returns in 1155 at Cluny, sevenfold around 1225 in Picardy, and reaches elevenfold in Artois 100 years later, scarcely less than in France in 1900. Everything happens in concert: population, cultivable area and production all expand and inflate. Between 1090 and 1220 we have before us 'the century of great progress'. Satisfied with these undeniable findings provided by manorial archives in England and elsewhere, the historian nevertheless cannot avoid some uncomfortable questions. Let us pursue these.

Mastering natural forces

As we have seen, the need to grow more and more grain to feed an ever-increasing population was placing pressure on villages to clear greater tracts of land. The area under cultivation was certainly expanding, but was this to the extent that animals were driven out of the woods? In fact, the increase in grain production was more a matter of increases in yield than of an expanding cultivable land area. The eighteenth- and nineteenth-century idea that arable farming was a Christian effort based on pious zeal must be abandoned. That would not have made the days any longer, and an uplifted heart does not always mean a stronger body. Let us also leave it to another century to prove conclusively that an optimal climate was fertilising the soil and fortifying the living. Let us confine our attention to techniques.

The situation, however, is not at all clear. First of all because it is possible to maintain, as every war unhappily proves, that inventions are more often consequences than causes; and second, because techniques only operate in one particular mode of production. Thus the watermill is described by Virgil and the heavy plough by Pliny, but a system reliant on slavery was not interested in those. The horse is certainly a better ploughing animal than the ox because its muscles enable it to extricate a ploughshare from the mud in sticky soil; but the horse is jumpy, delicate and expensive. To yoke two or four is only possible if there are replacements available. So people remained faithful to the ox in England, in Bavaria and in Burgundy up to about 1225, 1250 and 1275 respectively. If we add to this the fact that the medieval scribe struggled to translate into Latin the vernacular terms used around him,

Ploughing. The oxen pull the plough, two by two: the yoke is placed on the withers or between the horns. Horses, faster but more expensive to feed, only gradually superseded oxen in the thirteenth century. (Add. MS 41230, London, British Library.)

sometimes only in order to flaunt his elegant style, it will be understood why the disoriented historian can only advance cautiously.

One thing is certain, however: apart from some machinery such as the camshaft or the worm screw, which had not been seen in the ancient world – though this may be only because our sources are defective – everything that sustained medieval production came from the Graeco-Roman world, or from the Far East, especially India, and perhaps even China. The former supplied the technical treatises of Vitruvius, Cato, Columella and Pliny, a *compendium* of ancient thought. Then the Avars, Moravians and Khazars of eastern Europe seem to have transmitted to the West the procedures and customs which they themselves probably borrowed from their Asian neighbours. It does not lessen the achievement of the Middle Ages if we bestow the laurels for basic research and advance elsewhere; the medieval period deserves the credit for benefiting humanity by its practical adaptation and popularisation of such techniques. As a region rich in wood, water and iron, north-west Europe was ideally placed to transfer the 'inventions' of Heraclitus or Archimedes from theory to practice, in three areas.

First, the substitution of domestic animal power for the labour of a reluctant slave is an idea which dates from Neolithic times. But only when slaves were in short supply, as in Europe after the year 1000, did animal power come into its own. To be sure, thirteenth-century toll records still show us men carrying their burdens in sacks, in baskets hanging round their necks, on wheelbarrows or slung on poles, but everything else is in wagons furnished with a front-yoke for oxen, or a collar for horses or mules. These beasts would be harnessed in line in order to maximise their power of traction, and they would be shod in order to protect their feet and strengthen their legs. These practices probably developed in Scandinavia and Trier in the tenth century, and in Grenoble and Epinal some fifty years later, as in the Slav lands, but can also be seen earlier in the caravans of the Gobi desert and in the treatises of Pliny the Elder. But we still do not know the progress and extent of this development. In the England of William the Conqueror, a shire forged only 120 horseshoes a year, and an Angevin toll of 1082 still taxed a shod horse at double rate. But by about 1175 the use of animal power seems to have become ubiquitous.

281

Second, we see the substitution of animals by machines. This is a great step; so great in fact that Marx regarded it as the birth of a new mode of production, with the concomitant establishment of an entirely new set of relations between men. The outline is simple and familiar: the motor force of water, and eventually that of wind, could be harnessed by man to activate his machines without human labour. Again the ancient world had understood this, and Vitruvius knew quite well how a mill worked with a water race, just as Byzantine Asia Minor and Persia knew about windmills. But the unreliability of these natural forces in the Mediterranean, together with an abundance of slaves or of camels or oxen, meant that the harnessing of such energy was confined to the realm of theory or the level of a simple prototype. Again, just as with the example of team ploughing, the Middle Ages took this up and brought it into widespread use. The Islamic world, and much of the entire southern side of Europe from Spain to Syria, remained faithful to archaic methods right into the twentieth century: norias (buckets on a wheel) for irrigation, grain crushed underfoot by men or beasts, the drudgery of watering or grinding by hand – all this prevented any progress. In north-west Europe, however, with its abundant rivers, people built watermills on swift-flowing water courses, under bridge arches, and on races barred by sluicegates. The conversion of rotation on the vertical plane driven by the current or winds to rotation on the horizontal permitted the grinding of grain, husks, nuts and olives, while the force of a swinging movement could be harnessed for sawing wood or breaking stones, and connected to a mallet for striking iron or fulling linen, and of course for emptying water into irrigation channels. Nobody who sees the extraordinary variety of its uses can fail to understand that those who claim that the first mechanisation took place in the Middle Ages are justified in saying so, and that it is not until the era of the steam engine that this impetus is regained. There are traces, scattered but unmistakable, in the ninth and mid-tenth centuries, but it is after 1125 in the French regions of Picardy, Poitou and Berry, in England and the Rhineland, in the towns (Toulouse, for example, had forty mills) as well as the country, that machines loom into view. It was no mean feat to get hold of the oaks and elms, the axles and sails, the lead cogwheels, the monolithic millstones, the iron rims, not to mention the wages for the fitters, the costs of transport and the water itself. Wealth was indispensable. When we have a price, as for a mill near Amiens around 1200, it is that of 20 hectares of good land. Who could embark on such a venture apart from the master of the village? It was inevitable that he would seek reimbursement for his costs of by making the peasants pay for the use of the mill. By 1175 or 1200, this became obligatory, and resulted in society's rejection of anyone who could not pay his due to the miller, that execrable henchman of the lord. This was clearly a social as well as an economic shift.

Finally, we see the impact of metal. The history of humankind begins with the mastering of fire, because then people could work metal. But the quality of weapons, tools and ornaments depended on that of the metal or the firing. Iron is fundamental here; historians have noted the superiority of the metal resources in Germany and Brittany, which explains the quality of 'barbarian' weapons and the excellence of their firing, and also perhaps – as E. Salin maintains – the restoration of the north's superiority in arms and crafts. This cannot be detected with any certainty, however, before the mid-tenth century. Metallurgy suddenly seems to explode in Europe between 950 and 1075. In Catalonia, near the Harz, around Milan, in the Ardennes, in Yorkshire and Bavaria, perhaps even earlier in Bohemia and Moravia, seams of metal ore were opened up, forges established near woods or water, and eventually in villages or towns. This was an essential technical change without which neither clearances nor mills can be understood. But the man who worked with fire, even if he had lost a little of the magic aura that surrounded his ancestor in the time of the Nibelungen, remained the focus of the village: in his forge, villagers and lords alike came to consult the smith, the skilled metal-worker, the 'mechanic', as Georges Duby has called him, bringing him a weapon to be straightened, an axe to be hammered, a wheel-rim to be fixed, a horse to be shod. With jealously guarded status, like the miller's, and as the equal of the village priest, the smith remained the leading figure in the village until the beginning of the twentieth century. Inasmuch as the forge adjoined the mill, it is no misuse of language to speak of a pre-industrial plant in existence by the beginning of the eleventh century in the heart of Germany, and by the beginning of the twelfth century in the territories from Le Mans to the Pyrenees, from Asti to Verona. The records of commercial taxation provide the historian with a valuable tool with which to measure the progress of this industry between 1030 and 1160: it reached Cambrai and Poitiers, Léon in Brittany and Visé in the region of the Meuse, producing iron rods in the eleventh century, rough-hewn tools in the twelfth, and by the thirteenth century knives were being sold in the markets, along with nails and ferrules.

One major factor, however, continued to overshadow this important sector: the meagreness of the market. At the very time that Christian Europe seemed be achieving a higher level of craftsmanship, the renown of 'Frankish' weapons disappears from the Islamic texts; archaeology yields only debris. Production was henceforth concentrated entirely on local needs, and could only satisfy such needs by being stretched to full capacity, leaving no slack for exports. In other words, the shift from luxury production to utilitarian consumption, which seems to us such a promising development, had as its first consequence the local contraction of building and employment. It is thus not until after 1250 that we find Milanese arms in Cologne. For the moment, metal-working existed in a local or at best regional context, and those who worked it were as tightly controlled in their workplaces in the towns as were those peasants in the villages who carried their grain to the mills.

There was one exception, however, to this picture of alienation. The Cistercian order, growing up on the margins of established society, proudly isolated in its 'deserts', forested or otherwise, soon made metal-work its speciality. It may be that the historian is misled by the abundance of documents left by the white monks, but between 1140 and 1190 forges mushroomed on Cistercian estates, from Languedoc to the Rhine, from Yorkshire to Burgundy, and the sale of their products at fairs is undeniably the beginning of commercialisation on a grand scale.

Serving the land

I remarked earlier that it is not easy to find evidence of a theory of agriculture before the appearance of English manuals in the thirteenth century. But these interesting compilations for the wealthy landowners were doubtless inaccessible to the labourers themselves, **283** who had to rely on their own experience. The peasant 'had a feeling for' the soil and worked it accordingly. Before 1250, it was rare for a peasant to risk clearing mediocre soil, rare to plant crops that did not match the soil, rare to experiment with a single crop without being certain of the results. In this hard, titanic struggle, we can see men forced to adapt themselves to its needs. For two centuries they tried to mould their effort to the land.

Undoubtedly historians have not attached enough importance to work on the land itself. Anthropologists' encounters with rudimentary agricultural practices surviving into the twentieth century have shown us that it is precisely here that success or failure in mastering the soil lies. Through study of the *corvées* that were exacted and of the modest iconographic sources and, best of all, through examination of ancient farming patterns as preserved, for example, at Wharram Percy in England, we are able to mark the progress in breaking down and enriching ploughland. The verb *tertiare*, which suggests a third tilling after digging and turning, appears after 1120 or 1130 with reference to rich soils extracted from coppices; a fourth ploughing before sowing is detectable in Artois a little more than a century later.

It is surprising that more than forty years elapsed between the hypotheses advanced by Marc Bloch concerning ploughing conditions and the reconsideration of this fundamental topic of research. It is true that inquiries come up against the barrier of vague terminology and the silence, possibly due to ignorance, of church scribes. Nevertheless the question is an important one because on its answer depends – at least in part – the solution to the elusive mysteries of land division. We are increasingly convinced that the ancient 'crisscross' ploughlands – the furrows marked on a field in a grid pattern, encouraging the growth of little plots collected together, the *quaderni* of Italy or *aiole* of southern France – were gradually replaced by ploughing in long parallel furrows. Was it a change in farming technology that brought this about, as Bloch believed? Partly, perhaps, where the plough is concerned, but the animal must have played a key role, because the slow, heavy ox, which could adapt to disturbed terrain, was replaced by the horse, which was more difficult to guide in such circumstances. Was the division of estates responsible? But why then should this result in such awkward strips of land? Was individualism responsible for that? If so, then the parcels of land would be gathered together and enclosed, but we cannot see that this was the case. This remains an unsolved problem of agrarian history.

We are not on any firmer ground when we consider the problem of tools and equipment. Are we dealing with the *aratrum* of the ancient world, a simple cone of wood tipped with iron, which could be bent, as Pliny recommended, but which could not be expected to do much more than scratch the soil? Or are we dealing with a plough as we understand it, with an asymmetrical ploughshare and a coulter that traced a path for the mouldboard to turn the soil over much more deeply? The performance of these two tools was totally different. The heavy plough had little or no effect on the powdery soil of the Midi. It was thus probably Germanic in origin, or even Slav, if we are to judge by the oldest ploughshares so far excavated, from the ninth or tenth centuries. The two instruments could co-exist, as can be seen, for example, in Poitou or Lombardy up to 1130. But once again, our conclusions are rendered provisional by the pedantry of some scribes for whom all ploughing instruments

Sowing. In autumn, the sower scatters the seed, which he takes from a small box. The crows show interest in his activities. Add. MS 42130, London, British Library.

were necessarily *aratrum*, and by the vagueness of others for whom a *carruca* could be a heavy-duty wagon. The mists do not clear until 1125–50: then the heavy plough predominates north of the Loire and the Danube, with or without wheels, and distinctions no longer matter. It was drawn by six to eight oxen, or by two to four horses, depending on regional custom, and was able to deal with heavy, damp soil such as that recently reclaimed from the forests. The constraints imposed by such a heavy and complex piece of equipment – it was difficult to turn and needed at least two men to guide it – were compensated for by the fact that the grain could be planted deeper and was thus protected from frost or rotting. But although the soil was aerated, it received little in the way of artificial enrichment until about 1220 when practices such as marling, liming and the regular spreading of household manure are explicitly noted in leases. The soils of Wharram Percy have revealed traces of domestic manure carefully spread over the worked land. Such traces are also detectable in the Beauce, in Picardy, and in the Thames basin in the 1170s.

It was probably this enriching of the soil that made possible the gradual trend towards more frequent sowings, which would have been impossible on soil that was quickly exhausted. As far as we can judge, it seems that men sowed a good deal less than 0.7 hectolitres per hectare in the ninth century; by the late twelfth century, however, the figure was beginning to rise. Accounts from Cluniac and from manorial accounts in thirteenth-century England, the Ile-de-France and Picardy provide evidence which suggests a rise to between 2 and 2.5 hectolitres per hectare north of the Seine, between 3 and 3.6 hectolitres at Winchester and some 4 hectolitres close to Paris by the end of the thirteenth century.

One's first reaction to this is to suspect that, without modern methods of cultivation (especially the use of organic and inorganic fertilisers), the soil would quickly have been exhausted under wheat or other cereals with high nutrient demands. However, it was precisely to overcome this problem that we see another element of cultivation being adopted,

285

namely the regular 'resting' of the soil. This was a departure from the ancient custom of 'shifting cultivation' (moving on to new lands after the soil of old ones has been exhausted) and required a fundamental change to the way in which land was organised. Letting a field lie untilled, long recommended by Varro and Columella, could only be incorporated into a controlled cycle of cultivation made up of a series of winter sowings, spring sowings and a period of fallow, accompanied by ploughing and manuring, or, if need be, a system of alternating winter sowings and fallowing. All this implies that fields or parcels of land had to be placed into two or three groups, whether packed together or scattered does not matter, and a regular rotation imposed upon them. Without such a framework, this practice would have soon failed.

It is clear that such control of the soil is a world away from the timid efforts of the Carolingian period and that it was adopted only slowly. Some attempts to impose this sort of control can be detected in the middle of the twelfth century in Picardy and around Cluny but the first certain indications of it – although perhaps not all of the village's territory was affected – come from the Ile-de-France around 1248–55 (Vaulerent, Tremblay) and, some twenty years later, from Picardy and Flanders.

From 1100 to 1250 and beyond, the whole period of 'the leap forward' is marked by sustained effort. Did these efforts bear fruit? Here we face the problem of productivity. This is difficult because the sources at our disposal very rarely provide figures relating to both sowing and harvesting; only England in the thirteenth century, in areas such as Ely, Winchester, Ramsey and Glastonbury, allows us to make confident statements about the period before 1250. Elsewhere, in Bavaria, in Artois, in the kingdom of France, around Toulouse, in the Mâconnais and in Lombardy, there are only occasional glimmers. Furthermore, we often do not know the exact areas that were sown, or the quality of the crop, which makes a comparison with today's quintals per hectare (100 kg/ha) a risky matter. For this reason, estimates of productivity are generally in terms of the amount of seed sown, the grain returning so many times the original amount of seed. Making allowance for inevitable regional contrasts, we can at least discern an overall ascending curve. The incredibly low productivity of the Carolingian era – a twofold or threefold return (which would plunge even the most backward country into chronic famine) – was raised to four- or fivefold by the mid-twelfth century. Such a figure, at the lower end of what scholars accept as the average for the period 1175–1200, would certainly have removed the spectre of famine. But for the silt-laden soil of Swabia, the Thames and and Paris basins, the figures are much higher, seven- or eightfold; at the end of the thirteenth century and at the beginning of the fourteenth, in the Ile-de-France, Picardy and Brabant the returns reached eleven- or even twelvefold, a figure not far off the yield in rural France in 1900. Such a level can only have been reached in exceptional areas: but, with the reservations we have mentioned, a yield of thirteen to fifteen quintals per hectare (1300–1500 kg/ha) is certainly plausible. Elsewhere, which is to say across most of Europe, it would be safer to say that the yield was six or sevenfold during the height of medieval arable cultivation.

Let us focus on this average: it means that for contemporary kinds of white wheat, a hectare would produce 600 kilograms of flour. From this, the amount owed to the master

Byzantine mosaic of Christ Pantocrator in the Norman cathedral of Cefalù, Sicily, mid-twelfth century

Byzantine silk fragment, tenth to eleventh century (London, Victoria and Albert Museum)

Mosaic image of Christ with Roger II in the Martorana church, Palermo, Sicily, mid-twelfth century

Painting on wood of St Francis and scenes from his life by Bonaventura Berlinghieri, 1235 (Pescia, church of
St Francis)

must be subtracted, along with the tithe and the quantity that had to be sold in order to procure the cash needed for other payments, and of course for the seed needed for the next sowing. This means that we have to reduce the total volume by a half. If we reckon the daily ration of bread to be 400 grams, a hectare theoretically could feed a peasant for three years. But, in order to keep a family with five children above the hunger threshold, a man would need at least 1.5 hectares of sown land in order not to exhaust the soil, and to be able to rotate crops with his neighbours and feed his livestock. If he did not have that much land, he would have to rely on what he could gather, or choose crops that were more prolific but less nourishing.

The food harvest

In attempting to gather evidence of a 'traditional' system of food-production (as the geographers vaguely call it), we have tended to overlook one element that was fundamental to both the ancient and the medieval systems, namely the equal partnership of the forest and the open fields (the *bosc* and the *plain*, the mountain and the plain, the *saltus* and the *ager*, the outfield and the infield, as they are called according to time, place and language). This forest/farmland economy is difficult for us to reconstruct for three main reasons: first, we ourselves no longer encounter livestock grazing in the woods, feeding on shoots, beechnuts and acorns; second, the berries, windfalls, herbs and wild vegetables of centuries past have been reduced to only a few hedgerow species of chestnuts, blackberries or nuts; and third, hunting with decoys or nets is now subject to control. All these resources, however, were available to people in the twelfth century, and not only when circumstances led them to take refuge in the forest. Moreover, the woods of northern Europe with their beeches, chestnuts and oaks benefited people living in northern climates more than those living in the scrublands or maquis, the result, perhaps, of ancient devastation. Only the conifers, killing off the undergrowth, sheltered woodcutters alone; it was not until the fourteenth century that the prospect of profit in town increased the numbers of these trees (which today seem quite natural to us), from Latium to the Vosges, but which chased men and beasts from forests which had hitherto nourished them. At no time in the central Middle Ages can the extent of the outfield be measured; but it was everywhere, encircling the village clearing, existing as potential fallow land, a forest resource, a store of primary material. And there was no customary act of the twelfth or thirteenth centuries that did not establish with extraordinary care the precise conditions for its use, because in the end it was the least uncertain resource which nature offered to a still fearful and ill-equipped population.

We should not be surprised, therefore, by the parallel development of two initiatives, which at first seem contradictory: the attack on woodlands and then their protection. From the beginning of the twelfth century, there are clear signs of concern to preserve forests from felling abuses, of which I will say more shortly. From 1135 to 1180, the large massifs in central France such as those of Orléans, Marchenoir, Lyons and Yvelines were subject to temporary 'encampments', to areas being put out of bounds, to afforestations and fencings-off. Such areas allowed for re-growth after felling, but also served as game reserves and permitted the control of a rich resource from which concessions could be granted for services rendered. In this regard, nothing surpasses the royal forests of England: several million hectares withdrawn from economic circulation, woods, warrens, moors which the ruler reserved for himself, and over which he held absolute sway. Abuses, in the form of expropriations or of exploitation pure and simple, poisoned social relations, because in England as on the Continent, the availability of free access to the woods was a fiercely reiterated peasant demand. The concern to guard such closed-off areas with wardens (*forestarii*, *custodes*, *gruarii*) generally arose rather later, not before 1300 or 1320 in the Capetian realms, for example. We must take account not only of the short-term strategy practised by too many lords, worried about preserving intact an inheritance they were not maintaining, but also the legitimate desire to restore and select vegetation, the beginning of the forest legislation to come. Before the mid-thirteenth century, only the Cistercians had conceived of and applied a long-term forest strategy (felling every five or seven years, clearing the undergrowth and replanting), but their wealthy economy, so rich in potential was closed in on itself and did not lead to imitation.

With regard to the ploughed lands, there are two traits common throughout Europe, even if they are more marked in some regions than in others. First, cereal cultivation was by far the most important activity because the diet was based on carbohydrates: bread, gruel, pancakes, flour-based soups; the rest was merely an accompaniment, *companaticum*. Rations for monks and servants of between 400 grams and 1–2 kilograms per person per day, as in the ninth century, continued right up to the mid-thirteenth century, when information on nourishment reappears in our sources. Bread alone supplied 1,800 to 2,400 calories, much too high a level when there were no proteins to compensate, but it is salutary to remember that this level was maintained in France until 1900, and is still to be found in Sicily today, if not throughout Italy. Allowing for the different uses to which arable land is put across Europe today, the contrasts between medieval and twentieth-century cereal growing are not so very marked. Second, as discussed below, the development of mixed farming came to have a profound impact on the medieval countryside. First, however, we will look at cereals in more detail.

The range of cereals that we know today (except rice and maize) were present in medieval times, though there would have been many botanical variants. The cereals used were those that could be made into bread, i.e. *bladum*, the generic term which covered all the ears of corn: the soft-husked wheat (which, from Catalonia to Namur between 1000 and 1150 replaced the white wheats of antiquity) and spelt (with its hard husk and short stalk more rustic and scarcely any more prolific). Doubtless the best of the cereals – those that produced the whitest, finest, richest flour – did not succeed everywhere, especially where the soil had insufficient nitrates or was too dry. But, contrary to the traditional, ill-founded belief, wheat was never the exclusive property of the seigneurial table; payments in kind did not absorb everything that was produced. In the village markets wheat would always find buyers, and peasants sowed it for other reasons besides their master's pleasure. He willingly kept in reserve the cereal of the poor, the rustic rye which grew everywhere – in the thin soil of Italy, Castile or Poitou, the cold earth of the Auvergne, Brittany or the Rhineland,

and the stony ground of Bavaria. Rye was also grown alongside wheat, or sometimes mixed in with it. Its stalks were short, its flour bitter, and the poisoning that resulted from eating diseased rye bread was severe enough to trigger outbreaks of hallucinations across the whole of southern Europe after 1090. However, the yield was increasing and its survival was secure. As for barley – the wheat of the pharaohs, the cereal of the classical world – Italy remained faithful to it, but elsewhere it tended to be fed to animals rather than humans. It was oats, little appreciated by the Ancients, which saw the most marked changes in usage. First, it proved to be the best food for horses; its growth from 1040 to 1150 north of a line from La Rochelle to Venice mirrors that of the increased use of horses. Second, as a spring crop, it was more successful than barley in the March sowing, a key element in the rotation of crops. And oats were always an important ingredient in such foods as gruels or soup, in Saxon porridge, in the *gaumel* of Picardy, and for making the Celtic beer (long preferred to that made from barley). It was introduced in double sowing in crop rotations certainly before 1200, and in Bavaria there are even examples of places where oats were sown over two-thirds of the arable land.

All the same, the importance of these cereals should not obscure another side of an agricultural system that, until the fourteenth century, was more concerned with subsistence than with trade: systematic mixed farming. The aim of mixed farming – to provide for self-sufficient consumption without exchange – is the ideal of isolated or timid societies. Even during its great expansion in the thirteenth century, Europe could not free itself of this.

Where the growth of wheat was sparse and poor, as on the shores of the Mediterranean, wheat needed a back-up. There were other grasses, such as millet and sorghum (found in Castile, Sicily, Tuscany, Rouergue and as far as Orléans before 1190), but also pulses, such as broad beans, vetches, peas, and beans, whose tendrils wound round the stalks of wheat (or, less often, were trained round garden stakes). As fodder for animals and a basic ingredient of broth, these starchy foods were rich in calories. Pulses provide a good example of the constraints of medieval agriculture: without a specific place set aside for them, people had to sow them among other crops, notably wheat. To protect the peas and beans at wheat-harvest time, the wheat stalks were left standing tall; the gathering of stalks for animal litter and for thatching had to await the second harvest – that of the pea. In the meantime a second crop was left to the village poor. Techniques and necessities, utilitarian and social ends are closely mingled.

This form of mixed farming had a great impact on the face of the countryside and its traces can still be seen. If fruits and roots were no longer sought in the forest, if the 'little wheats' required special care, if cabbages, onions, leeks, everything we call 'greens' could not be obtained naturally in sufficient quantities, a part of the land had to be put aside for these secondary crops. Harvesting of these crops was women's work and this area was enriched more than others with the droppings of the seigneurial pigeons or human excrement. These conditions were perhaps only met in small areas, near houses in the middle of villages – or even in towns: *ferraginalia* and *orticelli* in Italy, *rivages* and *viridaria* in Languedoc, the Provençal *horts*, *huertas* in the Spanish Levant, *hardines* and *hortillons* in northern France. These fertile areas, irrigated before any others, carefully watched over, **289**

The harvesting of millet, the flour of which was used in making black bread. (*Theatrum Sanitatis*, Codex 4182, Rome, Biblioteca Casanatense.)

and indeed taxed, formed a ring around most settlements. They came into being before 1080 or 1100 in southern Europe, a little later in the north.

Now let us turn to the vine. No product of the soil has given rise to such extensive historical literature; none has given rise to such excessive claims. The reputation of wine, especially in Christian Europe, certainly owes much to its role in the Eucharist, and also, no doubt, to its superiority over polluted water, over beer that was pungent and indigestible, and over sharp, unfermented ciders or perries. But too many historians, following Roger Dion's work, have built up the myth of a production and trade that surpassed that of any other produce. In fact, growing vines was a difficult, disappointing and risky business; plantations in the thirteenth century in latitudes as absurd as northern England and Denmark suggest that the harvests would be of poor quality. Medieval wine scarcely kept a year, and if two litres a day were consumed, by women and monks as well as peasants, we can be sure that it had a very low alcoholic content. Besides, it is clear that before the 'strong wines' of the fourteenth century, there was no search for a profitable crop: vines were planted even on wasteland, near town or castle walls, near a waterway so that barrels could be easily transported, without any concern about soil type or an optimal site. Of course it is a privilege to drink one's own wine, and if the vineyard is not too large, one man can work it. But I am prepared to say that the success of the vine in the Middle Ages, so striking after 1020–50 in southern Europe, around 1150–80 or so in the north, was the result of changing social conditions. Almost everywhere the vine was *promiscua*, that is, mixed in with other crops, especially with the Mediterranean olive, the *oylata* of Provence or Languedoc; it then covered from 10 to 20 per cent of the land area, sometimes over 30 per cent in Catalonia. The share-cropping lease – which included a long period when the vines were planted and tended without charges, and then divided between the lord and the tenant as the vineyard came into production – greatly encouraged the peasants in a search for free-holdings, even for a term of thirty years. This was often one of the essential aspects of taking new lands into possession or renewing an old plot.

Animals and fields

The lack of animal protein in the diet caused deficiencies in muscular and nerve tissues, and upset the balance of the blood system. If people are omnivorous, as they were originally, they still remain carnivores par excellence. They have to be able to get hold of meat.

The problems involved in medieval animal breeding, about which, as usual, we are better informed at the end of our period than at the beginning, emerge from curiously formal texts: the number of pigs a forest could feed, taxes according to livestock population, tolls graduated according to draught animals or, at best, a head-count on an English manor. There is nothing, or almost nothing, concerning the animals themselves, their feeding or their fate. Following the example of the chaotic lists in the *Domesday Book*, it is as if no importance were attached to these questions at all. However, we do know that, from 1130, St Bernard interested himself in cross-breeding, that stud farms were set up in the Perche, Roussillon and the Vendôme, and that the lord of Rohan paid a great deal in Spain for stallions. If archaeology, in bringing to light many bone deposits of domestic and wild animals in village sites in Baltic Germany, has shed some light on diet, it is for periods earlier than those we are studying here. Let us try to establish some essential points.

The prestige of mounted warriors and the qualities readily ascribed to the horse seemed to give it pride of place as a mount, as a working animal in northern Europe, and as a draught animal almost everywhere. In fact, we do not know much about breeds, or the potential use of this animal. The only thing we know for sure is that its value increased, as we can tell from the trade rates and the selling prices. If round-ups or tributes exacted in horses stopped before 1100–25, no doubt it was because the animal was becoming less rare. However, in England – which did not take to horses – there were still seven oxen for every horse in 1197. In Picardy, the Chartrain and Bavaria, there were plenty of horses after 1165–80 and it was fairly common to find four of them in a modest stable. Between the 1160s and 1250, however, prices tripled, reaching five or six livres, or the price of a hectare of good land. This led to a marked difference in value between the pack-horse used for haulage or carrying pack-saddles, and the better cared for war-horse; shoes or their absence also came to indicate differences in value. The horse that was not shod became tired and crippled; once it had outlived its usefulness, nothing remained except its hide. Despite a lingering, pious notion to the contrary, archaeology has established that horse-meat was eaten, at least in north-west Europe.

Raising sheep was a source of prosperity in the English countryside and in the Iberian mountains: their wool was the basis of the textile industry; their milk was turned into cheese; their salted meat could be preserved. (Annunciation to the shepherds, detail from a bas-relief in the cathedral of Chartres.)

We do not have any more detailed information about oxen, of which there were still plenty in Saxony, Scotland and the Bessin around 1125. Often used as objects for exchange, oxen were also put to a variety of uses: for milk and fattening up on Hercynian soil or on Alpine massifs, as draught animals elsewhere. But this was a far cry from the speculative breeding of the fourteenth century. The ox provided very little meat, and its value did not increase in the same way as the horse's: although its price doubled from 1180 to 1250, it did not reach more than six to ten sous per head. It was the pig that sustained everyone's diet, with its fat and its flesh. Released into the woods, these animals did not resemble the pig of today. Their grazing was minutely regulated from the thirteenth century, but we have no idea of their numbers. We do know that in December they ended up slaughtered and salted, one being sufficient to feed a household throughout the winter.

Ten sheep to every cow in England, twenty in Poitou, thirty-five in Languedoc – the wool-producer, whose meat was not eaten, emerges as the dominant element in the livestock population. It did not play a food-producing role; it appears here because of its special breeding conditions. The passing of a flock of sheep, mixed with goats, was disastrous for vegetation, and the woods were forbidden them as a rule; they could fertilise unsown land while they grazed on it, but the sheepfold had to be moved constantly, because the greedy animals would gobble up all the wild grasses. Moors and scrublands could not sustain them; it was better to move by gradual stages in search of fresh grass in the summer months. Transhumance, even in the form of movement from valley sides to mountain pasture, became a problem which affected food crops because herds wandered across cultivated land and grazed where they liked, while their roving shepherds were used to living without laws and had no respect for the villagers. The *manades* and *bacades*, as they were called, from the Pyrenees to Provence, in theory followed fixed routes, known as *drailles* in Gascony, *canadas* in Iberia, *tratturi* in Lombardy. Anywhere with cropped grass was fine, such as the *frosts*, *herms*, and *causses* of central France, which were often the common land for the settled population. Regulations were made early: from around 1090–1120 in Savoy, the Dauphiné, in Apulia, and later in Spain in the wake of the Reconquest. No doubt there were clashes, too, although the archives are not forthcoming on this score. We know that the breeders gathered into associations with powerful political backing – like the Castilian *mesta* between 1254 and 1273, and the *escarterons* of the Briançonnais – while the peasants blocked the *drailles* and rough-handled the sheep. This was the resumption, after a lull, of a conflict that was well known to the ancient world.

As far as cattle were concerned, which at the outset were mixed with the sheep in their transhumance, another development can be observed. Once the areas of forest undergrowth began to dwindle, the cattle needed somewhere else to graze. Meadows beside rivers and streams, unsuitable for wheat, were very old; they were closed off after 1125 and their land price rose. But to extend them meant reducing the arable land area which directly nourished the population. This problem was identified around 1225 in the Brie, Bresse, Maine, in 1235 in England, in 1240 in Beaujolais and a little later in the north of the Paris Basin. Princes were obliged to limit the 'parks' sliced from village land; and they themselves were not unaware of the advantages of rearing cattle outside the woods on supervised pasture. The Cistercians, at first in England after about 1260 or so, set an example, but this time it was a bad one. For a while the *vaccariae* (cattle-farms) and the *bercariae* (sheep-farms) of great landowners seemed to pose no threat to the food-producing system; royal and aristocratic developments were initially sited on dunes, foreshores, *pacquis*, hunting land, and stony scrublands. But it was a great temptation to convert their own lands into pasture lands for their animals. Pasture and its enclosure loomed on the village horizon.

The remedy represented by stabling (Italian *stabbiatura*) was not suitable either for sheep or even cows; on the other hand, the influx of pigs into sheds, besides its effect on space, altered the forest landscape and the domestic economy. Pigs were fattened at home with household scraps, bran and the September acorn harvest. Henceforth, having a pig at home was a sign of affluence: winter could be survived and hunger staved off.

Transformation and diversification

If I had labelled the developments to be described in this section 'The birth of craft industry', I might have surprised the reader. This, however, is a matter of terminology, as with crop rotation. I call 'craft industry' that stage of production which is transformed due to techniques, rules and a regular rhythm which together create a special economic atmosphere of market-led activity. I am thus excluding the home-produced artifacts and all forms of manufacturing during the slave period. Of course jewellery, ships and garments of the classical period can be compared with their medieval counterparts, but they did not come from a working-class sector, and even large public workshops did not produce an intentional surplus for the market. It was precisely this which slowly developed in medieval Europe, especially in the period under consideration.

From hut to workshop

Carolingian texts have a large vocabulary for alluding to the quarters on estates where the women and slaves worked; the words do not seem to have been interchangeable and refer variously to a weaving shed, a press-house, or a small forge. But if we stick to the ideal plan of Saint-Gall, we may imagine these annexes as being carefully organised, specialised, 'functional', in 'streets' where workers in a particular craft lived, as Hariulf described ninth-century Saint-Riquier. Once again, archaeology has upset this ideal, not only for high-status sites (imperial palaces like those of Tilleda or Werra), but more importantly, in the more modest villages of England, the Rhineland and Thuringia, where archaelogical excavation has revealed the structure of the *genicia*, *spicaria* and *camerae* which we read about in the texts. Because of their appearance and foundations, archaeologists have labelled as huts the buildings of about 12 square metres where people worked; the furniture attests to a great variety of uses for these huts, and a fairly short period of occupation (perhaps 100 to 200 years). Their location varied, but they were all enclosed within the master's walls. The fact that they were built on and served estates makes it clear that this was a matter purely of domestic craftsmanship.

The same texts, however, are often silent about certain kinds of activity: metal-work, for example, or even milling. Obviously there were natural constraints to developing some activities: some needed to be near sources of fuel or running water. But this was true for beer cauldrons and they are almost always present in inventories. Thus certain activities escaped the master's control, though we do not know when this happened. The craftsman who worked outside this lord's sphere acquired a fame which probably owed more to his freedom than to his art. The weapon-maker was in this league – dexterity was associated with the magic of fire, and the swords he worked for the heroes of Germanic epic or romance obviously could not have been the product of servile hands. Perhaps there was a memory – still a reality in Venice and Milan in the tenth century – of public control over certain (apparently) essential crafts: weapon-making, baking and minting coins, which the State had long kept in its own hands and refused to abandon to the control of the great landowners. If this was the case, it explains how a free craft sector could succeed a public one.

Throughout the tenth and eleventh centuries then, two forms of manufacturing coexisted. One was domestic or subsistence work, answering the needs of master or villagers; it continued, as the few sites excavated from the eleventh century show, on the outskirts of the estate or of the peasant household; sometimes, in the latter case, in the open air, because the family hearth was not yet the centre of the household. The other form was more artisanal – individuals or small groups, masters of their trades, who always did the same kind of work. They were often based in the woods, or anyway far from settlements.

This is why the tremendous growth of the 'hermit' movement in the eleventh century, as in Byzantium, must indicate the development of an 'unofficial' artisan class, alongside that in the great estates, working in basketry, joinery, glassblowing, pottery, and forged metal. The fact that there was a moral dimension to the participants' rejection of the world does not cancel out their economic character.

As we have now come to expect, the key turning-point is concealed: we have only glimmers. In the first place, the Church ceased casting aspersions on manual work: it maintained the requirement of *sacrum otium* reserved for the souls of the élite, but the Cistercians, Carthusians and even regular canons undertook manual labour between 1080 and 1120. Was this a way of winning back the labouring hermits? Of blocking the paths to dissent or heresy along which the outcasts travelled so easily? Or was it simply because the disappearance of slavery had effaced the idea that work equalled debasement? The lay world did not lag behind: before 1100 in western France certain activities, such as the those of the blacksmith or tile-maker, even if inside the master's 'house', were considered dignified enough to be held in fief. Elsewhere, archaeology bears this out: 'huts' become scarcer, and disappear by the end of the eleventh century. This was the period when people were forming communities, and in Italy and in Languedoc, it has been noted that a first nucleus of settled artisans was forming around the motte or *rocca*; and in the wake of the *Reconquista* in Iberia, the same phenomenon appears between 1070 and 1100.

The twelfth century thus saw artisans settled in the villages. Certainly the relics of old arrangements remained: the charcoal burners and the potters went on with their work in the woods, but they had a bad reputation and were thought to be heretics. On the other hand, in the castles, women spun and sewed for the *familia* of the master who continued to demand that he be provided with certain goods, such as stakes, poles and thick woollen blankets, the *keutes* of northern France, but his household very rarely employed a domestic workforce. In the village itself specific activities were established based on materials acquired by the artisan in town or from travelling merchants: 'bundles' of iron, as the toll lists record, logs, lead ingots, skeins of spun wool. If the establishment of seigneurial control or the very high cost of the machines had not confined them to the master, who soon had the monopoly, the mill and the wine-press would have been shared. The men who shod the animals, renewed wagon wheels, sawed up planks or wove greatcoats were people from the village; they were also peasants, working the soil as well as practising their craft. We can pick them out in witness lists after 1100, climbing gradually up the social hierarchy, hot on the heels of the village priest or knight. As already noted, the smith was of the first rank because he inherited the prestige of men who tamed fire. But he, like the joiner, the clog-maker, the weaver and indeed the butcher (who smoked, salted and sliced the meat), saw his destiny linked to technical progress. Indeed the growth in the number of artisans parallels the advances in technology: 1070–1140 for most of north-west Europe, though towns, as we shall see, permit some variation in this crude chronology.

This major phase of economic development naturally contributed to the gathering and settling of the country population, which we have discussed above. It did not exclude the continuation of parallel activity on the estates, especially in the sectors where work **295**

The butcher killed livestock, salted and smoked the meat: goat-kids, sheep, pigs, poultry. The growth in meat-eating encouraged the development of this trade. (Hrabanus Maurus, *De Universo*, Monte Cassino Abbey.)

required a diversification of successive tasks which could be taken up, at the master's pleasure, in the domestic world of his household. Textiles were the most obvious candidate for this; in fact there is evidence that in Germany and in Champagne until around 1130–50 the production of fabric or woollen or linen cloth was largely done on estates and, after all, the famous picture of Ywain coming across the workroom where a hundred virgins were spinning, is set in a castle. We can suppose that this kind of activity, rarely concerned with market sales, declined during the twelfth century, not only at the same time as the seigneurial 'house' contracted, but also as the quality of work carried out in a village workshop at a low price made the castle's work superfluous. This point was reached when the rural craftsman devoted himself entirely to his work of transforming his raw materials, engaged an assistant, perfected his tools and extended his range. Once again witness lists are important: they show that after 1150 a growing number of smiths, potters and butchers in the village were not part of the original local population. Coming from the towns, were they the first sign of a reversal of the ancient tendency of the town being supported by the countryside? Or were they specialists trained in a region where there were plenty of others, trying their luck elsewhere? In both cases, whether getting hold of raw material or recruiting help, the town market played an essential role. Let us therefore move on to the towns.

The organisation of work

From the outset, almost by definition, the situation in towns was different. This difference was not simply qualitative; of course one could purchase in towns the sort of rare or costly object that would never be available in a village: finely worked leather, silk, rare timbers, chased gold. But most of this merchandise came from elsewhere, the result of trade, not of craft industry. Outside this sector, industry in the town did not differ greatly from that in the country – work on the estate of a bishop or count, followed by the opening of independent workshops where the client came with his request and inspected the process. But two characteristics soon distinguished the town from the village. First, the influx of new artisans took on the aspect of a gathering of relations or neighbours living in a tightly knit network of mutual support. The result of this was a certain degree of homogeneity in the make-up of the various urban professions, itself the result of the original settling of craftsmen next to water, walls, or a palace, according to whether they were tanners, butchers or goldsmiths, for example. It was also a consequence of the gate by which the first immigrants entered the town and through which their neighbours followed them. This gave a town a familiar lay-out, not always respected, of course, but surviving to some extent even in our mechanised cities. Thus there was not just one smith, weaver or joiner to be found in a certain street, but several. This did not mean, however, that there was a climate of competition from which a client would suffer or profit: the constant concern for good quality merchandise maintained an equality of price at least, which cancelled out the potential effect of neighbouring workshops. On the other hand, the presence of artisans, employing a few assistants, meant that they needed to maintain good relations, associations and mutual aid which had no equivalent in the countryside.

I will return to this essential aspect of the social fabric, but we should mention here some of its characteristic features. The first is that these men very quickly gained a defined role in urban society. The craftsmen played their part in the urban movements of the eleventh and twelfth centuries, and not only because they were economically necessary – their relations with local power-holders often influenced the administrative development of the town or its political orientation. I have already remarked that in the village the blacksmith was set apart from the husbandmen. So, too, inside the urban workshop the division of labour, which is essential to developing a means of production, was beginning. As ever, we have no firm reference points before 1080. When did the organisation into masters and workers come into being? When did fixed-term hiring begin? When did apprentices appear? When did the barrier go up between the craftsman and the patron who employed him? Here and there vague and partial answers emerge: the oldest texts regulating relations within a 'craft' – *métier* in France, *arte* in Italy, *Handwerk* or *Geselle* in Germany – date from the very end of the eleventh century and the beginning of the twelfth.

They still have something of the air of charitable or friendly meetings, with an annual banquet, the *potacio*, and subcriptions to cover costs; but there was already an élite of men with their own places, and a mass of men who hired themselves out. The latter might have been non-specialists, when that was all that was required or, on the contrary, real masters of

The carpenter was the craftsman in wood, a ubiquitous and precious resource. He put up the frames of houses, built ships and made furniture. It was not until 1371 that a corporation of cabinet-makers was founded, a group that saw itself as clearly distinct from the less-specialised carpenters. This is a massive oak cupboard, from the twelfth century. (Abbey Church of Aubazines, Corrèze.)

their tools and art, sufficiently reputable to be sought out and to have their salaries negotiated. If they were registered in a craft, the hiring lasted for the length of the work ordered, but would be renewed: no need now for the master to go to the Grève in Paris, to the Ponte Vecchio in Florence or outside St Mark's in Venice to look for a worker. He only did so if he needed extra staff, and drew on the group of ill-equipped and not very reliable men who hung around waiting to be hired and who, it goes without saying, were anxious and discontented. This was not, however, a pre-capitalist system because, once hired, the 'servant' (*valet*, *Knecht*, *puer*, *serviens*) was lodged, fed at his master's table, often paid in kind, and given the raw material for his work, although not the tools, which each worker owned. If he managed to save up, with his master's consent he could display a 'masterwork' of his craft and attach himself to a new patron. But there is no trace of this process, this possible promotion, before the thirteenth century. On the other hand, the presence of adolescents, sometimes of children between six and fourteen years old, who had been given a place in order to learn a craft, was certainly not a new idea; common sense dictated it. The master was paid for the apprentice, who could be put to use everywhere. There was still a domestic air about this arrangement, especially if the apprentice was a son of the master, and his likely successor.

This conservative and rather rigid organisation existed before its first appearance in our documents. When the 'companions', the workmen, joined with the beggars of Milan around 1045–50, or demonstrated in Toulouse by taking an enormous shuttle round the town, they must have had a 'social history' behind them. In the light of all this, it is plausible to suggest a final characteristic specific to the urban artisans. While at this time the village smith or clog-maker was free to make articles in whatever manner and whatever quantity he wished, and to decide where they would go, in the town the 'regulations' which governed the material conditions of work also governed those of production: its volume, quality and costs were fixed in advance, and in the interests of public order, local author-

298

ities made sure that the regulations were respected, even if this meant burning a sheet that was too short, or throwing badly baked bread into the river.

Thus conditions of work were affected by only three variables during the relatively stable period dealt with here: the effects of demographic changes on hiring, variations in the cost of manufacture, and the state of the market. The dimensions of the first problem are easy to see. The steady influx into the towns of immigrants who had few special skills, except rural-based ones such as working in the woods, weaving, or producing food, led to an ever-growing stream of workers joining the 'natural surplus' labour force which was the result of urban population growth. From 1100 to 1250 this combination continued. It was a good trend for the masters: they were free to raise the cost of entry into a 'craft', particularly if it was 'pledged' (i.e., carried guarantees of hire and production) as in about one out of three crafts in Paris around 1255. This increased the casual labour sector, and the masters could thus refuse large wage increases. On this last point our information, even after 1200, is uncertain, because we do not know the extent of benefits-in-kind conferred on the workman, let alone the different rates paid according to the degree of skill required. If we estimate the range of payment around 1140–50 to be between eight and twelve deniers per day, then we do not see its being doubled for over a century; the wage of a skilled worker was double that of an assistant, one of those ill-equipped and ill-trained men who were being hired in greater numbers.

If the continuous pressure on supply could be more or less satisfied, this was because production costs did not markedly increase. If the product to be processed did not arrive in sufficient quantities, whether because of economic disturbances or because of unexpected demand – for example, in intensive preparation for a crusade – or if there was a fear of shortages a town would quickly decide to procure the goods by whatever means necessary. When Venice established itself on *terra ferma* from the eleventh century onwards, or when Arras relaxed its toll on certain products in the twelfth century, or when Siena launched its raids on the surrounding countryside in the thirteenth century, this was in order to control access to wood, iron, salt and wool, as had already occurred in times of scarcity. Under these conditions, prices never suffered the ups and downs that later characterised an overheated economy. In other respects the positive state of the market, which acted as a regulator, warded off potential drawbacks: the pressure of demand did not slacken, and the market always needed to be replenished. Obviously we can observe only the wealthier classes: the Church which put back into commercial circulation money from securities sold because their owners had not reclaimed them; the aristocracy, which was forced by the social pressures of the thirteenth century into squandering its wealth to preserve its prestige; and the urban élite, merchants or intellectuals, who were beginning to ape the nobility. There lay the fault-line, faint as yet, between the rise of prices and the rise in wages.

Equipment and diversification

There were few crafts whose progress in terms of the volume of production or the refinement of techniques was not affected by the introduction of more varied equipment or the **299**

Progress in techical equipment. In a French bible of the thirteenth century, the millstone which Samson turned, whipped by his guard, is oddly depicted as a contemporary mill. The way it moves horizontally and the wheel turned by the man are meticulously drawn. (François Garnier's Bible, *c.* 1220–30; Vienna, National Library, Codex Vindobonensis 2554.)

extension of sources of supply. Paying closer attention to these will provide us with the best way of examining the stages of pre-industrial progress. Unfortunately, we can take the pulse only of the town, even though it was in the countryside, for the most part, that innovations first appeared.

This was certainly the case for anything dependent upon fuel. The fuel in question was necessarily wood; although the first mentions of coal in Yorkshire, Languedoc and Hainault occur between 1177 and 1206, it cannot be that this marks the dawn of competition. The potter's and tiler's kilns were on the edges of forests or near the sea, as were the first forges. What archaeology reveals in this regard, in Germany by the Rhine, in Catalonia, Burgundy and the Saintonge region, are veritable batteries of forges which can be dated to the beginning of the eleventh century. We can be certain, however, beyond the formal indications of toll lists, that sales were an urban matter, in places such as Paderborn, Mersebourg, Cologne, Liège, Barcelona, Milan, Brescia and Bergamo. And the same could be said for metal. Naturally the lodes were in the countryside; and there are rural (and ecclesiastical) texts which in 1120 and 1135 refer to galleries that caved in, to miners buried in the Dauphiné, Swabia and the Ardennes. But it is from the towns that we get the first hints of organised mining and trade, in the form of 'mining rules', of which those of Massa Maritima in Tuscany and of Iglau in south Germany from the mid-thirteenth century are the most famous and complete, but not the earliest.

I referred earlier to the development of mills. Here competition was fierce: a watermill up to the end of the twelfth century could be sited in a town or in a wood. The problem is to

300

work out at what moment, and where, its mechanism was adapted to diversified work. The connecting rod–crank system, and the camshaft, which were the bases for the swinging movement, whether horizontally as in weaving, or vertically as in grinding, were certainly in use around 1080 or 1100. When we see the multitude of devices described and drawn at the end of the twelfth century by Herrad of Landsberg in his *Hortus deliciarum*, the 'encyclopaedia' of the time, we may suppose that these were very familiar techniques. There were mills for hammering iron perhaps as early as 987 and 1010 in Germany, 1085 in Le Mans, but they became widespread from the beginning of the twelfth century (1104 in Catalonia, 1116 in Issoudun for the oldest examples, and between 1203 and 1237 in Champagne, Auvergne, by the Rhine and in the Dauphiné); mills for tanning were certainly earlier (around 1140–60 in Lombardy, the Ile-de-France and Normandy); mills for fulling can perhaps be detected in the eleventh century, and certainly before 1170. This last example, however, is the most interesting of all, because the work of a fulling mill was equal to that of forty men – forty unskilled men who had simply been required to trample the woven wool in a vat filled with a fixing solution. What could these men do now except migrate to the town or, if they were there already, seek to be hired for low pay as unskilled workers? Here in the town they would swell the numbers on the fringe of society, or, as happened in England between 1235 and 1240, form bands who went round breaking up mills, provoking legal proceedings and fines that were impossible to enforce. The same things can be said about the stages of making woollen cloth. We are not sure about the use of the spinning-wheel in Picardy before 1280 or 1285. On the other hand, the craft of treadle-weaving probably started at the beginning of the thirteenth century, permitting the production of lengths of cloth, *panni*, up to 15 metres long. The scale of production does not matter to us here so much as the increasing marginalisation of common labour. It is true that the spinning-wheel confined the woman to the house, and to some extent it was alienating work, but at a stroke the field labour in which women had taken part, such as haymaking or gleaning, became the province of the poor, the unskilled, or the outcasts from family life and was considered humiliating. It is also true that the craft of weaving, while giving rise to unemployment, also permitted – as we can see from 1150 – an extraordinary variety in the textiles on the market: brown, scarlet, barruly, russet, vair and so on – names which not only referred to their colours but also to their weave, fineness, and their cost (from 2 to 18 pounds for a length 2 metres by 10 metres in Genoa around 1200).

All these examples concern cloth because, as I said, it was the only semi-'industrial' form of medieval work where social tensions were first discernible. But the same phenomena can be found elsewhere, in work with wood, for example. The hydraulic saw, familiar in the Jura around 1268, made it easy to cut up tree-trunks. It was perfected in relation to naval armament and, in fact, the strength of ships increased in relation to tonnage before 1300 in the Mediterranean and the Baltic. If we consider that the construction of a galley of 400 tons with a life of eight or ten years required the felling of twenty oaks, forty beeches and twenty pines for the various components of the hull, the bridge, the masts and the oars, then we can understand the role played by improvements in technology in the European 'take-off'.

The rise of Europe: 1100–1250

The four pillars of Europe

This survey would be incomplete if we did not add a note on that regional concentration which, whether as cause or effect, for the 100 years between about 1125 and 1225 marked out on the economic map of Europe those areas of production and dispersal whose identification is indispensable to any study of trade, and which to a certain degree underlay urban development, and thus the shaping of the political map also.

It would seem indisputable that the first such grouping was established from the Pas de Calais: the London Basin, Picardy, Flanders, the region around the Meuse, Lorraine and the mid-Rhineland. This area encompassed regions of high agricultural productivity, certainly the highest in Europe at the time. It was rich in fundamental raw materials with iron in the Der, Argonne, Bessin and Harz, copper in the Ardennes, tin in Cornwall, and salt in Picardy and Lorraine; there were abundant woods; good quality leather and wool were plentiful; there was native flax and hemp; the English and Norman fisheries were the most active in the northern seas. In addition, this area supported a first-class cloth industry, combining the fine or coarse wools of England and Picardy, the centres of Flanders, Artois and Rheims, the woad of Picardy and ash from the Ardennes. So it is not surprising that there was a dense concentration of towns here, a high population, and the first movements towards emancipation. But we should also note that this was essentially a region divided between political powers jockeying for supremacy. Furthermore, although the landscape was mainly accessible, the natural axes for traffic – the Rhine, Scheldt, Meuse and Somme – ran roughly north–south, or south-east to north-west, which meant that products had to travel diagonally with frequent and expensive breaks for loading. Finally, this highly populated and much-worked area (it contained twenty of the sixty-five cities of Christian Europe with over 10,000 inhabitants before 1300) on the one hand consumed most of what it produced, and on the other hand was virtually self-sufficient, except in products that were anyway of secondary importance: oil, silk, furs, spices. Ash replaced alum, the wine was medicocre but drinkable, and could be supplemented by beer; and pottery was still rudimentary, but iron and wood supplemented it. We thus arrive at a basic conclusion that few items went beyond north-west Europe. This is a point that is not always sufficiently stressed, especially after Paris began its rise at the beginning of the thirteenth century. Fabrics and woollen cloth did go south, but in much smaller quantities than one can see in Saint-Gilles or Genoa around 1125, together with some ironwork and a little salt. What it did was to draw other regions into its orbit.

Staying in the north, we have to go some way to find an area of newly established commercial importance around 1250. This was the southern coast of the Baltic, with Hamburg in the west, Novgorod in the east, and a long coastal strip that was for a long time the point of contact for the Scandinavians of the ninth and tenth centuries and for nascent Germany. We are a long way from the mouth of the Scheldt. Here there was simply a transit strip, a sort of 'colonial' series of ports as in the Levant, of modest size and very different character, of which perhaps only one, Lübeck, had as many as 10,000 inhabitants. The others were merely assembly points for products from the interior: hundreds of thousands of pelts

– fox, squirrel, sable, ermine, mink – from Russia, fish and resinous wood from Scandinavia, flax and pitch from Pomerania, wheat from Poland. All this was in German hands. This was the domain of the German Hanse or of the Prussian Teutonic knights. But this area did not live on what it produced, it had to export its goods to London, Bruges, Rouen, Duisburg or the Slav principalities in central Europe. In exchange, it imported salt and wine from Poitou and cloth which was resold to Russia; this was an intense, vital but fragile traffic.

Turning south, northern Italy attracts our attention. Compared with north-west Europe, it offers obvious similarities but also startling differences. It sustains the same dynamism, variety and population density, with the addition of an ancient urban tradition that also provided it with more than twenty cities of over 10,000 people between Friuli and the Arno. But here, too, the region was not self-sufficient: wood from Istria, Illyria or the Alps and iron from Novara or Elba was in good supply and stone was good, but the region lacked leather and sufficient wool. Salt came from Latium or the Veneto, wine, oil and dairy products were to hand in sufficient quantities, but the great lack was grain, the old Roman problem. Most cities did not have enough grain in the fields around them for more than six months' consumption, despite their enviable technical proficiency. To complicate things still further, between the contiguous areas of Lombardy and Tuscany, there was an inconveniently large mountain chain. Thus nature drove the Italians either to the coasts or to the hills, to sell what they alone were able to purchase in the East (silk, alum, sugar, cotton), or their surplus oil and light cloth, gaining wheat in return. They got as far as Champagne on foot in the twelfth century, as far as Flanders by boat in the thirteenth, and acquired in exchange for Muslim and Greek riches (untreated wool or heavy cloth), salt and skins they did not have. To move on from this and establish permanent agents and make progress in the techniques of commercial association was just a step which, once taken by the Italians, advanced them beyond other Europeans.

The political and economic spheres alike were dominated by those cities which controlled the surrounding countryside; even Venice controlled its own *terra firma*. In Italy, the State was the city. Over the Alps, to the west, the scene changes again and this fourth economic area has its own characteristics, both more diffuse and more subtle. This zone consisted of the Rhône valley, the Velay, the Causses, Languedoc and Catalonia, half coastal, half continental, a region split among a dozen princes, none of whom dominated the others, without major cities (fewer than ten had 10,000 inhabitants), but which was midway between Italy and the north. Like the latter, it had quite enough raw materials and food products: mountain wood, iron from the Pyrenees, salt from Languedoc and Provence, wool and skins from transhumant livestock, pastel, saffron, and also wine, oil and grain. But, like Italy, it suffered from the difficulty of communications, the temptations of coral, brocades and skins from Spain, gold and wool from Africa, not to mention the eastern routes which may have been inaccessible from part of its inhospitable coast, but which found starting-points from Barcelona, Aigues-Mortes and Marseilles.

There were certainly other regions in thirteenth-century Europe where the potential for economic expansion looked hopeful: Poitou and around Bordeaux, for example, where fish, salt, wine and silver were all be found together; or in central Germany and Bohemia with their cloth, glassware, precious forests, and iron and silver mines. But in each of these areas, as in others, there was not the concentration of men, goods and activities that there were in the four main 'pillars' of Europe. Various observations can be made here. To what extent was the absence of economic support on this level detrimental to political structures, or in the other cases, did economic solidity serve as the basis for such structures? It is important to note here that the fragile Angevin Empire found itself pushed back by the mid-thirteenth century to the Bordeaux region and England, that is to say, to its two main areas of economic activity. As for the German Empire, torn between its Baltic shores, its Rhineland fringe and its Italian mirage, yet economically very weak at the centre, wasn't its collapse after 1250 broadly similar? But at this very time Milan, Venice, Genoa, the Count of Barcelona, the king of Aragon or the ruler of Toulouse, the Capetians and the princes of the Low Countries were all continuing to push their advantages. This transfer of the main areas of activity, in production or consumption, whether accomplished by human will or not, had obviously created a break with the past: the compartmentalisation which had hitherto only been penetrated by pedlars or the occasional wanderer was a thing of the past. We can say, therefore, that together with the internal development of society from the seigneurial cell, the economic explosion in Europe hastened the setting up of the market economy.

The market

Nineteenth-century bourgeois historiography, with its passionate interest in city liberties, spent much time surveying the renaissance of commercial trading in towns, which it took to be a sign of general progress. Then it moved on to a search for causes and, ever since the theories advanced by the Belgian historian Pirenne sixty years or so ago, historians have rambled on, arguing for or against the foreign origin of merchants (Pirenne's 'dusty-footed vagabond travellers'), or trying to mark out the stages and routes of international trade by examining currency hoards, chieftains' graves, and allusions made by Jewish or Arab travellers. We have thus arrived at an outline for the trade of the tenth and early eleventh centuries that is fairly well defined: in the north, the great flow of trade stretching from Ireland to the Caspian Sea, and dominated by the Scandinavians; in the south, Mediterranean piracy but, in the first half of the eleventh century, if not earlier in Catalonia, trade over land and sea from south of the Ebro, from Sicily to Alexandria and Byzantium; some famous places such as Amalfi, which Ibn Hawqal admired in 977; a few German merchants venturing to Prague, Cracow and as far as Kiev. But between the two arms of this enormous ellipse, nothing – nothing but anonymous pedlars, wanderers, and those on commissions for their masters in the cities. But the roads and rivers, and later the sea, became more lively after 1060–80. Traffic increased, trade revived, currency circulated; after 1100 Europe was engaged in the business of inter-regional trade, indeed international trade. This is the classic picture; and yet, it seems illogical.

Our contemporaries, like our predecessors, with their eyes fixed on figures, or all too **304** easily given to making syntheses, have thus committed the same error in method as

Pirenne: they see commerce in terms of the circulation of spices and their sale in towns, without being sufficiently concerned with the basket of eggs displayed in the square in front of a country church, which is equally revealing about trade. The explanation for this is quite simple: the historian has nothing to say about such activity because it was usually unregulated, and therefore no estimate of the figures involved has survived. Yet it is the basis of all other activities.

The primacy of circulation

Everyone has given the Romans credit for imposing on the Europe which they dominated an important network of paved roads and then has lamented their eventual deterioration, which is seen as a characteristic of medieval barbarism. Such a view takes no account of the sufferings endured by Gauls, Iberians or Bretons in constructing, for the exclusive use of their masters, these 'Works of the Romans'. Further, let us correct the prejudice which claims that the roads fell into disuse: in fact they were still used in the seventh century. Later scribes were rarely mistaken when they identified a road as Roman; the terminology employed was quite different from that used for other roads: *via publica, ferrata, calceata, strata*. Moreover, most of the great military engagements which required the moving of troops used them: Cassel, Legnano, Bouvines, Crécy, Poitiers; many long-distance journeys still made use of them, even as late as the fourteenth century. That said, we cannot deny that the network itself was not maintained and largely disappeared. It had been conceived with two precise intentions. One was to join up strategic or urban points by the straightest possible line. In western Europe generally, this was in two orthogonal directions: from Italy to Brittany and from the Rhineland *limes* to the Mediterranean. If the Middle Ages found that some of these routes continued to be useful to traffic, then the roads were preserved; if not, there was no point in maintaining them. They would have no economic function; their courses, their slopes, their surfaces were not appropriate either for hauling goods or for local transport; they may have been useful to pedestrians and riders, that is to say, couriers and soldiers, perhaps, but not to peasants and traders. Hence my earlier observation: in the Middle Ages, the village took precedence over the town, and haulage was developed. The roadways became almost impossible to use, except by troops of soldiers, which was what they had been built for. So let us leave aside these relics, ill-adapted to contemporary use, remembering that in the twelfth century people had sufficient sense to avoid impractical routes, and to make use of those where a ford or bridge existed. Sometimes the only function of these old roads was in defining the limits of parishes.

In many cases the Roman engineers had made good use of paths that existed before their arrival. Those came back into use, flanked by those which the villagers had constructed round them, once the land had been reorganised. This was now a network adapted to one basic and specific end – getting to and from the fields and the areas cleared for cultivation. For the most part, these roads are those we use today, and this medieval labour was fundamental. It is impossible to know when or how they first appeared. Moreover, on closer examination, we realise that any one route consists of a series of thread-like paths on the ground, indicating a given direction rather than rigidly following a fixed course – according to the state of the land, the nature of the vehicles, the desire of the traveller, the wish to avoid a toll, one path goes that way, one goes another. This interlacing produces such a blurred picture that it seems certain that, as in Flanders in the twelfth century, for example, after the crops' first ripening the riverside peasants were told to close off their fields to avoid damage, as was done elsewhere when the transhumant flocks went by. Obviously, when the lie of the land or water dictated a crossing, there was no choice. But one has the impression that even there the building of a fixed bridge in place of a ferry or a movable bridge of boats was not at first the rule; for a long time these were made from wood, even in towns, which meant that they were constantly catching fire (the bridge at Angers caught fire six times between 1032 and 1206). Stone bridges represented such an effort and expense that people were slow to build them across wide rivers: the one at Le Mans in 1034 is one of the oldest; but people often waited much longer, until around 1130–70 in western and southern France, for instance. The enterprise could be undertaken by bands of volunteers, as at Avignon, Pont-Saint-Esprit and Cavaillon. Elsewhere, building bridges required expert engineers. The erection of the St Gotthard bridge in 1237 is a feat as noteworthy as that of the construction of railway tunnels much later; commercially, the effect was the same. As for the fording points, much more frequent than today when we have often restricted the course of a river, they often presented several possible choices.

The poor quality of medieval 'roads' has undeniably obscured the picture of technical progress which was being accomplished through innovations in transport at this time. The taxation lists which crop up in the period from 982 to beyond the thirteenth century give us a fairly clear idea of the way goods were transported, once we sift through their stereotyped lists. There is no doubt that carrying things 'round the neck', that is, in a pouch or by a pole, in the manner employed in Asia, was the most frequent mode; there are references to baskets carried on the back, poles and wheelbarrows before 1200 or 1220; animals with pack-saddles are a constant feature. But what matters to us are the vehicles: carts with one or two axles already known to Antiquity (*biga*, *quadriga*), but whose efficiency (though not until 1275) was increased by improved coupling, yokes to support the leading animal, swingletrees and toughened ropes for coupling in a line, which increased the traction force instead of dispersing it as in Antiquity.

On the other hand, a shoulder harness for a horse and a frontal yoke for an ox meant that each beast's bone structure took the weight rather than its its neck, which had previously restricted their efforts: this can be seen from perhaps the tenth century onwards in the Rhineland and from 1100 in Spain and Normandy if we can believe the tapestries of Gerona and Bayeux. The movable front-axle permitted the useful development of the wagon (late thirteenth century); finally, there was the development of the famous horse-shoe, on which scholars cannot agree, as we saw earlier.

The main thing is to get some idea of the results of these innovations. The progress represented by the substitution of the horse for the ox, donkey or man has been calculated in terms of the speed and efficency of transport. Properly harnessed in a line and shod, four horses could pull a wagon with thirty sacks of English wool – 4.5 tons – at a rate of 5 kilo-

The costly construction of stone bridges, which replaced the wooden ones in the twelfth century, was linked with the development of trade. The tower stood sentinel over the waters. (Bridge at Orthez, Pyrénées-Orientales, thirteenth century.)

metres an hour. That would have taken eight oxen, sixteen donkeys or a hundred and thirty men; harnessed as they were in the early Middle Ages, animals could only shift a sixteenth of this load. This represents a revolution in transport.

All the same, one has the impression that waterways, rivers in this case, were preferred by many travellers despite being much slower and despite the fact that haulage by oxen or horses was necessary, and that the unpredictable condition of the river banks made progress difficult. What was more, it was easier to watch out for and tax barges than wagons, and obstacles such as weed, mills, and ferries with their ropes, made barges subject to delays and detours. So the preference for them must have arisen from two factors: first, security – these routes offered fewer traps (ravines and forests) than roads, and certain products were susceptible to damage from being jolted over the roads (especially wine, salt, and oil which could escape from split barrels); and second, the greater tonnage per load. Of course the barges (*sandalae, lambi* or *chalani*) known on the Seine, the Rhine or the Tiber since the eleventh century could not carry more than 30–50 tons, but that was a great deal more than a wagon could manage. After 1095 or 1100 the number of piers, quays and landing places increased, enabling the freight to be unloaded, either in towns or at roadsides for transhipment onto wagons. Thus a certain number of fairs or large markets grew up at these nodes in the transport network. In Flanders, locks were developed even on fairly fast-flowing waters but this seems to have been exceptional (1150–90).

And lastly, the sea. I mentioned above the progress made in deep-sea navigation before 1250, mainly by the Nordic peoples. Clearly this means of transport was the exception, not the rule; it had nothing to do with local trade, even where – as in Italy – coastal navigation would have helped when the land routes were poor and difficult. The freight capacity of a medieval ship, even if it seems ridiculously small to us today (the entire tonnage of the Venetian fleet in 1300 has been estimated at less than 100,000 tons – the capacity of one small oil-tanker today), greatly exceeded the freight requirements of a single region. For medieval maritime trading to be profitable, vessels had to carry products over long distances, especially goods that were of high value or of great weight; such ships also attempted ventures that put them at the mercy of storms and pirates – so putting such enterprises beyond the reach of almost all merchants, except perhaps the Italians. On paper, sea transport appears far superior to that on land: it has been calculated that 300 tons of sea freight could be carried a distance of 180 kilometres per day; such a shipment by land would require 100 wagons and take two months at an average speed of 20 to 25 kilometres per day. But this extraordinary difference, which has so impressed many medieval historians, should not give rise to any illusions: not all the ships could be guaranteed to arrive and, when assessed over a longer period, I believe that the size of their total cargo would have been much less than that transported by the thousands of wagons, mules and carriers that continuously criss-crossed the land.

Buying and selling on the spot

The levy made by the lord on his men's work (whether in kind or in cash) – the main resource of 'feudalism' and the justification for the master's protection and justice – has been very variously estimated by historians, and we will return to this point. It is enough for now to stress the fact that it is this levy, after the establishment of the seigneurial framework, that forms the basis of the market economy. Once his needs were met and his gifts distributed, the master disposed of what remained. It is obvious that, depending on the size of his household, his tastes or his social standing, he retained varying quantities of wine, grain, poultry and animals; but there is no doubt as to the mechanics of the process, revealed as early as the tenth century in saints' lives from the Ardennes, codified in Spain at León in the eleventh century, and more generally in the twelfth century. The lord would set about selling the surplus in the village, in the bailey, or in the castle farmyard. The sale of wine had priority, but almost always in combination with the peasants' products. This was the Spanish *mercadol*, generally held once a week. If we can believe the accounts of the Bishop of Winchester, this prelate sold 48.5 per cent of the wheat, 28 per cent of the barley and 17 per cent of the oats which had been harvested from his lands during the year (1208) or which came from indirect revenues. If we consider that a peasant couple, in order to have a saleable surplus (once they had allowed for their own consumption, saved some seed and paid off their tallage, rent or fines), needed at least four to six hectares of good land, and that it has been estimated that no more than a third of the peasants had such areas of land, then we see that the trading 'pump' was essentially primed by the lord in the twelfth century.

According to some Iberian records, animals were the most frequent item sold, ahead of produce and tools. These records indicate proportions of 44 per cent, 23 per cent and 12 per cent for these three basics, an interesting testimony to the bases of wealth. A special place in this economic sector must be given to the Cistercians, who provide an example of direct exploitation without seigneurial intervention. This took the form of the resale of over-production. Not constrained by the customs which to some extent curbed the arbitrariness of lay lords, the white monks (who did not have to account to anyone at this level) often played a decisive role in the local markets and prices, sometimes stock-piling certain foodstuffs, sometimes flooding the market with them; this was often the case with the three basic products that they controlled: wool, wine and iron.

With little money to spend, the peasants were themselves sellers. The transactions in village markets were not very extensive, but were of interest to various members of the more prosperous classes or their agents. The neighbouring town, however, besides its own requirements for produce, was the place where the lord, having sold his wine or his animals, was most likely to find and buy what he was looking for: expensive garments, finery, a trained horse, or simply some skilled artisan whom he would pay for a specific task. In this way, the urban *foro* was closely linked to the country *mercadel*. It is possible that at one time the town merchants themselves made the journey to the village, but one has the impression that before 1250 they limited themselves to offering bits of hardware to the peasants. The serious business was done in the towns. It was thus a natural development for many peasants who were not too far from a city to go there and directly offer to the citizens what they wanted to sell. The famous fresco by Lorenzetti in Siena, although later in date, shows this influx of country people into the town as symbolic of 'good government'; they bring eggs, a goat, cloth, firewood, milk, all of which the town lacked. Except in Italy, where it extended its economic control and requisitions into its *contado* (the surrounding countryside), the town had to buy such produce at retail prices, or go through professional dealers in meat and grain.

The urban market resembled ours only in appearance: a square, perhaps formed where two streets met, or an enclosed space (*foro cluso*) overlooked by the body of the town, with a market, public scales, and a loggia where disputes could be settled. But sales were made most often in little shops, at the base of each house, marked with a sign: the produce or the craft itself were visible to the customer; shutters were raised and stalls were laid out to protect and display the merchandise. Until the mid-thirteenth century, as in the towns of the Muslim world, there were probably streets that specialised in certain products or crafts, the result of the association between workers in the trade (for there was no competition in price, which was forbidden) and the presence of conditions essential to production (water for tanners, or space for unloading wood for clog-makers and cabinet-makers, for example); some of our streets and neighbourhoods still retain the signs of this, though we cannot always be sure that the enterprises held a monopoly within the town. Furthermore, it is difficult to date the setting up of this internal trade network. We know that specialised suburban market towns existed in Italy from 1080 or 1100 onwards, and within the town walls the trading streets were localised, for example the *merceria* of Venice and the *inferno* of Milan for hardware and armour; the dates are a little later for the 'streets' described by Hariulf in Saint-Riquier in 1125, or the surrounding of market squares in central Europe, the 'Grosse Ring' in Lübeck and the 'Rynek' in Cracow.

The fair: symbol of the Middle Ages

The peasants who brought their grain or the dealers who drove flocks to town to dispose of there were 'merchants'. When we evoke that social type, however, we tend to think of those who went by road or river – those vagabonds who carried their pouches, or rode mules – or of the richer sort who accompanied a line of wagons on horseback. These figures in fact were often going elsewhere, to the fair, and this quintessential medieval social gathering must detain us for a moment.

The meeting of vendors offering products of distant origin, not to local men but to other vendors, is a form of 'big business' that can be found in almost all periods. The West, however, refined its appearance. Sometimes these *feriae*, these periodic *nundinae* had religious roots, like the feast of St John for the Lendit fair centred on the Abbey of Saint-Denis, which dated from at least since the ninth century, or that of Holy Week at Pavia. Sometimes they were simply a result of geographical convenience: a place where goods had to be unloaded (as with the post-Carolingian *portus* or *wiks* in the region of the Meuse or northern Europe), or a crossroads like Chappes in Champagne, Visé, Thurout or Huys in Belgian lands. On occasion they stemmed from the will of a prince with a fiscal motive, giving advantages to travelling merchants, as in the case of the Duke of Brabant or the Bishop of Liège on the Meuse road. Sometimes there is evidence that such a will had to compel a reluctant geography: the *tractoria* or *conductus* given after 1137 by the counts of Champagne to merchants who wanted to get to a town market, and who had to be escorted by men-at-arms could be expected to provide the impetus for a gathering.

The principle of the medieval fair was to organise, outside the town but under its auspices and 'guard', a gathering of people and goods over an extended period, some two to five weeks, during which the protection of their goods and operations was guaranteed. The meeting took place in tents, rarely in halls, alongside a 'lodge' which was occupied by supervisors whose business was to determine the duration of the fair, decide on the days of 'issue' and supervise the settling of accounts. During the time of the fair there was more display than actual buying, promises of reciprocal transactions before the final clearing of accounts. It is not surprising that gradually the richer merchants obtained houses and cellars in the town, or conversely, that prohibiting the sale at stalls in the centre of town of certain goods while the fair lasted meant that citizens would frequent the *nundinae*. However, none of the apparatus of the fair – the proclamation or 'cry' of the value of the money used, the regulation of the sale of drink, the checking of products' quality – was established at a stroke. For a long time the situation remained uncertain: in 1127, in Bruges, on hearing the news of the assassination of Charles, Count of Flanders, the merchants packed up their goods and fled. Progress was slow, and fairs were often the basis for specialisation: wool in Northampton, Winchester, Stamford, St Ives and Boston; livestock

Big business was conducted in the towns: the covered market, usually situated in the centre, was open to peasants and craftsmen. (The Saint-Pierre-sur-Dives market, Calvados, thirteenth century.)

in Languedoc and Spain, in Montpellier and Medina del Campo; metals in Milan, Frankfurt, Novara and Nuremberg; light cloth and hardware at Saint-Denis, Rheims, Pavia, Saint-Gilles. Between the appearance of the fair at Visé (982) and the early twelfth century there thus sprang up a variety of bustling centres and in cases such as Metz, Toul, Liège, Verdun, Cologne and Genoa, between 1010 and 1080, it is difficult to distinguish the town, riverside or seaside market from a real fair.

The case of the Champagne fairs is exceptional: after all, as we have seen, it was easier to travel between northern Italy and the northern seas if one followed the Rhine, or to travel via the Meuse or the Oise and Yonne to reach the Saône, than to cut across Champagne, which had little to offer. Trade in Provins has been traced back to 999 and in Troyes to 1100; but the Italians we see north of the Alps, in Bruges in 1127, in Paris in 1140, come from elsewhere and are not found in Champagne on a regular basis until 1170. By that time the counts had encouraged the opening of fairs in Troyes, Provins, Lagny and Bar-sur-Aube, generally between 1145 and 1160. The Champagne gatherings are original in that they established a pattern of two a year in each town, in winter and summer, in a specific, properly protected area, which allowed an uninterrupted cycle of gatherings. This new phenomenon was enough to attract – albeit artifically – travellers to south and south-west Champagne, and to encourage distant merchants to expect a fixed and regular occasion, competently supervised, with barns for storage, and gradually also to use the local accounting procedures, which were more sophisticated and less risky than settlement in cash. This stage was not reached by Siena, Piacenza or Catalonia until around 1245–70; it must be

311

emphasised that the Champagne fairs played a key role in the evolution of monetary commerce by this device.

On the other hand, it is harder to measure the effect of fairs on the development of traditional urban markets after 1200. The presence of large, regular trade gatherings, especially in areas where there was considerable local produce, tended at first to strengthen the fiscal position of whichever prince or town welcomed them: charges levied on men and goods, particularly for the offer of protection or a guard during the period of the fair, meant that market activity was frozen for that period. In Italy there was even a *divieto*, a ban at least in principle on the export of local produce into the surrounding countryside during a fair. Probably many city markets rose from modest origins to the level of a fair, whether this was inside the town walls, or marked off by a palisade, or by some other means, as in Liège. From this there was an increase in the town itself of lodges or *fundaco*, reserved for one or other 'foreign' group, which tended to alter the fabric of the town. This was particularly striking at the end of the period under discussion, especially where the German merchants of the Hanse were concerned, in London as in Venice, but there were others too in places as different as Lübeck, Geneva, Douai, Barcelona, Lerida, Montpellier, Metz, and of course in the towns of Champagne, Troyes and Provins.

The emergence of the merchant

'The rise of the middle-class' is an indestructible cliché; this rise has been detected everywhere, in ancient Greece as well as in the nineteenth century. On the other hand, the figure of the professional merchant is difficult to make out in Antiquity, while it is very characteristic of the Middle Ages. I refer here to the merchant who was integral to local society, an element of the city, a permanent cog in the economy, and not the Syrian merchant of the seventh century, the wandering *mercator* of the ninth, nor even the 'dusty-footed vagabond' of the eleventh, a rootless pedlar who was persecuted or exploited. These marginal figures predominate before the main period of expansion in the eleventh century for two reasons. First, long-distance trade (leather from Cordoba, silk from the East, Czech glassware, perfumes, purple dyes) had been reduced in volume and in the size of its clientele and so such eagerly awaited trade was mainly confined to an élite market. Second, these outsiders, even if the title *amicus* was conferred on them, as it was by the Count of Bergamo in 1021, were defenceless, and could be threatened, robbed and expelled without too much risk, as they were by the bishops or archbishops of Turin, Cremona, Cambrai, Worms and Cologne between 900 and 1010. This small group of outsiders, who had no firm roots, not even distant ones, had a great capacity for survival but after 1150 they fade from the records; in Genoa, the last 'foreigner' to ply his trade, a Syrian, Ribaldo di Saraphia, died in 1175.

By this time the urban merchant class had been developing for over 100 years. Perhaps such people were originally agents of the bishop or count, or factors established in town by great rural lords, particularly ecclesiastics. Perhaps there were immigrants too, those like Godric of Finchale and others, to whom Pirenne attributed a fundamental political role.

It is fairly easy to follow the formation of this 'socio-professional' group, as we would call it today. Many settled in the new quarters of towns, the *burgi* which grew up beyond the walls after 1010–40, indeed on new sites, the *portus* or *wiks* of northern Europe. Their main characteristic at first was their tendency to group together, to join forces, no doubt because they were all too aware of their vulnerability. The first not exclusively religious associations of which we have written record concern merchants: fraternities (*fraternae, keures, compagna*) in north-west Europe and in Italy, at Tiel, Saint-Omer, Aire, Cologne, Würzburg, London, Barcelona, Genoa, Venice and Piacenza between 1027 and 1090. At this stage, of course, it was simply a matter of mutual assistance. But some contemporary groupings did have an economic dimension. Whether it was a case of borrowing from Islam – unlikely, however, before 1100 – or rather an imitation of Byzantine practices, there developed in Venice from 950 to 980, considerably later in Tuscany, and even in southern Italy and Norman Sicily, contracts of association. These were entered into by several interested merchants: *rogata*, a simple agreement, perhaps even verbal, of mutual aid when voyages were shared; *fraterna* or *societas*, which kept a family air but consisted in the pooling of efforts and money; *colleganza* and *commanda*, more precise arrangements, which settled the proportions due to each of the participants when the profits (or losses) were reckoned up, either *pro rata* for the capital provided, or as a function of the risks taken. Usually one of the associates, the one who brought in the more modest savings, actually ran the risks while the other, the sleeping partner, remained at home, but collected two-thirds or three-quarters of the profits. This may seem rather a one-sided contract, but fitting out a ship or equipping a mule-train was a considerable investment; its loss was an enormous risk which legitimised the profits of security. Conversely, a small owner would stagnate financially if he could not enter into such a system. Y. Renouard is right to see this flexible practice as the basis for and justification of Italian economic supremacy over a long period.

Moreover, a further step could be taken. From 1109 in Venice and 1143 in Genoa, *societates maris* became 'companies', adopting an ancient term which was used to describe the groups charged with equipping the fleet each year, as had been the practice in Genoa since 1090. This time the contract, which had a domestic dimension and a fixed term of one to six years (further renewable), consisted in rallying the base capital (the domestic *corpo*), each participant (*consors*) being jointly responsible for undertaking the task in hand. But it also called upon a *sopracorpo*, individual contributions from 'shareholders' who took a share in the enterprise and expected a yield from the profits, generally 8–12 per cent – quite an advantageous investment, higher than the average capital return and equal to what might be expected from a tithe, which was not available to everyone. These practices took a long time to catch on in northern Europe: the merchants preferred to help each other and to draw on the support of their native town rather than seek help from outside. The Saxon and Norman 'guilds' which one paid to enter (*geld*, money, is probably the origin of this Scandinavian word), and the German Hanse on the Continent had not gone beyond the stage of non-religious brotherhoods, with dues, banquets, a common chest, consuls in charge of the members' lot, a moral dimension in reciprocal charity, and controlled markets and monopolies of sale. Again, these did not develop in London, Lincoln, **313**

Winchester, Liège, Huy, Cologne, Rouen and Paris until after 1140 or 1160, and were taken over by groupings of a semi-national sort, such as the large Baltic Hanse at the end of the twelfth century, or that of the 'eighteen towns', controlling the sale of cloth from the Low Countries to the Champagne fairs.

Historians are increasingly convinced that these spontaneous groupings preceded the intervention of merchants in public life, after having believed for a long time that the 'law of the merchants', the *jus mercatorum*, the *Kaufleutegerichte* had, at the behest of the prince, particularly in Germany, unleashed that phenomenon. Actually we have no concrete proof of protective regulations peculiar to merchants, a private or public law which was theirs, before 1135–65; the fact that they were still being persecuted at the end of the eleventh century shows the ineffectiveness of any special legislation. Exemptions from laws, as in Ghent or Tours around 1045 or 1050, the granting of safe-conducts along the length of the Meuse or around Arras, or at Pisa again about 1130, remained revocable, subject to a prince's whim. On the other hand, after the mid-twelfth century the ascendancy of the merchant group seems indisputable in the towns, even when its activities were concentrated outside the walls, in the markets or fairs. Merchants were generally represented in the the body of the town where they established themselves, in various ways according to location, as we will see later. But they had their own organisation: 'consuls' specially entrusted with their business or a provost to whom the public authority – the count in Flanders and Catalonia, the bishop in Liège, Milan and Cologne, the king himself in Paris and London – delegated commercial law (for example in Arras in 1111, Genoa in 1122, Pisa in 1161, Milan in 1185). They had not yet reached the stage of having a royal master's protection, as in France in 1288, but this was a logical development.

Of course one cannot explain this growing ascendancy without adding that if the commercial risks, especially at sea, were great, the profits could be vast. Merchants' fortunes astonished their contemporaries both by their size and their speed of acquisition: by the eleventh century, the Pantaleone of Amalfi could present decorated bronze doors to their cathedral, to San Paolo fuori le Mura and San Michele di Gargano; in the twelfth century Inigo della Volta in Genoa and Romano Maiano in Venice quadrupled their original capital in five years, only to collapse a little later; in the thirteenth century, Florentine money-lenders and businessmen like the Bardi or the Peruzzi had a turnover of several hundred thousand florins per annum. Skilful management was involved, because the distribution of such capital reveals a prudent diversification of investments: at his death in 1268 the doge Ziano left a fortune of which 48 per cent was invested in maritime or armament contracts. He had a hand in 132 businesses – 25 per cent in buildings, 18 per cent lent at interest, and only 8 per cent in liquid assets.

Power and commerce

How did the merchant, who did not appear in the ideal pattern of an ordered society, manage to arrange his relations with the traditional power-holders, the guarantors of a social system with divine origins? This problem cannot have a single answer over a span of

Trade and lending were not favourably regarded by the Church. On this twelfth-century capital, in the cathedral of Autun, the devil is depicted with a bag of money in his hand.

two centuries; it was obviously a matter of evolution which, as is apparent from some of the preceding remarks, operated to the merchant's advantage, but only gradually.

This slow progress was due in part to a considerable obstacle: the Church, supported by Holy Writ, could not endorse mercantile activities. Whether the activities involved making a profit from some hapless purchaser, on the pretext that to acquire the commodity had taken a great deal of effort, or – and this was worse – from the interest charged on a loan, in both cases the proceeds depended on the passing of time, which was essentially a divine element. This might just have been permitted for a sailor who took the risks of a voyage, but not for a merchant who remained in port. I need not go into the reasons, easy enough to guess, behind the Church's gradual move to a more understanding position. From 1074, we see Gregory VII complaining about the Capetian King Philip I who let merchants be robbed; the author of the *Deeds of the bishops of Cambrai* referred to the death, in the general affliction of 1109, of one Werimbold of Cambrai, who had done many pious works. Moreover, gifts made on the verge of death, indeed the donning of the habit *in extremis*, while they may reveal a real feeling of guilt on the merchant's part, could soften the wrath of a hierarchy whose members, particularly monks, did not disdain to dip their hands into business. When, in 1198, a saint was made of Homobono, an anonymous merchant of Cremona, a threshold was crossed.

This feeling of being on the margin of true Christian society, however, may have helped to create a feeling of greater solidarity among the merchants, resulting in their organising themselves in order to resist pressure from holders of official authority. This was done partly by means of the companies mentioned above, but also by their training and educating themselves, not just relying on common sense or experience. The appearance of commercial schools for the sons of merchant families represented not only a major turning-point

315

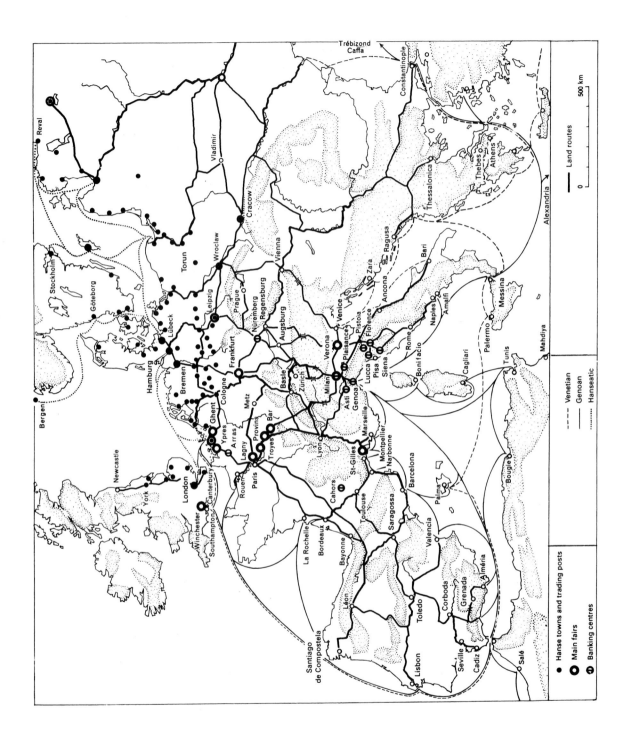

Trébizond
Caffa
Constantinople
Trézibond
Reval
Vladimir
Stockholm
Göteborg
Cracow
Wroclaw
Torun
Vienna
Thessalonica
Bergen
Leipzig
Prague
Nuremberg
Regensburg
Ragusa
Bari
Zara
Ancona
Athens
Thebes
Lübeck
Hamburg
Bremen
Cologne
Frankfurt
Augsburg
Verona
Venice
Pistoia
Florence
Naples
Amalfi
Rome
Lucca
Pisa
Siena
Bonifacio
Cagliari
Palermo
Messina
Newcastle
York
London
Canterbury
Winchester
Southampton
Ghent
Ypres
Arras
Lagny
Bar
Provins
Troyes
Metz
Basle
Zürich
Milan
Asti
Genoa
Marseille
Montpellier
Narbonne
Lyon
St-Gilles
Rouen
Paris
Cahors
Toulouse
Barcelona
Palma
Valencia
Almería
Grenada
Corboda
Bougie
Tunis
Mahdiya
La Rochelle
Bordeaux
Bayonne
Léon
Toledo
Seville
Cadiz
Salé
Lisbon
Santiago
de Compostela
Alexandria
Plaisance

500 km
0

——— Land routes

- - - Venetian
——— Genoan
· · · · Hanseatic

● Hanse towns and trading posts
○ Main fairs
⊕ Banking centres

in the history of learning, but a sign of a will to progress, and of the emancipation of the merchants: in Ghent and Bruges in the first half of the thirteenth century, and Lübeck, Breslau, and Erfurt between 1252 and 1269.

In sketching the birth of the basic economic areas of the Middle Ages, I gave a glimpse of the great routes travelled by long-distance trade; it is worth recalling the chief ones here. The sea routes can be classified on the basis of the three most travelled routes; first, from Venice, Genoa, Pisa, Marseilles and Palermo towards the Levant, Egypt and the Black Sea; this was the route for wood, arms, iron and woollen cloth in exchange for alum, silk, cotton, wheat, sugar, spices. Between 1113 and 1153, the towns of Liguria made themselves masters of the whole Tyrrhenian coast as far as Narbonne by means of commercial agreements; they could thus go and search out or carry the goods that fed these first flows of trade.

Moreover, it was there that the second route finished up, a route whose traffic was essentially one-way, from the Maghrib to the Balearic Islands, Barcelona, Montpellier, Naples or Sicily: this was the route for skins and gold, with leathers, wool and coral in Spain; but an intermediary, usually Jewish, was needed between Islam and the Christian world. It is hard to see what the Europeans could offer in exchange: saffron, light cloth, glassware, perhaps silver metal. The third route linked Bordeaux to Riga via the English Channel and the Baltic: this was the wine route (700,000 hectolitres annually to England in the thirteenth century, but also 200,000 to the Baltic in 1255), and also the route for salt, fish and woollen cloth, taken as far as Novgorod, the *koggen* departing again with wood (the first ship loaded with Norwegian wood reached Grimsby in 1230), furs, grain and more salt (500,000 quintals to Lüneburg in 1205). From 1104 to 1110 the Baltic was under German control, as was the North Sea from 1158 to 1170. Actually there was also a fourth sea route, but a much shorter one, from one side of the Channel to the other: English wool (around 1220, 30,000 'sacks' of more than 160 kilograms each), steel, tin and fish were exchanged for woad, iron, woollen cloth and copper. As for overland or river routes, four predominate, with some diversions. The Meuse route, which led into Germany as far as Paderborn and Leipzig, was the route for copper, woollen cloth and salt in one direction, and for iron, silver and wheat in the other; the path through Champagne, from the Somme to Mont-Cenis or to the Simplon, was the axis for fine cloth and delicacies; the route from Bavaria via the Brenner or St Gotthard passes brought the products of the East to Germany, together with Italian iron and woollen cloth in exchange for silver, jewellery and furs. The western route which went along the Loire for some distance, the threshold of Poitou, and from there became either the path towards Languedoc, or the roads through the Pyrenees in the direction of Spain, from Roncevaux to Saint-Jacques or from Perthus to Valencia, was the pilgrim road but also a road for cloth, lace, woollen cloth and salt going south, and for copper, fish, wine and perhaps gold going north.

Such a broad outline is intended to show the great axes that were open to long-range

Opposite:
Map 14. Trade flows in Europe, *c.* 1000–1250.

At the fair, women buy silk, rugs, leather goods, jewellery. The merchandise often came from the east. (*Cantigas* of Alfonso X, late thirteenth century, Madrid, Escorial Monastery.)

trade, and which were dictated by zones of demand or production and where those in power were concerned, not to check such movement, but to get hold of the profits. Historians often stress the burden of medieval taxation, referring to the paralysis it caused, and denounce it for stifling a spirit of enterprise. Nevertheless, even when princely taxation was at its worst, at the beginning of the fourteenth century, this levy rarely exceeded 13 per cent of the product's manufacturing cost, which approximates the level of indirect value-added tax in France. But the men of the eleventh, twelfth, and thirteenth centuries were not used to the idea of taxes, and were quick to protest against the variety of tolls levied at cross-roads, at unloading places, at fords, bridges and passes, under the pretext of a *conductus* or *salvamentum*, sometimes by the master of a tower, sometimes by a prince's agent. It is diffi-cult to count up these places where payment was made, and we know almost nothing except the listings left to us, a valuable source for traffic flows, despite the inevitable archa-isms and the frequent ignorance as to the total volume collected during a year. This grid of control and levies was put in place along with the formation of seigneurial cells. Before 1035–80, we know of a number of payment points on the Meuse, the Po, the Rhône, and along various routes in Flanders, Picardy and Poitou. We have an impression that taxes were adjusted, upwards of course, after 1150 until about 1200–10; there are altered scales of charges for Carcassonne, Nîmes and Montpellier, for Baupaume, Arras and Saint-Omer, and for Milan, Novara and Bergamo. Given that control was obtained over human traffic as well as over goods, the tolls assumed great financial and political importance.

This is revealed by the interest that was quickly shown in them by territorial princes, particularly in the city-states of Italy, and elsewhere by the thirteenth-century sovereigns. It is striking to note how, as fast as the royal domain expanded in Normandy, Picardy and Anjou, Philip Augustus was equally fast in securing the taxation points as well as the fortresses. For his part, King John of England, also short of money, tried in 1205 to levy a general tax on the important trade in wool, especially at the ports of embarkation where the sacks were loaded (Hull, Southampton, Ipswich and Dover), but without much success. But the idea that there was a source of income that was much more certain than the occasional feudal 'aids' (the tithes extracted with difficulty from the Church or the income from estates), rapidly gained ground. Commercial activity was the origin of public taxation.

Still, one cannot blame the merchants for trying to avoid it – and not only by exemptions and privileges, but also by fraud. Naturally sea trade did not lend itself so easily to this avoidance, though we do have evidence of clandestine landings and of contraband among the coastal inhabitants of Brittany, the Basque country, Pomerania and Picardy. But traffic overland offered much better chances of avoidance: as I have said, roads were not fixed, and it was always possible to try another route, to skirt a customs point, to try another ford. But the Rhône could not be crossed just anywhere, any more than the Alps or even the hills of Burgundy; in addition, there were toll-collectors on horseback who patrolled a wide area hunting out the evaders. We will never know how many were lucky enough to avoid them.

Gold and silver

If currency was not abundant and its minting difficult to control, it was nonetheless indispensable to a market economy such as grew up in Europe in the second half of the twelfth century. The matter of currrency has cropped up a number of times already in this study. Throughout the whole of the early Middle Ages, the chief weakness of the Christian West, compared with the Byzantine and Muslim worlds, would seem to have been the lack of a monetary instrument, confining the economy to the level of barter and hoarding. This was obviously ill-suited to sustaining growth. Carolingian efforts here, so often seized on by historians, seem in fact to have been an attempt at clarification and adaptation to neighbouring systems rather than a stage of quantitative progress; nevertheless, they deserve credit for two elements that were to remain valid up to the twelfth century, monometallism (the minting only of a silver *denarius*) and a scale of value, the product of a combination of Roman, Lombard and perhaps Anglo-Saxon usage. There was one pound (livre) of 491 grams, worth twenty *solidi*, and a *solidus* of twelve *denarii*, the only coins used in this restricted circulation. It is thought that these values were not imposed definitively until later – in 1015 perhaps in Germany – and that moreover, from that point a portion of a livre, the mark, was preferred as this permitted the precious metal to be cut. Today all writers are agreed that the problem of currency and the attempted solutions are a crucial element in European expansion. Maurice Lombard even went so far as to talk of an 'injection of

Military, civic and religious buildings required enormous sums of money. (MS Cotton Nero D.I., British Library).

Muslim gold' into Europe to explain the acceleration of progress. If this theory is no longer admissible – or only for certain areas bordering on Islam (for example, Catalonia, but not Campania) – and it had no impact outside them, at least we can agree that breaking the monetary encirclement of the dirham, the bezant and the dinar was a basic condition of resuming trade.

The silver revival

At the beginning, however, around 1010–50, when we can discern the dawn of a revival, the situation was not propitious. In the first place, Europe was not well provided with silver-bearing lodes. They were confined mainly to the Asturias, Canigou, the Melle country, Normandy and above all Rammelsberg and the Harz in Germany; and the ores yielded only 400 grams per tonne. Thus it could be said that only technical progress, systematic prospecting and improved extraction would enable people to overcome this obstacle. Progress was slow enough, though: between 1130 and 1170 the lodes of Carinthia and Styria, and those of Scotland, provided 1 kilogram per tonne. But it required 500 steres of wood to treat the ores and obtain a tonne of good quality silver. Nevertheless, progress was made: whereas 25,000 denarii were struck annually in Pavia around 1050–80, that is about 30 kilograms of silver, a hundred years later the Abbey of Cluny could demand about 400,000 from its men, and in England the value of 30 tonnes of silver coins was struck.

A second factor slowed down progress: the Carolingians had reasserted the public nature of minting, but they themselves had initiated a process of delegation or neglect which resulted in hundreds of mints appearing in Europe by about 1020 (for example, twenty in

Picardy, fourteen in Berry) in the hands of the royal family, counts, bishops, abbots, municipalities and seigneuries. This disarray came to affect the weight given the basic mark, which oscillated between 230 grams and 255 grams, and even the scales of monetary value, because the quality of the small change was a function of its usage, so that the Anglo-Hanseatic coinage, sterling (from 'Österlingen', the people of the East), was worth four times the coins of Tours, and those were worth four-fifths of Paris coins, but one-and-a-quarter times those of Vienne's, and so on.

Thus the competition established between the metal tokens was matched by increasingly urgent currency needs. Products often needed to be purchased in bulk when they were insufficent locally (such as wine or grain, and particularly luxury goods). Buying equipment (military and agricultural machinery and materials) and the paying of ransoms, workers' salaries, and the costs of pilgrimages all required ready access to currency. The most burdensome cost, however, was that of military, civil and religious construction: it absorbed 32 per cent of the Count of Flanders' expenses in 1187. The rearrangement of estates which accompanied the setting up of the seigneurial framework also swallowed up enormous sums in purchases and transactions: 1,000 livres for Cluny over twenty years, and 4,000 livres over fifty years for Saint-Amand in the mid-twelfth century. Obviously the lords or the town corporations placed the heaviest demands on currency. They strove to extend the profits of justice, proposed the buying-up of *corvées*, and tried to raise the ground-rents. But in order to meet these new demands, which they thought scandalous (*malae consuetudines*, bad customs), peasants and citizens also needed to use denarii, which they raised with difficulty from their slender sales on the local market.

There were three ways of breaking this vicious circle: first, an increase in extraction, as already mentioned; second, for the Church and private individuals to stop hoarding precious metals which were frozen in their private treasuries; and third, the extension of trade with countries possessing gold and silver. This led to the Germanisation of the Slav countries, which meant pillaging Polish treasures and seizing the mines of Bohemia and Silesia, and to Baltic expansion which liberated treasures amassed by the Vikings; it led to Iberian raids where prizes were bought back by Muslim princes for heavy ransoms or *parias*, and to the reconquering of the sea, from Genoa or Gaeta as far as Palermo or Mahdiyya, and then eastwards. All these elements were connected and can be roughly dated.

The gold from the *parias*, paid in Muslim coins or in ingots, streamed into Castile from 970–80 at the rate of about 40 kilograms a year, which enabled King Alfonso VI to pay Cluny an annual rent of between 1,000 and 2,000 dinars. The operations in the Mediterranean, as we have seen, took place a little later, c. 1040–90 in the Tyrrhenian Sea, and 1100–50 in the East. By then the Germans had occupied the Baltic and reached the Oder. It is also possible, however, to follow these stages within Western Europe itself by looking at the penetration of currency beyond the dominant class. It was after 1040, and especially from 1100 onwards, that in Picardy the proportion of demand for payments of dues in cash outstripped those in kind. In 1080 Cluny gathered in 200 livres from its peasants but by 1155 such sums had risen to 2,000 livres; in 1020 the Abbey of Farfa in Italy collected 20 per cent of its revenues in cash and 60 per cent two generations later; and in

Catalonia the proportion of currency transactions – in gold – rose from 30 per cent in the year 1000 to 53 per cent in 1030 and to 77 per cent in 1080. The situation was the same in towns, whether in the form of merchant taxes paid in money, or in forfeits levied to meet the cost of unexpected needs for weapons or building. The farming of merchant rights in Lincoln thus rose from 30 pounds in 1060 to 100 in 1090, 140 in 1130, and 180 in 1180. In Venice after 1139 the principle of loans in kind (*annonario*) was dropped in favour of *imprestedi* in money, in theory repayable; Pisa followed suit in 1162, Siena in 1168 and Lucca in 1182.

There is no doubt that a new stage was reached in the middle of the twelfth century, especially in its last quarter. The importance of liquid assets, already evident in the loans granted to Crusaders, can be measured by the volume of business handled and discharged in a single place of commerce (for example, the 6,000 livres brought into Genoa by drapers from Arras around 1180, or the 30,000 livres amassed by the Milanese for military purposes before Legnano in 1176), or by the sums of money paid by rural tenants, such as the 4,000 marks paid to Cluny in 1155, to which we have already referred.

From silver to gold

It is doubtful whether this upheaval in the economic machinery over roughly 100 years had only positive effects. The hunger for silver could be assuaged in the ways I discussed above. Also, though perhaps not deliberately, the currency could be allowed to slide towards depreciation. Before 1200, this phenomenon is not well attested, first because we do not have sufficient twelfth-century coins to 'assay', which would enable us to estimate their weight and standard; and then because the tangled confusion of systems and areas of circulation prevents us, without explicit evidence of a prince's intentions, from judging the effects or the causes of currency manipulations. We thus have to rely on isolated cases: while *deniers provinois* were minted in Rome (the quality of which was justified by the flourishing state of the fairs), the *Pavia denaro* was judged to be good only for the working out of divisional sums, and a system of double accounting was introduced: strong deniers, the new ones, and weak deniers, the old ones known as *brunetti* – 'black money' – because they had too large a portion of impure alloy. From 1180 onwards in central Italy good money was hidden and hoarded, an early example of Gresham's law, illustrating that bad money chases out good. Comparable phenomena may be seen elsewhere: in Languedoc, the 'black money' (the *brunos*, the *nigras* of Mauguio) resisted the *raymondin* of Toulouse which only prevailed once it had been debased. Where there are sufficient coins, the rate of depreciation can be more accurately observed: the royal workshops in Paris around 1100 produced deniers weighing 1.36 grams, 1.28 grams in 1170, 1.17 grams in 1192, and 1.02 grams in 1220. Obviously an intrinsic loss of about 20 per cent over fifty years cannot be seen as a major 'devaluation'. It demonstrates, however, that in the face of a growing demand the old system had to be revised. As one might expect, it was Italy that provided the model. It is clear that the paying of ever-increasing prices with small coins of insignificant value would have a paralysing effect on exchange. When a war-horse cost 5 livres, it took 1,200 one-denier coins to pay for it, and naturally, especially in the Levant countries, the acquisition of a caravan load was even more difficult. In 1192 the doge of Venice, Enrico Dandolo, had produced new coins, known as 'matapans' after Cape Matapan in the Morea, which he had sailed around. This coin was worth two solidi (i.e., 24 Venetian denarii of the period). This example, although followed by Verona in 1203, remained isolated for some time. But Florence in 1237, followed by Lucca in 1242, and then by almost the whole of Italy between 1250 and 1260, issued *grossi* to the value of 12 denarii, that is, one solidus. This trend crossed the Alps somewhat later: in 1266 Louis IX had *gros tournois* minted in France, at 4.22 grams – the same weight of the gold solidus of Constantinople or of the bezant (theoretically), but in silver. This coin was very successful, indeed it drove out the other Italian *grossi*, and was a severe blow to the seigneurial coinage, as lords were not allowed to mint it; it has been noted that around 1275, some 40 per cent of the dues paid to the Holy See were paid in this coin. Moreover, the example set by the Capetian king was followed in Montpellier in 1273, in Barcelona in 1285 by the king of Aragon, in 1275 by the Count of Flanders with the *groat*, in 1279 by the English king with his *great*, in 1278 and 1300 by Wenceslas of Bohemia and Poland with the *groschen*, and in 1285 by the imperial work-shops with the *grossen*. An especially noteworthy innovation accompanied the royal *gros*: twelve fleurs-de-lys formed a crown round the edge, which represented an attempt at reintroducing the notion of a value engraved on the coin, a commitment to or hope of using a coin that would henceforth be stable and reliable. The establishment of types and the gradual elimination of marginal issues accompanied this monetary development; but we cannot see effective results before 1310 or 1315.

Another door to the growth of exchanges and the sale of very costly goods remained open: the recourse to gold, whose value in relation to silver ranged from 1:7 to 1:12 according to locality, in the bimetallist areas such as the Islamic world. Again, the European situation was not initially a favourable one. The continent was not well provided with veins or flakes of gold and for a long time in the early Middle Ages, most gold was 'frozen' by being converted into works of art, in the wake of Roman pillaging of the East. At the very most, a little gold reached Europe because of commercial transactions without a return freight, or through seizures, for example in the Scandinavian region, in southern Italy, and between England and Spain. Some gold coins were struck in England around 1016, and some in Sicily and Naples after the Normans came; Greek bezants can be detected before 1100 in Florence, in Hainault, and in Chur in Switzerland. For obvious reasons Spain was a natural place for the circulation of gold coins. I have mentioned the effect of *parias* that were settled in dinars after 1000 by the Berber princes. They were used in the Christian Iberian states, and circulated along the entire Tyrrhenian coastline. At the beginning of the twelfth century, the Normans in Sicily, particularly Roger II, struck *tarinos*, copies of the Kufic Muslim *taris*; similarly in Portugal in 1139, and in Castile in 1175 under Alfonso VIII, *maravedis*, 'morabotins' (the name perhaps derived from the conquering Almoravids of the Maghrib) were put into circulation, and are found in Provence from 1160, and in Marseilles in 1220. Moreover, the Franks' States in Syria, deep in the 'gold zone', must also have struck bezants, for example from 1135 to 1150 at Ascalon, Antioch and Jaffa, which had such a

The golden écu of Saint Louis. On the reverse it bears the inscription: 'Christus vincit, Christus regnat, Christus imperat' ('Christ conquers, Christ reigns, Christ commands'); on the obverse, it bears the fleurs-de-lys. The king imposed his currency on his vassals, and it was current throughout the realm.

bad effect on Byzantine issues that the Komnenoi, unable to refuse these coins, were forced to revalue their own solidus, which was brought down to 18 carats, i.e. 75 per cent gold. The hostility, to put it no stronger, between Greeks and Latins, which continued to increase after 1170, is clearly linked to this slow asphyxiation of Greek trade. An event like the sack of Constantinople in 1204 can be seen as an episode in this 'financial war' being waged in the East. In any case, in taking home with them some 60,000 marks (15 tonnes of gold), the Venetians at a stroke made up for a hundred years of trade deficit with Byzantium and could expect to mint several million bezants.

Still, these were only stop-gaps, or the result of particular circumstances. Within western Christendom, truly Christian gold was neither abundant nor minted. At this time the potential sources of a regular flow were either the lodes of Ethiopia, 'the gold of Saba', or the Senegalese flakes from the Bambuk country, from the Soninke country near Bamako, 'the gold of Ghana'. Access by the Nile, or rather through Chad then the Nile, was controlled by the Egyptians; and, not surprisingly, the long period of hostility between Islamic Egypt and the Christians, from Saladin's time to 1250 and beyond, blocked off that route. To the west, the Berber caravans, those of the Makkari, reaching Senegal at Awdaghast then Sijilmasa, and from there moving either to Morocco and Spain, or to Tahert and coastal Algeria, were predictable and easily located; the raids of the Norman Roger II on the Maghribian coast were launched with this in mind. For their part the Jews of Algeria, Ceuta, Almeria and Barcelona, together with those of the Balearic Islands or Palermo, could perfectly well play the role of 'smugglers'. With the establishment of Almoravid domination at the end of the eleventh century, and that of the Almohads fifty years later, the whole region of western Africa and the Maghrib from Gao to Bougie, Morocco and central Spain came under the same rule, and the gold trade (together with that in salt) received a new impetus: by the end of the thirteenth century, it is estimated that the flow of gold to the Mediterranean shores was 30 tonnes a year. With or without the aid of the Majorcan Jews, it could be sought on the spot, and we have evidence that this was done at Mers-al-Kabir from 1120. Since the scarcity of silver greatly lowered the ratio between the two metals in Morocco, it became relatively easy and advantageous to establish an exchange on this basis: Senegalese gold was to be found in Palma from 1225, and in Palermo in 1232 (the date at which Frederick II struck handsome medals called Augustales and appended gold bulls to some documents, just like an emperor). In 1226 Marseilles obtained the right to mint gold, but seems not to have taken the risk of actually exercising it. Italy, as always, was the pioneer: Lucca in 1246 with a golden *gros*, Genoa in 1252 with a *genovino* at a value of 240 denarii, that is to say, of 1 livre. The Florentine *fiorino d'oro* appeared in 1254 with a weight of 3.56 grams, pure

The king's servants collecting taxes, Canterbury, *c*. 1148. (MS R 17.1, Trinity College, Cambridge.)

titration, also with a value of 1 livre in silver denarii, and a ratio of gold to silver of 1:9.2 or 1:9.5, then common in the West. Milan followed with the *ambrosino* in 1265, Siena with the *saneso* and in 1284, oddly late, the Venetians minted their ducat at the arsenal, the Rialto *zecca*, from which the name 'sequin' was derived. North of the Alps, as with the *gros*, there was a definite time-lag: the English gold penny of 1257 and Louis IX's écu in 1266 were not successful, and were soon withdrawn from cirulation as the florin flourished. It was not until 1290–1310 that the minting of the 'crown' or 'royal' in France, of the 'noble' in England, the 'chaise' in the Empire and the 'royal' in Castile demonstrated the successful spread of bimetallism.

Once again, however, the advantages of the new system brought in their wake constraints whose increasing pressure resulted in the difficulties that became apparent from 1270–80 onwards. Keeping the coins of both metals in a steady relationship and preserving their base value depended on two factors: first, a steady supply of precious metal which could match increasing demand; and second, economic and social stability which could survive intolerable fiscal demands or excessive public expenditure. The bimetallic system was therefore only stable for a short time, fifty years at most, from 1240 to 1290. After that date, the supply of African gold began to slacken due to tribal conflicts in Mali and the diversion by the Mamluks of Egypt of some of the traffic towards the north. The strengthening of princely and municipal authority diverted a large proportion of cash towards the urban wage-earning class as well as towards the costs of administration and seigneurial taxation. On the market, the value of the mark climbed steadily; the value of the silver mark, established at 54 sous tournois in 1266 was 55.5 in 1285, 58 in 1289 and 61 in 1295. Smuggling developed in Languedoc and in Venice as a result of demand in the East from the Mongols and even the Mamluks. Sources refer to 400,000 marks which happened to 'disappear' from Beaucaire in 1310. As for gold, despite the efforts of Venetians and Lombards who were in Alexandria to buy gold at a reasonable price between 1305 and 1311, its rise was even steeper: the mark rose from 28 livres in 1285 (which indicates a ratio with silver of 1:9) to nearly 40 livres in 1295 (a ratio of more than 1:12). In 1290, therefore, the 'hunger' for the precious metal reappeared, but without finding any of the stop-gaps of 100 years before: it was necessary either to manipulate the coinage, or to make war, in the hope that this would be profitable, or journey in Asia and Africa, searching for the metal at source.

The effects of growth

In the build-up to this economic strangulation, the combination of demand and a certain tightness in the market explain the appearance in our sources of social problems that hitherto had been masked by the sluggish exchanges. First, there was a rise in prices, which we cannot appreciate except as nominal values because we do not know the exact values of the coins which were actually used to pay them. England provides the most data, and I am therefore using it as a general model on the understanding that there were undoubtedly contrasts and differing trends in other regions. Whether it was a case of there being a large amount of cash, or of its poor quality or of a scarcity of products to match demand, there was a clear general trend upwards from 1140 onwards; in the course of the next fifty years, land, always in demand, increased in price by 30 per cent per acre, and then by 50 per cent over the next fifty years. Its price stagnated after that, however – a slow-down that was not experienced on the Continent until considerably later, around 1260–80. Sales of grain, livestock and wool do not seem to have fluctuated before the end of the twelfth century, but prices then began to take off, with a growth of 75 per cent between 1180 and 1230; later there seemed to be a gap between food products (which increased by 60 per cent before 1300) and raw materials (which went up by 25 per cent). So we see a major, steady thrust between 1180 and 1230, and another beginning after 1270, but over a long period the rate is modest, an increase of between 200 per cent and 265 per cent, according to the products chosen, over 150 years: we cannot call this an 'explosion', even if we take into account contemporary manipulations of the coinage.

General impressions, however, only make sense when they can be related to the consumers' means of payment. The wage-earning class is the most accessible 'barometer' and it begins now to make its appearance. When there was seasonal fieldwork – haymaking and grape harvesting, for example – there were numbers of English cotters, French labourers and Italian smallholders who were looking for additional income, but obviously one cannot base precise calculations on what they were paid for this work, outside their usual employment. In town we do not fare any better, because what the worker gained in kind – lodging, eating at the master's expense, and the loan of tools – does not allow us to estimate the real level of living standards. Nevertheless, there was a definite rise in wages: in Flanders an unskilled worker, assistant to a joiner or a fuller, for example, saw his wage increase from 12 to 24 to 36 denarii per day between 1210, 1240 and 1300 (i.e., it tripled); in the English countryside a reaper could expect 3 denarii in 1230, 6 in 1260 and 9 in 1290 (the same rate of increase). Clearly there was a great difference between wages in town and country which was a strong motive for emigrating to the town. All the same, if at first sight the common 'standard of living' seems to counterbalance the rises, this optimistic view stands in need of correction: of a wage of 36 denarii for a household, it has been estimated that food would account for 50 per cent of the total, which would never allow for putting aside a sum for household equipment or quality items for personal use. The wage-earner, with the exception of those who owned their tools and were thus readily hired (silversmiths, weavers, cabinet-makers), remained physically alienated in the town; and in the country, as he was only one unit among many, he remained subject to the vagaries of production and seigneurial taxation, even when, as a specialist in vines or sawing, he could hope for long-term employment.

This increase in revenue, however, was matched by the growing pressure of taxation from the lord, the town or the prince, to which I have already referred. In the country, if land rents could not be easily raised, this pressure took the form of heavy commutation taxes; in the thirteenth century the bishops of Ely fixed their total land rents at 20 per cent, and after 1265 Alphonse of Poitiers came up with the principle of payments by 'instalment', collected by the lord or suzerain when goods passed into the hands of the Church. This fiscal pressure also took the form of legal taxes which were inevitably accompanied by protests in the village communities. In the towns, the practice was frequently individual taxation, the *estime* on a fortune, as it was known in Toulouse. The sums obtained seem enormous: in Pisa the total increased from 2,400 to 40,000 livres between 1230 and 1280, and the Paris figures for the end of the thirteenth century were around 1 million livres. We can grasp the scale of this new burden when we see that a great number of French towns had to give up managing their finances themselves after 1256 because they had become so encumbered with debt.

Naturally enough, therefore, 'prosperity' led to trade in money itself. The great variety of currencies meant that there had to be exchange handling in all the market places. The 'money-changer' thus became an essential part of the medieval economy. This was not a well-regarded activity, and it could only be undertaken after a large security deposit (5,000 livres in Lille around 1300) had been made. It was also not particularly renumerative in itself, since we estimate the total commission received by the money-lender as being only 4–5 per cent. At his *banco*, his *tavola*, *taula*, in his *loggia* or *casana* (according to the terms used along the Tyrrhenian seaboard), the professional money-changer was for a long time simply someone who handled currency, perhaps a broker, such as Fremault de Tenremonde in Flanders or Thibaud de Heu in Metz, in the early thirteenth century. Moreover in 1206, at the Champagne fairs, the permitted total of operations was fixed at 12,000 livres. But from the middle of the century, as the books of Scriba the notary show, there was a change from simple manual exchange to the drawing up of bills (*instrumentum cambii*). From this point the money-changer was able to collect amounts which he would keep, waiting for their eventual, profitable exchange; he became a *banchiero*, as in Genoa.

Henceforth, the way to speculation lay open. In effect, the deposit of money intended to yield a profit, already implicit in the principle of trading contracts, could now be extended into the realm of pure commerce; after 1260 people such as the Arrighi in Siena, the Tolomei in Genoa (who were sometimes active outside their city), and the men from Piacenza in Champagne, all received sums that were intended not only for the settlement of trading operations but were to be 'banked'. The rate of return could reach from 9 per cent to 17 per cent with the Peruzzi and the Alberti in Florence, and their compatriots the

For a long while trade in money was the preserve of the Jews, as they were not subject to Christian laws. In this miniature, Genoese Jews lend a sum and the total is entered in a register. In the background there are various objects left as security. Note the motif, on the table, of the swastika. (Add. MS 27695, London, British Library.)

Frescobaldi held 122,000 livres. These 'banks', generally located in a particular quarter of a town – the Halle d'eau in Bruges, the Or San Michele in Florence, the Rialto in Venice and the Piazza Bianchi in Genoa – did not act in isolation. They were closely associated with the exchange operations because they could guarantee cover for operations undertaken elsewhere in a different currency, the first condition for the birth of bills of exchange; they were also associated with long-distance enterprises in which they had shares; and lastly, with advances and credit.

The other side of growth is indebtedness. Not everyone enjoyed the rise in the standard of living mentioned previously. It is not easy to fix the threshold of economic poverty. It has been set at under 4–6 hectares of land per household for the countryside, but around 1300 this was the situation of two-thirds of the peasants in the Saint-Bertin area. It is thought that in the towns an income of about 2 sous per day represented poverty, and less than this was earned by 70 per cent of Parisian workers. Were they driven into destitution? Perhaps not, if they had access to other food sources such as from gathering and poaching in the open country, or access to work in the 'black economy' in the town. Many people resorted to borrowing, as did the lords when faced with unexpected expenses. Lending, under a thundercloud of religious disapproval which never actually exploded into lightning, thus became an occupation. Loans were made on personal chattels or, for those with few possessions, on land; loans were granted by the Jews for one or more weeks, as well as by the Italians in Asti, Piedmont and Susa, by the Lombards, by the men of the south-west, from Cahors, but also by money-changers such as Colin le Gronnais in Metz or William Cade of

Arras before 1200. The bankers entered into this sphere later, after 1250, by lending against the harvest, or against tax revenues, as those of Piacenza did for English tolls, or as the German bankers in Cologne, Nuremberg and Lübeck did against taxes which the city handed over to them. Generally the calculation of interest was done in a roundabout way, in order to avoid Church sanctions; the 'mortgage', still condemned by Alexander III in 1163, provided for the repayment of exactly the sum borrowed, but the gain came from receiving produce and land revenues during the loan. The sale 'a remere' allowed the arranged repurchase of the land involved, but at a sum higher than its estimated value at the beginning of the transaction. Alternatively, especially for personal loans, the security (*gage*) was deliberately estimated at two-thirds or even a quarter of its real value, which offered a substantial guarantee in case of eventual non-redemption. These practices began early, at the very same time as the economic awakening necessitated borrowing for equipment, seed and construction. It has been discovered that 30 per cent of Catalan wills before 1025, and 60 per cent in the course of the following twenty-five years, mention debts to be recovered. This trend developed still further in the twelfth century, during the Crusades, and spread to the aristocracy. In the thirteenth century, the princes themselves were in debt to such an extent that there was almost no hope of their being able to recover those parts of the fisc given to lenders: Henry II of England borrowed 12,000 livres from Aaron of Lincoln, 6,000 from William Cade in 1185; St Louis owed 100,000 livres to the Sienese, and his brother, Charles of Anjou, 250,000; Philip III added 200,000 livres to the debt in 1276. The sums exceeded the ordinary means of princes: the profit from royal *prévôtés* was not more than 100,000 livres around 1250. In such circumstances there were thus no resources except currency manipulation, despoilment or war.

With the initial euphoria of an indisputable 'take-off' into economic growth, the thirteenth century, which for so long was seen as a prosperous period within the Middle Ages, now stands revealed as full of shadows and dangers. This was indeed the era of cathedrals and universities; but the former were not completed and the latter were divided in conflict. The 'good times of St Louis', which would later be fondly evoked by the contemporaries of the last Capetians or the Valois, are a deceptive image; it is not simply a facile play on words to see this period as a 'belle époque'.

8

The structuring of society

Several times in this book – indeed at the very outset – I have had to criticise the stereotyped image of the 'anarchic' Middle Ages. In fact, few other periods have done so much to increase the bonds between men. The twelfth and thirteenth centuries saw the grafting of a horizontal network of mutual obligations on to old and still solid dependencies. This firmly attached the strong to the weak and so put the finishing touches to the social fabric of adolescent Europe. All social levels were affected – all ages, all occupations, in fact the whole organisation of daily life and thought. But if we must assign a great part in this *encellulement* (cellularisation) to the power of constraints – such as the need for protection, mutual aid and subsistence which a harsh and ill-equipped society demanded, or to the fear of being alone in a world where mental structures had no place for the isolated individual and gave little opportunity for a solitary destiny, or finally to the burden of tradition – we cannot eliminate the powerful moral aspiration which drew men together into a *koiné*, a group, in which they clearly perceived elements in unity. The spiritual dimension, especially that which inspired a concern for salvation, underpinned all their efforts, for, as the poet of *Garin le Lorrain* said: 'The heart of a man is worth all the gold in the world.'

The family and the household

In the social formation of medieval Europe powerful currents met, stemming from the tribal, familial and dynastic customs of the Graeco-Roman, Celtic, Germanic and Scandinavian worlds; we have already seen that they fused in some places, and remained separate in others. The family was the basic framework, however, where individuals took shelter, where the sexes came together, and where primary economic activity was based. It is important, therefore, to trace the profound modifications of the family, distinctly typical of the 'classical' Middle Ages, when a synthesis was achieved between the diverse tendencies and common burdens forming it up to that point.

The transformation of family structure

As we know, nothing is more vague than the concept of the medieval *familia*, which is at the same time a group of people of the same blood (the *consanguinei*) – the 'cousins', extended to those who could claim a common ancestor (the *cognati*) – but also close relations (*proximi*), friends who were called 'kinsfolk', in order to establish a physical link among all those who frequented the house, the *mesnie*, the *familiares*, *vicini*. The 'family' is something of a great jumble whose limits are uncertain and which might range from the tribe (*Sippe* in German) to more authentic kinship links (*Geschlecht*), down to the more restricted group revolving round the couple (*Haus*). Furthermore, after the eleventh century, Roman and 'barbarian' law, together with those who glossed and practised the law, introduced into the concept of kinship some theoretical outlines of patriarchal ascendancy (agnatic lines) or collateral connections (cognatic lines) which obscured family patterns rather than clarifying them.

It is commonplace to recall that a family structure reflects the state of society or a stage in the economy; commonplace too to recall the unequal development of social groups as a function of the role they play in production and in relation to authority. The fragmentation of the enormous estates of the early medieval period, the disintegration of the old units of common exploitation such as *mansi*, the establishing of pioneers in cleared areas and the technical progress that permitted an increase of population on old lands – common sense tells us that all these developments must have encouraged the decline of familial interdependence and thus made the family group more flexible. But these phenomena were accompanied by the grouping together of people in villages, freely or by compulsion as circumstances dictated, and by constraints such as opposition to marriages outside the community, all of which tended to have the opposite effect. The masters of men and land, on their side, could only gain their freedom of action by shaking off the guardianship of a father or brother; but other than trying their luck in the Levant – as many did – they had to have land. To divide land, however, was to weaken their power; it was better to tighten the bonds of the family line, rather than loosen them, and to count on only one heir in order to avoid splitting up the inheritance, but with the equal risk of losing the heir in an accident and thus cutting off the line. These observations have two purposes: first, to emphasise that the history of the family in any period does not lend itself to a simple outline of development and that it proceeds by stages, second-thoughts and contrasts, which do not make the historian's task any easier; and second, to make it clear that the setting up of the seigneurial mould in the eleventh century, parallel with the urban expansion and the establishment of villages – all events which established a new structure of life – created the choices which confronted the family group and made them particularly decisive.

At first sight, there are good grounds for thinking that almost the whole of contemporary economic and social development inclined towards the dissolution of the 'large' family, and that what we know about population movements, which I have mentioned above, concerns isolated individuals or couples. The methodology most often used to gauge the decline of the power of the clan is based on the study of the twelfth-century legal practice of *laudatio parentum* (the approval, whether given immediately or after compensation, by the family members, close and distant, of a property deal made by one of their relatives, for example a gift or sale to the Church). As many examples of this type of document have survived, our evidence is quite substantial; it is true that it concerns those with property, not the less well-off, but it is precisely among the wealthy (the masters) that we would expect to find the family group resisting most strongly. The pattern is clear: the percentage of approvals or objections, and of lawsuits – for our purposes, they all indicate the feelings of the group – clearly fell. In Latium, in each fifty years between 1000 and 1200, they fell from 46 per cent to 25 per cent, 20 per cent and 15 per cent; in Picardy they fell from 36 per cent to 21 per cent, 23 per cent and 15 per cent; and in the Mâconnais they rose from 49 per cent to 70 per cent, but then fell to 50 per cent and 25 per cent. Observe the contrasting trends due to the different rates at which men or lands were gathered in, and equally, the variable results (though this is the realm of scholarship). The trend is plain: after 1150, the *consorzio familiare*, the large household of the early Middle Ages, was in retreat. And the trend became even more clear in the thirteenth century with 8 per cent (1200) and 2 per cent (1250) in Picardy, 3 families out of 47 in the region of Namur in 1247, but still 45 per cent around St Bavo of Ghent in 1212.

Nevertheless, we must not settle this problem too quickly. First of all, our argument cannot take into account gifts or sales which failed to come into effect (because they do not leave any trace in the documents), especially those which the *retrait lignager* (the right of family members to have first claim to family land), then at its height, allowed the families to invalidate in the name of the patrimonial interest of the group. We must also except some land which by its nature could not be reduced or divided up – the *honores*, as they had been called since the ninth century, the duchies and the earldoms, for example, which could only be held undivided (*una manu*). Detectable from 1100 in Anjou, and especially among the Normans in the Holy Land, this custom became the dominant rule under Barbarossa, around 1153–9; such a custom was more in the interest of the prince than of the family. In any case, this only affected a minority. There are, however, three points of resistance which prevented the complete effacing of the power of the clan.

In the first place, the twelfth century saw a sharpening of the idea of nobility in chivalry, and a development of the idea of vassalage, as we have seen above. This movement awoke in the aristocracy a cult of the family, of the family tree, the *stirps*. Was this an imitation of the trend set by the twelfth-century kings in tracing their legitimacy back to the vanished Carolingians, or was it an 'aristocratic' reaction, a concern with purity of blood which justified domination over others? Or was it a case of a heightened reverence for ancestors and the family tomb? Whatever the cause, there developed a very powerful literary and political movement, proclaiming the antiquity, purity and glory of the ruling families. From this 'genealogical literature', written by hired chaplains (such as Lambert of Ardres or Anselm of Bisato at the end of the twelfth century) and anonymous men or even princes (such as Fulk Rechin himself, Count of Anjou), some instructive facts emerge. First, it appears to have been impossible to go back in family memory beyond a certain threshold (875 or 925 depending on social level), which suggests that it was at that time that tribal organisation broke down and family lines emerged. Second, there was a desire – supported by legends and inventions – to enhance by a magical totem (an animal or a hero), by Carolingian or 'Trojan' descent, by the intervention of a fairy such as Melusine, or some other fabled origin, the epic saga of the family, which also gained lustre at this time from the building of ancestral shrines. No doubt the same concern is responsible for the practice of adopting a surname, a sobriquet to characterise the members of a group and to be handed on, such as 'Plantagenet' or 'Capet', on the highest social level right down to the most humble, such as 'Wheatfield'. These trends were effectively confined to the ruling class, which had many other motives for wishing to mark out and solidify its trunks and branches – be they kings, counts of Flanders or Anjou, lords of Amboise or Guines – but probably also affected its lower ranks, who founded collegial churches in the hope of commemorative masses for themselves and their ancestors.

A second trend, however, was not confined to this élite. This was the development, parallel to the general decline of large groups, of co-operation among groups in response to specific circumstances: this includes common interests that involved closer economic ties (transhumance, draining or clearing land), or closer military ties (guarding passes, defending borders) between members of aristocratic families, but also often between people of the lower orders. Such groups are the Flemish *faides*, the *bandas* of Biscaye, the Castilian *hermandades* and the *parçonneries* of central France. Furthermore, the developments in inheritance – and this again affected various social classes – led to *fraterne*, in which heirs, brothers for example, would keep holdings in common, undivided over several generations if possible: the principle of common exploitation of the inheritance. But this solution brought its own problems in the shape of the inevitable disputes among the wives or children of brothers, and the only apparently viable form of these family arrangements was the kinship network which – and this was true only for the aristocracy – covered vast areas with a tightly woven web of relationships: for example, in Picardy *c.* 1215–20 five family groups held more than eighty seigneuries.

The third aspect of kinship, about which I shall have more to say later, is of a different order of importance, at least in towns; I refer to the gradual blending at the humblest level of the ties of blood or friendship with the bonds of clientship. Of course the latter had always existed, but they had been veiled by a mask of reciprocal affection. This new type of *familia*, however, was no more than a crowd of dependants grouped around one or more branches of the same family. It is difficult to give an exact date for the extension of family ties into the world of the household, but some time before 1150 seems probable. After the assassination in 1127 of Charles the Good, Count of Flanders, the hunt was on for more than 260 members of the *familia* of the Erlembaldi, the murderers; most of these were in fact probably clients. These *parentes minores*, as they were called in Spain, the *seguiti* of Italy, the *Dienstmannen* of Germany, the wearers of 'liveries and badges' of England, were more like servants than down-at-heel kinsmen. But they bore the name of the family which employed and sheltered them, they were *degli Doria* if not Doria. This was a debased form of the extended kin-group which, if it yielded little in the shape of affection or money, could be relied on as a source of muscle-power in violent business.

333

The model of marriage. This wonderful statue of St Louis and his wife, Margaret of Provence, sculpted around 1290, shows a happily united couple. St Louis had a tender affection for his wife, who followed him to the Holy Land and bore him eleven children. The king is represented here as a Crusader, carrying a model of the Holy Sepulchre and holding a shield with the three fleurs-de-lys.

The establishment of the couple

'Therefore shall a man leave his father and his mother, and shall cleave unto his wife: and they shall be one flesh.' Was the ancient biblical precept to be fulfilled at last? Historians remain divided over this fundamental question of social structure; not over polygamy, which was more or less eradicated after the tenth century, nor over the existence of couples apparently living outside the control of their kin, visible from the early Middle Ages onwards, but over the stages and conditions in which the 'conjugal model' was established as the essential nucleus of people's lives. It is not a matter of a simple negative image of the preceding observations: the problem is marriage itself. At the beginning of the twelfth century, around 1125–50, when Hildebert of Lavardin, St Bernard, the canon lawyer Gratian and Pope Alexander III launched a general offensive in favour of making marriage a sacrament, the situation seemed impossible.

On the one hand, marriage was a relic of tribal society, the guarantee of a straightforward and secure handing on of material goods, and a matter that depended on reason rather than emotional attraction. It took the form of union between blood relations, endogamous union, up to the limits of the incest taboos, fundamental since prehistoric times, of parent and child, brother and sister; a union which required negotiation between the fathers, financial or property guarantees, feasts to highlight the public and solemn character of a union involving families, whose end was procreation. Future intentions were not important, and the contract could be terminated by sterility. Yet marriage had another aspect: an idea of spontaneous *consensus* and *dilectio*, of an engagement by oaths before witnesses, a priest if necessary, but without publicity or contract; nor was copulation necessary, as this was only a concession to lust. The only requirement was the absence of any kinship connection up to the seventh degree, as laid down by canon law; this union was indissoluble.

The Viscount of Béziers gives his daughter in marriage to the young Godfrey, Count of Roussillon. (*Libro de Feudos*, late twelfth century; Barcelona, Archives of the Crown of Aragon.)

Opposing both of these, there was the negation of any promise, whether public or not; the lively anti-matrimonial movement of the eleventh century, fed either by a disdain for the flesh which had heretical overtones, or by a delight in free union, combined with contraception; both attitudes were founded on a degree of disdain for the present world and the one to come.

Obviously the aristocracy, anxious to strengthen and tighten its ranks, encouraged the first type of marriage; the Church supported the second; and the third got nowhere. The populace followed whatever local custom was current, the *mos patriae*, the *consuetudo civitatis*, without much concern for principles: sometimes there was a lawyer registering a dowry in the Roman fashion and a *donatio propter nuptias*, a Romanised form of the Germanic *Morgengab*, forerunner of the dower; sometimes there was the exchange of vows, a kiss and rings in the presence of relations; and sometimes no notice was taken of forms or law and there was general concubinage, as in Normandy, *more Danico*, in the Danish fashion. The Church was to win the day, and although it had to make some concessions, this was a fundamental turning-point in human history. We are still living with its consequences.

Undoubtedly it was the eleventh-century Gregorians who initiated this trend, for example in their stress on the *societas* aspect of marriage with the exchange of ritual formulae, often of pagan origin, the breaking of which amounted to false vows (1096). But the second half of the twelfth century and the beginning of the thirteenth marked the essential stage in its formation, between Gratian's *Decretum* and the achievement of Gregory IX (between 1145 and 1235).

The *consensus* was necessary, in order to limit the chances of repudiation; copulation was equally necessary, to counter the anti-procreative tendency of the eleventh century which the Cathars were to take up. The announcement of the marriage (the 'bans') was indispensable in order to indicate the family links, but the prohibition on grounds of consanguinity was brought back to the fourth degree (second cousins) in 1214. Second marriages could take place after the death of one of the partners. The presence of a priest was desirable, but the spouses remained ministers of their mutual sacrament, and for this reason the Church placed it far behind baptism, penance or confirmation. In extracting this compromise, but encouraging individuals at the expense of the group, the Church had done positive work and delivered a decisive blow against the tutelage of the clan, if at the cost of innumerable battles with the aristocracy. That is why this war of the married couples has sometimes been regarded as simply an episode in the struggle for influence within the ruling class, the Church taking its revenge on the warriors who had subjugated it in the tenth century. Nevertheless, a decree does not change centuries of custom: the relations' consent remained necessary in Toulouse and Provence. The exclusion from all inheritance of dowered daughters, devised in Normandy, ended by spreading even to lands under Roman law around 1180–90. Not all the impetus came from the Church, therefore, but its contribution was to be decisive.

It reinforced, moreover, a matrimonial structure that was quite different from ours. The 'model' constructed by demographers for the pre-fourteenth-century period is based, in effect, on the conjugal nucleus uniting a girl – married off as soon as possible, perhaps before puberty, in order to encourage many pregnancies (the 'natalist' model often presented as one of the causes of the population explosion of these centuries) – with a man who had been waiting for 'promotion', a bachelor sometimes until he was thirty, which obviously posed problems of social and physiological regulation with regard to prostitution, adultery and homosexuality. In any case, we are dealing here with a couple joined in a sacrament, with a union in which the partners have at least a ten-year age difference, with a relatively brief duration of marriage (twenty years at the most), a rapid succession of pregnancies, very early widowhood from which it was difficult to emerge, an absence of paternal grandparents, and thus the important role played by the maternal uncle, whose age was more relevant than the father's in establishing emotional relations with his nephews; finally, around the young woman, attached to a greybeard, there was the watchful and enticing circle of the still unmarried *juvenes*.

To this marital structure, so different in concept from our own (as are the kinds of emotional attachments), we can add three other components: first, heavy infant mortality, a threat for all children up to the age of five or six years; second, the precocious entry into active life – a very early age for marriage for girls, while boys became warriors, ploughboys or apprentices at fourteen or fifteen; and third, the almost universal absence of grandparents. In this way, 'childhood' is effectively reduced to a brief episode of ten years. This is too short a time for the juvenile personality to blossom, or to have any impact on the matrimonial framework, between the moment when it escaped the claws of death in infancy and that when, still an adolescent, it was catapulted into adult activities. Equally, as we have

Recumbent stone figures, with hands joined:
the tomb of the Greenes at Lowick.

seen, the word *juvenis* had no connotation of age, but only of social status, that of a person still not 'established'. The slender place thus allotted to 'youth' in the modern sense, and the loss of an older generation that could act as go-between obviously deprived family life of two fundamental elements in its natural balance. Relations between husband and wife, between adults and adolescents, could only be sharper and briefer. The Church had succeeded in laying the foundations of the nucleus which still forms our emotional organisation, but many other aspects of this world were very different from our own.

The power of woman

Married at sixteen to a man of thirty who was old enough to be her father and often acted like it, always breastfeeding unless trying to conceive again, 'bought' in the aristocratic world by the family of her future husband (or sometimes consenting, but without entirely comprehending), destined for the convent or for humiliation if she remained on the shelf, threatened with the prospect that her dowry might be squandered during her marriage and her dower contested by her own children when she was widowed, pursued by the Church more rigorously than a man if she stumbled into adultery or homosexuality, excluded from religious offices, kept strictly to one side if she gained some political responsibility, maltreated as a little girl, shoved into marriage as quickly as possible, threatened as a widow or spinster by male lechery, not able or not daring to express her sexuality, her fantasies, her emotions, her energies through art or writing – did the woman of this period play an active part in society? One might doubt it after the foregoing list, which is by no means exhaustive. Indeed, I have omitted the opinion of the clergy, for whom Woman, responsible for the Fall, was a temple of Evil, a compendium of fleshly and monetary temptations, who demeaned Man, and who was weak, envious, disobedient, quarrelsome, cruel, extravagant and a symbol of lust; commerce with her was nothing but a source of sin and and represented a deplorable 'blot' on Creation.

Recumbent effigies holding hands, smiling Virgins carrying the Christ Child on the pillars of cathedrals, knights setting out on incredible feats of prowess or self-denial for the reward of one kiss, troubadours who risked hanging in order to 'lie beneath the blanket', the *lais* of Marie de France, the weaving-songs, the women's rooms in castles, queen mothers and queens, harsh countesses, wives of bankers who kept the accounts, reapers, spinners, embroiderers, sales-women in town and country, matrons who beat their husbands, young wives who betrayed them with vivacity, the feminine objects that clutter excavations, skeletons of both sexes mingled in tombs, the transmission of nobility, as well as servitude, *per ventrem*, the influx of names from the maternal line – no, women were certainly neither mere objects nor martyrs. It was to women that the risen Christ first showed himself; he spoke at length to the woman from Samaria, to Mary Magdalene, to Mary; and the company of strong women in the Bible effaces St Paul's suspicious misogyny.

For the past 100 years or so, and especially in the last generation, the social and moral position of women in centuries gone by has preoccupied historians, and it evokes an emotional modern response. Nevertheless, the *Frauenfrage* has clear answers in the twelfth and thirteenth centuries, even if their interpretation remains open to debate. Two general observations ought to be made at the start: first, estimating the progress or decline of a social group only makes sense in comparison with another social context; secondly, the interest taken in a problem of this sort by those who were aware of it at the time can only help the debate develop. As regards the first point there can be no uncertainty: the woman of 1220 had neither the rights nor the role of the woman of the late twentieth century; nevertheless, her situation was not only superior to that in preceding medieval centuries, but also to what it would be from the fifteenth century right up to the nineteenth – and this applies to all classes of women. As for the second point, besides the possibility of finding women who speak for themselves, which had hardly been seen before (except for cases such as Herrad of Landsberg and Héloïse and Marie de France), there was also a remarkable outburst from men taking radical positions concerning the place and role of women. We can recognise a 'feminist' current fed by Robert of Blois, Rupert of Deutz, St Bernard or Philippe de Novare, as well as the misogyny of the Church or of clerks such as Abelard, Beaumanoir or Jacques de Vitry.

Three areas seem to me to bear witness to what I myself have no hesitation in calling the 'matriarchal phase' of Europe's history. The first is legal in nature. The guarantees offered to the wife by the new marriage conditions, which I referred to above, by the chance of reclaiming dowers that had been dipped into (the Church gave a ruling on this in the thirteenth century), by the gradual strengthening of her claim to her part of an inheritance (that 'reserved portion' which we can see, from *c.* 1140–5 to the mid-thirteenth century, increasing to up to a third, the Italian *tercia*), by the maintenance of her rights of guardianship over her children, and finally by the solidity of the female lineage in genealogies. This final point relates to the fact that the woman, taken in marriage by a less well-off man, was very often the source of social promotion, sometimes indeed of accession to the nobility, and so had to be treated gently. Doubtless one could set against this arsenal of normative texts – as against any other – its theoretical and intentional character. Or one could stress that the male dominance in the management of a couple's property (and this was even truer in the handing on of offices in the military sphere) offered plenty of opportunity to whittle down such guarantees. One cannot deny, however, that a legal defence had been constructed whose breach, always possible but henceforth illegal, involved not only the moral sanctions of the Church, but those of public justice, indeed the vengeance of an injured kin.

More difficult to gauge, but much closer to the realities of everyday life, is the economic and social position of women, which seems to have improved. I have said that the man remained head of the household. The activities which take up most room in our archives are masculine by tradition or necessity: war, farming or manufacturing labour, long journeys. But beyond the evidence from those sectors which were from this time onwards mainly feminine (textiles, gleaning, horticulture), as revealed by archaeology and by hagiographical or romance literature – from the works of the nun Hrotsvitha to the spinners of *Yvain* complaining of their low wages – we must grasp, despite the ancient tradition of denigration, the essential place filled by domestic work in a society where feeding the group was the centre of all activity. There was nothing servile or humiliating in being the 'mistress' of the house, the nucleus of this primary cell in society. Let us stop despising the stove and the larder, as the bourgeois of the nineteenth and early twentieth centuries did. It is difficult to make firm pronouncements here because exhaustive studies have not yet clarified who owned the land, how the fief was handed down, aristocratic titles or even toponomy, from which we could gauge the importance of the female *manus*.

It seems to me that the third area, even if I reduce it to a few sentences, is even more revealing. Suspected by the Church of being more vulnerable than men to the temptations of the flesh, and encouraged to preserve their chastity or, at the very least, a proper continence, women were carried into the twelfth and thirteenth centuries in a whirl of sexual liberation that historians have real trouble in following and explaining. First of all they are deafened by the indignant denunciations uttered by the clerks; then the sudden silence of the Church, which confined itself to recalling certain limits that should not be overstepped, is no less astonishing. As guides to this delicate area, veiled by modesty, penitential legislation and anxiety for social stability, we have only literary or normative works before 1300. At least they are sufficient in number and agreement to permit a few observations. Between the long list of deviations and aspects of sexual behaviour compiled by the Bishop of Worms, Burchard, at the beginning of the eleventh century, and the success of translations of Ovid, from the *Liber Gomorrhianus* to the amorous exploits of Lancelot, much ground had been covered. In principle, of course, sexual relations were still confined to purposes of procreation. But from the mid-twelfth century onwards Peter Lombard and Gratian catalogued the procedures being used to avoid procreation. Naturally, they condemned them, but in vain; after 1220 and 1265, via Montpellier or Salerno, there appeared Muslim treatises on contraception, induced abortion and *coitus interruptus*. Albert the Great and Raymond of Penaforte, around 1250, were reduced to imagining motives for such behaviour – poor health, poverty, violence – not in order to accommodate them, but to explain their existence. The doctors of the Church, Thomas Aquinas among them, were driven to

339

advise not the heroic self-restraint advocated by St Bernard 100 years earlier, but positions or precautions intended to stifle pleasure, at least for women. And, if she experienced pleasure nonetheless, she had to confess it and purify herself. Perhaps the awareness of a new sexuality – of an eroticism too (in masculine terms), which paintings and sculpture of the period reveal – is the origin of an undeniable leniency towards prostitution. The increase in thirteenth-century towns of *prostibula publica* ('bordellos', *châteaux gaillards*, and the like) in the very neighbourhood of religious institutions cannot be fortuitous; the poor prostitutes, the *meretrices*, whom the Church eventually reclaimed as servants, nurses, and even as nuns, had a social and regulatory role as regards the world of matrimony, notably in limiting the rapes committed by bands of men – the external, masculine mark of the sexual pressures of the time.

Approved unions and mercenary ones, although they were by far the most common type, were not the only type of union in this period. The twelfth century shows every sign of being able to challenge the late nineteenth for the dubious honour of being the high summer of adultery; here too, the structure of marriage took its share of responsibility. But the most surprising feature is the astonishing flowering of romances and lyrics which, from the southern troubadours to the romances of the Round Table, exalted the conquest, always platonic, of the married woman; *cortesia* lent to sexual service the airs of vassalage. Kissing and caressing were obviously not enough for the *juvenis* or the roving knight in his quest for 'joy', and for every Percival or Tristan, there was a Lancelot or Jaufré Rudel! The Church, however, remained silent in the face of this apologia for adultery: an indulgence like that of Jesus for Mary Magdalene? But if so, why only in the twelfth and thirteenth centuries?

Physical punishments usually took the form of public humiliation, except in a serious case such as that of the daughters-in-law of Philip the Fair; there were also lengthy penances. But one has the feeling that the Church, under severe pressure, and confronted also with the heretical asceticism of the Cathars, let things pass. St Bernard, in two sermons on the female body, declared that if Eve had ruined the human race in tempting man, the 'new Eve', Mary, would save the work of the Creator.

Where did people live?

As long as the settlements remained unstable, even itinerant, and were essentially rural, we must look to archaeology to help us understand the daily life and social structure contained therein. Excavations have uncovered the foundations of huts and great halls, and also revealed the contents of rubbish dumps. It is useful again for the period between the fourteenth and sixteenth centuries when a number of sites fell into ruin, leaving remains or foundations far from settled villages. Unfortunately, for our period from the eleventh to the thirteenth centuries, we are stranded without inventories of furniture, without the prospect of recovering tools, without realistic iconography and, in the town as well as in the country, faced with later dwellings built on top of those that matter to us here. Obviously, in common with so many textbooks, I could fall back on the castle, the dwelling

The coffer met the necessities of a nomadic life: it served as a cupboard, seat and a trunk when moving; cloth, documents, jewels and weapons were kept in it. This coffer could have belonged to El Cid (1043–99). (Burgos Cathedral.)

of the master: it was a settlement, collective by its nature, undeniably essential to the developed countryside, and it has left us with much eloquent evidence. But equally, it was a military construction, with specific functions, whose organisation was dependent on the constraints arising from its various purposes and from what it contained. I will say a few words about it, nonetheless, but without embarking on a technical study of its defensive elements, which are not my concern here.

In the first place, the castle was a lodging before it became an instrument of war; its location does not always make sense in terms of the latter consideration. It was a symbol, *signum*, of power, judicial rather than military, economic rather than political. The famous description of the castle of Ardres bears this out: the cellars, larders, grain stores, storerooms and windowless kitchens, buried in a mixture of earth and stones; above them, the hall, *aula*, sometimes of nearly two hundred square metres as at Loches, the place where the *familia* gathered, and where kinsfolk, servants, and retained vassals slept on straw mattresses; then above that, the *camera*, the real chamber, where the couple slept, where they perpetuated their line, and where, beneath the curtained bed, they kept the chest where they stored furred clothes, documents, finery and money-bags; next to it, the *secretarium*, where there was a fire, because children or the sick were bedded down there, and where the women could retire to spin, listen to the hurdy-gurdy and the psaltery, or to a wandering troubadour, or, if they were allowed in, to old soldiers, greybeards past being dangerous, who, like Joinville, came to recount their past exploits. Then, accessible by wooden stairs which would be cut off in case of attack, the *solarium*, the level with the boys' dormitory where people could come and go, and the girls' chambers, a treasure which by contrast was locked up and watched over; below this again, the garrison, and, if it was not set apart, the chapel. We are, then, definitely dealing with a house, one extended by the elements that were necessary to the life of the group which huddled inside a wall further away, in the courtyard, the bailey: a few artisans' or servants' houses, secret cellars which we still call 'dungeons', stables, an orchard, a reservoir if possible (often a necessity, as in the Holy Land).

All specialists in military architecture have observed the progressive development over two centuries of the seigneurial house towards a complexity that reflects its civil rather than its military role. From 1100 or 1120 these houses for the masters were built in stone; **341** they changed from being square (as at Loches, Colchester, London or Langeais) to circular (as at Dover, Gisors, Houdan, Etampes or Conisborough), but always extending their structure to take in all the annexes. At the end of the twelfth century, as in the Holy Land where the village populations were forced to gather together when the Muslims raided, a double wall flanked with towers enclosed the whole, and part of the quarters seemed to be grouped around an interior court, before progressing towards light and comfort. This was the case with Château-Gaillard around 1195, with Angers, La Fere, and Carcassonne before 1240, and then with later constructions influenced by local custom, such as Castel del Monte in Apulia, and Conway or Harlech in Wales. We thus end up with a type of 'fortified palace', as doubtless the first Louvre in Paris was, and as the castle of Ghent is, in an austere style. The best examples are perhaps those of Yèvre, Coucy or Bothwell (1230–80), all constructions that represent the apogee of the concept of a princely residence, one decorated with tapestries and panelling, divided inside in a very complex way, but whose essential military role should not be overlooked, even if one notes the relative ease with which so many of them were surprised or taken during the baronial wars of the thirteenth century.

But let us leave aside the castle, which is the shining exception, and consider the houses where most people lived, in more or less compact groups. Given the scarcity of documents, what can be said? In the first place, there gradually developed a difference in structure between the town and the country, a difference which we consider entirely natural today, but whose origins go back no further than this period; and it happened even in the Mediterranean regions, where stone villages with adjoining houses seemed to mimic the neighbouring town. If I turn first to the lowland village, it is not only because the majority of people lived there, it is also because what is new there is very striking. The grouping of houses around the church or castle that marked the first phase of taking possession of land in the West dealt a fatal blow to the types of settlement of the early Middle Ages: the last pit-dwellings in Hohenrode are from the very beginning of the twelfth century, like the round huts of Pen-er-Malo in the Morbihan. We can still see on certain sites in England such as Chalton or Hangleton, or Hausmeer in Germany, great wooden halls, supported by pillars dividing them into aisles; but such structures, evidence of an earlier stage of family and social life, are merely relics. Henceforth the size of the rural house seemed to be reduced, 50 square metres at the most, and fixed; at Wharram Percy, a model English site, eight dwellings, slightly different in orientation or foundation, have been superimposed on the same place of settlement between 1150 and 1500. On the whole, there was a general evolution towards internal divisions in the peasant dwelling: one can see it in England as well as in Rougiers, in the Var. On the one hand there was henceforth an almost total separation of the 'hall' and the stable, since the hearth had been put back into the house and warmth from animals was no longer so necessary. The 'hall', the main room, was the place for cooking, meeting, spending the evening; it was where the dead were laid out and the newly born were nursed, where trestles and benches were set up. All the same there is no evidence, before the thirteenth century in Burgundy, of a hearth covered by a hood, the sign of a log fire which was more efficient and less smoky. The storerooms gave on to the main room, because the foundations generally did not allow for a basement of pressed earth; a few flat slabs delineated the area of the hearth. A second storey appeared in the mid-thirteenth century, with bedchambers and storing space for precious possessions such as grain and clothes for feast-days. But furniture consisted almost entirely of the holdall chest, the bed being the only important object as it housed up to three or four sleepers, several children, heaped with furs and covers, and we cannot be sure that beds with panelling and curtains date from this time.

The problem of materials raises more questions here. Naturally their selection was governed by what was available locally; it has been calculated that around 1250 in Yorkshire, the cost of bringing in the stone accounted for 60 per cent of the total cost of building a house in stone. Elsewhere, on the other hand, especially in the Mediterranean regions, the lack of different types of wood meant that dry-stone construction was preferred, without mortar. The general impression, however, is of a preponderance of wood; in this respect, the remarkable technical progress made in using mortice and tenon joints and panelling – perhaps partly stemming from boat-building – could only encourage *Stabbau*, *Holzbau*, building with planks, indeed with logs, pegged or piled up. The fire-risk is obvious, but so is the advantage of insulation, and contemporaries were aware of this. Despite all this, the use of cob (straw and mud) or of clay (gravel, mud and sawdust), the whole supported by wicker-work and half-timbering built on to an upper floor of stone, was still used almost as commonly as wood. On the other hand, stone was slow to be taken up, and moreover, in northern Europe at least, was a sign of wealth, given its cost. At Wharram Percy, there is even evidence that this was abandoned in some houses at the end of the thirteenth century. The roofing, on the other hand, did not change at all: thatch, and if this was lacking, tiles or roofing stones; examples of wooden shingles are very rare. Whatever material was used, whatever the lightness of the roofing, it is striking how few and narrow the openings were, both doors and windows. Was this due to the difficulty of closing them? Or because the inhabitants wanted protection from variations in outside temperatures? Or because of the greater importance attached to living in the open air rather than indoors? This has been debated. We may observe that, if the major step had been taken in establishing a country dwelling around a hearth, the arrangement of the dwelling had not yet reached the stage separating it from what geographers would describe as the 'traditional rural house'.

Progress seems clearer, however, in the towns. No doubt the urban traditions there, less burdened by ancient social structures, permitted a more rapid evolution. Of course thirteenth-century houses in towns are not like ours, but the essential structure is established. This can be seen first of all in their collective character. There were of course residences belonging to one man, but he housed servants and lodgers as well as his family. In this regard the calculation of household size, until the appearance of tax documents, is more problematic for the historian than such calculations in rural areas. This factor also meant that the urban house was a less flexible arrangement: generally rectangular, the smaller side giving on to the street, with a surface of about 100 square metres at the most, opening on to the road, the hall, workshop, storeroom or shop. It was lit by an opening whose shutters when raised served as a canopy, and when lowered made a stall; on the next storey, or storeys, as there were frequently three, were the main room and bedrooms. The hearth-fire

Romanesque houses in Tournai.

heated the ground floor, but the pipe went up to the next floor, along walls on which, if one had the means, hung woollen cloth or tapestries for insulation. Planks rested on joists which supported the pillars of the lower room, so that if the owner were to be banished (condemned to 'pull down his house'), he could do so relatively easily. No windows, no window panes even, before the fourteenth century. There were water-tanks for washing, if well-water was not too far away; latrines were outside, giving on to the courtyard, the street – or the house next door; behind the house, a bare space or a vegetable plot ringed by out-houses, these two elements sometimes constituting up to half of the land.

The building materials were much the same as in the country – wood, clay and cob. But here the fire-risk was so great (Rouen burnt down six times in the thirteenth century) that the use of stone grew much more rapidly than in the country; in Italy, stone was in regular use from the tenth century onwards. In order to gain more space on the upper floors, and also because the structure tended to subside, the houses were bulbous and often needed a row of props outside to support the upper storeys, but the traditional image of facing houses which touched at the top and darkened the street below was very rarely true. This very traditional image, which I have given here, needs a counterweight: when we begin to get hold of a small number of urban fiscal documents, the difference in quality among houses and their occupiers is striking. This, among other things, explains the boom in monographs on urban life in the fourteenth and fifteenth centuries. Obviously the differ-ence between a house valued at 10 livres and a grand bourgeois townhouse at 130 livres can be explained by reference to the furniture, varnished tiles and household equipment, and of course by all those constructional features that heighten the differences between, say, a stone residence with mullioned windows, sculptured entrance and decorated pillars, and a small wooden shop. In this respect the houses built on bridges – some sixty of them on the Pont Notre-Dame bridge in Paris – were the most sordid and the least solid; but every situation had its advantage: at least getting rid of all kinds of waste posed no problem!

The sheer bulk of the castle was the most obvious sign of social differentiation in the village; among the peasant houses of around 1300, there was only slight variation. By contrast, the town was already displaying the same scale of differentiation in construction and sale value that we experience today. Given this kind of social reorganisation, socio-professional differences were likely to nurture social conflicts, as we shall shortly see.

The village and the urban neighbourhood

The house was the basic economic nucleus. In the country, production remained a 'family' affair, even if one interprets family in its broadest sense. This was certainly one of the reasons for the absence of specialisation of labour, characteristic of a subsistence economy, apart from the obvious differences within the family due to age and sex. In the town it was a different matter as craft industries required a series of discrete processes in the making of the final product – particular groups of craftsmen were employed at different stages in the process. The workshop, however, retained a certain family aspect, as did the commercial firms: contemporaries referred to 'companions', 'company', 'brotherhoods'. Thus the basic group framework was certainly the family and the household. But the material conditions of daily life, uncomfortable and unsatisfactory even for the lord or the well-off bourgeois, were giving way to other forms of social life, of conviviality, which were just beginning to take shape and which have not entirely disappeared from view today.

Social patterns in the village

It is natural perhaps to turn to the church and the castle in order to find the central themes of village social life: the performance of the liturgy and its offices in the parish church, funeral rites in the cemetery, works and defence tasks in the castle. However, I shall use these activities only as a means of illuminating other forms of communal life.

Clearly, Sunday services – if followed, which a few preachers doubted was the case – and liturgical processions were ways of meeting. But the church, which was sometimes actually a fortified building, as in the Auvergne, the Alps and Lorraine, was also a community hall, a place for meeting when there were important farming decisions to be made, a centre of the village 'peace' since the eleventh century and thus the place where villagers took oaths in front of the 'peace-keepers' (the *judices pacis*, as they were called after 1170 or 1200 in Rouergue and Languedoc). The disappearance of the great parishes of the early Middle Ages, the *plebes*, ringed with *oracula* or *cellae*, had given birth to a tightly meshed network, preserving from village to village a link of common devotion, sometimes to the same patron saint whose feast-day would radiate out into processions and festivities shared among peasants over a large area. Faith would seem to be the basis of these gatherings. But when one sees in the mid-twelfth century in Picardy and Germany the weapons taken up and kept by the inhabitants of villages all under the same patron, or the imperial 'peace'

345

(*Landfrieden*) being extended to scattered country groups, one must perceive a secular dimension beyond the religious ritual.

The cemetery played the same role, but had a more concrete concern with the hereafter. Moreover, it was fixed in place – as archaeology keeps proving – before the church was erected: the dead forced the living to settle. But, being thus summoned by the dead, people became more and more attached to their memory, to their totemic influence, to the possibility of their return. Here the Christian religion gave way to pagan intermediaries: ghosts, vampires, goblins who haunted the burial grounds, and whom soothsayers, the simple-minded and the witches knew how to consult. The supernatural world of the dead shadowed the village of the living, and the *atrium*, the churchyard, was the meeting-place for them both. In Germany, Italy and the Celtic lands the cemetery was not only the domain of spirits and ghosts at night, but also a place of refuge and meeting in the daytime, where the market could be held as well as endless discussions with the lord – and it was one of the few places where the two sexes could meet, publicly, on equal terms.

It was only the men who were to be found working in the castle ditches, which had to be cleaned out, or in the groups patrolling the wood clearings, led no doubt by a hard-bitten cynical sergeant. And it was only the women who queued outside the master's mill and were obliged to listen to the fine words of some mendicant friar sent there by his order for the edification of the gossips, a method of forced preaching strongly recommended after 1250. In both cases, no doubt, complaints linked the participants together. But the presence of seigneurial power did not always arouse this negative, hostile aspect. The justice given by the master was another occasion for a gathering. We know that the characteristic form of the establishment of power was the erection of a great heap of earth and stones, the 'motte', the *dunio*, at least until around 1180, after which date the fragmentation of judicial authority saw it reduced from the level of the *firmitas* (the *munitio*, the *Hauptberg*) to the level of the simple stronghold. These command points, which are currently being surveyed, have one characteristic which is significant here: whether it was raised by *corvée* or by paid workers, the 'motte' represented the heart of seigneurial authority. It had to be built even if a natural rise – *pech*, *podium*, *colli*, *rocca*, as it was called in the Mediterranean region – existed and could have spared the master this task. Thus it played as much a symbolic role as a military one. Indeed, in the eighteenth century one can see the lord climb from his neo-classical mansion on to the abandoned 'motte' of his ancestors in order to pronounce sentence from it, because it was the emblem of justice. These 'mottes' were everywhere: 300 have been counted in Swabia, 100 or so in the countryside of Caux or around Agen, to take only scattered examples, and were of all heights. It was there that the master held his court, the *placitum*, there that he settled disputes, seated on a stone on his platform. Seigneurial justice is particularly difficult to discuss because, outside Italy or Spain, it did not give rise to written texts. But we can take it as likely that these meetings of all the men of the village, headed by the blacksmith and the priest, represented the most solid cornerstones of rural community life; it was there, even if afterwards one went to take an oath in the cemetery, that the rights and duties of everyone were established and agreed upon.

Common prayer, ghosts, gossip, judgement: these may seem rather austere motives for

A wooden Norwegian church, in the midst of its graveyard (Urnes, early twelfth century).

The castle of Chambois, Orne, twelfth century. Simple earthmounds were no longer sufficient for military needs. Protection now had to be provided not simply for a district, but for provinces, even kingdoms: on occasion large garrisons had to be accommodated and skilful sieges resisted. The thickness of the walls, the sparse openings, the increased number of crenellated towers added to the defensive capabilities.

meetings. We do possess more entertaining examples, but the ludic rites of the countryside remain so deeply anchored in a pagan past that the suspicious Church denounced them as survivals of magic. In the thirteenth century, the itinerant preachers, who were mostly Dominicans, like Stephen of Bourbon, set out the edifying catalogue of these 'deviations' which they desired to correct. It would be straying too far from my subject to linger on them here, especially in decoding their magic significance, but it must at least be remembered that the feast was part of communal life, that it was the expression of the unity of the social body, that the dances were a physical communion, that the fires that were lit purified the whole group and ensured its security and fecundity. Whether it concerned the spring festivals in May, a symbol of agrarian renewal, with their processions of young people disguised as woodland gods, the new plantings, imprecations and sprinkling of the fields (which the Church drew on for the rites of Rogation), or whether it concerned the firebrands intended to drive away evil spirits, the fires of St John, Easter and autumn, where people leapt over the embers, all were a sign of disarming the spirits. And the encirclings of the grain-threshing area were fecundity rites often accompanied, in fact, by illicit couplings; all these irrepressible manifestations, which went beyond the sphere of the Church, and with which it was forced to come to terms, were surely both a sign of a persisting rural dynamic and a means of asserting a communal life.

Caerphilly castle, thirteenth century, near Cardiff. The thick ramparts backing on to the buildings are flanked at the corners by strong round towers projecting outwards, which ensure better protection. But the interior arrangements gradually became more complex with rooms being added to satisfy the demands of the family for comfort.

These folk practices, which are becoming better understood thanks to the fact that contemporary anthroplogy is finally studying them seriously – and not before time! – do not seem to have taken any account of the social or legal status of those who indulged in them; age and sex were the only relevant criteria. There were occasions for meeting, however, that were specific to particular groups: we know a lot about those attended by warriors, especially the *juvenes*. These were the *torneamenta*, the tournaments, whose origins appear to lie in north-west France, which involved teams of young warriors led by a champion opposing each other in real 'manoeuvres', progressing from castle to castle in the summer months and gaining money by winning prizes. They were occasions for stout blows and profitable takings, initiation exercises for war, diversions in which women and money played a key role, and where blood flowed too, which explains the Church's categorical but ineffective condemnations (Lateran Council, 1179). They were also the scene of drinking bouts, sexual excesses and violence which seem an inordinate reaction to the vassal's being cooped up for several weeks in his lord's castle. And what a source of revenue for a skilful man! William the Marshal, a star on the mid-twelfth century tournament circuit, made 203 'captures' in three months, and amassed a profit of 1,000 livres.

One would like to know more about the 'alternative' villages, those which escape every kind of text: the houses of the summer shepherds, isolated in their pastures where they reproduced the social and hierarchical structure of villages; or the inhabitants of subterranean villages, that replication, which we are only just discovering, of houses on the surface in a series of galleries, cavities and storerooms where a part of peasant life unfolded, at least as late as the eleventh century. Archaeological investigations show that their reputation as temporary shelters does not suffice to explain the many traces of permanent occupation that are now being revealed.

Social patterns in the town

Despite their anachronistic nature, and the way in which their pure spectacle obscures their original significance, popular processions and urban celebrations are still held in many towns, especially in Italy and the German regions. These are a dim reflection of a fundamental type of urban sociability, best known through documents of the fourteenth and fifteenth centuries, but already old even then, since Gregory of Tours in the sixth century left an account of it. This relatively extensive documentary evidence permits both a more logical study of these communal phenomena and a deeper examination which together justify the sort of sociological observations that are not permitted where the countryside is concerned.

Let us leave aside for the moment the role of the Church in the towns, particularly the cathedrals. A study of its role would reveal a larger version of the rural scene: buildings capable of holding more than the entire population of the town, which they dominated by their bulk, as at Chartres, Rheims or Beauvais, acting as a place of assembly and also of theatre with spectacles mounted by the clerics themselves at the Christianised feasts, with dancing and mime; all very different from what one would expect of dignified canons. Let us leave aside too, the 'palaces' and the 'towers' where over 1,000 places were set for the guests at dynastic feasts to celebrate marriages, burials, and totemic feasts, as in Florence in 1268, and where the unashamed display of banderoles (striped cloth hung from the windows), the harnessing of animals or palanquins, and cavalcades in the streets provoked sumptuary laws in Italy in the fourteenth century. These were family phenomena to which I shall shortly return.

At the other end of the social scale, there were two centres of assembly: first, the tavern where people generally played more than they drank and which acted as a meeting-place for men. Here they could be hired, discontents aired, and beggars and unemployed could gather. But they were dangerous places – councillors kept a wary eye on them – and were increasing rapidly in number: more than 200 have been counted in London in the fourteenth century, and in France, St Louis had to issue decrees against gaming with money, which was at the root of brawling, and order that taverns be emptied by curfew. We know very little about the steambaths before 1330 or 1350. They were a rare phenomenon in the medieval town, where ignorance of the benefits of bodily hygiene was rife. Is there some link with the baths of Antiquity? This is doubtful, but like them, they were a place to meet and talk rather than to exercise. These public baths, where both sexes crowded together, soon earned a bad reputation – and in the baths at Avignon there were indeed more beds than tubs; they were compared to *maisons de passe*, 'nunneries' and other bordellos which proliferated nearby, along the quays, near bridges or washing-places. Here it must be emphasised that the 'matrimonial model', which I discussed earlier, made prostitution a social regulator. This explains the high number of prostitutes (1.5 per cent of the population in fifteenth-century Dijon), the municipal protection they enjoyed and the resigned acceptance by the Church which lived in hope of a 'reclamation' (always possible as the women aged). Indeed the Church did not hesitate to acquire, gather together and watch over the *maisons de passe*. But if this social trend, common to all civilisations, is not surprising, it merits inclusion here because it was combined – as in Antiquity, in Greece at least, or closer to our own age, in the *Belle Epoque* – with a hierarchy of fixed-price pleasures, which raised some of these places of bliss to the level of *salons* with *courtisanes de luxe*.

But it was the square or the street, in good weather or bad, which offered the natural theatre for urban gatherings. It has been said that 'popular culture' was born there, and we shall return to this point. The games played there, the processions and the parades that clogged these spaces, were of an astonishing variety: in 1210–55 in northern France and Lotharingia there were theatrical events inspired by religion, lively tableaux taken from the scriptures or from saints' lives, ancestors of the 'mystery' plays of the fifteenth century, and which Innocent IV tried to regulate in 1264. This rudimentary form of theatre, urban as in Antiquity, was played out in front of the church, sometimes inside it or in the nearby churchyard. But the little comical plays, the bourgeois *behourds* of Flanders in which the aristocratic tournaments were mimicked, the jousts and *soule*, medieval football, needed space: thus they were played on the *prata*, the *non aedificandi* area which, in theory, was clear of the city wall – in London, Salerno, Pisa and Paris. It is not difficult, moreover, to perceive beneath these collective amusements rivalries between neighbourhoods, between followings, as well as the origins of political groupings. The streets, however, were for everyone, and the shows were given everywhere, the neighbourhoods combining or taking turns. These were the rites of the Spring or May Festivals or the Rogation Days transferred to the town, and here was the Carnival, emasculated today, but then squeezed into the eve of Lent by the Church, like an echo of ancient Saturnalia: sexual liberation together with a temporary reversal of the social order. Clearly these were worrisome for clerics and aldermen, already anxious over public dances, the lewd versions of Morris dancing, and the bacchic dancing in rings, and the plays, as they were called in York, the processions of 'madmen', young people in disguise, perched on carts and poking fun at the powers that be. Far preferable, however, even if they were ruinously expensive, were the visits of princes which became occasions for drinking bouts, costly decorations and generous almsgiving, but where the fractious aristocracy came together; such ceremonies displayed submission to authority, sometimes hospitality in the ancient style, and homage to the established order.

The birth of the village community

With their eyes fixed on the town, believing that the roots of 'democracy' were to be found in urban communities. nineteenth-century historians, and a number in the twentieth century, disregarded the emanicipation movement in the countryside. At best they saw it as a reflection of that in the towns, merely an imitation. They did not take any notice of the chronological gaps, nor of the essential difference in the nature of these phenomena: even when peaceful, the 'commune' was insurrectionary because it was defined suddenly, and against an existing situation. It gave a moral character to a social body, hitherto excluded from scholars' social formulations. The territory subject to the rural *échevins*, however, was built into the seigneurial framework; it was the fruit of long, slow evolution. And if, in fact, the occasional urban text has been accepted which gives something of bourgeois life to country bumpkins, this is because there was no need to write anything different when the desired advantages were comparable and because the oppositions between town and country were not as clear to contemporaries as they appear to us. Marxist historians, however, are ready to detect in the setting up of these groupings an important turning-point in the opposition between the dominators and the dominated and have seen in this, more than in the oligarchies of blood or wealth which ruled the communes, a major step in social progress.

The difficulty – perhaps the cause of the long neglect – comes from the awkwardness of a documentary approach. The deliberations of village groups, let alone their procedures of accountability, do not come to light, for example in Hainault, until the very end of the thirteenth century. The 'laws', the 'assizes', the charters of franchise, or more simply the records of respective rights established with the local lord, 'records of custom' as they were called in the Meuse region (the German *Weistümer*, the *firma burgi* of Normandy and Le Mans, for example), all these are numerous during the period 1160–1220, but they are concerned with particular cases of achieved emancipation, not with the general situation. The latter, like everything else in its first stages of development, remains in the shadows, and I rely here on common sense rather than proofs. Let us see what basic points we can establish.

The coming together of the peasants, once a basic settlement had been established, was obviously facilitated by the parish: the house of God and the churchyard were meeting-places and also places for celebrations; I have already discussed this and will not go back over it. But we must stress the absolutely secular nature of the consciousness that stemmed from having a fixed residence, from belonging completely to the village group. The inhabitant (the *manant*, the *villanus*) was *par excellence* a part of a whole, and this tie already excluded the stranger, the passer-by, but by no means the village priest, the artisan, or even the lord. Essentially, this was the birth of the same sort of feeling that in towns affected people living in the same neighbourhood, or the same street: the groups of houses (*linea*, row, or *coron* according to region – Iberian, Anglo-Saxon, Picardian) were perhaps not as strong a fabric as an urban *consorteria*, but their identity was apparent, for example, in England when the reeve came to make his inquiries in the village. On this level, the construction of a fence, a simple palisade (*etter*) to discourage unwanted guests, or sometimes even of a wall or earthworks, strengthened the feeling of unity. In Mediterranean regions, where the process of group-formation in the tenth and eleventh centuries was often accompanied by fortification, the *castro* was surrounded by a stone wall against which the houses were built.

One imagines that this early effort, mostly pre-1020 or 1050, received a renewed impetus during the great phase of expansion of inhabited lands or the reorganisation of grain sowing which accompanied land clearance and the extension of farming land: the new villages in clearings, those built along a single street (*Strassendorf, Waldhufendorf*), the Gascon *sauvetés* or Italian *villafranca* (built on a geometric plan, round or square, but always walled), and the Christian *aldeas* of Castile, represent coherent groups on which privileges could be bestowed without any more difficulty than on towns. It was in this phase, essentially from 1075 to 1160, that modifications were introduced, which generally proved to be basic and durable. The most striking feature here was the village, whether new or old, whose focus was the power of a castle which generally formed a rival nucleus to that of the church and the cemetery. These 'castle villages' over the whole of western France, the *castelnaus* of the south-west, had their counterparts throughout Europe: the *castro* flanking a fortified *rocca* in northern and central Italy, the *castilion* of southern Italy, the *klaat* of reconquered Iberian lands, the *burgo* of Aragon, the Polish *opole*, the German *Hofburg*, the Anglo-Saxon *burh* or *borough*. There was always something authoritarian, military rather than legal, in the development of this type of village: the land, the *destret*, the *salvament* was thought of more as an area under protection than an area to be worked. In these circumstances the lord's influence was extremely strong and the development of communal elements very slow; moreover, in many regions such villages represented a large proportion of the total, from 65 per cent to 70 per cent in Normandy, Maine and England, almost half in Poitou, Gascony, west Germany and peninsular Italy. If, moreover, he found himself in a resettlement zone, the lord could argue for the absolute necessity of a wall and garrison of his own, as seen in the *bastides* (fortified places), many of which were erected after 1200 on the borders of Capetian lands, and those of the Plantagenets in Aquitaine.

Unlike these 'castle villages' where production was aimed at satisfying the needs of the castle, the villages that were simply 'rural' and 'ancient' seem to have been economically less constrained: the simple German *Dorf* or *Wohnburg*, the *poblaciones* of Old Castile, the Christian *aldeas* and Mozarabic *alqueiras* of La Mancha, the Levant and New Castile, the *pazzos* of Asturias, the *castro*, the township of northern and eastern France, all these had slowly attracted cottage industries and a varied market. Here the clients for joiners, smiths, butchers, wheelwrights and haberdashers were mostly villagers; in the thirteenth century one even discovers, around Namur and Hainault, *mercatores bladorum*, grain merchants, urban intermediaries.

My earlier remarks about the local *mercadel*, the weekly market, particularly apply to these villages: there we find hides, yarn, flax, balls of carded wool, pots and pans. Of course the area on which this drew was only a few kilometres at most; but the money that circulated gave them some bargaining power with the lord, if an opportunity of gaining privileges arose. Thus it seems likely enough that the first communal groupings would have been of an economic nature: teams responsible for fire-watching in the woods of Scandinavia or the Black Forest, or for keeping the dykes in good repair in Flanders and Frisia (*wateringen*). The pastoral areas, those where there was a simple shift to the mountains in season (Navarre, Savoy), and also those where there was extensive transhumance

353

Rural landscape (left). The castle is situated in the middle of its lands; the village houses border the green which leads to the castle. Communal life is lived within the seigneurial framework. (Castle Bolton, Yorkshire; Cambridge University Collection.)

A hill village (right). Built on the side of the mountain exposed to the sun, situated below the church, the village clings to the grey granite; the placing of the houses follows the irregularities of the terrain. (Eus in Roussillon.)

An aerial view of the new town of Grenade-sur-Garonne. Created at the behest of a sovereign or lord, the new towns had a regular layout, usually a rectangular grid as here. Their foundation stemmed from political, economic or sometimes strategic motives, and was accompanied by the granting of privileges (freedoms) to the population which was attracted to settle there.

(the Dauphiné, upper Provence, the Iberian *meseta*, Béarn and Causses), were particularly driven to form groupings which were obviously imposed by the need to assemble the herds in *bacades*, *madaes*; the *escarterons* of the Briançonnais, the *fruitières* of the Jura, and later the Castilian *mesta* represented the developed forms of shepherds' organisations. Lastly, where the hand of the seigneur was not so heavy, some autonomous military activity was allowed to supplement his own; carrying arms was authorised here and there, in Picardy or the Rhineland around 1145 or 1155, obviously under the guise of peace patrols. In the Apennines, where the extensive family structures were strong, in the Gafargnana for example, we know of associations of armed peasant groups, *communia militum*, albeit organised by nobles.

Two elements, finally, also helped to consolidate the bases of village self-management. One was basically spiritual (initially at least): these were pious groups, the 'confraternities', associations of devotion and mutual aid which gradually, thanks to subscriptions from their members entered on a register (a 'matricule', *matricularii* = churchwardens), built up sufficient capital for the purchase of common land (*terrae francorum*, *Allmende*, *communia*), and tools which could be lent or rented out. Undoubtedly, after 1250 and perhaps earlier, the more important villagers were able to exercise a form of economic control, not to say guardianship, over their less fortunate 'brothers', and indeed over those peasants who were not on the register, by renting tools to them at a cost and time of their own choosing. But the history of this peasant divide does not concern me here. What matters about the birth of these confraternities (dates unknown: the beginning or end of the eleventh century?) is that they gave the populace common property, the 'lands of Holy Saviour', of 'Corpus Christi' and so on, that is to say, economic power. In excluding first of all the lord, then out-siders and foreigners (the *Gäste*, *Landsassen*) and probably also unfree men, the confrater-nity became something that belonged to the *manants* (the inhabitants), the framework in which the villeins met. In this respect, it is striking that in villages of intensive agricultural activity and in open-field country, the confraternity was the first body to develop notions of collective responsibility concerning the land – of being careful not to let plots run to seed or to fall into the hands of strangers (*adjectio sterilium*, as it was called in Antiquity when the allocation of uncultivated plots by the authorities constituted a powerful motivating force for union); also, at least in the *communia*, mutual agreement among the farmers over a coherent policy of crop rotation and land management occurred within the framework of the confraternity. Firm evidence for the first of these elements does not appear until fairly late, 1162–93 in Picardy for example, and for the second until even later, in the second half of the thirteenth century.

The second element already hints at the presence of rudimentary internal organisation; indeed it suggests the delegation of justice, which implies an accommodation with the master. There is hesitation over the origins of the right to judgement being given to the *meliores* and *prudentes homines*, to *probi homines*, *prudhommes*, the 'good men'. Was it a case of extending the manorial courts, as is suggested by the presence of the lord's agent at the head of these sittings (*dinge* in the Low Countries, *Hofrat* in Germany) together with the fact that they were limited to transactions concerning the land, *cognitio fundi*, as the lawyers call

The exercise of justice: a false witness is condemned to have his tongue pierced and to parade through the town. (MS from Cîteaux, thirteenth century, Bibliothèque d'Agen.)

it? Or was it rather a delegation of the power of the *bannum*, that is to say, an agreed withdrawal from public justice, the lord reserving for himself only the most important cases? Here again, the terms designating the sitting peasants, in French *écoutètes* (Latin *scultetus*) and *échevins* (Latin *scabini*), and also the fines for small penal offences – blows, abuse, theft – make us think that the latter was the case. In any case, this stage was essential and was reached by 1120–30 in northern France and western Germany, not much before 1160–85 in central Europe, but perhaps much earlier in the region of the Pyrenees and Iberia (1070–1100 in Béarn and possibly Aragon).

The passage to the next stage, that is, the master's official recognition of the village's own organisation, generally began after 1130: we do not have any record of the Iberian rural *fuero* before that time, but it may have existed; 'laws' were granted in northern and eastern France and in the Low Countries from 1120 onwards (for example, Florennes 1121, Brogne 1131, Cavron 1141). Certain texts listing in some detail the privileges or the burdens of communities had more than local application, such as that of Lorris-en-Gâtinais, granted by Louis VII (1155), which was adopted by ninety localities, or the Count of Hainault's for Prisches (1158), and above all William Archbishop of Rheims' charter for Beaumont-en-Argonne, which spread to nearly 500 communes in the former Lotharingia. On the whole, the basic phase of the blossoming of rural *échevinages* in this area with fixed-price justice – for example, the confirmation of customs, the fixing of a ceiling for dues, the selling-off of demands for labour and the suppression of arbitrary demands, to name just a few – took place between 1170 and 1220 alongside a very strong contingent of similar urban charters of privileges. It is very likely, in fact, that the vast majority of seigneuries thus delegated a certain degree of power to the peasants, perhaps not always in writing, but certainly in exchange for money: the *villes batiches* of Hainault (towns with no commune), like the *bans* of Lorraine or the *universités* of Normandy and Berry contented themselves with merely the privileges of law. There were many attempts to go further, as seen in the grouping into leagues of the village 'communes' of the Laon region around 1174, or the efforts at military organisation in Picardy between 1219 and 1229. In all these cases the

357

military aristocracy was able to crush such tentative stirrings. It did not intend to go beyond small concessions in exchange for money; retaining military superiority and keeping control of higher justice and equipment was fundamental; and in the country, it had nothing to fear from violent confrontation: the discontented peasants of Ponthieu, Bray or Normandy, for example, who took up axes and pitchforks in 1226, 1249 and 1256, were not animated by the revolutionary spirit of their tenth-century ancestors; and there was no urban militia capable of defeating mounted knights in battle.

The case of the Mediterranean areas of Europe, excepting the *fueros* of Spain, is less interesting; the feebleness of the peasant movement, or rather its atrophy on the level of economic concerns (I have already referred to the pastoral groups) is not easily explained, given the parallel decline of seigneurial authority at the end of the twelfth century, and the absence of full state power. Elsewhere, in Italy, and indeed in Provence or Languedoc, urban control over the *contado* might have stifled the peasants' impulses, but this was not the case for central France or Aquitaine. I think that this must be attributed to the less dynamic nature of the peasantry stemming from the dominance of crops that were more 'individualist' – vines, olives, *ferragina*, and so on – and perhaps also to the scarcity of middle-sized villages; we see few examples of compact villages that did not become little towns after the *incastellamento*. The granting of written privileges, *statuti*, in Italy, in the Vivarais, around Toulouse and Lyon, was generally quite late, well into the thirteenth century, and in some cases was quickly challenged in the fourteenth century; the term *échevin* was replaced here by *syndic*, and this semantic shift is important because it represents an elimination of legal responsibility in favour of simply representing economic interests. There was certainly a demand to go further, notably in the Rhône valley between 1247 and 1252, and to obtain, among other concessions, that of bearing arms; but this effort was the result of the particular circumstance surrounding Emperor Frederick II who was anxious to create a 'social' distraction in the Capetian camp while he was in difficulties in Italy; besides, the movement died out of its own accord without bearing any fruit.

Urban structures

Beginning my narrative in the last decades of the eleventh century frees me from having to deal with the irritating problem of urban continuity in Europe since classical times; after the year 1000, the renewal of urban activity cannot be disputed, even if it is not easily placed in the scenarios dreamed up by scholars. Nevertheless, in order to grasp the stages and variety of forms of urban growth, it is necessary to attempt a classification within the period that concerns us.

The first basic element concerns immigration into both ancient and newly created urban centres. Today we are sufficently advanced in urban prosopography to be able to discern the rural provenance and continuing links with the country of many 'bourgeois' families; it appears that the natural demographic growth of a nucleus of officers and artisans whose roots went back many generations and who surrounded the bishop or count is not enough to account for this rapid urban development. There had to be a contribution from outside:

Pre-Romanesque statue of St Foy in gold-covered wood, late tenth century (abbey treasury, Conques)

Wood statue of the 'black Virgin', Catalan, eleventh century (Dorres, south-west France)

Margrave Ekkehard and his wife Uta, polychrome statues in the cathedral of Naumberg, Germany, mid-thirteenth century

The coronation of the Virgin, polychrome ivory, thirteenth century (Paris, Louvre)

people who worked on the lands but whose links with it were snapped as the old manorial system broke up; naturally enough, these were often younger sons of peasants, affected by the disintegration of large families after 1200, and less certain than before of finding a patch of land to put to good use; but they were also people who counted on finding in the town a better legal status or social level than in the country. As an offended master could pursue a runaway serf there, at least within a certain time limit (usually a year), the town was perhaps not such an attractive place for liberty as the famous German phrase suggests: 'Stadtsluft macht frei' (town air makes free), at least not before the thirteenth century. Even then, in Italy (for example, in Assisi in 1210, and Bologna in 1257) the unfree received by the town were heavily taxed. All the same, illusions are stubborn, and it may be that the urban law, the *Stadtgerichte*, seemed to offer a guarantee; it was only in the Spain of the *Reconquista*, to which I shall return, that, given the circumstances, people did not look too closely into the past of those newly arrived. The peasants who did arrive in towns, usually young and without tools or special skills, came from nearby: it has been estimated that in Arras, around 1150, 72 per cent came from less than 10 kilometres away. Such a short range probably explains the strength of the links between the new town-dweller and his village birthplace. If he was successful, the immigrant would no doubt extend his operations to his family village. This in turn explains the relative ease with which, in the fourteenth century, bourgeois landholding could return to the countryside: the Hucquedieu, Louchard or Wagon of Arras were, from 1220, landholders in the villages from which their forebears had come. This feature was even more pronounced if a landed aristocratic house kept a large part of its family group in the *distretto*, that is, the land near the city: in Venice the Foscari, the Contarini, Orseolo, Ziani and Morosini based their fortunes on their estates in the Terra Ferma, as did the Guidi and Alberti in Florence; masters of part of Genoa, the Fieschi and the Grimaldi were very often in the Apennines; and the Orsini, the Colonna, the Frangipani, the Ottaviani or Caetani were more often to be encountered in their Latium *castelli* than in Rome. One should emphasise, however, that there was a necessary stage of waiting outside the ramparts before being admitted to the town, and sometimes the waiting lasted for centuries: the *serranos* who came down from the Pyrenees towards the Ebro, or the beggars (*panosi, patarii*) attracted to Milan or Novara in the mid-eleventh century by the hope of paid work crammed the town ditches, masses ripe for the revolutionary movements of the eleventh century.

It is useful to introduce here a clear distinction between at least two types of towns whose reactions to the human groupings were quite different. Some, those of the former *Romania*, often had a long history, and had remained intact or been revived in periods before the year 1000. Their nucleus, usually the count's palace and the episcopal seat, formed the heart of the city, enclosed by walls mainly dating from the repairs of the tenth century; the inhabitants were mostly agents (*ministeriales*) of public or religious power, representatives of aristocratic families, of artisans and bailiffs; they prided themselves (for the most part, mistakenly) on their ancient family lines and gave themselves ancient titles (*cives, curiales, quirites*), affecting to respect what remained of ancient municipal life, a model revived during the Carolingian era with a palazzo (a public tribunal or urban assembly). If, **359**

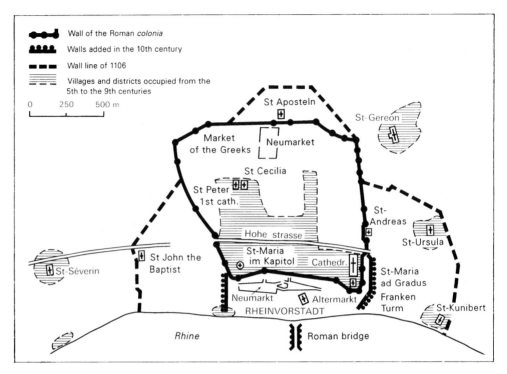

Legend:
Wall of the Roman *colonia*
Walls added in the 10th century
Wall line of 1106
Villages and districts occupied from the 5th to the 9th centuries

0   250   500 m

St Aposteln
St-Gereon
Market of the Greeks
Neumarket
St Cecilia
St Peter 1st cath.
St-Andreas
Hohe strasse
St-Ursula
St-Maria im Kapitol
St John the Baptist
Cathedr.
St-Séverin
St-Maria ad Gradus
Neumarkt
Altermarkt
Franken Turm
St-Kunibert
RHEINVORSTADT
Rhine
Roman bridge

Map 15. Plan of twelfth-century Cologne.

however, there was an apparent break with ancient times, as in Provence or in Languedoc, then there was more of a 'feudal' colouring; the families called themselves 'knightly' (*boni homines*, *castellani*), but the spirit was the same: a rejection of newcomers. On account of this it was alongside the walls, but sometimes at quite a distance, that the immigrants clustered – in the Italian *borghi*, the *barri* of Languedoc, the *bordaria* of Aquitaine, the Iberian *barrios*, the *bourgs* of Poitou or the Paris Basin, and the Rhineland *burgum*; the birth of this phenomenon (980–1060 in general) took place around suburban monasteries, crossroads or defence towers. The movement affected Cologne and Regensburg as much as Soissons, Cambrai and Chartres, Poitiers, Toulouse and Narbonne, Barcelona, Segovia or Sepulveda, Florence, Genoa and Milan. An essential part of its importance came from the parallel establishment of commercial elements in these satellite towns. In general, it was not until the mid-twelfth century that the old cities absorbed the new cells into a new common enclosure: 1132 in Pisa, 1152 in Genoa, 1176 in Florence, 1145 in Toulouse, 1157 in Avignon, 1180 in Beauvais, 1192 in Amiens, 1200 in Paris and Liège, 1175 at Regensburg, and 1180 in Cologne. At that moment they achieved a unity which the other urban type had possessed, in principle at least, from the beginning.

Europeans, mesmerised by Islamic towns, take too little notice of a similar diversity and scale to be found in their own creations. Once again this second type might be an ancient **360** foundation, emptied of its inhabitants, voluntarily or not, and repopulated by decree; this type of *repoblación* accompanied by the distribution of lots amongst the inhabitants (*repartimiento de suertes*) was typical of Spain in the *Reconquista*; some towns were ancient, such as Salamanca, Tarragona, Valencia, Cordoba and Seville, others had grown up in the early Middle Ages: Ubeda, Jaén, Baeza. Alternatively they might be royal creations (Burgos, Oviedo, Vich, León), or ecclesiastical foundations (Jaca, Urgel, Lerida, Estella, Sahagun) to confine ourselves to northern Spain. In both cases, establishment in the midst of an agricultural region, the *alfoz*, calculated to be able to provide food for the inhabitants, was accompanied by the assignment of special quarters, either on ethnic and religious grounds (Jews, Mudejares), or on commercial grounds ('Francos', Genoese); the remainder was divided into quarters for *caballeros* and for *peones*. These authoritarian practices were maintained to the end of the *Reconquista*, as in Murcia, Seville and Valencia between 1232 and 1243. The Iberian example offers a particularly clear case of towns subject to tight public control which, while quick to grant certain privileges, also took great care to maintain surveillance. The situation was roughly the same throughout the villages of the Mediterranean zone.

This form of populating and repopulating was not peculiar to Spain, and in the German zone of Poland one can find similar examples: after all, Hanseatic towns such as Lübeck (1158–61) were structured in the same way. Nevertheless, over the whole northern face of Europe the situation was more complicated. Since the era of large-scale Scandinavian–Slav commerce in the ninth and tenth centuries, enclosed and defended trading posts had grown up, stamped by their various ethnic origins, *wik*, *hampton* or *gorod*, *portus* and *emporium*, as at Hedeby (Haithabu), Birka, Bardowik, Quentovic, Duurstede. The decline of Scandinavian activity had generally resulted in the total ruin of these nuclei. A second generation, however, had taken over the role of the Scandinavians and often their very sites, just a few dozen kilometres away, which were now under German, Flemish or Lotharingian control, as with Hamburg, Lübeck, Bremen, Bruges, Huy, Tiel, Maastricht, Lille, and sites which had been occupied for even longer, such as Antwerp, Brussels, Caen, Ghent and Douai. This expansion occurred in the tenth or early eleventh century; it did not rule out the development of self-generating *bourgs*, as at Ghent or Douai, but these towns showed a social homogeneity that was related to their almost exclusively commercial origins. In the interior of the Continent, however, in the non-Romanised part of the Empire, beyond the Rhine or the Danube, it was a matter of deliberate creation (as in Spain) but for different reasons. The Saxon and Salian rulers of the tenth and eleventh centuries, in their anxiety to make their authority felt over the secular Church (*Kirchensystem*) and their own landholdings (*Reichsgut*), created towns of all sizes: in theory, according to the classification of German historians, forty episcopal towns, twenty monastic towns, twelve palatine towns and forty-eight princely towns. These foundations could not have been made without systematic immigration, designated locations and legal privileges. But there was no rigid organisation such as that favoured in Spain. In these towns, as well as in those which originated as trading posts, the term *burgenses*, in the sense of *viri hereditarii*, was current before its late eleventh-century appearance in the old Roman centres such as Cologne.

The welcome offered by the town

The preceding survey runs a certain risk: intended to underline the variety of urban structures, it contradicts in advance, at least in principle, the observations which follow and which are supposed to be generally applicable. I trust that the reader will find them useful all the same.

In fact, whatever their origin, the twelfth- and thirteenth-century town-dwellers, like those of Antiquity, lived outdoors. What I have already said about the material conditions in their dwellings explains this. It is rather difficult for us to grasp the importance of this life in the open air, in the midst of our mechanised cities where the street is merely an axis for traffic; nevertheless, the southern part of Europe – Spain even more than Italy – offers us a medieval spectacle, when the heat of the day has subsided, a spectacle which the city dwellers provide for themselves; in France one must go to a small town to find in the town squares of Provence or Languedoc something of this outside life; I do not need to go back over the kinds of spectacles for which the medieval street was the usual setting. In this respect, moreover, it should be pointed out that before the opening up of well-defined squares – generally in the fourteenth century – the *piazza maggiore, plaza mayor, grosse Ring, grand'-place*, in front of the building of the 'seigneurie'(the town hall or Rathaus), our ancestors needed strong nerves to tolerate the state of the streets: generally there was only a dirt road, divided by a channel in the centre, rutted by cart-wheels, cluttered with pieces of equipment, household slops and dead animals, threatened by the overflowing private latrines, scattered with chickens, empty barrels, sticks, and above all by herds of swine, presumably useful for consuming everything that was edible, and which come to mind, among hundreds of anecdotes, as the cause of the fatal accident in Paris to the elder son of Louis VI. Numerous decrees went out to encourage neighbourly concern; Philip Augustus was said to be disgusted by the stink of the streets in the heart of Paris and had several hundred metres paved; this example was followed in a few northern towns such as Ypres and Calais, and then by some in the east, such as Troyes, Rheims, Cologne and Nuremberg, before 1270, but was practised quite widely in Italy where Roman roads had left sufficient models and sections intact. As for drains, they lay in the future.

The street was not simply the place where people met and heard speeches or watched shows. It brought together people with the same skills. At least this was the case until the end of the twelfth century during the main phase of influx into the towns; naturally enough, the newcomer would be drawn to the house of a compatriot who might be able to find him work in the same trade. Subsequently, a reorganisation of the professional structure of the streets undermined this state of relative unity, to which Muslim towns or a few street-names in our own cities still bear witness. In speaking earlier of the artisan class, I touched on the origin and development of professional groupings. As with the rural assemblies, historians have investigated the first stages of these friendly societies; they have reminded us of the role of the confraternities, particularly of the importance of the *convivia, potaciones, drykkia*, that is, the drinking sessions held in honour of the feast of the patron saint of the craft; the meeting-place, often a cellar in the street where the artisans gathered (*Keller*, *Stube*), could thus become their common premises, and indeed, around 1150, there are examples of *Morgensprach*, professional meetings being held there. Apart from some information about individual merchants, we do not have documents on the subject prior to 1127–30 (Würzburg, Strasburg), after which they become more plentiful (Saragossa, Cologne, Oxford, Winchester, Rouen, Toulouse). It is thought, however, that most of these groups had been in existence since 1030 or 1060 in Italy, and about fifty years later to the north of the peninsula. Possibly the gradual hardening of the internal organisation of the artisan class came initially from its geographical explosion. In raising the level of entry to a craft, especially for those which were defined as such at a later date (not before 1212 for the butchers of Genoa, 1244 for the wool merchants; and in Toulouse, nothing before 1181), or in reducing the number of apprentices, and above all in making it more difficult to produce the 'master work' which opened the way to being a master craftsman, those running the crafts were only following the traditionally anti-competitive, conservative policy which seemed to them vital for maintaining the social order. Their actions had two effects bearing on the study of groups in the towns: on the one hand they eliminated a large proportion of qualified workers, driving them to work on the side, in private, or into unemployment, which was the root of the acute disturbances which shook the towns from 1245 to 1250; on the other hand, they led to growing urban specialisation by weeding out products which could not find local outlets: in England, people began to work on skins and fabric more than on wool or metals, in the German Rhineland leather or iron replaced cloth, in Italy cloth, furs and products from the East replaced metal and glass. This 'specialisation' does not surprise us, and need not have harmed social relations; but in social terms it tended to increase the mass of workers who had a reduced number of outlets and, in the absence of any power to find them employment (because the medieval economy did not have the necessary flexibility) it led them to unite in groups that were clandestine and anti-establishment, outlawed and harried, 'bands', *consortia*, of which the first recorded examples appeared in 1255–60 in the Rhône valley, a new tear in the urban social fabric.

Medieval towns were small. Remember that we cannot count many more than sixty around the beginning of the fourteenth century that had over 10,000 inhabitants, or five or six with more than 50,000 (Paris, Milan, Florence, Genoa, Venice and Palermo), and even this is disputed. Despite their modest size, medieval towns were much more familiar than modern towns with the concept of organisation according to district (*quartier*). No doubt this, rather than the street, offered a framework for a group's self-awareness. Of course some of them, the Italian *consorterie*, the *pariages* of Lorraine, drew their sense of unity from belonging to a household, to a *casa* or *albergo* which owned the houses, contributed to building the church and built a family palace. But, even under this guardianship of merchants or nobles, a unity was created: clients or those with obligations to the family (*sicarii* armed to defend the 'towers' which overlooked the neighbourhood), stood together. Moreover, there was a degree of social homogeneity: it has been noted that, no doubt in order to keep the maximum number of artisans or simple 'bourgeois' under their thumbs, the dominant families maintained low rents for most of their houses, scarcely more than

3–6 per cent of a Parisian worker's wage in the early fourteenth century; this policy might have had the desired effect but, as we can still see today, a fall or stagnation in rental values sooner or later means deterioration, first of all of the actual fabric of the housing, and then of its social standing. It must be said that we know nothing about these sociological nuances before 1300, but we can safely imagine them. Other groups drew their sense of unity from a dominant professional activity: the *Socherie* (clog workshops) of Metz, the *Merceria* in Venice, the *Mezel* (butchers) in Chambéry, the *Inferno* (metal workshops) in Milan, the *Fusterie* (cabinet-makers) in Geneva, etc. In these various examples the choice of the main craft was often linked to the material conditions imposed by the relevant technique: water for tanning, treating fine skins and fulling, access to primary materials that came by river for woodworking, isolation for abattoirs, and so on. These contingencies could be further complicated by the requirements of potential customers: palaces drew silversmiths and lawyers, famous convents or cathedral cloisters attracted students, those who sold skins, and innkeepers, which helped in the mingling of various populations. To find simple homogeneity again, one has to turn back to those 'reserved' neighbourhoods to which I referred with regard to Spain, and especially to the Jewish quarters.

This form of block organisation, which did not follow the lines of the urban parish network, was signalled by very visible material objects such as chains across the streets and the emblems of the governing craft or family, and organised patrols under a bourgeois captain. The names by which these groups were designated, for example on the occasion of a march or procession, are based on all or some of these roles: they were the 'banners', the *bannières* (Paris), the *gonfalonerie* (Florence), the *enseignes* (Lyons), the *connetablies* (Low Countries, Germany), and so on. These groups were not only a social reality but also a political one, as the storms inside Italian towns demonstrated in the fourteenth and fifteenth centuries. But at the date my study ends, no official framework, such as the *quartiers* of Paris, was yet in place.

Finally, I cannot conclude this rapid survey of the locations and forms of gatherings in towns without mentioning the town wall. Its construction and maintenance was, financially speaking, the great business of the town involving everyone – and in times of repair, it was capable of absorbing the town's finances for several years. The defence of the walls, and especially the gates, was also the business of all the town's 'citizens'. If a garrison existed, it was concerned only with protection of the castle itself; it was the townspeople who ensured that the piece of the wall abutting their street was properly guarded, and this responsibility does not seem to have raised any protests. The ramparts and their surroundings were also a microcosm of the town, where, as in a caricature, polluted water, the filth of the streets and of public latrines, runaways, prostitutes, taverns, bear-keepers and wandering minstrels all came together; festivals and games started from here too, and it was in the shadow of the walls that fairs were held. Some villages in southern Europe, of course, had walls but these enclosures were often just the back walls of houses and would have earned the scorn of the towns. The city dweller (and this certainly has not changed) despised the countryman – for each viewed the world from a different perspective. As early as the fifth century, St Augustine recognised this when he maintained that what made

The outstanding feature of the town was its wall, which was a means of defence, a symbol of power, and an expression of urban art and architecture. (Gate and towers of the walled town of Laressingle, Gers.)

towns was not ramparts but minds: *non muri sed mentes*. Recently an English historian added to the file on this ancient conflict a very striking comparison of rural and urban crime in England after 1250 through a study of the court rolls, a comparison which could not be made for another hundred years for the Continent. One can see from this that if occasional aggressive offences were more numerous in the towns, which is always the case, there was no greater likelihood of murders, and that such murders were more often motivated by notions of defending honour than by covetousness, and took the form of solo attacks rather than group action, and that as regards insults, the countryman who wanted to show that his target was outside the group would call him a 'pagan', a 'Jew' or a 'Saracen', while in the town, people preferred to humiliate someone inside the group rather than exclude him from it, by insults revealing an 'anal fixation' or 'sexual obsession', with a vocabulary echoed very precisely by our own contemporaries.

Towards the commune

'Commune – a new, detestable word', wrote Guibert of Nogent, canon of Laon, *c*. 1125, for he had been witness to the violent events in his town. However, eye-witnesses must be regarded with suspicion: often they understand nothing of what is going on. Guibert was no exception, but his prestige has remained so great up until this century that the communal movement is still seen through his eyes, with the Bishop of Laon murdered in a barrel. This prelate well deserved his fate, and in any case, it was almost the only bloody episode of the whole period. I said earlier that urban emancipation had been insurrectionary. This is not to say that it was explosive and violent; it varied a great deal in its manifestations, depending on the situation of the active elements in the town, and their power and determination varied from place to place. So we must now examine those.

The landholding aristocracy, indeed the aristocracy who held posts around the count or the bishop in the town, represented the primary element because, before 1100 and even up to 1150, it was the richest and strongest. These were the *magnati*, the *ricos hombres*, the 'men of inheritance', as they were called in Italy, Spain and the Low Countries; only to this fraction could the contentious word 'patricians' be applied, dusted down from Antiquity, and which, as it referred to a *gens*, a *familia*, was not suitable for bankers. This inheritance from Pirenne has to be rejected. There were not many of these men at all, and as mentioned earlier, they often lived in the country. But their *case*, their *alberghi* extended to the towns, where they had clients, friends and relations. Numbers are impressive: the Doria 'clan' had 300 members, the Spinola 'clan' in Genoa had 400; in Pisa, in the census of 1228, 2,250 individuals out of 4,270 were members of these *consorteries* (*conzorzi familiari* as they were called in Italy); but this phenomenon can be seen elsewhere too: in Liège from the eleventh century the bishop's *familia* numbered 4,000 people; in Metz there were assocations of 1,500 to 2,000; in Bordeaux the associations known as *oustaus* contained several hundred people. These families held urban land, perhaps the remains of the fisc snatched from some now-forgotten public office, or perhaps ecclesiastical property seized in the tenth century under cover of an advocacy or a lay abbacy, or simply purchased land. In general, like lords, they claimed the right of taxation, and went on to confiscate urban land that was not built on; moreover, their military power guaranteed them, as if by right, a castle and garrison whether this was a case of genuine delegation to them as viscounts (as in Milan, with the suggestive name of Visconti, the Buonsignori in Siena, the Este in Ferrara, the Malaspina in Parma) or through straightforward seizure (for example, the Embriaci in Genoa, the Guidi in Florence, Utenhove in Ghent, Zorn in Strasburg, and Luskirchen in Cologne). And lastly, they nominated priests in the parishes under their sway, and indeed canons: in York, Southampton, Cologne and Lübeck, in Laon and Jaca.

Their importance in the town was measured in material terms by the towers they erected above their houses, as a symbol of power rather than defence. There were 135 of these in Florence around 1180, 300 in Avignon in 1226, and 80 in Regensburg; they were to be seen everywhere, in Basle, Frankfurt, Trier, Metz, and some can still be seen today in Bologna or San Gimignano. Also they were in charge of strongholds such as the city walls of Toulouse and the arenas at Nîmes and Arles. The concerns of this aristocracy were simple: it wished to retain military and judicial control over the town; the rest did not matter. In effect it was master of the countryside, it had vassals, it dominated the *rocce* or the villages, it had infiltrated the confraternities and was ready to participate in economic expansion, which it fed by the sale of products from its estates. Doubtless this explains the deliberately open nature of this class; right up to the mid-thirteenth century it accepted the rise, by marriage for example, of new people from rustic or administrative backgrounds, such as the Dandolo and Barbarigo families in Venice, the Spinola and Doria in Genoa, the Albizzi and Pazzi in Florence. The 'Golden Book' of the *case, vecchie e nuove* was not closed in Venice until 1286; such developments tightened the 'noble' grip: there were 180 families in Venice, 46 in Lübeck, 95 in Arles, and 25 in Barcelona around 1230. Thus they could bring pressure to bear on the *contado*, indeed on the narrower *distretto* surrounding the town, the *pourchainte* as it was called in northern France, for a distance of up to some seven leagues; and through the *capitanei* or associate members of the *consorzio* they kept an eye on anything of importance in the town, while retaining their grip on key legal and financial levers of power.

The situation for the religious aristocracy was very different. Even if the links between the warrior dynasties and the episcopacy in the eleventh century had become so closely intertwined that it took a long struggle to undo them (as in Languedoc and Provence), the Church did not have access to the same means of action as the landholding aristocracy. Of course its estates were just as extensive as the latter's; moreover it had at its disposal, especially in the old Roman cities, comital rights or their equivalent. In Pisa, Milan, Pavia, Cologne, the prelate also held a large area of land; men-at-arms gathered round him, as in Narbonne, Cremona, Milan and Liège, the *milites majores*, as they called themselves, as opposed to the *milites castri* of the local nobility. But these means were often countered, during the phase of the 'peace of God' by the nobility: the viscounts of Languedoc, the *gastaldi* or *capitanei* of Lombardy, the *advocati* or *Vogts* of Lotharingia and Germany escaped the prelate. At the beginning of the twelfth century the situation of the bishops in towns was precarious, as was that of the monasteries in the small market towns, undermined by the progress of craftsmen and merchants. In order to keep physical control over men, the Church was forced to refuse any concessions in administrative or judicial matters; military problems escaped its control, and the economy was merely an area where the two sides met. If the claims of the populace impinged on sensitive areas, the Church could only, even if its pastoral role suffered, reject them and take harsh measures.

The populace in question – *minores, popolo minuto, poulares*, 'common people' – obviously formed the majority; but it was divided, first of all between masters and servants, then between skilled servants and unregistered workers, then between crafts that were highly regarded (those with a wealthy clientele, such as wool, silk, gold, silver) and the others, and lastly between artisans and tradesmen, the latter being on the margins, dynamic, quick to gather together and dangerous. The populace had a right to take part in the large regular gatherings (*Bauding, balia, arengo, mallus*) where it expressed its opinion by shouts that had no effect on those who 'consulted' it; it only existed through the charitable associations of the neighbourhood or the craft, which I have mentioned and which were all limited in aim, but without resources for action. Sometimes, for example in the Rhineland of the eleventh century and in Cologne in 1103, parishes had a *Burmeister* who could head a body of men; in 1066 at Huy, the Bishop of Liège entrusted the *castrum* to the guard of *burgenses*; in 1063   **367** in Palermo the inhabitants were required to join in a military campaign, and in Spain this was considered quite natural. This mass which called itself *cives* in the Roman regions, *burgenses* elsewhere, was not totally disorganised: from 1014 in Florence there are references to the *capitanei plebium*, in Pavia in 1020 to the *universitas civium*, as in Lucca and Cremona; this was particularly the case in Spain, where the *caballeria* and the *peones* formed a *communia* whenever there were military sorties.

The term 'commune' was launched, but for a long time it had various meanings: *communa militum* for Apennine villagers (early twelfth century), while the merchants of Cardona in Spain formed a *communa commercialis* (1102) and there was a *communio* of rebellious peasants around Le Mans (1070), and a *compagna communis* of Genoese shipowners (1099). It signified 'union', no more; but it quickly came to embody the idea of an assembly of town-dwellers. It was this that combined the efforts of the various elements outlined above. It seems to me that a geographical survey would be more useful here than a misleading synthesis; but it is good, too, to emphasise at the outset, that in following the stages by which communes were established, one common characteristic emerges which has been long rejected by historians in the name of 'urban democracy': the aristocracy was the mainspring of this movement; it was the aristocracy which triggered it or harnessed it, not always in the same way or at the same time, but certainly everywhere. We are far from Pirenne's 'vagabonds'; far too, I believe, from the group of *cives*, the clients of the bishop or rural immigrants, who have been presented, and are still being presented, as the principal engine of this emancipation.

The consulates

Italy is a good illustration of this observation. It was the families of the *consorterie*, interested in maritime expansion or control of the countryside, who took the initiative: the rapprochement between all the *curiales* and *boni homines* of their parties and a handful of episcopal officers abandoning their master's cause was the origin of the appearance of courts of justice which they dominated and which were under the direction of the *consules primores*, in Cremona (1030), Venice (1035), Milan (1045), Piacenza (1070), Verona, Parma and Pisa (1080), Genoa (1099) and Bologna (1105). This movement certainly prompted, here and there, the formation of economic groupings, and commercial ones in the maritime towns. Thus the Genoese *compagna communis* of 1100 was an extension of the consulate of the preceding year, but its ringleaders were the same heads of the *consorterie* turned shipbuilders. In some cases, such as Venice, exceptional as usual, the attack on all local hereditary or permanent power (including that of the doge in this instance) meant that the only remaining force was that of the *magnati*. The seizure of various organs of political pressure or economic organisation followed this first stage, often accompanied, as in Genoa in 1156 or Pisa in 1162, by imperial privileges confirming the *fait accompli*, with the consular council forming a veritable 'seigneurie', and with the crafts and trades being represented by delegates who were called priors in Florence, and who came from the principal professions and trades, the *arti maggiori*, which I have mentioned.

Alongside them, organised according to their districts, which were represented by the *gonfalonieri*, the banner-holders, were the people and their 'captain', who in theory retained some rights over the co-opting of priors or consuls, and who were grouped in a general assembly, *la balia*, where steam could be let off but little was accomplished. Where can we glimpse 'democracy' in all this? There was only one attempt, and that was a notable failure. It occurred in Rome, thanks to the disappearance of the pope and the Germans, under the 'popular dictatorship' of Arnold of Brescia, who dreamed of restoring his city to its ancient glories, recreating a Senate and unleashing the *popolo* of the *rioni*, the districts of the city (1144–45), on the palaces of the nobles. The visionary tribune had his moment of triumph, but the fickleness of the *populus Romanus*, the underhand activity of the nobility and finally the arrival of Barbarossa re-established the old order; Arnold was captured and executed (1155). Complete municipal organisation, in fact, took quite a long time to get established in developing towns, which were often split between various interests and without any overall control once the imperial power disappeared in the thirteenth century. This extremely confused period in the peninsula's history was marked by internecine wars between families, the ancient landholding families pitted against those whose fortunes were built on the sea. There is not much point in going into these in detail, but two features emerge: on the one hand a phase of recourse to control and arbitration by an external agent, theoretically representing the empire, the *podestà*, usually a stranger to the town, indeed to Italy, having a palace and a garrison but keeping himself at a distance. The rare examples of a dictatorial seizure of power, those of Boccanegra in Genoa (1256–62), the Della Torre in Milan (1266), or of Ugolino della Gheradesca in Pisa (1282–4), were generally swallowed up in revolt. The second feature was the political mask with which the battling clans covered their struggle for control of the economy. Some labelled themselves enemies of the Germans and drew closer to the pope or the princes of southern Italy; these were the Guelfs (an echo of the earlier Welfs of Bavaria who, in the eleventh century, had fought against the Teutons); the others responded by calling themselves Ghibellines (from Weibelingen, a patrimonial estate of the Swabian emperors). In general, they simply aspired to a little more order, but the preference for the Germans failed to prevail: everyone called themselves Guelfs after 1250. These conflicts went on everywhere, from 1216 in Florence and 1217 in Genoa; their revival was not just a matter of politics, because the ups and downs of the course of events involved a gradual expansion of the power of the commercial element at the expense of the oldest families; in Florence the uprisings of 1223, 1237 and 1250; in Genoa those of 1217, 1241 and 1262; in Pisa those of 1254 and 1270; and in Milan those of 1214, 1266 and 1277, all prepared the way for entry to the rank of prior (indeed of 'consul') for the *arti minori* which had neither merchants nor aristocrats. The threshold was crossed in Florence in 1293: the 'Ordinances of Justice' adopted there excluded from government some 147 ancient families, such as the Guidi and Alberti, requiring each inhabitant to register in a trade (Dante chose that of a grocer!) and opening the rule of the city to twenty-one trades. This sort of upset, while on a very large scale in Florence, was general throughout the peninsula: Siena, Viterbo and Bologna as early as 1281, Genoa in 1309 and Milan in 1311, all took the same path. One must not conclude that this was anarchy; on the contrary, it was a quest, painful and muddled, for a major stage in urban history, such as the city of Antiquity had tried to achieve so long ago: that of the city-state, mistress of the *contado* and the economy, free from all sovereignty. The fifteenth century tried to give substance to this dream through the person of the urban prince, which was quite another thing. Nor was this a time of powerlessness, let alone anarchy; first of all this was an important phase of increasing Italian prosperity; further, these 'bourgeois' – a large number of whom were men of war – were soldiers. Barbarossa, who had already, like his predecessors, suffered from Roman obstinacy in the defence of their city, had the bitter experience at Legnano in 1176 of finding that the militia of the towns of Lombardy were nothing like the rustic footsloggers on the other side of the Alps; there he saw his army of German knights crushed in defeat.

There is no more intriguing and surprising story than that of the Italian towns of the Middle Ages: here we find, as if in a laboratory, the seeds of political parties, of the role played by public opinion, of the clash of business and public interests, of the question of labour relations, the hazards of a representative regime. The fertility of the Italian mind, well versed in the craft of the law, the liberty enjoyed by a land that was so much coveted that foreigners' designs upon it cancelled each other out, help to explain this unique story. And it was unique; elsewhere, as I will briefly explain, things were simpler. The Tyrrhenian littoral had its own distinctive characteristics. First, political disorder and economic powerlessness had kept it in a prostrate state up to 1000 and beyond; later the control of the Italian merchant towns, the establishment of locally energetic seigneurial powers together with a strong demand in town for rents or lodging had slowed down development. But the aristocracy, here with military rather than landholding roots, was, as in Italy, solidly in command of the armed forces and the land, while the spread of literacy from Turin, Genoa and Lombardy encouraged imitation of the peninsula: the notaries, the *causidici*, the *juris periti* appeared after 1058 or 1060 in Provence, in Languedoc and indeed as far as Poitou; they developed the judicial centres whose appearance almost always coincides with that of administrative bodies: 1129 in Montpellier, 1138 in Arles, 1175 in Toulouse and 1190 in Limoges. As for the latter, they were set up more rapidly than across the Alps, but also less freely: the local counts or viscounts preserved a certain control over the *milites*, the *cabalarii* installed in towns; moreover the merchants, often Jews or Italians, were more active than the artisans (I have already mentioned the slow development of trades): their *communitas*, as it was called in Montpellier from 1110, was ready to come to friendly agreement. The effect of this simpler situation is that the birth of the southern *consulats* occurred later and was well-balanced. There was frequently an equal number of noble and 'popular' consuls, merchants for the most part, with public control usually uncontested, at fairly late dates: 1129 (Avignon), 1138 (Arles), 1141 (Montpellier), 1144 (Nîmes), 1152 (Toulouse), 1178 (Marseilles) and 1189 (Agen). The two main towns of Languedoc, those on which the comital authority weighed heaviest, given the power of the houses of Saint-Gilles and of Barcelona, took time to recover from a false start when their ambitions, particularly their military ones, were checked, but the following dates can eventually be added to our list: Toulouse (1189) and Montpellier (1204). Even without the military dimension of

Lombardy, the towns of Languedoc had obtained considerable control over their *contado*, as seen, for example, in the extension of urban commercial legislation (Toulouse 1182–9). This is explained, no doubt, by the lack of resistance in village communes. One can also put this down to a relatively calm climate within the cities: while Italy went through incessant ups and downs, Languedoc, with the exception of brief demonstrations by textile-workers in Montpellier around 1175, experienced only one revolt (in 1248 in Toulouse), with some others occurring in the first third of the fourteenth century. It is true that the phenomenon of Catharism and the long repression which accompanied its defeat (from about 1215 to 1270) meant that there was severe external control over all this region, which gradually became royal.

Over the Pyrenees, the same characteristics appear but stretch back to an earlier time, as here there was constant warfare, traffic in gold, immigrants coming and going. The military aristocracy was in the hands of the count or the king, after several attempts at emancipation prior to 1070 or 1080. Moreover, there were also knights in the country; there were no such categorical distinctions as obtained elsewhere. Besides, in a town that had been recaptured the law had to be laid down immediately. The *fueros* issued by the prince display as much concern with private arrangements as with administrative organisation: the 'customs' of Barcelona, elements of which dated back to perhaps 1064 or 1077, had inspired a great number of charters; Jaca from 1080 (?), Cardona (1102), Sepulveda (1104), Compostela (1136), Tortosa (1149) and Teruel (1179) were given *concejos* which designated the judges (*alcades*) and organised the militia. The participation of different social strata varied but, as later in the north, the part assigned to the nobility was generally equal to that of the 'people'. Was the iron fist that gripped the towns a cause of inertia, approaching that of Languedoc? Perhaps the cause was the phase of economic expansion which accompanied the *Reconquista*. It was not until this ended at the foot of the Sierra of Granada around 1260–5 that the social climate of Iberia changed. But it changed violently. The insurrection of Berenguer Ollier in Barcelona in 1285 and the terrible repression that followed showed, as in the fourteenth century, that the social demands of the Catalans had been suppressed too long. By contrast, even in its state of continual upheaval, which was almost contemporary with this, Florence knew how to avoid such an ordeal.

The communes

North of the Loire and the Alps lay quite a different world: a land of strongly established villages, without such a strong urban tradition, with princes closer at hand if not stronger, and with craft activity firmly anchored to local production. The aristocracy played a key part on this stage: no imitation of Venice was possible here. Merchants were outsiders, relatively weak, rather marginal figures as they had been for a long time: no Genoa here either. As for the Church, it was strong, assured of royal support, and clinging to its meagre judicial weapons: this was thus nothing like Milan. This is not to say that the situation evolved uniformly, and in fact three areas are quite distinct.

First, there was the 'cradle' of the communes, from the Seine to the Rhine, with a great

Corporation seals of the thirteenth century: glovemakers, fishmongers and weavers.

central core of new or ancient towns established on rich land, the regions of Artois, Flanders and the Meuse, from Amiens to Liège. It was here that the earliest professional associations came into being; on the other hand, the relative weakness of district organisation reveals that the hold of the family was weaker than in southern Europe. It was here, too, that the the *portus* – the market town – developed, becoming the focus for regular merchant activity. The eventual claims of these social elements did not really undermine public order: they made no military demands, or even judicial ones, but simply desired guarantees of protection and economic liberties. Thus it was a slow movement, but it began early, with the development of the market towns or the grant of the first charters for confraternities or trades; this takes us into the tenth century, or rather the beginning of the eleventh, in Liège (1002), Ghent (1013), Saint-Omer (1027) and Brussels (1047). An oligarchy of *burgenses* with the support of an aristocracy remaining in the countryside set in motion negotiations to obtain the right to oversee taxation and the markets. At Worms in 1073, Cologne in 1074 and Cambrai in 1077, these demands appeared within the parish framework. They were premature and failed. Their failure was due first of all to their being addressed to the bishops, and if the Bishop of Liège was happy to entrust the *castrum* of Huy to the townspeople (1066), it was because this in no way weakened his power; but the Bishop of Cambrai could not agree to anyone imposing a 'council' on him, and only left his town in order to return to it with military backing. Secondly, the more radical popular elements were also part of the movement, wishing to recreate in one of their former centres the revolutionary atmosphere of the pre-1050 period, and in doing so they committed abuses that chilled the zeal of the affluent. The failure gave rise to the idea of a stricter union of *burgenses*: a sworn brotherhood for mutual aid, a *conjuratio*. Obviously this was not acceptable to the Church, which had control over any oath-taking, and for whom it was a religious, sacral matter (*sacramentum*, oath). Henceforth the pattern was simple: *burgenses* and local aristocrats took oaths, conditions of self-management were negotiated (or purchased), and a charter may have been drawn up. In physical terms, the inhabitants would have their palace, their *hôtel* (town house), their tower like those of the nobility, their bell like that of the church, and their seal; in judicial terms, they would designate – obviously this was only among the notables – the *échevins* and the mayor, in a mixture of legal and manorial terminology, who were in charge of public works, tax assessment and the lower law courts. Usually the armed forces and the castle remained under the lord's control, along with the higher courts and various taxes. This was the essential element for him, as a rural lord, more so than in Italy; if he got round to conferring the guarding of the walls and the right of watch and guard to the townspeople, it was because this posed no great risk for him; prior to the fourteenth century, footsoldiers did not play a decisive part in battle. If the lord was a territorial prince, the business was quite quickly settled, as in Saint-Quentin (1090), Arras (1108), Valenciennes (1114), Amiens (1119), Ghent (1124) and Bruges (1128). If he was the king, and thus a quasi-sacral figure, it was more a case of closely watched freedoms: the Capetians encouraged emancipation abroad rather than at home, and Paris had a royal *prévôt* without having a commune. If the prince was a powerful ecclesiastic, he acted in much the same way, retaining control over essentials, as in Liège, Rheims and Metz. But if he was a bishop with fewer resources, then there were hesitations, trickery, delays (as in Strasburg 1105, Noyon 1109, Cologne 1112, Worms 1115 and Beauvais 1125), and sometimes drama (Laon 1112).

What is striking about this far from exhaustive list is the very brief span of this development, 1090–1130, scarcely more than a generation, and much shorter than in Italy or the south of France; but I hope the reader has understood that this 'explosion' was in fact the end product of social groupings that had been long in gestation. This explains why the later history of these towns, without matching the complexity of the Italian cities, especially as regards institutions, was very rich in terms of judicial and social developments. The rivalry between great houses was not pronounced here because, as I explained, the hold of the aristocracy was less firm and one suspects that up to the beginning of the fourteenth century it was nearly always the same families who shared the authority and the profits. If there was no direct equivalent to the Italian *podestà*, to a certain degree royal authority made up for that. The Capetians' interventions, particularly where private or commercial rights were concerned, increased after 1224–39 with decrees on public order, the sale of drink, guard duties and revision of the trade statutes, such as Etienne Boileau's in Paris in 1246 and, again in Paris, reduction of exemption privileges in cases of fraud. Even in 1256, in a certain number of towns in his domain, Louis IX was to impose control over urban finances by means of a local bailiff which severely diminished the communes' autonomy. The mid-thirteenth century was, furthermore, the time when widespread economic difficulties and tensions within social classes gave rise to demands, in reaction to rising prices, higher thresholds for entering the trades, the difficulties of hiring, and all-too recognisable economic pressures. The northern regions were the main theatre for this, such as Arras in 1225, 1253 and 1260, and particularly Liège, where in 1253–5 a popular leader (*ductor populi*), Henry of Dinant, advocated the seizure of noble and ecclesiastical property under the slogan which was taken up again by the Flemish Peter De Koninc in Bruges in 1302: 'Everyone must have as much as each other.' The Liège episode was a bloody one, as were minor explosions here and there (the mayor of Pontoise was murdered in 1267), but it was not until after 1280, and especially 1302, that these demands broke out everywhere. But this is, as in Italy, another part of urban history.

373

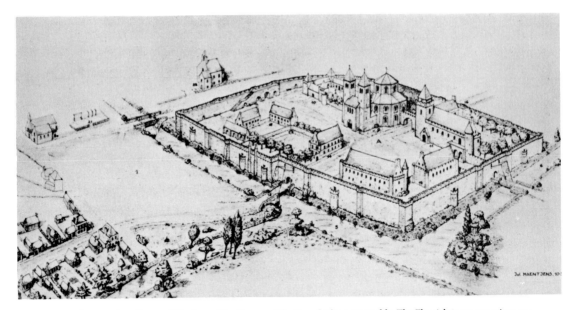

Bruges: the old core of the town. The Burg and the Grand-Place are visible. The Flemish town was given an autonomous administration in the twelfth century. A century later, thanks to the canal built in 1180 between Bruges and its outer harbour, it had become a centre of international and maritime trade. (After the drawing by the architect J. Haen Tyens.)

Across the Rhine one has the same impression as across the Pyrenees: the controlled, public aspect of the movement is clearly discernible, and the benefits conferred are less. The emperor and the princes increasingly tended to focus on the towns. In the mid-twelfth century this was true for Barbarossa, as for the Zähringen of Swabia, the Wittenburgs of Bavaria and the Babenbergs of Austria. Perhaps only the Baltic towns escaped this heavy presence. On the other hand, the development of new towns, with their planned districts and their assembly places (the *Dom*, the *Markt*, the *Ring* and the *Pfalz*), their control over the *Burg* or the *Munz* (the cathedral), the commercial quarter, the main square, the prince's palace, the fortress and the mint, was usually peacefully accompanied by the grant of means of self-management, but almost exclusively economic – control of toll-gates, of exemptions, of the movement of merchants – though sometimes judicial too, concerning the rights of merchants and liberty for newcomers. An entire hierarchy took part in fixing rights and obligations: those of the prince, the count, or an advocate (*Vogt*); those of the masters of each district (*Burmeister, Schultheiss*); those of the *burgenses*, that is to say the descendents of the officers of the local court, the merchants and masters of trades – since the populace (the *pestilens multitudo*, the *Muntmannen*) was kept at a distance. A *Rat* (a council), which was not sworn, was set up, composed of provosts representing geographical rather than professional groups. As so often in Germany there was a time-lag and, apart from the example of Freiburg (1120), this movement did not get under way until after the mid-century: Regensburg (1156), Augsburg (1157), Lübeck (1159) and Hamburg (1189). Under these conditions, there were no social upheavals before the fourteenth century or even later; but on the other hand, we can establish a classification, even if it is a

374

somewhat theoretical one, according to the degree of emancipation achieved: the further west they were, towards the region of communes, the more the towns were 'free'. Thus along the Rhine, along the *Pfaffenstrasse*, the 'priests' road' – Cologne, Mainz, Worms, Speyer, Aachen, Frankfurt, Strasburg, Basle, Constance – the towns were considered to be 'free', self-managing. But it must be noted that they were sworn to the emperor, which Strasbourg had tried in vain to avoid in 1273; they owed *Heerfahrt* (war service) and the burden of shelter and tax (*Steuer*). Others were only 'imperial towns', such as Regensburg, Nuremberg, Augsburg, Lübeck and Goslar, that is to say, under the control of a count or a head of a garrison.

These seem only moderate advantages when compared to those of the communes. But how happy the townspeople of England, Normandy and Aquitaine would have been to possess them. Here there is a vacuum which, if not surprising, is at least disconcerting, because it confirms the economic backwardness of the Atlantic coast and plays a part in the failure of the 'Angevin Empire'. The Anglo-Norman case is not surprising. As far as that goes, besides the upheaval of the conquest in 1066, we have here the strongest royal power in northern Europe; the sheriffs were established in towns that were quite small and scattered; the rulers, particularly the Angevins, were determined to support trade groups, and the English guilds prospered. Even when, because of political circumstances, Richard the Lionheart granted privileges to Rouen (in 1195!), it was not at the same level as the enfranchised towns of the Capetians. What is surprising, however, is the backwardness of Aquitaine, a region that had long been without much public authority. Was this a sign of economic weakness? But salt, wine and the passage of pilgrims or knights on their way to Spain must have encouraged a strong merchant establishment; towns such as Poitiers and Bordeaux had civic traditions. Nevertheless, there was no take-off: the privileges of Rouen were extended to Bordeaux (1206) and La Rochelle (1214); not much of a prize for such towns as, their subsequent history confirms, revealing by their almost inexplicable case-histories the dangers of trying to produce a generalised picture of the medieval town.

The powerful and the powerless

Moving from the village to the town, or vice versa, the historian of the 'classic medieval period' encounters organisational structures and social relations which, no matter how sophisticated, do not contradict the fundamental fact that the 'seigneurie' was the framework for human relations; this brought the dominant and the dominated, the powerful and the powerless face to face. Orthodox Marxist historians employ the term 'feudalism' – which I myself persist in challenging as an awkward, not to say erroneous term – to characterise the nature of the relationships of interdependence typical of the tenth to fifteenth centuries. Let us try to define the social groups.

Wealth

In order to have power over men, it is necessary to possess some exceptional quality and to have unchallenged material resources; the other elements of power, law and force, are nothing without these, and flow from them. We are thus concerned here with a fundamental area of historical research. As far as wealth goes, there is little disagreement or obscurity: whether it was a matter of inherited patrimony, land received as a fief, purchases or various acquisitions resulting from a marriage, or a good business deal, this wealth was first of all property, land and buildings. I have already discussed the growth of fortunes founded on the profits of personal capital in Italy at the end of the thirteenth century. These were exceptional cases among city dwellers, merchants, minorities. The amassing, or, to put it another way, the grouping of landholdings in the hands of the warrior aristocracy or of the Church went through quite clear-cut chronological stages. The first stage covers the first half of the eleventh century, when people were gathered together, dwellings were reorganised and the nucleus of the seigneurie was established. The second stage is roughly the period 1125–75, which tallies with the massive penetration of cash into the countryside and with the phase of the extension of arable land and the expansion of Christianity. It was a stage in which laws of a 'mercenary' nature, exchanges and sales, make up some 35–40 per cent of our documentation. The subject of these contracts (such as mills, rights of use, fisheries, ironworks and tolls) bear witness to an increasing interest in operations that we might call 'profitable'. As for the lands themselves, transactions often concerned very large areas (100 or 150 hectares, for example). The third stage, from around 1220–30 up to 1270–80, offers another aspect: it could take the form of recovering tenure by a return to direct exploitation, as in Lorraine and northern France, a 'seigneurial reaction' which was a response to the low returns on land rent; or it could appear as the seizure of pastureland (in Spain for example, around 1240, when the Sidonia and the Sotomayor began to establish the bases of an enormous monopoly on transhumance, which was to become the *Mesta* in 1273) or common land, which in England resulted in the countermeasures of the Merton statute (1253), the first step in a long series of measures against 'enclosures'. The numerous aquisitions by the Church, notably the land agreements made during the Crusades, can be brought into the same phase. One of the fiscal effects, as I said earlier, was to encourage the princes to set up a system of controls on grants to the Church, amortisation (1265), which spread throughout France in the time of Philip the Fair, together with a requirement that a statement of recent acquisitions be drawn up (1295–1300), a boon for historians of Church property.

We have no way before 1300 of estimating the property holdings of the rich, whether lay or ecclesiastical. The scattered examples furnished by censuses or secular land surveys deal with a very large range, from properties of 100 hectares to those of 4,000 or 5,000 hectares. One has the impression that of a unit of about 2,000 or 3,000 hectares, roughly a third of the land was under the master's direct control; this would generally include the woods, water, hunting grounds and some enclosed fields, at a time when less and less free manual labour was becoming available through the system of *corvée*. Moreover, the internal structure or balance of these great estates would not always have been the same. In some places dispersal of the plots hampered setting up a farm; in others, revenues could not be collected because of the distances involved; elsewhere, the expenses were hardly covered by the returns, reinvestment was entirely frustrated and ready money was lacking, paralysing the treasury. These difficulties of the seigneurial regime were neither widespread nor obvious at the time this account ends. They become, however, apparent and fundamental to the explanation of the period that was to follow.

Undoubtedly the ideal of the historian of this period is to be able to grasp the scale of the 'feudal levy' – the burden imposed on his men by the master. This must remain an ideal, because the second panel of the diptych (peasant production) is missing. Let us try to sketch some outlines. Let us put ourselves in the position, common enough if not 'classic', of a lord, a *dominus*, endowed with public rights, which he alone exercises over a seigneurie of some 4,000 hectares, occupied by about sixty households, which gives him a village of 250 to 300 souls, a good average number. The part of the land which he owns, over which his ancestors rather than he himself established control, and which he has rented out, is no longer of great economic viability by the thirteenth century. The land rent, frozen by custom, lost value through the rise in prices; it has been calculated that the returns on landed capital must have declined, after 1210 or 1220, to a mediocre rate of 5–7 per cent; the abrupt interruption in the passing on of tithes to churches shows that these (a yield of 9–12 per cent by definition) were reckoned to be a better return; in Italy, the growth and success of the *loca* at 8 per cent for commercial business points in the same direction. Obviously the revenue brought in this way was connected to the amount of the land rented out, but at Saint-Denis, in 1230, the total was not even 1 per cent of all the receipts; elsewhere proportions of between 6 and 12 per cent could be attained, but that remains very small. On the other hand, it was possible to count on the profits from the dues charged on transfers of property, the *quint* for lands given in fief (1239), *lods et ventes* for common land, to a value of 8.33 per cent in the Ile-de-France, 12.5 per cent in the Bordelais, and up to 25 per cent in the Lyonnais. Altogether the average of the disseisin–seisin rose to 1 sou or 1.5 sou per lot around 1225–30. However the rise was so keenly felt that protests against these bad new customs, *malsusos* as they were called in Castile, were heard again as they had been in the eleventh century. From the pulpit, Jacques de Vitry thundered against 'the devouring wolves'. Such indignation was excessive: after 1225–30, with lands subject to such dues having become customarily hereditary, though the dues were not very frequently collected, there was massive fiscal evasion; all the same, our estimates readily show that such dues from transfers equalled a decent income from rent, rising from 8 to 13 per cent. Since the produce coming directly from the estate, at least that which was not used but sold – grain, wine, poultry, wood – does not seem to have increased beyond this level either, we see that the basic seigneurial revenues rested on three elements which were also the essence of the lord's superior social position: the rights of protection, of justice, and the control of production.

The first can be seen in the total amount of the tax demanded, in principle, for the guaranteeing of the peace, which was, *par excellence*, the task of the warrior: *questa, tolta, tallia, tonsio, bede, Steuer* – the number of terms is enormous. It is important to note that one of the main concerns in the formation of village communes was to limit the scale of this tax, a movement that was general throughout north-west Europe between 1150 and 1180, and a little later in the south, sometimes not until the thirteenth century in regions where serfdom was strong (Ile-de-France and Champagne around 1220–50). The amount of this tax was, unhappily, variable: 40 sous per man at Cluny in the mid-twelfth century, 5–8 sous in Poitou around 1200, less than half that in Picardy in the middle of the century, and insignificant in Italy. All the same, one can see that in general such a levy could mean a regular annual income of at least 15–20 livres, and for the peasant four to five times his rent. As for justice, that *magnum emolumentum*, which was also a very strict moral obligation for the master, it is perfectly clear that this was a gateway to wealth. While custom could freeze the rent, and tax could be fixed by agreement, fines could easily proliferate. A great English lord around 1270 drew £1,000 pounds per annum from fines, the value of 70,000 days' labour; the Bishop of Ely, his contemporary, succeeded in collecting fines worth 28 per cent of his total income, but within a century this had risen to 62 per cent. There were also taxes exacted for use of the mill and the oven, cash substitutes for *corvées* or obligations of hospitality. In northern France around 1277, such seigneurial rights can be estimated at 6–24 deniers for the *corvées*, and several sous for the rest, an income amounting to about 15–20 per cent of the master's total.

All these observations lead to two comments: seigneurial demands were many; they were not crushing except for the ill-equipped peasant or for someone isolated from the village agreements. We are right, therefore, to discern among the peasantry a rift, initially economic in nature but which could become legal, between one group able to meet the levies, and another threatened by destitution. On the other hand, the stability of seigneurial wealth could only be assured, especially for the very rich, by constant pressure in demands of law and lordship. If these were the only things to be relied upon, at the very time when the role that they justified – to control and to judge – was passing gradually into the king's hands, there was a potential threat (though for the local squire rather than the prince) of rejection by some of the peasantry who could see that the 'feudal contract' had been broken.

Nobility

The master, however, had not simply to live, but to live well, to squander and spend, make a show, in order to fulfil the other aspect of his role, leading a 'noble life'. In both town and country public opinion conflated the two ideas: the wealthy, the *rikes homes*, the *divites*, the *ricos hombres*, the *viri hereditarii*, were also the nobles, the *magnati*, the *proceres*, the *nobiles*, the *optimates*.

At the beginning of the twelfth century the confused situation over origins was clarified, as I have said: the nobility was not always a well-defined judicial category but a social class whose wealth was the common denominator and upon which there converged various currents, though historians are still divided as to which was primary. Freedom, blood-line, membership of an outstanding family, the powers of lordship, military prowess, all were mixed together, and the strong interest in genealogy had no little bearing on the matter. Of course this fusion was not achieved simultaneously everywhere: knighthood and nobility were still distinct around 1170–80 in Picardy, Brabant and the Namurois, even more so among the servile knights of Germany, around 1250–60, and in the Ile-de-France or in Aragon, while confusion existed in Italy from 1100 onwards, perhaps from an earlier date in southern France. Abandoning a nickname in favour of a name taken from one's land or castle thus became the fashion, and then the general rule. The handing on of this rather abstract mark of distinction tended to be a masculine concern, because of the growing predominance of military activity in the group.

One problem, however, still remains. This is the question of relations of nobility with feudal-vassalic links. Obviously no one doubts that the two structures were extremely close to each other. All the same they were distinct in law. Personally, I remain convinced that the feudal world proper, that is, the one subject to all those rules and rituals which we have discussed above, only represented a minority of the rich, a fraction of the nobility, and that the 'freeholders' were therefore more numerous. Of course, it cannot be denied that in our documentation the number of feudal cases, or simply the use of feudal vocabulary, increases: even in a region which resisted feudal customs for a long time, such as Picardy, this percentage went from 4 per cent between 1050 and 1100 to 9 and then 12.5 per cent in the first and then the second half of the twelfth century, falling off somewhat after that; around 1100–25 on the Canche, out of 100 deeds, only 25 per cent concerned fiefs as against 35 per cent concerning allods, and this area was strongly feudal. At the beginning of the thirteenth century or at the end of the twelfth, there were 60 vassals on 500 square kilometres around Ailly in Picardy, 2,800 on 30,000 square kilometres in Normandy, 2,000 on 10,000 square kilometres in Champagne, 20,000 on the 500,000 square kilometres of the Empire; the Count of Flanders who promised feudal aid of 100 vassals could only round up 50. It must be admitted that all these figures are not reducible to the same fraction; sometimes the figure is low (in Germany 4 per 100 square kilometres), sometimes average, from 9 to 12 along the Channel coast, or high, as in Champagne. But in all these cases, it seems to me, we are dealing with a lower proportion of 'nobles' than is usually reckoned to be plausible before 1200, about 4 or 5 per cent of the population. It is true, on the other hand, that the development of the feudal world offered considerably enhanced possibilities of joining the nobility to those who were not authentically noble and thus wished to substantiate the idea: partly because of the increase in types of fiefs without lands and thus without services (especially military) to provide. Such were the 'money-fiefs' (*fiefs-rentes*) which appeared in Fulda in 1048, in England after the conquest, in Normandy and Flanders in 1079 and 1087, and which were doubtless of interest to military figures, but also to town-dwellers, the *Burgmannen* who had no intention of taking up arms. But concessions were also made to the feudal lords who had to cope with the heavy expenses of armed service (around 1135 military equipment cost 20 livres, the value of 150 hectares of land!), in the form of a tax, *adjutorium*, *adoha*, *écuage*, payable annually. The kings, who set the example, especially the Angevins after 1153, relied on it to pay mercenaries, who were efficient and more manageable. By the end of the twelfth century the practice had become widespread: it consisted of a horse, saddled and fully equipped and led to the lord's host as a substitute for the service of the warrior himself. It is easy to see the danger in the spread of the custom of multiple homages (of which there are examples in the Vendômois around 1046, in Catalonia in 1077, and the extraordinary cases in Germany, like that of one particular lord in 1229 owing forty-eight homages!). At Roncaglia in 1154, Barbarossa tried to soar above this confusion by exacting a form of liege homage to himself, but to no avail, even in Germany.

In the course of the thirteenth century the nobility experienced contraction and redefinition, the causes of which were diverse: some of the family groups suffered from the concentration of economic resources of which I spoke earlier; a number of the features which marked out their superior social status underwent a shift and were sometimes given up, for example the upkeep of a castle in favour of a simple manor; the expenses of the dubbing ceremony led to its being confined to a single son, the eldest, and then to its becoming unaffordable altogether, forcing the poorer nobles to be content with the position of squire. Even within the feudal group, the increasing financial demands imposed by the lord, and indeed the suzerain, became unbearable: in 1133 in Normandy and later elsewhere, the establishment of what was in effect taxation by the lord, in the form of 'aid' for a daughter's marriage, for the knighting of a son, for his own ransom, and for his departing on a crusade, led to the sale of lands. The German vassals had to cope with the ruinous *Romfahrt*, which everyone tried so hard to get out of that, in order not to have to set out for Italy entirely on his own, the emperor Barbarossa had to modify it (1156). There were also the burdens of 'relief' which seem to have been crushing: tradition fixed this *Verlief*, this *koop*, as it was called in Germany and the Low Countries, at the rate of a year's revenues from the fief to be relieved; but the value of the castles held was added (1170), and sometimes the sum was fixed at the lord's will, if there was competition for the succession. In this way Philip Augustus very usefully filled his coffers with 50,000 marks imposed on Baldwin of Hainault, applicant for Flanders (1192), as well as with the 20,000 marks wrested from King John, claiming the continental inheritance of his brother Richard the Lionheart (1200). In order to recover this, John in his turn levied a fixed *heriot* in England of some £100–£125 in 1214. It must be added that the disastrous Malthusian practice of the nobility in matrimonial matters – of having only one married heir – also certainly contributed to the biological extinction of a number of branches: around 1230–40 in Picardy, nearly 30 per cent of the lines were new.

All this was accompanied by a reduction in numbers. It has been calculated that the 120 family lines in the Westphalia of 1150 fell to 98 in 1200 and 64 in 1250, while the figures for Picardy at the same period are 100, 82 and 42 respectively. The economic decline or even ruin of certain lines, and the rise of others, sometimes by new paths (royal ennoblements after 1250), led to the introduction of distinctions and a hierarchy which now reflected not origins but social level. In the Empire, such distinctions were charted with an almost excessive precision: the *Heerschild* in the twelfth century, the 'mirrors' drawn up by jurists or systematisers, like Wolfram von Eschenbach and his 'Mirror of the Saxons' (*Sachsenspiegel* of 1225), determined the ranks, from the imperial princes to the servile knights, those *Dienstmannen* of whom some were to make a brilliant career. This example was copied, for instance in France by Philip of Novare. But more than these categories, it was in fact the status, the *brazo* as it was called in Spain, of the nobles that separated them

Sovereign power was recognisable by its attributes: the coronation glove of the kings of Sicily. (Vienna, Kunsthistorisches Museum.)

from others; they were knights, the rest were squires; they were *domini*, lords, the rest were *domicelli*, *donzeaux*; they were tenants in chief, the rest were vavasours, *vassi vassorum*; they were 'peers' in the Low Countries, the others were simply 'men'. In itself this separation was not fundamental; nevertheless, it rested on one essential element: the holding of power over others.

Power

The exercise of authority in the twelfth and thirteenth centuries, despite the opposition which obviously appeared, was not basically different from what we know ourselves: its favourite instruments were, as always, law, force and patronage; its material bases were economic, even if the revenues for a long time belonged to the prince personally. It is not the same in as far as the aura or charisma that surrounded the anointed king is concerned, since there are no traces of that today. That said, I do not want to deny the differences: first of all, in the period we are studying, even the idea of the public institution, the 'State', was no more than embyronic; the *res publica* was, as the etymology suggests, the 'common good', rooted in a collective consent to order, an eminently conservative concept.

Moreover, kings, even those who called themselves Caesar, took their examples more readily from the Bible than from Antiquity. There was thus a curious mixture of religious concern – leading the people to salvation, maintaining the rule of God by the royal *professio* taken at the coronation on holy objects – and a public concern of an office, a *ministerium* to be fulfilled. From this arose the two facets of royal power: because the king belonged among the ministers of the sacred, everything which upheld his authority, the integrity of his person, the symbols of his power, what we call the *regalia*, was untouchable; and **381** because he had to lead a Christian people, he had to give laws and provide himself with the means by which obedience to his word, the *verbum regis*, was overseen. In these conditions, the dream of a *dominium mundi*, the employment of force to master the Church and its Roman head, exceeded the limits of the role devolved upon the king. Neither the canon lawyers, nor even the Roman jurists could accept this vision; the German sovereigns tried in several ways to impose this view, but all failed miserably.

There is no question here of sketching the individual European monarchies of the twelfth and thirteenth centuries, or narrating episodes from their political history. But royal power, like many other social elements, adapted itself to circumstances, and a survey of its various aspects seems necessary. Royal power was essentially a family group, a 'house', a line, a *stirps*, like any other noble structure. The king was the noblest of the nobles, no more. But the life of his clan, the use he could make of its members to extend his authority, clearly was an exceptionally important tool. We do not know a great deal about medieval monarchs; it is hard to judge them through their official biographers, or by examining their laws which, however, even when unsuccessful, do sometimes reveal the scale of their plans. The twelfth and thirteenth centuries are not known for really extraordinary personalities. Some, by what we know of their character and their political sense, were a credit to their family, but rarely without some shadow on their memory: the Capetian Philip Augustus, the Plantagenet Henry II, the Swabian Frederick Barbarossa, three contemporaries; before them, the Norman Roger II of Sicily, and at the end of our period, the Castilian Alfonso X, the Emperor Frederick II, and Philip the Fair of France. But Louis VIII of France or Henry VI of Germany lived for too short a time, Henry V and St Louis for too long. What is important is to highlight the following characteristic: these princes counted on their wives, their brothers and their children to help them to survive; like Louis VII, they did not hesitate to divorce in the hope of having a male heir, or, like Louis IX, to grant dangerous privileges, the *apanages*, to their brothers; most of them associated their eldest son with themselves in power. But of all these clans, only one attained its aims without upset: the Capetians. While the Angevins tore themselves apart in endless quarrels – husband imprisoning wife, son rebelling against father, brothers hating each other, murderous uncles – in the French family complete calm reigned, which enabled it to experience two minorities without any threat to the dynasty. This was no doubt a matter of luck, with elder sons ready to rule without making a fuss, active regents and obedient uncles. At this high level, however, it was not only a matter of chance but of skill.

In order to rule, the prince needed the Church. It provided him with security and manpower: the Capetian king, once free from the temptation to traffic in episcopal sees, could count on twenty-six subject bishops and sixty-seven royal monasteries; he enjoyed the revenues of ecclesiastical offices during a vacancy, he protected the clergy, he could obtain pecuniary assistance (the 'tenth'), he surrounded himself with prelates and later with friars. Even if he led a questionable private life, which could earn him excommunication, Rome trusted him, and popes who were expelled came to him for support and refuge. This was a great resource at the very time when first the Norman and later the Plantagenet rulers of England were increasingly aggressive towards prelates whom they saw as recalci-

A royal dynasty: Frederick Barbarossa (1152–90) and his sons Henry and Frederick. (From the *Welf Chronicle*; Hesse, Landesbibliothek.)

trant, and opposed to new burdens. To control them Henry II imposed on them his friend Thomas Becket, who soon changed his attitude. The consquence is well known: exile in France, pardon, return, murder, public penitence and the weakening of royal power (1159–72). The case of the Empire is different: the sovereign set great store by the Church; he even practised what was called the *Reichskirchensystem* in which he was supported by those sees to which he had appointed strong allies; to lose this support would be to lose himself in the princely quagmire of an enormous Germany. Thus the Salian emperors obstinately refused any papal intervention in these nominations, the investitures; when the Geman ruler, Henry V, had to compromise at Worms in 1122, the Germans did not give up, and Barbarossa pursued the same policy in attacking the Church at the top to make it surrender. He was thwarted, albeit by the Lombard militia rather than by Pope Alexander III, whose stirrup he nevertheless humbly held in Venice in 1177. To succeed where his grandfather had failed, Frederick II needed time, money and allies, but he too met defeat in his turn.

Could one count on the 'faithful men', on friends and vassals, in the event that the Church, whose views sometimes differed from the monarch's, shied away? In the twelfth century, at least in the early years, this 'feudal' vision was upheld. The territorial princes were the delegates of the king; their vassal mentality kept them from the path of treason, **383**

The King of France, Philip Augustus, falls from his horse at the battle of Bouvines (1214); he is recognisable by his crown and shield with the fleur-de-lys. (Matthew Paris, *Chronica Maiora, c.* 1255; Cambridge, Corpus Christi College.)

and indeed, no one would ever have dreamed of getting rid of the monarch; if they fought him, it was because they sincerely believed themselves to have been betrayed. The situation, however, could be delicate as in Flanders, Champagne, Burgundy and Toulouse, on occasion, as well as in less important regions. Obviously some conflicts broke out, as in the disputed successions in Flanders (1071, 1127, 1191), family quarrels in Champagne, and the Albigensian venture which meant that a rather reluctant king and his brothers got involved in Languedoc. But generally, around 1270, the situation was fairly secure, except in the west which, although rather an isolated region, covered a good half of the realm. Earlier William the Conqueror, then his son Henry, both dukes of Normandy and kings of England, had tended to be troublesome; but these episodes were only skirmishes, and Flanders, Anjou and Aquitaine could be counted on. But everything changed when the same man, Henry Plantagenet, united England, Normandy, the Loire valley, Brittany and the whole of the south-west, from Poitiers to Béarn (1151–4); moreover, as king he was not disposed to pay homage. What saved, or at least preserved, the French king (for the Angevins never wished to reject him, although they could have done) was of course the discord among the Angevin princes, the apathy of King John, the defeat of his allies at Bouvines (1214), the English rebellions, the daring of Philip Augustus, the moderation of St Louis, and also the extreme fragility of the Angevin 'Empire', the incompatibility between a strong England and continental possessions that were difficult to defend. Stable by 1259, the situation then began to deteriorate again, but was this really rivalry between a king and a prince?

Such rivalry was the case in the Empire, where a development at a slower pace than elsewhere had resulted in the carving out of large 'duchies' (*Stämme*) along ethnic, fiscal and customary lines, in Saxony, Bavaria, Lotharingia, Franconia, Alemannia, Swabia, and the 'marches' created in the east during the process of Germanisation in Brandenburg, Lausitz, Meissen and Austria. German policy followed two divergent paths. The first was to attach the *Reichsfürsten*, the chief princes, closely to the person or the family of the king of Germany, if necessary going so far as to guarantee inheritances or yield them the *regalia*;

Barbarossa thought to strengthen the feudal hierarchy by this means. Unfortunately the imperial dynasties were not long-lasting; promises and appointments had to be constantly renewed, while some princes, instead of keeping to their duchies, expanded and put out tentacles in every direction, such as the princes of Lotharingia who expanded as far as Italy, or like the Welfs of Bavaria in the eleventh century, or the Saxon Henry the Lion who was active from Lübeck to Leipzig, in Alsace and in Switzerland. So another strategy was necessary, that of breaking them by force, which Barbarossa eventually succeeded in doing to Henry the Lion; but there again, Frederick II, who spent too much time in Italy, failed to sustain the policy.

It was a much better policy to surround oneself with paid servants. Government by the family, the feudal hierarchy, had its good points, but so too did having agents and taking the advice of experts. This time it is England that provides the model. William I extended the Saxon system of sheriffs (shire-reeve); he built up around himself a *curia*, which the Angevins took up, perhaps copied from the Flemish model, consisting in direct vassals, clerics, a financial service (exchequer) and a chancellor (1129); from 1106 judges travelled throughout the realm, a justiciar (supreme judge) stood ready to deputise for the king on whichever side of the Channel the king was absent. This was not enough though – there had to be legislation and accounting. From 1130 the king had kept a record of payments and receipts; henceforth there were 'assizes' for feudal lords and clerics, as at Clarendon (1166) and Northampton (1176), and assizes for arms and forests (1181 and 1184); the *curia* sent out royal orders, the 'writs'. All this required an organisation of some 2,000 people in 1177. Nevertheless, this kind of government tended to be placed in the hands of technocrats – experts, often from the Continent, in law or finance, such as Ranulf Glanville and Walter Map. As fiscal demands increased, the lesser nobility – there were no princes here – demanded to be consulted: in the aftermath of his defeat in 1214, John had to submit to their demands. *Magna Carta* of 1215 laid down that the barons and clergy were to be assembled when a tax had to be levied; they would hold a *parlamentum*. The king's sincerity was not necessarily handed down to his heirs: Henry III steered this 'parliament' towards a judicial role, to be watched over by his officers; he himself set up a personal council, the wardrobe. This had the same end results as before: fiscal abuses, a preponderance of foreigners (especially from Provence who surrounded his wife), military defeats, and revolts (including a very serious one in 1258 because it had as its leader Simon de Montfort, Earl of Leicester, grandson of the conqueror of Toulouse). There was a call for councils, for control by the lesser nobility, the development of county courts – in fact, a real purge. Henry III backed down but consulted Louis IX of France who supported him (1264); strengthened by this, he returned in force to crush the barons, killing their leader and cutting him to pieces. Nevertheless, Simon de Montfort's rash actions precipitated long-lasting changes; parliament gathered and inquests into government continued. England had a solid administration.

At that time, nowhere else was such an administration to be found; Capetian France can offer only a pale reflection of these innovations. The *curia* existed, a descendant of the Carolingian 'palace'; but the princes seemed to be concerned only with their own domains. **385**

It was Philip Augustus who, after having left unfilled the two court offices that he considered most dangerous, that of chancellor (1187) and of seneschal (1191), developed the idea of having roving (later permanent) investigators, *baillis*, paid in wages, whose role Louis IX extended after 1254. But the specialisation of the *curia*, from which developed a court of justice, the *parlement*, later an accounting section, was far from equalling the English *curia*. In practice it was not until the time of Philip the Fair that the richest and most powerful of the western kingdoms was governed by more than a handful of clerics and lesser nobles. Of course there was some turbulence, but the 'baronial' movements during Louis IX's minority (1229–43) were superficial. There was no overall design in these egotistical and isolated demands of the nobility. Elsewhere, either anarchism triumphed, as in Germany, where even Frederick II could not manage to impose either fiscal organisation or establish ministerial agents, let alone meetings of a *Reichstag*, between 1235 and 1242; or, by contrast, everything was done at once, but in an extraordinary atmosphere of war and foreign influences. This was the case in Spain, where the kings established a *curia* and a fisc in the twelfth century, and above all in Sicily under Roger II who, powerful throughout the country, set up fiscal offices directed by a 'logothete' (tribunals presided over by an 'archonte') and an army under the command of an 'emir'.

The failure of the Germans, the success of the English, the resistance of the Capetians had one and the same source. Medieval power in effect had one fundamental basis: revenues. If they were lacking, every effort depending on men, clerics, kinsmen, princes, and agents was likely to be in vain. However, the revenues could no longer be in the form of taxes – Europe had too long been unfamiliar with them. When Frederick II tried them in towns in 1232, he failed completely. Wealth lay in the estates, where the king was allowed to 'live of his own', to be independent. But Germany did not have this foundation. The *Reichsgut* certainly existed. At Barbarossa's accession, it consisted of some fourteen palaces, thirty-five castles, fifty rural estates and property or rights in 1,400 localities; to this were added the revenues of the reigning family. It was by no means sufficient. However the practice of automatic re-infeudation (*Leihezwang*) imposed on the Salians prevented their being able to count on escheats; they had to hold on to what little they had. By contrast, in France the Capetian ruler had at his disposal the Carolingian fisc, and he made purchases, exchanges, acquired inheritances and developed it. While it is not certain, as Conan of Lausanne reported, that the personal domain of the king brought him in 228,000 livres in 1179, and 438,000 in 1223, there were in 1125 in any case twenty-four *prévôtés*, that is, administrative units for legal and fiscal matters, fifty-six in 1202, and 106 by the end of the thirteenth century. The structure of the English royal domain was somewhat different, as its origins lay in confiscations, William I having appropriated some 16 to 18 per cent of the land (basically regions to be exploited and passed through – the 'forest', although this term did not always imply a wooded area). Subsequently Henry II around 1180, and then Henry III by a writ of 1244 increased the land area; this was not so much a matter of procuring revenue, given the nature of the land, as of building up a reserve of possible fiefs, or providing a form of separation between two powerful lords who had become dangerous. In this outline, one could say that the domain served the English Plantagenet for government and the French Capetian for sustenance. And surely these are the two great concerns of the powerful.

The question of judicial freedom

Among the powerless, there was an additional preoccupation, that of liberty, of freedom. And it was liberty before the law that was of prime concern, distinguished not just by the right to move freely, to take a spouse or to leave an inheritance, but also by the right to attend the 'public' court, to have one's own tools and equipment, to be called to the host, to pay the *taille* (symbol of the protection given only to men worthy of the name). Perhaps not enough has been made of the moral and psychological side, which may have been the most keenly felt: the right not to be whipped in public, not to be forbidden to marry, not to be rejected by the Church, not to be attacked by dogs. To conceal such humiliations, plenty of men did not hesitate to abandon everything and go off where their badge of shame, handed down to them by their mothers, would not be known.

The problem of the importance of a lack of such freedoms has given rise to interminable debates, which still continue. There is one point of agreement, however, albeit marginal: pure slavery, such as that of Antiquity, did not disappear from Europe; on the northern and southern fringes of the continent it still flourished, with slaves destined for Islam if they were Irish or Norwegian, or for Christian use from the Tyrrhenian region, especially from Spain and Provence. Between 1240 and 1280, the price of slaves, mostly blacks, rose in Barcelona from 3 to 10 livres, much more than for the Muslims employed by religious orders in Aragon. Marseilles seems to have been another centre, but it developed later. Obviously this was a secondary phenomenon, but still worthy of interest. A second, more important point of agreement, concerns the old theory of Marc Bloch (which one is astonished to encounter even today in textbooks some fifty years on) that all peasants were serfs. This has now been universally abandoned. It is most regrettable that Western historians continue to use the word 'serf' in the Marxist manner, just as they do 'feudalism', without specifying its meaning. They know perfectly well that this is a misuse of the term, since it implies economic alienation when there was no question of anything but legal alienation in the Middle Ages, at least before 1300.

But even after establishing these points, differences of opinion abound. Were there 'specific burdens' of serfdom? In northern and eastern France, and in the Empire, the seizure of a large part of the inheritance of a bondsman (of one's 'own man' – a *quotidianus, Tageschalk, Leibeigen*) could still take place, even up to the mid-thirteenth century. The *Besthaupt* or *Buteil* was a tax on movables, cattle, money or chattels. But these practices were sometimes inflicted on men who otherwise bore no signs of servitude, for example in Champagne and Berry. Only the total seizure of inheritance, the escheat, was the mark of alienation. But such acts were rare and the risks involved made more than one master hesitate: what good would it do to work hard if one lost everything in the end? Such demands therefore tended to disappear. Around 1250 the Church began to introduce into custom the idea of a transmissible portion, for example, a third of movables, a fifth of land. The

387

obstacle to freedom of marriage, the expensive *formariage* (a tax paid for the privilege of marrying a partner from outside the lord's estate), also represents a tax paid by free men, as in Artois for example. There remain only the head taxes, such as the *chevage* (*questa* as it was called around Toulouse), which was still going strong around 1210–20, levied at the lord's discretion in northern France, and customary in Spain, which would be an admission of servitude. It has been emphasised, however, that its original sum of 4 deniers per head bears a strong resemblance to the emancipation tax of Antiquity. There is no lack of categories of men whose particularly deprived situations tempts one to rank them among the serfs, the *censuales* in Germany, for example, as well as most of the English 'villeins'. But the latter, at least, appeared at the manorial court and were subject to the 'common law'; in my opinion, it is wrong to call them serfs. Personally, then, I tend to think that serfdom was only residual, always uneven in its manifestations, more of an archaic survival than an actually existing status. The numerous 'manumissions', individual or collective, which appeared in the Ile-de-France, in the royal domain from 1230 and especially from 1250 onwards, undoubtedly contributed towards the removal of legal serfdom from the areas in which it was weakest, such as Berry, the Nivernais, Franche-Comté, Flanders, Thiérache, Vermandois and Languedoc, while it survived within the realm of France, thus affecting scarcely 8–10 per cent of the population.

This freedom concerns the freedom of men, but land also could be free. This is another area of heated scholarly debate. The 'allod', land with no other master than the man working it, who offered neither taxes nor services, could be noble or peasant land. The former, probably very widespread before the year 1000, had been mostly subsumed into the feudal system: a 'return' to the status of fiefs was common throughout Europe. For the latter, the same mechanism, a return to tenure, would seem to be a natural conception. The problem is to follow the fates of the lands and their masters who resisted this consequence. By definition it is a difficult search because it concerns precisely those who escaped either the Church or the feudal lords, the sources of our documentation. Nevertheless, the prevailing opinion is now that there were many more such 'allods' than was once thought. The decline in the number of allods in the eleventh century was reversed with land clearances, the foundation of new villages and the contraction of some seigneurial powers. At the beginning of the twelfth century, the number of documents mentioning this category of property falls in Picardy from 17 to 3 per cent, but in Champagne *c.* 1150 it stays at 17 per cent and in the Chartres region at 33 per cent; the figure rises a little before 1200, but then seems to decline. At the end of this period, however, the signs of resistance increase. In legal terms the Roman law of southern Europe encouraged this, as did some kinds of contract elsewhere; one example of this is the Catalan *aprisio*, which envisaged the transfer of the right of ownership to the cultivator at the end of a fixed term. On the judicial level in Hainault, in Germany, the comital courts which the *Gemeinenfreien* attended, are evidence of the existence of such a social group. We do not have many ways of measuring its influence; but it is very significant that a sector of free landholders, even if they were under attack everywhere, could be maintained up to the eve of the upheavals in property-owning at the end of the Middle Ages, particularly where this concerned peasant workers.

Estate *corvées*: under the watchful eye of a supervisor, the peasants have to undertake manual labour for the lord's benefit.

The question of economic freedom

Obviously what was fundamentally important to men of the time was knowing to what extent they were free to dispose of what they produced. It could be argued that the seigneurial framework and the master's levies represented constraints which excluded any notion of 'freedom', but this is to play with words, because by that count no one was free except those who wandered the forests.

While we can describe some peasants as economically 'free' against a background of seigneurial power, this definition incorporates all sorts of nuances and qualifications. But the obverse of this is that serfs themselves could have a degree of economic freedom. The conditions of tenure here play an essential part. It has long been thought that the fixed rent, with its origin in custom giving it protection from increases (except for some scandalous attempts to jack it up), must have been favoured by the peasants; the sum total was not high, certainly, but there are extraordinary irregularities which resist explanation: in the Ile-de-France around 1260, fixed rents for open fields rose from 2 to 12 deniers per acre, while those for vines rose from 4 to 60 deniers per acre. And the attempts at fixing a uniform sum according to area, as in Chaource (Champagne) in 1276 – a sou and a measure of oats per field – met with no success. One can see why the levying of dues payable as a proportion of the harvest (which was a safeguard for both parties) was such a tempting prospect, especially on new lands. In the south the *agrière* and *tasca* were set at a quarter or a fifth of the produce from the land, while in Italy the levy went as high as a half, whereas in northern France (where it was known as the *champart*) it fell to perhaps one-eighth. After 1220 or 1230, what is most striking is the quest for contracts covering several lives, namely, tenant farming. Its beginnings in the Ile-de-France, England and Flanders between 1235 and 1260 have been thoroughly studied; the interest of both parties (farmer and tenant), at least at the start, seems certain, but the undertaking did lead to some resistance on the part of the peasants; one could say that the practice of tenant farming risked increasing the difference in economic freedom between the farmer and the tenant farmer. There is no

389

evidence of hostility in the countryside over this matter until the end of the thirteenth century, but there was certainly an imbalance.

The disappearance of estate *corvées*, with their drain on the peasants' time and bodily strength, yet without much real profit for the master, is obviously an element of this freedom. In general, their decline as a result of the substitution of cash payments is plain: around 1234 the *corvée* was reduced to two days for haymaking in Picardy; in Provence it fell from six to three days and then disappeared altogether between 1198, 1260 and 1277. There was, however, a simultaneous counter-movement on the part of the lords: some masters, often men of the Church, wanted to reassert the value of manual work in their service and tried to demand 'free' days, for example those at Saint Bavo of Ghent around 1210 and at Saint-Denis around 1240. There was certainly an upsurge in the Lyonnais, the Bordelais, Sologne and Champagne in France; and in England too, where the Bishop of Ely increased them between 1221 and 1251. This seigneurial reassertion came up against both inertia and ill-will. Between 1250 and 1257 at Saint-Denis and at Péronne, the corvées were deliberately sabotaged. The famous protest of Verson in Normandy, which dates from this time, is good evidence of the bitterness of the relations between those who owed corvée and their supervisors. There was so much bitterness that, from 1250–60 (around 1251–6 in the Low Countries and 1280 in Luxemburg), cash commutations became widespread. Peasants, at least the richer ones who were able to afford the large amounts required for such compensation, gained time, which was more precious than money.

Under favourable conditions, large-scale peasant holdings could be established. By means of seigneurial land records, it is possible to attempt an examination of this distribution, especially for the period around 1300. Even before this date, in Tuscany, the Sabine country, Bavaria, Catalonia, Picardy, near Winchester and Ely, there were farms or *censes* of 100 to 150 hectares built up by 'husbandmen'. The relative loosening of the land market may explain this, but so may the break-up of the mass of peasants which squeezed those left behind by economic progress on to cramped patches of land while the rest of the land fell into the hands of a successful minority. The example of the Namur region, or of Picardy, around 1259 and 1280, can serve as a reflection of such developments; one might note here that 35 to 60 per cent of the workers (assuming that they did not have other plots on neighbouring land) worked less than 1.5–2 hectares, which was only half the amount considered the minimum for survival in these fertile lands; some 25 to 40 per cent worked 3–10 hectares, the survival line cutting the group roughly in half; the remainder worked more than 10 hectares (perhaps up to 60 hectares). Simplifying things somewhat, in view of the master's demands, I can repeat here the statement I made earlier, that out of ten peasants, four lived in financial difficulties or in misery, four lived modestly, but in some security, and two lived in comfort.

Outsiders

Some people were even more unfortunate than the poorest peasants discussed above. A man was not an outcast solely because of material poverty, but above all because he was

The outsiders: after judgement, the guilty are led to prison. (Munich, Bayerische Staatsbibliothek.)

not perceived as belonging to a group, as being isolated, vulnerable; it was in judicial rather than economic terms that he experienced this vulnerability. Certainly there was no lack of beggars and their situation had worsened since the disappearance of the idea of giving hospitality to one who had perhaps been sent by God. At the gates of the abbeys bread was still distributed, along with eels and beer, and a monastery such as that at Cambrai still devoted 6–8 per cent of its budget to this. But the beggars increasingly became 'professionals': in Italy they were *immatriculati*, registered; in Nantes, Paris and Lille at the end of the thirteenth century some formed a 'trade' or guild, with right of entry, badges of identification and reserved places. Or they gathered in the hospices, apparent in south-east France and Italy from the tenth century, and which increased in number after 1171–85 (as in the diocese of Paris, where their number grew from 4 in 1150 to 29 in 1200 and 83 in 1250). If they were wanderers, they were soon suspected of spreading heresy; and it is true that many followed some visionary, like the 'master of Hungary', or those 'pastors' who scoured the countryside between 1235 and 1250, without our being able to tell whether or not they were bearers of some social message. Elsewhere they mingled with those who had chosen a life of poverty, like the Lombard *umiliati*, after the sermons of Peter Valdes around 1170, or the disciples of Peter of Verona after 1245, the *laudesi* of Florence who sang and begged. Was this not the Franciscan ideal? When their presence grew excessive, they were cooped up in one district or forcibly enrolled as labourers, as in Poitiers. We would like to be able to estimate their numbers. We have some figures (for example, 3,000 in Toledo, 6,000 in Milan and Montpellier, and 5,000 in Ghent, between 1239 and 1265), but these *pannosi*, these beggars excluded from trades and the land, might in fact be unemployed or casual labourers, or as in Languedoc, newly migrant peasants, who had not been

391

admitted to the town – the people of the *tosca* (the scrubland), the Tuchins of the fourteenth century.

Social rejection turned many into brigands. They met up with the charcoal burners in the forests, with runaway serfs, banished town-dwellers or demobilised soldiers; they thus lost any legal status which they may have had. As outcast subjects of suspicion they formed bands of beggars who, in towns, were driven into one district at night and kept under surveillance, and who, in the country, were carefully watched and hanged without trial at the first opportunity. Before 1300 these were only a few unimportant bands who with each 'terror', each 'commotion', burst like fetid bubbles on the surface of a society in uproar. But if they were enlisted or courted by others, this fringe could become a dangerous class.

This was not the case for the 'living dead', the lepers cut off from any contact with others and whose number rose disquietingly in the thirteenth century. In the diocese of Paris there were eight lepers' hospitals in 1150 (the first dating from 1106), twenty in 1200 and fifty-three in 1250 – indeed, such a disquieting rise that the figures are suspect. However, it has been suggested that this reflects contact with the East where the illness was certainly endemic. But the presence of innumerable lepers reminds us of forms of skin lesions – eczema, impetigo – which are not contagious but which might carry the suggestion of leprosy. *A posteriori* the abrupt disappearance of the plague – it is last mentioned in France in 1317 – could justify this notion, because there were no prophylactics to speak of, and the tuberculosis which followed the leprosy did not hold sway until after 1350.

Cut off from the community by their sickness or by their activities, the leper and the beggar were deliberately excluded; some others did not count simply because they were 'others'. These were the mad, the idiots, the simple-minded, through whom God might express himself, and whom contemporaries were perceptive enough not to lock up. But there were also the *mudejares*, Muslims enclosed in Christian lands, tied to the soil (the *exari-cos* of Spain), ruled separately (Teruel, 1176), probably not ill-treated, but irremediably separated by their faith, even when they could prove themselves to be of Gothic or Iberian descent. In the twelfth century they were numerous even in the lands long since reclaimed from Islam, amounting to some 35 per cent of the population north of the Ebro.

Indomitable, numerous, hopelessly excluded by their race, their language, their faith, by law and custom, the Jews encapsulated all the disadvantages. But in a way, they also encapsulated all the advantages because they depended exclusively on the prince ('my Jews', as Philip Augustus called them). They were part of the fisc and were protected just as the fisc was. Of course they paid for this 'liberty' in the contempt with which they were generally treated by Christians; but the latter did not intend to ban the God-killers, since, apart from their practical usefulness, their presence in the heart of the New Testament bore witness to the Old, and presented the face of the damned to comfort the believer in his faith. The Jewish communities, a legacy from Antiquity, were established particularly around the Tyrrhenian sea: in the eleventh century there were 500 families in Naples; Benjamin of Tudela found over 400 in Narbonne, Lunel and Montpellier; during the retaking of Toledo in 1085, Alfonso VI of Castile had 3,000 at his side; but we also know they lived in Arles, Vienna, Lyons, Mâcon, Mainz and even in Brussels and Regensburg. Traditional historiography has portrayed them as money-lenders or doctors. But before 1150 they ploughed, harvested grapes, irrigated their land, bore arms; in Languedoc they controlled the trade in salt, leather and slaves; in the Balearic Islands and Spain they served as trading agents for African gold, or as trading agents for Sicily. Their situation was very stable: although they mingled with Christians, they were ruled by their rabbis, judged according to their own law and openly practised their religion; between 1090 and 1140, in Spain, Toulouse and Languedoc they were known as tax collectors, treasurers, owners of manors and even viziers (in Valencia). As they provided abundant and regular sources of revenue for the princes, by means of all their economic activities, they were protected from persecution; in the country or town fairs they were insulted or mocked, and every Sunday priests thundered against the 'perfidious Jews', but these born middlemen doubtless managed to endure such miseries because we do not see them running away, nor converting. Through them, the beliefs of the ancient world and that of Islam, the gold of Africa and the herbs of the East reached Salerno, Barcelona, Palermo and Montpellier. It is true that they were kept at a distance from any form of integration, familial or economic, but six or seven centuries of tolerance seemed to guarantee their existence.

Unhappily, the religious intransigence that accompanied the Gregorian renewal of the Christian faith exposed the Jews to unquenchable hatred. Some ignorant visionaries, like Peter the Hermit, launched crusading bands of countryfolk against the Jews. In 1096 in Cologne and Mainz (but not in Worms or Frankfurt), they were burnt in their synagogues. At the same time – as a consequence of this perhaps – parallel dogmatic intransigence hardened divisions in the rabbinic world: the Ashkenazim of Germany, rigorous and devout, confronted the Sephardim of Spain. The Jews withdrew into themselves, and were encouraged to gather together in separate districts, the ghettoes which were now enclosed (for example, the *chancel des Juifs* near the Bretonnerie in Paris and the Giudecca in Venice).

In Christian iconography the physical type of the Jew now appeared in caricature: small in stature with a hooked nose, curly beard and dark eyes. The Jews were excluded from the army, even from the Spanish *caballeria villana*; their lands were seized, they were refused access to trades, their only avenue was to become money-lenders and dealers. They thus became figures of hate to the poor. A first wave of expulsions and confiscations marked the period 1144–5 in France and England, and then, from 1175 to 1182, spread throughout western Europe, even to Castile. This was the time when many Jewish communities withdrew into central Europe, to Pomerania and Silesia, or to the fringes of the Christian world, Venice, Sicily, the Levant. In 1215 the Lateran Council confirmed the ban, and imposed the wearing of the cap and the sign of the Star of David; worship could only be clandestine. In 1237, in his devout zeal, St Louis permitted the massacre of Jews in Paris, enforced the wearing of the infamous costume, had copies of the Talmud destroyed, generated 'miracles', vigorously encouraged conversions, stripped the assets of the recalcitrant and expelled them in 1240 and 1244. All this was then imitated by the weak Henry III of England. Thus there evolved round the Mediterranean the remarkable groups of Marranos, Jews who proclaimed their conversion to Christianity in order to go on practising medicine, pharmacology or astrology, but who continued to practise their faith in

393

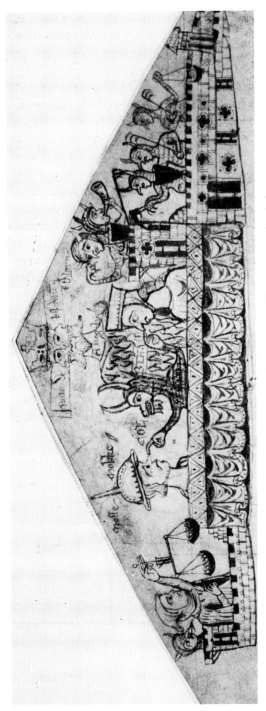

An English anti-Jewish caricature. (Tallage Roll for the year 1233; London, Public Record Office; reproduced with the permission of the Controller of HMSO.)

secret, while running the risk of being burnt at the stake. Only Spain still remained a refuge; the new confiscations and expulsions of 1290 and 1306 led to a flood of exiles, settling particularly in Andalusia and the Levant, which had become, along with Poland, the new promised lands.

It has often been noted that the mid-thirteenth century, in most of the developments we have discussed, represented a kind of levelling-out, sometimes a tailing off: techniques had been acquired, markets conquered, structures were established. Territorial or commercial expansion drew to a close, the hazards posed by sea and climate had been conquered. However it was also the moment when perspectives altered. Failures seemed possible and some were evident. The infiltration of a cash economy gradually sapped a system of production which was exhausted, at a time when the State, or indeed the town, seemed ready to assume or resume control of a world that had been profoundly rural for nine centuries. But what strikes the observer most vividly is the split in the social order. Already forms of association or simply custom itself had put an immense distance between the rulers and the ruled; those who could cross it, spur-wearing merchants, or wine-drinking bourgeois, were only admitted by merging their interests with those of the 'nobility', while the power of the latter appeared less and less in the prestigious form of judge or warrior, and more and more as an abuse of their strength or powers of taxation. And divisions became apparent even among the mass of workers: masters against assistants, assistants against the unemployed, merchants against masters, ploughmen against casual labourers, those doing their master's bidding for reward or for nothing. These tensions were still masked by the continuing growth of population, general prosperity, the enhanced dignity of kings and the triumph of orthodoxy. The first half of the thirteenth century is a period of achievement in the history of Europe. There was a community of spirit, faith and expression. We must now enter into this *koiné*. We have examined Europe; we must now turn to Christianity. This may prove to be a delicate matter.

9

A strict normalisation

For Western Christianity the tenth and eleventh centuries had been a turbulent era, a time of questioning and innovation. Out of suffering and sorrow a new power structure had been born: feudal society. The Roman Church had sought to free itself from the tutelage of the Empire and had taken charge of a reform movement that aimed at freeing the spiritual from the grip of the material. In the twelfth and thirteenth centuries, this raging torrent was becoming calmer. Not that this period was less troubled than the preceding one, but in every area there was a tendency towards stabilisation and the period's events were either the outcome or the prolongation of processes initiated before 1120.

The hierarchy restored

This was particularly evident in the Church which, as we have seen, concluded a series of pacts with the secular powers at the beginning of the twelfth century in order to put an end to the conflicts which had pitted it against them during the past decades. Prolonging those would risk putting in question the very bases of social order and risk encouraging anarchy. The clerics who were most attached to Gregorian principles and reforming ideas were in fact hostile to everything at home or abroad that might overturn the established order. For them, as for most of their contemporaries, there was a strong feeling that there existed an order fixed by Divine Providence, in society as in the physical universe, and that each individual belonged to a stable group, having its rights and its duties, situated in a hierarchical order which it was not up to that individual to question. To disturb earthly society, according to William of Auvergne (d. 1248), was the same as attacking the heavens themselves.

To evoke the transcendent models of the Middle Ages is generally to evoke this sense of immobility. Differing from our society, which is centred on change and which looks to a future that it hopes will be better, the society of the twelfth and thirteenth centuries exalted stability and considered the mutability of things human a consequence of original sin. The

The Wheel of Fortune or the vicissitudes of the human condition: he who is king or emperor today may be a beggar tomorrow. (Cantonal and University Library of Lausanne.)

theme of the Wheel of Fortune, so frequently pictured in the iconography of the period, did not illustrate the richness of historical evolution but the weakness of man, plaything of his passions and ambitions. The only progress possible, in the eyes of contemporary clerics, consisted in restoring the Church and Christian society to their primitive perfection, that ancient original splendour, a nostalgia for which had spurred on so many of the reformers.

Order and the law of God

But once the great problems which had triggered the Investiture Conflict were settled, at least on the level of principle, the Church could not help but draw closer to those powers which it had just opposed. This tendency was more or less pronounced depending on the country. With the Empire, which had not renounced its universalist claims, relations remained difficult for a long time, and renewed confrontations took place in the reigns of Frederick Barbarossa and Frederick II. But it was quite another matter with the national monarchies, as we can see in France, where the Abbot of Saint-Denis, Suger, was the chief counsellor to Louis VI and Louis VII. Everywhere rulers surrounded themselves with prelates and monks who were their most faithful collaborators and often their most enthusiastic historiographers. Despite local conflicts such as that in England which ended in the murder of the Archbishop of Canterbury, Thomas Becket (d. 1170), the dominant trend was towards a closer and closer association of throne and altar, which Ivo of Chartres, around 1100, had already called for and which was to remain one of the characteristic traits of the Ancien Régime.

One of the causes of this rapprochement between the two hierarchies, which was particularly noticeable at the local level, was undoubtedly the fear of seeing the masses call into question their situation of dependence and subordination as regards the ruling class. Since the first decades of the twelfth century, the Church had forbidden laymen to set themselves up in judgement of their pastors. If priests behaved themselves in a manner unworthy of their calling, henceforth it was up to the bishops, and them alone, to punish them. Counter to the arguments which had prevailed in Gregory VII's time, and which had been taken up and enlarged by some of the popular religious movements, it was formally affirmed that the validity of the sacraments had nothing to do with the moral integrity of those who celebrated them, from the moment that the latter were validly ordained and consecrated. Worried by the success of heterodox preachers such as Peter of Bruys or Eon de l'Etoile, the clergy closed ranks and drew closer to the seigneurial aristocracy, whose favour and generosity were indispensable to it.

In many regions, especially in northern France and Italy, the communal movement began, and very often asserted itself at the expense of the bishops' power. We know of the invective of the monk Guibert of Nogent, during the insurrection in Laon, against popular 'conspiracy' and the undertakings of merchants and urban craftsmen. These movements took hold, however: in the towns as well as in the country there developed aspirations towards liberty which were often accompanied by overt hostility towards a clergy that was both dominant and unenlightened. This was perhaps nowhere so marked as in Rome, Pope Eugenius III being chased from the city in 1146 by a revolt aimed at ensuring the autonomy of the city in relation to the Holy See. It was a cleric, Arnold of Brescia, who led the movement and who was a great success with his demand that the Church renounce its temporal powers and wealth everywhere. The papacy called on the new emperor, Frederick Barbarossa, for help, and he repressed the communal movement in Rome and brought about the flight, and then the death, of the reforming tribune. It was a significant alliance between the two powers – the papacy and the Empire – who were to oppose each other over subsequent decades, but who presented a common front at any sign of subversion.

Even if the Church softened some of its demands and showed itself more accommodating towards secular power, it did not entirely break with the spirit of Gregorian reform. In the eleventh century it had struggled to gain its freedom and loosen the grip of the laity, at least on its higher levels. In the twelfth and thirteenth centuries, it put more emphasis on the priority of the spiritual over the temporal and tried to strengthen its influence over society at large. Since Gregory VII, in fact, the objective pursued by the most conscientious clerics was not so much the establishment of a few fervent communities which might ensure the salvation of their benefactors by their prayers, but the realisation in the here and now of a Christian society, truly anticipating the Kingdom of God on earth. Of course monasticism remained active and flourishing throughout the twelfth century, as proved by the spectacular growth of the Cistercian order, which over several decades spread throughout the West under the impetus of St Bernard. But the new characteristic of this period is the renaissance of the secular church, linked to the new concept of religious life. To plagiarise, while also adapting, a famous formula, it was no longer a matter of interpreting the world but of transforming it. Action stole a march on contemplation, without of course eliminating it. From this perspective, monasticism was no longer the only model for the religious life. Besides, in returning to its origins, monasticism became increasingly distant from society. Henceforth established in the 'desert', that is in the heart of forests and marshes, the monks came to emphasise personal asceticism and escape from the world rather than pastoral activity. The latter was gradually taken on by the regular canons, whose development was encouraged by Urban II and his successors, and especially by the bishops who, purged of their more doubtful elements, returned as key figures, after a long eclipse. Between the first Lateran Council (1123) and the fourth (1215), the Latin Church had changed its face. After the death of St Bernard in 1153, the monks ceased to play a key role, while the bishops' prerogatives were strengthened and more clearly defined. The dioscesan framework, dislocated in many a region by the process of feudalisation, now regained a certain coherence thanks to the movement for the restoration of churches and tithes from the laity. Almost everywhere, after 1150, firmer organisational structures were set up, which allowed the clergy better control over the religious lives of the faithful.

This renewal of ecclesiastical structures and institutions was particularly perceptible at the top of the hierarchy. Gregorian reform had ended up by exalting the functions and prerogatives of the pope. Endowed with the insignia of power in his coronation, where he received the tiara (two, then three superimposed crowns which symbolised domination over the Church and over the world), he behaved increasingly like a sovereign, both temporal and spiritual. The papacy, in linking itself to the cause of reform, had really become, according to Gregory's own words, 'the head and centre' of the universal Church. Its legates had precedence over archbishops; they could call for and preside over regional or national synods, forcing bishops to demote and excommunicate rulers whose moral behaviour did not conform to its laws.

In fact the Church in this period equipped itself with normative codes that became more and more precise, with a universal scope. Between 1125 and 1140 a monk from Bologna, Gratian, drew up a canonical collection, that is, a systematic compendium of Church law, known as the *Decretum*, which rapidly became authoritative. This text, which is a direct offshoot of the Gregorian movement, defines clerics as beings both separate from the mass of the faithful and superior to them by reason of their supernatural mission. It also emphasised the autonomy of Church law – for this was a period in which official tribunals developed in **399**

The insignia of ecclesiastical power. Left: the pope's tiara (Innocent III, thirteenth-century fresco, Subiaco, lower church). Right: a bishop's mitre, showing the martyrdom of Thomas Becket, Archbishop of Canterbury. (From Seligensdadt, Munich, Bayerisches Nationalmuseum.)

each diocese and judged clerics and laymen for offences against the moral or religious order – and its coercive power through the expedients of canonical sanctions (refusal of Christian burial, excommunication and interdict).

At bottom, Gratian's conception of the Church was that of a centralised monarchy in which the bishops were subject to the pope and in which the metropolitans or other primates had only limited powers of presidency and control. This work has rightly been seen as the synthesis of old law (the canons of the great councils of the first Christian millennium) and new law, consisting in the decisions of the most recent popes. This development was strengthened in the pontificate of Pope Alexander III, himself a jurist trained in Bologna, who gave the force of law to papal decretals, that is, to the decisions taken by himself and his immediate predecessors with regard to specific problems submitted for their consideration. These texts, assembled in official collections from 1234 on the initiative of Gregory IX, were henceforth authoritative, and the new law, established by the will of the pope, would do away with local traditions and customs, which the canon lawyers were busy discrediting. Thus, well before secular society, the Church was provided with a unified law; henceforth there was only one central authority to legislate in the last resort and to have the power to dispense with the rules which it had created itself.

In practice, however, papal pretensions to universal authority came up against serious resistance. If the clerics generally submitted quickly enough to the new law, which increased their privileges, the German emperors and their allies in Germany and Italy opposed the establishment of theocratic power with all their strength. Frederick Barbarossa (1153–90), and above all Frederick II (1208–50), for their part sought to strengthen the ideological foundations of their authority by themselves adopting the universalist concepts of Roman law, which exalted the role of the prince as the source of all legislation. Other powers, too, such as the Italian communes and national monarchies, had no desire to submit in everything to the will of the Roman pontiff. This was soon seen in 1201, when Innocent III, with the decretal *Novit*, endeavoured to intervene in the conflict between Philip Augustus of France and his adversary, John, King of England and Duke of Normandy. While the sovereign pontiff maintained his right to intervene in the affairs of princes 'because of sin', the King of France rejected this claim and maintained his absolute autonomy in the temporal sphere. But the failures of papal strategy must not obscure the influence exercised by the Holy See on forms of government. From the first third of the twelfth century, the pope was surrounded by a real court, the Curia, and he had at his disposal sophisticated services such as the Chancery and the Apostolic Chamber (finances), whose efficiency was soon feared. This evolution of the Roman Church was only just beginning in the twelfth century, but it was already sufficiently advanced to arouse the criticisms of a man as respectful of ecclesiastical institutions as St Bernard who, in a treatise addressed to his former disciple Pope Eugenius III, was indignant to see Peter's successor in the 1150s living like a king, surrounded by administrators and courtiers. In advance of most states, with the exception of Sicily and perhaps England, the Church provided them thus with a model, that of a centrally administered monarchy, which they then endeavoured to imitate.

The common culture of the rulers

In the face of pressure from the clerics, whose advance in the fields of scholarship and law was so striking, the other ruling group, the lay aristocracy, reacted by providing itself with a homogeneous system of values and images. We can see these emerging in the last decades of the eleventh century and flowering between about 1100 and 1250, spreading throughout most of Christendom. This evolution was not the work of princes, even of those who were influential. The royal courts, such as those of the Hohenstaufen and the Capetians, existed as centres of traditional culture where the Church's influence remained predominant. They developed activities of a liturgical and musical order, within the framework of the royal chapel, and genres of literary scholarship: for example, hagiography, historiography and Latin poetry. The new initiatives, in fact, came from the bottom up, that is, from the world of the *milites* (knights) and vassals, who made up the largest group within the aristocracy, but whose situation remained precarious for a long time. For, contrary to what Marc Bloch believed, we now know that, save for exceptional cases such as those of Normandy or England after 1066, the old Carolingian nobility had not disappeared by 1000 after the 'iron century'. The ducal or comital families who were in power in the eleventh century did not merge with the group of military vassals, those free men who had the means to fight on horseback, nor with the adventurers who, through armed prowess and skilful marriages, had gained mastery of a tower or castle commanding one or more villages. But, to the extent to which their power in fact became hereditary and the concession

401

A knight. Thirteenth-century aquamanile. (Florence, Bargello Museum.) In a civilisation in which war was an everyday matter, he was above all a fighter on horseback, armed with a long lance, protected by a helmet and shield.

of fiefs by the powerful in exchange for their loyalty increased that power, these knights tended to blend into the aristocratic group. A seigneurial class was created which sought to distinguish itself from other social groups by establishing barriers making impossible either the decline represented by a return to the land and manual labour or the entry into the ruling class of new elements: bourgeois *nouveaux riches*, plunder-rich rustics or mercenaries. In the course of the twelfth century a new nobility was established, to which one could not belong unless one followed a way of life distinguished by certain distinctive signs and rituals which were the basis of the ideology of chivalry.

This common culture was built up by a double process. The first was the extension to the whole of the seigneurial class of habits and concepts which had originally belonged to a restricted élite. Thus the 'royal model', which the German and French princes had made theirs in the tenth century, subsequently continued to percolate to the lower levels of the aristocracy: the dynastic idea, the sense of lineage, the veneration surrounding male ancestors had only been the province of a very small number of great families around the year

Dubbing. For a long time a purely secular ceremony, it took on a religious character under the Church's influence. The ritual consisted of several stages: here the new knight receives his sword. (MS Roy. 20 D XI, The British Library, London.)

1000. In the twelfth century, the popularisation of these concepts profoundly marked all the seigneurial clans, who sought to organise themselves on the basis of lineage in such a way as to emphasise the process of 'descent' of authority down to the lowest level, that of the landholding seigneurie. From then on one can define as nobles the group of men who shared the privileges and customs which had been the king's several centuries earlier.

But this evolution was not only effected from the top downwards. It is noticeable, for example, with regard to the spread of dubbing. This rite of passage which simply marked entry into adulthood was current among the *milites*, but the high aristocracy seems to have been unaware of it for a long time. By the mid-twelfth century, on the other hand, there was scarcely a prince's son or even a king's who had not been dubbed, because the ceremony had become an attribute of nobility and a much sought-after honour. In fact, it was around the warrior values particularly adopted by knights that the new aristocractic culture was built. This was especially in evidence on the occasion of great assemblies which took place on feast-days and at tournaments. The more the extension of the peace of God limited the possibility of private wars, the more these extremely bloody encounters – in which champions confronted each other in a closed field in front of an audience of connoisseurs – were appreciated. It was the same with gatherings of the seigneurial court, where figures were created to match knightly aspirations, especially the *juvenes*, that is, the 'young men', those who had not yet settled down, and the bachelor squires, who were champing at the bit under their father or elder brother's authority, awaiting the chance of promotion.

The wandering minstrels addressed a more popular public than that of the troubadours. Here, two minstrels who are conjuring form the letter 'H' in an early twelfth-century manuscript of the *Moralia in Job*, from the Abbey of Cîteaux. (Dijon, Bibliothèque municipale.)

If the framework within which the new aristocractic literature in the vernacular was created was much the same everywhere, its expression was noticeably different from region to region. In northern France, from Normandy to Anjou and Champagne, it was above all the clerics living alongside the lord of the manor who composed the poems that were then recited by the *jongleurs* before an audience that was attentive, indeed fascinated, but passive. The *chansons de geste* or stories of chivalry tackled problems that were very meaningful for their audience, such as the cases of conscience arising from multiple oaths as vassals or the vengeance required by felony. Through a process of sublimation, founded on a recourse to a more or less mythical past (the era of Charlemagne) and to an unreal area, often Mediterranean (from Roncevaux to the Alyscamps via Narbonne and Orange), this exaltation of militarism ended up in the service of the Lord God. By contrast, in the Midi (south of the Loire), the new literature was embodied in the concreteness of actual existence, because the cultural context of creation and performance was quite different. The authors of the vernacular songs were mostly secular figures, who spoke of themselves in the first person and equally played a part in the presentation of their works.

The audience, a more restricted group from which clerics were excluded, did not remain passive, as its members intervened successively to play a creative part and to express directly if not an original sensibility, at least an authentic culture. The southern texts were thus shorter, less military, more lyrical, and relied upon sophisticated metrics and complex melody. They sang of love, above all, *fin amor*, although war and adventures were not lacking. The poetry of the *trobadors* was the expression of a more civil, urban and secular aristocracy than that of the North. The difference reflected the past of these regions, but especially the relations between the clergy and the laity. In the lands from Limousin to Provence, Gregorian reform was principally translated into a renewal of monasticism, and the secular clergy, little affected by the movement, seemed not to have tried too hard to Christianise the society around them. This resulted in a clearer separation than elsewhere between the sacred, identified with a flight from the world, and the profane, where festivals and *joie de vivre* reigned.

The message which emerged from the songs in the *langue d'oc* was quite clear: men appeared as equals before love (at least within the group of knights), but nobility of the soul was encountered among the minor lords and the 'young', the *juvenes*, who merely lived in hope, more than among the wealthy and the well-to-do who readily cultivated avarice and who contented themselves with purely sensual love – conjugal union within the framework of legal marriage or amorous adventures with the servants – which implied no quest for merit. Courtly love did not rule out possession, but those who celebrated the former knew that the latter was very difficult in practice. Crammed into the lord's court, the knights of course coveted his daughters or dreamed of committing adultery with his lady, their *domina*. But the suitors, those whom the *trobadors* called the *lauzengiers*, were so numerous that they cancelled each other out and none of them, even if fortunate, could pretend to reign solely over the heart of his lady. What the courtly man could hope to gain from his love and the efforts he made was honour, above all. This was, however, granted by the ladies, who could thus raise above his rank a poor knight or a valorous young squire.

The origins of courtly poetry have been much discussed. Some people have discerned Christian influences (the cult of the lady could be a secular reflection of Marian devotion), as well as Arab or Latin. None of these hypotheses should be excluded, and it is true that poetry in Latin, with the rediscovery of Ovid, in some twelfth-century works expressed a concept of love that in certain respects is quite close to that of the troubadours. But that is not the essential source. As has been shown, the birth of this secular literature in southern France, and the success it then found in the rest of France, Italy and the Germanic world, were not unrelated to the the permanent state of tension between the lower nobility and the high feudal lords in their common life at court, and to the historical necessity of neutralising by means of a common ideal the essential differences between the two groups. The paradoxical love which was the basis of the courtly system – renouncing immediate delight in order to acquire more merit in the eyes of the lady one wished to win – was perhaps the sublimated projection of the aspirations of minor vassals who, having neither fiefs nor money at their disposal, sought to assert themselves by gallantry and seduction.

We might wonder why this literature, which was formed in the midst of the minor lords of southern France, was valued by greater lords, such as William IX, Duke of Aquitaine, the oldest known courtly poet and one of the most original. What interest could the high nobility have in making their own the aspirations and fantasies of a group of newcomers who were in any case their inferiors? Doubtless they understood that it was necessary to

Devotion to the lady and the Marian cult. A knight kneeling before the Virgin and Child. (Twelfth-century manuscript, Saint-Omer library.)

strengthen the loyalty due from a vassal because of his personal oath, by other, more subtle links. Love and loyalty figure among knightly values. Would it not be worthwhile to exalt them so that they would become the bases of an ideological consensus within the aristocracy? It has rightly been observed that the great age of troubadour literature coincides with the second feudal period: that in which real links lose their supremacy in lord–vassal relations and in which relations within the aristocracy are founded principally on personal relations. Certainly the lord no longer had land to offer. But in bringing up his vassals' children at his court, strengthening the slender links between himself and the vassals by conviviality and frequent gifts, exalting the values of fellowship, he contributed to the establishment of a model order, founded at one and the same time on love and a respect for distance, which would constitute a powerful factor in social integration. Thus, in the *canço*, the internal tensions of the aristocracy were commuted into aesthetic tensions, and the pleasure in beauty dimmed the mind to the disappointments of existence, as well as the irreversible nature of the evolution which would deepen daily the abyss between the great and small lords. In the North, as in the Midi, the thematic content of the courtly works quickly became conventional: at the end of the twelfth century, the King of France did not treat his vassals in the way that King Arthur treated his table companions, the knights of the Round Table. South of the Loire, under the influence of Roman law, the vassal's contract became more demanding and the oath took the place of the promise. As for the 'adventure' so praised by Chrétien de Troyes through the figures of Lancelot, Percival or Gawain, it proved to be increasingly illusory or disappointing. But the fashion for courtly literature did not slacken for all that, and for a long time chivalry still worked its enchantment in works that softened the harshness of the time, creating an imaginary world in which a community of the nobility, at all its various levels, still seemed possible.

The emergence of this aristocratic literature is an important event in the history of the medieval West. For the first time, a culture was formed in the vernacular that was not based on the religious and moral values of Christianity. To monogamous, indissoluble marriage, which the higher clergy and the monks had tried to insist upon among the laity from the end of the eleventh century, the nobility opposed its own concept of love, founded on *de facto* polygamy and disregard for matrimonial ties. From the Marian cult, then in full bloom, there followed devotion to the lady, object and centre of a veritable liturgy. Alongside the traditional concept of the woman as procreator and worthy of respect as a mother – that is, the source of the family line – the idea was asserted that what was really at stake in relations between men and women was pleasure.

Undoubtedly this took the form of a game, and perhaps we should see in it a simple inversion of an infinitely less pleasant reality. Nevertheless, a whole society took up this game, recognising itself in this idealised vision and revelling in its artistic expression. Courtly literature thus soon became a real code of behaviour for all the élites of western Christendom. Around 1200, the son of a rich merchant of Assisi who aspired to live as a knight, St Francis, was singing love-poems in French. And even after he gave himself to the service of Dame Poverty, he continued to show the greatest respect for aristocratic values such as liberality and magnanimity. To live in the courtly manner was also a way of distancing oneself from inferior social groups, the bourgeois and the peasants, who were unable to stand back from desire and money. Beyond all the internal differences within the seigneurial group, courtliness (*courtoisie*) presented itself above all as a refusal of all forms of 'baseness', that is, in the last analysis, of the culture and behaviour of the subordinate classes.

The triumph of writing, the suppression of other cultures

On the linguistic level, the major development of the twelfth and thirteenth centuries was the emergence of vernacular languages and their promotion as vehicles of a dignified, written literary culture. Seen earliest in the Germanic lands, complicated in England by the traumas of the Norman conquest, the phenomenon became firmly established above all in France, and later in Italy, Catalonia and Spain. The Church lost its cultural monopoly, and Latin, while it retained its strong position, after 1250 was only the technical language of abstract thought (theology, philosophy, law). It is not certain, however, that we can speak of a general promotion of lay culture. In a society as compartmentalised as that of the Middle Ages, the laity was far from constituting a homogeneous group. If the knights showed themselves anxious to withdraw from the tutelage of the clergy, they were nevertheless still under their influence and felt closer to them than to the peasants or craftsmen. Moreover, from the end of the eleventh century, in many regions of the West the lay aristocracy was concerned to give its children, or at least some of them, a minimum schooling, as the examples of Abelard or Guibert of Nogent demonstrate. So we see that the nobility soon went beyond the simple quest for physical prowess and warrior exploits – rather, they

The cult of the dead: a twelfth-century *lanterne des morts* (literally, lantern of the dead) in Fenioux (Charente-Maritime). The *lanterne des morts* was a hollow stone pillar with a lantern at the top, symbolising the souls' eternal life; inside, there was a spiral staircase; at the foot, the base covered an ossuary.

sought *prud'homie*, that is, an equilibrium between valour and a certain wisdom learned from books or at least from the texts read. This development contributed to a gradual distancing of the nobility from what we might call the folk culture, which remained the province of the coarse.

That secular, basically peasant culture had been attacked and neutralised by the Church since the early Middle Ages, an era in which we can only glimpse this culture through conciliar condemnations, the penitentials or hagiography deriving from the clergy. When some authors do transmit a few fragments, their component parts are almost always misrepresented in order to make them inoffensive. From the eleventh century onwards, the influence of folklore strengthened or, rather, the pressure it exerted on the learned culture became more evident, as is shown by the developments of the cult of the dead, the increase in formulas for blessing or cursing and the widespread use of the ordeal.

The literature of chivalry made some borrowings from these oral traditions in the twelfth century, especially in Germany and England, before the success of the courtly genre came to submerge these relics and to unify the expressions of aristocratic culture by means of its own set of themes. Thus in the *Nibelungenlied*, an epic German poem put into writing at the end of the twelfth century by Bavarian clerics, there reigns an atmosphere of bloody violence and profound pessimism which is linked to the primitive heroic traditions of the Germanic peoples and to Scandinavian mythology. In these stories, inspired by the family rivalries amongst the Merovingians and by the vicissitudes of the Burgundian kingdom of Worms, some pagan concepts come to light: the inextinguishable nature of vengeance, the superiority of women over men, the absence of all sentimentality. These are traits whose survival in the midst of the Middle Ages attest to a psychology and scale of values that were completely different from Christianity. One could say the same, or almost, with regard to the *Matter of Britain*, that collection of fables and stories of Celtic origin full of marvellous folklore, on which the twelfth-century authors of chivalrous romances largely drew. The role of Melusine has been rightly highlighted: the fairy who brought to knights their lands, castles and lineage, and who became the symbolic and magical incarnation of their ambitions.

The study of *Yvain, or the Knight of the Lion* by Chrétien de Troyes (*c.* 1180), which was such a success, shows the importance of the theme of the forest, this world of marginality and disorder where strange beings proliferated – werwolves and wild men – incarnations of the popular belief in the existence of a continuity between man and the animal kingdom, and indeed the vegetable kingdom, which the Church countered with the opposing idea of man made in the image of God and in his likeness. In his *Life of Merlin*, the English cleric Geoffrey of Monmouth presented the wild man as the fruit of a coupling between a mortal woman and a demon incubus. Other twelfth-century English authors, such as Gervase of Tilbury and Walter Map, also reflected popular traditions which the Church had not yet obliterated and which continued to lead an underground existence. But on this level, the bloomimg of courtly culture was in the end more harmful than beneficial to the lower classes. In giving birth to a written literature, it helped to plunge into obscurity and to marginalise a whole group of oral traditions that did not resurface until they were given voice by the victims of the Inquisition. One could say the same with regard to the birth of a 'bourgeois' literature, which began to develop in the late twelfth century in the large towns of northern France, especially in Arras, and in central-northern Italy. If satire on the clergy was not lacking, and if the world of the nobility was an object of more or less irreverent parody in this literature, it was still the villein, the stupid, gross peasant, who was the favourite target of these authors, who were concerned to distinguish themselves from the country bumpkins they themselves had often been, having only recently emerged from the rural world.

In the twelfth century, however, there were still bridges between the various milieux that we have marked out, and the cultural landscape in reality was less compartmentalised than it was later to become. In certain areas, one could even find a common stock of attitudes that transcended the socio-cultural divides. Thus the clergy of this period, for example, manifested a sense of the concrete and a credulity which is not very different from that of the people. At all levels, what had not been seen or experienced was beyond belief: but people believed everything they saw, and the attitude of the Church with regard to miracles evolved over a long period and only at the highest levels. Abstractions had no hold over such minds. Thus sanctity, before it was conceived as a set of moral qualities, was widely perceived as an efficacious power and a beneficent influence. The same literalism impregnated the ascetic ideal of the hermits or the aspiration towards poverty of the evangelistic movements as much as the grammarians' efforts to find the realities behind words by means of their etymology and roots. Moreover, certain intermediary groups ensured a link between the world of the schools and that of the streets and woods. Thus the Goliards, an ill-defined group of non-conformist poets, succeeded in combining in their poetic works elements of antique culture, the inheritance of their clerical training and village traditions, such as the myth of the Land of Cockaigne, or sensual pleasure, where abundance and youth lived eternally, the peasant version of the Golden Age. It is even possible that the rediscovery of ancient paganism, either directly or through Arab intermediaries, led some scholars to a

409

better understanding of folk culture, as the success of bestiaries, lapidaries and astrological treatises would seem to show. But it was above all in those areas where the Church had not yet clearly defined its dogma that traditional concepts continued to flourish. The main area was that of the Four Last Things: Death, Judgement, Heaven and Hell. The absence of dogmatic precision on this subject until the fourteenth century encouraged the display of beliefs and behaviour which, under cover of sacred texts such as the Book of Revelations and of learned speculations on the end of the world, expressed the survival of millenarian dreams and messianic hopes. The same problems were posed with regard to the Beyond, that obscure world populated by ghosts who were believed to return in order to trouble the living and whom it was necessary quickly to seal up in Purgatory. And finally, there was the question of the existence of devils, which the clergy evoked so often in their fight against usury and all forms of immorality, but with which many of the laity did not hesitate to make pacts, at the risk, like Theophilus, of jeopardising the salvation of their soul.

With regard to culture, it was in the religious domain, however, that the fiercest tensions between the clergy and the laity emerged. A particularly durable barrier was erected around holy writ by the Church; the clergy, far from breaking it down, were jealous guardians of this treasure, which they considered as their own possession. Translations of the Bible into the vernacular were forbidden, out of fear that the laity would interpret difficult passages of the Scriptures incorrectly and thus slip into heresy. This was not an imaginary risk, as was shown in the late twelfth century by the Cathar *Perfecti*, who offered a dualist, gnostic interpretation of the Gospels. The result was a dichotomy between theological thought, the province of a small number of specialists with university backgrounds, and the spontaneous expression of popular religious feeling, which became increasingly common as the thirteenth century advanced. From Flanders to the lands of Liège, from the Rhineland to Saxony, a literature of mysticism came into being, the work of women, often from lowly backgrounds, who explored the ways of union with God using the language of everyday life. In 1232–3, the Flemish Cistercian nun Beatrice of Nazareth wrote an autobiography which crowned a brief treatise, *The Seven Steps of Love*, the first mystical writing by a woman in the vernacular. A few years later, a beguine from Anvers, Haedwych, composed in her native dialect a work that touched the heights of religious lyric poetry. This movement grew, especially in the German lands, and naturally aroused anxiety among the clergy, who regarded with suspicion this show of popular mysticism over which they had no control. The feeling was expressed very clearly by a German Franciscan, Lamprecht of Regensburg, when he wrote:

> This art has arisen since yesterday
> Among the women of Bavaria and Brabant.
> What is this art, then, Lord God,
> Which an old woman understands better
> Than a learned and scholarly man?

The Church also tried to control the distribution of these texts and subjected them to theological censorship, before condemning the beguines at the beginning of the fourteenth century on the pretext that they had been contaminated by heretical influences. Thus they suppressed one of the most fertile and innovatory forms of expression in medieval culture, one whose concerns were above all with the laity and women.

Progress in legal scholarship

From the early Middle Ages, the West no longer had a uniform system of civil legislation imposed on all the subjects of a prince. After the barbarian invasions, the system of personal law had prevailed, varying according to a person's ethnic group and social rank. Then, with the disappearance of all state-controlled, centralised justice, there was an even greater diversity. After the establishment of the seigneurial and feudal framework, the notion of law disappeared and gave way to custom, which was usually not written down. 'There were nearly as many laws as houses', said a lawyer from Bologna in the twelfth century, recalling just such a period. But in the whole of Christendom, Italy was where the idea of law had been least forgotten. Its towns, more than any others, had retained their roles as administrative centres for the surrounding regions, and judges gave sentences according to Lombard law, itself strongly impregnated with Roman influences. Moreover, in the eleventh century, the northern and central regions of the peninsula belonged to the Empire and, despite the difficulties experienced by the German rulers in achieving obedience, the idea of a superior public authority survived there better than elsewhere. Much the same was true of Rome, where papal power remained uncontested. This explains the existence, attested very early in these regions, of notaries who could draw up formal documents by virtue of imperial or papal authority, and before whom deeds had to be registered in order to be valid. To train these practitioners there were schools for notaries, recorded in Parma and Ravenna, where they could acquire some idea of the law. It was from these modest beginnings that, from the late eleventh century and especially in the twelfth, a renaissance in civil law and legal studies took place, centred on Bologna. Its main architect was a master of the school in the town, Irnerius, whose main achievement was to make civil law an autonomous discipline, distinct from the framework of liberal arts and equipped with its own techniques, particularly the gloss. Under his influence, and that of his pupils, there was a remarkable renaissance of legal studies in the course of the twelfth century, which resulted in the gradual rediscovery of authentic texts of imperial Roman law – in particular, Justinian's *Digest*, which had only been known in fragmentary collections littered with later interpolations.

We should consider the reasons for this recourse to sources that had been dispersed and forgotten. Of course it is due, to some extent, to the desire to return to Antiquity and its more reliable traditions which characterised all areas in the twelfth century. But above all, it was the renaissance of economic activity in the markets and towns, earlier in Italy than elsewhere, which encouraged the search for a law, especially where contracts were concerned, that would transcend local circumstances and diverse customs. To this was added the desire of some idealist intellectuals, devotees of logic, who aspired towards a single authority enforcing a common law. Towards the mid-twelfth century, the professors of law

411

at Bologna thought they had found a harbinger of this in the person of Frederick Barbarossa, who was then endeavouring to establish imperial authority over Italy. In exchange for supporting his claims by affirming that the only source of law was the will of the prince, they received a number of privileges from him in 1158, which helped to strengthen their prestige and influence. But this belated rediscovery of Roman law could not end in a pure and simple return to Justinian's legislation. Centuries of history could not be obliterated, and furthermore the vicissitudes of Barbarossa's reign, particularly his final defeat at the hands of the cities of the Lombard league, were enough to show the anachronistic nature of this restoration. At the Peace of Constance in 1183 the Italian communes gained recognition of their right to make their own laws, and a little later began to draw up communal statutes which differed noticeably from town to town. Roman law retained its prestige and was raised above other laws, but did not suceed in doing away with them. To the end of the Middle Ages, the judicial situation in Italy would be characterised by the co-existence of civil law, Roman law (*jus commune*) with the law of a particular community (*jus proprium*). But this should not mislead us: the communes' statutes as written down in the thirteenth century were not simple practical or empirical rules, as the customs of the seigneurie might be even when they were set down in writing, but genuine municipal legislation, sanctioned and ratified by political bodies.

The spread of Roman law was almost as early and rapid in southern France. In these regions, customary law had remained quite close to Roman law and the use of written law had never disappeared. From the 1140s, Toulouse and Montpellier welcomed schools of law where jurists were trained who were influential in the consulates and the courts of the most powerful lords. It was they who, to the scandal of the troubadours, introduced south of the Loire the practice of a vow sworn on the Gospels or relics, which replaced the simple promise in feudal-vassal relations and in judicial contexts: were the nobility no longer to be believed on their word alone and their relations ruled by the *convenientia*? To swear or give guarantees was good only for merchants and villeins. But, despite the fulminations of a Peire Cardenal, contractual relations were transformed at all levels and surrounded by new judicial guarantees. In an indirect and diffuse way, Roman law influenced local custom and helped it to evolve in a more rational manner, restoring the value of forgotten notions such as equity. In Italy, it even made its mark on a number of *libri feudorum*, which were then rewritten. More than a group of texts, this was a conceptual tool which allowed a new approach to legal and social problems, with a language which soon became the preserve of a special class of practitioners.

In northern France, Roman law did not enjoy the same fortune. The Capetians, suspicious of texts that exalted the predominance of the emperor, forbade their being taught in Paris, which did not prevent their being studied in Orléans from the late twelfth century. But the northern regions did not remain entirely insulated from the legal renaissance. The recording of oral custom is detectable first of all in the west (the Norman *Customal*, compiled *c.* 1200, the *Assizes* of Count Geoffrey of Brittany), and then it extended to central France (*Usage* of Amiens,1249; Pierre de Fontaine's *Enseignements*, 1254; the *Livre de justice*, 1265). There was an identical movement in Germany, when Eike von Repgow compiled the *Sachsenspiegel* (The Mirror of the Saxons) around 1221–4. As scholars have shown for Flanders, what then appeared in these regions was a new type of penal law, aimed at removing from criminal offences the private nature which they had in German feudal law. In order to legitimate the active intervention of public authorities in matters of blood justice, the clergy of the comital entourage had vigorously to reinstate the notion of a public order of which power was the guarantor. Thus crimes became in principle transgressions of comital authority, which was empowered to punish them, and repression became a public service. Communes, for their part, did the same. A sworn peace between the bourgeois forbade feuds, or private vengeance, disputes were made subject to the obligatory arbitration of the commune's 'prosecutors', who made offences a matter of public law. Trials gradually ceased to be combats between individuals, in which authorities merely played the role of witnesses, and became debates between an individual and a representative of the public powers, who replaced the offended party. The ancient process of accusation, too, gave place by the late twelfth and early thirteenth century to a process of inquiry. A private complaint was enough to bring about legal proceedings on the part of the count's *bailli*, subsequently assisted by feudal civil law courts. The appearance of what was in effect a 'public ministry', responsible for engaging in legal proceedings on its own initiative against criminals, was one of the chief creations of the Middle Ages. We could say more about the development of the system of proofs. The Germanic system of ordeal by fire or water or judicial duel was replaced in the second half of the twelfth century by a more rational and objective system in which judges played an active role, since it was up to a commission of *échevins* to investigate and listen to the witnesses in a position to provide legal proofs. It was the same for the Church, for which recourse to ordeals was forbidden by the fourth Lateran Council of 1215. This whole movement towards the rationalisation of justice and the expansion of the law bore fruit mainly in the thirteenth century. Directly or indirectly, it proceeded from the growing influence of legal scholarship – in Roman law and in canon law, which borrowed considerably from the Roman.

Its repercussions in the political sphere were no less important, given the extent to which it contributed to the renaissance of the idea of the *res publica*. For John of Salisbury, the great English scholar who became Bishop of Chartres and reflected current thinking on contemporary political problems, the prince was 'a public person and a public power'. In France and in England, the expression 'the Crown' began to be used, which implied a continuity transcending the succession of individual sovereigns. The king, from being the dispenser of justice which had hitherto been his primary role, now became legislator. In France it was St Louis who was the innovator, after a lapse of several centuries, in legislating by ordinances valid throughout the realm. The feudal framework remained, and the sovereign decided nothing without having consulted his peers. But the monarchic order was already looming on the horizon, and it was not long before the jurists of the Capetians would proclaim that 'the King of France is emperor in his kingdom'.

The crushing of dissent

After 1120, we see the increase in the West of popular religious movements challenging the power and wealth of the Church. The latter had emerged from the Investiture Conflict stronger and wealthier. Great and lesser lords, rattled by threats and canonical sanctions, began to restore those parts of the Church's worldly property that they had carried off in preceding centuries: churches, tithes, taxes crept back into the hands of the clergy, and especially the hands of the monks, who were the main beneficiaries of largesse donated, very often, *in articulo mortis*.

Popular movements between challenge and heresy

At the same period, however, the best Christians, clergy as much as laity, were influenced by the ideal of the apostolic life, characterised by a desire to return to communal life and by the renunciation of private property. In order to fully realise these aspirations, some of the laity joined the religious in various manners, like the south German peasants who, if we are to believe Bernold of Constance, flocked to place themselves in obedience to the monks of Hirsau and joined them as lay members, that is as servants and agricultural workers. But many, despairing of ecclesiastical institutions and convinced that they would never be reformed, drew apart from them and engaged in violent polemic against the clergy, urging the faithful not to pay tithes and to refuse to receive the sacraments, especially baptism and marriage. With Peter of Bruys and Henry of Lausanne we have the denial of the Church itself, together with its rites, the sole requirement being that of a purely spiritual faith.

Even when they did not go to these extremes, many of the faithful expected the Church, in its material aspect also, to conform to the poverty of Christ and his disciples. It was in the name of this ideal that Arnold of Brescia demanded that the Roman Church renounce its temporal power and its riches (1151–5). His failure and tragic end only strengthened his supporters' idea that the hierarchy was an obstacle to the spread of the Gospel. Many of the laity, because of the lives of poverty and asceticism they had adopted, also thought themselves qualified to preach. The Church's ministry, however, was restricted to the clergy alone.

For all these reasons, the atmosphere of understanding and co-operation – created in the eleventh century between the reformist élite in the clergy, gathered around the pope, and the popular religious movements – was only a memory by the mid-twelfth century. In reinforcing the privileges of the clergy and emphasising their separation from the secular world, the Gregorians had prepared a difficult future for their successors. The gulf was widening between a Church which was developing its structure and strengthening its legal armoury on the one hand, and the apostolic movements on the other, who were tending towards an ever more extreme spiritualism. The history of Peter Valdes and the Waldensians illuminates these tensions clearly.

According to contemporary sources and the Inquisition manuals of the thirteenth century, the sect of the Waldensians, or the Poor Men of Lyons, had been created by Valdes, a rich citizen of Lyons. This man, after seeing the light, abandoned all his goods and decided to live in poverty and evangelical perfection, following the apostles. He then made a translation into the vernacular of the Gospels, some books of the Old Testament and some passages of the Church Fathers. Having thus acquired direct knowledge of the word of God, he began to preach in the street and public places, gathering in many men and women whom he sent in their turn on missions to towns and villages. The first episode must have taken place around 1170–6. In March 1179, a delegation from the small community went to Rome, lead by Valdes himself, who wanted their way of life approved by Pope Alexander III and the third Lateran Council. By this period they were certainly in difficulties with the clergy of Lyons, who confronted them with the canon law forbidding the laity to preach, especially when, as was their case, they had no fixed abode. We are lucky to have a record of the reaction of the Englishman in the *curia*, Walter Map, who assisted the penitentiary cardinal responsible for examining their request:

We saw the Waldensians, simple, unlettered people, thus called from the name of their leader, a citizen of Lyons on the Rhône . . . They earnestly requested that they be given authorisation to preach, judging themselves educated in fact, while they are barely half–knowledgeable . . . Like the pearl before swine, would the Word be given to simple minds whom we know to be unable to receive it, let alone able to hand on that which they have received? This cannot be and they must be dismissed . . . These people have no fixed abode; they go around two by two, barefoot, dressed in wool, possessing nothing, having everything in common with the Apostles; they follow naked the naked Christ. They begin very humbly, because they have not yet got a foothold. If we let them, it will be we who are pushed aside.

An attitude characteristic of a haughty and self-important cleric, crushingly scornful of the uneducated laity, who felt himself threatened in his monopoly as the licensed intermediary between the word of God and men.

Nevertheless, the reaction of Pope Alexander III was at first more clear-sighted than that of his advisers: Valdes received oral confirmation of the religious way of life he proposed to observe, along with an authorisation, perhaps only for himself, to preach if the local priest agreed. In practice, however, difficulties were not slow to appear. The new Archbishop of Lyons, Jean de Bellesmains, certainly sought to take control of the movement. Not having succeeded, he withdrew from Valdes and his companions the permission to preach. The latter would not submit, and replied that 'it was necessary to obey God before men'. This did not mean that the Waldensians rejected the hierarchy or thought it worthless: they simply judged it impossible to renounce their calling, which was to spread the Gospel. Thus they were expelled from Lyons and excommunicated, first of all by the archbishop in 1182–3, then by Pope Lucius II in 1184. This did not prevent the spread of the movement; on the contrary, it extended first to Languedoc and Lombardy, then to other regions of France and Italy in the late twelfth century. For all that, we should not over-estimate the excommunication of 1184. Even where it was known, many of the clergy and laity continued to regard the Waldensians as good Christians: after all, they lived in poverty, according to the Gospels, and preached an orthodox doctrine. Moreover, they shared with the Roman Church an aversion to Catharism, against which they argued as fervently as the Roman Catholic apologists. Finally, the disciples of Valdes for the most part belonged to the bourgeoisie and common people. They were thus rarely in contact with the ecclesiastical hierarchy and continued to go to church, in as much as they were not expelled from parish communities. This is clearly seen in Metz in 1199, where Pope Innocent III had to intervene, at the bishop's request, to condemn the intrigues of groups of Waldensians who were inciting the faithful against a clergyman whom they reproached as inadequate: 'Some of them', said the pope, 'have nothing but contempt for the simplicity of their priests and, when these offer them the word of salvation, they secretly murmur that they find better doctrine in books and that they are capable of expressing it better themselves.' As we see, the debate always revolved around the same problems: should the laity, given their cultural inferiority, real or supposed, have contact with the word of God only through the intermediary of clergy duly authorised by the hierarchy? The Church maintained that, even if the priests were not equal to their task, the faithful were not to judge them nor to establish sects or small clandestine groups which would destroy parish unity. Finally, it was out of the question for the laity to assume the right of preaching themselves, because it was specifically the function of clergy within the Church.

At the same time, in Lombardy (which was both the domain of communes and the 'receptacle of all heresies', as an orthodox author expressed it) the Humiliati movement was developing. It first appeared in Milan around 1175 and rapidly spread to all the large towns on the Po plain. The *Chronicle of Laon* (*c.* 1220) presents them as 'town-dwellers who, while remaining at home with their families, have chosen a certain type of religious life: they abstain from lies and lawsuits, contenting themselves with simple dress and engaging in the struggle for the Catholic faith.' But this text, interesting as it is, tells us nothing about the origins of the movement, which must have sprung up among artisans wanting to follow the apostolic way of life. Like the Waldensians, they refused to take oaths and above all they claimed the right to preach. Many of those who entered the movement were married. Couples vowed themselves to continence, and some of them assembled in houses where men and women co-existed in separate communities, vowed to work and prayer, while others remained in their homes. In the beginning, manual labour was a necessity because most of the adherents came from modest backgrounds. There was nothing heretical, as we can see, in these practices; but the affirmation that the laity, while remaining in the world, could lead a religious existence and bear witness to the Gospels seemed scandalous to most of the clergy, who were inclined to condemn all the popular movements under one heading.

Mortal danger: Catharism

Much more dangerous to the Church than these spiritualist groups, whose structure did not call into question essential doctrine, was the growth of Catharism. It has long been discussed whether this set of beliefs was introduced into the West from the East, or whether it was of indigenous origin. This debate does not greatly interest historians today. It is virtually established that the Bogomils, that is, Manichaeans who came from the Balkans, were present at the first meeting of the representatives of the Provençal Cathar communities in 1164, at Saint-Félix de Camaran, and it is certain that the graft would not have taken had there not been minds receptive to the message. This message was presented as an effort to realise the full and entire Christian life, as it had been revealed in the New Testament. The

Catholic Church was accused of having disguised the revolutionary truth of the Gospel, which resided in the following dualism: God, seen as Good and the Spirit, is opposed throughout eternity to Satan, the principle of Evil and master of Matter. The Devil, whom official theology saw merely as a fallen angel, dangerous and deceitful of course, but not the creator of the material world, was a divine power for the Cathars. Between these opposing forces there was a battle whose outcome was uncertain and which each person experienced within him- or herself, since people were essentially bodies (matter) filled, to a lesser or greater degree, with spirit. It followed that the object of the religious life was an ascent, a human effort to disengage from corruption in all its forms. In order to make this effort, it was necessary to follow the example of Christ, who was not a person of the Trinity for the Cathars, but the greatest of the angels – or the best of humans – whom God had made his son. Everything the Church said about him was false: his body and his death were only appearances, and it was not his Passion that saved mankind, but his teaching as found in the Gospels, and above all in St John's. Of course even within Catharism there were various levels, and beside the absolute dualism we have just outlined, there was also a modified dualism, which insisted primarily on the role of the angel Jesus sent by God to reveal to man what was right within him and to offer a possibility of salvation through asceticism and a rite of union with God, the laying on of hands or *consolamentum* administered at the point of death. For the absolute dualists, on the contrary, deliverance from the bonds of matter could not occur until the end of a process of reincarnation, the souls of those who had done the right thing in life passing by metempsychosis into superior beings.

It is not certain that the followers of Catharism, of whom there were soon large numbers in south-west France and Italy, knew and understood all the subtleties of Cathar dogma. The strength of the latter lay in its presentation as a syncretism of which the Gnostic aspects could satisfy demanding or subtle minds. Its obsession with the flesh linked up with old traditions of Mediterranean folk culture. Above all, it was perceived as a Gospel movement since it completely rejected the Old Testament, the work of a wicked God, and exalted spiritual values. Its doctrine was severe, but the distinction between the 'Perfecti', whose asceticism drew the admiration of the masses, and the simple believers, who were not constrained to renounce sexual life and work, allowed everyone to hold to it to some degree. Finally, Catharism served as a vehicle for virulent anti-clericalism, which was not displeasing to many of the laity. At a period in which knights saw the Church as imposing a restrictive sexual morality, in which merchants fell under the blow of the sanctions of canon law with regard to usury, and in which women could not hope to play an active role in Christian communities, one sees why a movement which rejected the mediation of institutional priesthood would have been sympathetically received in many circles. Liturgy, churches, tithes – what were they all for, if not to maintain a catholic clergy without prestige, the corrupt offshoot of an initially pure community whose doctrine was false and whose sacraments were no longer effective?

For the first time in the history of the Middle Ages there was, in certain areas of the West such as southern France or the large towns of Lombardy and Tuscany, a church on the margins of the official Church, with its own hierarchy and structures. From Toulouse to

Cremona, from Béziers to Florence, the Cathars or their sympathisers took pride of place and did not hesitate to challenge Catholics in public controversies, where they had no shortage of arguments for denouncing the inadequacies and ignorance of the clergy, as well as the wealth of monks and prelates, confronting them with the rigorous asceticism and holy way of life of the Perfecti. Within Christianity itself, a counter-society had now been born which grew to question the foundations of the existing order and even the basis of dogma, the Incarnation.

The Catholic Church slowly became aware of this situation. For a long time the Cathars, whose doctrine was partially secret, were not clearly distinguishable from the swarm of other dissident religious movements. It was not until the last decades of the twelfth century that treatises (generally titled *manifestatio*) appeared, bringing to light for the priests and faithful those aspects of their beliefs most opposed to Catholicism, and it was only in the thirteenth century that some clerics undertook to refute them in a systematic way. The only force that the hierarchy found to oppose them at first came from the Cistercians, who then established themselves near the northern Italian towns and went there to preach, as St Bernard had done several decades earlier against the 'Manichaeans' of Aquitaine. But the effectiveness of these missions was limited because these monks, coming from a rural background, were scarcely equipped to confront urban audiences, with their aggressive and subtle challenges. The first condemnations of heretical sects, pronounced in 1184 at Verona by Pope Lucius III, were ineffective. They also showed little knowledge of the phenomenon of heresy, because they were aimed indiscriminately at several recognised movements, such as the Waldensians or the Humiliati, whose doctrine was not essentially different from that of the Church, as well as at others, like the Cathars, which had nothing much in common with Christianity.

Recovery

Faced with this rapidly deteriorating situation, which called into question the ideological hold of the Church over western Christendom, Pope Innocent III (1190–1216), one of the strongest personalities of his time, opposed it with a double reaction: on the one hand he tried to reintegrate into Catholicism the popular religious movements which did not question the fundamental doctrines of Christianity; on the other hand, he embarked upon an unrelenting battle against the Cathars, which he endeavoured to associate with the public authorities in order to gain maximum effectiveness.

Innocent III, in fact, was intelligent enough to realise that there could be something valuable and positive in the religious aspirations of a number of the lay groups which the bishops and priests often tended to confuse with the Cathars and persecute without distinction. In 1201, he recognised the Humiliati of Lombardy as legitimate by granting them a rule which consecrated most of the habits they had practised for several decades, integrating them into a traditional canonical order. The primitive fraternity gave birth to three religious orders: the first was formed of brothers and sisters consecrated to God, who lived a conventual life; the second was formed of laity, men and women, living in double communities; and the third, by far the most original, incorporated those who continued to live at home with their families, according to a rule of life, or *propositum*, centred on penitence and work. To win over the Humiliati to the Church, Innocent III had to yield on two points: first, he recognised the legitimacy of their refusal to take an oath, a principle to which they were firmly attached, and second, he granted them the right to preach anywhere, except in churches. Their homilies, however, were to be confined to the area of morals and were not to encroach on matters of dogma, which were reserved for the clergy. This distinction was based on the idea that there were two kinds of text in the Scriptures: the *aperta*, relating to life and action and directly comprehensible to everyone, and the *profunda*, those passages requiring exegesis which could only be given by clergy with theological knowledge and training. Having done this, the pope defused a potentially explosive situation and opened the way to new experiments, such as that of St Francis and his companions. The Humiliati were not slow in taking adavantage of the possibilities now available. Visiting Milan in 1216, Cardinal Jacques de Vitry wrote about them: 'These people, who have abandoned everything for Christ, gather in various places, living by the work of their hands, often preaching the word of God and readily listening to it. Their faith is as deep as it is strong, and their activities are effective.'

This open papal policy, which attempted to bring back into the Church the orthodox elements of popular religious movements, was not so successful with regard to the Waldensians. In 1207, at the end of a 'colloquium' held at Pamiers in the presence of the Castilian bishop Diego of Osma and probably of St Dominic (one of the leaders of the Waldensian movement), Durand of Huesca was converted along with some of his disciples. Innocent III received them in Rome in 1208 and took them under his protection. Under the name of Poor Catholics, they continued their existence as itinerant preachers, arguing against the Cathars and preaching the Gospel. In fact they had also been granted the right to practise the ministry of preaching and of living in poverty. In return, they submitted to the authority of the local ecclesiastical hierarchy and the Roman Church. The impact of these conversions was limited, however: most Waldensians did not follow the example of Durand, not being utterly convinced that the Catholic Church would recognise their apostolic vocation and respect their right to preach. Rather than submit, they chose to endure many centuries of persecution, with the result that the Waldensian church still exists today, especially in Italy.

The poor man of Assisi

Much more far-reaching were the consequences of Innocent III's approval of a group of penitents from Assisi, led by the son of a merchant, Francis, who went to Rome to see him in 1210. This brotherhood did not yet have a large number of members, but they attracted the attention of their contemporaries by their desire to live by the letter of the Gospel. This aspiration had already inspired various twelfth-century religious movements, most of which had ended up in dissidence or heresy. But Innocent III discerned the profound orthodoxy of St Francis, his desire to submit to the Church, in particular to Rome, as well as his

Francis of Assisi. (Subiaco, fresco in the chapel of San Gregorio, thirteenth century.)

zeal to save souls. Thus he had faith in him, and gave oral approval to the rule – a simple collection of passages from the Gospels – which Francis submitted. Some years later, in 1223, his sucessor Honorius III gave formal approval to a new rule which would govern the order. By this time, the order had taken the name of 'Friars Minor'.

One cannot help being struck by the originality of this new organisation. Even the name which the founder had chosen was significant: *minores* (minors) in the writings of the time meant the lowest social categories, especially the powerless people in the towns, the world of exploited workers or the unemployed. By referring to a socially deprived group and to the virtue of humility in the name of his new community, St Francis was already breaking – without a fuss but in a profound way – the link between the religious State and the seigneurial condition. The monks of his time, even those who, like the Cistercians, declared themselves anxious to flee the world, were in fact great landowners. The monasteries constituted a kind of collective seigneurie, managing, defending and increasing their considerable patrimony, both real estate and movable property. In the mind of the laity, especially of the poor, they belonged to the aristocratic world, even if there were individuals among them who were extremely saintly and practised poverty to a very great degree.

The Franciscan order, however, in the spirit of its founder, was characterised by a complete rejection of wealth and even of any form of possession. St Francis abhorred money, and his behaviour with regard to material goods was always marked by contempt and revulsion. He also forbade his companions and followers to possess or covet material goods – the Friars Minor had to be on an equal footing with the poorest of men. Like the destitute and in the image of Christ, 'who had no place to lay his head', they were not to keep reserves or provisions and were to abstain completely from the world of buying and selling. To meet their daily needs, he and his first companions trusted in Providence and in the work of their hands (begging was only envisaged as a supplement, when it was impossible to find enough to live on by working). From the same perspective, the 'poverello' would rule out possessions of any kind, collective as well as personal. All appropriation implied in their eyes a refusal to share, and thus exposed man to the sin of avarice. They were also aware of the fact that

The fourth Lateran Council condemned the Cathar heresy in 1215. In this drawing, the Fathers of the Council count the archbishops, bishops and abbots present. (Matthew Paris, *Chronica Maiora*, Cambridge, Corpus Christi College.)

religious communities which accepted goods were soon caught up in a system of violence: 'If we owned things, we would have to defend them,' he responded one day to the Bishop of Assisi who was astonished by their poverty. The spirit of ownership was, in their eyes, the source of discord and hate. Thus those who wished to live according to the Gospels had to abstain from all forms of ownership.

The new fraternity was equally distinct from previous religious orders in terms of its structures and way of life. The first Friars Minor in fact lived as itinerant preachers, without a home, and not in convents or monasteries. When they stayed somewhere temporarily, it was either in simple huts or in modest houses put at their disposal by clergy or laity. Even when they began to be settled in permanent establishments, for example in Bologna in 1220, they frequently went out to preach or beg and did not lead a cloistered existence.

More revolutionary still at this time was the fact that, within the order, clergy and laity met on an equal footing. This situation was a clear break with monastic forms of organisation, which were strongly marked by the spirit of feudal hierarchy: with the Cistercians, for example, monks and lay brothers certainly lived in the same monastery, but they formed two distinct groups, each having its own life, the former attending to divine office, the latter to material tasks. The barrier separating them was both cultural and social: the choir monks, from the aristocracy, knew how to read Latin; the lay brothers, usually recruited from the peasantry, were illiterate. St Francis wished to transcend these gulfs by giving to all members of the brotherhood the same rights and the same duties, the essential in his eyes being a common way of life, without compromise regarding poverty.

He himself, for canonical reasons, had to take the tonsure which made him one of the clergy. But he took care to make as little of this as was possible, in order not to be cut off from the plain brothers, and never received more than minor orders. His greatest concern was to abolish within the order all distinctions founded on learning or social rank. The only difference he admitted between clergy and laity was that the former had to read the office each day, while the latter could simply recite the Paternoster. This way of life soon proved to be enormously successful and, by 1230, the order had several thousand members and several hundred establishments. A few decades later, it was solidly established throughout Christendom, exercising considerable influence in all spheres.

At the same time, but in a very different context, another religious order was born and developed, on which the papacy would come to rely heavily in the fight against heresy and the reconquest of society: that of the Friars Preacher, instituted in 1216 by St Dominic, a **421**

Spanish canon. This time it was a matter of priests not laity, or more precisely. of regular canons, as had existed since the late eleventh century. But the novelty of St Dominic's foundation lay in its apostolic objectives: unlike canons or monks, the new religious were not to be shut away in cloisters. If they lived a conventual life, they sought above all to reach men by going out into the world to proclaim the word of God. St Dominic and his companions first established themselves in Languedoc and tried to combat the Cathars on their own territory. They too chose to live in poverty and to own nothing collectively, contrary to the monastic orders. Learned in doctrine, they did not hesitate to confront their adversaries in public controversy, for which a solid knowledge of the Scriptures was necessary. It also brought them some success. But this peaceful means of confrontation did not have time to develop in Languedoc, because Innocent III, angered by the murder of his legate Peter of Castelnau, launched what is called the Albigensian Crusade in the region.

The developing order thus retreated to the main university centres of the time, Paris and Bologna, where it attracted many recruits. Its founder had understood that the ignorance of the clergy in religious matters had frequently allowed heresy to flourish. He therefore stressed the importance of theological training, in order to provide the Church with a body of specialist preachers of a very high standard. This initiative was just what the papacy had wished for, and it supported Dominican efforts. After 1220, the order of preaching friars was firmly established in the large towns, especially in Italy, providing the Church with valuable support in the defence of orthodoxy.

Repression

The other wing of the religious strategy of Innocent III, as of his successors, was the armed struggle against heresy, undertaken alongside the 'recovery' of popular religious movements. Convinced that he could get nothing out of the Count of Toulouse or the lords of the Midi, many of whom were openly or secretly Cathars, in 1208 he chose the path of crusade. This serious decision had weighty consequences. It implied, in fact, that there were entire areas of Christendom which were as estranged from the faith as the lands of pagans or Muslims. But the pope did not hesitate, convinced that the 'anti-Church' of the Cathars must be destroyed before it triumphed. To obtain this end in Languedoc, he relied on the lords of the north, such as Simon de Montfort and the Duke of Burgundy, drawn to the Midi by purely religious motives. The Albigensian Crusade has had a very bad press. It is undeniable that the pitiless massacres perpetrated by northern barons in the south, at Béziers, at Carcassonne, at Toulouse from 1209 to 1212, followed by the crushing of Peter II, King of Aragon, who had also tried his hand, at Muret in 1213, set the southerners against the northerners, and dealt a savage blow to the original structures and culture of southern France. All the same, the Capetian intervention after Simon's death (1218) managed to rally a large part of the aristocracy and the bourgeois to the cause; it is thus excessive to see in the campaigns nothing but a manifestation of royal conquest and imperialism, pushing its power as far as the Mediterranean. In 1229, the Count of Toulouse had to give in and promise his loyal co-operation in wiping out heresy. The last Cathar castles, like that of

Almost contemporary with the events it illustrates, this drawing evokes the capture of Béziers (1209). On the left, the Crusaders' camp; on the right, within its ramparts, the town dominated by the cathedral's tall tower. While the knights make their charge, some footsloggers have already crept in, despite the watch, by one of the gates. Pillage and massacre are about to begin. (*La Guerre des Albigeois*, thirteenth-century manuscript; Paris, Bibliothèque nationale.)

Montségur, were brought down in the reign of St Louis. But nothing was gained as long as this heresy maintained its reserves and support intact at the local level. By an effective policy of intimidation and sanctions, the Inquisition tribunals (1233), in which the Dominicans played a very active part, patiently tracked down the heretics, and by the end of the thirteenth century Catharism existed only in remote mountain valleys, and in the popular forms where dualist myths were combined with folk beliefs, such as we can observe in Montaillou in the early fourteenth century.

In Italy, given the different political and social context, repression took other forms. The autonomy enjoyed by each commune frustrated general measures, such as the imperial constitutions against heresy promulgated by Frederick II in 1224 at the request of the Holy See. Moreover, conflicting powers and abilities among the municipal authorities and the bishops, which existed in many towns, created a climate favourable to heretics, who also enjoyed the protection of the Ghibellines, enemies of the Church's temporal power. The

423

papacy thus tried to insert these constitutions, town by town, into legislation. It relied on the mendicant orders for help in this. Their great popularity led, in some regions, to their being given full powers to reform the communal statutes in a way hostile to heretics. This was the case in Bologna and Verona in 1233, when the Dominican Giovanni of Vicenza, once he was given full powers, had a number of Cathars burned, and again in Lombardy, where the Franciscans did the same. But these episodes were short-lived, and the popularity of these religious stars waned after a few months. The mendicant orders then undertook, with papal support, the creation of groups of pious lay people, as a Catholic party and clerical militia, who not only took the lead against supporters of heresy and the Ghibellines, but also tried to gain power at the municipal level so that repression could become effective. The most outstanding example in this regard was that of the Dominican St Peter Martyr, great preacher and inquisitor, who created in Florence in 1247 the Society of the Faith and ended by being murdered by those he had fought against. By canonising him in 1253, a year after his death, the papacy was clearly indicating the approved path for the defenders of the faith, clergy as well as laity. The result of all these efforts was effective. After the fall of Frederick II in 1250 and the elimination of his descendants, the political triumph of the pope was accompanied by a complete and definitive liquidation of heresy, which succumbed to the blows of an Inquisition which the heretics no longer had any possibility of escaping.

Towards conformity

From the last third of the twelfth century onwards, the Roman Church, having ensured recognition of its primacy, could devote itself to the realisation of the second part of its reform programme, which was aimed at ensuring the triumph of religion not only at the top of the social pyramid but also at its base, in each of its elements. In fact conditions had changed a great deal since the eleventh century, and it was no longer enough for the people to be organised by Christian leaders and made to pay their tithes to the clergy. The masses, in every area, were emerging from their passive roles, as the success of the heretical movements had demonstrated. At the very heart of Christianity the fight was on a new front: that of the winning over of the inner person, whose first witness and inspirer was St Bernard. Soon this battle came to the foreground and required even greater energies and resources than the armed struggle against the infidel. The progress of Catharism in particular obliged the papacy to react promptly, for fear of widespread subversion. This led to an enormous effort, initiated at the third Lateran Council (1179) and reaching a climax at the fourth (1215), designed to make the beliefs and practices of the faithful conform to the demands of the Church.

The pastoral offensive

This pastoral turn of events, which led the clergy to interest themselves more closely in the religious lives of the simple faithful, was not confined, as was often the case, to simply reorganising ecclesiastical structures. It was rather a matter of a fundamental change in catechetics founded on the value of words as instruments of mediation and persuasion. Rather than getting the laity to partake of its written culture, the Church preferred to adapt itself to the essentially oral culture of the former. The result was an extraordinary growth in preaching. This might seem unremarkable to someone in the twentieth century, accustomed to associating sermons with religious services. But in fact it represented a profound change because, during the early Middle Ages, the religion lived and practised by the great majority of those baptised had been reduced to a set of ritual signs and gestures. The language of the liturgy, even in the areas of Romance languages, had become incomprehensible to the faithful. The bishops, for their part, had plenty of other things to worry about besides talking to their congregations about God. Even so, when they went to the trouble of preaching they were not always understood by their flocks, who in any case looked to them primarily to protect them from famine and to carry out exorcisms or miracles. But, little by little, the religious demands of the masses were mounting. The secular clergy had never been able to satisfy their expectations, which explains among other things the success of the heterodox movements. The hierarchy and the clergy who were more aware of contemporary problems understood that, in order to win them back, it was necessary to speak to them in their own language. Neverthless among the peasants, who made up the greater part of the population in the West, there remained, as we have seen, whole layers of folk culture that the Church had not succeeded in dislodging. Some monks, especially the Cistercians and the mendicant orders, understood this very well and tried to 'tame' their audience by using in their sermons secular themes and stories. This led to the fashion for *exempla*, short colourful stories taken from tales or legends and ending in a 'moral', which they did not carry in themselves but which the preacher skilfully grafted on to them. On the other hand, the clergy who were concerned with indoctrinating the urban population became aware of the fact that 'the Christian people', as it was then called, was no more a single unity than society was tripartite. The old distinction between warriors, men of prayer and workers no longer corresponded to social reality, which was much more diverse. Thus if one wanted to reach all groups and social backgrounds, one had to meet them at their particular centres of interest. To this end the Church inaugurated, at the end of the twelfth century, a pastoral outreach to various kinds of people, or more precisely, extended to the working world that effort of adaptation which it had undertaken for nearly a century with regard to the knightly class. Alongside the military saints, exalted in the preaching and religious iconography of the twelfth century, artisan and merchant saints now made their appearance, as protectors of the trades which were increasing in the towns. Innocent III ratified this development by canonising in 1199 St Homobono, a draper from Cremona who had died two years earlier. And in 1261 the Archbishop of Pisa, Federigo Visconti, did not hesitate to say in a sermon given to businessmen: 'It must be very pleasing to merchants to know that their colleague St Francis was himself a merchant, and that he was sanctified in our era!' The same tendency to favour the trade and status of people is found in the confessors' manuals which flourished at this period – here one can see a powerful effort being made to Christianise the notion of work and professional ethics.

These efforts to bring religion closer to people's lives were not always successful, for the very reason that there were incompatibilities between clerical and lay cultures. Even when they had merely a veneer of Latin learning, priests and monks were convinced of their superiority to the faithful. Even if they preached in the local idiom, the message they transmitted remained rather crushing. Their listeners in fact, unlike today's congregations, had no access to the sources of this teaching and no way of controlling it. Also the clergy's addresses, larded with biblical or literary references, aroused less spiritual support than impassioned reactions ranging from delirious enthusiasm to vehement protest. So too the attention given by the clergy to problems of social life had more to do with strategy than a change of attitude towards secular realities and work. Ecclesiastical culture continued to favour basically rural values, and even a great Dominican preacher like Humbert de Romans, in the mid-thirteenth century, continued to set the peasants, who were naturally excluded from the world of violence and money-making and atoned for their faults by manual labour, against the bourgeois and artisans of the towns, who had every chance of being corrupt because they did not live by natural products but by the exchange of goods and wealth.

In order to understand both the extent and the limits of the thirteenth-century pastoral offensive, we should ask ourselves what its objectives were. The aim of the mendicant orders and the clergy (who were concerned with the care of souls, the *cura animarum*), was not so much the struggle against unbelief, which was an unusual condition and limited to a few exceptional minds, as the eradication of false beliefs. In short, they wanted to get people to believe the right thing and act in the right way. Many of the faithful had been swayed by the influence of heterodox movements; others continued to be attached to practices which the clergy, coming from the schools or universities, were quick to describe as magical or diabolical. Between heresy and superstition, preachers sought to define for their listeners a middle way, by conveying a few essential doctrinal ideas and above all by imposing devotional and pious practices that were uniform. Among the latter, the Church thus placed most value on the sacraments, and especially on confession. This was the particular importance of the famous Canon XXI of the fourth Lateran Council (1215), which made it obligatory for all the faithful to confess and take communion at least once a year. For this reason, most of the sermons of the period addressed to the people were given in Lent, which was the main season for both preaching and penitence. Terrible threats were uttered against those who neglected their religious obligations, and we know how much medieval iconography drew on the theme of the death of unrepentant sinners, of misers and the lustful, frequently represented in cathedral carvings.

The long-term effects of this insistent chorus were remarkable. Religious practice became uniform. Devotion to the Virgin and to the humanity of Christ became the universal language of Roman Christianity. The liturgy itself became more homogeneous as the new orders spread throughout Europe the usages and calendar of the Roman *curia*. It was not just the problem of the last agonies that became, under the effect of the new catechetics, one of the principal concerns of all the faithful. From the twelfth century onwards, some clergy had maintained that there was a place where bodily pains earned by sin could be expiated after death. We know how important this was to become, in sermons as well as in Western consciousness – the theme of purgatory which was to find its literary expression with Dante in the *Divine Comedy*.

Measuring the effectiveness of this attempt at fixing and homogenising religious beliefs is difficult. Attempting to appreciate the impact of the new catechesis by trusting the complaints that abound in the normative texts of the age would be as misleading as trusting the demonstrations of remarkable spiritual vitality which may be observed amongst some fervent groups of penitents or beguines. Neverthless, we have to say that in the thirteenth century, through confraternities and the Third Orders, a devout élite was formed which was not simply recruited from the ranks of the higher aristocracy. Members of the laity, among whom women were the most numerous, showed themselves capable not only of maintaining a dialogue with the clergy on an equal footing, but even of impressing them on a spiritual level, as in the case of St Elizabeth of Hungary-Thuringia, or of St Louis of France. But this concerned a minority only, and the bulk of the laity, outside the transient popular movements, seemed to remain relatively indifferent to the religious programme that the clergy was proposing, which could only reflect the practices and spirituality of the latter. Everything in fact happened as though the ultimate objective of this pastoral offensive had been the clericalisation of the laity and not its promotion. This inadequacy was the consequence of the cultural situation. The pastors, increasingly marked by scholasticism, claimed to be the only ones who knew what real Christianity was, and tended to regard the minds of their flocks as malleable material, to be moulded as they saw fit. This was the period when the Church defined the field of belief with ever-increasing precision, and when ignorance began to be classified as error. The growth of preaching was contemporaneous with that of the Inquisition. Through their desire to impose a religious model which implied support of their own culture and system of values, the clergy ended by marginalising a large section of the faithful and by provoking the exasperation of many others, who were no less Christian than they were, but who wanted to be Christian in their own ways.

The death of tolerance

The period stretching from the beginning of the twelfth century to the middle of the thirteenth is characterised by both a diminished sense of tolerance and a worsening of conditions for ethnic and religious minorities. This development was particularly noticeable in Italy, where the Norman conquest had brought under a single dominant power peoples who spoke Greek and followed the Orthodox rite, together with Arabs and Jews, and also in Spain, where the *Reconquista* advanced after the victory of Las Navas de Tolosa in 1212.

In fact, the relative tolerance which reigned in these regions and which had made them from the mid-eleventh through the twelfth centuries a melting-pot of cultures and civilisations was an exceptional phenomenon, being mainly the result of a balance of powers rather than ideological choice. In southern Italy and in Sicily, the Norman rulers, especially Roger I and Roger II, had to rely on all sorts of force and to guarantee privileges and respect for the customs of local populations in order to impose their authority. Furthermore, for political ends, they had understood all the advantages to be gained from the support of Greek clergy, who did not submit to the pope and were trained to respect the power of the monarchy. As for the Muslims, there were many of them in Sicily and they had to be reckoned with. Further, their contribution on a cultural level, like that of the Jews. was considerable, and the court of Palermo owed much of its brilliance to them.

In Spain, the situation was somewhat different, but the fact that a number of Mozarabic Christians were living in Muslim emirates in the south obliged the architects of the *Reconquista* for a long time to treat carefully those of their new subjects who remained faithful to Islam. After 1150, however, these subtle balances deteriorated and the minorities were increasingly harried. The Crusades were certainly a factor in this. In leading the Christian masses to see the Muslims as the enemies of the true God, and the Jews as the murderers of Christ, they created and sustained a growing climate of hostility. The return of hostilities on a grand scale in the Holy Land at the end of the twelfth century profoundly disturbed the consciousness of the Westerners, who dreamed of nothing but 'avenging the honour of God', and for whom any tolerance with regard to Islam had become weakness or treason. St Louis aligned himself exactly with this new attitude when he stated that one must not argue with such people, but rush upon them. As for Christians who did not belong to the Roman Church, developments were no more favourable. The disdainful if not hostile welcome reserved for the Crusaders by the Byzantines, especially during the second Crusade, left the Westerners with deep resentments which, skilfully exploited by the Venetians, resulted in the capture of Constantinople in 1204. Even more than the schism in 1054, this saw the opening up of a gulf of contempt and sometimes hatred between Latins and Greeks, which was to last for centuries.

Even before this, the strengthening of hierarchical structures within the Roman Church had been conducive to the gradual Latinisation of the clergy and the liturgy. Starting in Sardinia, where Greek monasticism had been important since the tenth century, this process developed in southern Italy in the second half of the twelfth century. It was encouraged in Sicily by a large influx of Italians. The balance between the ethnic communities was destroyed, and under the last Norman kings, William I and William II, Greeks and Muslims lost the relatively favourable position they had held. The former managed to survive in a few regions where there were enough of them to form a bloc, the latter ended up by revolting at the beginning of Frederick II's reign. Beaten and decimated, they lost their traditional autonomy and lingered on as part of the mass of the Christian population. It was the same in Spain at a later date.

This phenomenon of closure and rejection may be found even more plainly in relations between Jews and Christians. Of course the legal status of the Jews, since the early Middle Ages, had relegated them to the margins of society. But apart from certain brief and localised periods of tension, under the Merovingians and Carolingians the situation of the Jews in the West had not in fact been particularly unfavourable. Placed under the protection of the bishops, for whom they provided important economic and financial services, they benefited from a degree of autonomy and could practise their religion without hindrance; we

have discussed earlier what economic or political place they could claim. Moreover, before

Jews praying in a Spanish synagogue, fourteenth century. (MS Or. 2884, London, British Museum.)

the twelfth century, not all of them lived in towns, and Jews could be found in the country, where some of them were involved in agricultural activities. But the growth of commerce and the renewal of exchange required their concentration in urban settings. They often formed large and autonomous communities, ruled by their own leaders and having one or several synagogues as well as rabbinical schools, as we might note in Rouen and Paris, or in the large episcopal cities of the Rhine valley. They were connected to each other by a constant traffic of travellers and correspondence. Jewish merchants and scholars coming from Muslim Spain and even the East often visited their co-religionists in the West, and it was thanks to these economic and cultural exchanges that links survived, in the tenth and eleventh centuries, between the two shores of the Mediterranean.

In this period Jews and Christians, though perfectly distinct, maintained some contact. In the towns, the Jewish quarter was at first like a parish grouped around the synagogue rather than a ghetto. The influence was mutual, especially on the religious and cultural level. Moreover the Jews served as interpreters, particularly in relations with the Muslim world, and monastic exegetes, especially among the Cistercians, did not hesitate to consult rabbis about the original text of the Bible, and search for solutions to the obscurities of the Vulgate in the *veritas hebraica*. It is significant, on the other hand, that Abelard employed a Jewish intellectual – the incarnation of rabbinical scholarship and attachment to the Law – in his famous *Dialogue between a Philosopher, a Jew and a Christian* of 1140–2. Finally, we know about the intellectual influence of the Spanish Jews in the transmission of the works of Antiquity to the West, especially the works of Aristotle. All this implies an advanced level of exchange, at least at the level of the cultivated élites. But this situation which, without being idyllic, at least allowed the Jews to live in relative tranquillity, was not slow to deteriorate. Here again the Crusades mark a turning-point, and we have referred above to the appearance of pogroms and expulsions, the source of exile and retreat for these communities.

Confronted by these outbreaks of violence, the authorities adopted an ambiguous attitude. The ecclesiastical hierarchy and the papacy defended the Jews, stating that it was up to God, not man, if need be, to take vengeance for harm done to his Son. The Jews, said St Bernard, were witnesses to the Passion of Christ in our midst, and their presence was useful to Christians. But the protection given them by the bishops became more and more dubious. By the end of the twelfth century, the Jews had been forced to weaken their contacts with Christians; any form of proselytising was forbidden them, while measures were taken to encourage those Jews who wished to convert to Christianity. As for the lay authorities, they sought above all to profit from the situation, making use of popular hostility to sell their protection dearly, and periodically taking expulsionary measures against the Jews, notably in France from the time of Philip Augustus, quickly followed by periods of tolerance, each heavily financed by the leaders of the Jewish community. But insecurity constantly increased: in England and then in France accusations of ritual murder (the murder of a Christian child by Jews) began to appear on to which, in the thirteenth century, were grafted accusations of profanation of the Host (an example is the miracle of the Church of Les Billettes, in Paris, where the profaned Host began to bleed). All this resulted in the Jews

Montségur castle (Ariège), the religious centre of the Cathars for fifteen years, 1230–44

Ortenburg castle, lower Rhine, thirteenth century

Chateau Gaillard, Richard the Lionheart's fortress at Andelys (Eure), late twelfth century

Castle Trim, Ireland, thirteenth century

being surrounded with an aura of superstition and making them the designated victims of all sorts of violence, whether from the unleashed crowds or the authorities, who were very happy to use them as scapegoats.

Thus between 1100 and 1250, manifestations of dissent and the right to differences in the religious domain gradually disappeared. At the end of this process, Roman Christianity had become a homogeneous cultural entity, and minorities and dissidents were reduced to living in its shadow. Within it, the Inquisition tracked down heresy to its final refuges. Outside it, the West in its broadly expansionist way sought to impose its rites and beliefs everywhere. In the East, the Church installed a Latin hierarchy wherever it could. It was only able to conceive of a Christian unity – as we can see by the first council of Lyons and especially by the second council (1274) – in the form of complete submission of the 'schismatics' to all the demands of the papacy.

A uniform expression

The fiction of a stable thirteenth century, of a sort of golden age, the 'time of my lord St Louis', the era of the great universities and cathedrals, has long since been challenged. First of all, the last decades of the century cannot be included in such a fiction, since we see in each one the indications of a crisis in growth; and secondly, the entire first half of the century, as we have seen, was marked by storms and rumblings. Nevertheless, the angelic vision of a community joined in prayer and study is not entirely erroneous. The essence of that century (with the year 1200 at its centre) which has come down to us, speaks of peace and light; we forget the wars, usury and spiritual repression, ignore the crushing of popular culture, the triumph of the rich, the blind pride of the Church. Perhaps the common memory, in letting this sediment settle, is more just than that of the professional historian; we should end with the following picture of the Christian world, the balance sheet of an adolescence finally entering maturity.

The scholarly explosion

One of the great cultural innovations of the twelfth century was the rapid expansion of urban schools. Not that monastery schools suddenly disappeared: in the imperial lands, in England and in Italy, they retained a certain standing right up to the era of universities. But it was no longer in them that new forms of learning were developed, forms that went beyond ecclesiastical circles to touch increasingly large groups. Their success was linked, of course, to the expansion of the towns, whose population and extent were rapidly growing at the time. It was also supported by the development of the countryside, which provided bishops and chapters with material resources not only for constructing fine cathedrals, but also for engaging some teachers on a permanent basis. The papacy encouraged this movement in the hope of raising the level of learning among the clergy. From 1079, cathedral chapters were obliged to open and run a school. A century later, Alexander III required each bishopric to pay for the services of a master in theology who was to devote himself entirely to the study and explication of the word of God. Because these schools remained Church institutions, they were placed under the direction of a canon of the chapter, supervisor of the school or chancellor, who sometimes did the teaching himself or, more often, gave this task to others, the *magistri* (masters), who specialised in the profession. In the best centres of scholarship, it was soon the custom to call on clergy from outside the town or the region who were renowned for their learning. The pupils enjoyed the legal status and the privileges of clerks. There were certainly future priests among them, but most of them did not see themselves as priests nor even as taking minor orders. Since teaching was considered as a ministry of the Church the teachers were obliged to be celibate, which is why Héloïse refused Abelard when he proposed marriage to his pupil, in order to atone for the wrong he had done her. As she genuinely loved him, she did not wish marriage to destroy a potentially brilliant career. Alongside these episcopal schools, there developed in the twelfth century those of the regular canons, of which the most famous were Saint-Victor and Sainte-Geneviève in Paris.

As the twelfth century advanced, the tie binding schools to the local ecclesiastical structures was lengthened and relaxed. The influx of students meant that the chancellors had to authorise a growing number of masters to teach, but could only exercise distant control over them. Teaching did not yet become secular, but the masters benefited from greater freedom of expression, the more so as they became skilled at making profitable use of the diversity of eccesiastical institutions. Thus in Paris most of them established themselves on the Left Bank, answerable to the canons of Sainte-Geneviève and the monks of Saint-Germain-des-Prés, and thus were exempt from episcopal authority. It was there that the Latin Quarter – as it was called from the thirteenth century – grew up.

Faced with the reluctance of some prelates, Pope Alexander III adopted a liberal policy in the granting of teaching licences (*licentia docendi*), which allowed the opening of a school. Chancellors had to grant this without payment and could not refuse it to any clerk who could prove his competence and aptitude in teaching. These measures allowed the number of masters to multiply and gave rise to a veritable scholastic 'explosion', which touched all social groups by the end of the twelfth century. The demand for instruction was very high everywhere: alongside the schools with international reputations, like those in Paris or Bologna, many middle-sized towns in this period created scholarly institutions for instruction at an elementary level. In Italy and Flanders we even see the opening of schools independent of the Church, where notaries and merchants were trained. Latin remained the basis of instruction, but these schools also taught practical subjects in the vernacular, useful for merchants and the wealthier peasants. In England, in the mid-thirteenth century, a certain number of villeins were perfectly capable of keeping account books or drafting rural leases.

Excepting these small, specialised schools (which we would call technical schools today), whose operation we do not in fact know much about, the contents of instruction and the study programme were in principle the same everywhere. The academic organisation, which went back to the Carolingian era, was inspired by both the concept of Christian **432** knowledge which St Augustine had defined and the classification of the seven liberal arts

The expansion of knowledge: the astronomer with his astrolabe (used to measure the height of the stars above the horizon), the clerk and the calculator. (Illustration from the *Psalter of St Louis and of Blanche of Castile*; MS 1186, Paris, Bibliothèque de l'Arsenal.)

inherited from late Antiquity. The subjects taught, considered to be auxiliary to the *sacra doctrina* (the knowledge of the Scriptures and Christian revelation), were divided into the *quadrivium* (arithmetic, geometry, astronomy and music) and the *trivium* (grammar, rhetoric and dialectics). But this was more a matter of theoretical classification than of an obligatory programme of study. Outside certain centres such as Chartres and Seville, the study of the *quadrivium* was neglected almost everywhere. Even a great mind like Abelard had no interest in mathematics and natural sciences. It is true that in Antiquity these were also not very highly regarded, and that for a long time they had a rather fantastic, if not magic aspect (herbals, treatises on stones). In the majority of cases, the interpretation of the material world scarcely went beyond the cosmological theories inspired by Genesis or Plato and Aristotle, for whom, as we know, the modern distinction between philosophy and natural sciences did not exist. Only a few curious minds such as the Englishmen Adelard of Bath or Daniel of Morley showed particular interest in the sciences. They still tackled the study of natural sciences in an empirical and technical manner.

The knowledge dispensed in the medieval schools, then, was essentially literary and very much influenced by classical models. Teaching itself was based on texts from the Psalter (from which people learnt to read) to the Latin authors such as Cicero, Ovid or Boethius, or the Greeks translated into Latin such as Plato and Aristotle, who were gradually rediscovered in this period. The master was no more than the interpreter of these

433

authorities, but in the twelfth century his commentary became more extensive and ended up as a text in its own right, to be written in the margin of the other. Masters were no longer content merely to explain difficult words, they tried to extricate the deeper meanings of the text or its doctrinal content. The boldest masters did not hesitate to adopt a critical attitude with regard to the great thinkers of Antiquity and the Fathers of the primitive Church.

To be master of one's 'thought'

Although the Church had harshly hammered home and jealously guarded its teachings, it had not completely stifled the search for knowledge and the practice of meditation and contemplation. Indeed, it was the men of the Church themselves, rather than the illustrious monks, who were striving to extend the body of knowledge. Such knowledge came from the 'Gentiles', the Ancients, but also from the Muslims, who transmitted the message enriched by their own reflections. Against the closed and militant religious orders, where 'holy ignorance' was preached by figures such as St Bernard, we see the openness of mind and thought of men like Peter, abbot of Cluny, who dreamed of having the Koran translated. Others saw more clearly just what the faith could gain from a confrontation with the knowledge of others; at the beginning of the twelfth century, the 'Bible' of Guiot of Provins, which reflected the hopes of Parisian clerks, cursed the 'stinking, horrible' times of isolation, and Honorius Augustodunensis declared, 'For man, ignorance is exile.'

Hugh of Saint-Victor, Ivo of Chartres and Peter the Venerable were among the famous prelates or abbots who courageously grappled with the new study of Plato, Aristotle, Seneca, Pythagoras and Ovid; in the thirteenth century the Dominicans, wisely following these examples, ensured that they had the decisive weapon, with regard to secular masters as well as also heretics, of comparative knowledge of dogmas and metaphysical systems. It was the period – right in the middle of the Crusades – in which Christianity opened itself to the lessons of the Muslims: a flood of 'Arab' treatises reached the Sicily of Roger II, Catalonia, Languedoc and Provence, Campania and Venice. The mathematical works of al-Khwarizmi, the medical treatises of Avicenna, al-Razi and al-Battani were translated and read; after 1220 or 1230 the commentaries of Averroes on Aristotle and the reflections of Maimonides reached beyond the Pyrenees. Far from succumbing either to contempt or adulation, the thinkers, doctors and geometricians of Palermo, Salerno and Montpellier examined, criticised and absorbed these works. The flame of reasoning blazed again.

The use of reason, the dialectical method, played a great part in the 'liberal arts' as taught in the cathedral schools. In the early twelfth century, William of Champeaux in Paris used it to criticise Aristotle, the philosopher *par excellence*. But the authorities feared the corrosive effect on faith and dogma of Aristotle's writings on physics or metaphysics, where the material world slipped away from the divine; and in Paris, again around 1210, teaching Aristotle's ideas was theoretically forbidden. But all this was too late: the man of 1130 or 1150 already felt himself an artisan quite exceptional in Creation – a man at work on the world, a *homo faber* in the likeness of God – and his curiosity could not be suppressed. In their disorderly, provocative demonstrations, the Goliards attacked the whole established order, showing in their own way a desire to shake off the yoke of dogma.

There was still a shortage of men to set an example for this revolution in thought. In France, this was the role of Peter Abelard, the first 'professor'. This Breton clerk, indifferent to the futile subtleties of a straightforward reading of the Scriptures, was the first to break with the traditional teaching of the cloisters. In open revolt, after 1120, against the Bishop of Paris, he drew his captivated followers to the Latin Quarter. Here he came to be persecuted for his private life by the jealous, and for his faith by the mystics; the hostility of St Bernard obliged him to retire to Cluny where, up to his death in 1142, Abbot Peter treated him with respect and charity.

However, in his masterpiece entitled *Sic et non* (*Yes and No*), Abelard presented and tested a method which enabled him to surmount the contradictions that existed between the authorities themselves. As for Alan of Lille, he went so far as to write that 'authority has a nose of wax', which is to say that citing an authority was merely a formality which did not impede. Thus, one of the most important advances of the intellectual and cultural renaissance of the twelfth century, at least on the level of general culture and the development of mental attitudes, was the rapid expansion of logic. While monastic learning had above all valued rhetoric (the art of language and discourse), the great masters of the twelfth-century school emphasised dialectic, which one can broadly define as the art and manner of judging everything on the grounds of intelligibility and truth. The first person to apply this method systematically was Abelard himself, but he was only responding to the expectations of his listeners: 'My students required human and rational reasons and they needed intelligible explanations rather than citations from authorities. They claimed that it was useless to speak unless what one said was also explained and that people could only believe what they had first grasped through understanding, and that it was ridiculous for a teacher to lecture others on what neither he nor those he taught could understand' (Abelard, *History of my Misfortunes*, ch. 9).

Under pressure from his students, the 'knight errant of dialectic' did not hestitate to turn his rational speculation to revealed truth. His aim was to construct a 'theology' – a new word which scandalised traditionalists like St Bernard, who characterised as impertinence an intellectual approach which consisted of applying categories of the human mind to the divine world. Nevertheless, it would be wrong to interpret the conflict between the Parisian master and the abbot of Clairvaux as a simple opposition between rationalism and spiritualism. The former never maintained that his comparisons were exact equivalents of the reality of dogma or that they could plumb the profound mystery of God. It was rather a clash between two kinds of learning: monastic exegesis, literary and Scripture-based, oriented towards prayer and contemplation, and scholastic philosophy, which wanted to put at the service of the faith the potent curiosity and investigatory power of reason. Abelard, condemned in 1140 by the Council of Sens, was for the moment a defeated figure. But in fact he was the real victor because it was his method, cleared of his rather glib and sometimes conceited optimism, which was to become the basis of medieval scholarship. **435**

Furthermore, with him appeared a new type of man of learning: the intellectual, who would soon be called the academic. Of course previous ages had known knowledgeable men and thinkers of a very high standard, like Bede or St Anselm. But their activity had been primarily hermeneutic: within ecclesiastical society, their role was to devote themselves to the analysis of sacred texts, studying the words, searching for hidden meanings, truer than the literal ones. By these efforts they hoped to discover the key to an understanding and explanation of history and society. Biographers of saints, chroniclers, authors of biblical commentaries, these clerks had a unified, world-wide vision of learning and life which they sought to transmit smoothly to suceeding generations. With Abelard, this global vision and tranquil certainty disappeared. The field of knowledge was broken up, specialisation appeared and a critical attitude became the rule. Paris was set fair to be the new Jerusalem. Emerging from the bosom of the Church and its encompassing vision, the intellectuals were led to set up new forms of solidarity in order to exercise freely an activity which was becoming separate from religious authority and drawing closer to other professions.

The nascent university: humanism?

In some of the more important centres of learning, which were first called *studium generale*, we see what were in effect universities appearing between 1180 and 1230. These took the form of professional associations (the word *universitas* referred to any organised trade in the Latin texts of the period) – assemblies of masters and students.

They were not formed in the same way everywhere: in Paris, universities emerged from the initiatives of secular masters, who had become numerous and who were trying to escape the chancellor's supervision. They united with their students to defend their corporate rights against the civil and local Church authorities. In Bologna, on the other hand, where law was the main subject, it was the students who came from other countries to learn the new disciplines who formed an association, or guild, drafting the law and negotiating with the commune in order to obtain for themselves and their teachers privileged status. Their efforts were suported by Emperor Frederick Barbarossa, who took them under his protection in 1159. For their part, the Parisian academics received support from the papacy, which clearly saw in this new institution a way of by-passing local and national particularities and of training clerks, especially theologians, who would be able to explain and defend Christian doctrine against its detractors. They were also supported by the king, who was not displeased by the idea of limiting the power of the bishop: the Parisian masters received a concession from Pope Celestine III in 1194, backing from the king in 1200, the personal protection of Innocent III in 1205, and statutes were finally granted in 1215 by the legate Robert de Courçon, and ratified in 1229 by the regent, Blanche of Castile. Other universities were created at the beginning of the thirteenth century at Orléans (literary studies and civil law) from 1227 to 1268, at Montpellier (medicine and law) from 1225 to 1256, and at Oxford (1214–40).

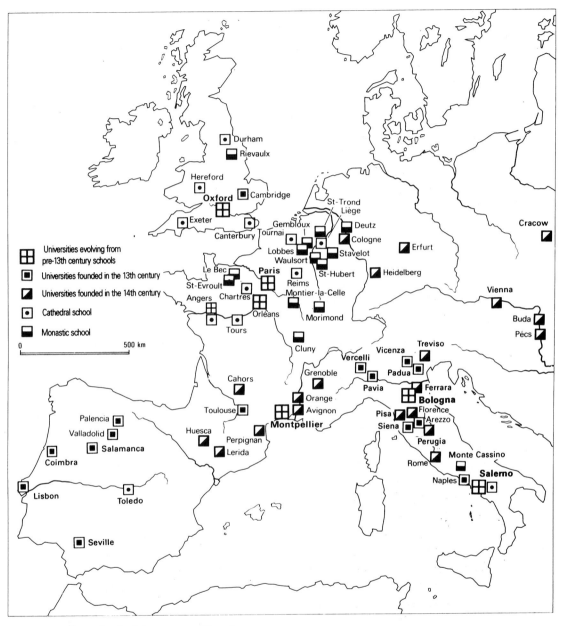

Map 16. Intellectual and religious centres of learning.

These were specialist centres, and people came from great distances to study there. Like the mendicant orders, the university assembled men from all levels of society and all the lands of the West. It had independent legislation, statutes guaranteed by the highest religious and civil authorities, and it gave rise to a new social group, the *ordo scholasticus*, which transcended the traditional distinction between clergy and laity. Even though the academics benefited from the privileges of clerks, they were not tonsured and only a very small proportion of them would go on to an ecclesiastical career. Most of those attending university sought a higher qualification in order to gain access to the upper echelons of the State or society. Stemming as it did from the unpremeditated assembly of intellectual workers, and not simply from the wish of a prince or pope, the university was from the outset a highly self-conscious institution. From the thirteenth century, legends circulated in Paris according to which Charlemagne had transferred the higher learning (*translatio studii*) from Rome to Paris, and, in Bologna in 1229 a false document was discovered, which was taken as authentic, according to which the creation of its law schools dated back to one of the last Roman emperors, Theodosius II. These were no more than fables, but the university, conscious of having formed itself, took the stance of being a third power, founded on knowledge and science, alongside the Church and the State. Moreover, from the thirteenth century the professors of law at Bologna demanded to be called *domini* and claimed knightly status, extolling the sciences which made them, according to Ceno da Pistoia, 'the fathers and brothers of princes'.

In return for their recognition by religious and secular wings of the established order, the universities had to accept a common discipline, from provisions regulating dress, ceremonies and communal rites to the organisation of studies into a coherent programme (*ratio studiorum*), which in Paris was fixed at the beginning of the thirteenth century. The era in which masters taught independently of one another in front of students who departed when they thought they had learnt enough was past. Professors were grouped by faculty (art, theology, civil and canon law and medicine). The arts constituted a sort of foundation course which had to be followed (probably between the ages of fifteen to twenty) in order to enter the other faculties. A minimum period of study was laid down: eight years for theology and civil law, six years for canon law. The stages of an academic career, marked by a series of grades, took shape. One began as a 'bachelor' before gaining a doctorate and a degree, which allowed one to practise as a 'master', i.e. teacher. At each stage it was necessary to pass examinations and especially to provide proof of the ability to master a question in an oral exposition and a 'dispute' (*quaestio disputata*). In the presence of masters from the university, a candidate used the dialectical method to overcome the contradictions between the authors or theses which were the subject of his commentary. From the late twelfth century there was a concern with organising into a doctrinal body the different *quaestiones* debated in the schools. This effort produced works such as Peter Lombard's *Book of Sentences*, which outlined the main problems of theology and indicated the solutions proposed by the Parisian masters. In the field of law, there appeared major works of commentators, like the *Glossa ordinaria* synthesised by Johannes Teutonicus or the *Summa Codicis* of

Azo (*c.* 1230–40) which served as the basis of civil law teaching until the end of the Middle Ages.

Under the influence of these teaching structures and 'summas', there developed in the universities a mentality common to all who attended them, even if they were organised in 'nations'. This new scholarly learning was founded mainly on the use of texts, because instruction took as its point of departure the commentaries of authoritative writers. As books were costly, the students who could not afford them copied them page for page from a reliable copy held at the university bookseller's. Little by little the book lost its sacred or prestigious character and became a working tool. Gothic writing became cursive and uniform, and abbreviations increased. This was a far cry from the sumptuous calligraphy of the monastic *scriptoria*. The academic manuscripts of the thirteenth century are all alike and no longer display the finely decorated capital letters or coloured illuminations. Even the originality of the teaching tended to decline from the years 1250–70. The universal curiosity and intellectual boldness of the preceding era was blunted; the masters were above all trying to organise knowledge and synthesise it into compendiums offering a coherent and unified vision of the whole domain of knowledge. Encylopaedic ambitions, an intellectual and bookish approach to problems, a desire for rationality – these were the characteristic traits of the scholarly culture developing in the universities. This 'scholasticism' was quite different from what had flourished in the monasteries and even the cathedral schools in the eleventh and twelfth centuries.

Teaching at this time was not essentially for professional ends, unlike the other forms of association of the period. The student might become a master in his turn, but that was not the student's aim; rather, he was learning, honing his mind. There was no subscription to pay, and no salary was received either; there was no place of learning, not even a library; the student followed the master to whom he had attached himself, wherever it pleased him to give his commentary. The advantages of this absolute liberty are as plain as its inconveniences, because either the student was rich, which established a regrettable process of selection, or else his poverty led him to angle for a benefice, some work, a place in one of the 'colleges' where a patron lived, such as that of Robert de Sorbon in Paris. As for the master, he too had to fish for some remuneration and, from 1220, the competition from the preaching orders (by definition untroubled by these secular needs) risked stealing his listeners, because the Dominicans did not take payment.

All this did not prevent the university from appearing – from 1220 to 1270 – as the ideal crucible for early 'humanism', which was emerging as a fragile and delicate synthesis of faith and reason. Paris, which was gradually assuming the role of capital of Christendom, saw an influx of foreign masters wanting to make their contribution: the Englishmen – Alexander of Hales (d. 1245) and a bishop of Lincoln, Robert Grosseteste (d. 1253), defenders of experimentation; the Italian Bonaventura (d. 1274), and the German Albert of Cologne (d. 1280), whose lectures in the mid-thirteenth century served as the basis of the *Summa Theologica* of St Thomas Aquinas (d. 1274), also an Italian, and, like Albert, a Dominican. This high point of Christian metaphysical thought, however, was attained

439

Map 17. The Romanesque and Gothic in the West.

amidst serious difficulties. These arose from the rivalry between the brothers and secular masters, from the eviction of poor students, and from anxious authorities. This is why we might say that the blossoming of the universities occupied a very brief period, although that does not detract from the value of its example. In fact, under the influence of the academics, discourse about God very soon tended to become unintelligible to non-specialists. St Bernard's exclamation that 'people discuss the Holy Trinity at every crossroads and

440

the simple claim to have access to the most secret mysteries of the faith' was no longer valid a century later. Theological speculation had become a subject for examination in the schools, and the subject unfolded in a coded language.

This is why, from the beginning of the thirteenth century, things began to change within the academic world. If the theologians continued to play a major role, especially in Paris, they were in close competition with the lawyers, whose influence extended not only to the Church but to the whole of society. From the end of the twelfth century in Italy, canon (eccelesiastical) law was separated from theology and came under the influence of civil law. In Bologna at the time of Johannes Bassianus, the first doctor *utriusque juris*, of Azo and Accursius, a Roman-canonic law was created that would be widely disseminated. This convergence was not obvious and from the council of Tours (1163) to Honorius III (1219), the Church strenuously tried to forbid monks and clerks to learn and teach civil law. But canon lawyers were aware of the precision of Roman legal language and borrowed extensively from it between 1190 and 1215. Furthermore, the papacy found in it confirmation of its rights to promulgate laws. At a time when it was making the pope its emperor, the Roman Church could not long ignore these texts, which showed the prince as superior to laws (*legibus solutus*) and as a sovereign law-giver. At the same time Roman law was opened to the influence of Christian morality and secular constitutions bore the signs of this. Ecclesiastical and legal authorities henceforth spoke the same language, based on the *Digest* and Gratian's *Decretum*, and blended in Church and State.

In the thirteenth century a new language, that of the jurists, was imposed on society; and in its turn it came to exclude all those, mainly the bourgeois and peasants, who could not penetrate its mysteries. Thus began the rule of the men of law and the doctors of the schools.

The art of numbers and light

There is nothing artificial in associating artistic expression with philosophical thought: they are simply the two faces of the same mastery and the same need. Born, as it were spontaneously, in various regions between 1060 and 1130, Romanesque art drew its powerful originality from the fact that it was the first genuinely independent form of European feeling. It has been said earlier that its principal characteristics fully express the emotional life of the time: a return to the human form but with a 'folk' or magical background; magnificent commissions executed according to a long-matured and unified plan; the predominance of massive structures, balanced with a kind of restrained power ready to thrust towards the heavens. These aspirations went beyond the mid-twelfth century, not only in Provence and Italy, which were then fractious components of the Empire, but also in Burgundy, Auvergne and Poitou. A number of buildings, notably monastic ones such as those at Vézelay, Saint-Savin or La Charité, were not completed and decorated until after 1150.

At that time a new form of expression had already been born, so stupidly described as 'Gothic' or 'barbaric' by the neophytes of the renaissance of Antiquity. This time, this art

Gothic art: the main portal of Bourges cathedral (*c.* 1165).

had a cradle, the Ile-de-France, which earned it the name in the Middle Ages of *opus francigenum*, 'French work'.

It was a royal art, linked at the beginning with the Capetian triumph, but also conceived as such in England, in Castile, in central Germany. It was an urban art, perhaps because after 1175 or 1200 it was in the towns that the need for construction or reconstruction was strongest. It did not take its specific style from architecture, unlike the Romanesque innovations: the buildings had identical plans, often comparable shapes. Some of its characteristics that the profane eye happily recognises – the diagonal ribbing under the vaults, the

442

galleries, the broken arches – had been known and used here and there since 1100; even the flying buttress was no more than a means of support enabling the thrust of the vault to be higher. On the other hand, it was precisely this concern to soar upwards, the striking progress from walls to the glass cages of the Sainte-Chapelle or Saint-Urbain de Troyes, which broke with the Romanesque; mere figures were not the key difference (48 metres in height being the record elevation at Beauvais) as there were more impressive heights in the East. And there was also a concern with mathematical balance, which was difficult to calculate, and with light. In this supreme embodiment of Christian art there was a metaphysical dimension which was close to the philosophical thought of the time.

Another similar trait was to be seen in the way the decoration (not only the sculptures which spilled over the entire surface of buildings, but also the frescoes, stained glass, even the miniatures on parchment) rejected the fantastic or symbolic so dear to the Romanesque artists; proportion was respected, the human face became more naturalistic, on effigies as well as in scenes taken from the Scriptures. Expressions relaxed into smiles; instead of the often vengeful and suffering mood of the Romanesque there were tranquil scenes with familiar, secular motifs. In other words, while it was of course the glory of Christ, and that of the Virgin, which was to be magnified, we also see man in his seasonal labours, his trades and his local devotions.

It was natural that the first building sites should appear in Capetian territory, all the more so as Romanesque art had not been outstanding there: the royal abbey of Saint-Denis in 1135 was the first of a series, although some scholars would want to slip in Sens and Durham around 1128, not that it matters much.

In concentric circles of increasing radius, the most accomplished of these buildings emerged slowly from the ground: Chartres, Laon, Noyon by 1155; Paris, Canterbury, Lincoln by 1175; Chartres again, Bourges and Le Mans around 1200, Amiens in 1220, Rheims and Beauvais in 1225; Salisbury, Dijon, Strasburg, Angers; then, far from the initial cradle, Burgos and Toledo by 1225, and Bamberg, Magdeburg and Naumberg. Italy held out, from St Mark's in Venice and Torcello to Anagni and Spoleto. An original form was sketched there which would be sampled only later in the north. For the moment this art smacked of Byzantium, the Maghrib and ancient Rome: it was not at all 'Gothic'.

Christian Europe perhaps never again attained a level of unity comparable to that which existed between 1225 and 1250. This generation did not experience food shortages and large-scale conflicts; the pressures of population growth were not yet a threat because commerce was full of vitality and land was still there for the taking. In smothering many of the drives which might have been fruitful, the Church held the reins of social order – yet this order was not sustained by terror and injustice. One body of thought, one language, a common form of expression was recognised among the members of the Europe that had finally been born. And it was this same generation who saw the decline, retreat and humiliation of the two proud civilisations of the East which had hitherto dominated the scene, and whose collapse marked a major break in the history of the world.

443

Left: The western façade of Chartres cathedral (mid-twelfth century). Right: The columnar statues on the central portal of Chartres cathedral.

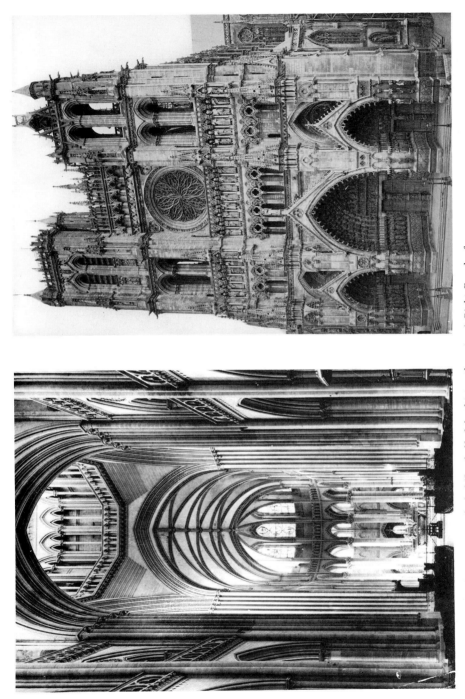

Left: Choir and cupola of Coutances cathedral (first half of the thirteenth century). Right: Façade of Amiens cathedral (mid-thirteenth century).

The path taken by Christ to Golgotha, in Jerusalem. Theoretically the symbol of Christian unity, Jerusalem has been the pretext for many ambitions, hatreds and settlings of accounts. The Crusades only briefly strengthened Muslim unity, which had ceased to be 'Arab', while they dealt a fatal blow to the moribund Byzantine Empire.

PART 3

The East in Decline: 1100–1250

Islam dethroned 10

The establishment of the Fatimids in Egypt and Syria at the end of the tenth century profoundly altered the make-up of the Muslim world in the Near East; the relative harmony of the Abbasid caliphate in the political and religious spheres was followed by division and rivalry. Moreover, the economic dominance of the caliphs of Baghdad had been shattered by the Fatimids through their occupation of the Syrian and Egyptian outlets to the Mediterranean. Claiming to be the only legitimate heirs of the Prophet by their direct descent from Fatima and Ali, the Fatimids had tried to wipe out the Abbasid caliphate; their temporary capture of Baghdad in 1059 briefly raised their hopes. In fact, the intervention of Tughrul's Seljuk Turks on the caliph's side turned the situation around: the success of the Seljuks not only allowed the re-establishment of the Abbasid caliph in Baghdad, but also pushed the Fatimids back to the confines of their bases in Syria, whence the Seljuks tried to dislodge them little by little, without being able to chase them from Palestine altogether.

The ailing East under attack

The battles that took place in that region proved to have important consequences – above all, they spurred the western Christians into coming to liberate the Holy Land from its belligerent inhabitants. The arrival of the Seljuks in the Near East must also have strengthened the position of the Sunni Muslims against the Shi'ite Fatimids, highlighting the shift of the Abbasid caliphate towards the role of spiritual head of the Muslim community, to the detriment of its role as temporal lord. This had already begun under the Buyid viziers at the end of the tenth century and the beginning of the eleventh.

The Seljuk expansion westwards, first successfully towards Syria, then towards Egypt, **449** finally turned in the direction of Armenia, which necessarily entailed a confrontation with the Byzantine emperor. The battle of Manzikert in 1071, when the emperor was defeated and taken prisoner, besides initiating a period of ten years of internal conflict in the Greek Empire, gave the Turkish tribes access to Asia Minor, and some were not slow to take advantage of it. From this point the fate of the Near East was transformed, the Turks playing an essential role for many centuries. These transformations affected not only the realm of politics, but also human, social, religious and economic life. Just as in North Africa where Arab domination had given way to that of the Berber rulers, so in the Near East it gradually declined to the benefit of the Turkish sultans. The Arabic-Muslim civilisation did not, however, disappear: adopted by the newcomers, it still flourished and displayed creative energy in literature, sciences and art. As for the Crusades, which were finally to fail in both political and religious terms, they fostered the development of economic relations already established, and the Italian merchant cities, notably Venice and Genoa, learnt to take advantage of the fortunes and misfortunes of the Frankish presence in the East.

Two irreconcilable powers

At the dawn of the twelfth century, two powers dominated the Muslim world of the Near and Middle East: the Fatimid caliphate of Egypt, and the Seljuk sultanate which controlled Khurasan, Iran, Iraq, Syria and stretched towards Asia Minor. Eastern in their origin, their conception and exercise of power, their internal institutions, religious choices and economic role, these powers confronted each other directly as well as across the Latin states of Syria and Palestine. When, during the course of the twelfth century, the Seljuk baton in the provinces was taken up by the Zangids, and later by the Ayyubids, this was a continuation of the Turkish momentum, but in an Arabised-Kurdish guise, which extended to Egypt and gave to a part of the Near East a degree of political and religious unity.

Although Fatimid authority was challenged at a local level, the dynasty (henceforth established in Cairo) controlled the whole Mediterranean coastline, directly or indirectly, from Morocco to northern Syria during the first half of the eleventh century. Politically and economically, it represented a considerable force, but its political influence, as we have seen, aroused resistance from the Berber tribes of the Maghrib and from Syrian emirs who were hostile to any external power; the religious split also failed to attract popular sympathy for the Fatimids because of occasional persecutions; finally, Fatimid authority was exercised through the intermediary of an army in which Sudanese, Turkish, Armenian and Circassian mercenaries had an increasingly large presence and which tended to play a political role in the second half of the eleventh century. Nevertheless, Fatimid power was far from exhausted at the end of that century, and its privileged position on the Mediterranean coast between the lands of the Indian Ocean and those of Mediterranean Europe gave it enormous economic advantages.

On the other hand, in less than a century, the core territories which then made up the domains of the Abbasids in the East passed into the direct control of the Seljuk leaders. These leaders took the title of sultan (so, in practice, becoming the holders of temporal

A Seljuk caravanserai. Their place of origin, as well as their dynamism, confirmed the Seljuks' natural intermediary role in trade with India and China. A number of caravanserais emerged in Turkey in the twelfth and the thirteenth centuries. Among them was the very handsome caravanserai of the Sultan Han (1229) at Aksaray, near Konya. Note the scale of the stones.

power), leaving the caliph of Baghdad only his role as religious head of the Muslim community, in the name of the faithful Sunnis opposed to the Shi'ite Fatimids. The authority established by the Seljuks in Khurasan, Iran, Iraq and then eastern Asia Minor was heir to the tribal traditions of the Turks, the Khurasanian administrative system, and Arab and Iranian political culture; its practical expression was the *Siyasat-Nameh* (*Book of Government*) of Nizam al-Mulk, vizier to Sultan Alp-Arslan (1063–73) and Malik-Shah (1073–92). The arrival of the Seljuks in the Near East, then of other Turkish and Turcoman tribes, not only altered the political situation in the region, but also introduced an absolutely new human and social factor: dynamic religious behaviour, embodied in the activities of warrior brotherhoods like that of the *ghazis*, affecting an entire economic area (important for its produce and its location between Europe, India and China). The control of Syrian and Palestinian ports thus appeared to be at stake in the confrontation between Seljuks and Fatimids, but the issue was postponed by the Crusades and their consequences.

By its very nature the whole basis of the Fatimid regime was sacred. Its head had to be a descendant of the Prophet: he was given the title of *imam* (guide) and the imamate could not go outside the Prophet's family, each *imam* being designated by his predecessor, but not necessarily being the eldest son of the reigning *imam*. This succession functioned perfectly well until the end of the eleventh century when, on the death of the caliph al-Mustansir, **451** the designation of *imam* began to be contested, either by the family of the caliph or by important individuals at court, especially the vizier, or with increasing frequency by the caliph's guard, which was recruited from many regions and to whom the *imam*'s symbolic role meant nothing. The inability of the Fatimid caliphs to unite the Muslims under their authority to fight the Crusaders, or even to oppose them with their own forces, was a mark against the caliphs and the caliphate. Their unpopularity increased in the second half of the twelfth century, when the Fatimids went so far as to conclude an alliance with the Latin king of Jerusalem, whose influence could then extend as far as Cairo. It is thus not surprising that the elimination of the dynasty by Saladin aroused little opposition in Egypt.

Even before that, the caliphate's power had been undermined by the viziers. Initially they had been the executors of the caliphs' policies, but in the second half of the eleventh century, under the caliphate of al-Mustansir, Badr al-Jamali transformed the vizier's office. Circumstances led to Badr al-Jamali's being granted full powers: from simply being head of the Fatimid armies (*amir al-juyush*) he became head of the civil, judicial and religious administration. The viziers who succeeded him benefited from the same authority, imposing it on the reigning caliph by force if necessary; but, with this weakening of the caliphs' power, rivalries broke out at court and within the Fatimid government, and the viziers often suffered a tragic fate. As the twelfth century wore on, the viziership became increasingly unstable as the regime itself grew more anarchic. Remarkably enough, in a state so markedly Islamic in origin, several viziers were Christians, or former Christians (notably Armenians) converted to Islam. This suggests that in the first era of the dynasty in Egypt, there were opportunities for certain sectors of the Egyptian population other than Sunni Muslims to work with government authorities. The authorities relied on a very centralised, hierarchical administration, dependent on the caliph or vizier in power, and which, rivalling the Abbasid administration, can be considered a model of its kind. Christians and Jews were well represented within it and showed great loyalty towards a regime that brought them both material and spiritual benefits.

In a similar way, the Fatimid caliphs resorted to non-Arab mercenaries to form their personal guard and even a section of their army, which was one of the privileged elements of the Fatimid State. But during the twelfth century, realising its own importance, the army exerted increasing pressure on the caliph, the vizier and various branches of the administration; different elements of this army (Berbers, Turks, Sudanese) then began to fight each other with a view to controlling the regime, which was unable to resist it.

The Seljuks represented an entirely different system. While they were Muslims and applied the principles of the *shari'a* (the Holy Law of Islam) to their State, they were above all the inheritors of Turkish tradition, on to which Iranian and Arab elements had been grafted. The principal trait of the dynasty was the concentration of military and civil power in the hands of family members: the family recognised the eldest as its head, with the title of sultan and the task of conducting affairs of state, but important offices in the army and civil administration were distributed among his brothers, uncles and nephews. This system prevailed as long as the head of the family was seen to be a person of strong calibre, who displayed authority and aggression; conquests meant that the potential appetites of close or distant relations could be satisfied by allowing them a slice of power without the unity of the State being threatened. Such appanage carried within it the seeds of destruction for the Seljuk State. In fact, from the end of the eleventh century, a growing number of small independent principalities can be detected in upper Iraq, in the Jazira and in northern Syria. Theoretically placed under the control of a Seljuk prince, they were in fact governed by the *atabegs*, guardians of the young princes, who gradually assumed real power: the result was the weakening of the Seljuk sultanate in Iran, Iraq and northern Syria. The Seljuk sultanate in Asia Minor escaped this, however, even at the end of the twelfth century when the Sultan Kilij-Arslan II, having divided his realm among his sons, came close to destroying it.

The Near East divided in two

The Seljuks were Sunni Muslims: they were no longer troubled by theological questions, but they did conceive of religion as a fundamental element of the State, an element in government, order and morality; they only recognised orthodox Islam, and fought hard against the Shi'ite faith of the Isma'ilis. Their orthodoxy stemmed from Iranian Islamic tradition, especially from the synthesis by Abu Hamid al-Ghazali, the famous thinker, philosopher and theologian who had succeeded in reconciling faith and reason to the satisfaction of the Seljuk Turks. Like their Fatimid neighbours and rivals, they were very tolerant of non-Muslims, whether Christians or Jews.

Various other characteristics differentiated the Fatimids from the Seljuks. The power of the former, particularly from the second half of the eleventh century, was exercised mainly over Arab peoples, and to a much lesser extent over non-Arab or non-Muslim minorities. In practice, since the beginning of the eleventh century and more so after mid-century, the Maghrib had escaped Fatimid control and passed into that of the Berber dynasties, despite the invasion of Arab tribes (the Hilali) coming from Egypt. The Seljuks, on the other hand, dominated a very diverse collection of people – Turks, Iranians, Kurds, Arabs, and later Armenians and Greeks; the great majority of these people were Sunni Muslims and thus were not opposed to Sunni rulers. While there were some groups who were not Sunni, such as the Nizarites (the *haschischiya* – the 'Order of Assassins', who were ruthlessly hunted down) and a very small minority of Christians, until the Seljuks occupied Asia Minor the whole Muslim population recognised the Abbasid caliph as its head. As the sole legitimate authority, the caliph could delegate some of his power to the Seljuk sultan and thus confer on him, through this investiture, a legitimacy and power-base of his own. Although this power was initially confined to military and administrative matters, it gradually extended to judicial and religious matters, and the sultan gained considerable advantage from the struggle with the Fatimids. The definition of Seljuk laws which appeared in the *Siyasat-Nameh* was based as much on the temporal nature of Seljuk power as on the religious character of the power conferred on it by the caliphate. By the end of the eleventh century – and this became even more apparent in the twelfth – danger lay in the system of divided responsibility among the Seljuks: the enfeebled authority of the grand sultan in Iraq facilitated the rise of other sultans in Asia Minor and Khurasan. Although they officially recognised the Abbasid caliph as religious head and the sultan of Baghdad as head of the Seljuk family, they argued that they should appear as their legitimate representatives and, in consequence, should be granted local powers in all domains: political, administrative, judicial and religious. Possibly the ethnic diversity of the lands under Seljuk influence also facilitated the division of political power and the creation of these sultanates. Clearly, religious unity could not preserve political unity.

Under the Fatimids the fact that the caliph was not the spiritual leader of the great majority of people, and that he could not attract their loyalty, led to the growth of the authority of the viziers, who held very real political power without any religious implications. The excesses of some viziers and their agents (the mercenaries), together with their lack of resistance to the Crusaders, gave rise in the last third of the twelfth century to a strong return to Sunnism in both the political and religious spheres, and to a reconciliation between the ruling power and the populace. Unlike in the Seljuk world, the Syrian–Egyptian area was reunified (under Saladin), but only for a limited period.

The Mediterranean world and the Near East experienced important commercial shifts in the second half of the eleventh century, for various reasons. First among these were the political causes: the establishment of the Fatimids in Egypt and Syria, the reconquest of northern Syria by the Byzantines, the beginning of the Abbasid caliphate's break-up, and the upheavals resulting from the presence of the Seljuks and other tribes, from the shores of the Black Sea to those of the Aral Sea. Then there were specific commercial causes: the appearance of Italian merchants (already present in Ifrikiya) in Egypt and soon afterwards on the coast of Palestine and Syria; commercial links were established between the Fatimids and merchants from Amalfi, quickly followed by similar links with the Pisans, the Genoese and then the Venetians, producing a permanent European presence in the East; the increased role of Jewish merchants from Ifrikiya and Egypt; and finally, the Fatimid control over commerce with the Sudan and East Africa. Chance events, such as the destruction of the port of Siraf on the Persian Gulf in an earthquake (which effectively severed the link between Basra and Baghdad), also played an important part in maritime relations between India and Iraq. As we have noted above, the port's destruction and the appearance of pirates in the Gulf encouraged the diversion of a great part of this commercial traffic towards the Red Sea and Egypt. Finally, troubles in the Abbasid East and the instalment of a strong, stable regime in Egypt also had commercial ramifications.

By contrast, the northern part of the Near East, from Byzantine Asia Minor to Khurasan, suffered from a series of conflicts, both internal (as among the Greeks) and regional; moreover, the arrival of Turkish and Turcoman tribes brought some changes to the everyday life of local populations. Ethnic changes, changes in some of the traditional economic activities, and a lesser role for the capital of the caliphate – all this worked against the Persian Gulf–Iran–Iraq route, even if some of the commercial caravans continued to use it.

We cannot know for sure, but it is possible that the Seljuk sultans intended to restore commercial traffic over the lands they controlled, perhaps as far as the Mediterranean or Black Sea coasts. This would help to explain their attacks on the Fatimids in Syria and even in Palestine, and on the Byzantines in eastern Asia Minor. However, the arrival of the

Crusaders and their establishment on the shores of Syria and Palestine and in parts of the interior thwarted these Seljuk attempts.

At the end of the twelfth century, when the defeated Crusaders abandoned most of their positions, Muslim unity was only seemingly re-established. If Saladin and then the Ayyubids established their control over Syria and Egypt, Iraq escaped it (as did Asia Minor); the new situation prevailed for half a century until the sudden incursions of the Mongols into the Muslim Near East, who overturned the established order once more. But again we see the situation in the tenth and eleventh centuries repeated here: a division between the northern and southern zones, which sometimes broke into open conflict. This situation prevailed right up to the beginning of the sixteenth century, when the Ottoman sultans set about re-establishing the unity of the Muslim Near East.

Christian aggression

When the Crusaders reached the Byzantine and Muslim Near East, they found a region of division and strife. In Asia Minor the anarchy of the years 1071–81 had been followed by the stabilisation of power with the accession of Alexios I Komnenos; however, he had had to allow the Turkish tribes to establish themselves on the Anatolian plateau, and even in the coastal area of the Sea of Marmara. Thus the Seljuks under Suleyman I, and then under Kilij Arslan I, occupied the main towns on the Nicaea (Iznik)–Iconium (Konya) route; the Danishmendids occupied the Sivas–Kayseri–Malatya triangle; and the Artukids and Saltukids occupied east and south-east Asia Minor.

These tribes arrived in the wake of Alp-Arslan's victory at Manzikert (Malazgird) in 1071 over the Byzantine Emperor Romanos Diogenes. By stages they advanced across the centre and even westwards, taking advantage of the struggle for the succession among the Greeks – they either supported one of the candidates (as did the Seljuks) or established their own authority in place of the Greeks (as did the Danishmendids). Following the seizure of power by Alexios I, these tribes benefited from favourable circumstances: the emperor was preoccupied with the restoration of imperial power, the administrative and military reorganisation of the empire, and the struggle against invasion in the west by the Normans of southern Italy.

The weakening of Byzantine power was also accompanied by quarrels among the Turks. Suleyman aimed at ensuring his supremacy over all the Seljuks and engaged unsuccessfully in fighting his Iraqi cousin; his successor, Kilij Arslan, gave up the eastward expansion but was violently opposed to his neighbours and rivals, the Danishmendids, who were moreover permanently at war with the Armenian dynasty in the upper Euphrates. This explains why the Crusaders, disembarking in Asia Minor, did not meet with any great opposition and why their march through Nicaea, Dorylaeum and Konya as far as the Gates of Cilicia encountered few problems.

Having entered Syria after the long siege of Antioch (1098), the Crusaders had no difficulty conquering the main towns on the Syrian–Palestinian coast. This was also due to rivalries which, shortly before, set the Seljuks against the Fatimids in this region (the

While Islam misrepresented the ideological nature of the Crusades, Western imagery depicted the 'Saracen' with the devil's grin. (Luttrell Psalter, fourteenth century; The British Library, London.)

Fatimids had even taken Jerusalem from the Turks less than a year before the Franks took possession of it), which obviously made it impossible to form a united front against the invaders. The Fatimids had even sent an embassy to the Franks at the time of the siege of Antioch, and a Frankish embassy went to Cairo. On this subject, it has been said that there was a plan which would have given Syria to the Franks and Palestine to the Fatimids, but this is scarcely credible, given the aims of the Crusaders on the one hand, and the Fatimids' suppliant status on the other. The Crusaders' success up to that point would not have inclined them to such an arrangement; in any case, shortly after this, the Fatimids were in possession of Jerusalem (August 1098) and endeavoured to occupy the whole of northern Palestine, in the hope of keeping the Frankish threat at the greatest possible distance, along with the ever-present Seljuk threat. This attempt failed when, on 15 July 1099, the Crusaders took brutal possession of Jerusalem, and shortly afterwards of the coastal ports, which they occupied as far as Jaffa between 1100 and 1120. The Muslim divisions in Asia Minor, as in Syria and Palestine, thus worked in the Franks' favour. But in Asia Minor, they also found allies, willing or conscripted, in the Armenian states of Cilicia and Taurus, whose local rulers joined them or at least submitted to them. The Armenian prince, Thoros, ruler of Edessa, called on Baldwin of Boulogne to help him get rid of the Turks; but in the event it was he who was despatched, and Baldwin thus founded the first Crusader state in the East, the county of Edessa (March 1098).

The Crusaders thus invaded a region that remained deeply divided during the last years of the eleventh century. But we should note that, at the beginning of the Frankish expedition, the Muslims had no idea that they were seeing a different sort of invasion: for them, it was an attack by Christians from the north, of the sort to which they had been accustomed since the tenth century, and it seemed all the more familiar because there were Byzantine Christians among them, both in Asia Minor and at Antioch.

Their first reaction was to think of it as a temporary offensive with limited objectives, against which there would always be time to conclude alliances. It was not until they were faced with the persistent besiegers of Antioch, and above all by the invasion of Syria and

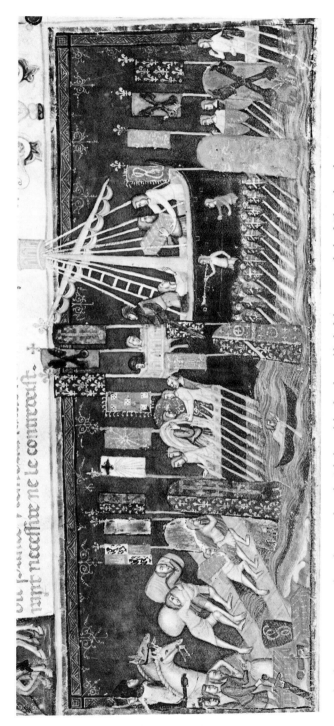

Faced with growing pressure from the Crusaders, the Seljuks mobilised and soon blocked their passage by land. Thus, from the beginning of the twelfth century, the Crusaders had to go by sea in their attempt to reach the Holy Land. (Thirteenth-century French manuscript: MS 4274, Bibliothèque nationale, Paris.)

then of Palestine, followed by the creation of a kingdom of Jerusalem, that the realisation hit them. But it was then far too late to repel the Frankish danger.

From the early twelfth century, however, a distinct form of resistance appeared, whose long-term consequences are indisputable. First of all, confronted by the second wave of Crusaders in Asia Minor, the Seljuks and Danishmendids joined forces to prevent them from crossing the country. Thus, in August 1101 the Lombards were defeated near Amasya, while a little later the Count of Nevers' troops were crushed near Ereghli, and the same happened to the contingents from Aquitaine and Bavaria. The central Anatolian plateau was firmly held by the Turks, and henceforth reinforcements could only reach the Holy Land by sea. As a result, the *atabegs* of the Jazira and the Seljuks of Iraq felt less threatened, while the Count of Edessa, who was continually harassed by his Danishmendid neighbours (to whom Bohemond of Antioch had fallen victim), could only expect support and reinforcement from the Crusader states in the Holy Land. Thus in Asia Minor the Muslim Turks managed to present a common front against the invaders; but once the danger had passed, they returned to the struggle for hegemony in the Anatolian plateau.

On the other hand, after the first defeats in Syria, the local princes, Seljuk emirs and *atabegs* from Aleppo, Hama, Homs and Damascus resisted all the Frankish attacks. The long siege of Antioch had shown that the Franks were not as invincible as once thought, and, depending on circumstances, the Muslims could either make temporary alliances among themselves against the Crusaders' attacks or conclude an accord with the latter if necessary. Thus they managed to hold on to the main towns of the Syrian hinterland, to protect the Aleppo–Damascus–Mecca route and to draw on aid, when required, from Mosul and Baghdad. But this was a matter of local, opportunist policy rather than a general movement of opposition to the Crusaders; it was nothing like a holy war, and in fact relations, especially of a commercial kind, were established whenever possible between the Muslim and Frankish merchants.

Further south, the Fatimids had lost Jerusalem and almost the whole of Palestine, but eventually they adapted to the Latin presence in the region and to the creation of Crusader States in the Holy Land. In fact, the presence of the Crusaders served to draw the attention of the Seljuks, and also formed a barrier between Turks and Fatimids. This suited the latter, given that the internal situation in Egypt was deteriorating and the Fatimids did not wish to fight with anyone; thus, for a while, maintenance of the *status quo* was sought from the Franks. Moreover, as the Fatimids held one of the routes to the Indian Ocean, they were able to offer Italian merchants advantageous commercial links – more direct and less risky than those pertaining in Syria and Iraq.

The Latin venture in the East

The episode of Latin settlement in Palestine and Syria continues to provoke much interest in the West, while in the history of Islam it can be reduced to a parenthesis whose effects, in the end, were practically nil. The interest of European historians, apart from the general theoretical problem ('the Cross versus the Crescent', early 'colonialism', and so on), arises from the very unusual nature of the experience (the imposition of a form of social organisation on a population which had not previously experienced it) and the richness of the documentary material generated by the effort at such organisation. The importation in its pure state of Western aristocractic society which remained fixed in its initial structure (without the evolution it naturally underwent in the West) means that the precise nature of vassal relationships, royal prerogatives and legal procedure can be better appreciated in law-books such as the *Livre au roi*, the *Assises de Jérusalem*, the *Assise de la cour aux bourgeois*, the work of John of Ibelin and the *Assise sur la ligece* than in most of the customaries of Europe.

The first and most important aspect concerns the number of men. The return home of most of the Crusaders, the inevitable losses involved in conquest until about 1120, the defeat of expeditions sent out to help, and the small number of Christian women present made Frankish domination almost impossible without the gradual adoption of various ad hoc measures. The difficulty was primarily a military one: it is estimated that there were approximately 1,500–2,000 heavy cavalry and 12,000–15,000 foot soldiers. These troops, a ridiculously small number for holding 80,000 square kilometres, were well supported by the annual arrival of armed pilgrims who came to fulfil their vows, but these men were generally not used to local conditions and suffered terribly from thirst and heat in their armour under a burning sun. The development of paid corps of native armed men, the 'turcopoles', was some help in overcoming the shortage of manpower, but betrayal was an ever-present threat. The establishment of the warrior-monk orders (Hospitallers and Templars) after 1112–20 provided a warrior élite, always available, but stubborn to the point of obtuseness and given to squabbles and arrogance. Mixing with Armenians, Greeks and even Syrians could only happen in the towns and, in the West, these figures with their robes and turbans were soon despised as more inclined to make peace than to do battle.

In the last resort, success rested on superior military tactics and technology: the terrifying charges to which the Easterners were not accustomed, the soldiers whose armour no arrow could pierce, the vast fortresses which were capable of sheltering, whether they liked it or not, the assembled villagers, and whose many extraordinary ruins still testify to their strength: Krak des Chevaliers, Saône, Beaufort, Montréal, Chastel Blanc, and so on. But what if the charge by great horses did not work, if the cisterns ran dry, if the heat was too intense for wearing armour? The Franks held on because they had total control over the seas, protecting their rear, and because the younger sons sent out to Syria in search of adventure often proved themselves to be exceptional captains, such as the Norman Tancred and Baldwin I of Boulogne before 1120, and later Fulk of Anjou and Raymond of Tripoli.

Danger lay not only in small numbers, but also in the aggressive behaviour of these predatory men, to whom the Church had promised salvation through blood. Although a single 'kingdom' of Jerusalem had been created in 1100, the Norman 'princes' of Antioch and Edessa, the Toulousain 'counts' of Tripoli, then the Poitevins, Provençals, and in the thirteenth century the men from Champagne, along with the Germans, were given over to incessant rivalry, which their retreat from the coast in the thirteenth century transferred to the towns. Italian or Catalan quarrels arose in each port where the merchants had obtained, as we have seen, privileges and markets (*funduq, fondaco*). The intransigence of

The Krak des Chevaliers. Because of the scant forces available and the need to hold certain key positions between the plateau and the sea, the Frankish knights built formidable fortresses, of which the Krak, in Syria, has remained the most famous example for over eight centuries.

both sides was not only turned on each other but also against the Christian minorities who could have helped them.

Conversely, it should be noted that the Franks had not found all the assistance and sympathy they had hoped for among the Christian peoples of Syria and Palestine; they were usually Orthodox, especially in northern Syria, and had little sympathy for the Latin Church's seizure of power in so many areas, spiritual as well as material. The intolerance shown by Western prelates and lords heightened this antipathy and not many rallied to their side, except among the Maronites, and if they did, it was a temporary, often individual, gesture. All the same, relations between Franks and eastern Christians, episodic as they were, had unhappy consequences for the latter because, after the Franks departed, the Muslim rulers visited on the whole Christian community punishments that had been incurred by only a few members.

These shadows continually lengthened. But they should not hide the enormous effort of acclimatisation attempted at least in the twelfth century. Realising that there could be only a tiny élite of masters, and also very careful of 'custom', the Franks contented themselves with collecting the land taxes or public revenues of the Muslim regime, the tithe (*zakat*), customs dues (*dogana*) and rent for land; they may have employed the Western terminology of manors and estates, but they left their government and judicial functions to the *ra'is* and the *qadi*, as before. It is thought that their relations with the country were very superficial,

460

Salah al-Din ben Ayyub, or Saladin. After having deposed the caliph of Cairo, he brought Egypt and Syria together and then undertook to pursue the struggle against the Franks. He regained Jerusalem, which provoked the Third Crusade (with Philip Augustus and Richard the Lionheart). While he eventually lost some of the conquered territories, he confirmed Ayyubid political and religious unity from Mesopotamia to Egypt. (Engraving, Book VIII, *Saladin Soldan d'Egypte* by A. Theuet.)

and aggression against the peasantry was rare. They made no attempt at conversion, or changing the law; they had simply transplanted, on to virgin soil, fiefs, homage and various services for their own benefit, but in a rigorous manner necessitated by the climate of war; there was a feudal hierarchy in the German or Spanish style, in which each person – king, prince, count, peer, baron, viscount, castellan, landed lord – was in his station. This was a conservative situation, of course, but also a protective one. It was only in the towns that existing organisation was greatly changed, which explains why the 'kingdom of Acre', almost entirely urban, experienced such disturbances in the thirteenth century. In this respect it was the Italians who did the most to introduce the administrative practices of their cities into the ports, setting up local administration by district (*ruga, vicus*), designating 'consuls' or bailiffs for each community, specialised commercial tribunals (*fonde*), and so forth.

The effect of this graft onto the body of Islam must not be exaggerated. Admittedly it offered Europe the certainty of regular and privileged access to eastern trade. But it was surely only a point of entry – Egypt and Asia Minor were the essential locations. Long before Saladin, territorial possessions, which were too small to play a decisive military role in the East, took second place to merchants' concerns. It was this that was to bring about the eventual defeat of the Latin conquest.

Saladin: saviour of Islam?

The first attempts at resisting the Frankish presence in Syria arose from local problems and rivalries between neighbouring Christian and Muslim territories: Edessa, Antioch, Aleppo,

Mosul, Mardin and Damascus. This was no holy war but quarrels between princes who were indifferent to the origins or religion of a potential ally. In the 1120s, the whole of northern Syria was shaken by the Frankish attacks on the main towns, and by the violence of the Batinians, heterodox Isma'ili Muslims, at Aleppo and Damascus. Despite often bloody defeats, such as the famous massacre of the Field of Blood (*Ager Sanguinis*) in 1119 between Aleppo and Antioch, the Franks managed to ensure control over the Gulf from Alexandretta to Sinai: they installed outposts along the Gulf of Eilat, and in Transjordan, such as the famous Krak de Moab. Merchant or pilgrim caravans were always at their mercy. Indeed, after 1160 the pirate ships went so far as to harass Jedda, the port of Mecca.

The emir of Mosul, Imad al-Din Zangi, set himself a twofold task after 1128: to reclaim from the Franks the lands of northern Syria, and to make Sunni orthodoxy prevail over Shi'ism in this region. In restoring lustre to the struggle against the enemies of the true faith, Zangi gave new life to the concept of the *jihad* (Holy War). However, in his own lifetime it was not a clear concept in the Muslim mind – his actions were various and widely dispersed, making it difficult for his contemporaries to discern his guiding principles. When he disposed of the Shi'ites and Batinians at Aleppo, and indirectly at Damascus, many Muslims were won over to his side, but he was too stern for the people of Damascus who, instead, drew closer to the Franks in Jerusalem. Furthermore, the retaking of Edessa in December 1144 was perceived throughout the Muslim world as a first, vital step in the battle against the Latins. Conversely, the fall of Edessa showed the Latins how fragile their settlement in the East was, a fragility that arose from the limited number of men in the region and from hostility on the part of Greeks and Arabs who, once the first surprise was past, mounted a strong counter-attack. The Crusaders needed reinforcements: Christian Europe had to show its strength and willpower. This was why the kings took part in the Second Crusade, preached by Bernard of Clairvaux. The Christians intended that their own holy war should oppose the Muslim *jihad*; we know that this Crusade (1147–9) did not match the success of the first, and its results on the ground were negligible.

Thus a new situation developed in the East, where henceforth the Franks were on the defensive in northern and central Syria, and where the Muslims under Nur al-Din, son and successor of Zangi, gradually achieved unity from Mosul to Damascus. This was patient work in which Nur al-Din pursued his father's aims by fighting both Muslim heretics and Latin Christians and succeeded in making the Turkish, Kurdish and Arab emirs of the Jazira and Syria recognise his authority. From his accession in 1146 to his death in 1174, Nur al-Din constantly appeared as the Muslim believer *par excellence*, not only because he knew how to foster and make effective the spirit of the *jihad* against the Franks, but also because his activities contributed in part to the annihilation of Shi'ism in Syria and to the reinforcement of Sunnism. This was done partly by developing places for meditation and encouraging the spread of Muslim orthodoxy, and partly by marginalising and isolating the Fatimids of Egypt, who were guilty of having concluded an alliance with the Latins in Jerusalem. Nur al-Din was recognised as the head and protector of the Muslims, with the immediate consequence that they were unified under his authority, while the Fatimids were eventually eliminated. Egypt was re-integrated into the group of orthodox Muslim countries in the Near East, and the Frankish kingdom of Jerusalem was destroyed. The

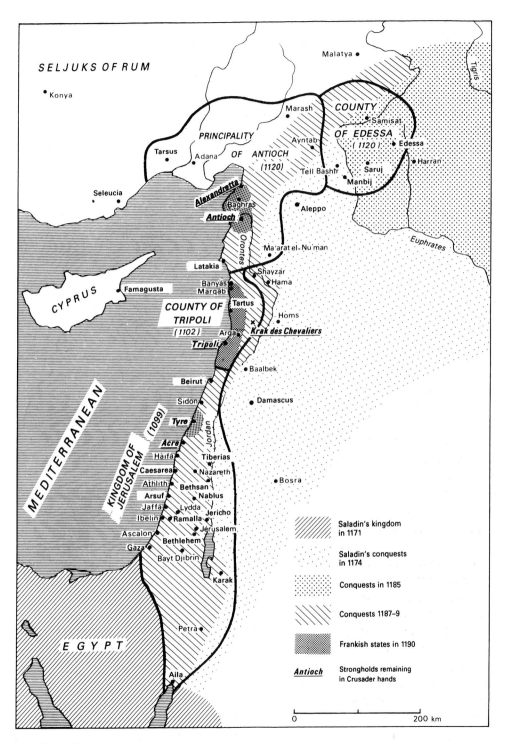

SELJUKS OF RUM

• Konya

• Tarsus

Adana •

Seleucia •

PRINCIPALITY

OF ANTIOCH
(1120)

Malatya •

Marash •

Ayntab •

Tell Bashir •

• Samisat

COUNTY

OF EDESSA
(1120)

• Edessa

Saruj •

Manbij •

• Harran

Alexandretta

Baghras

Antioch

Orontes

Latakia •

Banyas •
Marqab •

Tartus

COUNTY OF
TRIPOLI
(1102)

Arqa •

Krak des Chevaliers

Tripoli

CYPRUS

Famagusta •

• Aleppo

Ma'arat el-Nu'man •

Shayzar •
Hama •

Euphrates

Tigris

• Homs

Beirut •

Sidon •

Tyre

Acre

Haifa •

Caesarea •

Athlith •

Arsuf •

Jaffa •

Ibelin •

Ascalon •

Gaza •

MEDITERRANEAN

KINGDOM OF
JERUSALEM
(1099)

Jordan

Tiberias •

Nazareth •

Bethsan •

Nablus •

Lydda •
Ramalla •

Jericho •

Jerusalem •

Bethlehem •

Bayt Djibrin •

• Baalbek

• Damascus

• Bosra

Karak •

E G Y P T

Petra •

Aila •

Pattern	Description
Saladin's kingdom in 1171
Saladin's conquests in 1174
Conquests in 1185
Conquests 1187–9
Frankish states in 1190
Antioch	Strongholds remaining in Crusader hands

0   200 km

Map 18. Saladin's conquests.

architect of these last events was Salah al-Din ben Ayyub, called Saladin by Western historians.

In the mid-twelfth century, Egypt seemed to be one of the essential components of the Near East. The fruitless efforts of the vizier Tala'i against the kingdom of Jerusalem were followed by negotiations with envoys from Nur al-Din, Emperor Manuel I and King Baldwin III. The final stages were triggered by the disintegration of Egypt's internal political situation: quarrels among the viziers, chaotic intervention by various sectors of the army, conflict and rebellion in several provinces – these all led both Nur al-Din and the new king of Jerusalem, Amalric I, to contemplate bringing Egypt into their respective camps. Amalric's two unsuccessful expeditions in 1161 and 1162 were followed by an attack in 1164 led by the Kurdish emir Shirkuh, acting on behalf of Nur al-Din at the request of a former vizier, Shawar, who had taken refuge in Damascus. Once Shawar was restored to his post, he refused to carry out the promises he had made to Nur al-Din and sought help from Amalric. An initial expedition took place in July 1164, and a second in 1167, with the help of the Greeks, in the wake of an invasion by Shirkuh's troops; eventually both adversaries withdrew. A renewed attack by Amalric in 1168 provoked reactions from Nur al-Din and Shirkuh; despite his shrewd policy of balances and promises, Shawar was finally despatched in favour of Shirkuh, who had already forced the Franks to retreat, in January 1169. The new vizier drew closer to the Fatimid caliph, but his death a few weeks after his accession enabled his nephew, Saladin, to inherit the title of vizier and the command of the army. He resisted two attacks by Amalric and finally, on the death of the Fatimid caliph al-Adid, re-established Sunni orthodoxy in Cairo. In September 1171 the name of the Abbasid caliph was pronounced in the *khutba* (the Friday sermon, which included a prayer for the ruler of Islam). Until the death of Nur al-Din (1174), relations between him and Saladin, which had at first been cordial, were embittered by Saladin's desire to maintain his independence in Egypt and the areas around the Red Sea, his policy here being guided by economic considerations.

The death of Nur al-Din and quarrels over the succession enabled Saladin to launch expeditions into Syria and the Jazira. However, it was not until the end of 1180 that he was officially invested by the Abbasid caliph and became, not without local challenge, the real leader of the Near East, achieving the union for which Nur al-Din had hoped. The Latin position was thus severely weakened; to the insubordination of one warlike 'baron' or another was added the powerlessness of the king of Jerusalem, Baldwin IV. He was paralysed by sickness, by acute jealousy among the warrior families, and by the double-dealing of the Byzantine emperors. These emperors, having been re-established in Antioch and Cilicia since 1137–59, coveted Egypt and entered into subtle intrigues with the Armenians and the Turks, their ambitions arousing deep disquiet in the West, especially in Italy. In 1187, having captured the Frankish army and its king at Hattin, Saladin took Jerusalem and the coast, except for a few places such as Antioch, Tyre and Ascalon.

The union was completed with the incorporation of Palestine into the Ayyubid territories. The Third Crusade (1190–2) allowed the Franks to regain some of the Palestinian coast, from Tyre to Jaffa, but ultimately only confirmed Saladin's triumph – an end to the

464

kingdom of the Holy Land and a restoration of the power of the Ayyubid realm, which extended over upper Mesopotamia, Syria, Palestine and Egypt. Here, with Sunnism having definitively supplanted Shi'ism, we see a political union underpinned by religious unity. This unity was not the work of Arabs but of the Turks and Kurds who were at the forefront of the military, political and religious struggle: 'Arab' power, properly speaking, thus disappeared for several centuries in the Near East.

The capture of Jerusalem, the ending of schism in eastern Islam, the freeing of the Red Sea, the resumption of cargoes of gold and slaves on the Mediterranean and of links with black Africa make up the remarkable balance-sheet of Saladin's activities. Nevertheless, at his death in 1193, the durability of these sucesses was in doubt: the caliph had broken with the sultan of Egypt, ports remained in Christian hands, the Turks were not united, and from the Far East to Europe routes were being sketched via Anatolia and Turkestan that bypassed Egypt.

In fact, an earlier Muslim unity had been created in Asia Minor out of the Danishmendid emirate and the Turcoman tribes at the expense of the Byzantine Empire, and to the profit of the Seljuk Turks: the sultan Kilij-Arslan II triumphed over his Danishmendid rival (1164–74) and inflicted a severe defeat on the emperor Manuel I Komnenos at Myriokephalon in November 1176. This repeat of the battle of Manzikert destroyed all Byzantine hope of reconquering the lands of Asia Minor, ensured Seljuk authority over the whole of the central plateau and established the political and religious power of the Seljuk sultanate of Konya. Turkish power had become a reality, to the extent that a chronicler of the Third Crusade already gave the name 'Turchia' to Seljuk Asia Minor. Thus, at the end of the twelfth century, the Muslim Near East had undergone an irrevocable development, with the rise and victory of new peoples.

Grounds for hope?

The Fatimid failure to hold Baghdad and to suppress the Abbasid caliphate had direct political and economic consequences. First of all the Fatimid caliph, al-Mustansir, saw his authority considerably diminished and he had to turn to a strong man, the vizier Badr al-Jamali, to restore the State's prestige; this measure inaugurated the period during which power was in the hands of the viziers – as had been the case with the Abbasid regime a century earlier. Next, in order to undertake the expedition to Iraq, al-Mustansir had to dig deep in the treasury coffers, which were henceforth almost empty, while the army was riven by internal quarrels and mutinies among the Turkish and Sudanese troops, and a horrific famine preyed on Egypt for several years.

A prosperous Egypt, pivot of eastern trade in the twelfth century

Badr al-Jamali, besides bearing the title of vizier, also had that of *amir al-juyush* (commander of the army), and introduced new ideas into the Fatimid State. The most important of these was the fact that the person of the vizier could supplant that of the caliph and take **465** military, civil and even religious powers into his hands. Moreover, being of Armenian origin and having formerly been a slave of a Syrian emir, he built up an Armenian (Christian) guard which enabled him to strengthen his authority, especially over various sections of the army, by eliminating unruly elements (Sudanese and Turks) or sending them to Ifrikiya (Berbers); as for the caliph, he was more or less interned in the royal palace, emerging only for official ceremonies.

The centralisation of power, already marked under the first Fatimid caliphs of Cairo, was thus increased by Badr al-Jamali and his successors: provincial governments were directly dependent on Cairo, where the *diwans* (government departments) managed the administrative and financial life of the country from the vizier's or caliph's palace, and the civil and military agents were ranked in a precise hierarchy reflected in their salary, their insignia and their place in ceremonies. These functionaries, mostly resident in Cairo, were both a support and a danger to the Fatimid government – there was intense rivalry among them, and the search for important and well-paid posts and for the vizier's patronage fostered jealousies and conflict. However, under Badr al-Jamali, as under his successors al-Afdal and al-Mamun, the vizier's authority was unchallenged, an authority strengthened by the fact that social and economic life was flourishing.

Although Christians suffered harassment under the caliph al-Hakim at the beginning of the eleventh century, and later under the vizier Yazuri, the conditions for non-Muslims returned to normal from Badr al-Jamali's time. Christians were employed as government servants – and some of them became important ones, such as the Coptic monk Abu Najah who, in 1129, became counsellor to the caliph al-Amir (who got rid of the caliph al-Mamun) – and we know that some viziers were Christian. But it also appears that Jews named as viziers were converts to Islam. Christians and Jews were active participants in the economic revival and, for its part, the government, especially under the viziers al-Afdal and al-Mamun, encouraged the celebration of religious feasts and instituted a number of ceremonies, granting official financial support for Christian celebrations and the restoration or construction of churches and monasteries. This liberal policy towards Christians led to gradual assimilation, and it is around this time (the eleventh and twelfth centuries) that one can see Arabisation proceeding apace, a development also due to the fact that the Arabs were probably in the majority, while noting the decline of the Coptic language, which tended to become basically a liturgical language.

Towards the mid-eleventh century there was an anti-Christian reaction in the time of the vizier Ridwan Ibn Walakhchi, marked by severe measures (eviction from the administration, confiscation of property and even executions). This policy did not last, however, and until the end of the dynasty, the Christian and Jewish communities were not the object of any great prejudice; such difficulties, if they existed, were the result of the political disorder which began in Cairo and led eventually to Saladin's taking power.

If the economic life of Egypt was in a bad state before the arrival of Badr al-Jamali, the measures he took rapidly improved it. Not only did he restore order, but he also restored confidence to the peasants by decreeing a tax reduction for three years, and to the merchants by borrowing rather than confiscating sums which he promised to return. This renewed security encouraged production and trade, as well as the paying of taxes and duties, and in consequence encouraged the whole effort of construction and art that centred round the new city of Cairo. It is remarkable that the political disintegration of the twelfth century did not noticeably affect economic growth, even when external circumstances brought about the ruin of fabric manufacturers in Tinnis and Damietta in the Nile Delta and their transfer to Fustat and Cairo. Few documents concerning the administration of land have survived, but we know that the system of traditional taxes (*kharaj*, tithe) in use under the Abbasids continued under the Fatimids. It is possible that pious endowments (*waqf*) were more extensive than before as the creation of religious establishments and buildings would be supported by these funds, but such income was essentially an urban resource (from the shops, markets and baths, for example). The system of *iqta* seems to have been established already, under strict state control.

As far as agriculture is concerned, Egypt seems not to have experienced any fresh natural disaster after that of 1062–9; production was therefore both steady and abundant, allowing sufficient supplies to be distributed to the inhabitants and shops, and providing the government with considerable resources through taxes and various levies. The main products were wheat, barley, vegetables (especially broad beans), sugar cane, crops for animal fodder and, among the industrial crops, flax and cotton. Wood, however, was rare and not of good quality, and thus had to be imported from the West through the Italian merchants, and was used chiefly for shipbuilding. Another source of wealth was the gold brought back by explorers from Nubia to the mint at Fustat (replaced in 1122 by the mint at Cairo); Egyptian coinage thus preserved its value and this continued under the Ayyubids when Saladin re-established the links with Abyssinia and Chad.

The government exercised strict control over traders and craftsmen, as can be seen in the case of the weaving workshops; it collected large taxes on products for export. According to al-Muqaddasi:

The taxes are particularly heavy in Tinnis and Damietta. No Copt can weave a length of material in Chata without getting the government's seal for it; it can only be offered for sale by brokers recognised by the State, and a State official records it on a sale register. Each length is given to an employee who rolls it up, then gives it to another who ties it up with palm fibre, passes it to a third who puts it in a box, and then to the fourth who ties up the box, and each of these employees collects a fee. At the end, another tax has to be paid. Each of the taxes is recorded by the signature of each of the employees on the box and checked by inspectors on board the exporting ships.

Other products of Fatimid industry acquired a great reputation: objects made from ivory and rock crystal, pottery and leather had given rise to an export economy.

The Fatimids had developed good trading relations with various ports and towns in Italy since their establishment in Ifrikiya; these were maintained after their settlement in Egypt, and Jewish merchants and artisans certainly played a part in these commercial activities. This emerges clearly from the Genizah archives, deposited in the synagogue in Cairo and recently brought to light and studied. These documents reveal not only the role played by the Jews of the Maghrib (who settled in Cairo from the end of the tenth century) in the

The renovation of Cairo. Towards the end of the eleventh century, Badr al-Jamali gave Cairo the city walls which still exist in part today, notably the Gate of Victory, where we see that a round tower, more effective for defence, replaces the square tower. (Watercolour by David Roberts, 1839.)

western Mediterranean trade, but also that played by the Muslims of the Maghrib who extended Egyptian links in the direction of Arabia and India from the eleventh century.

This extension of trade to the Indian Ocean was connected with the anti-Abbasid policy of the Fatimids and with the policy of agricultural and industrial development in this era. A key element was the construction of a fleet intended to sail the length and breadth of the Red Sea and along the east African coast. Trade via the Red Sea was gradually replacing that via the Persian Gulf, especially as the Abbasid world was continually troubled. Commercial ports were established at Aydhab and Qusayr, and control of the Yemen meant that they could use the navigational skills of the Yemenis. As we have seen, Egypt thus became a market and entrepôt between the world of the Indian Ocean and that of the Mediterranean. Towards the last quarter of the twelfth century we see for the first time the Karimis, merchants who were specialists in the Red Sea and western Indian Ocean trade, who reached their peak under the Ayyubids.

This expansionist trade policy touched the eastern coast of Africa, and soon the coasts of Sind, Gujarat, Baluchistan and India, and was shadowed by a policy of religious expansion, as some Egyptian Muslim merchants were also missionaries and propagandists for Shi'ism, or travelled the lands of the Indian Ocean in company with Shi'ite missionaries. This establishment of Arab merchants on the coasts of the Indian Ocean benefited the Fatimids, who had made Egypt the most important staging-post between the East and the West: they collected heavy taxes on the merchandise (often luxury items) as it came into and went out of the country. The main port was Alexandria, whence the merchants of Italy, Amalfi, Venice, Pisa took the road to the East; in exchange for sugar, fabrics, spices (all products from Africa and India), they brought wood, iron and even wheat, according to demand. This trade began during the reign of the caliph al-Mustansir, which explains his fantastic expenditure, and the buildings he instigated which were the wonder of travellers, notably the Persian Nasr-i Khusrau.

Cairo and Fustat thus overflowed with the wealth that made the caliphs' fortunes, but also with government servants, merchants and artisans of every sort. Buildings multiplied: Cairo became a true capital and eclipsed Baghdad and the towns of Syria; the luxurious tastes of the caliphs gave a remarkable impetus to all the arts, and what we might call 'Fatimid art' spread throughout the Muslim world. The building of the al-Hakim and al-Azhar mosques indicates the extraordinary development of both monumental and decorative arts. On one hand, the Fatimids borrowed extensively from Abbasid art of the Samarra period (for example in their use of circular minarets in descending scale); on the other, it seems that they also drew on local artistic sources, especially that of the Copts who surely inspired their figurative iconography, with processions of animals, people, scenes of hunting, drinking and dancing. Wood and ivory panels, and what we know of fabrics, ceramics and bronzes all indicate a very high degree of technical skill. But these were also signs of a prosperity which aroused the admiration of Muslim travellers.

This abundance of wealth required a government that was strong and steady in its exercise of power, but the weakness or the incompetence of the twelfth-century caliphs, and the rivalry among the viziers, opened the way for internal struggles and the demands of the mercenaries. The battle for power finally profited Saladin and his successors, but their attempt at unity could not prevent Ayyubid Egypt from separating itself clearly from Syria and forming the undoubted successor to Fatimid Egypt.

Egypt comes to a halt: the Ayyubids in trouble

Successors to the Zangids and, more distantly, to the Seljuks, Saladin and the rulers who followed him in Syria and Egypt brought noticeable changes to the political, social and economic life of both lands. The first was obviously the type of regime set up by Saladin, who introduced a system of appanages (an entirely family-based conception of power) under the authority of one of the family members recognised as the chief emir, often with the title of sultan. This system could have entailed the splitting up of territories united by Saladin. Some feeling of solidarity prevailed, however, and even if squabbles broke out, a member of the Ayyubid family (al-Malik al-Adil, al-Malik al-Kamil, al-Ayyub for example) was always found to restore family unity. Nevertheless, the apannage system, which led to various provinces of the State being governed by close relations, led in its turn to the creation of lesser appanages and then, in so far as the army constituted the element of force under the Ayyubid princes, to the creation of *iqtas* under military supervision. This system of appanage was not, however, applied to Egypt itself.

The *iqtas* had been developed, under the Seljuks in particular, in the form of assigning the revenues from a given area to an individual (*muqta*), generally a military man. The need to win the army's loyalty, especially towards the end of the dynasty, led them to increase the *iqtas*, and sometimes also to expand them to the extent that they were not much different from appanages; later the Zangids, without any official declaration, accepted the hereditary right of the holders of an *iqta* although in theory they were only a personal gift for life. Because the situation in Syria, with the Frankish presence there, obliged the Ayyubids to build up a strong army, the system of the *iqta* spread throughout the country. All the same, it remained under the supervision of the *diwan al-juyush* (army office), both for the granting of *iqtas* and for the collection of revenue in money or kind due from the *muqta*; the employees of this department were specially responsible for the cadastre, which was indispensable for determining the *iqtas*. In addition, the *muqta* had to provide from the revenues of his *iqta* a certain number of soldiers (10, 20, 100, or whatever) according to the size of his income. In Egypt, this system which existed in a flexible form under the Fatimids was not as extensive as in Syria and was seen as strengthening the strict administrative and financial control of the State, which preserved the ownership of more than half of the land.

Such control required a large number of administrative personnel; the greatest number of posts were occupied by the Copts at all levels in the hierarchy, the Armenians having lost the pre-eminence they held under the Fatimids. Under the Ayyubid princes, the non-Muslim peoples – Christians and Jews – were treated with tolerance in both Syria and Egypt; when the Jews returned to the Sunni fold, Shi'ism practically disappeared with the last Fatimid caliph. Saladin himself was extremely devout and respectful of traditional Muslim laws, and abrogated all the legal decisions that were contrary to Muslim law, which led to

470

Government servant or messenger, this man mounted on a camel would certainly be one of the numerous personnel employed by the administration and merchants to maintain the links necessary for the political and economic organisation of Egypt. (Egyptian gouache drawing, twelfth century; Paris, Louvre.)

some complications. Under his reign and that of his successors, there was a great expansion of the *madrasas*, that is, the institutions where religious and judicial instruction was given, and where religio-judicial and administrative personnel were trained; this expansion was important in Syria and the Jazira, less so in Egypt. As for the army, composed mainly of Turks and Kurds, it suffered from a loss of unity that encouraged rivalries among the princes; gradually the army was taken over by the Turks, especially in Egypt where Malik al-Kamil began massive recruitment among slaves of Turkish origin (the Mamluks), who seized power in 1249 and placed at their head one of themselves, al-Muazzam Turan-Shah, thus inaugurating the regime known as the Mamluk sultanate, which would govern Egypt until 1517.

The seemingly rapid and almost accidental disappearance of the dynasty is evidence of the ossification that seems to have set in in Egypt at the beginning of the thirteenth century. Here we must give due weight to the military difficulties that were occupying the attention and resources of the sultans. As we remarked earlier, the reduction in the Latin possessions to a series of ports in the Levant – but soon backed up by Cyprus and possessions in the Aegean – did not suddenly settle the military problem of the Frankish presence. On the contrary, it was clear that Egypt would henceforth be the target for the West. Cairo was aware of this and there the prevailing policy was one of temporisation and entente. The benefits from Mediterranean trade, the scale of which we will see shortly, were well worth some sacrifices; there was thus a succession of truces and commercial treaties in 1198, 1203 and 1215. When the Christians of the 'King of Jerusalem', John of Brienne (actually based in Acre), attacked Damietta in 1217, al-Kamil went so far as to propose the restoration of the Holy City; if he managed to avoid such a deal that time, it was because of the folly of the Crusaders, who found themselves cut off by the Nile flood outside al-Kamil's camp (1221). The offer was accepted, however, in 1229 by the German Frederick II, who was moreover pro-Islam and Arab-speaking. This enormous concession was also motivated by the constant threat to Syria, not only from the quarrels between the Ayyubid princes and the Frankish attacks (for example between 1239 and 1241), but also from pressure from the

Khwarazmians who ravaged the coasts and ransacked Jerusalem in 1244. The assault led by Louis IX in 1248 from Cyprus towards the Delta was a grave threat to Egypt. Again, it was undoubtedly the carelessness of the Crusaders that led to defeat at Mansura in December 1249, a defeat aggravated by the capture of the king. But it is clear that the sultans had left it all to their mecenaries, notably to Baybars, who now began his brilliant career which was to lead him to the sultanate (1260) and to the reconquest of Palestine and Antioch. In this situation of constant alarms, it is not surprising that the Mamluks should seize power.

This had no bearing on the personal prestige of the sultans. They were largely supported by Egyptian opinion, which was willingly pacifist. The Ayyubids gave great encouragement to the *sufi* religious movement (especially in Syria and upper Egypt), which promoted a mysticism of retreat and humility. A number of convents (*khanaqah*) were established, a distant echo of Eastern monasticism in its early centuries. But the development of *madrasas* was also maintained: Aleppo and Damascus, rather than Cairo, replaced Baghdad as cultural centres. Although in general the Abbasid tradition held sway, the decorative arts quickly turned towards the Fatimid tradition: animal scenes, Kufic inscriptions, and a proliferation of floral decoration.

Economic stability maintained

In the economic sphere, Ayyubid Egypt seems to have continued along the lines laid down by the Fatimids, or perhaps even earlier, so far as internal finances were concerned: the text of the *Minhadj* by al-Makhzumi is typical in this respect. Taxes on non-Muslims (*jawali* or *jizya*) distinguished, according to the *shari'a*, three categories of contributors based on their wealth: the rich, the moderately rich and the poor. It would seem that in late twelfth-century Egypt there were not many in the first category, the majority of subjects falling into the third; in Fayyum there exists a calculation for a uniform tax of two dinars per head, but this appears to be an exception. All the organisation of tax assessment and collection was the job of specialist government servants (*hushshar*, *adilla*, *hussab* etc.). Statements were drawn up every ten days, then every month and at the end of the year.

The *zakat* – the legal tax payable by the Muslims – was levied on grain, animals and the products of major trading (imports and exports). The beneficiaries of the *zakat* were the *amil* (tax collector), the destitute, volunteers for the holy war who were not on the *diwan* list, and some other minor categories. The *kharaj* or land tax was determined by the nature and yield of the crops on the land (liable or not liable to flooding), which implies the establishment of a precise cadastral list; moreover, it seems that the tax on cereals, broad beans, peas, lentils, and so on were collected in kind, while that on fruit trees and some manufacturing crops (flax, cotton, cane) and kitchen vegetables were paid for in cash. There were various other levies and taxes. State properties, dwellings and shops, for example, were subject to levies (*riba*). Taxes paid in coin were banked by the *jahbadh*, those in kind were gathered into the State granaries and stores.

This fiscal system was run by a large number of people and was subject to local modifications, following the lines of previous arrangements, sometimes of very long standing. Not all the arrangements current in Egypt were suitable for Syrian conditions, though a number of them were transferred.

It is unlikely that Egypt experienced an economic boom under the Ayyubids. The causes for stagnation can be sought in the consequences of the Crusaders' presence in the Near East, and the battles and invasions that followed. But we should not conclude that there was a decline either, because favourable conditions still prevailed. Good relations with the Franks encouraged the resumption and development of commercial relations not only with Italian merchants, but also with those from southern France and Catalonia, and the ports of Alexandria, Damietta and Latakia (the outlet for Damascus and Aleppo) benefited from this. These good relations continued until the mid-thirteenth century; there was undoubtedly major international trading activity: the text of the *Minhadj* shows that Egypt formed the focal point of this trade in the Ayyubid world. Damietta exported flax, cotton, skins, fish, spices, sugar, alum, grains, salt and luxury fabrics, while Tinnis exported goods such as gold, silver, silk, material, putty, wood, iron and pitch. Egypt became even more central because access to the Red Sea was forbidden to the Franks – especially to the Italians – and the Ayyubids controlled the Yemen. It was at this time that the group of merchants called the Karimis (whose name has given rise to several hypotheses as to its origin) flourished and practically monopolised trade in the Red Sea, to the detriment of non-Muslim merchants (including the Jews). The Karimis were not just merchants, traders or ship-owners, they were also bankers who constituted trading groups, usually family-based; above all they controlled the trade in produce coming from India and the lands of the Indian Ocean, and were established in Arabia, the Yemen, Alexandria, Damietta and Cairo, but also in Syria where they had contact with the Frankish merchants.

The Karimis were probably the most important providers of customs revenue: they were scarcely affected by the Ayyubid regime and their activities continued under the Mamluks. Their role as well-established intermediaries on the trading route betwen East and West gave them an importance they knew how to use – for the good of the sultan as well as themselves. In the mid-thirteenth century neither the Mongolian threat nor the new Crusades threatened their economic hegemony.

In Syria and Palestine the establishment of Italian merchant colonies in the coastal towns, together with non-aggressive political relations, facilitated trading relations: Italian merchants even got as far as Aleppo and Damascus. If the Egyptian trading route gave access to the Indian Ocean, the Syrian route linked them with Iraq, Iran and the countries of Central Asia. The absence of strife in northern Syria and the Jazira, at least until the Khwarazmians arrived, favoured the export of products from the Middle East (silk, skins, and so on). It is worth noting that the first third of the thirteenth century saw a marked increase in the presence of Frankish merchants in the East. Not only were they in Constantinople, from where they reached the lands round the Black Sea, but they also penetrated Seljuk Asia Minor, as well as Syria and Ayyubid Egypt. They went even further: merchants and also Franciscan and Dominican missionaries endeavoured to push as far as the Mongol world, which was accomplished by the end of the century. There is no doubt that

473

the Ayyubid era, like that of the Seljuks in Asia Minor, facilitated such expansion. The advent of the Mamluk regime in Egypt and Syria in no way hindered the dynamism of the West, which moreover benefited the new masters of these regions.

The birth of 'Turkey'

The political and social fragmentation which occurred under the Seljuks in Iran and Iraq did not affect the Seljuks in Asia Minor, despite a serious crisis in the late twelfth century, at the end of Kilij-Arslan II's reign (1154–92), and after his death.

This branch of the Seljuk family, which settled in Asia Minor after the battle of Manzikert, also carried the name of the Seljuks of Anatolia (from Anadolu, the Turkish name for Asia Minor) or of Rum (from the word 'Roman', as applied to the Byzantine Empire, which claimed to have inherited the former Roman empire). These Seljuks, for most of the twelfth century, had maintained their unity partly thanks to the political and religious struggle against the Byzantines, partly because of local rivalries and the struggle for domination over the Anatolian plateau, which pitted them against the Danishmendids. Victory over the latter in 1173, and then over the Byzantines in 1176, marked the triumph of the Seljuks; hardly had this been won than Kilij-Arslan instituted in his state the system of appanage, giving each of his twelve sons command over a region. For more than fifteen years, Anatolia experienced a situation much like that in the other Seljuk sultanates, but eventually Suleyman II (1196–1204) and Kay-Khusraw I (1204–10) re-established the dynasty's unity and power. The first sixty years of the thirteenth century were a particularly brilliant and prosperous period for the Anatolian Seljuks.

The weakening of the Byzantines – temporarily reduced to the empire of Nicaea (which maintained good relations with the Turks) and the empire of Trebizond (which had to cede the port of Sinope) – facilitated the consolidation of the sultanate of Konya, the town which the Seljuks had made their seat of government, in the interior as well as along the frontiers. On the southern frontier, the Armenians and Franks from Cyprus had to abandon the fortresses in the Cilician Taurus and the ports of Pamphylia, Antalya and Alaiyya; to the east, Seljuk territory spread as far as Erzurum, but Kurdistan, although temporarily conquered, ultimately could not be incorporated into the sultanate. These conquests and reinforcements, accomplished especially by the sultans Kay-Kavus I (1211–20) and Kay-Qubad I (1220–37), had two other consequences. One was to prevent, for the time being, the Turkoman tribes entering Seljuk territory as they were driven westwards by the Mongol advance; the second, thanks to the peace and security which reigned under the Seljuk sultanate and to its consequent prosperity, was to encourage contacts with Italian merchants, notably the Venetians, who could henceforth travel across Asia Minor at no great risk and who concluded commercial agreements with the Seljuks.

Domestically, too, there was consolidation. The Seljuks knew how to build up a state that was well organised politically and administratively, where people of different origins and religions could live together without conflict. This resulted in a pronounced development of urban and rural life, and a real surge of cultural and artistic achievement.

The sultan of Rum maintained his authority over members of his family, to whom in principle he delegated power in the provinces, but with the aid of the army chiefs (the *beys*, who were directly under him) and the administrators (the *valis*, representing the *sahib-i diwan* or vizier, responsible for civil administration, and himself responsible directly to the sultan). There was thus a degree of centralisation of power. The question of influences on this state has long been discussed: were they Byzantine, Iranian, Arabian, or even Turkish? In fact, whatever influences there were, it should be remembered that the Seljuk sultanate was of Turkish origin, if not Turkoman; tribal traditions were maintained, particularly the pre-eminent role of the family and the personal links with other chiefs. After the Danishmendids had been despatched, there was no more fighting with other Turkish groups in Asia Minor until the arrival of the Turkoman bands around 1235–40. The Seljuk state was also a Muslim state and thus followed its rules, acknowledging the *shari'a*, the Holy Law of Islam. But because there were only a small number of suitably qualified Turks, the sultans turned to Iranians and Arabs to fill positions in the civil service; thus the Arab language was important in the administrative sphere (all official texts and inscriptions were in Arabic), while the cultural sphere was dominated by Arabic and Persian. The Turkish language was not abandoned, of course; it remained the language of common use and found expression in popular literature, but it remained basically an oral language. Byzantine influences also appear in the local adaptation of jurisdiction, as in social and religious contacts, the Greeks being numerous in Asia Minor and probably constituting the majority of the population.

Turkish penetration at the end of the eleventh century had two main aspects. First, although it did not involve a large number of individuals, they were tightly grouped and within those groups solidarity was the rule, as with all minorities. The second was that the struggles within the Byzantine Empire had led some people to turn to the Turks in a number of places in Asia Minor, including western Asia Minor. The struggle between Byzantines and Armenians, and among the Armenians themselves, facilitated the penetration and settlement of the Turks in various central and eastern regions: Danishmendids, Saltukids and Mengucheks for example. One could almost say that the settlement of Turks in Asia Minor came about less through their desire to conquer than through opportunities provided by local rulers. The result was that the populations did not undergo political upheavals or a series of changes due to war. One can also add that the Greek or Armenian population remained in place, in the towns as in the countryside; the only inhabitants to leave were the great landowners and some of the Byzantine higher government servants, civil or religious, who had gained land from the Greek Empire. The pressure they exercised on their subjects did not make their departure a matter for regret, and Seljuk taxation was probably no heavier than Byzantine. There were no religious problems: the Turks left the existing Orthodox hierarchy free to exercise their religion, and the Monophysite Greeks and Armenians, the Orthodox patriarchs having gone, gave a warm welcome to the new arrivals, who permitted the free practice of their religion.

It took a long time for these lands to become Turkish and Islamic, a humane process which was the consequence of Turkish and Turkoman peoples occupying part of the 'open'

475

country, and then settling down and entering into relations with the indigenous peasantry; mixed marriages, the number of which we cannot estimate, acted in favour of the development of what was Turkish and Islamic. In the towns, it seems that a certain number of Christian Greeks and Armenians voluntarily converted to Islam, with the intention of preserving the advantages they had already acquired or, given their social or intellectual standing, of gaining administrative posts. We cannot guess at the extent of such conversions, nor should they be exaggerated, but the undeniable fact is that at the end of the twelfth century Asia Minor had a markedly Turkish character; Westerners who travelled across it gave it the name 'Turchia' (while Muslim authors still called it 'the land of Rum'). The Muslim aspect was apparent in the development of guilds on a religious basis or linked to specific groups (artisans, various companies, the military). Among the Turkoman tribes, there was a superficial assimilation of Islam to old traditions from Central Asia; in the fourteenth century the Turkoman spiritual leaders or *babas* seemed to direct the movements challenging official civil and religious powers. Evidence of Islamicisation was also provided by the increased number of mosques as well as of other religious buildings – *madrasas*, tombs, hospitals – some of which were markedly original in their decoration.

The Seljuk tax system was much like that of other Muslim states; the *iqta* was perhaps less extensive and better controlled by the government, and it was only in the second half of the thirteenth century that it became really important through the disintegration of central power. The Seljuk state directly administered a great part of the conquered territories, whose taxes, duties and various revenues were collected locally by the finance officers under the *sahib-i diwan*. In the towns the inhabitants were subject to traditional taxes while trade was subject to import and export duties, market taxes, transaction taxes and so forth.

The towns constituted an important element in the social and economic life of the Seljuk sultanate. This was partly because the military, government servants, monks and Turkish artisans, Iranian and Arab government servants (in the largest towns), Greek, Armenian and Jewish tradesmen and artisans all lived cheek by jowl. In the professional guilds Turkish artisans possibly worked alongside non-Turks, but information on this subject for the period is scarce and we cannot rely on observations made about later periods: the *futuwwa* (*fütüvvet* in Turkish) probably existed, as did the religious brotherhood of the *akhi* (closely linked with the artisans), but both were really fourteenth-century phenomena. Relations were established between Muslim and Christian religious personnel, and a little later one finds evidence of this in the audience and works of the Turkish mystic Mevlana Jelal ed-din Rumi.

Economic life, undoubtedly restricted and compartmentalised for the whole of the twelfth century because of the fighting and troubles that dominated Asia Minor, received fresh impetus once political unity and security were established at the end of that century. Local production (agriculture, cattle breeding, wood, carpets, honey, alum, gold, copper) increased noticeably. Exports grew, facilitated by the fact that the Seljuks, in the first quarter of the thirteenth century, were masters of the outlets to the Black Sea (Sinope, Samsun) and the Mediterranean (Alaiyya, Antalya).

Italian merchants landed at the Mediterranean ports, Greek merchants traded from the

A mosque-hospital. Besides the 'cathedral-type' mosque, there were a number of buildings used for daily prayers. Other buildings could be annexed to them, such as *madrasas*, hospitals and so on. Such complexes were developed especially in Turkey in the twelfth and thirteenth centuries. The mosque-hospital of Divrigi (1228–9) is counted among the most handsome examples of this type.

Black Sea ports, Armenian merchants traded with Iraq and especially Iran, the Byzantines of Nicaea in the time of John Vatatzes traded with the Turks. Asia Minor was criss-crossed by caravan routes along which were built staging-posts, the caravanserai or *khans*, which were also to be found in the larger towns. The main routes connected the Mediterranean ports of Antalya and Alaiyya with towns in the interior: Konya, Akshehir, Ankara, Aksaray, Kayseri, Sivas and Erzurum (the transit route towards Iran). This exchange and transit trade was particularly beneficial for the Seljuks, who collected customs duties, tolls, entry and exit taxes.

Little is known about the intellectual world of Seljuk Asia Minor except through the religious and mystical writings of Mevlana Jelal ed-din Rumi (1207–73), author of mystical works written in Persian and Arabic, and only rarely in Turkish. His son, Sultan Veled, and his disciples founded the brotherhood of Mevleni dervishes (or 'whirling dervishes') in his honour and to his memory. Literary works were written in Arabic and Persian, and they remained scarce until the fourteenth century.

On the other hand, there was a rich and original artistic culture. The Turks brought to Anatolia a distinctive art, initially borrowed from the Iranians and Arabs but now adapted to local geographical and social conditions, with perceptible influences from the Byzantines and Armenians (we know the Greek names of the architects of Seljuk mosques). This art

477

was manifest in the mosques (Ala ed-din Mosque in Konya, mid-twelfth to early thirteenth century; Ala ed-in Mosque in Nidje in 1224; the great mosque of Divrigi of 1229; the great mosque of Malatya in 1247), in the *madrasas* (in Konya, Kayseri, Erzurum), in polygonal or round tombs (Divrigi, Niksar, Konya, Kayseri, Sivas), in palaces – of which, unfortunately, almost nothing remains but a memory – and in a number of caravanserai, the remains of which can still be seen along the old caravan routes. These constructions were evidence of the prosperity of the country, and of their builders having the confidence to leave their mark, not only on a religious level. There was a feeling for decoration, whether on the portals and façades with their geometrical, floral or lettered motifs, or inside buildings with their blue, black and white tiles. Seljuk art was not grandiloquent, but it was on a human scale and expressed a simple and direct taste.

The Ottomans who later pursued and extended the work of the Seljuks found that the latter provided a model they could use and develop. It was more through the Seljuks of Asia Minor than through those of Iran or Iraq that the Turkish world learnt to take its place in the Muslim world of the Near East.

The final flowering of Persia

The power that the Seljuks of Iraq had established over the whole of the Middle East, from eastern Asia Minor to Khurasan, was immediately subject to the internecine struggles which engaged the energies of the heirs of Sultan Malik-Shah shortly after his death in 1092. The family unity established by the Great Seljuk sultanate was fragmented through the covetousness of the princes, not to mention that of their tutors and guardians, the *atabegs*; each wanted to ensure domination over a piece of the sultanate, and thus principalities were formed, sometimes quite small, whose rulers seemed to have only one aim – fighting each other. This break-up, accentuated in Syria by the arrival of the Crusaders, was mainly due to the appanage system under the Seljuks, and to rivalries that had broken out even in the top echelons of the State before the death of Malik-Shah. It is equally likely that those who held appanages in their turn increased the assignment of *iqtas* in order to ensure the support of a military faction, but the increasing weakness of the princes permitted the transformation of these temporary, life-long grants into hereditary personal property. Moreover, some *atabegs* leaned heavily on the local populace – Iranian, Arabian or Kurdish, according to the region – in order to build up their own power. The tribes, who until then had more or less supported the authority of the Seljuks, cast off this yoke and in effect gained their independence.

In Baghdad, profiting from this disintegration of the Seljuk sultanate, the caliph al-Nasir (who reigned from 1180 to 1245) came forward and exploited his role as caliph. He sought to surround himself with the different components of the Muslim world, including the Shi'ites; he also turned to political, corporate, social and cultural groups, such as the *futuwwa*, which he transformed into a source of support for the caliphate, especially in Baghdad where it henceforth consititued the dominant element in the city, run by the bourgeois and military circles devoted to the person of the caliph.

478

In this confused political situation, and against the backdrop of an economy that was gradually weakening because of the diversion of the main trade route either to the north or across the Iranian plateau, it is suprising to encounter a continuation – one might even say the climax – of an intellectual and artistic sophistication which was easily the equal to that at the end of the tenth century or in the eleventh. But it had shifted eastwards, gradually abandoning Baghdad for Shiraz, Isfahan and Harat. As this 'orientalisation' increased, Iranian, Bactrian and even Hindu influences swept through Persian art, giving it a second life. This was not merely a veneer; these influences penetrated as far as the design of religious buildings, introducing the use of the central court flanked by four *iwans*, enormous alcoves reserved for prayer, each flanked by two slender minarets, the new type of 'Turkish' or 'Indian' mosque, but also obviously based on the design of the Sassanian or even Achaemenid palaces. The twelfth and thirteenth centuries also saw increased Asiatic influence on decoration: historiated pottery with incised scenes, polychrome faience with floral or fantastic patterns in which we see many of the elements of the Far East.

The *madrasas* of the eleventh century had encouraged an intellectual upsurge unmatched in the West. By contrast, the twelfth and thirteenth centuries give the impression of consolidation or of taking stock. Al-Ghazali, who died in 1111, was the embodiment of the pessimistic tradition in Persian thought: his book 'The confusion of the philosophers' was a rigorous critique of innumerable systems of thought handed down from Antiquity and the beginning of the Muslim world. In his desire to return to a life of purity, isolation and faith, which the *Sufis* had been demanding for a century, he looks to us like a Muslim precursor of the great movement towards a simpler life which disturbed the Christianity of St Francis a hundred years later. But this hope of spiritual renewal was underpinned by an optimistic tradition in Persian thought: al-Ghazali was answered by Suhrawardi (d.1191) who, sweeping away the rubble of sects who were always internally divided, tried to leave a syncretic, almost Neoplatonic message, dominated by the idea of a complete wisdom that assimilated all that had gone before. As for literary expression, that also took on a *fin-de-siècle* appearance: the 'assemblies', the *maqamat*, which portrayed daily life in racy, ferocious or lyrical little plays, were the fashionable genre at the end of the thirteenth century. These have given us miniatures rich in picturesque details, exercises in linguisitic viruosity, but are evidence of a society that had run out of fresh ideas. Few works of universal value appeared but, at a time when mortal danger threatened this sophisticated culture, there is something poignant about the most illustrious of court and city poets, Sadi of Shiraz (who died in 1290, at the age of nearly a hundred), devoting his most beautiful works to the description of roses.

Thus, after suffering violent internal fighting between the partisans or so-called defenders of the Abbasid caliphate and those of the Fatimid caliphate, and after the confrontations with the Franks in Palestine and Syria, the eastern Muslim world found an apparent unity. There was now only one caliph, the caliph of Baghdad, and Sunnism was triumphant, the Shi'ites and heterodox religious believers having been defeated or eliminated. This unity was, however, only apparent; in fact, new states under the name of sultanates were being established in politically and geographically well-defined regions: Asia Minor, **479**

Syria–Palestine, Egypt, Iraq, Iran, not to mention the distant areas where other dynasties emerged, such as those of the Khwarazm-Shahs, and the new wave of Turkomans spreading eastwards.

Moreover, power henceforth passed from Arab and Persian hands into those of other peoples who had hitherto been their subjects, such as the Kurds and the Turks, who had adopted Islam and were more or less adapted to the situation around them. Here Arab culture and traditions were easily maintained, the Persian substratum or the new Turkish input imposing compromises that led to regional differentiation.

It should be noted that in the mid-thirteenth century the Muslim states of the Near East seemed to have triumphed over their many difficulties and installed apparently solid and well-run regimes. Furthermore, closer contacts with the Franks had encouraged the development of trading relations and an expansion of economic life in general, even if, in some regions, traditional structures were overturned by the arrival of nomadic or semi-nomadic tribes. But only the disintegration of central power in Asia Minor, in western Iran for example, could bring about general collapse.

Around 1230–50, then, the most significant feature is the fragmentation of the eastern Muslim world. It was only the dominant Arab and Persian influences in the spheres of religion, power, literature, science and art, that held the disparate areas together.

The Mongol catastrophe

Beyond the easternmost Muslim outposts, north of the caravan trail joining Samarkand and Bukhara to northern China, nomadism was the traditional way of life. From this 'melting pot' of the Steppes, the clans of Huns, Avars, Turks and Magyars broke out in search of fresh pastures, either towards China or towards the Volga, as far as Iran. In the ninth century, if not earlier, Islam had reached the western fringe, the almost untouched lands of the Uigur Turks, provoking two movements: the influx of mercenaries as far as Iraq, followed eventually by the strong tide of Seljuks and the Turkoman infiltrations. In the opposite direction there came the merchants and the fugitives – Nestorian Christians and Mazdakite Persians seeking refuge as far away as Lake Baikal. A parallel phenomenon was taking place in northern China where the yellow-skinned Tartars and Khitans settled in Peking, adopting Chinese ways and converting to Buddhism. Travellers and pilgrims thought little of the pastoral tribes who continued to wander between the Gobi and the Siberian taiga. What we know of their funerary art, however, and of their effective military organisation indicates a significant level of development; although their animism or the simple worship of *Tengri*, Heaven, seemed to leave them entirely indifferent to the monotheistic religions of their sedentary neighbours.

In the last decades of the twelfth century, the actual Mongol or Turco-Mongol clans living between Lake Baikal and the upper reaches of the Amur took some steps towards federation, from time to time putting a *khaqan*, a great chief or supreme *khan*, at their head. This might have been a new attempt at amalgamation as a prelude to a move towards China rather than towards the west, where the Khwarazmian Turks (Uigurs) and the Khitay (both converts to Islam) seemed little inclined to yield them ground. Yesügei's clan, which came from the region of Qaraqorum, south-east of Lake Baikal, managed to put together one such union on the basis of 'fraternal' oaths and marriage alliances. Yesügei's son, Temujin, probably recognised as *khaqan* around 1195, was able to imbue his tribe with military organisation and discipline which, after a dozen years of raids and pillage, gave him supremacy over the peoples of the east (the Tartars and Merkit of northern China) and the south (the Kerait and Naiman tribes), before he finally wheeled west, around 1212, on the Uigurs and Qarluqs settled in Islamic territory.

As ruler, he took the title of Chingiz (Genghis) Khan, and established a system of organisation in the conquered lands that was entirely new for an empire based on a steppe without towns: regular assembly meetings (*quriltai*) of tribal chiefs, a hierarchy of military ranks with a regular system of promotion and specific functions for each, and appointment of governors responsible for levying the tribute (*darughachi*) in the regions occupied by non-nomadic peoples. The government of the whole rested with the khan, but his family could receive a grant (*ulus*) of power over lands conquered or to be conquered. An efficient courier system enabled Chingiz Khan to be kept informed of any possible insubordination on the part of a son or 'brother', i.e. another tribal chief.

It is almost impossible to know what motivated Chingiz Khan (and after his death in 1227, his sons Ogedei, Chaghatai, his grandson Güyük and his great-grandson Möngke, who was elected Great Khan in 1251) to go so far beyond the traditional nomad areas of the Mongols. Indifferent to religion, for a long time unskilled in administration or taxation, untouched by any interest in either urban life or agriculture, the Mongols of the mid-thirteenth century seemed to have acted in the manner of the Huns in previous centuries: pillaging in order to seize provisions or horses, destroying in order to avoid any reprisal, occupying in order to increase their grip. Such a rudimentary concept of 'government' obviously depended on having a sufficient number of warriors at their disposal, probably less than 150,000 mounted men altogether, but they were light, mobile, excellent archers, trained to all the hunter's tricks; moreover, they knew how to use the weapon of terror, skilfully backed by savage reprisals. As had been the case with the Huns, since all resistance or surprise attacks triggered a systematic slaughter of the conquered people and the exhibition of corpses as trophies, any sign of a Mongol raid aroused extreme panic and brought about immediate submission. But the disorder unleashed among sedentary peoples was not confined to psychological upheaval or even death: the Mongols, by burning down towns, filling in canals and destroying rural habitation, stifled the economic activity of entire regions, dispersing the population, wiping out the élites and crushing religion.

Eastern Islam suffered grievous damage. Already in 1220–3 a disastrous campaign had ruined Bukhara, Samarkand, Kabul, Balkh, Ghazna, Nishapur and Rayy before it moved on to the Ukraine and Crimea. Between 1233 and 1241 another campaign, led by the remarkable tactician Sübötei, devastated the whole of Iran, the Kurdish lands and Armenia, before striking the Armenians in Cilicia and the sultan of Rum, who could only escape by submitting to the Mongols. Sübötei then crossed the Caucasus, subjugated the Kipchaks of the Volga and Vladimir's Russian principalities of Kiev and Moscow; he burnt down Novgorod

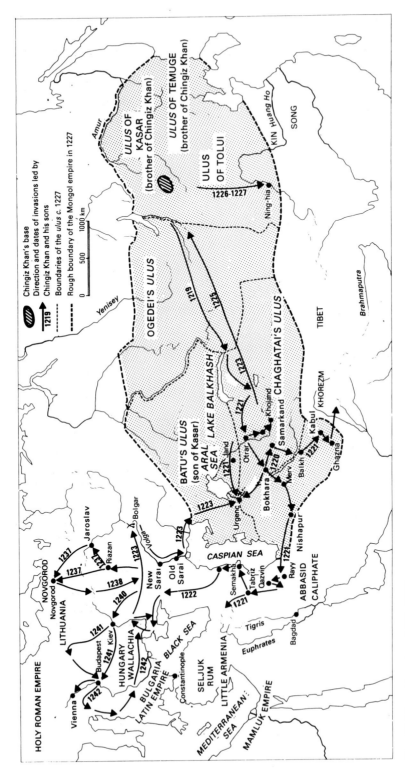

Map 19. Mongol invasions, 1219–1250.

near Lake Ladoga before advancing on Poland and Hungary, devastating the region of Vienna, then withdrawing to the Adriatic in an atmosphere of apocalypse – an atmosphere that spread through Europe owing to the horrifying tales of the Slav and Danubian Christians. A third campaign in 1256, undertaken by Hülegü, also a grandson of Chingiz, was aimed this time at Iraq and Syria: in 1258, Baghdad was taken and the Abbasid caliph stuffed into a sack and trampled by horses, a pitiful end to the dynasty. Only Baybars' Mamluks managed to stem the tide in 1260, when it tried to turn towards Sinai. If we add to all this the wandering troops of Turkomans and Khwarazmians, fleeing in panic from extermination or slavery, who managed to turn the life of the Near East upside down (for example when they sacked Jerusalem in 1244), we can easily appreciate the appalling and unforeseeable disaster which Islam suffered in one generation.

It should be conceded that worship was not forbidden, holy places had not been profaned, and Kurdish Egypt remained safe. Even in subjection, the Anatolian Turks constituted a strong force and, as we shall see, the *pax Mongolia* had its advantages for merchants and missionaries. But the glowing hearths of Muslim culture, which had burned for five centuries, this melting pot where the heritage of Antiquity, of Iran, of Hinduism and Hellenism had met to enlarge the human spirit, were now extinguished. We have to wait until the latter half of the twentieth century for Syrian, Mesopotamian and Persian Islam to reawaken – and in a very different form.

The Maghrib on the move

The power of the Almoravid Empire should not make us forget that the eleventh and twelfth centuries were generally a period of territorial retreat for western Islam. Christian cities and states, their economies and societies, were all expanding and, in the end, proved to be the more dynamic force. The chronicles of the Hispano-Maghribine dynasty are mostly an account of constant effort, not always crowned with success. Laborious and expensive mobilisation of great armies were required to check the progress in Spain of an enemy whose socio-political organisation, feudal in part, favoured progress at the expense of Muslim society. The latter, in its urban and rural forms, was organised on quite different lines, insufficiently militarised and unable to provide from its own ranks the forces necessary for its defence.

It is important to note that it was during the first half of the eleventh century that the first manifestations of this Islamic inferiority to Christendom began to appear. This was the era of the crisis of the Cordoban caliphate, which enabled Castilian and Catalan warriors to intervene in the internal affairs of Muslim Spain and to bring back from their expeditions the dirhams and dinars which would henceforth haunt the dreams of Christendom's adventurers. To see the very first signs of the relative decline of western Islam, however, we should perhaps go back a little further, towards the end of the tenth century, to the period when Andalusian piracy was declining, when the base at Fraxinetum (La Garde-Freinet) was destroyed and when Christian mercenaries were already being recruited in great numbers for the caliph's army.

The political divisiveness of the *taifas* is perhaps not in itself a cause of Islamic weakness. The Christian states in the north of the peninsula were also divided, and it would have been difficult to predict, in the first decades of the eleventh century, that the powerful kingdom of Toledo would be absorbed by the Castilian–León bloc, or that poor, minuscule Aragon, penned in by mountains, would finally take over the huge, rich valley of the Ebro, with its prosperous towns, its irrigated crops and its infinitely superior economic and cultural life. Rivalry between the Muslim rulers was probably only one of the causes of the inferiority of the *taifa* kingdoms relative to their Christian adversaries, an inferiority that showed itself in the economic and political dependence that became obvious with the payment of *parias* in the second half of the century. There are doubtless other, deeper, unknown causes which also explain the divison and then the collapse of Sicily under Norman attack from the south of Italy. In Sicily, as in Spain, political disorganisation and military weakness were apparent before the mid-eleventh century. The Byzantines regained a foothold on the island from 1038 to 1040, when the unified state of the Kalbi dynasty in Palermo was disintegrating. Between 1061 and 1091 the Normans occupied the island, while in Spain the Christians began their territorial advance, no longer content with the profit to be had from imposing tribute on the politically subordinate Muslim states. The first conquests were the work of King Fernando of León-Castile, at the expense of the kingdom of Badajoz in the north of what is now Portugal (Lamego and Viseu in 1057–8, Coimbra in 1064). In 1085 his successor, Alfonso VI, entered Toledo and at the same time, Valencia became for nearly twenty years the seat of a large Christian army. In the east, the Aragonese took Huesca in 1096. In the Mediterranean, it is above all the growing strength of the Italian cities that attracts our attention.

Considered as a whole, these factors reveal an indisputable military decline in western Islam during the eleventh century, as it faced the power and increasing dynamism of the Christians. Perhaps we should also refer to the internal causes of this decline. We know that some documents from the Cairo Genizah seem to show that there was a difficult situation in Zirid Ifrikiya from the first half of the eleventh century: a letter written around 1040 by a Tunisian Jew congratulates his correspondent on his intention to settle in Egypt, because 'the whole of the West will henceforth be worth nothing'. This remark confirms the arguments that an economic and social crisis was developing even before the Hilali invasion of the Maghrib.

The Hilali: a catastrophe?

Fierce controversy rages around this problem. The historiography of the colonial era tended to make the 'Hilali catastrophe' the major turning-point in the history of the medieval Maghrib. These Arab nomads, despatched by the caliphs of Cairo to 'reconquer' Zirid Ifrikiya for their own benefit, had thrown off the Fatimid yoke. By their arrival in 1051–2 they provoked a fatal imbalance in this urban, sedentary civilisation with its Roman traditions, a civilisation that was particularly vulnerable because of the ecological conditions in the country. The defeat of the Zirid troops at Haydaran in 1052 marked the beginning of end for the Kairouan state. The Zirid dynasty, from 1057, had to retreat to Mahdiyya, abandoning the interior to Bedouin raids. The same process was repeated several years later in the state of the Banu Hammad, where the emir al-Nasir in 1068–9 had to leave his capital, Qal'a, which was too exposed to the Hilali, to establish himself on the coast in the newly founded town of Bougie. Nomadic forms of life thus developed throughout most of the eastern and central Maghrib at the expense of settled agriculture and hitherto prosperous towns, which survived with some difficulty by adapting to the development of a countryside largely beyond their control. Politically the country fragmented into a number of autonomous local governments of varying kinds: urban oligarchies, Arab tribal chiefdoms, petty local principalities in the hands of a *qa'id* playing at being an independent lord – they all sprang up spontaneously in an anarchy that contrasted sharply with the well-ordered and centralised large states of the preceding period.

Some of the elements of the general picture sketched here cannot reasonably be doubted. The political fragmentation of the second half of the eleventh century is undeniable, as is the growing Bedouin influence over the countryside. The picture of the central Maghrib painted by al-Idrisi in the first half of the twelfth century is convincing enough. There is a striking contrast between the prosperity of Bougie and the surrounding plains and the difficulties experienced by areas in the interior, beyond the chain of the Bibans, 'to which the raids of the Arabs stretched'. In the region of Qal'a, for example, 'the inhabitants live with the Arabs in a state of truce which does not prevent conflict arising between them, in which the latter usually have the advantage'. Four days' journey to the east, Mila is 'a handsome town, well watered, surrounded by trees which bear plenty of fruit. It is populated by Berbers of different tribes, but the Arabs are the masters of the countryside.' This last example, however, suggests that we should not exaggerate the scope of the 'devastation' wrought by the tribes coming from Egypt in the mid-eleventh century. In many places a balance was struck between the Arabs and the natives, citizens or peasants, as at Constantine, 'a populous and commercial town, whose inhabitants are rich, which has advantageous treaties with the Arabs and co-operates with them in cultivating the land and reaping the harvests'.

The spread of the new eastern ethnic element in many parts of the Maghrib had a variety of consequences, whose impact it is often difficult to judge. The Hilali invasion has been blamed first of all for 'the disappearance of a good many cities established in Antiquity as well as more recent creations, such as the temporary capitals of the Banu Hammad, Qal'a, Achir, Tihert, along with the annihilation of a good many villages, and the sadness and desolation of much fertile countryside'. Without discounting such 'destruction' in the interior regions, some studies have stressed the effects of the arrival of the Hilali on the monetary economy; 'On the one hand, the Hilali invasion dried up the influx of Sudanese gold, and on the other the anarchy was such that Ifrikiya was driven to buy grain in Sicily. As the Normans demanded payment in gold, one can see a positive haemorrhage of the yellow metal. Hence at Mahdiyya, a shortage of gold, the need to secure it in order to pay for grain, the necessity of privateering (seizure of precious merchandise, gold pieces and Christians who could be ransomed for gold).' 'Anti-colonialist' authors, for their part, detect **485** clear signs of economic and social malaise in the western Maghrib before the Hilali arrived, so that they merely accelerated a process that had already begun. Such authors tend to emphasise the difficulties caused by the way trading routes veered towards Spain, and by the increasing Christian power in the Mediterranean. For some Maghribian authors, the advent of the Hilali even has a positive general effect, 'since it transformed and regenerated the Maghrib, disseminated Arabic in the rural areas and hastened linguistic unity. It established relations between town and country that were very often peaceful and fruitful, gave the country an effective military presence and prevented medieval Christianity from gaining a foothold in North Africa.'

In fact, the historiography of the period is shot through with prejudices and value judgements. We lack precise studies that would allow us to judge the manner and timing of the disintegration of urban life, which affected the interior but not the coasts, where the city-states of Mahdiyya, Bougie and Tunis remained, along with a number of secondary centres that were more or less independent. Should we see the towns everywhere becoming 'entrenched camps isolated in the midst of a depopulated countryside'? At least we should note that neither the Arabs' progress in the hinterland nor the military and commercial growth of the Christians in the Mediterranean prevented the large coastal towns from prospering; around them state structures were preserved. After the Almohad episode, it was around one such centre, Tunis, that the Ifrikiyan State of the Hafsids reorganised itself. They managed to restore the political unity of the eastern Maghrib in a flexible and realistic way, on the basis of allowing a large degree of autonomy to the Arab tribes, the Berbers in the mountain regions and, at times when the dynasty was weakened, to the many cities and territories in the south and west. Not all the dynamism and constructive force of State structure had disappeared from these territories if we are to judge by the fact that even in the fourteenth century on three occasions 'the master of the dissident state of Constantine, by taking Tunis, forcibly recreated Hafsidic unity'.

The Almohad interval

The initial expression of the Berber revival was at least as surprising as that of the Almoravids in the eleventh century, and just as brief. Muhummad ibn Tumart, the defender of the oneness of God (al-muwahhid, hence the name Almohad), a Berber from the Masmuda tribe in the Moroccan Atlas mountains, had been a zealous disciple of al-Ghazali in the East, and like him was convinced of the need to return to his roots. Around 1120 he began to attack in Marrakesh the jurists, the *fuqaha*, the Jews, the ungodly, all those among the Almoravids whom he suspected of laxity and duplicity. Forced to take refuge in Tinmal in the mountains around 1125, he founded a militant community there, had himself proclaimed as the Mahdi, and sent his disciples out to the plain even before his death in 1130. In the space of fifty years, either in the form of individual raids or, after 1145, raids by army corps made up of united Berber tribes, the Almohads took over the whole of the Maghrib. Fez (1160), Marrakesh (1147), Bougie (1152) and Kairouan (1160) fell into their hands in an atmosphere reminiscent of the Fatimid outburst of the tenth century, but in which

486

certain canny commanders, such as the Norman Roger II of Sicily, took part by stepping up their landings and raids in the territory from Tunis to Mahdiyya. After 1145, the Almohads also crossed into Spain: Cordoba (1148), Seville (1149), Granada (1154) and Valencia (1171) were all occupied. Yaqʿub Yusuf, the grandson of the Mahdi, then Yusuf Yaqʿub, his great-grandson, managed to occupy Almoravid Spain, and the Castilians, who were alarmed, were firmly resisted at Alarcos (1196).

Almohad domination is rich in contrasts. On the one hand these austere 'reformers' whose art was systematically severe and abstract, lost little time in spending extravagant sums on their palaces and mosques. It is to their period, if not to these very men, that we owe some of the most beautiful minarets still standing in western Islam: the Hasan tower in Rabat, the Kutubiyah in Marrakesh, the Giralda in Seville. On the other hand, these systematic minds, hostile to pagan philosophy, to gnosis and to Jews (whom they persecuted), produced the three most confidently original systems of thought in the Maghrib of the time. The first is that of Ibn Bajjah (Avempace as he was known to Christians), a doctor in Fez then in Seville (d. 1138) and the first commentator on the *Metaphysics* and *Categories* of Aristotle. He was the teacher of Ibn Rushd (1126–98), known to the Christians as Averroes, who became their intellectual beacon in the thirteenth century. Hostile to al-Ghazali, convinced of the need for reasoned dialectic to support dogma, Averroes is a fundamental link in the introduction of rationalism into European thought. Our third orginal thinker is Maimonides (d. 1204), a persecuted Jew, who was one of the most active propagators of Aristotelianism within the Jewish community – and, as we know, the Jews played a key role as intermediaries between the Islamic and Christian worlds.

The collapse

During the summer of 1212, having forced the passes of the sierra Morena, the three Christian kings – Alfonso VIII of Castile, Sancho of Navarre and Pedro II of Aragon – inflicted a severe defeat on the Almohads at Las Navas de Tolosa. The Berber domination of the straits had already been weakened by rebellions among the chiefs. Between 1235 and 1265, the Christians swept the Muslim garrisons from Spain: the Portuguese were at Beja in 1235, the Aragonese were at Valencia in 1238 and in the Balearics in 1235; the Castilians reached Cordoba (1236), Murcia (1243), Cartagena (1244), Seville (1248) and Cadiz (1265). It was the complete and irrevocable collapse of Islam in Iberia: there were only the shreds of Malaga and Granada left, the jewels of Muslim art that glowed until the end of the fifteenth century.

The disaster spread like an epidemic: in Ifrikiya the Hafsids settled in Tunis, relying after 1226 on the pirates of the Balearics, and after 1236 the Ziyanids settled in the central Atlas region. In Morocco itself, the Berber revolts increased, especially in the Zanata where the clan of the Banu Merin (the Merinids) occupied the plain and settled in Marrakesh in 1269. Maghrib unity was broken in three, and only the superficial Ottoman influence in the modern era restored it.

However, as with the collapse of eastern Islam, the collapse of western Islam did have some positive aspects. Small but vital groups were reassembled in areas where they had undisputed historical and geographical roots, in Morocco in particular, and in Egypt. The collapse freed the commercial gold routes to the Sudan, which henceforth ran to the Mediterranean without the obstacles of universalist or fundamentalist influences; and the Saharan trails, those gates to black Africa, were opened to trade just as Anatolia and the shores of the Caspian were opened under Mongol control. In the short term, however, the outcome seemed disastrous. On the point of regaining Toledo and of taking Constantinople at the end of the eleventh century, the Muslims in the mid-thirteenth century had been entirely driven from the sea, cut off to both the east and the west from territories essential to their domination; and the only ones among them who were prominent in the following centuries were Muslims of a very different sort. Islam was to slumber for seven centuries, a longer period than its entire previous existence.

The death throes of Byzantium: 1080–1261

11

The great defeat at the hands of the Turks in 1071 did not change the empire overnight. It was only gradually that weaknesses came to light and, as has been rightly said, a journey through Byzantine territory at the end of the twelfth century would in fact have revealed an extraordinary stability in people's lives, especially in the countryside. The same is true of the very structure of the empire; while it is obvious to us that it was gradually retreating to its European territories, it is doubtful that contemporaries were aware of this and, at least until the end of Manuel Komnenos' reign in 1180, the regaining of Asia Minor was an essential part of the imperial plan.

The loss of Anatolia after the battle of Manzikert was not in fact inevitable. The victor, the sultan Alp-Arslan, had no real intention of establishing himself there; his aim, as a very orthodox ruler, was to get rid of the heretical caliphate of the Egyptian Fatimids. In fact it was the internal upheavals of the empire combined with a serious under-estimation of the danger posed by the Turks that sealed Asia Minor's fate.

Behind the façade

The death of Romanos IV Diogenes in 1071 was followed, in the reign of Michael VII Doukas (1071–8), by a series of military uprisings in Asia. The protagonists, whether Greek or Norman, regularly relied on support from the bands of Turks who roamed the country, while the government itself, mistakenly believing the sultan to be the basic danger, introduced these same bands into the area around the Straits. The new Seljuk sultan, Malik-Shah, sought in vain for entente with Byzantium.

The latter did not believe he was sincere and instead took into its service one of Malik-Shah's cousins, Suleiman. Under cover of working for Byzantium, Suleiman was already in control of the shores of the Sea of Marmara by c. 1080 and he came into direct confrontation with Malik-Shah in the conquest of eastern Anatolia. The empire was equally blind with regard to the West: in rejecting the advances of Gregory VII it threw him

Livestock turned loose, crops devastated – the empire was powerless before the raiding bands of Turks in the Anatolian countryside. (Greek MS 135. Paris. Bibliothèque nationale.)

into the arms of the Normans, thus forcing him into tacit approval of the Norman offensive in Albania in 1081–5.

Byzantium confined to Europe

Central authority, however, recovered its stability in 1081, with the *coup d'état* which brought Alexios I Komnenos to power. Despite his talent, the new emperor clearly demonstrated that Byzantium could no longer keep fighting on several fronts. The gravest danger was that which overshadowed the Balkans. First of all there was the attack by Guiscard on Albania, which could not have been countered in 1085 without the help of the Venetian fleet; then there were the Pechenegs, who surged across the Danube from 1086 to 1091. The Byzantines' own efforts gradually pushed them back but they came so close to Constantinople that, for the first time, the emperor was obliged to ask for help from a Latin lord, the Count of Flanders, Robert the Frisian. During this period, the Byzantine armies were virtually inactive in Asia. Their only intervention (and an inept one at that) was to repulse Malik-Shah who, in trying to eliminate his rebellious cousins, was actually doing the empire's job – for not content with attacking places such as Nicomedia, the local emirs were using pirate fleets to carry out raids around the Aegean. In 1092, however, the emperor finally seemed to grasp the situation and agreed to an alliance with the great sultan whose death the same year would allow Suleyman's descendants to regroup slowly.

The main event of Alexios' reign, the First Crusade, sheds light on the resources and aims of the empire. Around 1095, the empire was at peace for the first time in twenty years, but its recent trials had weakened it to such an extent that there was no question of its launching an offensive in Asia Minor with its own forces alone. If there could be no question of calling on the Latins for help, which the situation no longer warranted, Byzantium could dream of taking them into its service in the form of mercenaries, which it had been doing anyway for more than half a century. It was probably what the Byzantine envoys requested at the Council of Piacenza in 1095. We know that the Westerners, particularly Bohemond, an old enemy of Byzantium, had no intention of limiting their activities to regaining power on the emperor's behalf. We also know that the Crusade gave birth to political units built on territories that had once belonged to Byzantium, especially in Edessa and Antioch, so giving rise to confrontations between Greeks and Latins until 1104, and which, thanks to Bohemond, produced material for a programme of propaganda implying for the first time that the Greeks were traitors and allies of the Turks. Bohemond, returning to the West, profited from this by carrying the fight into the Balkans. The second Norman Albanian expedition, in 1107, ended in a defeat which obliged him to recognise Alexios as his lord for the principality of Antioch, but he died in 1111 and his successors renounced this subordinate status. The Crusade could only complicate the overall position of Byzantium in Asia Minor, adding Latin enemies to its old Muslim adversaries. From the point of view of the Greeks, who had difficulty in seeing how it differed from Norman attacks, the Crusade constituted a constant threat to their western borders, something unknown to them until then. Combined with the nomad advance on the Danube and the

491

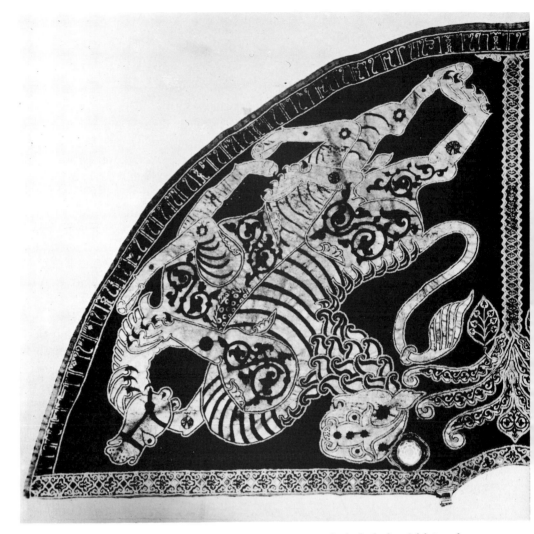

The coronation cloak of Roger II of Sicily. Son of the Norman Roger I Guiscard, who had taken Calabria and Sicily from the Muslims, Roger II was crowned king in 1130. This splendid cloak of silk and gold, studded

birth of new Slav states such as Raška and Zeta, it encouraged them to deploy the core of their hard-pressed forces in protecting their Balkan territories. This was the main feature of the reign of Alexios' son, John II Komnenos (1118–43). Until 1135 he defended his western borders against Pechenegs, Serbs and Hungarians, and when confronted by the renewed Norman threat after the accession of Roger II of Sicily, his response was to integrate the empire more closely into the Latin political system, tightening his links with Venice and Pisa and even allying himself with the German Empire. It was only in 1137 that he managed to get the prince of Antioch to recognise his sovereignty, but this was renounced in 1142, and it was on an expedition aimed at crushing the eastern Latins that the emperor died, in April 1143.

with pearls and precious stones was made in Palermo by Egyptian craftsmen.
(Vienna, Kunsthistorisches Museum.)

The 'sick man of Europe'

No doubt it was the inactivity of the Turkish world that masked the very Western character of John II's work, and the same is true of the greater part of the reign of his son, Manuel
I (1143–80). The great undertakings of the latter in the West seem to be those of an empire
that was once more on the offensive and sure of its eastern borders, but in fact they testify
to a recentring of the empire on its Balkan territory and to the grave need to regain control
of the Adriatic and the Ionian Seas. More than the Second Crusade which, while it alienated the empire from France, left the German alliance mostly intact, it was the Sicilian
threat that marked the first years of Manuel's reign.

In 1147, Roger II captured Corfu and raided Greece, taking with him most of the silk-workers from Thebes and Corinth. This orientation towards the Adriatic explains why, at the same time, Byzantium sought to exert increasingly tight control over Serbia and Hungary which rebelled in 1149. Venice, which was aware of presenting itself as a vulnerable target, helped Manuel to regain Corfu the same year, but the siege of the town was the occasion for the first significant clash between Greeks and Venetians. The latter saw their fears confirmed when Manuel, profiting from Roger's death in 1154, regained a foothold in Italy and subjugated the Marches and Apulia; he was expelled in 1156 and had to make peace two years later, so marking the end of Byzantine claims to Italy but not of those directed towards the Adriatic. In 1161, Manuel imposed his candidate for the succession to the throne of Hungary and profited from this by winning power over Croatia, Bosnia and, most significantly, Dalmatia. When the emperor also received the submission of the Grand Župan of Serbia (Stephen Nemanja), Byzantium – once again master of its western seaboard – became all too real a threat for Venice, as well as for the German emperor (Frederick Barbarossa), the king of Sicily and even for the pope and the maritime republics of the Tyrrhenian Sea (Genoa and Pisa). Thus while Manuel was confiscating Venetian property within the empire in 1171, a large coalition of all these powers came together between 1169 and 1177.

The calm on the eastern borders, however, should not disguise the renewal of Turkish power in this period. The Anatolian sultanate, the sultanate of Rum, centred on Konya (formerly Ikonium), had already been roused in 1159 by one of the rare acts accomplished by Manuel in the East, namely his reaffirmation as suzerain of Antioch and the tacit recognition of his supremacy by the kingdom of Jerusalem. Besides, even here Western influence was present, because it was likely that Barbarossa's diplomacy had something to do with the breaking-off of the treaty between Sultan Kilij-Arslan and the emperor in 1162. From 1175 this break was confirmed and it was in the course of the campaign that followed that Manuel was crushed (on 17 September 1176) at Myriokephalon.

From 1180, when Manuel died, to the fall of Constantinople in 1204, Asia Minor, still Byzantine to a line running roughly from Amastris to Miletos, seemed fairly quiet but this was the time when a number of military nobles carved out more or less independent domains for themselves, which added further to the general disorder. Everything that mattered happened in Europe, and what happened was a series of catastrophes for Byzantium. The internal political history was a sequence of *coups d'état*: the seizing of power by Andronikos I, Manuel's cousin, in 1182; the fall of Andronikos and thus the end of the dynasty in 1185; then the weak reigns of the Angelos emperors, first Isaac II, then Alexios III, his brother, who had Isaac blinded and imprisoned in 1195. Under these conditions the empire could not prevent the disintegration of its Balkan domains: in 1181–3 rebel Serbs and Hungarians raided Macedonia and Bulgaria which, under the leadership of the Asen brothers, in 1185–7 regained an independence they had lost for nearly two centuries. Henceforth Byzantium had no access to the Adriatic except by the coast of Albania whose princes, while independent, remained loyal to the empire for fear of Serbian expansion. Even a cultural challenge to Byzantium arose as a threat in this area. In 1202 Vukan of

Serbia recognised papal supremacy and, in 1204, Kaloyan of Bulgaria even received his crown from Pope Innocent III. Henceforth the empire saw two Slav powers on its borders which inflicted on it a series of defeats and indeed threatened (in the event of a new Latin attack) to make a pact with them. In 1185 the Normans of Sicily had returned to the offensive and had even succeeded in taking and plundering Thessalonica, the second city of the empire. Although they were pushed back, they were quickly followed by the Third Crusade in 1189–90, in the course of which Barbarossa, assured of support from the Serbs and Bulgarians, came close to attacking the capital itself. Byzantium in fact only lost Cyprus, conquered by the English under Richard the Lionheart. But Henry VI, Barbarossa's son, who inherited not only Sicily (by marriage) but also its traditionally hostile attitude to Byzantium, put together a plan for the conquest of the empire that was only cut short by his sudden death in 1197. The idea was henceforth rooted in the West, and it reappeared when the Crusaders of 1204 decided to put an end to the 'sick man' of Europe – the Byzantine Empire.

Thus the focusing of the empire on the Balkans brought about its downfall. Given the alteration in its structure and mental outlook, however, such refocusing was the only possibility for renewal, and it was on the same basis that rulers of the Laskaris and the Palaiologos dynasties, in the thirteenth century, founded their attempts at restoration. Moreover, if the Komnenoi had failed, it was not because they had not seen the need for far-reaching internal reforms, despite the criticism usually levelled at them on this score. One cannot help observing that the real imbalance here was not revealed until the mid-twelfth century, when Manuel I broke with the defensive tradition of the empire in order to launch an aggressive military policy that was ill-suited to a political structure which was still firm but had greatly weakened resources.

Mercenaries, masters of war

It would be quite wrong to see, in the era of the Komnenoi, simply the triumph of a military caste to whom all the State's resources were subordinated.

Certainly, a military *coup d'état* brought Alexios Komnenos to the throne in 1081, and his principal support was indeed the old ruling class, the military and landowners, who had possessions in Asia. Thus his seizure of power did have the appearance of class revenge on the new dominant strata, the administrators and bourgeoisie. But Alexios' personality suggests that he was hardly the bearer of a new ideology. Even allowing for the hagiographical dimensions of the work of his daughter, Anna Komnena, she was writing at a time when the memory of her father was still fresh, and she could not have been entirely untruthful when she praised him for having 'peacefully ordered matters which are naturally ordered by war and iron', and when she reminded readers that the greatest success is that achieved 'neither by blood nor by combat'. She offers real insight into the mentality of the period when she mentions that young men were brutal because 'they had not tasted the miseries of war'. It was by no means only his general hostility to Manuel Komnenos that made Niketas Choniates sternly reproach the emperor for having responded to the peaceful

495

overtures of the Second Crusade with openly hostile measures. In Manuel's time, we might even think that the old pacific mentality was confirmed by the constantly warlike policies of the emperor, the more so because most of his campaigns were conducted against Christian peoples, which was seen as scandalous. Anna Komnena reminded readers that the divine will desired that everything should be forgiven between Christians, and Alexios himself had put an end to the war against the Serbian prince of Diokleia in order to avoid 'civil war'. As for Niketas, he praised John II for having decided against forcing his way into Antioch because he was 'totally opposed to a war between Christians'. The reluctance of the Byzantines to set off for war was evident on many occasions; in 1158, at the time of an Armenian expedition, Manuel summoned troops from the theme of Seleukeia, but nobody came. Besides, the fact that the era of the Komnenoi saw the widespread use of mercenaries offers little support for the idea of a militarised empire. At the time of the first Norman attack on Albania, we already find Macedonian Slavs, Turks, Saracens, Russian Varangians and Norman contingents in the imperial army, and we know that the imperial guard itself included Germans together with Anglo-Saxons who had fled their country at the time of the Norman Conquest. Alexios and John Komnenos continued to recruit from among these peoples, but it was Manuel who made systematic use of them: not only was his army made up of French, Germans, Anglo-Saxons, Normans from Sicily and Alans from the Caucasus, but his vassal states in the West sent him contingents of Serbs, Hungarians and Vlachs, while the Frankish states in the Levant procured Armenians, Turks and French knights for him. Obviously all this shows that he had difficulty in recruiting soldiers in the usual way. We might wonder whether the agrarian and tax reforms which characterised this period were aimed not so much at raising a 'national' army but at better ensuring the rapid payment of troops recruited abroad.

Certainly, by the end of the eleventh century the old *stratiotai* system, by which certain lands were obliged to provide soldiers or their equivalent in cash, had completely disappeared. The fragments of the Theban cadastre from this period no longer mention *stratiotai* lands. No doubt driven by the need to recruit a growing number of mercenaries, the State had made out of the *strateia* – originally a substitution tax for those who could not or would not serve personally – a tax which affected the whole population. In the public documents of Michael VII and Nikephoros III Botaneiates it was included in the long list of taxes from which people asked to be exempt. That is to say, as with some taxes in our own time, the profit from the *strateia* no longer had to be specifically assigned to military ends, but was just one of the general Treasury sources.

Nevertheless, it remained very important and the charters of exemption, which must have always been considered as exceptional favours, cannot disguise the care with which the State ensured its collection. In this respect the age of the Komnenoi, at least until the reign of John II, did not produce any innovations: a charter of Alexios for the monastery of Patmos, dated April 1089, shows the emperor confirming the exemption of new inhabitants on the island, repopulated by its founder Christodoulos, but imposing the tax on the peasants on the lands which the saint had previously possessed in Kos, and which he had ceded back to the fisc in exchange. The difficulties in recruitment, at least until about 1130,

The tax collector. At the end of the eleventh century, the taxes paid by the subjects of the State gradually supplanted former systems, without entirely getting rid of them. This did not prevent the government servants from being very careful in collection, nor the tax-payers from being despondent.

show both the inadequacy of the old system and how slow the Komnenoi were to appreciate that it had to be replaced. Throughout the twelfth century foreign military colonies were established in the empire, of Pechenegs, Hungarians and Serbs; although this was a traditional practice, it could only serve as an insufficient stop-gap.

The stepping-up of military grants

The real reform, which can be dated from the reign of John II and which was promoted by his minister John of Poutze, was in fact itself merely the codification and generalisation of practices that had been current for a long time. It cannot be understood without taking account of how far rural structures had evolved and of the existence of legal models whose application had originally been to a strictly limited area.

The Komnenoi did not want the rural communes to disappear. We know that they were already in a very bad state before 1080, and the sources show that although they continued to exist, their decline had become irrevocable. The *chorion* and its inhabitants (*choritai*) were still referred to, but the last mention of the rural community dates from 1098, and it is likely that these two terms should be translated after that date as simply 'village' and 'villagers'. It was villages such as these that, under Alexios III, the Athenians sought to take over near their city, and certainly the *choria* in near-contemporary Crete must be understood as having a very limited meaning. No doubt the powerful, a term which covers not only the great landowners and dignitaries, but also the wealthy inhabitants of the towns,

497

were chiefly responsible for this decline, but it also followed a policy consciously pursued and traceable for at least a century. We know that it consisted in settling peasants on land belonging to the fisc, so that these *demosiarioi* were henceforth the direct dependants of the State. The Komnenoi had not initiated this, but they expanded and systematised the process so that by the mid-twelfth century the *demosiarioi* formed a great part, perhaps the majority, of the inhabitants in the countryside. It should be noted that the State continued to operate a rigorous quota system for the settlement of peasants on private estates, especially on those belonging to monasteries. In 1175, Manuel made the monks restore peasants who had been wrongfully settled, and the weak Isaac II did the same in 1186. Moreover, towards the end of his reign Manuel had passed a measure that repeated Nikephoros Phokas' legislation, guaranteeing the properties belonging to the monasteries but forbidding them to increase it or add to the number of peasants attached to them.

The situation in the countryside in the twelfth century, then, is quite different from how it is usually presented. In taking ever more extensive control over land and men, and limiting the expansion potential of private property-owners, the State risked freezing all possibilities of investment in land, at the very time when, as we shall see, business was prospering but not sufficiently to absorb all the capital accumulated in the towns. This freeze must have been all the more irksome in that the dynasty had to reward, especially in its early days, the old aristocracy to whom it owed its rise, and to provide for princes, princesses and family relations, within the framework of a policy that put the main offices of the State into the hands of its kin group. The Komnenoi, like their predecessors, thus distributed grants that were often very substantial, including hereditary grants of land plus the revenues produced by those who cultivated it, which could obviously only apply to lands directly dependent on the fisc. Such a system did not involve anything new in legal terms, it simply extended the great landed estates belonging to laymen and reduced a certain number of *demosiarioi* to the status of private *paroikoi*. The Komnenoi, however, went further, doubtless so as to avoid excessively diminishing their fiscal patrimony. From 1084, Alexios granted to his brother Adrian, in the Kassandra peninsula, a certain amount of state land in full ownership together with the tax revenues of other lands on the peninsula which were in the hands of private owners, the most important being the Lavra monastery of Mount Athos. In this latter case, the beneficiary obviously would not be the owner of the lands whose revenues had been granted to him, he simply replaced the State as collector of taxes, and the status of the tax-paying owners themselves was unchanged. Nevertheless, that some dangerous innovation was suspected here is shown by the fact that the landowners reacted by demanding that the State declare categorically that their rights remained undiminished. The monks of the Lavra did this in 1084. In practice, the new beneficiary would install his own tax administration in the district allotted to him. This was the case with Adrian Komnenos, and was also the case with a daughter of John II, Maria, who, in the second half of the century, had her own tax collectors (*energontes*) in the district of Hierissos. Clearly this new system did transform the relations between administrators and administered since between these two now stood the figure who held the concession. Even

if the latter only possessed fiscal rights – because there was no question of abandoning other regalian rights to him, especially that of justice – he tended to act as if he were the real owner, and the small and middling tax-payers, unlike the powerful Lavra monastery, did not have the means to counter his abuses.

We must not exaggerate the extent of these grants, but evidently they constituted a juridical model on which a new system of management could be built – the military system of *pronoia*, which had two inseparable aims: to improve troop recruitment and to tap unemployed capital for this purpose. While the earliest mention of the term *pronoia* concerns the concessions arising from the system of *charistike*, it is striking that the first firm reference to this institution comes from the reign of John II. A source from the Lavra, dating from 1162, mentions a *pronoiarios* whose ancestors had been *stratiotai*, a term which by then no longer related to the old *stratiotai* system and designated precisely those who held *pronoia*.

We already know that the *strateia*, one tax among others, had proved to be ineffective. No doubt its profits were still retained, or at least part of them, by the local administrations responsible for the recruitment and maintenance of the armies. The yield from it must have been disappointing, but there was gradual reform. Apparently it was John II who took the decision to transfer to the treasury the profits of a part of this tax, namely that which came from the maritime provinces and was intended for the construction and equipment of the fleet. But it was not until Manuel I's reign, if we are to believe Niketas, that all the profits of the *strateia* were concentrated in the central funds. This meant that a replacement had to be found. Such a replacement became available from the moment that a great section of the peasantry, the *demosiarioi*, were answerable to the State, while there gradually evolved, within the framework of large imperial grants, a system of concession of revenues which did not imply any right of ownership. What this means is that the military *pronoia* was simply the grant of a certain amount of revenue, usually levied by the State's agents, to individuals who, in return, owed armed service and were thus called 'soldiers' (*stratiotai*). We must emphasise here that this was not a matter of a land grant; the texts speak of 'grants of *paroikoi*', which must obviously have been *demosiarioi*, whose fiscal profits – clearly not the person – were given over to the holder of the concession. These peasants, who henceforth paid their levies to the *stratiotes*, and by the same token the villages in which such peasants lived, were henceforth considered as 'subject to the army' (*estrateumenoi*), which is not to say that they themselves were soldiers, but that the taxes they paid were designed to maintain their *stratiotes*.

The importance of the *pronoia* has been much exaggerated, and in particular it has been seen as evidence of an important shift of power towards the aristocracy within the empire. It seems, however, that the *pronoia* was not in fact greatly extended under the Komnenoi: in 1152, in the list of estates given to a Thracian monastery by the *sebastokrator* Isaac Komnenos, we see only two villages 'subject to the army', alongside fifteen estates (*proasteia*) and thirteen villages of the classic type. Twelfth-century sources in general do not suggest that the *stratiotai* were powerful lords. Documents from the Lavra, spanning the period 1162 to 1196, instead sketch a picture of restless, aggressive individuals of limited means: we see them renting out their lands to the monastery, even if they did so with bad grace. Moreover, the *pronoia* was a grant for life at most, so the State could remove it at will

A view from Mount Athos. A monastic fief long favoured by the emperors, the peninsula nevertheless did not escape fiscal inconsistencies. This was the case in the twelfth century when Alexios Komnenos granted his brother the revenues from a monastery of Kassandra, while he was trying to curb the ambition of other such privilege-holders who acted as though they were the true owners.

from the holder. In these conditions, the *pronoia* would scarcely have been attractive to the great landowners or powerful government servants, and this is what Niketas says when, at the time the system was decisively established by Manuel, he lists the people who snapped up the 'grants of *paroikoi*': they were 'people who plied the needle, and gained their livelihood with pain and difficulty, others whom fortune had made stable-boys, yet others who earned their bread in the dust of the brickyards or the sweat of the forges'. In other words, the *pronoia* theoretically had the double advantage of strengthening the army and providing an outlet for the lower classes, especially the town-dwellers, who had a certain amount of capital but not enough to buy land. It even seems, according to the sums of money Niketas instances as given by potential *stratiotai* to recruiters in order to obtain *pronoia*, that this was a matter not of some bribe, but of a tax to be handed over in the normal run of things in order to obtain possession of 'imperial letters', which conferred taxation rights, a practice conforming to old Byzantine customs. Thus the system had the additional advantage of putting quite substantial sums into the coffers of the State.

Consequently, the *pronoia* system in itself had little influence on recruitment for the army.

First of all, it did not restore a 'national army' to counterbalance the ever-increasing mercenary force, since a *stratiotes* could easily be a foreigner, like the Cuman *stratiotai* mentioned in documents from Mount Athos at the end of the twelfth century; moreover, these same documents, which record contemporary practice, show the great difficulty experienced in making the incumbents fulfil their obligations. Benjamin of Tudela doubtless exaggerated somewhat when, on visiting the empire in 1167, he remarked that the Greeks were no longer militarily active. It is true, however, that John and Manuel Komnenos were mainly concerned with fiscal matters, specifically with concentrating in the State's coffers sums of money that had hitherto been badly managed or under-employed in the provinces and to which they would add the payments from the *stratiotai* on recruitment. In this sense the *pronoia* could have a military effect in that it made available for paying mercenaries money that had previously been frozen, while preserving at least the semblance of a Greek army. But the consequences were negative in the long term. While the additional resources allowed the State to sustain its military potential for longer, at a time of constant war, the system was full of dangers for those living in the countryside, already exposed to the abuses of magnates and monks, and now subject to petty tyrants, who were all the more inclined to exert pressure because they themselves were not among the very rich. We might think that, up until the death of Manuel Komnenos, the State remained sufficiently strong to check these dangers; it is even likely – as the documents demoting those *stratiotai* guilty of injustices show, even at the very end of the century – that the administration continued to work well while the central government under the Angelos rulers became weaker and weaker. But the foundations of future developments had been laid and, after the chaos of 1204, the major holders of privileges and the minor *stratiotai* forgot the origin of their titles and tried to pass off their fiscal prerogatives as authentic rights of ownership, thus diminishing the status of the peasantry yet again.

The empire of the Komnenoi, then, was increasingly guided by military requirements (especially from the mid-twelfth century), rather than by military strategy. No real symptom of the militarisation of Byzantine society is observable, but trying to meet the needs of an army of mercenaries resulted in an ever-growing drain on the vital resources of the State. And this draining away of the empire's life-blood was increasingly the work of intermediaries – tax-farmers, high-ranking landowners and *stratiotai*; with the grip of central authority weakened, the empire was in danger of dissolving into innumerable independent groups with no stabilising hierarchy, for Byzantium had no experience of a truly feudal system.

Towards the death throes

The employment of mercenaries, the granting of *paroikoi* to private landowners and to the Church, the system of *pronoia* and the settlement of foreigners on imperial territory – none of this indicates healthy population growth. Increasingly people became scarcer than land, and in the great effort to dominate the peasantry, the desire to control its muscle-power played at least as big a part as the desire to collect the profits of taxation.

The East in decline: 1100–1250

The countryside in decline

The empire of the Komnenoi was necessarily a less populous state, given that it was cut off from a great part of Asia Minor. Naturally there could have been a decrease of population in the lands occupied by the Turks, but the extent of this should not be exaggerated because a peasant does not leave his land unless the situation has been made quite unbearable, and this was not the case in the sultanate of Konya. Kinnamos shows that the Greek population continued to live on under Turkish domination, while Niketas in fact tells us that some Greeks living in imperial territory willingly settled in the sultanate, attracted by the tolerance and promises of the Muslim ruler. Moreover, the fall of the Italian provinces only involved the emigration of a very few members of the upper classes. And finally, the settlement of foreigners in the empire was limited to a restricted number of military colonists, so that the Byzantine population was reduced to its natural growth rate which, under medieval conditions, meant stagnation at best, and most likely a decline. Natural disasters were not very important in this reckoning. Plagues and earthquakes seem to have been extremely rare in Byzantium in the twelfth century, whereas Italy, Sicily and particularly the Frankish and Muslim areas of Syria were badly hit. The history of famines and dearth has yet to be written, but we do not have the impression that they were either frequent or serious under the Komnenoi. In my opinion, we must look for the origin of this undeniable fall in population primarily in the wars of the time.

The most serious military episodes, from the demographic point of view, were no doubt those in the first period, between 1081 and 1118, and at the end of the century, between 1180 and 1204, because, unlike the campaigns of the Macedonian era, they directly affected imperial territory; Turkish raids in Asia, Pechenegs and Cumans in Europe, Norman expeditions, devastating Crusades, Bulgarian and Serbian rebellions were all marked by plundering, massacres and the uprooting of whole populations. By contrast, in the period of conquest in the reign of Manuel I, war was once again waged on the frontiers, at least up to 1176, and was carried out mainly by troops of mercenaries, probably without much loss among the empire's own population. But, paradoxically, this period of nearly half a century – a period of 'peace' between two wars, when people attempted to enjoy a peace which they hoped would last – saw no increase in the birth-rate. Anna Komnena, who was writing around 1130, did not miss the opportunity to criticise her contemporaries who, 'having never known war', did not know how to occupy themselves in any but the most futile ways.

It is very difficult to chart the consequences of this population decline with any precision. It is certain, however, that the countryside paid the heaviest price since, already burdened by taxation which increasingly escaped state supervision and exposed the peasants to the threat of losing their very status as free men, the peasants were also the first victims of war and invasion. The struggle which engaged the State and the great secular and ecclesiastical landowners for the control of manpower reveals both the falling birthrate in the countryside and the flight of peasants from it. The sparseness of population in the countryside had other disturbing consequences; for example, the Greek population was concentrated in

Tree of Jesse window in the royal abbey of St Denis showing Abbot Suger, mid-twelfth century

The Balfour ciborium, English, enamel and copper gilt, 1150–75 (London, Victoria and Albert Museum)

The Gloucester candlestick, English, gilt and base metal, early twelfth century (London, Victoria and Albert Museum)

Southern rose window, Notre-Dame, Paris

the areas most suited to cultivation, leaving less productive zones, especially in the mountains, open to non-native groups, often pastoralists, who were not easily controlled by the State and who, when there was an invasion, might either rebel or even aid the invaders. Thus it was that the Vlachs came to play a vital role in the Bulgarian revolt of 1186. In Asia Minor, in the provinces where Byzantine power had been restored by the first two Komnenoi, the reconquest drove the Turks from the plains and valleys, but it did not wipe them out and allowed them to regroup in the plateaux, where they sometimes formed thickly populated centres, resistant to assimilation, and must have made the future dismemberment of Asia Minor all the easier. Finally, in the regions where the Greeks had always been in the minority, their lack of dynamism favoured the expansion of non-native peoples whose growth had hitherto been stable. This was the case in Illyria, where the Albanians reoccupied the plains from which they had been expelled, and it was the same in Macedonia and Bulgaria. This situation was serious because these were border regions where the Greek or Hellenised population increasingly grouped together in towns, which appeared as islands without strong connections to each other and without sufficient resources to make an impression on the surrounding territory.

The fact remains that the old imbalance between Europe and Asia was only worsened in the course of the twelfth century, as demonstrated by the efforts at repopulation, particularly evident under John and Manuel Komnenos. When John deported Serbian prisoners to Asia Minor, it was with the intention of putting abandoned lands back into production and so making them a source of revenue; the same was true of Manuel's settling of Christians from Philomelion at Pylae, in Bithynia. It is not surprising that these increasingly empty lands gave rise, at the end of the century, to large territorial units over which high dignitaries lorded it in total independence.

The currency collapse

This very disturbing background has not always been sufficiently emphasised. Instead, the tendency has been to see the Komnenian era only through its urban civilisation, which appeared to show a remarkable brilliance and vitality. This was demonstrated by the great number of copper coins (*follis*) in circulation: the excavations in Corinth and Athens have yielded an enormous quantity for Alexios' reign and especially for Manuel's, and large hoards have also been found in the Argolid, Macedonia, Bulgaria, Illyria and throughout the perimeter of the Aegean. However, we should not rush into seeing this as a sign of great prosperity. While the abundance of fractional currency certainly indicates local trading activity, it seems that its horizons became increasingly limited. The uncommon number of types of *follis* under the Komnenoi tends to suggest the existence of trading zones which, while not being entirely closed, functioned more and more as independent units. Thus the great majority of the Athenian and Corinthian *follis* were struck locally. Similarly, the silver currency of Alexios Komnenos seems to have been destined especially for Trebizond, the Transcaucasus and, to a lesser degree for the Pontic coasts, and very seldom reached the Balkans. This undoubtedly reflects a slackening of inter-regional relations, a 'provincialisation' of commercial activity, which certainly contributed in large measure to strengthening autonomy, especially after 1180. Moreover, even if this can be explained in part by the fact that the largest number of excavations have been undertaken in the Balkans, the twelfth-century currency seems to have been mainly European, which again confirms the growing relative importance of the western regions. The monetary reform of Alexios Komnenos in the years 1096–8 resulted in the establishing of four mints for gold currency (at Constantinople, Nicaea, Trebizond and Corinth). That at Corinth, the latest one because it does not seem to have produced much before 1105–6, in fact probably issued at least half of the new kinds of coin.

Large-scale internal trade could hardly avoid being disrupted by the confusion which affected the standard currencies in gold and silver, especially after 1071. Unlike the reforms of Monomachos, the monetary adjustments in the reigns of Michael VII and Nikephoros Botaneiates had resulted in a severe debasement in the weight and alloy content of these currencies, which betrayed an evident crisis in the treasury. While Monomachos' contemporaries do not seem to have been aware of alterations in currency, from the end of the eleventh century onwards sources do begin to reflect people's complaints; there was a crisis of confidence and people hoarded good coins, a trend which could only be strengthened by the wars, rebellions and invasions. Thus when the Komnenoi gained power, the situation was extremely confused and it seems that, at least for the first fifteen years of his reign, Alexios I was entirely concerned with military needs and did not have the time to consider monetary reform. This was a time of expedients, as seen in the confiscations from the Church as well as from those of the laity opposed to the new emperor, and also in the spread of former bad practices, such as that of demanding a tax in sound currency and ensuring that payments were made with devalued coins. Not only were the tax-payers overburdened, but the fiscal administration no longer knew exactly what criteria to apply in the collection of taxes. Alexios' reform, at the end of the eleventh century, thus had two aims: to acknowledge plainly the currency devaluation, so that henceforth a gold piece would be two-thirds silver, and to establish a new parity between the two metals, so that the *nomisma* would then equal four silver *miliaresia*.

Circumstances, however, conspired against this desired stabilisation. On the one hand, the 'hunger for silver' which struck the whole of the East at this period meant that the *miliaresia* disappeared and were replaced by a sort of improved *billon* which only had 6 per cent white metal in its composition. On the other hand, forms of currency multiplied, each with its own specific purpose. The 1136 charter (*typikon*) of the monastery of Christ Pantokrator in Constantinople, founded by John II and his wife Eirene, lists a considerable number of coins, each to be used in very precise circumstances: the high dignitaries of the monastery were to be paid in 'gold *nomismata*', their subordinates in 'new *nomismata*' while the silver *trachy nomisma*, which no doubt corresponded to the new *billon* (*skyphatos*), was to be used for running costs and alms. Whatever this meant, it does not indicate a healthy financial situation, and the merchants, especially foreign ones, increasingly scorned the imperial currency and carefully specified in their contracts the particular coinage in which transactions were to be conducted. It follows that these monetary confu-

504

sions greatly complicated internal trade. This was a period in which foreigners, especially Italians, were increasingly necessary commercial partners. The scarcity and confusion over currency naturally led to their being sold more and more products in order to get hold of rare coinage, but the empire could buy less and less in exchange. The Venetians were fully aware of this and in the twelfth century they tended to bring with them their own low-value deniers rather than products which they would have found difficult to sell. In the same period, they tried to drain off to the West the sound gold currency which still circulated in the empire, and contracts, particularly those going through Epiros, were specifically targeted at buying this currency with the small Venetian deniers. The monetary situation proved that the imperial economy was on the road to becoming 'colonial', and the privileges granted to the Italians could only accentuate this up to the end of the twelfth century.

Trade in decline

The first real wound to the empire's trading economy was essentially self-inflicted. In 1082 Alexios Komnenos granted certain privileges to Venice as a reward for her intervention during the attack on Albania by the Normans. Among other things Venice was granted the freedom to trade throughout most of the imperial territory (except for the Black Sea and the larger islands of Crete and Cyprus), and exemption from all commercial taxes. The Venetians were also given a district in Constantinople, including a church, buildings and wharfs. We should not exaggerate the immediate importance of this privilege. Venice, at the end of the eleventh century, was only a modest trading power, with a relatively small fleet dependent on private initiative (the Arsenal was not created until 1104) and slender financial means. Venice's wealth at this stage lay in its land; trade was of secondary importance, at least until the mid-twelfth century. Thus the city of the lagoons only gradually began to exploit the extraordinary advantages it had been granted. Moreover, contemporaries for a long time remained unaware of the dangers these advantages harboured; indeed it was thought that the Byzantine merchants were doing well out of the whole affair because the Venetians, no longer paying customs duties, could henceforth offer them better prices for their products (as was true of the big landowners from whom Venice bought its wheat and oil).

In the event, Venice soon came to consider the empire as its private preserve. In 1106 the Venetians captured Pisans near Rhodes and refused to release them unless they promised to give up trading in the Aegean. Perhaps the imperial government had begun to realise the danger of letting the Venetians establish a monopoly. The lesser privilege granted to the Pisans in 1111, which gave them a reduction in customs duties from 10 per cent to 4 per cent, could only have been aimed at encouraging competition with Venice. The same agreement also shows that the emperor was trying to protect his own traders because he specified that if the Pisans bought goods in one province of the empire for resale in another, then they would be liable to the same taxes as the Greeks, particularly to the *kommerkion*.

Venetian merchants. These peaceful but already properous traders were fast becoming the worm that was to gnaw at the edifice of Byzantine commerce and consequently at the foundations of the empire itself. If the call to a crusade in 1199 was greeted without much enthusiasm by the European princes, various circumstances, including the increasing greed of the Italian merchants, lay at the root of the capture of Constantinople. (Marco Polo's *Book of Marvels of the World*, fourteenth century; Paris, Bibliothèque nationale.)

This role of counterbalance which devolved upon the Pisans becomes clearer when one sees the true extent of Venetian progress at the beginning of John II's reign. When he tried to avoid renewing the privilege of 1082, Venice unleashed a plundering expedition in the Aegean islands, so that the emperor was compelled in 1126 to recognise the advantages Venice had acquired and even add to those the privilege of access to the great islands, which previously had been denied them. Perhaps John II believed that he still had the resources to defend his subjects. The act of 1126 provided for exemption from the *kommerkion* for those Greek merchants engaged in selling to the Venetians. This was in fact a very dangerous arrangement: it encouraged preferential sales to the Venetians at the risk of starving the Byzantine consumer, and above all of putting small and middle-sized traders out of the running, so that their decline was then inevitable. Soon there was only room for those producers who preferred to market their goods directly, and the whole Byzantine merchant class gradually fell into a state of lethargy. The rise of the Italians thus had at least two serious consequences: instead of a prosperous and relatively homogeneous class of merchants, it gave rise to a muddled group of small local traders and grand exporters who, in order to ensure their sales, constantly tried to increase their domination over the land, so that this in turn contributed to the increase in great estates and the enslavement of the rural classes.

The downward slope

From 1130, therefore, there was general discontent with the Latins. The ruined traders were joined by the peasantry and the townspeople, all worried about their subsistence. While Venice posed the greatest threat, it was the other Italian merchants who were the most bitterly resented. All that the government could do, however, was try to set one Italian city against another. Although the emperor needed a lot of persuading and sought, vainly, to obtain undertakings from Pisa against the Western Empire, Pisa's privileges were renewed in 1136 and 1170, while Genoa obtained the same advantages in 1155, and also had them renewed in 1170. But the Latins grew more and more arrogant. As early as 1149, while they were helping Byzantium to regain Corfu from the Normans, the Venetians staged a gross parody of imperial ritual and, after witnessing the arrival of the Genoese in Constantinople shortly after 1155, Pisans and Venetians rose up in 1162, and pillaged the district occupied by their rivals. It is interesting, in this latter case, to see a certain number of Greeks taking part in the pillaging, happy to despoil the Latins even if alongside other Latins whom they detested still more.

In these conditions, the government tried to find new weapons. With the Pisans and Genoese, who were accustomed to a feudal system, the government could make use of the ties of vassalage, as Alexios I had done with the crusading lords. But with regard to Venice, which was always resistant to feudalism, it could not play on this and such allegiance as did exist was already very uncertain. In Constantinople, the Venetians had overflowed their district even before 1150 and had become entirely uncontrollable. Manuel had thus conferred 'burgess' status on them, which carried the obligation to take a life-long oath of fidelity to the empire. This was not a perfect solution, since it affected only Venetians settled on imperial territory, not the traders who went to and fro and who were often the richest; they were only bound by the measures of 1082. As for the heavy taxes levied on the Latins by the Jewish minister Astaforte, they also only affected the merchants settled in the empire and irritated the Italian republics without greatly reducing their resources.

Only force now remained. Venice, around the beginning of 1171, once again defied imperial authority by pillaging the district the Genoese had just reoccupied. On 2 March, Manuel ordered the arrest of all the Venetian merchants in the empire and confiscated all their assets. The loss, estimated at 400,000 *nomismata*, was enormous for Venice, which had been accustomed to concentrate its capital in Constantinople in order to invest it in its trade with the East. Moreover, if driven out of the empire, Venice would have to reorient its network around the Latin and Muslim Levant where its competitors, Pisa and especially Genoa, had enjoyed uncontested superiority since the First Crusade. The emperor, however, must have soon realised that he could not remain on bad terms with Venice at a time when Barbarossa continued to be hostile. In 1171 Venice had raided the Aegean islands and in the following year, along with the Germans, had taken part in the siege of Ancona, the last Greek foothold in Italy, before allying itself by a treaty in 1175 with the worst enemies of Byzantium, the Normans of Sicily. Besides, breaking with Venice did not resolve the Latin problem; Pisa and Genoa were profiting from the Venetian absence to enlarge their **507**

Floating platforms. Despite, or perhaps because of, its imminent fall, the empire consolidated certain defensive sites along the coast. These platforms, armed with battering rams, acted as fire ships to be launched against attackers. (*De Machinis Bellicis*, twelfth century; Rome, Vatican Library.)

ventures in the empire, to the point that, around 1180, Eustathios of Thessalonica estimated the number of Latins in Constantinople to have reached 60,000. It seems that Manuel, shortly before his death, had agreed to accept a new treaty with Venice which made provision for heavy compensation for the losses suffered in 1171.

With the Latins having commandeered the Byzantine economy, central power could only decline after Manuel's death. William of Tyre went so far as to write that the period when the Latin Empress Maria of Antioch was regent, between September 1180 and April 1182, was the golden age for what he called 'our faction'. The regency relied on two forces whose interests had long been closely linked: the Latins and the 'powerful' landowners, that is on the complex of producer-buyers who by-passed the urban classes and especially the Greek merchants. It is understandable, therefore, that in April 1182 when the regent fell and Manuel's cousin, Andronikos I Komnenos, came to power, there was a general massacre of Latins in Constantinople, although the new emperor had not wished it. Yet the western merchants could not be by-passed, and Andronikos found himself having to make overtures to the only Latins who had not suffered in the massacre. The Venetians, absent from the empire since 1171, were henceforth installed again. This rapprochement, together with the Norman attack in 1185, obviously helped to bring down Andronikos, who had thus alienated the anti-Latin party which had brought him to power.

508   The Angelos dynasty (1185–1204) had no choice but to resume the policy of striking a precarious balance between the various communities. Venice obtained new privileges from Isaac II in 1187, putting the Pisans and Genoese on the defensive; the latter received new advantages in 1192, the Pisans becoming the main support of Alexios III after 1195, until 1198 when Venice extorted from Alexios a chrysobull which, in opening up to it the whole of the empire, from Albania to Bulgaria and Cilicia, granted its citizens unheard-of legal privileges, which allowed them for the most part to escape imperial justice.

Such a situation could only lead to disaster. The Greeks were angry, gathering only crumbs from their own trade and seeing the Latins behave like conquerors in their land. In 1192 the Genoese went so far as to jeopardise the empire's foreign relations by capturing a Venetian galley which was sailing from Egypt to Constantinople with the ambassadors of Saladin on board; meanwhile Pisan ships took up positions at Abydos, at the entrance to the Dardanelles, in order to plunder all their competitors' ships sailing towards the straits. Such excesses reveal the ill-will of the Latins who, subject to the vagaries of a capricious policy, wished to control Constantinople even more tightly, even if they had no intention of a political take-over. In the first years of the thirteenth century the idea became current, especially in Venice, of putting an emperor on the throne who would be the West's creature, and who therefore could refuse them nothing.

A tempting prey

The Italian economic invasion explains the paradoxical aspects of urban life in Byzantium in the twelfth century. It had all the appearance of prosperity, and even seemed to reach a high point in Manuel's reign. In fact the Italians penetrated further and further into the country, looking for local products, and this activated old markets and initiated new ones. For example, the Venetians continued coming to Greece to buy silk in Thebes, oil in Sparta, fruit and wine in Modon; but the privilege of 1198 shows that they then extended their network to the continental regions where foreigners had scarcely ventured previously. In Macedonia, we find them at Nish, Skopje, Pelagonia and Prilep; in Thrace at Didymoteichos and Adrianople; and in Bulgaria at Philippopolis where they bought wine, grain and stock-feed; this was also the case in Epiros (Kastoria) and Asia Minor (Nicomedia). Here we must remember that we usually see only the brighter side of such trade, not the serious disorganisation it caused to local trade structures. For example, now that the Italians could go directly to the sources of trade in Macedonia or Epiros, they by-passed the merchant class in the large ports such as Thessalonica and Dyrrachion and so reduced their role to being mere landing stages. Constantinople herself was no longer really the mistress of Thracian commerce and the straits no longer provided the only access to the Bulgarian market, which the Italians could reach from their position in the Aegean. Moreover, the very configuration of the towns now revealed insecurity and relative contraction: over the old core, generally walled (*kastron*), was imposed a fortified redoubt with a purely military purpose (*akropolis*), clearly separated from the rest by an intermediary wall (*diateichisma*). This was how towns such as Corinth, Argos, Patras and Nauplion appeared to the French conquerors after 1205. But this trend towards fortification should not be exaggerated as it was far from being general at the beginning of the thirteenth century. The *Chronicle of the Morea* tells us that most of the Peloponnesian towns, from Patras to Modon, were towns of the plain and that some, such as Andravida or Nikli, were not even fortified. At strategic points, however, the process of building forts which had no urban function was in full swing, such as those which commanded the narrow passes of Skorta, in the central Peloponnese. These fortified towns and castles were naturally the anchor points for local dynasties who, by the end of the twelfth century, increasingly defied the central authority – Leo Sgouros at Corinth, Doxpatres at Skorta, Theodore Mangaphas at Philadelphia and even Theodore Laskaris at Nicaea. If there were still Greek suppliers in these towns who flourished thanks to their Italian clients, the rest of the populace, small and middling traders as well as artisans, gradually lost their traditional means of existence. These were the classes in distress who, especially under Manuel Komnenos, set off in search of the fiscal resources which the *pronoia* system assured them.

The military and economic ventures of foreigners, then, had caused a profound trauma which also affected the cultural sphere. Of course, despite general dislike, the culture of the West had often become the model; however, the taste for tournaments, chivalrous customs, and indeed the courtly romance, did not go much beyond the narrow circle of the court. In general, Byzantine culture sought to close itself off from external influences and seemed desperate to maintain, in form and content, what had been acquired in the 'belle époque', even going so far as to eliminate those elements which, being authentically Greek, might disturb the fine balance of Christian Hellenism. It is significant that the reign of Alexios Komnenos was marked, at the outset, by the condemnation of Psellos' most brilliant pupil, John Italos. With this, Platonism was overshadowed for two centuries by an official, anaemic Aristotelianism, to the extent that what one understands by Hellenism in this period has little to do with ancient thought; above all, it concerns a passionate effort to find an ever purer language, and admittedly it was in twelfth-century Byzantium that the most perfect Greek was written. Reading historians such as Niketas Choniates or orators such as George and Demetrios Tornikes, Michael Italikos or Nikephoros Basilakes, one cannot escape the impression that this archaic language studded with pedantry must have been restricted to an élite, at a time when the people spoke a language that was continually evolving. In fact it was in the twelfth century that numerous neo-Greek dialects began to be established throughout the empire and they won out two centuries later: right at the end of the twelfth century, Michael Choniates, archbishop of Athens, gave examples (which he found upsetting) of the dialect forms current in Attica. Nevertheless, the age of the Komnenoi was sometimes aware of the riches of the vernacular or demotic; writers such as Manganeios, Michael Glykas and above all Theodore Prodromos used in their lengthy and often satirical and exuberant poems savoury details from daily life. We should note that the language of these poems was an artificial pastiche of the vernacular, which ordinary people themselves probably understood no better than the archaicised language. Moreover, these works were addressed to the emperor and his circle, and were about as authentically popular as the peasants' slang in Molière. When we consider that, for its part, the Church managed to transcribe into scholarly language everything in the liturgy that still savoured of the popular, we can only be sceptical about that extension of culture to a wider public with which the

Komnenoi are generally credited. Of course this is not to say that their accomplishments were negligible; even if its achievements remained sealed off from the masses, the twelfth century at least brought to perfection a remarkable instrument of culture, forged in reaction against everything foreign, and which later centuries, after having given it new life, knew how to use brilliantly to affirm the strength and vitality of Hellenic values.

Under sentence of death

The last decade of the twelfth century had seen an acceleration in the internal dismemberment of the empire. Everything worked towards this: the dispersal of tax resources, exemptions, grants of land to the sovereign's relations and allies, the provincialisation of the economy and culture. Before 1204 it is clear that whole regions of the empire had broken away from it to a greater or lesser extent, both in Europe and in Asia Minor: a Mangaphas in Philadelphia, or a Sgouros at Corinth and Argos behaved like minor kings. The basic principle that had never been seriously questioned in Byzantium – namely, the sacred unity of political power – became gradually more hazy in people's minds, because the new dynasties had nothing in common with the claimants to the throne in previous centuries. While Bardas Skleros used his command to acquire supreme authority, Sgouros aimed only at carving out for himself an independent 'principality' in central Greece.

1204

A new Latin assault on Egypt (ardently desired by Innocent III after Saladin's death had given hope of a better outcome from the mediocre Third Crusade – and even considered for a time by the son of Barbarossa, Henry VI, who was also heir to Sicilian Norman claims), was planned from 1198. It would have to be attempted by sea as the weak state of the Greek Empire ruled out any support: the fall of the Komnenoi, the rivalry between Isaac Angelos (brought to power by the masses) and his brother Alexios (who soon succeeded him), the intermittent uprisings of the people of Constantinople against Latin merchants, the rebelliousness of local leaders – all this argued for keeping a distance from the Balkans. But a strong counter-current drew the Westerners there. Although occupied with a dispute over the crown of Germany, Philip of Swabia, brother of Henry VI, did not forget that he had married Isaac's daughter; for their part, the Montferrats of Italy and Saint-Jean of Acre argued for gaining a secure hold on the Aegean, playing on the growing hostility of the West towards the 'perfidious' Greeks.

Launched in 1199, the call to the Crusade roused little enthusiasm. Too many princes were returning from the Holy Land. The Count of Champagne, the designated leader, died prematurely, and the Crusaders were forced to seek help from the Venetians whose doge, Enrico Dandolo, exacted a high price: in 1201 he charged 85,000 marks to transport Boniface of Montferrat, who had become the leader of the Crusaders, and when payment was delayed, the Crusaders had to promise to capture the town of Zara, which Venice had recently lost. Did the flight of Isaac's son Alexios IV Angelos to the court of Philip of Swabia, and his subsequent voyage with the Crusaders and the doge, play a role in the decision to **511**

call in at Byzantium, after the departure of the fleet in October 1202? Did the Venetians secretly intend to settle their account with the dying empire? Were the Italians and Germans pushed into the venture? This is still under discussion nearly eight centuries after the event. The Latins, ill-received by the Byzantine crowds, staged a military demonstration outside Constantinople to frighten Alexios Angelos into flight in August 1203, and they then enthroned his nephew of the same name. This first stage prepared the way for what followed: a hard winter for the Crusaders, increasing misunderstandings with the Greeks, sedition in the city, and the victorious assault of 12 April 1204 on the hitherto inviolate walls of the New Rome.

The burning and plundering of the city demonstrated the extent of the admiration and hatred it had aroused: theft, brutality, sacrilege, rape and profanation accompanied a systematic plundering in which the skill of the Venetians was wonderful to behold. Besides the fabrics, icons, books and ivories destroyed or torn to bits, these strange Christians, themselves stupefied by the extent of the plunder, shared what has been estimated at nearly 300 tonnes of gold and silver. Then, all authority apparently having disappeared, the Crusaders, after lengthy deliberations, decided that the Count of Flanders, Baldwin, should be crowned as emperor, and that the Marquis of Montferrat should get the whole of the northern peninsula as his consolation prize. Other Crusaders – from Champagne like the Villehardouins or from Burgundy like the La Roches – went off to settle in the Peloponnese and in Athens. Venice took the rest: the islands, including Crete, the castles along the coast and roughly half of the capital!

The break-up and the scramble for spoils

The division of the empire was purely theoretical. Besides the rivalry between the Frankish barons, external dangers threatened: in 1205, Baldwin was defeated and captured by the Bulgarians.

While Thrace and the greater part of Greece passed effectively into Latin control, the years 1204–5 saw the dismembered remains of the empire regrouping around three poles of varying importance: the little empire of Trebizond (where the Komnenoi had been installed from before the fall of Byzantium), the state of Nicaea (whose ruler, Theodore Laskaris, had himself proclaimed emperor in 1205, just as the legitimate sovereign, Alexios III Angelos, was captured by the Marquis of Montferrat), and the Despotate of Epiros (where Michael Angelos Doukas set himself up in the same year). In this complex game, made even more complicated by the intervention of the Bulgarians under King Kaloyan and the Turks of Rum, the two main Byzantine powers of Nicaea and Epiros shared one aim: to drive out the Latins and assure themselves of the imperial throne by recapturing

Opposite:
The capture of Constantinople. The artistic quality of Delacroix's famous painting reflects the importance of the event. On 12 April 1204, the walls of the New Rome fell to the combined assault of the leaders of the Fourth Crusade and the Latins, after which they indulged in a systematic sacking of the city. (Delacroix, *Entrance of the Crusaders into Constantinople*; Paris, Louvre.)

Constantinople. At first Nicaea was directly exposed to Latin attacks, and twice – in 1205 and 1207 – it was only Bulgarian attacks on their rear that forced the Latins to withdraw from territories in Asia Minor. Whatever the reasons, the Latins were driven back and a sense of confidence in the future was expressed in 1208 when Theodore had himself solemnly crowned in Nicaea by the patriarch of Constantinople, who had just been reinstated there. Moreover, having repulsed the Turks and annexed a part of the Trebizond Empire between 1211 and 1215, Theodore could present himself as the legitimate emperor. His prestige reached even as far as the Balkans where, in 1219, Sava, the first autocephalous archbishop of Serbia, asked to be consecrated by the patriarch of Nicaea.

Epiros, however, which under Michael I had been content to unify and organise the territories from Dyrrachion to the Gulf of Corinth, became a real rival with the accession to power of the ambitious Prince Theodore in 1215. Theodore launched a lightning attack against the Latins and in 1224 overran Thessalonica, where he crowned himself emperor shortly afterwards. Meanwhile Theodore Laskaris had died in 1221, leaving power to his son-in-law John III Vatatzes, against whom the dead ruler's brothers rebelled. The two rivals marched on Constantinople, where Latin power was no more than a shadow. By 1225, Vatatzes had made himself master of several of the larger Aegean islands and parts of Thrace, including Adrianople. Theodore of Epiros, however, allied himself with the Bulgarians, but he wanted to move too fast and, already seeing himself as master of the capital, made the mistake of unexpectedly breaking the alliance; in 1230, he came up against the troops of Asen II at Klokotnitsa, where he was defeated and taken prisoner. Epiros survived as an independent state but its rulers, by admitting towards the middle of the century that they bore merely the title of *despotes*, implicitly recognised that the only legitimate power was indeed at Nicaea.

The settlement of Latin barons in a small part of the empire eventually proved to be a development of some significance. Admittedly, in the northern part the permanent threat from the Bulgarian King Kaloyan, which extended to the very outskirts of Constantinople, put the Westerners constantly on the defensive: Baldwin's brother and successor, Henry of Hainault, wore out his considerable gifts as warrior and administrator in defending himself against Nicaea, against the Bulgarians and against Boniface and his successors in Thessaly. When he died in 1216, Latin domination was confined to the coast, from Byzantium to Thermopylae, the Venetians having fortified the ports leading to the straits of Corfu without worrying about the interior. This self-interestedness coupled with systematic hostility to all other Italian powers, especially Genoa, had a disastrous effect on the fate of the Latin Empire: it drove all the forces hostile to the Venetian republic into the arms of the Greeks of Nicaea. The accession to power of the Courtenay family in Byzantium, without authority or support, smoothed the way for the Greek princes.

While the results in the north were so disappointing, elsewhere there were very surprising and long-lasting successes on the part of the barons who made for Athens and Thebes, which became seats of principalities and duchies, and for Argos, Patras, Nauplion and Corinth, strongholds in the Morea (1205–12). A strategy of alliance by marriage, notably between the Angelos and Villehardouin families, the vigilant presence of the Venetian garrisons on the edge of the Peloponnese (at Modon and Coron), the entirely theoretical

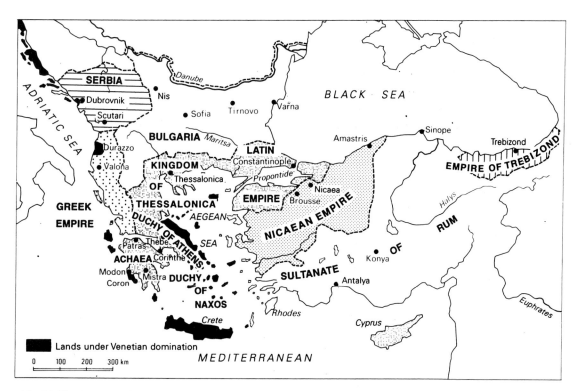

Map 20. The East in 1214.

nature of their dependence on the Latin princes of Thessaly or Thrace, all ensured the Franks in the Morea a security no longer known in the north. The Byzantine presence did not disappear, it is true, because between the loss of their last stronghold, Monemvasia, in 1248 and the events of 1261 (soon to be discussed), there was only a short interval. But the Latin settlement, while numerically very weak, succeeded in putting down roots thanks to a skilful – or perhaps inevitable – policy of reliance on the local Greek aristocracy. Overall, however, these preoccupations prevented the Franks from making any direct intervention in the threatened straits areas and made possible the reconquest by the rulers of Nicaea.

John III Vatazes (1221–54), one of the last great Byzantine rulers, could thus patiently pursue his ends in Europe, despite problems with the Bulgars, who switched their allegiance with the Greeks and Latins several times. The death of Asen II in 1241 eliminated this problem, especially as it was quickly followed by the Mongol invasion of Europe and Asia. Bulgaria was permanently weakened by this and the sultanate of Rum was forced to submit to the conquerors, which greatly profited Byzantium, whose territories they had not reached. Master of Thessalonica and of Macedonia in 1246, Vatatzes pushed the Epirots ever westwards and in 1252 forced their ruler, Michael II, to send his son and heir, Nikephoros, to the court in Nicaea. On his death in 1254, Vatatzes bequeathed his son, Theodore II, an empire that was sufficiently strong to repel the Bulgars and make further progress into Epiros. In desperation, Epiros could see no alternative but to throw itself into

515

the arms of the Latins by joining a quadruple alliance with Venice, the king of Sicily, Manfred, and the prince of the Morea, William Villehardouin. After the emperor's premature death in 1258 and the usurpation of Michael Palaiologos, it fell to the latter to crush the alliance at Pelagonia in 1259 and, with the help of the Genoese, finally regain Constantinople in 1261. That same year, Michael imposed on William Villehardouin, his prisoner since Pelagonia, a treaty which recognised his possession of the four cities of the Morea. Among them was the fortress of Mistra, key to the whole of Laconia, from which he soon began a reconquest of Greece that would take nearly two centuries.

Upheavals in the population

The fact that Byzantium was now a European state can be seen in the Franks' behaviour after their conquest: it was not until the end of 1204, when it was too late, that they attempted the conquest of Asia Minor. In the last quarter of the twelfth century, there had been a remarkable strengthening of the Byzantine presence here. Admittedly, the eastern frontier regions were becoming more and more deserted.

During the campaign of Myriokephalon in 1176, Manuel Komnenos found the region of Philomelion to be deserted and unproductive. This was a vast area, from Dorylaion in the north down to Attaleia on the south coast, which had been depopulated not only by the Turkish raids but also by the policy of the Komnenoi, which had been to transfer the Greek population from this area to the western provinces. This practice had two advantages: it put the invaders in difficulty, because they could not obtain supplies in the deserted region, and it meant that the Greek population in the west was constantly increased by large Hellenic contingents from the Aegean islands. In this well-controlled region, the Komnenoi had undertaken a large-scale programme of urban fortification, which offered protection to the peasants in the event of raids. The programme was not interrupted even by the advent of the Angeloi and was rigorously carried out under the Laskarid dynasty, especially by Vatatzes, but it was not enough: it left the countryside without defences and even encouraged an exodus. This is why Manuel Komnenos, who was certainly more concerned with Asia Minor than has generally been thought, completed the work by fortifying the villages themselves. This gave more security and greater stability for the rural classes and consequently a return to some prosperity in the countryside as well as in the town. This was what Vatatzes was doing when Skoutariotes describes him as fortifying the towns which 'because of their small size and obscurity should be called fortresses rather than towns'. We must thus suppose that there was a certain increase in the Greek population of Asia Minor before the fall of Constantinople. That event, however, drove out on to the roads and seas the population of the capital, of which a large part found refuge beyond the Bosphorus. This no doubt provided an important reinforcement of the Hellenic element without which the success of the Laskarid dynasty would be hard to understand. Moreover, by keeping their capital in Asia Minor even after the reconquest of Thrace and Macedonia, they clearly demonstrated that the provinces of Asia Minor would remain the living heart of their empire.

In Europe the situation was more complicated and did not encourage optimism. The
Frankish conquest was a bloody affair. In the Peloponnese, the *Chronicle of the Morea*

The site of William of Villehardouin's castle at Mistra. These bare ruins, of which only a part date back to the age of chivalry, commanded the whole defensive system of the Morea. It was fifty years before the Byzantines succeeded in retaking it. The castle then became the residence of the *despotes*, son or brother of the sovereign.

stresses the disasters that the war entailed, particularly the loss of men, which meant that many women would never marry or would remain as widows. In the Greek lands to the north, the situation was even worse, because it was there that the Latins, Nicaeans, Epirots and Bulgars confronted each other. The Bulgars, especially in the campaigns of 1205, 1230 and 1237, caused appalling havoc in Thrace, and it was not for nothing that Kaloyan was known as 'Slayer of the Romans'. As for the confrontation between Epiros and Nicaea, it transformed Thessaly, Macedonia and Epiros into a permanent battlefield between 1225 and 1260, certain areas being taken and retaken three or four times by one adversary or another. Unless sheltered in walled towns, the Greek population of Macedonia and Thessaly undoubtedly fell in numbers, to the benefit of the Slavs and other ethnic groups. Significantly, Thessaly was known from the thirteenth century as 'Greater Vlachia', following the unstoppable influx of Vlach immigrants. Epiros, however, seemed to be an

517

exception. Not only did a great number of the refugees from Constantinople retreat there, but Frankish and Bulgarian brutality drove a number of Macedonian Greeks in that direction, especially after 1205, to the extent that we can certainly think in terms of a re-Hellenisation of the provinces of Acarnania and Aetolia, and even of population growth there. Again it should be noted that this population was very unevenly distributed: as John Apokaukos, bishop of Naupaktos, shows, the coasts of the Gulf of Corinth, exposed to raids by the Franks of the Morea, were absolutely deserted in 1220–30. This means that people had emigrated to the interior in search of protection, a movement which affected both the social structure and population of the countryside. The result was a marked growth in the inhabited centres, which had been quite small until then, as in the case of Ioannina, a small town (*polichnion*) before 1204. Michael I of Epiros made it into a strong town in order to receive the refugees, and their influx must have been considerable because it unleashed a counter-movement on the part of the people already there, who felt they were being swamped. We should, however, be cautious in drawing conclusions here. The dislocation of 1204 also encouraged the expansion of non-native peoples. The princes of Epiros were thus forced to accept the existence of the Albanians, who prevented them from controlling central and northern Illyria and north of Berat, while the Bulgarian expansion in eastern Macedonia had irrevocably 'barbarised' the region of Ochrid at the very time when the Epirots undertook its reconquest after 1215. In general, these regions which suffered most in demographic terms, and where the Hellenic element was on the defensive, were those which the rulers of Nicaea regained after 1225. One cannot help thinking that this was one of the reasons for the defeat of the Palaiologoi who, returning to Constantinople in 1261, wished to reconstruct these disparate and weakened provinces as the heart of a new empire.

The triumph of the aristocracy

Both society and the economy were better organised and more healthy in Asia Minor. Naturally there were common features; one of the most important was the increasing pace of the process by which the rural classes came under the control of the powerful. The great exodus after 1204 displaced into Asia Minor as well as Epiros a number of peasants who had lost everything; and the dispossessed aristocracy also took this route (for example, the great landowners of Thrace, who had suffered at the hands of both the Latins and the Bulgars). Whether they wanted to or not, the rulers of Nicaea and Epiros were forced to rely on these great families, which could only lead to a gradual lessening of state control over the peasants; similarly they were forced to climb down when confronted by the holders of *pronoiai*. It is true that the Laskaris family, taking the traditional line, was automatically hostile towards ownership of large inheritable estates; and grants of sole ownership remained very rare, as they did under the first Palaiologoi. But a new and significant feature, the disorder of the years 1180–1205, caused the collapse of the middling landowner, at whose expense the 'powerful', who had long been unchecked, enlarged their estates through cheap acquisitions. This made the rulers concerned to enforce the pre-eminent rights of the State over lands placed under *pronoia*. In 1233, Vatatzes repeated the prohibition on selling these lands, reminding his subjects that 'the lands given in *pronoia* always remain under the State's control'. All the same, the records of the great monastery of Lembiotissa, near Smyrna, prove that from before 1261 some holders of *pronoiai* had succeeded in passing on their rights to their descendants. After 1261 the State reclaimed *pronoiai* with increasing frequency, but the movement had begun and could not be halted. State control remained effective, however, in the empire of Nicaea, which even tried to reconstitute a prosperous peasantry by reviving the old *stratiotes* system of the Macedonian era; moreover, even if they had become *paroikoi*, the peasants remained aware of their rights and did not hesitate to take action in the public tribunals against those they still found difficult to call their 'lords'. Despite the scarcity of our sources, it seems likely that the process of 'aristocratisation' was even more rapid and brutal in the Despotate of Epiros. From the 1230s, *pronoia*, in theory a purely fiscal measure, seems to have become attached to land and even to lordship. John Apokaukos tells us of a *pronoia* 'made up of *paroikoi*, fields, and oak woods', and of holders of *pronoiai* who claimed levies in kind from the peasants and did not hesitate, if they complained, to put them to death.

For the future, it is important to emphasise that an even more profound 'aristocratisation' marked the regions that fell under Latin control and which later reverted to Byzantine rule. In the Morea, the Franks certainly had not made a deal with those whom the *Chronicle of the Morea* calls the 'great men' (*megaloi anthropoi*), such as Sgouros, who were eliminated. But they had welcomed – because there were too few Franks to control the country without help – the group of notables, or *archontes*, the great majority of whom chose to collaborate with them. This had grave consequences. In contrast to the rules of Byzantine law, which considered all men to be free and equal, even if they were in fact separated by enormous economic and social gulfs, Western practice raised an insuperable legal barrier between the *archontes*, who tended to integrate with the feudal class, and the class of the common people (*koinon*) reduced to the status of 'villeins'. Thus the Greek *archontes*, generally kept on their own lands, had a stronger right to dispose of both the lands and the people on them than on Byzantine land. With the reconquest, the Palaiologoi had to take this situation into account and guarantee the acquisitions that had been made. Moreover, profiting from Frankish ignorance as to the true status of the lands, in a country where all the administrative texts and especially the cadastre were in Greek, many holders of *pronoiai* managed to convert precarial (short-term) holdings into heritable property. Thus the social structure of the Morea henceforth differed greatly from that in the rest of the empire, which surely had a bearing on the genesis, in the fourteenth century, of the Greek Despotate of Morea.

What survived

The economy also demonstrated the pre-eminence of Asia Minor. In the west, in the Latin areas as well as the Greek, the Italian presence continued to grow and so intensified the colonial aspects of the economy. In the Morea, the merchant colonies of Patras and Klarentza furnished all the supplies for the princes' and barons' courts, reducing the role of the local artisans to almost nothing. In Epiros, the birth of an independent Greek state had even weightier economic consequences: it broke the traditional land links which led from Dyrrachion towards Macedonia, Constantinople and Greece. In this sense, the privileges granted to Ragusa by Asen II of Bulgaria in 1230, and by Manuel Angelos of Thessalonica in 1234, were invitations to trade rather than evidence of real activity. Significantly, Venice did not even try to obtain privileges from the princes of Epiros. The few Venetian merchants who stopped at Dyrrachion only came to buy the local wheat. This was also the case with those from Ragusa, even though they obtained privileges from Michael I and had them renewed and extended in 1237 and 1251. The local produce – wheat, salt, wool – was the only object of their trade. This indicates that maritime trade, dealing only with raw materials, had conclusively replaced the former traffic in commodities from the East which the Westerners procured directly from Constantinople and their possessions in the Aegean. A local merchant class, whose members served as intermediaries between the great supplying landowners and the foreign merchants, now grew up, but it was parasitic and merely emphasised the colonial nature of trade, as practised in Dyrrachion and equally at Arta.

In Asia Minor, the situation was different. Admittedly, Theodore Laskaris, who distinguished the Venetians' interests from those of other Latins, granted Venice a privilege in 1219 which confirmed all the advantages they had obtained in 1198. But this act, motivated more by political than by economic considerations, certainly did not foster a Venetian invasion; moreover, at an uncertain date, Vatatzes took a series of measures which had the effect of making it almost a dead letter. Seeking to create the conditions for real economic independence in his empire, he absolutely forbade the importation of luxury products, whether from the East or from Italy, so that everyone should be content with 'what the Roman soil produces and with what Roman hands make'. The emperor set to work on a programme of agricultural restoration which benefited from the renewed sense of security, moderate population increase and the still fairly extensive liberty of the rural classes.

Nikephoros Gregoras shows how the emperor made his estates into model farms and how this example spread through the countryside. The empire had at its gates a perfect client, the Turkish sultanate of Konya. From the beginning of the thirteenth century, the inter-Anatolian traffic was remarkably active, as witnessed by the dense network of caravanserais (*khans*) which had been constructed, and through which circulated the caravans of the Anatolian route (encouraged no doubt by the decline of the Levantine coast and the growing role of the Cilician kingdom of Lesser Armenia). Since the Turks of Rum were almost permanently in need of more food supplies, they came to exchange their gold and produce for Byzantine provisions. This became one of the major assets of the Nicaean economy, especially when, after their defeat at Köşe Dağ in 1242, the Turks were at the mercy of the Mongol invasion. Under these conditions, it is not surprising that the Nicaean finances were very healthy and that the currency of the Laskarid rulers was incomparably better than that of their predecessors or their competitors in Epiros. Without these resources, Vatatzes would not have been able to conduct his victorious campaigns and to assemble, as at Magnesia, in Lydia, the money, arms and precious goods that Skoutariotes lists for us.

The prosperity of Nicaea explains, finally, how it became the repository of Byzantine thought and culture. The representatives of high culture, such as Niketas Choniates, took refuge there, and a new generation worthy of them was trained there, best represented by the historian George Akropolites. The texts stress the support given by Vatatzes to learned

Nicaea, now Iznik in Turkey: the scene of the last act of the Byzantine tragedy in the thirteenth century. It was the refuge of Theodore I Laskaris, who founded his realm there and gave the city, later to become the capital, a fortified wall following the outline of a wall dating from the third century, traces of which are visible in front of the towers.

men and the care with which he assembled in the capital an ever-expanding number of manuscripts. In the west, there was also a cultured group of emigrants, the most remarkable representative being the great archbishop of Ochrid, Demetrios Chomatenos: he and others were able to revive, in their entourage, a desire to match Eastern culture, but Western Hellenism was much more modest in its achievements than the Nicaean movement. In both places, this was a culture on the defensive, probably communicated orally within a restricted élite, because even the most enthusiastic advocates of the empire of Nicaea have to admit that its school system was almost non-existent.

The heritage was preserved nonetheless. Moreover, the crisis of 1204 may be seen as a general rehearsal for the great diaspora that was to follow in 1453. This was when a considerable number of educated people, artists and artisans chose to take refuge in the Slav countries, and especially in Bulgaria which, between 1204 and 1206, looked as if it were the only true home of orthodoxy. This was a doubly important fact. Not only did it entail a new diffusion of Byzantine art amongst the Slavs – recognisable, for example, in the frescoes of Bojana, near Sofia (1258–9) – but above all it was a witness to the formation of a real 'orthodox front', despite the bloody clashes between Greeks and Slavs, for whom the principal enemy came from the west. The politics of this 'front' mattered, but even more important was its culture.

521

The horses of Venice. Part of the booty carried off by the Venetians after the sack of Constantinople in 1204, these four gilded bronzes formerly adorned the famous Hippodrome of the Byzantine capital. Six centuries later, Bonaparte in his turn carried them away to adorn the Carrousel. They were returned in 1815, not to Constantinople but to Venice, where they still adorn the façade of St Mark's.

The pilgrims' path to the shrine of St James at Compostela. From the eleventh century the tomb of the apostle attracted pilgrims from all over Europe. Legend had it that St James had lived in Spain and that his remains had been miraculously discovered thanks to a star, from which the name Compostela arose (Campus stellae, field of the star).

523

This curious labyrinth, with the cornerstone of Amiens cathedral at its centre, has given rise to various interpretations, some of them esoteric, the most popular being that penitents would trace its paths on their knees on Good Friday. An inscription on the cornerstone records in a mixture of Old French and Picardy dialect the names of the architects, Robert of Luzaches and Thomas Cormant, as well as the foundation and completion dates of the cathedral (1223–88).

Select bibliography

Note: This bibliography has been revised for English readers, although a number of books in French have been retained as a guide to sources used in the original text.

THE CHRISTIAN WEST

GENERAL HISTORICAL SURVEYS

Barber, M., *The Two Cities: Medieval Europe 1050–1320*, London, 1992
Barraclough, G., *Eastern and Western Europe in the Middle Ages*, London, 1970
Bartlett, R., *The Making of Europe*, London, 1993
Bautier, R.–H., *The Economic Development of Medieval Europe*, London, 1971
Boutruche, R., *Seigneurie et féodalité*, 2 vols, Paris, 1968–70
Brooke, C. N. L., *Europe in the Central Middle Ages, 962–1154*, 2nd edn, London, 1987
Cipolla, C. M., *The Fontana Economic History of Europe*, vol. I: *The Middle Ages*, London, 1972
Contamine, P., *War in the Middle Ages*, Oxford, 1984
Duby, G., *The Early Growth of the European Economy*, London, 1974
Fossier, R., *L'enfance de l'Europe*, 2 vols, Paris, 1982
Genicot, L., *Le XIIIᵉ siècle européen*, Paris, 1968
Holmes, G., *The Oxford Illustrated History of Medieval Europe*, Oxford, 1988
Kula, W., *An Economic Theory of the Feudal System*, London, 1976
Le Goff, J., *Medieval Civilization, 400–1500*, Oxford, 1988
Matthew, D., *The Medieval European Community*, London, 1977
Mundy, J. H., *Europe in the High Middle Ages, 1150–1309*, 2nd edn, London, 1991
Poly, J.–P. and Bournazel, E., *The Feudal Transformation, 900–1200*, New York, 1991
Southern, R. W., *The Making of the Middle Ages*, London, 1953

GENERAL SURVEYS OF THE ECONOMY AND SOCIETY

The Cambridge Economic History of Europe, vol. 1: *The Agrarian Life of the Middle Ages*, 2nd edn, Cambridge, 1966
The Cambridge Economic History of Europe, vol. 2: *Trade and Industry in the Middle Ages*, 2nd edn, Cambridge, 1987
The Cambridge Economic History of Europe, vol. 3: *Economic Organization and Policies in the Middle Ages*, Cambridge, 1963

Select bibliography

Duby, G., *Rural Economy and Country Life in the Medieval West*, London, 1968

Latouche. R., *The Birth of the Western Economy*, London, 1961

Pounds, N. J. G., *An Economic History of Medieval Europe*, 2nd edn, London, 1994

Singer, C. et al., *A History of Technology*, vol. 2, Oxford, 1956

THE FRAMEWORK OF DAILY LIFE

MAN AND THE ENVIRONMENT

Cipolla, C. M., *The Economic History of World Population*, 7th edn, Harmondsworth, 1978

Duby, G., *The Europe of the Cathedrals, 1140–1280*, Geneva, 1966

  The Three Orders: Feudal Society Imagined, Chicago and London, 1980

Goetz, H.–W., *Life in the Middle Ages*, Notre Dame (Ind.) and London, 1993

Le Goff, J., *The Medieval World*, London, 1990

Le Roy Ladurie, E., *Times of Feast, Times of Famine: A History of Climate since the year 1000*, London, 1972

Russell, J., *Late Ancient and Medieval Population*, Philadelphia, 1958

  'Population in Europe 500–1500' in C.M. Cipolla (ed.), *The Fontana Economic History of Europe*, vol. 1, London, 1972

  Late Ancient and Medieval Population Control, Philadelphia, 1985

LAW AND THE FAMILY

Brooke, C. N. L., *The Medieval Idea of Marriage*, Oxford, 1989

Brundage, J. A., *Law, Sex and Christian Society in Medieval Europe*, Chicago, 1987

Duby, G., *The Knight, the Lady and the Priest*, London, 1984

  (ed.) *A History of Private Life*, vol. II, *Revelations of the Medieval World*, Cambridge (Mass.) and London, 1988

  Love and Marriage in the Middle Ages, London, 1991

Duby, G. and Le Goff, J. (eds.), *Famille et parenté dans l'Occident médiéval*, Paris, 1977

Ennen, E., *The Medieval Woman*, Oxford, 1989

Heers, J., *Family Clans in the Middle Ages*, Amsterdam and Oxford, 1976

Herlihy, D., *Medieval Households*, Cambridge (Mass.) and London, 1985

Noonan, J. T., *Contraception: A History of its Treatment by the Catholic Theologians and Canonists*, Cambridge (Mass.), 1965

Olivier-Martin, F., *Histoire du droit français des origines à la Revolution*, Paris, 1948

Power, E., *Medieval Women*, Cambridge, 1977

Radding, C. M., *The Origins of Medieval Jurisprudence: Pavia and Bologna 850–1150*, New Haven, 1988

van Caenegem, R. C., *The Birth of the English Common Law*, 2nd edn, Cambridge, 1988

White, S. D., *Custom, Kinship and Gifts to Saints*, Chapel Hill and London, 1988

ECONOMY AND SOCIETY

REGIONAL MONOGRAPHS

Abel, W., *Geschichte der deutschen Landwirtschaft vom frühen Mittelalter bis zum 19. Jahrhundert*, 2nd edn, Stuttgart, 1967

Abulafia, D., *The Two Italies*, Cambridge, 1977

Beech, G., *A Rural Society in Medieval France: the Gâtine of Poitou in the Eleventh and Twelfth Centuries*, Baltimore, 1964

Bloch, M., *French Rural History: An Essay on its Basic Characteristics*, London, 1966

Bonnassie, P., *La Catalogne du milieu du Xe à la fin du XIIe siècle*, 2 vols, Toulouse, 1975–6

Darby, H. C., *Domesday England*, Cambridge, 1977

Davies, N., *God's Playground: A History of Poland*, vol. I, Oxford, 1981

Duby, G., *La société aux XIe et XIIe siècles dans la région mâconnaise*, Paris, 1953

Evergates, T., *Feudal Society in the Baillage of Troyes under the Counts of Champagne, 1152–1284*, Baltimore and London, 1975

Fossier, R., *La terre des hommes en Picardie jusqu'à la fin du XIIIe siècle*, Paris, 1968

Fournier, G., *Le peuplement rural en Basse-Auvergne durant le haut Moyen Age*, Paris, 1962

Hallam, H. E., *Rural England, 1066–1148*, London, 1981

Haverkamp, A., *Medieval Germany, 1056–1273*, 2nd edn, Oxford, 1992

Hyde, J. K., *Society and Politics in Medieval Italy*, London, 1973

Larner, J., *Italy in the Age of Dante and Petrarch 1216–1380*, London, 1980

Lennard, R. V., *Rural England, 1086–1135*, Oxford, 1959

Nicholas, D., *Medieval Flanders*, London, 1992

Paterson, L., *The World of the Troubadours*, Oxford, 1993

Poly, J. P., *La Provence et la société féodale 879–1166*, Paris, 1976

Reilly, B. F., *The Medieval Spains*, Cambridge, 1993

Rösener, W., *Peasants in the Middle Ages*, Cambridge, 1992

Sawyer, B. and Sawyer, P., *Medieval Scandinavia*, Minneapolis and London, 1993

Toubert, P., *Les structures du Latium médiéval*, 2 vols, Rome, 1973

Van Houtte, J. A., *An Economic History of the Low Countries 800–1800*, New York, 1977

Wickham, C. J., *The Mountains and the City: The Tuscan Apennines in the Early Middle Ages*, Oxford, 1988

SOCIAL GROUPS: THE ARISTOCRACY

Arnold, B., *Princes and Territories in Medieval Germany*, Cambridge, 1991

Bloch, M., *Feudal Society*, London, 1961

Brunner, O., *Land and Lordship*, Philadelphia, 1992

Cheyette, F. L. (ed.), *Lordship and Community in Medieval Europe*, New York, 1968

Contamine, P. (ed.), *La noblesse au Moyen Age*, Paris, 1976

Duby, G., *The Chivalrous Society*, London, 1977
   The Legend of Bouvines, Cambridge, 1990

Ganshof, F. L., *Feudalism*, London, 1964

Keen, M., *Chivalry*, New Haven and London, 1984

Mayer, T., *Adel und Bauern im deutschen Staat des Mittelalters*, Leipzig, 1943

Mittlis, H., *Lehnrecht und Staatsgewalt*, Weimar, 1933

Reuter, T. (ed.), *The Medieval Nobility*, Amsterdam and Oxford, 1979

Reynolds, S., *Fiefs and Vassals*, Oxford, 1994

Structures féodales et féodalisme dans l'Occident mediterranéen (Colloque de Rome, 1978), Rome, 1980

Les structures sociales de l'Aquitaine, du Languedoc et de l'Espagne (Colloque de Toulouse, 1968), 1969

Select bibliography

SOCIAL GROUPS: OUTSIDE THE ARISTOCRACY

Bader, K. S., *Studien zur Reichsgeschichte des mittelalterlichen Dorf*, Weimar and Cologne, 1957–73

Blumenkranz, B., *Histoire des Juifs en France*, Toulouse, 1972

Bonnassie, P., *From Slavery to Feudalism in South-Western Europe*, Cambridge, 1991

Cam, H. M., *Liberties and Communities in Medieval England*, Cambridge, 1944

Fossier, R., *Chartes de coutume en Picardie (XIᵉ–XIIᵉ siècles)*, Paris, 1975

Fourquin, G., *The Anatomy of Popular Rebellion in the Middle Ages*, Amsterdam and Oxford, 1978

Hilton, R. H., *Bond Men Made Free: Medieval Peasant Movements and the English Rising of 1381*, London, 1973

Reynolds, S., *Kingdoms and Communities in Western Europe 900–1300*, Oxford, 1984

Stow, K., *Alienated Minority: The Jews of Medieval Latin Europe*, Cambridge (Mass.) and London, 1992

Verlinden, C., *L'esclavage dans l'Europe médiévale*, vol. I, Bruges, 1955; vol. II, Ghent, 1977

Werner, F., *Pauperes Christi*, Leipzig, 1956

Wickham, C., *Land and Power: Studies in Italian and European Social History 400–1200*, London, 1994

THE COUNTRYSIDE

Aston, M., Austin, D. and Dyer, C. (eds.), *The Rural Settlements of Medieval England*, Oxford, 1989

Aston, T. (ed.), *Landlords, Peasants and Politics in Medieval England*, Cambridge, 1987

Beech, G. T., *A Rural Society in Medieval France*, Baltimore, 1964

Beresford, M. and Hurst, J. G., *Deserted Medieval Villages*, 2nd edn, Gloucester, 1989

Bois, G., *The Transformation of the Year 1000*, Manchester, 1992

Brown, R. A., *English Castles*, London, 1976

Chapelot, J. and Fossier, R., *The Village and the House in the Middle Ages*, London, 1985

Dion, R., *Histoire de la vigne et du vin en France*, Paris, 1965

Dyer, C., *Lords and Peasants in a Changing Society: The Estates of the Bishopric of Worcester, 680–1540*, Cambridge, 1980

Fossier, R., *Peasant Life in the Medieval West*, Oxford, 1988

Fournier, G., *Le château dans la France médiévale*, Paris, 1978

Genicot, L., *Rural Communities in the Medieval West*, Baltimore and London, 1990

Hallam, W. E. (ed.), *The Agrarian History of England and Wales*, vol. II: *1042–1350*, Cambridge, 1980

Hensel, W., *Méthodes et perspectives de recherche sur les centres ruraux chez les Slaves*, 1962

Higounet, C., *Paysages et villages neufs du Moyen Age*, Bordeaux, 1975

Histoire de la France rurale, vols I and II, Paris, 1975

Kenyon, J. R., *Medieval Fortifications*, London, 1990

Langdon, J., *Horses, Oxen and Technological Innovation: The Use of Draught Animals in English Farming from 1066 to 1500*, Cambridge, 1986

Menant, F., *Campagnes lombardes de Moyen Age*, Rome and Paris, 1993

Miller, E. and Hatcher, J., *Medieval England: Rural Society and Economic Change 1086–1348*, London, 1978

Slicher van Bath, B. H., *Yield Ratios 810–1820*, Wageningen, 1963

Titow, J. Z., *Winchester Yields*, Cambridge, 1972

Unwin, T., *Wine and the Vine. An Historical Geography of Viticulture and the Wine Trade*, London, 1991

White, L., *Medieval Technology and Social Change*, Oxford, 1962

TOWNS AND TRADE

Barel, Y., *La ville médiévale*, Grenoble, 1977

Beresford, M., *New Towns of the Middle Ages*, London, 1967

Beveridge, W., *Prices and Wages in England from the Twelfth to the Nineteenth Century*, London, 1939

Boussard, J., *Nouvelle histoire de Paris*, vol. I, Paris, 1976

Carus–Wilson, E. M., *Medieval Merchant Venturers*, London, 1954

Chapin, E., *Les villes de foires de Champagne des origines au début du XIVᵉ siècle*, Paris, 1947

Dollinger, P., *The German Hansa*, Stanford, 1970

Ennen, E., *The Medieval Town*, Amsterdam, New York and Oxford, 1979

Gimpel, J., *The Medieval Machine*, London, 1977

Gouron, R., *La réglementation des métiers en Languedoc au Moyen Age*, Paris, 1958

Herlihy, D., *Pisa in the Early Renaissance: A Study of Urban Growth*, New Haven, 1958

Heyd, W., *Histoire du commerce du Levant au Moyen-Age*, 2 vols, Leipzig, 1923

Hilton, R. H., *English and French Towns in Feudal Society*, Cambridge, 1992

Hodges, R. and Hobley, B. (eds.), *The Rebirth of Towns in the West AD 700–1050*, London, 1988

Le Goff, J., *Your Money or Your Life: Economy and Religion in the Middle Ages*, New York, 1988

Lopez, R. S., *The Commercial Revolution of the Middle Ages 950–1350*, Cambridge, 1976

Miskimin, H., Herlihy, D. and Udovitch, A. L. (eds.), *The Medieval City*, New Haven and London, 1977

Mundy, J. and Riesenberg, P., *The Medieval Town*, Princeton and London, 1958

Petit-Dutaillis, C., *The French Communes in the Middle Ages*, Amsterdam and Oxford, 1978

Platt, C., *The English Medieval Town*, London, 1976

Renouard, Y., *Les hommes d'affaire italiens au Moyen Age*, 2nd edn, Paris, 1968

　　Les villes d'Italie de la fin du Xᵉ au début du XIVᵉ siècle, 2 vols, Paris, 1969

Reynolds, S., *An Introduction to the History of English Medieval Towns*, Oxford, 1977

Rörig, F., *The Medieval Town*, London, 1967

Spufford, P., *Money and its Use in Medieval Europe*, Cambridge, 1988

Verhulst, A., *Rural and Urban Aspects of Early Medieval Northwest Europe*, Aldershot, 1992

Waley, D., *The Italian City-Republics*, 2nd edn, London, 1978

Wolff, P., *Histoire de Toulouse*, Toulouse, 1958

　　L'âge de l'artisinat, Vᵉ–XVIIIᵉ siècles, Paris, 1960

THOUGHT, POWER AND POLITICS

POWER AND POLITICS

Abulafia, D., *Frederick II*, London, 1988

Baldwin, J. W., *The Government of Philip Augustus*, Berkeley, Los Angeles and London, 1986

Bates, D., *Normandy before 1066*, London, 1982

Duby, G., *France in the Middle Ages 987–1460*, Oxford, 1991

Dunbabin, J., *France in the Making 843–1180*, Oxford, 1985

Folz, R., *The Concept of Empire in Western Europe from the Fifth to the Fourteenth Century*, London, 1969

Fuhrmann, H., *Germany in the High Middle Ages c. 1050–1200*, Cambridge, 1986

Gillingham, J., *The Angevin Empire*, London, 1984

King, E., *Medieval England 1066–1485*, London, 1988

Leyser, K., *Communications and Power in Medieval Europe*, London, 1994

Select bibliography

MacKay, A., *Spain in the Middle Ages: From Frontier to Empire, 1000–1500*, London, 1977

Matthew, D. *The Norman Kingdom of Sicily*, Cambridge, 1992

Mitteis, H., *The State in the Middle Ages*, Amsterdam and Oxford, 1975

Tabacco, G., *The Struggle for Power in Medieval Italy*, Cambridge, 1989

THE CHRISTIAN FAITH AND CHURCH HIERARCHY

Bolton, B., *The Medieval Reformation*, London, 1983

Brooke, C. and Brooke, R., *Popular Religion in the Middle Ages*, London, 1984

Brundage, J. A., *Medieval Canon Law and the Crusader*, Madison, 1969

Chenu, M.-D., *Nature, Man and Society in the Twelfth Century*, Chicago, 1968

Cohn, N., *The Pursuit of the Millennium*, 2nd edn, London, 1970

Cowdrey, H. E. J., *The Cluniacs and the Gregorian Reform*, Oxford, 1970

D'Avray, P., *The Preaching of the Friars*, Oxford, 1985

Delaruelle, E., *La piété populaire au Moyen Age*, Turin, 1975

Dobiache-Rojdesvenski, O., *La vie paroissiale en France au XIIIᵉ siècle*, Paris, 1911

Emmerson, R. K. and McGinn, B. (eds.), *The Apocalypse in the Middle Ages*, Ithaca and London, 1992

Hamilton, B., *The Medieval Inquisition*, London, 1980

   Religion in the Medieval West, London, 1986

Head, T. and Landes, R. (eds.), *The Peace of God. Social Violence and Religious Response in France around the Year 1000*, Ithaca and London, 1992

Lambert, M., *Medieval Heresy*, 2nd edn, London, 1992

Lawrence, C. H., *Medieval Monasticism*, 2nd edn, London, 1992

   The Friars, London, 1994

Le Goff, J., *The Birth of Purgatory*, London, 1984

Magnou-Nortier, E., *La société laïque et l'Eglise dans la province ecclésiastique de Narbonne de la fin du VIIIᵉ à la fin du XIᵉ siècle*, Toulouse, 1974

Mollat, M., *The Poor in the Middle Ages*, New Haven, 1986

Morris, C., *The Papal Monarchy: The Western Church from 1050 to 1250*, Oxford, 1989

Moore, R. I., *The Formation of a Persecuting Society*, Oxford, 1984

Robinson, I. S., *The Papacy 1073–1198*, Cambridge, 1990

Southern, R. W., *Western Society and the Church in the Middle Ages*, Harmondsworth, 1970

   Saint Anselm: A Portrait in a Landscape, Cambridge, 1990

Tellenbach, G., *The Church in Western Europe from the Tenth to the Eleventh Century*, Cambridge, 1993

Vauchez, A., *Religion et société dans l'Occident mediéval*, Turin, 1980

FORMS OF EXPRESSION

Baldwin, J. W., *Masters, Princes and Merchants: The Social Views of Peter the Chanter and his Circle*, 2 vols, Princeton, 1970

Benson, R. L. and Constable, G., *Renaissance and Renewal in the Twelfth Century*, Oxford, 1984

Bloch, R. H., *The Scandal of the Fabliaux*, Chicago, 1986

Bolgar, R. R., *The Classical Heritage and its Beneficiaries*, Cambridge, 1954

   (ed.), *Classical Influences on European Culture*, Cambridge, 1971

Bumke, J., *Courtly Culture*, Berkeley, 1991

Clanchy, M. T., *From Memory to Written Record*, 2nd edn, Oxford, 1992

Cobban, A. B., *The Medieval Universities*, London, 1975

Crocker, R. and Hiley, D. (eds.), *The Early Middle Ages to 1300*, vol. II, *The New Oxford History of Music*, Oxford, 1990

Crombie, A., *Augustine to Galileo: The History of Science AD 400–1650*, 2nd edn, London 1961

Ferruolo, S., *The Origins of the University: The Schools of Paris and their Critics, 1100–1215*, Stanford, 1985

Francastel, P., *L'humanisme romain*, Paris, 1970

Gameson, R. (ed.), *The Early Medieval Bible*, Cambridge, 1994

Knowles, D., *The Evolution of Medieval Thought*, London, 1962

Leclerq, J., *The Love of Learning and the Desire for God*, London, 1978

Le Goff, J., *Intellectuals in the Middle Ages*, Oxford, 1993

Murray, A., *Reason and Society in the Middle Ages*, Oxford, 1978

Nelli, R., *L'érotique des troubadours*, Toulouse, 1983

Page, C., *The Owl and the Nightingale: Musical Life and Ideas in France 1100–1300*, London, 1989

Radding, C. M., *A World Made by Men: Cognition and Society, 400–1200*, Chapel Hill and London, 1985

Rashdall, H., *The Universities of Europe in the Middle Ages*, 3 vols, Oxford, 1936

Smalley, B., *The Study of the Bible in the Middle Ages*, 3rd edn, Oxford, 1983

ART

Aubert, M., *High Gothic Art*, London, 1964
  French Sculpture at the Beginning of the Gothic Period 1140–1225, New York, 1972

Avril, F., Barral, X., Alte, I. and Gaborit-Chopin, D., *Le temps des croisades*, Paris, 1982
  Les royaumes d'Occident, Paris, 1983

Dodwell, C. R., *The Pictorial Arts of the West 800–1200*, New Haven and London, 1993

Duby, G., *The Age of Cathedrals: Art and Society 980–1420*, Chicago, 1981

Focillon, H., *The Art of the West in the Middle Ages*, 2 vols, London, 1963

Grodecki, L., *Gothic Architecture*, London, 1986

Lasko, P., *Ars Sacra 800–1200*, Harmondsworth, 1972

Mâle, E., *Religious Art in France: The Thirteenth Century*, Princeton, 1984

Martindale, R., *Gothic Art*, London, 1967

Mayr-Harting, H., *Ottonian Book Illumination*, 2 vols, London, 1991

Wilson, C., *The Gothic Cathedral*, London, 1990

THE BYZANTINE WORLD

GENERAL SURVEYS AND POLITICAL HISTORIES

The following list is in addition to the relevant section of the bibliography in volume I.

Ahrweiler, H., *Etudes sur les structures administratives et sociales de Byzance*, London, 1971

Angold, M., *A Byzantine Government in Exile*, Oxford, 1975
  The Byzantine Empire 1025–1204: A Political History, London, 1984

Chalandon, F., *Histoire de la domination normande en Italie et en Sicile*, 2 vols, Paris, 1907

Fine, J., *The Early Medieval Balkans*, Michigan, 1983
  The Late Medieval Balkans, Michigan, 1987

Select bibliography

Kazhdan, A. P. and Epstein, A. W., *Change in Byzantine Culture in the Eleventh and Twelfth Centuries*, Berkeley and London, 1985

Magdalino, P., *The Empire of Manuel I Komnenos, 1143–1180*, Cambridge, 1993

Matthew, D., *The Norman Kingdom of Sicily*, Cambridge, 1992

Obolensky, D., *The Byzantine Commonwealth*, London, 1971

Oxford Dictionary of Byzantium, 3 vols, Oxford and New York, 1991

Portal, R., *The Slavs*, London, 1969

Runciman, S., *A History of the First Bulgarian Empire*, London, 1930
> *The Emperor Romanus Lecapenus and his Reign*, 2nd edn, Cambridge, 1988

ECONOMIC AND SOCIAL PROBLEMS

See the relevant section of the bibliography in volume I, in particular the works of P. Charanis, D. Jacoby, G. Ostrogorsky and J. Starr; and on town and country, the works of H. Ahrweiler, H. Antonianis-Bibicou, L. Boulnois, P. Grierson, P. Lemerle, R. S. Lopez, C. Morrisson and N. Svoronos.

The *Travaux et mémoires du Centre de recherche d'histoire byzantine de Paris* publish many articles on these topics; see in particular the volumes for 1976 and 1979.

Bratianu, G., *Le commerce génois dans la Mer Noire*, Paris, 1929

Harvey, A., *Economic Expansion in the Byzantine Empire*, Cambridge, 1989

Hendy, M., *Studies in the Byzantine Monetary Economy, c.300–1450*, Cambridge, 1985

Jacoby, D., *La feodalité en Grèce médiévale*, Paris, 1971

Ostrogorsky, G., *Pour l'histoire de la féodalité byzantine*, Brussels, 1954

PROBLEMS ARISING FROM THE CRUSADES

Balard, M., *La Romanie génoise*, 2 vols, Rome, 1978

Brand, C. M., *Byzantium Confronts the West 1180–1204*, Cambridge (Mass.), 1968

Hamilton, B., *The Latin Church in the Crusader States*, London, 1980

Lilie, R.-J., *Byzantium and the Crusader States*, Oxford, 1993

Longnon, J., *L'empire latin de Constantinople et la principautée de Morée*, Paris, 1949

Nicol, D. M., *Byzantium and Venice*, Cambridge, 1988

Thiriet, L., *La Romanie vénitienne au Moyen Age*, Paris, 1959

CULTURE AND RELIGION

In addition to works cited in volume I, see:

Dvornik, F., *The Photian Schism*, Cambridge, 1948
> *Byzantine Missions among the Slavs*, New Brunswick, 1970

Every, G., *The Byzantine Patriarchate 451–1204*, London, 1947

Hussey, J. M., *Church and Learning in the Byzantine Empire, 867–1185*, London, 1937
> *The Orthodox Church in the Byzantine Empire*, Oxford, 1986

Lemerle, P., *Cinq études sur le XIᵉ siècle byzantin*, Paris, 1971

Le millénaire du Mont Athos, 963–1963, 2 vols, Chevetogne, 1963–4

ISLAM

In addition to the general works cited in volume I, see:

Hourani, A., *A History of the Arab Peoples*, London, 1991
Sourdel, D., *Medieval Islam*, London, 1983

REGIONAL PROBLEMS

The Near East, Turkish and Mongol zones
Cahen, C., *Pre-Ottoman Turkey*, London, 1968
Grousset, R., *Conqueror of the World*, Edinburgh and London, 1967
   The Empire of the Steppes, New Brunswick, 1970
Hitti, P. K., *History of Syria, including Lebanon and Palestine*, London, 1951
Holt, P. M., *The Age of the Crusades: The Near East from the Eleventh Century to 1517*, London, 1986
Kennedy, H., *The Prophet and the Age of the Caliphates: The Near East
   from the Eleventh Century to 1517*, London, 1986
Morgan, D., *The Mongols*, Oxford, 1986
Richards, D. S. (ed.), *Islamic Civilisation 950–1150*, Oxford, 1973
Saunders, J. J., *The History of the Mongol Conquests*, London, 1971
Thorau, P., *The Lion of Egypt*, London, 1992
Vryonis, S., *The Decline of Medieval Hellenism in Asia Minor and the Process of Islamicisation from the
   Eleventh through the Fifteenth Century*, Berkeley and London, 1971
Wiet, G., *L'Egypte arabe*, Paris, 1937

The West
Bonnassie, P., *La Catalogne du milieu du Xe à la fin du XIe siècle. Croissance et mutations d'une société*, 2
   vols, Toulouse, 1975–6
The Cambridge History of Africa, vol. 3: *From c.1050 to c.1600*, Cambridge, 1977
Cheine, A. G., *Muslim Spain, its History and Culture*, Minneapolis, 1974
Fletcher, R., *Moorish Spain*, London, 1992
Golwin, L., *Le Maghreb central à l'époque des Zirides*, 1957
Idris, H. R., *La Berbérie orientale sous les Zirides, X^e–XIIe siècles*, Paris, 1962
Lacoste, Y., *Ibn Khaldun. The Birth of History and the Past of the Third World*, London, 1984
Latham, J. D., *From Muslim Spain to Barbary*, London, 1986
Prieto, A. and Vives, Y., *Los reyes de taifas. Estudio histórico-numismatico de los musulmanes españoles en
   el siglo V de la Hégira*, Madrid, 1926
Reilly, B. F., *The Contest of Christian and Muslim Spain 1031–1157*, Oxford, 1992
UNESCO, *General History of Africa*, vol. IV, *Africa from the Twelfth to the Sixteenth Century*, Paris, London
   and Berkeley, 1964
Urvoy, D., *Le monde des ulémas andalous du Ve–XIe au VIIe–XIIIe siècles. Etude sociologique*, Geneva,
   1978

The Crusades
Atiya, A. S., *Crusade, Commerce and Culture*, Bloomington (Ind.), 1962
   The Crusades: Historiography and Bibliography, Bloomington (Ind.), 1962

Select bibliography

Cahen, C., *La Syrie du nord à l'époque des Croisades*, Paris, 1940
   Orient et Occident au temps des Croisades, Paris, 1983
Ehrenkreutz, A. S., *Saladin*, New York, 1972
Eliséef, N., *Nûr ad-Dîn, un grand prince musulman au temps des Croisades*, 3 vols, Damascus, 1967
Kedar, B. Z., *The Franks in the Levant, 11th to 14th centuries*, London, 1993
Kedar, B. Z., Mayer, H. E. and Smail, R. C. (eds.), *Outremer: Studies in the History of the Crusading Kingdom of Jerusalem, Presented to Joshua Prawer*, Jerusalem, 1982
Lyons, M. C. and Jackson, D. E. P., *Saladin*, Cambridge, 1982
Maalouf, A., *The Crusades through Arab Eyes*, London, 1984
Mayer, H. E., *The Crusades*, 2nd edn, Oxford, 1988
Newby, P. H., *Saladin in his Time*, London, 1983
Prawer, J., *The World of the Crusades*, London, 1972
   The Latin Kingdom of Jerusalem, London, 1972
   Crusader Institutions, Oxford, 1980
Richard, J., *The Latin Kingdom of Jerusalem*, 2 vols, Amsterdam and Oxford, 1979
Riley-Smith, J. *The Feudal Nobility and the Kingdom of Jerusalem*, London, 1973
Runciman, S., *A History of the Crusades*, 3 vols, Cambridge, 1951–4
Setton, K. M. (ed.), *A History of the Crusades*, 6 vols, Madison 1969–89
Sivan, E., *L'Islam et la croisade. Idéologie et propagande dans les réactions musulmanes aux croisades*, Paris, 1968

ECONOMIC AND SOCIAL PROBLEMS

Trade, town and countryside
Ashtor, E., *Histoire des prix et des salaires dans l'Orient médiéval*, Paris, 1969
   A Social and Economic History of the Near East in the Middle Ages, London, 1976
Cook, M. A. (ed.), *Studies in the Economic History of the Middle East*, London, 1970
Goitein, S. D., *A Mediterranean Society. The Jewish Communities of the Arab World as Portrayed in the Documents of the Cairo Geniza*, Berkeley, Los Angeles and London, 1967–88
Heyd, W., *Histoire du commerce du Levant au Moyen-Age*, Leipzig, 1923
Hourani, A. and Stern, S. (eds.), *The Islamic City*, Oxford, 1970
Labib, S., *Handelgeschichte Aegyptens in Spätmittelalter*, Wiesbaden, 1965
Lopez, R. S. and Raymond, I. W., *Medieval Trade in the Mediterranean World*, London, 1955

Art and thought
Cambridge History of Arabic Literature, vols I, II and III, Cambridge, 1983–90
Dodds, J. D. (ed.), *Al–Andalus. The Art of Islamic Spain*, New York, 1992
Hillenbrand, R., *Islamic Architecture*, Edinburgh, 1994
Hodgson, M. G., *The Order of Assassins*, The Hague, 1955
Kühnel, E., *Islamic Art and Architecture*, London, 1962
Lewis, B. (ed.), *The World of Islam*, London, 1976
Nicholson, R., *A Literary History of the Arabs*, Cambridge, 1930
Sourdel-Thomine, J. and Spuler, B., *Die Kunst des Islam*, Berlin, 1973

Der zwo bruder der do stach der hieß heintz
vnd was ein Galsurer

The making of a coat of mail required a great deal of care. Not only did it have to provide protection but, as Crusaders had to supply their own equipment, it also had to last several generations. (Nuremberg, Stadtbibliotek.)

The art of Portuguese ironwork: the grilles of the Lisbon cathedral cloister, thirteenth century.

Index

Note: A page number in italics indicates a text illustration.

Index

Index

Index